Making Precious Things Plain

Volume 12

New Testament Study Guide, Pt. 3

The Epistles and the Book of Revelation

Randal S. Chase

Making Precious Things Plain, Vol. 12:
New Testament Study Guide, Pt 3.
The Epistles & the Book of Revelation
(2nd Edition)

Send inquiries to:
Plain and Precious Publishing
3378 E. Sweetwater Springs Drive
Washington, UT 84780

Send e-mail: info@makingpreciousthingsplain.com

For more copies visit www.makingpreciousthingsplain.com

For a listing of all Plain and Precious Publishing products, visit
www.makingpreciousthingsplain.com
or call 435–251–8520.

Printed in the United States of America

ISBN: 978-1-937901-12-7

Cover: "St. Paul at His Writing Desk" by Rembrandt, 1629.

Making Precious Things Plain
Volume 12
New Testament Study Guide, Pt. 3
The Epistles and the Book of Revelation

Table of Contents

Acknowledgments

This book is dedicated to Church members everywhere who hunger and thirst for an understanding of the scriptures. It has been my privilege to teach literally thousands of such souls in gospel classes, as well as in CES Institute and Adult Education classes, over the years. They have all inspired me with their dedication to reading, pondering, and feasting upon the word of God. I have learned much from them in the process.

I acknowledge the help and encouragement of my sweet wife Deborah, who has assisted me in all of my endeavors to teach and to write concerning the gospel of Jesus Christ. I acknowledge the encouragement of many friends and students to write these study guides, the patient and meticulous assistance of my editor and son, Michael Chase, who has assisted in this work, and other Church scholars who have provided solid counsel about its form and substance, and who have offered invaluable insights on many topics.

I acknowledge other knowledgeable gospel scholars and teachers who have written similar study guides in the past, which I have quoted time and time again in this volume:

The Life and Teachings of Jesus and His Apostles, which is the New Testament Institute Student Manual [Church Educational System manuals, 1979] is an invaluable tool for all students of the New Testament, and many of the cultural, linguistic, and other ideas presented herein were first obtained from this manual.

James E. Talmage's *Jesus the Christ*, 3rd ed. [1916] has been a standard for years in understanding the life of Christ and the four Gospels. Bruce R. McConkie's *Doctrinal New Testament Commentary*, 3 vols. [1966–73]; *Mormon Doctrine*, 2nd ed. [1966]; *The Promised Messiah: The First Coming of Christ* [1978]; *The Mortal Messiah: From Bethlehem to Calvary*, 4 vols. [1979–81]; and *The Millennial Messiah: The Second Coming of the Son of Man* [1982] are also crucial to understanding the life of Christ and the Gospels. The *Studies in Scripture* series, Volumes 5–6 [1986–1988], edited by Kent Jackson and Robert L. Millet, provides excellent scholarly commentary on the New Testament from a variety of LDS researchers and authors.

Daniel H. Ludlow wrote *A Companion to Your Study of the New Testament* [1982], as part of a series of such companions to our study of all the scriptures. These perhaps come closer to the spirit of what this book is all about—making the history and revelations plain to those who just need a little help with their gospel studies. I have had some of Brother Ludlow's family in my classes, and I cherish his personal encouragement to me and a personally-signed copy of his *Selected Writings* that he provided to me a few years ago.

Many of the above-named volumes are now out of print. I am hoping that the portions of them that I have quoted in this volume will continue to spread their insights for years to come.

Foreword

The life and ministry of Jesus Christ, as told in the four Gospels, is so beloved of all Christians that it can overshadow the books that follow in the New Testament. But anyone who does not seriously read and contemplate these books is missing some of the most inspiring stories to be found anywhere in scripture. This period of the Church's history is breathtaking in its worldwide scope, as the Apostles obediently took the word of God to places as far-flung from Jerusalem as India and Spain, Russia and Libya. Gospel blessings were extended to people and races who had previously been ignored or shunned. And the growth of the Church presented challenges to the Apostles as they struggled to keep the doctrine and practices of the members pure. In all of this, the early Church became a metaphor for the very same challenges the Church has experienced in these latter days.

The book of Acts provides the historical background for the epistles of the Apostles. From reading both, we get the full context of each situation that brought forth the teachings in these letters. We understand better the struggles early leaders faced as they tried to bring together both Jews and Gentiles into the Church of Jesus Christ. And because their visits among the Saints were few and far between, we sense the urgency with which they wrote their letters to the Saints to try to keep them in the right way and to tamp down the rising tide of apostasy. The Apostles performed miracles, gave stirring discourses, and boldly proclaimed the risen Lord in every circumstance. And in the end, they paid with their lives for proclaiming the truth.

The Prophet Joseph Smith said, "Follow the labors of [Paul] from the time of his conversion to the time of his death, and you will have a fair sample of industry and patience in promulgating the Gospel of Christ. Derided, whipped, and stoned, the moment he escaped the hands of his persecutors he as zealously as ever proclaimed the doctrine of the Savior. And all may know that he did not embrace the faith for honor in this life, nor for the gain of earthly goods. What, then, could have induced him to undergo all this toil? It was, as he said, that he might obtain the crown of righteousness from the hand of God."[1]

Though fewer in number, the acts and epistles of the other Apostles and disciples are no less important. We observe these men and women of faith, after the resurrection of Christ, bearing fervent witness that they had seen and touched the resurrected Master. We read the letters of Paul, Peter, John, and others, as they struggle to fend off the forces of apostasy. And we see their prophetic gifts manifested in the many visions and prophecies they recorded concerning our own latter day and the restoration of the Gospel in the final dispensation of time.

President Harold B. Lee said, "As we review again the matchless and unselfish devotion of these early prophets and martyrs to the gospel of Christ, may we bow in reverence and repeat with a greater appreciation and comprehension as with the multitude in Jerusalem on the occasion of the triumphal entry the words: 'How blessed is he [the Apostles of the past and present] that cometh in the name of the Lord.'"[2]

The wording of the epistles can be challenging. Paul's intellect and schooling made him the "James E. Talmage of the New Testament." We need some help in understanding what he was saying. But we have many such helps in the Doctrine and Covenants, the teachings of the Prophet Joseph Smith, and the commentaries of Bruce R. McConkie and other faithful scholars. This author's sincere desire is to make the acts and epistles of the New Testament as plain as possible to every level of reader.

How to Use This Book

To facilitate learning, students and teachers may use this study guide in a variety of ways. I have suggested two below, in no particular order of preference. Choose the method that works best for you, but whatever method you choose, complete the assigned scripture reading for each week's lesson *before* you go to class.

Option 1. Prayerfully read the scriptures associated with the current lesson *first*, and then read the chapter in this book that corresponds to those scriptures.

Option 2. Carefully and prayerfully read the scriptures associated with the current lesson, using this study guide as a reference to help you understand the context and consequences of the scriptures *while you are reading them*. To do this, you would keep this book open and use it as a guide and commentary alongside your scriptures.

This study guide comments on many, but not all, of the scriptures in the New Testament. Rather than a verse-by-verse analysis, I have provided a summary restatement of events, divided into scripture blocks with attached explanations and quotes. An example of how these scripture blocks and comments are organized is shown below:

- **2 Thessalonians 2:7–8 Satan will eventually be bound.** The phrase "he who now letteth will let, until he be taken out of the way" (v. 7) is a prime example of how Old English can be torturous to understand.

  At the time the Bible was translated, to "let" meant to "restrain" or "hinder."[3] Thus, Paul is saying that "he who now possesses and restrains the Church (Satan, through apostasy) will eventually be restrained himself. Satan has and will continue to cause misery, unhappiness, and sin throughout the world. But he will eventually be "taken out of the way"—bound by the Lord at the beginning of the Millennium.[4] Satan will be revealed for the evil being that he is, and the Lord will "consume [him] with the spirit of his mouth, and shall destroy [him] with the brightness of his coming" (v. 8).

Some Chapters Are Thematic, Not Chronological

While the order of presentation of these chapters on the New Testament is roughly chronological, it is not strictly so. There are a number of "topical" chapters that provide a more general understanding of the context within which events occurred, such as the introductory chapter on "Paul's Ministry, Methods, and Message." Also, chapter 32 teaches principles for "Living in the Spirit" which includes Galatians even though it was written later than the epistles that follow this chapter.

In every chapter, I have provided an historical setting for the scriptures discussed. I have also freely included other scriptural references that provide additional light on the topic. In the end, understanding the doctrine is more important than the history, though I believe it is possible to understand both, and it is better if we do.

Note to Teachers

For the convenience of readers, the chapters in this study guide are organized around the lesson topics for the Church's Gospel Doctrine classes. However, teachers should remember that this study guide is not intended to become a substitute for the official lesson manuals of the Church. Your lessons should follow precisely the organization found in your lesson manual, and should be centered on the assigned scriptures for each lesson. Teachers should read their lesson manuals first and take note of the main doctrinal points that are listed there. After doing this, teachers may use this book as a way of enhancing their own personal understanding of the events and scriptures covered in a particular lesson, just as any other gospel scholar might do. But you should never use this book as a guide to teaching your lessons.

Notes

1. *Teachings of the Prophet Joseph Smith*, sel. Joseph Fielding Smith [1976], 63–64.
2. In Conference Report, April 1955, 19.
3. *The Great Apostasy* [1909], 41–42.
4. *Doctrinal New Testament Commentary*, 3 vols. [1965–1973], 3:63.

Special Chapter

Paul's Ministry, Methods, and Message

(Introduction to Volume 12)

INTRODUCTION TO PAUL AS A MISSIONARY

A Physical Description of Paul

Bronze Medallion of Paul, 100 AD

In January 1841, Joseph Smith gave a detailed description of the Apostle Paul's physical appearance and mannerisms:

"Description of Paul:–He is about five feet high; very dark hair; dark complexion; dark skin; large Roman nose; sharp face; small black eyes, penetrating as eternity; round shoulders; a whining voice, except when elevated, and then it almost resembled the roaring of a lion. He was a good orator, active and diligent, always employing himself in doing good to his fellowman."[1]

Saul's Preparation for Missionary Work

By the time of his "first mission journey," Saul had already been involved in missionary work for 10 years. Following his conversion, he taught the gospel in Damascus and the surrounding area for three years. Then he "went up to Jerusalem" to receive his formal mission call (Galatians 1:18). Barnabas, a known and trusted Church member, introduced Saul to Church authorities at Jerusalem (Acts 19:26–27). Saul was then called by the Apostles to serve for several years as a missionary to his home city of Tarsus. After that, he and Barnabas journeyed to Antioch, teaching there "a whole year" (Acts 11:26).

PAUL'S MINISTRY

Paul's Ministry Was to Both Gentiles and Jews

- **Acts 9:15–16 "He is a chosen vessel unto me."** When the Lord told Ananias to go and restore the sight of the stricken Saul, Ananias was dismayed, for Saul had troubled the Saints much. But the Lord said: "He is a chosen vessel unto me, to bear my name before the Gentiles."

  Paul planted in the hearts of his fellow Israelites the message of the gospel. He taught them that, as a covenant people, they (like him) were obliged to share their witnesses and covenants with the gentiles.

The ministry of Paul was also to the gentiles of his day. His writings continued to "preach Christ and him crucified" to the spreading gentile nations of the earth long after his death (including us). Despite thousands of years of apostasy, Paul's testimony kept the teachings of Jesus Christ alive in the minds and hearts of millions of people through the dark ages, and have come down to us in our own time, when Paul's counsel has spread globally.

Paul's Special Qualifications for His Ministry

Paul was uniquely qualified for his ministry. No other missionary or Apostle was as well adapted to taking the message of the gospel of Jesus Christ to both Jews and Gentiles throughout the Mediterranean world. Consider the following.

- **For the Jews: he was an expert on Mosaic law.** Paul had been prepared for his mission as a young boy by studying the Mosaic law under Gamaliel (Acts 22:3). This would be essential to his reasoning with the Jews concerning Christ and how the law was fulfilled in Him. As a member of the Sanhedrin, Paul was well known for his scriptural mastery.
- **For the Gentiles: he was a multi-lingual speaker and writer.** Paul also learned multiple languages—Hebrew, Greek, Latin, and Aramaic. Since he would be traveling the known world, this multilingual ability would be essential to teaching people in all the nations surrounding the Mediterranean Sea. If he had come to them speaking only Hebrew or Aramaic, they would not have understood him or respected him as a teacher.
- **For his own protection: he was a Roman citizen.** Paul emphasizes that he was "born free," which means he had not purchased his citizenship. He was a naturally-born citizen of Rome, which helped him in numerous ways to serve the kingdom of God. He could not be mistreated by Roman authorities (Acts 22:25–28), and he could travel freely throughout the empire.

PAUL'S METHODS

Paul's Preaching Methods

- **1 Cor. 9:19-23 Paul adapts himself to different circumstances.** He viewed himself as a "servant unto all, that I might gain the more" (v. 19). "Unto the Jews I became as a Jew, that I might gain the Jews" (v. 20), and "to them that are without law [the Gentiles, who did not follow the law of Moses]" Paul became a Gentile "that I might gain them that are without law" (v. 21). And "to the weak became I . . . weak, that I might gain the weak" (v. 22). Thus, Paul was "made all things to all men, that I might by all means save some, and this I do for the gospel's sake, that I might be partaker thereof with you" (vv. 22–23).

  Elder Bruce R. McConkie said, "Paul here says he made himself all things to all men in an effort to get them to accept the gospel message; that is, he adapted himself to the conditions and circumstances of all classes of people, as a means of getting them to pay attention to his teachings and testimony. And then, lest any suppose this included the acceptance of their false doctrines or practices, or that it in any way involved a compromise between the gospel and false systems of worship, he hastened to add that he and all men must obey the gospel law to be saved."[2]

"PAUL AT ATHENS," COLLER, PROVIDENCE LITHOGRAPHIS CO., 1907

— **Acts 13:5, 15–16 Paul usually preached first to the Jews**. His practice was to enter into the local synagogue, where he would take the opportunity (always provided) for any man to offer "word[s] of exhortation for the people" (v. 15). Paul would stand up and preach Jesus Christ to the Jews (v. 16; see also Acts 14:1; Acts 17:1, 17). As a former member of the Sanhedrin, Paul was well-versed in Jewish beliefs and practices and would use these to reason with the Jews concerning Christ.

Even though the Church had declared by revelation that all worthy Gentiles could become members of the Church, missionaries would normally travel to places where there were established Jewish communities so they could take advantage of this practice and preach to their brethren of the blood of Israel.

Jewish communities could be found all over the ancient world from North Africa, Egypt, and the Arabian Peninsula, to Mesopotamia, Asia Minor (modern day Turkey), and throughout Greece, Italy, France, and Spain. Thus, the diaspora of Judaism was a worldwide phenomenon, and it facilitated missionary work in all these areas.

Paul's Writing Methods

REMBRANDT

Once Paul had preached to a group of Saints, he maintained contact with them through letters. It was the only method available to him in his day. But because Paul was a very literate man, his letters were powerful sources of doctrine, testimony, and reproof.

Paul's earliest epistles pre-dated the writing of the Gospels by Matthew, Mark, Luke and John. Thus, he was the first to commit to writing a witness of mission and Atonement of Jesus Christ. His epistles speak of things about Jesus' ministry, teachings, death and resurrection that comport completely with the accounts in the Gospels. Thus, he validates what the Gospels would later contain, and we know that these teachings and testimonies were circulating in the Church decades before the Gospels were written. The chronology of the epistles and the Gospels is as follows:[3]

Epistle:	Author:	Date:	Written From:
James	James	50–51	Jerusalem
1 Thessalonians	Paul	52–53	Corinth
2 Thessalonians	Paul	52–53	Corinth
1 Corinthians	Paul	57	Ephesus
2 Corinthians	Paul	57	Macedonia (Philippi)
Romans	Paul	57–58	Corinth
Galatians	Paul	58	Macedonia (Philippi)
Matthew (Gospel)	Matthew	60s	Antioch
Mark (Gospel)	Mark	60s	Rome
Colossians	Paul	61–62	Rome
Philemon	Paul	61–62	Rome
Ephesians	Paul	61–62	Rome
Philippians	Paul	62	Rome
1 Peter	Peter	62–64	Rome
Hebrews	Paul	65	Rome
1 Timothy	Paul	66	Rome
2 Peter	Peter	68	Rome
Titus	Paul	67-68	Rome
2 Timothy	Paul	67-68	Rome
Luke (Gospel)	Luke	70s	Rome
Acts	Luke	70s	Rome
Jude	Jude	80	Jerusalem
John (Gospel)	John	90-95	Ephesus
1 John	John	96	Ephesus
2 John	John	96	Ephesus
3 John	John	96	Ephesus
Revelation	John	96	Isle of Patmos

PAUL'S MESSAGE

Joseph Smith and the Apostle Paul: A Comparison

PAINTING FROM DEGUAROTYPE, MAUDSLEY, 1844

One useful way to summarize Paul's message is to show how comprehensively it impacted the mission and message of Joseph Smith. Paul's mission experiences were so similar to those of the Prophet Joseph Smith that he often compared himself to Paul. And he frequently used Paul's language and teachings in his own ministry. Here are two examples:

1. "Deep water is what I am wont to swim in. It all has become a second nature to me; and I feel, like Paul, to glory in tribulation; for to this day has the God of my fathers delivered me out of them all, and will deliver me from henceforth; for behold, and lo, I shall triumph over all my enemies, for the Lord God hath spoken it" [D&C 127:2].

2. "It was nevertheless a fact that I had beheld a vision. I have thought since, that I felt much like Paul, when he made his defense before King Agrippa, and related the account of the vision he had when he saw a light, and heard a voice; but still there were but few who believed him; some said he was dishonest, others said he was mad; and he was ridiculed and reviled. But all this did not destroy the reality of his vision. He had seen a vision, he knew he had, and all the persecution under heaven could not make it otherwise; and though they should persecute him unto death, yet he knew, and would know to his latest breath, that he had both seen a light and heard a voice speaking unto him, and all the world could not make him think or believe otherwise.

"So it was with me. I had actually seen a light, and in the midst of that light I saw two Personages, and they did in reality speak to me; and though I was hated and persecuted for saying that I had seen a vision, yet it was true; and while they were persecuting me, reviling me, and speaking all manner of evil against me falsely for so saying, I was led to say in my heart: Why persecute me for telling the truth? I have actually seen a vision; and who am I that I can withstand God, or why does the world think to make me deny what I have actually seen? For I had seen a vision; I knew it, and I knew that God knew it, and I could not deny it, neither dared I do it; at least I knew that by so doing I would offend God, and come under condemnation" [JS-History 1:24–25).

David Rolph Seely and Jo Ann H. Seely said:[4]

> The Prophet Joseph Smith must have felt a deep kinship with the Apostle Paul. Both began their service to the Lord through a life-changing vision. Both were true to the vision they received and acted with unrelenting faith and courage to fulfill their missions, bearing testimony to a skeptical world (see JS–H 1:24–25). And both sealed their testimonies with their blood as witnesses to the gospel they had so fervently preached throughout their lives.
>
> Joseph Smith read and loved the writings of the Apostle Paul. A scriptural index to the *Teachings of the Prophet Joseph Smith* lists over 1,000 references Joseph Smith made to Paul's writings in his own teachings.[5] The Apostle Paul's language can be seen in many of the Articles of Faith: in the first principles and ordinances of the gospel listed in the 4th article (see Heb. 6:1–2), in the Church officers listed in the 6th article (see Eph. 4:11), in the gifts of the Spirit listed in the 7th article (see 1 Cor. 12:8–12), and most notably in the "admonition of Paul" paraphrased in the 13th article (see Philip. 4:8).[6]

Dr. Robert J. Matthews[7] notes that in *Teachings of the Prophet Joseph Smith*, which contains only part of the Prophet's many writings and sermons, the following references to Paul and his teachings are made:

The following references are found under "Paul":	**Page(s)**
He was the author of Epistle to Hebrews	59-60
He was an example of industry and patience	63
He labored unceasingly in the gospel	63
A summary of life and labors of Paul	63-64
He did not seek honors of this life	64
He will receive a crown of righteousness at Jesus' second coming.	64
He had received the Second Comforter	151
He was visited and taught the mysteries of Godliness by Abel.	169-70

The following quotations of Paul were used by Joseph Smith: Page(s)

PAUL'S FAITHFULNESS

The Rigors of Missionary Work in Paul's Day

Missionary work in Paul's day was vastly different than it is today. The only means of transportation for missionaries was walking. Except for the rare occasions when they could travel by ship, their journeys were all walking, in all kinds of weather and through all kinds of terrain.

The stark reality of having to walk for thousands of miles across the known world in each of his three missions was made even more remarkable by Paul's infirmity—a painful hip condition that caused pain with every step.[8] He might have used it as an excuse, but he did not. He took the matter to the Lord and then accepted the Lord's answer.

PROVIDENCE LITHOGRAPHIC CO., 1901, #34

> And lest I should be exalted above measure through the abundance of the revelations, there was given to me a thorn in the flesh, the messenger of Satan to buffet me, lest I should be exalted above measure.
>
> For this thing I besought the Lord thrice, that it might depart from me.
>
> And he said unto me, My grace is sufficient for thee: for my strength is made perfect in weakness. Most gladly therefore will I rather glory in my infirmities, that the power of Christ may rest upon me.
>
> Therefore I take pleasure in infirmities, in reproaches, in necessities, in persecutions, in distresses for Christ's sake: for when I am weak, then am I strong [2 Cor. 12:7–10].

The Prophet Joseph Smith said:

> In Paul's last letter to Timothy, which was written just previous to his death, he says: "I have fought a good fight, I have finished my course, I have kept the faith: henceforth there is laid up for me a crown of righteousness, which the Lord, the righteous Judge, shall give me at that day: and not to me only, but unto all them also that love His appearing."
>
> No one who believes the account, will doubt for a moment this assertion of Paul which was made, as he knew, just before he was to take his leave of this world. Though he once, according to his own word, persecuted the Church of God and wasted it, yet after embracing the faith, his labors were unceasing to spread the glorious news: and like a faithful soldier, when called to give his life in the cause which he had espoused, he laid it down, as he says, with an assurance of an eternal crown.
>
> Follow the labors of this Apostle from the time of his conversion to the time of his death, and you will have a fair sample of industry and patience in promulgating the Gospel of Christ. Derided, whipped, and stoned, the moment he escaped the hands of his persecutors he as zealously as ever proclaimed the doctrine of the Savior. And all may know that he did not embrace the faith for honor in this life, nor for the gain of earthly goods. What, then, could have induced him to undergo all this toil? It was, as he said, that he might obtain the crown of righteousness from the hand of God.
>
> No one, we presume, will doubt the faithfulness of Paul to the end. None will say that he did not keep the faith, that he did not fight the good fight, that he did not preach and persuade to the last. And what was he to receive? A crown of righteousness. And what shall others receive who do not labor faithfully, and continue to the end? We leave such to search out their own promises if any they have; and if they have any they are welcome to them, on our part, for the Lord says that every man is to receive according to his works.

Reflect for a moment, brethren, and enquire, whether you would consider yourselves worthy [of] a seat at the marriage feast with Paul and others like him, if you had been unfaithful? Had you not fought the good fight, and kept the faith, could you expect to receive? Have you a promise of receiving a crown of righteousness from the hand of the Lord, with the Church of the Firstborn? Here then, we understand, that Paul rested his hope in Christ, because he had kept the faith, and loved His appearing and from His hand he had a promise of receiving a crown of righteousness.[9]

Notes

1. *Teachings of the Prophet Joseph Smith*, sel. Joseph Fielding Smith [1976], 180.
2. *Doctrinal New Testament Commentary*, 3 vols. [1965–1973], 2:353.
3. Adapted from *Charting the New Testament*, © 2002 Welch, Hall, FARMS Chart 13-2
4. "Paul: Untiring Witness of Christ," *Ensign*, August 1999, 22.
5. See *Scriptural Teachings of the Prophet Joseph Smith*, sel. Joseph Fielding Smith [1993]. The index of that book lists over 1,100 references to the epistles of Paul, only a few of which are listed on page 4 of this book (see above).
6. See J. Philip Schaelling, "Paul," in *Encyclopedia of Mormonism*, ed. Daniel H. Ludlow, 5 vols. [1992], 3:1070; and John W. Welch, *An Epistle from the New Testament Apostles* [1999].
7. This is Matthews' summary of the index to *Teachings of the Prophet Joseph Smith*, 422. It is quoted in Kelly Ogden & Andrew D. Skinner, *New Testament Apostles Testify of Christ*, [1998], 242–243.
8. An apocryphal source, the "Acts of Paul and Thecla" contains a description of Paul on page 100: "At length they saw a man coming (namely Paul), of a low stature, bald (or shaved) on the head, crooked thighs, handsome legs, hollow eyed; had a crooked nose; full of grace . . . Sometimes he appeared as a man; sometimes he had the countenance of an angel" (emphasis added to highlight the painful condition of his hips and things).
9. *Teachings of the Prophet Joseph Smith*, 63–64.

SECTION SEVEN

Paul's First Missionary Journey

(45 AD — 49 AD)

The events described in this section include those that occurred during the Apostle Paul's first missionary journey. On this journey, Paul departed from Antioch in Syria and traveled by sea to the Isle of Cyprus, then on to the area of modern-day Turkey. He then returned by sea to his home base of Antioch in Syria. This journey included the following ministries:

ISLE OF CYPRUS:	Salamis, Paphos
PAMPHYLIA:	Attalia, Perga
GALATIA:	Antioch, Iconium, Lystra, Derbe
JERUSALEM:	The Council at Jerusalem

The associated chapter of this book, corresponding to Gospel Doctrine lessons, is:

30. Paul's 1st Mission & Jerusalem (Acts 13–15)

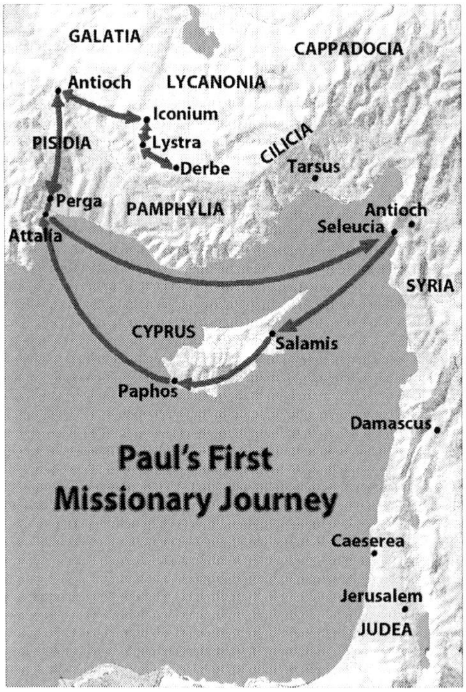

ADAPTED FROM MAP 19 IN THE LDS EDITION OF THE BIBLE

Paul's first missionary journey lasted about one year, from 47–48 AD. He traveled 1400 miles by sailboat and foot, visiting Antioch (Syria), Seleucia, Paphos, Perga, Antioch (Pisidia), Iconium, Lystra, Derbe, Samaria, and Jerusalem. His companions were Barnabas and John Mark (Mark; see Acts 13:13). During this mission, they baptized, confirmed, ordained, and healed. More than once, they had to flee for their lives. And they frequently were troubled with doctrinal questions.

The Significance of Paul's First Missionary Journey

Paul and Barnabas established branches of the Church in areas far removed from Jerusalem. Saul demonstrated his capacity as a missionary, a leader, and an organizer by entering towns with no members and where few had ever even heard of Christ, and, by the time he left, leaving behind small but thriving branches of the Church. Through this process, many heard and received the gospel message. Saul was eager to preach the gospel to all men. In keeping with the nature of his call—to take the Gospel to the Gentiles—whenever the Jews rejected the word of God, he turned to the Gentiles.

The following is a chronological list of events that took place during this period and the scriptures from Acts and the Epistles that tell the story.

Date	Events	Scriptural References
PAUL'S FIRST MISSIONARY JOURNEY (45–49 AD)		
45	Paphos, Cyprus:	
	Paul Curses a False Prophet	Acts 13:6–12
	Antioch. Pisidia:	
	The Savior Was of the Lineage of David	Acts 13:13–15
	The Gospel Is Offered to Israel	Acts 13:26–41
	Paul and Barnabas Teach the Gentiles	Acts 13:42–49
	Iconium, Galatia:	
	Jews Persecute Paul and Barnabas	Acts 13:50–52
	Lystra. Galatia:	
	Paul and Barnabas Hailed as Gods	Acts 14:8–18
	Paul Stoned, Revived, Preaches	Acts 14:19–28
48–49	Paul's continued labors in Antioch	Acts 14:26–15:2, 25–34
THE COUNCIL AT JERUSALEM		
49	Judea:	
	The Question of Circumcision	Acts 15:1–35

Chapter 30b

Paul's First Missionary Journey and Events at Jerusalem

(Acts 13–15)

INTRODUCTION

As mentioned in the introduction to this section of the book, Paul's first missionary journey lasted about one year, from 47–48 AD, during which time he traveled about 1400 miles round trip.

He departed by boat from Antioch in Syria, bound first for the island of Cyprus. His companions were Barnabas, John Mark (Mark; see Acts 13:13), and Silas.

In the coming year they would baptize, confirm, ordain, and heal. More than once, they would have to flee for their lives, and they would be frequently troubled with doctrinal questions.

But they would find and baptize such great stalwarts as Timothy. And they would devote themselves entirely to the work.

THEBIBLEREVIVAL.COM, #43

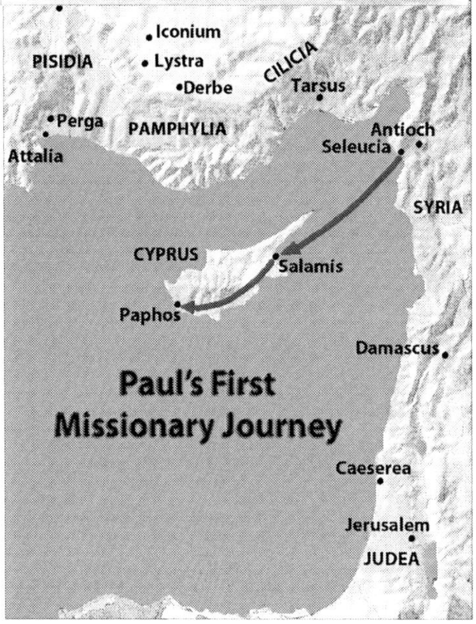

THE MISSION TO CYPRUS

A New Name for Saul

- **Acts 13:4–5** The missionaries sailed 130 miles from Antioch's port, Seleucia, to the city of Salamis on the island of Cyprus, probably around March at the opening of the sailing season. From Salamis, they journeyed overland to Paphos on the western end of the island—a distance of 100 miles—teaching as they went.
  - — **Acts 13:9 Saul becomes Paul.** Saul's name was changed to Paul while he was in Cyprus. "Paulos"

means "small," an apparent reference to his short physical stature. The Prophet Joseph Smith said he was about five feet tall.[1]

Cyprus was Barnabas' home, which is perhaps why they began their mission there. He would be preaching the Gospel to former friends and acquaintances. But most of them rejected his message, and continued in their idolatry and sin. As Gentiles, they worshiped the Goddess Venus, to whom they built a temple and offered sacrifices, sometimes accompanied by lewd and immoral practices in celebration of fertility.

The missionaries moved on from Salamis on the east coast of Cyprus to Paphos on the west coast. Paphos was the seat of power. The appointed Roman proconsul for the province, Sergius Paulus, lived there.

The Governor of Paphos Believes

- **Acts 13:7 They teach Sergius Paulus, the Roman proconsul for Cyprus.** He is described as a "prudent man" who had requested that Paul and Barnabas preach to him (v. 7). This was a significant opportunity to teach someone in authority, the governor of the island of Cyprus.

- **Acts 13:6, 8 Elymas seeks to dissuade Sergius Paulus from believing.** Elymas, whose name means "sorcerer," was a Jew and a false prophet as well (v. 7). He may have had influence with the governor, and seeing a threat to his livelihood, he "withstood [Paul and Barnabas], seeking to turn away the deputy [Sergius Paulus] from the faith" (v. 8).

- **Acts 13:9–11 Paul curses Elymas with blindness.** Under the influence of the Spirit, Paul "set his eyes on him, and said, O full of all subtilty and all mischief, thou child of the devil, thou enemy of all righteousness, wilt thou not cease to pervert the right ways of the Lord?" (v. 10). Paul then cursed him in the name of the Lord, saying, "thou shalt be blind, not seeing the sun for a season. And immediately there fell on him a mist and a darkness; and he went about seeking some to lead him by the hand" (v. 11).

  — **Alma 30:47–56** This incident is very similar to Alma's cursing of Korihor in the Book of Mormon, with the same results.

THEBIBLEREVIVAL.COM, #20

The Prophet Joseph Smith said: "When a man goes about prophesying, and commands men to obey his teachings, he must either be a true or false prophet. False prophets always arise to oppose the true prophets and they will prophesy so very near the truth that they will deceive almost the very chosen ones."[2]

Elder Bruce R. McConkie said, "Similar situations arise in the Church today. For instance, brethren who go forth today to preach and to confirm the Churches sometimes take it upon themselves to advocate political, educational, and social philosophies which seem right to them—on occasions even claiming such are essential to salvation—which in fact are not the voice of God to his people."[3]

- **Acts 13:12 Seeing the miracle performed by Paul, Sergius Paulus "believed."** He was "astonished at the doctrine of the Lord," as were, no doubt, others who also witnessed the miracle and believed. Thus, a small branch of the Church was organized in Paphos.

THE MISSION TO PERGA

Mark Leaves His Mission

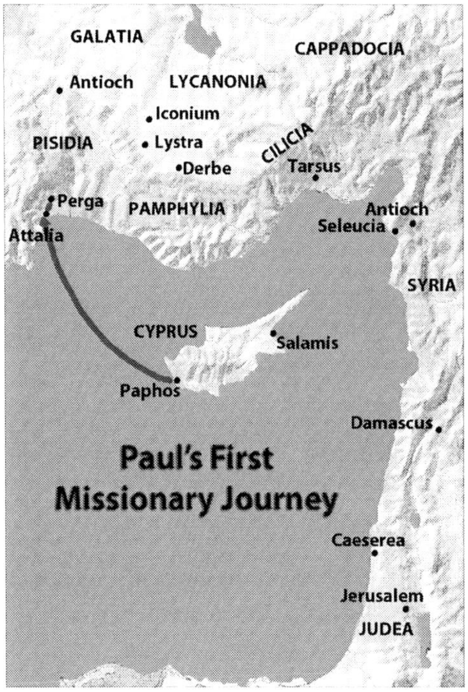

- **The Journey to Perga:** From Paphos they sailed 180 miles north to the port city of Attalia, in the province of Pamphylia, on the southern coast of modern-day Turkey. After arriving in Attalia, Paul, Barnabas, and John Mark walked inland to the city of Perga, about 12 miles to the northeast.

- **Acts 13:13 The departure of John Mark.** At this point in the journey, they lost one of their companions. Luke, the author of Acts, gives a rather matter-of-fact description of the event, saying only that "John depart[ed] from them [and] returned to Jerusalem."

  This departure by Mark produced some bitter feelings for a while (Acts 15:36–41), and there is no record of Mark's traveling again with Paul. But they were apparently eventually reconciled because Paul later called Mark "a comfort" and "my fellow worker unto the kingdom of God" (Colossians 4:10–11).

These events demonstrate the passion with which Paul pursued his missionary labors and the seriousness with which he viewed his call. They also demonstrate that Paul was human, as he himself observed when he later said to the people of Iconium, "We also are men of like passions with you" (Acts 14:15).

THE MISSION TO ANTIOCH OF PISIDIA

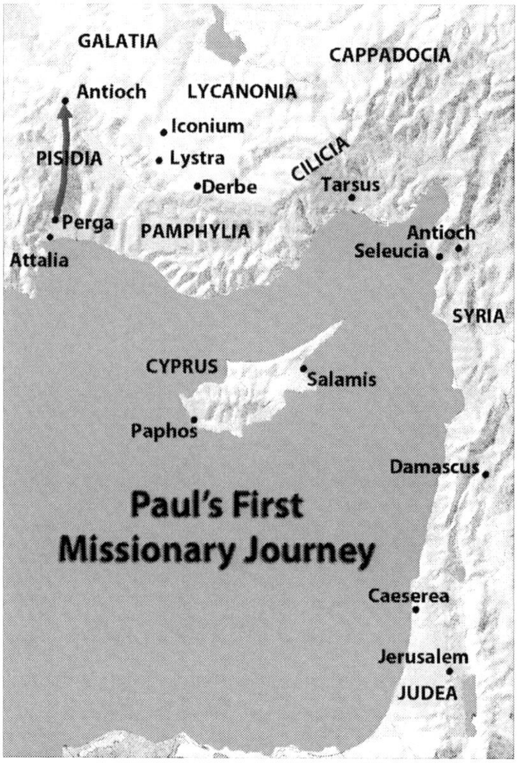

- **The Journey to Antioch of Pisidia:** This Antioch should not be confused with the Antioch in Syria, from which they had begun their mission. This journey would have required climbing nearly 100 miles from the coast up into the mountains of Pisidia, and would have taken 5 or 6 days to accomplish.

  In Antioch, we see the pattern that Paul followed when preaching to Jews and when preaching to Gentiles. In every city, he always started with the Jews.

Preaching to the Jews

- **Acts 13:14–15 The rulers of the synagogue invite Paul to speak at the Sabbath service.** This was the normal custom, and Paul took good advantage of it, speaking as a Jew to the Jews. Paul's discourse at that synagogue is one of the most carefully preserved sermons in the book of Acts.

THEBIBLEREVIVAL.COM, #20

- **Acts 13:23–41 Paul's message to the Jews** follows the same pattern as the sermon preached by Stephen. He rehearsed the history of the children of Israel from Moses to David (vv. 16–22), who they all recognized as their first great king. Then he made the following assertions:

  — Jesus is rightful heir to David's throne (v. 23)
  — His life & mission fulfilled prophecy (vv. 24-29)
  — He was resurrected (vv. 30–37)
  — He is the only source of salvation (vv. 38–41).

- **Acts 13:43 Many Jews believe their message.** Following this Sabbath meeting, "many of the Jews and religious proselytes followed Paul and Barnabas," and were persuaded to "continue in the grace of God." Note that a "proselyte" was a person who was not a Jew but was a believer in Jehovah and the law of Moses.

Preaching to the Gentiles

- **Acts 13:42, 44 Nearly the entire city came together to hear them.** After the missionaries departed the synagogue, "the Gentiles besought that these words might be preached to them the next sabbath" (v. 42), "and the next sabbath day came almost the whole city together to hear the word of God" (v. 44).

F. LAPORTA, 1908, IN THE BIBLE AND ITS STORY

- **Acts 13:48–49 Many Gentiles believe.** The missionaries' message made them "glad," and they "glorified the word of the Lord" (v. 48). Word spread quickly, and "as many as were ordained to eternal life believed."
  - — **JST Acts 13:48** Note the important change in the Joseph Smith Translation, footnote 48a: "and as many as believed were ordained unto eternal life."

"Lo, We Turn to the Gentiles"

- **Acts 13:45–47 Jewish leaders become jealous of their success.** The Jewish leaders sought to stop their preaching by "contradicting and blaspheming" (v. 45). Frustrated with their rebellion against Christ, Paul and Barnabas said, "Seeing ye put it from you, and judge yourselves unworthy of everlasting life, lo, we turn to the Gentiles" (v. 46).

THEBIBLEREVIVAL.COM, #25

- **Acts 13:50 The missionaries are expelled from the city.** The Jews then persuaded the influential and wealthy individuals of the city to expel the Christian missionaries.

  The Prophet Joseph Smith said: "After this chosen family had rejected Christ and his proposals, the heralds of salvation said to them, 'Lo, we turn unto the Gentiles.' And the Gentiles received the covenant and were grafted in from whence the chosen family were broken off. But the Gentiles have not continued in the goodness of God but have departed from the faith that was once delivered to the Saints, and have broken the covenant in which their fathers were established, and have become high-minded, and have not feared. Therefore, but few of them will be gathered with the chosen family."[4]

- **Acts 13:49–52 Paul and Barnabas dust off their feet as a witness against the city** (v. 51). The dusting off of feet is a priesthood ordinance, and is performed only by authorized servants of the Lord. Apostles are certainly authorized. When properly and appropriately performed, it is a testimony against those who willfully and maliciously oppose the truth. It is not used in anger or against those who simply reject the message of the gospel (see also D&C 24:15; D&C 60:15; D&C 75:20; D&C 99:4).

  I remember well how anxious some missionaries in my mission were to exercise this damning ordinance. Missionaries are sometimes caught up in emotional exchanges with those who oppose our Church, and having been personally hurt, they would "dust off their feet" against an entire city for the sake of a single insult. Thankfully, the Lord does not damn and destroy an entire city because a youthful elder wants to strike back against someone who has embarrassed him. As far as I can tell, this kind of thing is reserved only for Apostles and those ordained by them to represent the Twelve. We would do well to remember that all people are God's children and He is far more interested in saving them than destroying them. Paul and Barnabas had proper authority and good reasons to perform this ordinance. We usually do not.

  Elder James E. Talmage wrote, "The responsibility of testifying before the Lord by this accusing symbol is so great that the means may be employed only under unusual and extreme conditions."[5]

THE MISSION TO ICONIUM

Paul and Barnabas Are Apostles

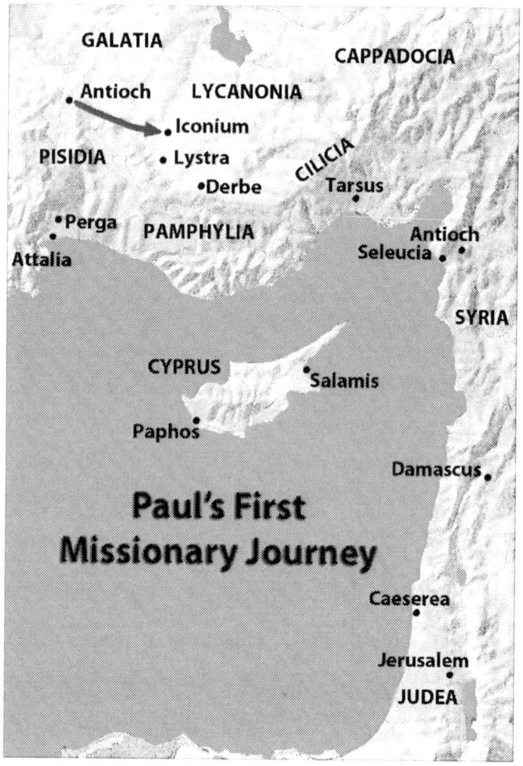

- **The Journey to Iconium:** The missionaries moved on to Iconium, 80 miles to the southeast, immediately entering the synagogue to teach the Jews of the city.
- **Acts 14:1–3 Paul and Barnabas find believing Jews and Gentiles in Iconium** (v. 1). But again "the unbelieving Jews stirred up the Gentiles, and made their minds evil affected against the brethren" (v. 2). Because of their faith, the missionaries stayed a "long time" in Iconium, and performed "signs and wonders" in their city (v. 3).
  - **Acts 14:4, 19 Paul and Barnabas are called "apostles."** This is the first mention of Barnabas and Paul as Apostles. When they became such is not clear, though it may have happened during their visit to Jerusalem. Paul himself declared that he was "an Apostle, (not of men, neither by

man, but by Jesus Christ, and God the Father. . .)" (Gal. 1:1), and continued to assert this throughout his ministry (1 Cor. 1:1; 2 Cor. 1:1; Gal. 1:1; Eph. 1:1; 1 Tim. 1:1; 2 Tim. 1:1; Tit. 1:1).

Because of the ambiguity of the precise time of his ordination, Paul's relationship to the Twelve has been debated by modern Christian scholars. But we believe, as President Joseph Fielding Smith said, that "Paul was an ordained Apostle, and without question he took the place of one of the other brethren in that council."[6]

President Joseph Fielding Smith also said, "We are extremely lacking in information in relation to many important details that failed to seep through the ages to our day, and we are left in darkness to know when and where Paul was ordained. . . . The fact may be correctly surmised that Paul did find time to mingle with his brethren [of the Twelve] and that through the divine inspiration the apostleship was conferred on him by their action. . . . We have no reason to believe that Paul received his ordination independent of the action of the other apostles."[7]

- **Acts 14:5–6 Paul and Barnabas flee to Lystra and Derbe.** As in previous cities, their success in Iconium brought forth opposition as well. It grew to the point that "there was an assault made both of the Gentiles, and also of the Jews with their rulers, to use them despitefully, and to stone them" (v. 5). When they were informed of a plot by their enemies to stone them, they "fled unto Lystra and Derbe" (v. 6).

THE MISSION TO LYSTRA AND DERBE

Worshiped and Stoned in Lystra

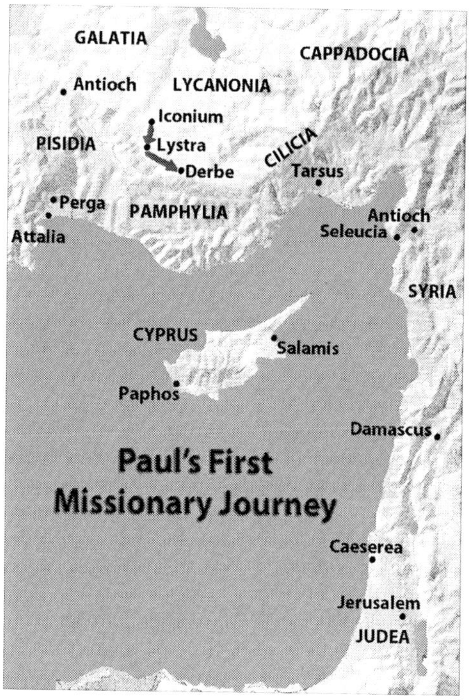

- **The Journey to Lystra:** Lystra was 25 miles south of Iconium in the region called Lycaonia. The Taurus Mountains border this region on the south. Phrygia borders it on the west, Cappadocia on the east, and Galatia on the north.
- **Acts 14:8–10 In Lystra they heal a man who was born lame.** He was "impotent in his feet, being a cripple from his mother's womb, [and] never had walked" (v. 8). As Paul looked upon him, he "perceiv[ed] that he had faith to be healed, [and] said with a loud voice, Stand upright on thy feet. And he leaped and walked" (vv. 9–10).
- **Acts 14:11–12 The people of Lystra believe the missionaries are gods.** Seeing what they had done for the crippled man, "they lifted up their voices, saying . . . The gods are come down to us in the likeness of men" (v. 11). They called Barnabas, "Jupiter," and Paul, "Mercur[y], because he was the chief speaker" (v. 12).

- **Acts 14:13–18 They seek to make sacrifices to Paul and Barnabas.** The "priest of Jupiter . . . brought oxen and garlands unto the gates" in order to do "sacrifice with the people" (v. 13). Shocked by this demonstration, "Barnabas and Paul . . . rent their clothes, and ran in among the people, crying out, . . . Sirs, why do ye these things? We also are men of like passions with you" (vv. 14–15).

COLLER, PROVIDENCE LITHOGRAPHIC CO. coller, provlitho

They explained that their purpose was to "preach unto you that ye should turn from these vanities unto the living God, which made heaven, and earth, and the sea, and all things that are therein" (v. 15). They said that the one true God had "in times past suffered all nations to walk in their own ways," and whether they believed in Him or not had "gave us rain from heaven, and fruitful seasons, filling our hearts with food and gladness" (vv. 16–17). It was to Him that they should sacrifice, not to false gods or men. Still, "these sayings scarce[ly] restrained . . . the people [from doing] sacrifice unto them" (v. 18).

President David O. McKay said:

> At Lystra, Paul and Barnabas found a people who were almost entirely heathen for they worshiped Jupiter and Mercury and other false deities, and knew little or nothing about the true God. There were Jews amongst them, but not of sufficient numbers even to build a synagogue. . . The country was wild and rugged, and the inhabitants were like the country. They were 'villagers of little learning, and rude in dress and manner.' Such people are usually shy of strangers, and slow to accept anything new. But once they begin to get confidence in the stranger, they may be easily swayed by him; not having very definite opinions of their own . . .
>
> [When the people saw the miracle, they proclaimed] 'the Gods have come down to us in the likeness of men,' and they named Paul and Barnabas after their gods. Barnabas was tall, so they called him Jupiter; and Paul, being short and a gifted speaker, they called Mercury, because Mercury was supposed to preside over learning and eloquence. Some time after the meeting, the priests of Jupiter, who officiated in the temple of Jupiter that was in the city, decided to offer sacrifice to . . . Paul and Barnabas. So with the people, they gathered at the gates of the city, brought oxen and began to prepare to offer sacrifice.
>
> When Paul and Barnabas heard of it, they ran among the people, and 'rent their clothes' in protestation against such sacrifice. To rend their clothes was to express intense feeling and the people so understood it. Besides doing this they cried: 'sirs, why do ye these things? We also are men of like passions with you, and preach unto you that ye should turn from these vanities unto the living God, which made heaven and earth, and the sea, and all things that are therein' . . .[8]

- **Timothy and Lois are converted.** Despite such idolatry, some very choice souls were converted at Lystra and Derbe. Among them was young Timothy, who later became Paul's "son in the faith" and a trusted missionary companion. He would also eventually would serve as a righteous and effective bishop.

  President David O. McKay said: "Some of the most intelligent comprehended the truth, and accepted it . . . In [Lystra and Derbe], out of the persecution and affliction heaped upon them by the ignorant and wicked, Paul and Barnabas brought to the faith some of the choicest members of the early Church. Among these were Timothy, whom Paul afterwards called his son; Eunice, Timothy's mother, and Lois, Timothy's grandmother, whose 'unfeigned faith' Paul commended in later years. Undoubtedly, the friendship alone of these noble people more than paid Paul for all the persecution he suffered during this first mission."[9]

Timothy was a faithful disciple who Paul referred to as "my son in the faith."

- **Acts 14:19–20 Agitators from Antioch and Iconium stir up a mob to stone Paul.** They had failed in their efforts to stone him in their own cities, but had followed the missionaries to Lystra with the intent of carrying through on their plot. These Jews "persuaded the people," and some of the people of Lystra who had once sought to worship him, now sought to kill him. "Having stoned Paul, [they] drew him out of the city, supposing he had been dead" (v. 19). But he was not. As sympathetic disciples "stood round about him, he rose up, and came into the city: and the next day he departed with Barnabas to Derbe" (v. 20).

  President David O. McKay said: "There were certain Jews there who had followed the missionaries from Antioch and Iconium, 'who persuaded the people' that Paul and Barnabas were deceivers, and that the miracle which had been performed had been done by the power of the evil one. These Jews swayed the people to such an extent that instead of worshiping Paul and Barnabas, they picked up stones and stoned Paul until he fell to the earth, apparently dead. Thinking he was so, the mob then dragged his body out of the city and left it . . . He had been stunned, but not seriously injured; so a little gentle nursing gave him strength to stand on his feet, and he walked back to the city."[10]

A Brief Mission to Derbe

- **Acts 14:21 The conversion of Gaius.** Though Paul had been thrown out of Lystra and left for dead, the next day Paul and Barnabas were on their way to Derbe—a journey of about 20 miles. And there they "preached boldly and effectively, and converted many to the truth, among them a man by the name of Gaius, who proved to be a staunch and true friend to Paul and to the Church generally."[11]

A RETURN JOURNEY THROUGH THE BRANCHES

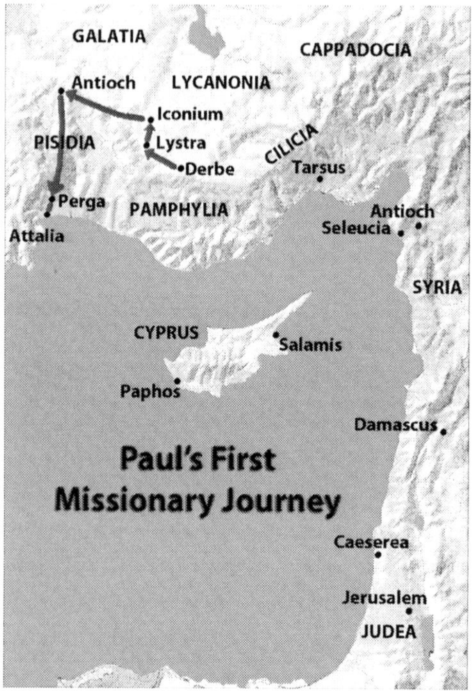

- **Acts 14:21–25 The missionaries return to the Branches to strengthen Church members.** They were on their way home, but took advantage of the opportunity along the way to re-visit the branches they had previously established.

  They returned first to Lystra, and then traveled 40 miles to Iconium and 60 more miles back to Antioch in Pisidia. In each placed they "confirm[ed] the souls of the disciples, and exhort[ed] them to continue in the faith" (v. 22).

  Paul would suffer all kinds of persecutions during his missionary journeys, as we will see. But Paul's privations provided an inspiring example to these new Christians who would, themselves, later face mobbing and death for the sake of their faith. Paul declared to them that "we must through much tribulation enter into the kingdom of God" (v. 22).

PROVIDENCE LITHOGRAPHIC CO., 1896, #30

  Paul did not know if he would ever see these cities or these Saints again, so he was anxious to strengthen them before he left. Paul and Barnabas "ordained . . . elders in every church [branch]" to provide ongoing leadership (v. 23). They also prayed and fasted with the members, and then "commended them to the Lord, on whom they believed" (v. 23). This pattern of strengthening new converts was repeated in the region of Pamphylia, where they revisited Pisidia and the port city of Attalia" (vv. 24–25).

President Gordon B. Hinckley said:

> Each year a substantial number of people become members of the Church, largely through missionary efforts. Last year [1996] there were 321,385 converts comprised of men, women, and children. This is a large enough number, and then some, in one single year to constitute 100 new stakes of Zion. One hundred new stakes per year. Think of it! This places upon each of us an urgent and pressing need to fellowship those who join our ranks.
>
> It is not an easy thing to become a member of this Church. In most cases it involves setting aside old habits, leaving old friends and associations, and stepping into a new society which is different and somewhat demanding. With the ever-increasing number of converts, we must make an increasingly substantial effort to assist them as they find their way. Every one of them needs three things: (1) a friend, (2) a responsibility, and (3) nurturing with 'the good word of God' (Moroni 6:4). It is our duty and opportunity to provide these things . . .
>
> The challenge now is greater than it has ever been because the number of converts is greater than we have ever before known. A program for retaining and strengthening the convert will soon go out to all the Church. I plead with you, brethren; I ask of you, each of you, to become a part of this great effort. Every convert is precious. Every convert is a son or daughter of God. Every convert is a great and serious responsibility."[12]

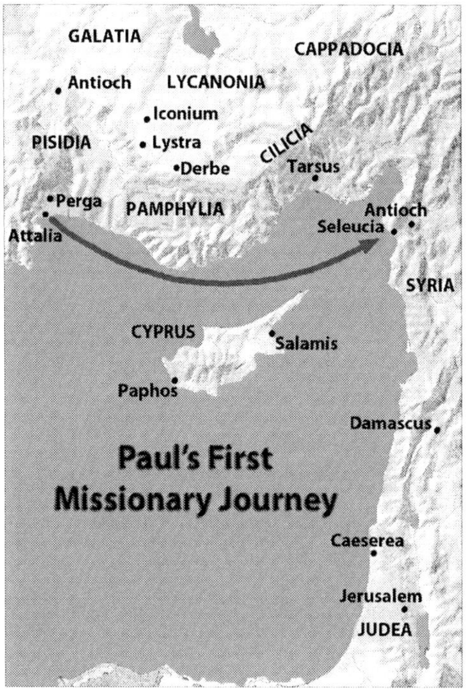

- **Acts 14:26–28 The Apostles return and report on their mission.** From Attalia, they "sailed to Antioch [of Syria], from whence they had been recommended to the grace of God for the work which they fulfilled" (v. 26). They "gathered the Church together, [and] rehearsed all that God had done with them, and how he had opened the door of faith unto the Gentiles" (v. 27), and then remained at Antioch for a "long time with the disciples" (v. 28).

THE JERUSALEM COUNCIL

A Dispute Arises Over Circumcision for Gentiles

Paul and Barnabas had reported to the leaders and members in Antioch, but it also became necessary to report to the Apostles at Jerusalem. This meeting has come to be known as the "Jerusalem Council," which was held in 49–50 AD. It had been 10 years since Peter converted Cornelius, and 14 years since Paul himself was converted.

Their success among the Gentiles had become well-known, and new questions were arising among Jewish converts about the need for Gentile members to live the law of Moses and to be circumcised. For the Jews, the ordinance of circumcision was symbolic of the entire law of Moses. A "circumcised man" was more than just a man who had been physically circumcised; he was a man who kept the law. Circumcision was instituted by Jehovah himself with Abraham and his descendants as a token of their covenant with God. It set them apart from all other men, symbolizing purity and promising eternal blessings to all who served the Lord in righteousness (see Abraham 2:8–11; Genesis 17:9–14). According to the law of Moses, every male child was to be circumcised when he was eight days old (Leviticus 12:3).

- **Acts 15:1–2 The dispute over circumcision.** In the days of Jesus and the Apostles it was common to refer to people as "of the circumcision" and "of the un-circumcision," when referring to Jews and Gentiles. (Gal. 2:7). Following the atoning sacrifice of Jesus Christ, the need for circumcision was removed, but some Jewish Christians still practiced it and wanted Gentile converts to practice it as well. The issue had become contentious and caused serious divisions in the early Church.

  After their conversion to Christ, some Gentiles at Antioch were confronted by "certain men which came down from Judæa [who] taught the brethren, . . . Except ye be circumcised after the manner of Moses, ye cannot be saved" (v. 1). Paul and Barnabas "had no small dissension and disputation" with these Jewish members" (v. 2).

  Elder Bruce R. McConkie said:

  > When Barnabas and Paul returned to Antioch they found disputations among the disciples regarding circumcision. Several Church leaders from Jerusalem had visited ' the thriving branch and had mistakenly sown the seeds of contention by instructing the male members that they needed to be circumcised if they wanted to be saved... They came from the headquarters of the Church, . . . and were good and acceptable brethren; but on the issue of circumcision they erred, teaching false doctrine and not being led by the Spirit.
  >
  > Since the Lord often leaves his servants to struggle with and work out solutions for difficult problems, before they finally receive his mind and voice by revelation, similar situations arise in the Church today. For instance, brethren who go forth today to preach and to confirm the Churches sometimes take it upon themselves to advocate political, educational, and social philosophies which seem right to them-on occasions even claiming such are essential to salvation—which in fact are not the voice of God to his people...
  >
  > Notice the ominous wording: these men 'came down . . . [and] taught the brethren.' They seem to have been good, honorable men, but they erred regarding circumcision."[13]

Paul and Barnabas Attend the Council

- **Acts 15:2–6 The journey to Jerusalem.** The Church members at Antioch "determined that Paul and Barnabas, and certain other of them, should go up to Jerusalem unto the apostles and elders about this question" (v. 2) Paul and Barnabas immediately departed for Jerusalem to seek an answer from Peter and the Twelve. This visit and this question were the primary reasons that the Jerusalem Council was convened (v. 6).

Their route to Jerusalem took them through Phoenicia (Tyre and Sidon), and Samaria (Caesarea). In these cities they "declar[ed] the conversion of the Gentiles," which brought "great joy" to those who heard them (v. 3).

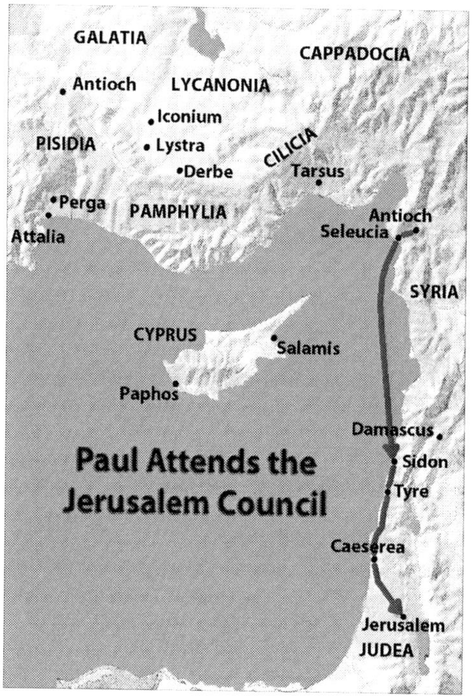

They took others with them to Jerusalem, including Titus, a Greek convert who was not a Jew and therefore a prime example of a faithful Gentile. With the success of Paul's Gentile mission, many non-Jews were now joining the faith and the Apostles needed to consider the effects of an ever-increasing percentage of the Church that was not Israelite by heritage.

"When they were come to Jerusalem, they were received of the Church, and of the apostles and elders, and they declared all things that God had done with them" (v. 4). Despite the joy of some members concerning the Gentiles, "there rose up certain [men formerly] of the sect of the Pharisees" who had been converted to Christ but believed "that it was needful to circumcise them, and to command them to keep the law of Moses" (vv. 4–5).

- **Acts 15:6–11 Peter presides and conducts the meeting.** Peter stood, bore his testimony, and reminded the Church that the revelation opening the gospel dispensation to the Gentiles had come from the Lord to him (v. 7). It was his right to decide matters of doctrine as revealed to him by God. As Elder Bruce R. McConkie said: "Peter [was] the president of the Church; he receive[d] and announce[d] the mind and will of Deity on all matters."[14]

  Peter did not believe that the old system of the law of Moses must be thrust upon Gentile converts. God Himself showed their acceptability unto Him by "giving them the Holy Ghost, even as he did unto us" (v. 8). He "put no difference between us and them, purifying their hearts by faith" (v. 9). "Now therefore why tempt ye God, to put a yoke upon the neck of the disciples, which neither our fathers nor we were able to bear?" (v. 10). He declared that "through the grace of the Lord Jesus Christ we shall be saved, even as they" (v. 11). Peter had learned that God is no respecter of persons or races or ethnicities; all are welcome to join the kingdom of God through baptism.

- **Acts 15:12–18 Barnabas and Paul report on their mission.** They "communicated unto them that gospel which I [had] preach[ed] among the Gentiles" (Galatians 2:2) and "what miracles and wonders God had wrought among the Gentiles by them" (v. 12). This was further evidence of God's acceptance of the Gentiles and their worthiness before Him without the need for circumcision.

- **Paul argues against the continued need for circumcision.** He believed that circumcision for either Jew or Gentile was done away in Christ. This was significant considering that Paul, before his conversion, had been among the most stringent of Pharisees with regard to keeping the law of Moses. But he now believed that the law had been fulfilled in Christ and it was no longer necessary to circumcise (see Romans 2, 3, 4; 1 Corinthians 7:19; Galatians 5:6; 6:15; Colossians 2:11, 3:11).
    - **Nevertheless, Paul had differing responses to it under differing circumstances.** As always, he was willing to adapt to the audience for the purpose of preaching. Rather than letting circumcision become a roadblock to either Jew or Gentile, he advised a different response for Timothy than for Titus.
    - **Acts 16:1–3 For Timothy (a Jew), Paul required it, to appease the Jews.** Timothy's mother was a Jew and his father a Gentile (v. 1). He was a faithful Church member, "well reported of by the brethren that were at Lystra and Iconium" (v. 2), but rather than let his split-heritage become an issue Paul "took and circumcised him because of the Jews which were in those quarters: for they knew all that his father was a Greek" (v. 3).
    - **Galatians 2:1–3 For Titus (a Gentile), Paul did not require circumcision.** He took Titus with him to the Jerusalem Council (v. 1), and decided that "Titus, who was with me, being a Greek, was [not to be] compelled to be circumcised" (v. 3).

- **Acts 15:13–18 James, the brother of the Lord, is a presiding officer at the council.** Though he had once opposed his Brother, James had apparently been converted when he saw the Lord after His resurrection (1 Corinthians 15:7). And now, these many years later, he had apparently become the presiding officer of the branch of the Church at Jerusalem (see Acts 12:17; 15:13; 1 Cor. 15:7; Gal. 2:9–12). In that responsibility, he had eventually replaced James, the son of Zebedee and original member of the First Presidency, who had been martyred by Herod at Jerusalem in 44–45 AD (Acts 12:2). He was also evidently an Apostle because he was one of the presiding officers at this council of Apostles.

ANONYMOUS MEDIEVAL ARTIST

James, Brother of the Lord & Author of the Book of James

James stood up and declared, "Men and brethren, hearken unto me: [Peter] hath declared how God at the first did visit the Gentiles, to take out of them a people for his name. And to this agree the words of the prophets" (vv. 13–15). He cited a prophecy that the Lord would rebuild the Jerusalem temple "that the residue of men might seek after the Lord, and all the Gentiles, upon whom my name is called" (vv. 16–17).

- **Acts 15:19–21 James declares the Twelve's decision.** In doing so, he confirmed the declaration of Peter. His advice was to allow Gentiles to abstain from Judaic practices but require all Church members to abstain from fornication and "the pollutions of idols" (v. 20). This included such pagan practices as eating the flesh of animals who had been strangled (a common practice among pagan peoples who intended to use them as sacrifices), and also from eating blood (v. 20). By this means they would avoid offending the sensibilities of Jews who could be found in nearly every city (v. 21).

- **Acts 15:22–29 The Apostles issue an Official Declaration to the Church.** They sent "chosen men of their own company to Antioch with Paul and Barnabas; namely, Judas surnamed Barsabas, and Silas, chief men among the brethren" (v. 22) with letters from the presiding authorities which declared:

> The apostles and elders and brethren send greeting unto the brethren which are of the Gentiles in Antioch and Syria and Cilicia:
>
> Forasmuch as we have heard, that certain which went out from us have troubled you with words, subverting your souls, saying, Ye must be circumcised, and keep the law: to whom we gave no such commandment:
>
> It seemed good unto us, being assembled with one accord, to send chosen men unto you with our beloved Barnabas and Paul, men that have hazarded their lives for the name of our Lord Jesus Christ. We have sent therefore Judas and Silas, who shall also tell you the same things by mouth.
>
> For it seemed good to the Holy Ghost, and to us, to lay upon you no greater burden than these necessary things; that ye abstain from meats offered to idols, and from blood, and from things strangled, and from fornication: from which if ye keep yourselves, ye shall do well. Fare ye well. [Acts 15:23–29].

- **Acts 15:6–31 The pattern by which decisions about Church policy and practices are made** was set by this process. In continues in the Church today.

  — Church leaders meet to consider the matter (v. 6).
  — They discuss the matter thoroughly (vv. 7–21).
  — They make a decision in accordance with the Lord's will (vv. 19–21).
  — The Holy Ghost confirms that the decision is correct (v. 28).
  — The decision is announced to the Saints for sustaining (vv. 22–31).

Elder Bruce R. McConkie said: "In this instance the decision apparently was both reached and ratified by following the revealed procedure used by the Prophet in translating the Book of Mormon. That is, the Lord's agent struggled and labored with the problem, searched the scriptures, sought for possible conclusions, and did the best they could to solve the problem on the basis of the sound principles which they knew. Having arrived at what they considered to be an appropriate solution—that is, adopting James' statements which were based on Peter's announcement of principle—they then asked the Lord if their conclusions were true and in accord with His mind. (D&C 8 and 9)."[15]

- **Acts 15:30–35 The Gentiles in the Church rejoice when they hear the word of the Lord delivered in the epistle** (vv. 30–31). The visiting brethren, Judas and Silas, who were "prophets also themselves, exhorted the brethren with many words, and confirmed them" (v. 32). Then after a short period of time among them, Judas departed "in peace from the brethren [and returned] unto the apostles" (v. 33), while "it pleased Silas to abide there still" (v. 34). "Paul also and Barnabas [also] continued in Antioch, teaching and preaching the word of the Lord, with many others also" (v. 35).

THE ARISTOCRACY OF RIGHTEOUSNESS

These issues continued to vex the Church. Despite the declaration of the Apostles, the issues of circumcision and the old law were not resolved in the hearts and minds of some members of the Church. It allowed Gentiles into membership without adopting Judaic practices, but did not sever Jewish Christians from their Mosaic heritage. This produced a dual system, with one set of rules for Jews and another for Gentiles. Upon Paul's return to Jerusalem years later (Acts 21), he found Jewish Christians still holding to the traditions of Judaism.

SCAFRICANAMERICAN.COM

Paul believed and taught that righteous and faithful persons of all races are accepted by God, who is the Lord and Savior of all who believe in Him (Romans 2:10–13). It is not now, nor has it ever been, about race; it is about righteousness. The only aristocracy the Lord recognizes is the aristocracy of righteousness.

We are not immune to the arrogance shown by Jewish members in Paul's day. We have seen similar problems arise over the abandonment of the practice of polygamy and later the giving of the priesthood to all worthy males regardless of race or ethnicity. Though these things were also declared by means of official declarations from the Prophet and the Apostles, some have rejected their counsel and hold to the traditions of their fathers.

Elder Hugh B. Brown said:

> The Gospel of Jesus Christ teaches the universality of God's concern for men, and that obedience is a universal fundamental law of progress, both temporal and spiritual. The aristocracy of righteousness is the only aristocracy which God recognizes. This leaves no room for self-righteous expressions in words or actions of being 'holier than thou.' There is a real unity in the human race, and all men have a right to equal consideration as human beings, regardless of their race, creed, or color.
>
> For any church, country, nation or other group to believe that it is the only people in whom God is interested or that it has special merit because of color, race, or belief, that they are inherently superior and loved by God, without regard to the lives they live, is not only a great and dangerous fallacy but is a continuing barrier to peace. This is demoralizing,

whether it is the exploded and presumptuous myth of an Aryan race of supermen or disguised in more subtle forms. Let us steadfastly avoid such demoralizing arrogance."[16]

- **D&C 1:34–35 The Lord is willing to accept any person who desires salvation and is willing to keep the commandments.** The Lord has declared that He is "willing to make these things known unto all flesh; For I am no respecter of persons, and will that all men shall know . . ."

  Elder Joseph Fielding Smith said:

  > It does not mean that the Lord does not respect those who obey him in all things more than he does the ungodly. Without question the Lord does respect those who love him and keep his commandments more than he does those who rebel against him. The proper interpretation of this passage is that the Lord is not partial and grants to each man, if he will repent, the same privileges and opportunities of salvation and exaltation.
  >
  > He is just to every man, both the righteous and the wicked. He will receive any soul who will turn from iniquity to righteousness, and will love him with a just love and bless him with all that the Father has to give; but let it not be thought that he will grant the same blessings to those who will not obey him and keep his law. If the Lord did bless the rebellious as he does the righteous, without their repentance, then he would be a respecter of persons."[17]

Notes:

1. Paul was only 5 feet tall (see *Teachings of the Prophet Joseph Smith*, sel. Joseph Fielding Smith [1976], 180).
2. *Teachings of the Prophet Joseph Smith*, 365.
3. *Doctrinal New Testament Commentary*, 3 vols. [1965–1973], 2:139.
4. Jackson, *Joseph Smith's Commentary on the Bible*, 150.
5. *Jesus the Christ*, 3rd ed. [1916], 345.
6. *Doctrines of Salvation*, comp. Bruce R. McConkie, 3 vols. [1954-1956], 3:153.
7. *Answers to Gospel Questions*, comp. Joseph Fielding Smith Jr., 5 vols. [1957–1966] 4:99–100.
8. *Ancient Apostles*, Lesson 27, First Missionary Journey (Cont'd)—at Lystra and Derbe.
9. *Ibid.*, Lesson 27.
10. *Ibid.*, Lesson 27.
11. *Ibid.*, Lesson 27.
12. In Conference Report, April 1997, 66; or *Ensign*, May 1997, 47–48.
13. *Doctrinal New Testament Commentary*, 2:139.
14. *Doctrinal New Testament Commentary*, 2:143.

15. *Doctrinal New Testament Commentary*, 2:144-145.

16. In Conference Report, April 1966, 119.

17. *Church History and Modern Revelation*, 4 vols. [1946–1949], 1:255.

SECTION EIGHT

Paul's Second Missionary Journey

(49 AD — 53 AD)

Paul's second missionary journey lasted about four years, from 49–52 AD. His companion was Silas. They traveled approximately 3000 miles. They departed from Antioch in Syria and traveled by land to Tarsus, then on to Derbe, Lystra, Iconium, and Antioch. From there, they traveled by land through Asia to Troas. They sailed from there to Philippi, then walked to Thessalonica and Beroea. Another sea journey took them to the capitol of Greek culture, Athens, and then on to Corinth. Returning home, they traveled by sea to Ephesus and then on to Caesarea. Then, after reporting to Jerusalem they returned to Paul's home base at Antioch. Paul wrote two epistles during this journey, both of them to the Thessalonians.

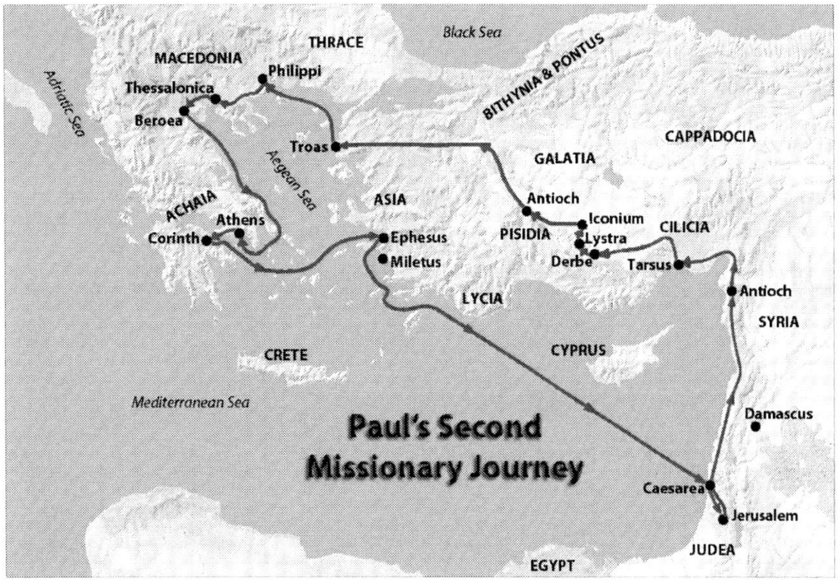

This journey included the following ministries:

GALATIA:	Derbe, Lystra, Iconium, Antioch (Pisidia)
ASIA:	Troas
MACEDONIA:	Philippi, Thessalonica, Beroea
ACHAIA:	Athens, Corinth
ASIA:	Ephesus

The associated chapters of this book, corresponding to Gospel Doctrine lessons, are:

31a. Paul's Second Mission (Acts 15–18).
31b. Paul's First Epistles (1&2 Thessalonians).

The Significance of Paul's Second Missionary Journey

This journey established a practice which was to continue throughout Paul's work as an Apostle: to "visit our brethren in every city where we have preached the word of the Lord, and see how they do." (Acts 15:36). On this journey they revisited some of the branches Paul had visited during his first missionary journey: Derbe, Lystra, Iconium, and Antioch. Paul did not always go in person to previously visited places on his missions; sometimes he sent Timothy or Titus or Silas.

During his second mission, Paul started the practice of following up his visits with letters of commendation or admonition. Paul wrote his first two epistles—1st and 2nd Thessalonians—from Corinth to the Saints at Thessalonica. This way of communicating with converts in branches he had previously visited became an important part of Paul's ministry and resulted in the many epistles of Paul that we enjoy today.

This was Paul's first entry into "Europe" as he traveled through the province of Macedonia while visiting Philippi, Thessalonica, and Beroea. As always, Paul preached to both Jews and Gentiles. Paul preached some of his most famous sermons at Athens, the capitol of Greek culture, including his famous sermon on the "Unknown God."

He and his companions were jailed at Philippi, but used the situation to convert a jailer and his family (Acts 16:16–40). They suffered other persecutions, having to flee Thessalonica, and being taken to court in Corinth. But as always, Paul demonstrated his perseverance in the face of difficulty and his absolute dedication to the cause of Christ. He was directed in his work by the Holy Ghost, receiving visions and instructions constantly. And as in his first mission, Paul demonstrated the power of God through miracles on several occasions (Acts 16:7–9, 26; 18:9).

The following is a chronological list of events that took place during this period and the scriptures from Acts and the Epistles that tell the story.

Date	Events	Scriptural References
PAUL'S SECOND MISSIONARY JOURNEY (49–53 AD)		
49	Judea:	
	Paul and Silas Become Companions.	Acts 15:36–41
	The Holy Ghost Directs Paul's Labors	Acts 16:1–15
	Thyatira, Asia:	
	An Evil Spirit Cast Out	Acts 16:16–18
	Philip, a Jailor, Receives Christ.	Acts 16:19–40
	Thessalonica. Macedonia:	
	Paul and Silas Flee Persecution	Acts 17:1–14
	Athens, Greece:	
	Paul Preaches the Unknown God.	Acts 17:15–34
51–52	Corinth, Greece:	
	Jews and Greeks Hear the Gospel	Acts 18:1–11
	The Jews Take Paul to Court	Acts 18:12–22
	1 Thessalonians written from Corinth.	1 Thessalonians
	2 Thessalonians written from Corinth.	2 Thessalonians
52	Jerusalem	
	Paul's fourth visit to Jerusalem	Acts 18:27–28
52–53	Antioch	
	Paul labors in Antioch	Acts 18:23

Paul's Second Missionary Journey

(Acts 15–18)

INTRODUCTION

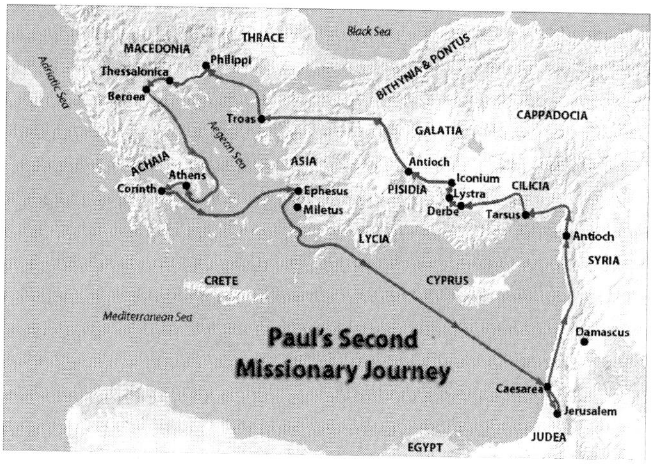

As mentioned in the introduction to this section of the book, Paul's second missionary journey lasted about four years, from 49–52 AD, during which time he traveled about 3000 miles round trip. His companion was Silas. They departed from Antioch in Syria, traveling through his home town of Tarsus on the way to cities in the provinces of Pisidia, Asia, Macedonia, and Achia. In the process, he would begin the practice of revisiting old converts, and of writing epistles to Saints in cities distant from his current location. In the coming year there would be moments of misunderstanding between the missionaries and moments of great triumph. They would be persecuted and imprisoned, but by miraculous means would be set free and continue their ministry. And as always, they would devote themselves entirely to the work.

Choosing a New Companion

- **Acts 15:36–41 Paul does not want Mark as a mission companion.** On his first mission journey, Mark had abandoned the work in Pisidia and returned home (Acts 13:13). His leaving produced some bitter feelings in Paul, which were now demonstrated. When Barnabas wanted again to "take with them John, whose surname was Mark" (v. 37), "Paul thought not good to take him with them, who departed from them from Pamphylia, and went not with them to the work" (v. 38).

- **Acts 15:38–41 Barnabas departs with Mark; Paul chooses Silas.** "The contention was so sharp between them [Barnabas and Paul], that they departed asunder one from the other" (v. 39). "Barnabas took Mark, and

F. HALS, 1625-30

A painting of John Mark author of the Gospel of Mark

sailed unto Cyprus; and Paul chose Silas, and departed" (vv. 39–40). Silas had, together with Paul and others, previously delivered to Antioch the decision of the Jerusalem Council (Acts 15:1–35). He is probably Silvanus, whom Paul mentions in three of his letters (2 Cor. 1:19; 1 Thessalonians 1:1; 2 Thessalonians 1:1). He was prominent among leaders of the church at Jerusalem, and was, himself, a prophet who preached the gospel (Acts 15:32).

President David O. McKay said:

> We know that later, this circumstance became a matter of sharp dispute between Barnabas and Paul, but just why John [Mark] wished to return we are not informed. Perhaps he had not intended to travel so far; or it may be that matters at home needed his attention; or he might have been over sensitive, and felt that "two were company but three were a crowd;" but whatever the cause Paul and Barnabas had to continue their journey without the young man Mark. Later, he resumed his missionary work traveling with Barnabas. There is no record of his traveling again with Paul; although the latter wrote of him later as 'a comfort, and a fellow worker unto the kingdom of God.'[1]

Elder Bruce R. McConkie said:

> Even Apostles and prophets, being mortal and subject to like passions as other men, have prejudices which sometimes are reflected in ministerial assignments and decisions. But the marvel is not the isolated disagreements on details, but the near universal unity on basic principles; not the occasional personality conflicts, but the common acceptance, for the good of the work, of the faults of others. It is not the conflict between Paul and Barnabas which concerns us, but the fact that they (being even as we are) rose thereafter to spiritual heights where they saw visions, received revelations, and made their callings and elections sure—the fact of their disagreement thus bearing witness that we in our weaknesses can also press forward to that unity and perfection which shall assure us of salvation."[2]

THE MISSION TO GALATIA

Lystra

- **The Journey to Lystra:** Traveling through Paul's hometown of Tarsus, the missionaries proceeded westward to Derbe, where Paul had preached during his first mission. From there, they traveled northwest to Lystra, where on his earlier mission Paul had been thrown out of the city, stoned, and left for dead. Nevertheless, there were faithful Saints in Lystra whom Paul wished to visit.

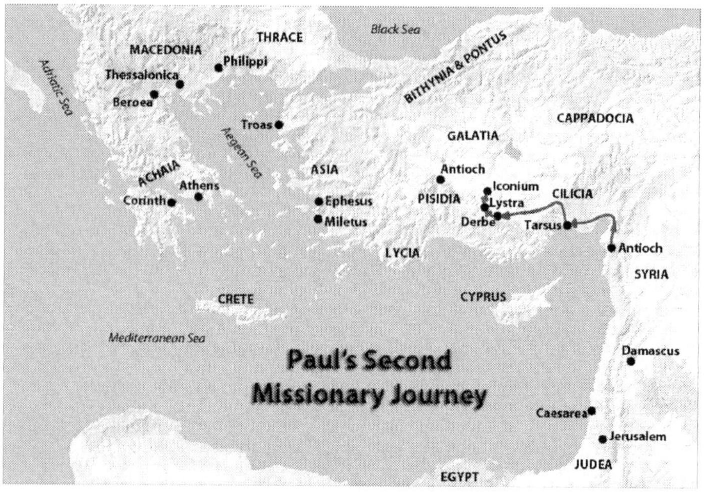

- **Acts 16:1–5 Paul chooses Timothy.** Timothy and his family were among the very choice souls at Lystra who had been converted during Paul's first mission. When Paul arrived this time, Timothy was "well reported of by the brethren that were at Lystra and Iconium" (v. 2). Paul invited him to join them on this missionary journey. Paul would later refer to Timothy as his "son in the faith" (1 Tim. 1:2), and Timothy would eventually serve as a righteous and effective bishop.

  Timothy's mother was Jewish and his father a Gentile (vv. 1–3). Though Paul had vigorously opposed circumcision at the Jerusalem conference, and the authorities had decreed that Gentiles did not need to be circumcised, Paul chose to circumcise Timothy, so as not to alienate the Jews.

THEBIBLEREVIVAL.COM, #30

Paul called Timothy "my son in the faith"

- **Acts 16:4–5 Preaching, teaching, and baptizing.** As Paul and his companions traveled through the cities of Derbe, Lystra, and Iconium, "they delivered [to] them the decrees [on requirements for Gentile converts] . . . that were ordained of the apostles and elders which were at Jerusalem" (v. 4). These faithful branches were "established in the faith, and increased in number daily" (v. 5).

THE MISSION TO MACEDONIA

Philippi

- **Acts 16:6–12 Paul is directed by revelation to Philippi:** Paul and his companions traveled on through Galatia, visiting Iconium and Antioch of Pisidia. Paul then wanted to go into the province of Asia (western Turkey on modern maps) but was forbidden by the Spirit (v. 6). They continued northwest-ward through the region of Mysia, where Paul wanted to go north into Bithynia but was forbidden by the Spirit (v. 7). So, they traveled west to the city of Troas on the coast of the Aegean Sea (v. 8). There, Paul

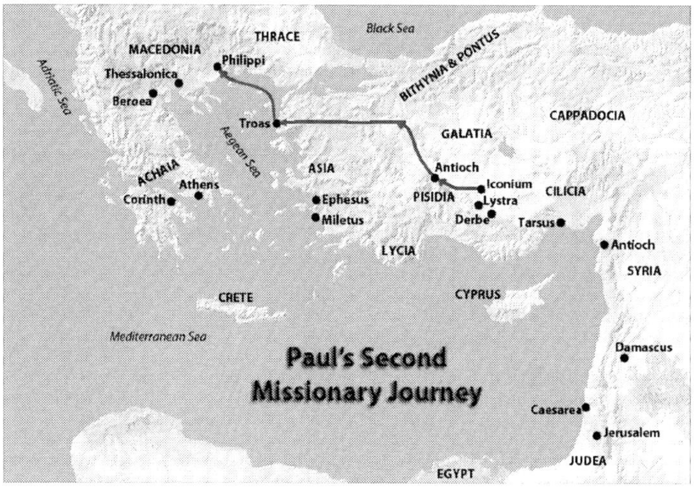

received a vision of a man of Macedonia, who stood before him and said, "Come over into Macedonia, and help us" (vv. 9–10). Macedonia, north of Greece, is part of what we today call continental Europe. This would be Paul's first visit to that continent.

While at Troas, they are joined by Luke, author of the book of Acts. Immediately obedient to the vision, Paul and his companions sailed northwest 150 miles to Neapolis, then walked the few more miles inland to Philippi (vv. 11–12).

Elder Thomas S. Monson recounted how, in our own time, the president of the Quorum of the Twelve changed his stake visiting assignment to a place where a dying little girl had prayed for him to come and give her a priesthood blessing. Neither the president of the Quorum of the Twelve nor Elder Monson knew about the young girl's prayer before the change was made.[3]

- **Acts 16:13–15 Lydia becomes the first convert in Europe.** The Israelites, like other societies in the ancient Near East, prized colored dyes—especially blue, scarlet, and purple. As with other things that are rare, such as gold and diamonds, these dyes were treasured because of the limited quantity that was available. Purple was extracted by the Phoenicians (Tyre and Sidon) from Murex snails, which thrive along the Mediterranean coast there and were used in textile dyeing. Lydia was a relatively prosperous woman who sold purple dye in Philippi.

On the Sabbath day, Paul and his companions "went out of the city by a river side, where prayer[s were] made," and sat down next to "the women which resorted thither" (v. 13). One of these women on this day was "Lydia, a seller of purple, of the city of Thyatira, which worshipped God" (v. 14). The Lord opened her heart and she, "attended unto the things which were spoken of Paul" (v. 14). She was baptized along with her entire household, and then "constrained" Paul and his companions to "come into my house, and abide there" (v. 15). Her faithfulness led Paul to call her a "yokefellow" in his epistle to the Philippians (4:3).

PROVIDENCE LITHOGRPAHIC CO., 1901, #34

- **Acts 16:16–18 In Philippi the missionaries encounter a spirit of divination, soothsaying, and sorcery.** This was very similar to the use today of horoscopes, palm-reading, crystal balls, curses, charms, Ouija boards, seances, etc. Soothsaying, or the practice of divination, was an ancient deceptive art (Isaiah 2:6; Daniel 2:27; 5:11), and was forbidden to the Lord's people (Deut. 18:9–14; Joshua 13:22). As Paul and his companions "went to prayer, a certain damsel possessed with a spirit of divination met us," who made money for her "masters" by soothsaying (v. 16).

This woman followed after Paul and his companions for many days, crying, "These men are the servants of the most high God, which shew unto us the way of salvation" (vv. 17–18). This testimony came from an evil spirit that had taken control of her body and actions. Then finally, Paul "being grieved, turned and said to the spirit, I command thee in the name of Jesus Christ to come out of her. And he came out the same hour" (v. 18).

We learn two important lessons from this incident. The first is that evil spirits are very real, and do in fact possess the bodies of some on this earth. We observed this in the ministry of the Savior, and see it again in this event among the Gentiles in Macedonia. I also have personally witnessed people possessed with such spirits, and have used Priesthood ordinances to cast these spirits away. One such incident involved my niece, who was rendered completely immobile and unable to speak except in unintelligible mumblings. After being set free of this influence, she immediately returned to normal functioning.

The second lesson we learn from this incident is that the use of divination of any kind simply invites such spirits into our lives and grants them permission to possess us. We must remember that Satan and his followers, being eternally denied the opportunity to have bodies of their own, vowed to seek to possess the bodies of others. We must, at all costs, avoid dabbling with horoscopes, palm-reading, crystal balls, Ouija boards, seances, witchcraft, and late-night scary stories of evil spirits. These are not harmless fun. They are invitations to be possessed.

- **Acts 16:19–28 Paul and his companions are beaten and imprisoned.** Those who had profited from this woman's activities were angry. They "caught Paul and Silas, and drew them into the marketplace unto the rulers, and brought them to the magistrates, saying, These men, being Jews, do exceedingly trouble our city" (vv. 19–20). They accused Paul and Silas of "teach[ing] customs, which are not lawful for us to receive, neither to observe, being Romans" (v. 21).

  Customs—the traditions of generations before—are cultural practices that people hold dear and defend at all costs. How dare these foreigners preach anything that disturbs our practices and beliefs? The crown grew angry, and the "magistrates rent off their clothes, and commanded to beat them" (v. 22). Then, "when they had laid many stripes upon them, they cast them into prison, charging the jailor to keep them safely" (v. 23). They were "thrust . . . into the inner prison, and . . . their feet [made] fast in the stocks" (v. 24).

  Though things looked dismal, Paul and Silas trusted the Lord to deliver them. They loudly "prayed, and sang praises unto God" (v. 25). Then suddenly, "there was a great earthquake, so that the foundations of the prison were shaken: and immediately all the doors were opened, and every one's bands were loosed" (v. 26).

  For the jailer, this was a catastrophe. With all of the prisoners set free, he would certainly be executed because, under Roman law, if prisoners escape, jailers were put to death. "He drew out his sword, and would have killed himself, supposing that the prisoners had been fled" (v. 27). But Paul "cried with a loud voice, saying, Do thyself no harm: for we are all here" (v. 28). Seizing the opportunity to teach, Paul and Silas did not flee.

- **Acts 16:29–36 The jailer and his family are converted.** Thankful for their charity, the jailer "called for a light, and sprang in, and came trembling, and fell down before Paul and Silas" (v. 29). He had witnessed the miracle of the earthquake and the loosening of their bands. He was convinced that they were servants of God, and asked them, "Sirs, what must I do to be saved?" (v. 30). And they said unto him, "Believe on the Lord Jesus Christ, and thou shalt be saved, and thy house" (v. 31).

PROVIDENCE LITHOGRAPHIC CO., 1902, #41

The jailer took them to his home and treated their wounds (v. 33). And there the missionaries taught and baptized the jailer and his entire family (vv. 32–33). The following day, word came from the magistrates to set Paul and Silas free, and he did so with a blessing: "depart, and go in peace" (vv. 35–36).

Some Christians use this instance to claim that belief on the Lord Jesus Christ is all that is necessary for salvation. But to do so would require that we read only the words of Paul and Silas at the jail, and to ignore what happened thereafter. The jailer was first taught and then baptized.

Elder Bruce R. McConkie said, "Belief alone is scarcely the beginning of that course leading to a celestial inheritance if it is isolated as a thing apart, if it is supposed that it does not embrace within its folds both baptism and a subsequent course of enduring to the end. (2 Ne. 31:15–21). And in the very case at hand, Paul and Silas teach the gospel to the whole group, baptize them, and without question give them the gift of the Holy Ghost, thus starting them out in the direction of salvation."[4]

- **Acts 16:37–40 In beating Paul, they had mistreated a Roman citizen.** This was forbidden under Roman law. So, upon hearing that their prisoners were Roman citizens, city officials attempted to reverse their injustice privately. That is why they sent word to the jailer to set them free. "But Paul said unto them, They have beaten us openly uncondemned, being Romans, and have cast us into prison; and now do they thrust us out privily? nay verily; but let them come themselves and fetch us out" (v. 37). When the magistrates heard this, they were quite afraid, but "they came and besought them, and brought them out, and desired them to depart out of the city" (vv. 38–39). Paul and Silas returned to the home of Lydia, "and when they had seen the brethren, they comforted them, and departed" (v. 40).

Thessalonica

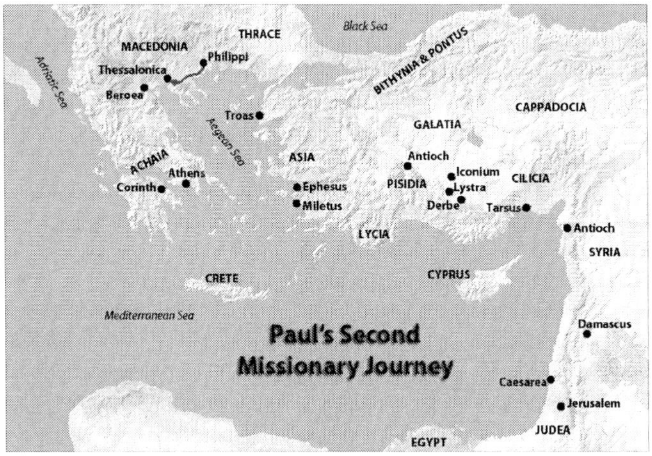

- **The Journey to Thessalonica:** The missionaries traveled southwest along the coast to Amphipolis, then west across the peninsula to Thessalonica, a journey of about 80 miles. Thessalonica was a city named after the sister of Alexander the Great, who was born near there.

- **Acts 17:1–4 Paul, "as his manner was," went into the synagogue of the Jews to teach.** For "three sabbath days [he] reasoned with them out of the scriptures, opening and alleging, that Christ must needs have suffered, and risen again from the dead; and that this Jesus, whom I preach unto you, is Christ" (vv. 1–3). In this case, "alleging" means to bring forth evidence or to present proof. Paul was an expert on the scriptures, having been taught at the feet of Gamaliel and serving as a member of the Sanhedrin before his conversion. This made him uniquely qualified to teach the Jews throughout the Roman empire.

  As a result of his preaching at Thessalonica, "some of them believed, and consorted [associated themselves] with Paul and Silas" (v. 4). Among these were not only Jews but "a great multitude" of "devout Greeks" and quite a few of the "chief women" of the city (v. 4).

DORE 1896

- **Acts 17:5–9 Jewish antagonists assault the home of Jason.** While in Thessalonica, Paul stayed at the home of Jason, an apparent relative of Paul (Romans 16:21) who later served in a leadership capacity in the Thessalonian Branch of the Church. After observing how many had believed Paul's words, some envious Jews, along with "certain lewd fellows of the baser sort . . . assaulted the house of Jason, . . . set[ting] all the city on an uproar, and . . . [seeking] to bring them out to the people" (v. 5). However, Paul and Silas were not there at the time, so "they drew Jason and certain brethren unto the rulers of the city, crying, These that have turned the world upside down are come hither . . . whom Jason hath received" (vv. 6–7).

The charge was that they "do contrary to the decrees of Cæsar, saying that there is another king, one Jesus" (v. 7). This accusation "troubled the people and the rulers of the city" (v. 8). But they could not beat or imprison a Roman citizen, so "when they had taken security of Jason, and of the other[s], they let them go" (v. 9).

Beroea

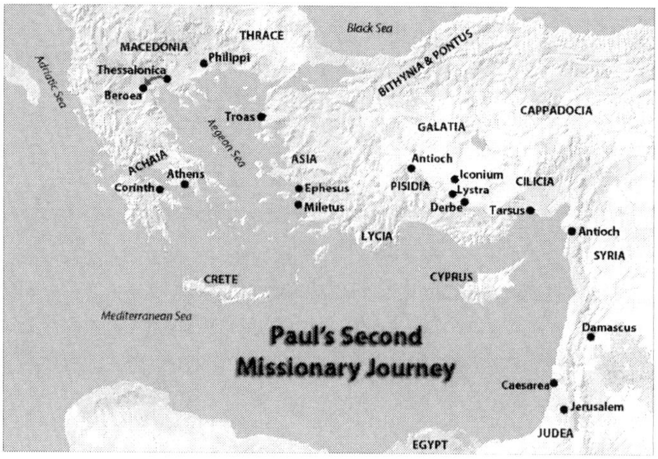

- **Acts 17:10–12 Paul and Silas are sent by the brethren to Beroea,** 50 miles southwest of Thessalonica (v. 10). And there, Paul and Silas "went into the synagogue of the Jews" (v. 10).

  These Jews "were more noble than those in Thessalonica, in that they received the word with all readiness of mind, and searched the scriptures daily, whether those things were so" (v. 11). And as a result, "many of them believed," including "honourable women which were Greeks, and of men, not a few" (v. 12).

- **Acts 17:13 Enemies from Thessalonica stir up trouble.** Not content to have expelled them from their own city, these "Jews of Thessalonica had knowledge that the word of God was preached of Paul at Berea," and "they came . . . and stirred up the people."

THE MISSION TO ACHAIA

Athens

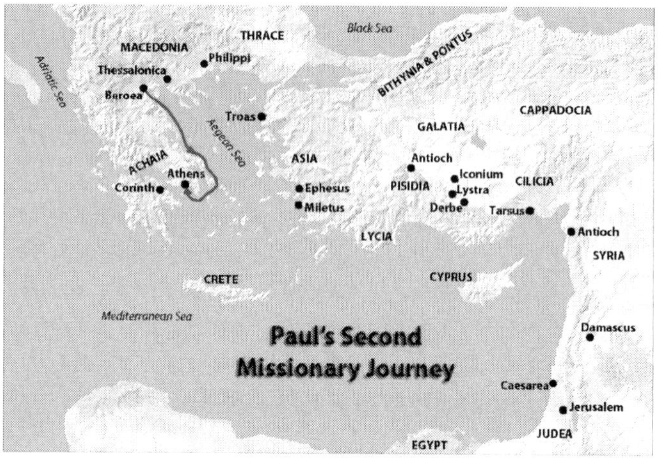

- **Acts 17:14–15 Paul sails alone to Athens.** To escape the mob at Beroea, Paul was forced to set sail immediately for Athens, while Timothy and Silas remained behind (v. 14). After a journey of 250 miles, Paul arrived at Athens, in the province of Achaia.

  Athens was a major center of world culture. Greek, the language of Athens, was the international language of the learned. Its philosophers viewed God as an abstract being or power, rather than as a literal Father of spirits. They worshiped God's creations rather than God Himself. And they replaced revelation with reason and debate, valuing the wisdom of men more than of God.

These are the Greek philosophies that eventually overtook the ancient Church. Most of these beliefs became the official doctrine of the fallen Church, decreed by councils of men who received no revelation and used reason to decide matters of doctrine. The connection to the Roman empire made them secure, and the adoption of Greek ideas made them popular. Thus the "whore of all the earth" overcame the Church and apostasy ensued.[5]

Nevertheless, as a place steeped in reason and open to public debate, Athens provided a setting where the gospel might be effectively preached, and Paul saw the opportunity. He sent for his companions to come "with all speed" to join him in Athens (v. 15).

- **Acts 17:16–18 Paul sails alone to Athens.** While Paul waited for his companions to arrive, "his spirit was stirred in him" (v. 16). He saw before him a "city wholly given to idolatry" (v. 16). He "disputed . . . in the synagogue with the Jews, . . . with the devout persons, and in the market daily with them that met with him" (v. 17). This "market" was the famed Agora, or Marketplace, where the chief men of the city gathered daily to hear debates and do business.

Greek philosophers did little else but debate

Those that gathered in the marketplace had primarily two philosophies:

— The Epicureans:

  - Believed the creation happened by accident.
  - Believed happiness (pleasure) is the goal of life.
  - Believed sorrow and pain are to be avoided.

— The Stoics:

  - Recognized a supreme governor of the universe.
  - Believed man is in a constant battle with nature.
  - Believed the body is vile and should be ignored.

When philosophers of these two schools encountered Paul, "some said, What will this babbler say?" (v. 18). "Babbler" is a Greek slang word that means "one who picks up scraps of information here and there." Essentially, they were accusing Paul of being unintellectual. Others said, "He seemeth to be a setter forth of strange gods: because he preached unto them Jesus, and the resurrection" (v. 18).

To the Gentiles, anyone who was crucified was considered a loser and not to be respected.[6] Jews also believed that if Jesus had been a prophet, God would not have suffered such an indignity to come to Him (Deut. 21:22–23). Furthermore, since Epicureans believed that sorrow and pain are to be avoided, He should never have permitted Himself to be crucified. And for Stoics, resurrection was not a good thing. They believed the body is vile and when the spirit is set free from it, it is better off.

- **Acts 17:19–21 Paul on Mars' Hill.** Greek philosophers "spent their time in nothing else" but philosophizing (v. 21). Thus, hearing Paul's new philosophy, as crazy as it sounded, was of great interest to them. They "took him, and brought him unto Areopagus" (v. 19). Areopagus (Ar-ee-AH-pagus) is Greek for "Hill of Ares," who was also known as Mars, the god of war. The council that met there was the highest court in Athens.

  The Greeks demanded to "know what this new doctrine, whereof thou speakest, is? For thou bringest certain strange things to our ears: we would know therefore what these things mean" (vv. 19–20).

"PAUL AT ATHENS," COLLER, PROVIDENCE LITHOGRAPHIC CO., 1901

- **Acts 17:22–23 Paul's sermon on the "unknown God."** Seizing the opportunity to teach in the most famous forum in all of Greek culture, "Paul stood in the midst of Mars' hill, and said, Ye men of Athens, I perceive that in all things ye are too superstitious" (v. 22). This does not seem to be a great way to start, insulting them. But actually the word "superstitious" in this instance should have been translated "very religious." It was a complement. And Paul was preparing them to hear the truth.

  Paul continued, "For as I passed by, and beheld your devotions [acts of worship], I found an altar with this inscription, TO THE UNKNOWN GOD. Whom therefore ye ignorantly worship, him declare I unto you" (v. 23). This was brilliant. They had built an altar to the "unknown god" just in case they had missed one of them unintentionally. Paul was therefore asking them to worship one of their own gods whom they did not know.

- **Acts 17:24–25 Paul teaches of the nature of God.** This God, Paul said, "made the world and all things therein," and so, since He is "Lord of heaven and earth, [He] dwelleth not in temples made with hands" (v. 24). Neither is He "worshipped with men's hands," because He needs nothing from us. In fact, "he giveth to all life, and breath, and all things" (v. 25). This is step one toward conversion—to know the nature of God and our relationship with Him.

Acts 17:28 Paul was familiar with one of the Greek's favorite poets. Here we see the value of Paul's extensive & classic education. He was well-read & familiar with philosophies of his day. He could converse well

- **Acts 17:26 Paul teaches of a prem[...]** [...] of one blood all nations of men for to dwell o[...] [...]ed the times before appointed, and the bo[...] concerning the premortal life—the "tim[...] earth and determined what nations woul[...] what Moses taught when he spoke of how [...], when he separated the sons of Adam," and [...] the number of the children of Israel." (Deut. [...]

  Elder Joseph Fielding Smith said, "If the Lord [...] their habitations, then there must have been [...] nations."[7]

- **Acts 17:27–28 Paul teaches that we are the [...]** [...] Paul invited the Athenians to "seek the Lord, . . . [and] haply . . . fe[...] him, and find him, though he be not far from every one of us (v. 27). "For in him we live, and move, and have our being; as certain also of your own poets have said, For we are also his offspring" (v. 28). Paul was quoting one of the Greeks' favorite poets, Aratus, who said: "Always we all have need of Zeus. For we are also his offspring."[8] Here we see the value of Paul's extensive and classic education. He was well-read and familiar with all the philosophies of his day—a man who could converse with the Gentiles in their own language and according to their own culture and beliefs.

  President Harold B. Lee said, "May I ask each of you again the question, 'Who are you?' You are all the sons and daughters of God. Your spirits were created and lived as organized intelligences before the world was. You have been blessed to have a physical body because of your obedience to certain commandments in that premortal state. You are now born into a family to which you have come, into the nations through which you have come, as a reward for the kind of lives you lived before you came here and at a time in the world's history, as the Apostle Paul taught the men of Athens and as the Lord revealed to Moses, determined by the faithfulness of each of those who lived before this world was created."[9]

- **Acts 17:29–30 Paul warns against idolatry: God will no longer "overlook" it.** Paul reasoned that since "we are the offspring of God, we ought not to think that the Godhead is like unto gold, or silver, or stone, graven by art and man's device" (v. 29). In times past, God had "winked at" mankind's worship of idols because of their ignorance, "but now command[s] all men every where to repent" (v. 30).

- **Acts 17:31 Jesus of Nazareth will judge all men on the judgment day.** Paul assured the Athenians that God "hath appointed a day, in the which he will judge the world," and that judgment will be done "in righteousness by that man whom he hath ordained" [meaning Jesus Christ]. And to give assurance to all men that this is so, God "hath raised him from the dead."

- **Acts 17:32–34 Some Athenians think that Paul is out of his mind.** Having preached that a carpenter from Judaea was God and that the human body would be resurrected to live forever, some of those present "mocked: and others said, We will hear thee again of this matter" (v. 32). Having delivered his message, "Paul departed from among them" (v. 33). Most would reject his teachings, but "certain men clave unto him, and believed," including "Dionysius the Areopagite, and a woman named Damaris, and others with them" (v. 34). "Dionysius . . . was the first convert after Paul's address to the Athenians [on Mars Hill], and he became the first bishop of Athens."[10]

Corinth

- **The Journey to Corinth:** The missionaries departed Athens and traveled westward about 50 miles to Corinth, the capital of the Roman province of Achaia, and its most important commercial center.

  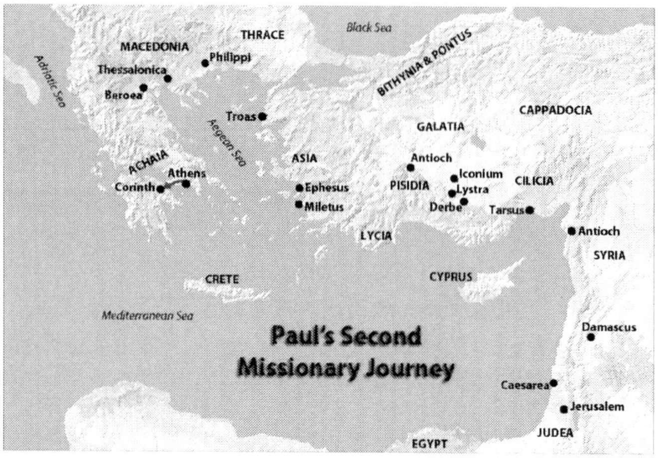

  There were approximately 20,000 Jews living in Corinth at the time of Paul. And they lived in the middle of one of the richest and most immoral cities in the world.

  The temple of Aphrodite, located on Acrocorinth (the high hill overlooking the city) had more than 1,000 ritual prostitutes who participated in immoral practices that were supposedly an act of worship for Aphrodite. As a result, the word "Corinth" became synonymous in that day with "fornication." Realizing this, Paul said he went to Corinth "in weakness, and in fear, and in much trembling" (1 Cor. 2:3).

- **Acts 18:1–4 Paul takes residence with a Jew named Aquila.** This man was "a certain Jew named Aquila, born in Pontus, lately come from Italy, with his wife Priscilla; (because that Claudius had commanded all Jews to depart from Rome)" (v. 2). The man was a tentmaker, and because Paul was of the same craft, they related well and he invited Paul to abide in his home (v. 3). Paul remained there for a while, "reason[ing] in the synagogue every sabbath, and persuad[ing] the Jews and the Greeks" (v. 4).

- **Acts 18:5–6 The Jews reject Paul's message.** After Silas and Timothy arrived from Beroea, Paul felt "pressed in the spirit, and testified [strongly] to the Jews that Jesus was Christ" (v. 5). His testimony was rejected, and when the Jews "opposed themselves, and blasphemed, he shook his raiment, and said unto them, Your blood be upon your own heads; I am clean: from henceforth I will go unto the Gentiles" (v. 6). This also meant that Paul had to find another place to reside.

- **Acts 18:7–8 Crispus, the chief ruler of the synagogue, believes.** Paul had taken up residence with Justus, a man "that worshipped God, whose house joined hard to the synagogue" (v. 7). And while living and teaching there, "Crispus, the chief ruler of the synagogue, believed on the Lord with all his house" (v. 8). As a result, "many of the Corinthians hearing believed, and were baptized" (v. 8).

G. FOXLEY, PROVIDENCE LITHOGRAPHIC CO., 1901

- **Acts 18:9–10 Paul receives a reassuring vision of Christ.** "The Lord [spoke] to Paul in the night by a vision, [saying] Be not afraid, but speak, and hold not thy peace: For I am with thee, and no man shall set on thee to hurt thee: for I have much people in this city" (vv. 9–10).

- **Acts 18:11 Paul remains in Corinth for one and a half years.** Encouraged by the Lord's visit, Paul decided to stay put and seek out the "much people" the Lord said were ready for his message in the city. "And he continued there a year and six months, teaching the word of God among them."

At this Point, Paul Wrote 1 & 2 Thessalonians from Corinth, AD 52–53

(These epistles are discussed in the following chapter.)

- **Why Paul wrote his epistles.** During his second mission, Paul began a practice that eventually produced all the epistles we have from him in the New Testament. After visiting a city, Paul was seldom able to return there, due to extreme distances and time. So, it became his practice to follow up such visits with letters of commendation or admonition —a method Paul used throughout the rest of his life. To deliver these epistles, Paul usually sent Timothy, Titus or Silas.

REMBRANDT

- **Acts 18:12–17 Gallio "cares not" about Jewish disputes.** Always agitating against Paul and his message, Jews who opposed him "made insurrection with one accord against Paul" and brought him to "the judgment seat" of "Gallio . . . the [Roman] deputy of Achaia" (v. 12). They accused Paul of "persuad[ing[men to worship God contrary to the law" (v. 13).

  THEBIBLEREVIEW.COM, #21

  Before Paul could even open his mouth in his own defense, Gallio said to the accusing Jews, "If it were a matter of wrong or wicked lewdness, O ye Jews, reason would that I should bear with you: But if it be a question of words and names, and of your law, look ye to it; for I will be no judge of such matters. And he drave them from the judgment seat" (vv. 14–16).

  Thus permitted to do whatever they wanted, "all the Greeks took Sosthenes, the chief ruler of the synagogue, and beat him before the judgment seat. And Gallio cared for none of those things" (v. 17).

- **Acts 18:18 Paul remains at Corinth "a good while" and then departs.** When it was time to leave, he sailed toward Syria, his home. He took with him Priscilla and Aquila, but "took . . . leave of the brethren" as he had done earlier when he came to Athens.

- **Acts 18:18 Paul's Nazarite vow.** Before leaving Corinth, Paul cut his hair as part of a Nazarite covenant with God. A Nazarite was a man or woman who took a voluntary vow to separate his life for the service of the Lord, or to live consecrated unto Him.[11] His life and all his efforts were completely and expressly dedicated to the Lord. In some cases, these Nazarite vows were for life, but more often they were for a specific period of time, after which the person returned to a normal life. This was apparently the case with Paul.

  A Nazarite always initiated such a vow by shaving his head, and thereafter, under this vow, three things were regulated: diet, appearance, and associations. This may seem odd today, but not if we consider that our missionaries today do these same things during the time that they serve.

  Other Biblical figures who seem to have taken such vows, or had parents who made the vows for them, include Samson (Judges 13:5), Samuel (1 Samuel 1:11, 28), and John the Baptist (Luke 1:15). Besides this one, Paul was involved in another instance of Nazarite vow-taking later in his ministry at Jerusalem (Acts 21:23–26).

A BRIEF MISSION TO ASIA

Ephesus

- **The Journey to Ephesus:** On their way home, Paul and his companions sailed out from the eastern port of Corinth and across the Aegean Sea to Ephesus.

  Paul had wanted to preach in this city when they were in Galatia, but had been redirected by the Spirit to Philippi instead. Now he had a brief opportunity to preach to the people of Asia.

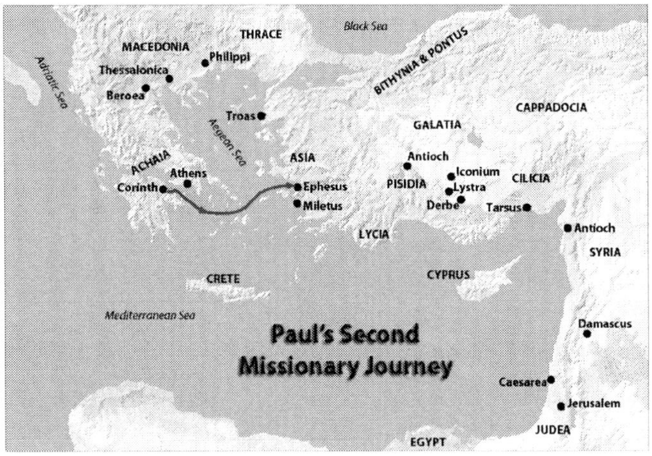

- **Acts 18:19–21 Paul teaches in the synagogue at Ephesus.** He left his female companions for a time and "entered into the synagogue, and reasoned with the Jews" (vv. 19–20).

  They were receptive and "desired him to tarry longer time with them, [but] he consented not" (v. 20). He "bade them farewell, saying, I must by all means keep this feast that cometh in Jerusalem: but I will return again unto you, if God will" (v. 21).

- **Acts 18:22 Paul returns to Jerusalem and finally to Antioch of Syria.** They "sailed from Ephesus" and "landed at Cæsarea." From there he went up "and saluted [visited] the church [at Jerusalem], reporting on his four-year mission.

  Then finally, "he went down to Antioch," his home. He would not be there long. Almost immediately he began his third missionary journey.

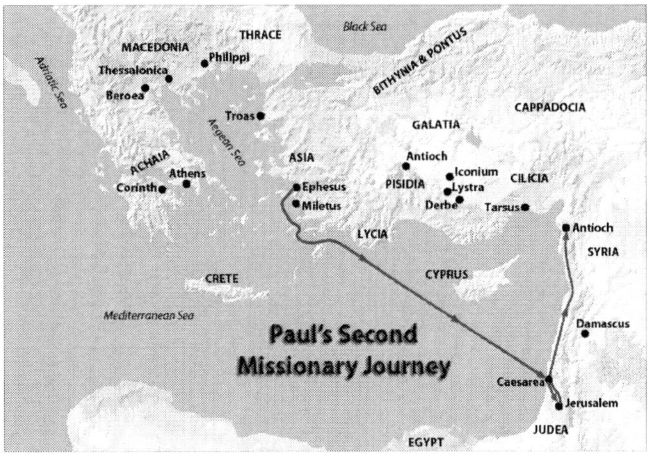

Notes:

1. *Ancient Apostles* [1964], Lesson 26, First Missionary Journey—at Paphos.
2. *Doctrinal New Testament Commentary*, 3 vols. [1966–1973], 2:145.
3. *Ensign*, November 1975, 20–22.
4. *Doctrinal New Testament Commentary*, 2:152.
5. See Tad Callister, *The Inevitable Apostasy* for what I consider to be the best summary of the apostasy available in print today.
6. See Dana M. Pike, "Before the Jewish Authorities," Chapter 7 in *The Life and Teachings of Jesus Christ*, 3 vols. [2003], 3:264, footnote 132.
7. *The Way to Perfection* [1949], 47.
8. Aratus, "Hymn to Zeus."
9. In Conference Report, October 1973, 7; or *Ensign*, January 1974, 5.
10. Eusebius, *History of the Church*, 67.
11. Keil and Delitzsch, Commentary, 1:3:34.

Chapter 31b

Paul's First Epistles

(1 & 2 Thessalonians)

INTRODUCTION TO PAUL'S EPISTLES

Why Paul Wrote His Epistles

During his second mission, Paul began a practice that eventually produced all the epistles we have from him in the New Testament. After visiting a city, Paul was seldom able to return there, due to extreme distances and time. So, it became his practice to follow up such visits with letters of commendation or admonition—a method Paul used throughout the rest of his life. To deliver these epistles, Paul usually sent Timothy, Titus or Silas.

When Paul Wrote His Epistles

REMBRANDT

The epistles do not appear in the Bible in chronological order, but we have a general idea when most of them were written. Most of them were written during Paul's second and third missionary journeys, from 50–60 AD. Some of the others were written during his two imprisonments at Rome, between 61–68 AD. Others may have been written toward the end of the first century, and one book, Hebrews, offers no clues to its dating, making it difficult to tell when the letter was written.

The epistles of Paul are arranged in our New Testament according to their length and their doctrinal significance. Thus, Romans, the longest, comes first; Philemon, the shortest, comes last. The book of Hebrews was placed after the others because the compilers of the New Testament questioned whether Paul wrote it. The following chart lists the epistles in their order within the Bible.[1]

EPISTLE	# OF VERSES	% OF EPISTLES
Romans	433	15.6%
1 Corinthians	437	15.8%
2 Corinthians	257	9.2%
Galatians	149	5.4%
Ephesians	155	5.6%

EPISTLE	# OF VERSES	% OF EPISTLES
Philippians	104	3.8%
Colossians	95	3.4%
1 Thessalonians	89	3.2%
2 Thessalonians	47	1.7%
1 Timothy	113	4.1%
2 Timothy	83	3.0%
Titus	46	1.7%
Philemon	25	.9%
Hebrews	303	11.0%
James	108	3.9%
1 Peter	105	3.8%
2 Peter	61	2.2%
1 John	105	3.8%
2 John	13	.5%
3 John	14	.5%
Jude	25	.9%
Total	2,767	100%

The following chart represents this author's best estimation as to the dates when the epistles were written. The justification for these dates is provided in the chapters of this book that contain them. The first section of the chart lists Paul's epistles in chronological order, and the second section lists the other epistles in that same order. It is interesting to note that the epistle written by James, the brother of the Lord, may have been the first ever written, and that his brother Jude's epistle was one of the last.

EPISTLE	WRITTEN FROM	DATE WRITTEN
1 Thessalonians	Corinth	52–53 AD
2 Thessalonians	Corinth	52–53 AD
1 Corinthians	Ephesus	57 AD
2 Corinthians	Macedonia	57 AD
Romans	Corinth	57–58 AD
Galatians	Corinth	58 AD
Ephesians	Rome	61–62 AD
Colossians	Rome	61–62 AD
Philemon	Rome	61–62 AD
Philippians	Rome	62 AD
Hebrews[2]	Rome	65 AD
1 Timothy	Macedonia	66 AD
Titus	Macedonia	67–68 AD
2 Timothy	Rome	67–68 AD
James	Jerusalem	50–51 AD
1 Peter	Rome	62–64 AD
2 Peter	Rome	68 AD
Jude	Unknown	80 AD
1 John	Ephesus	96 AD
2 John	Ephesus	96 AD
3 John	Ephesus	96 AD

THE EPISTLES TO THESSALONICA

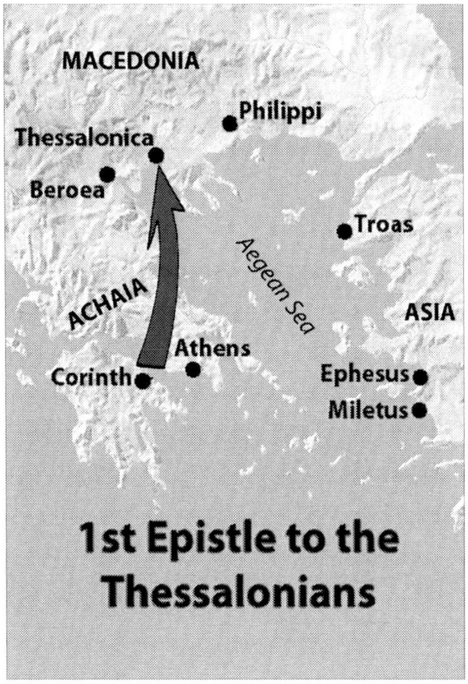

We know from information in the previous chapter that Paul visited Thessalonica early in his second missionary journey and taught them for 3 weeks. He and his companions were driven from Thessalonica by Jews who rejected their message of Christ's atonement and resurrection. Nevertheless, the gospel did take root there among some Jews and Gentiles.

Knowing of the constant persecution of members in Thessalonica, and being unable to go himself, Paul sent Timothy and Silas to check on the Saints there (1 Thessalonians 3:2; Acts 17:15; 18:5). When they returned, they brought a favorable report (1 Thessalonians 3:6). Paul therefore determined to write to them and commend them for their faithfulness, as well as to warn them against spiritual dangers.

First and Second Thessalonians are the first two (chronologically) of Paul's surviving epistles. These letters were, as nearly as can be determined, written from Corinth several months after Paul had left Macedonia, probably near the close of 52 or the beginning of 53 AD.

1 THESSALONIANS

The main theme of 1st Thessalonians is the Second Coming of Christ, about which the Saints at Thessalonica had several questions. Paul addressed those questions, but also wrote about several other important themes. We will explore these themes by topic rather than with a verse-by-verse approach, because Paul's comments on each of these topics run throughout these two epistles.

Paul's Affection for the Saints of Thessalonica

- **1 Thessalonians 1:1 Paul's typical introduction.** Paul's introductions to each of his epistles are all quite similar. They mention God the Father and (separately) His Son Jesus Christ. In this one he included greetings from Silas and Timothy who were with him at Corinth when he wrote this epistle.

- **1 Thessalonians 1:2–4 Setting a positive tone.** Paul set the tone for this epistle by offering praise for the faithfulness of the Thessalonians, despite significant affliction. He assured them that they were in his prayers (v. 2) and called them the "elect of God" (v. 4).

- **1 Thessalonians 1:5 Paul reminds them of how they received the gospel from him.** Paul and his companions did more than merely preach the word unto them. They did so "in power, and in the Holy Ghost, and in much assurance; as ye know what manner of men we were among you for your sake."

Paul preaching to the Thessalonians

- **1 Thessalonians 1:6–9 Their conversion unto Christ.** They became disciples of Christ "in much affliction, [but] with joy of the Holy Ghost" (v. 6). They were excellent examples "to all that believe in Macedonia and Achaia" (v. 7). Word of their faithfulness had spread not only to these places, but also to "every place your faith [in] God [has] spread abroad," making it unnecessary for Paul "to speak any thing" about it to others (v. 8). People in other places would tell them about the Saints at Thessalonica "and how ye turned to God from idols to serve[d] the living and true God" (v. 9).

- **1 Thessalonians 2:1–10 Paul summarizes how the missionaries taught them.** Though they had "suffered before, and were shamefully [treated], as ye know, at Philippi, we were bold . . . to speak unto you the gospel of God with much contention" (v. 2). "With much contention" here means "with much opposition."

  Paul seems concerned that the Saints of Thessalonica might be persuaded by those who would speak evil of the missionaries in their absence. He reminds them that they "did not use deceit, . . . uncleanness, [or] guile" in teaching them (v. 3). They did not seek to please men with their preaching, but to please God who had entrusted them with the gospel message (v. 4). They avoided flattering words, covetousness, and the seeking of glory from those that they taught (vv. 5–6). They were "gentle among you, even as a nurse cherisheth her children" (v. 7). And because of their love for the Saints, "we were willing to have imparted unto you, not the gospel of God only, but also our own souls, because ye were dear unto us" (v. 8). He asked them to "remember, brethren, our labour and travail: for labouring night and day, because we would not be chargeable unto any of you, we preached unto you the gospel of God" (v. 9). And he said that they are "witnesses, and God also, how holily and justly and unblameably we behaved ourselves among you that believe" (v. 10).

- **1 Thessalonians 3:1–5 Paul's tribulations keep him from re-visiting Thessalonica.** When it became obvious while they were at Athens that their difficulties would prevent Paul from being able to return to Thessalonica soon, he "could no longer forbear" knowing of their welfare and sent Timothy, "our brother, and minister of God, and our fellow labourer in the gospel of Christ, to establish [them], and to comfort [them] concerning [their] faith" (vv. 1–2).

  In saying this, Paul was not seeking that any man "should be moved by these afflictions: for [ye] yourselves know that we [all men] are appointed thereunto" (v. 3). When he was at Thessalonica, he told the Saints that he would "suffer tribulation," and since then "it came to pass, and ye know" (v. 4). But being anxious to know of their welfare, he "sent to know your faith, lest by some means the tempter have tempted you, and our labour be in vain" (v. 5).

- **1 Thessalonians 2:17–20 Paul desires to see them exalted at the Second Coming.** Paul lamented that he had been "taken from you for a short time in presence, not in heart," and said he tried "abundantly to see your face with great desire" (v. 17). He would have "come unto you, . . . but Satan hindered us" (v. 18). Nevertheless, he assured them that "our hope, or joy, or crown of rejoicing" was to see them "in the presence of our Lord Jesus Christ at his coming . . . For ye are our glory and joy" (vv. 19–20).

Becoming Sanctified

- **1 Thessalonians 4:3–5 God desires that all men and women become sanctified.** "For this is the will of God, even your sanctification, . . . That every one of you should know how to possess his vessel [body] in sanctification and honour" (vv. 3–4). To do this they must "abstain from fornication" (v. 3), and avoid "the lust of concupiscence, even as the Gentiles which know not God" (v. 5). Concupiscence is Latin for "passion" or "to desire ardently."

  Elder Bruce R. McConkie said, "To be sanctified is to become clean, pure, and spotless; to be free from the blood and sins of the world; to become a new creature of the Holy Ghost, one whose body has been renewed by the rebirth of the Spirit. Sanctification is a state of saintliness, a state attained only by conformity to the laws and ordinances of the gospel. The plan of salvation is the system and means provided whereby men may sanctify their souls and thereby become worthy of a celestial inheritance."[3]

PROVIDENCE LITHOGRAPHIC CO., 1901, #34

- **1 Thessalonians 4:6–12 What we must do to be sanctified.** Paul mentions a number of essential qualities.

  Sanctification requires purity. How often we hear those who lust seek to justify their behavior by saying, "It's natural. It's part of being human."

  Paul refutes that idea by saying, "God hath not called us unto uncleanness, but unto holiness" (v. 7). He did not "make us that way," as Satan would have us believe. We are not trapped in some predetermined behavior or impulse. It was Lucifer who proposed that we have no choice in this life; God insisted that we should be free to act and be accountable for those acts.

  Paul also mentions charity. If we become offended, we should not "go beyond and defraud [our] brother in any matter" (v. 6). He is speaking here of revenge, and he reminds us that "the Lord is the avenger of all such, as we also have forewarned you and testified" (v. 6). Holding a grudge is also offensive to God because "he . . . that despiseth, despiseth not man, but God, who hath also given unto us his holy Spirit" (v. 8).

  We must also love one another. Paul said, "as touching brotherly love ye need not that I write unto you: for ye yourselves are taught of God to love one another. And indeed ye do it toward all the brethren which are in all Macedonia: but we beseech you, brethren, that ye increase more and more" (vv. 9–10).

  Saints must avoid taking undue interest in other people's affairs and live lives of quiet dignity, honesty, and work. Paul counsels us to "study [learn] to be quiet, and to do your own business, and to work with your own hands" (v. 11). He also teaches that we must "walk [live] honestly toward them that are without [those around us]" and says that, if we do, we will "lack of nothing" (v. 12).

- **1 Thessalonians 5:11–13 We must love and sustain our leaders.** True Saints should "comfort ourselves together, and edify one another," which Paul observes that the Thessalonian Saints were already doing (v. 11).

  In connection with this, we should strive to "know them which labour among you, and are over you in the Lord, and admonish you; And . . . esteem them very highly in love for their work's sake. And be at peace among yourselves" (vv. 12–13). Rather than "evil speaking of the Lord's anointed," we are to learn to respect and love our leaders and not engage in criticism and gossip.

  Elder David B. Haight said, "When we sustain the President of the Church by our uplifted hand, it not only signifies that we acknowledge before God that

The Apostle Paul

he is the rightful possessor of all the priesthood keys; it means that we covenant with God that we will abide by the direction and the counsel that come through His prophet. It is a solemn covenant."[4]

President John Taylor said, "We hold up our right hand when voting in token before God that we will sustain those for whom we vote; and if we cannot feel to sustain them we ought not to hold up our hands, because to do this, would be to act the part of hypocrites. . . . For when we lift up our hands in this way, it is in token to God that we are sincere in what we do, and that we will sustain the parties we vote for. . . . If we agree to do a thing and do not do it, we become covenant breakers and violators of our obligations, which are, perhaps, as solemn and binding as anything we can enter into."[5]

Elder Jeffrey R. Holland said, "It is no small thing to 'sustain' another person. The word literally means to 'uphold' or, if you prefer, to 'hold up.' When we sustain life, we nourish it, we keep it going. When we sustain a friend or a neighbor or a stranger in the street, we give support, we share strength, we provide help. We hold each other up under the weight of present circumstance. We bear one another's burdens under the heavy personal pressures of life.'"[6]

- **1 Thessalonians 5:14–15 How we should deal with our fellow men.** Paul suggests all of the following:
  - — Warn them that are unruly.
  - — Comfort the feebleminded. "Feebleminded" means "faint-hearted"—those who lack courage or resolution to live the gospel.[7]
  - — Support the weak.
  - — Be patient toward all men.
  - — Do not be vengeful. "See that none render evil for evil unto any man; but ever follow that which is good, both among yourselves, and to all men" (v. 15).

THEBIBLEREVIVAL.COM, #30

- **1 Thessalonians 5:16–22 How we can improve our relationship with God.** Again, Paul lists a number of essential things:
  - — Rejoice evermore, which means to have a good and positive attitude (v. 16).
  - — Pray without ceasing, meaning regularly and without fail (v. 17).
  - — Be thankful. "In every thing give thanks: for this is the will of God" (v. 18).
  - — Quench not the Spirit. Always seek the Spirit's guidance, and respond to it (v. 19). "In the true Church there will always be powerful manifestations of the Spirit of God. Inclinations to bridle and submerge these is of the world."[8]
  - — Despise not prophesyings. Listen to the Apostles and Prophets and believe them (v. 20).
  - — Prove all things; hold fast to that which is good (v. 21). We have the Light of Christ which helps us to discern good and evil. We should reject evil and seek the good.

— Abstain from all appearance of evil (v. 22). We are not to "walk the edge" of what is appropriate, nor allow ourselves to be in unworthy places. We are not only to avoid evil, but even the very appearance of it.

- **1 Thessalonians 5:23 If we do all these things, God will sanctify us,** making it possible for our "whole spirit and soul and body [to] be preserved blameless unto the coming of our Lord Jesus Christ."

- **1 Thessalonians 5:26 Greet others with a holy salutation.** To "greet all the brethren with an holy kiss" means to greet them with a "holy salutation." We generally refer to other Saints as brother or sister—a "holy salutation" that reminds us of our eternal relationship to each other.

The Second Coming of Christ

- **1 Thessalonians 1:10 A promise of deliverance from the "day of wrath."** Paul counseled us to "wait for his Son from heaven" who would "deliver . . . us from the wrath to come." The "wrath to come" is "the desolation of abomination which awaits the wicked" at the Second Coming of the Lord Jesus Christ (D&C 88:85).

The Prophet Joseph Smith said, "It seems to be deeply impressed upon our minds that the Saints ought to lay hold of every door that shall seem to be opened unto them, to obtain foothold on the earth, and be making all the preparation that is within their power for the terrible storms that are now gathering in the heavens, 'a day of clouds, with darkness and gloominess, and of thick darkness,' as spoken of by the Prophets which cannot be now of along time lingering."[9]

President Brigham Young asked, "Are you prepared for the day of vengeance to come, when the Lord will consume the wicked by the brightness of His coming? No. Then do not be too anxious for the Lord to hasten His work. Let our anxiety be centered upon this one thing, the sanctification of our own hearts, the purifying of our own affections, the preparing of ourselves for the approach of the events that are hastening upon us. This should be our concern, this should be our study, this should be our daily prayer. . . . Seek to have the spirit of Christ, that we may wait patiently the time of the Lord, and prepare ourselves for the times that are coming. This is our duty."[10]

- **1 Thessalonians 4:13–15 Paul's teachings on the resurrection.** Paul said, "I would not have you to be ignorant, brethren, concerning them which are asleep [dead], that ye sorrow not, even as others which have no hope. For if we believe that Jesus died and rose again, even so them also which sleep in Jesus will God bring with him" at the Second Coming (vv. 13–14). The Lord had told Paul that "[those] which are alive and remain unto the coming of the Lord shall not prevent them which are asleep" (v. 15). His atonement and resurrection will bless both the living and the dead.

- **1 Thessalonians 4:16–18 Paul's teachings on Christ's coming.** "For the Lord himself shall descend from heaven with a shout, with the voice of the archangel, and with the trump of God: and the dead in Christ shall rise first" (v. 16).

  "Then [those] which are alive and remain shall be caught up together with them in the clouds, to meet the Lord in the air" (v. 17). This is what the Christian world calls "the rapture." It will be rapturous indeed to be caught up with the Lord—whether we are at that moment alive or dead—and to descend with Him at His Second Coming.

  And if we are among those who are deemed worthy to be caught up to be with Christ, "so shall we ever be with the Lord" in His celestial kingdom (v. 17). Whatever our present circumstances may be, we are to "comfort one another with these words" (v. 18).

"MESSENGER OF THE COVENANT," ©JOSEPH BRICKEY, USED BY PERMISSION

- **1 Thessalonians 5:1–10 Paul's teachings on preparing for the Second Coming.** People in Paul's day as well as our own are curious as to when the Lord will come again. Paul said, "But of the times and the seasons, brethren, ye have no need that I write unto you. For yourselves know perfectly that the day of the Lord so cometh as a thief in the night" (vv. 1–2). "Day of the Lord" is an Old Testament phrase meaning when God will come with judgment—in other words, the Second Coming.

  Paul says He will come "as a thief in the night." This means "unexpectedly." JST Luke 12:44 shows that Jesus Himself used this expression. He will come when people are not expecting Him.

  People who do believe in His coming will speak of "peace and safety" in their day. But "then sudden destruction cometh upon them, as travail upon a woman with child; and they shall not escape" (v. 3). These are what Paul calls the "children of the night"—the people of the world who dwell in darkness. They will not "see" [acknowledge] the signs which indicate the approach of His Second Coming. The "day of the Lord" shall be a dreadful day for them.

Righteous Saints, however, "are not in darkness, that that day should overtake you as a thief" (v. 4). "Ye are all the children of light, and the children of the day: we are not of the night, nor of darkness" (v. 5). The "children of the day" are those who dwell in light and truth. They will "see" the warning signs and prepare themselves spiritually for the Second Coming of Christ. For them, the "day of the Lord" will be a day of great joy.

Paul cautions us not to grow weary of waiting and become numbed to the day of His coming. We must "not sleep, as do others; but . . . watch and be sober" (v. 6). We have been given the signs of His coming, and as we observe them taking place we should have renewed faith that He will, in fact, come.

President Joseph Fielding Smith said, "I do not know when He is going to come. No man knows. Even the angels of heaven are in the dark in regard to that great truth. [See Matthew 24:36–37.] But this I know, that the signs that have been pointed out are here. The earth is full of calamity, of trouble. The hearts of men are failing them. We see the signs as we see the fig tree putting forth her leaves; and knowing this time is near, it behooves me and it behooves you, and all men upon the face of the earth, to pay heed to the words of Christ, to His Apostles and watch, for we know not the day nor the hour. But I tell you this, it shall come as a thief in the night, when many of us will not be ready for it."[11]

While the wicked "sleep in the night; and . . . are drunken in the night," the Saints should be "sober, putting on the breastplate of faith and love; and for an helmet, the hope of salvation" (vv. 7–8). We do not need to fear because "God hath not appointed us to wrath, but to obtain salvation by our Lord Jesus Christ" (v. 9).

Christ atoned for all of God's children, whether dead or alive, and provided the means by which they may "live together with him" after His coming (v. 10).

2 THESSALONIANS

Paul's first letter to Thessalonica did not resolve all their questions about the Second Coming. He had also learned that persecution of the Church in Thessalonica was still strong, but the members had followed his counsel and rallied around each other (2 Thessalonians 1:3–4).

Paul said he "gloried" over the patience and faith with which they were enduring their trials (v. 4), and assured them that these trials would make them "worthy of the kingdom of our God" (v. 5). And the Lord Himself will punish the wicked for their evil (v. 6).

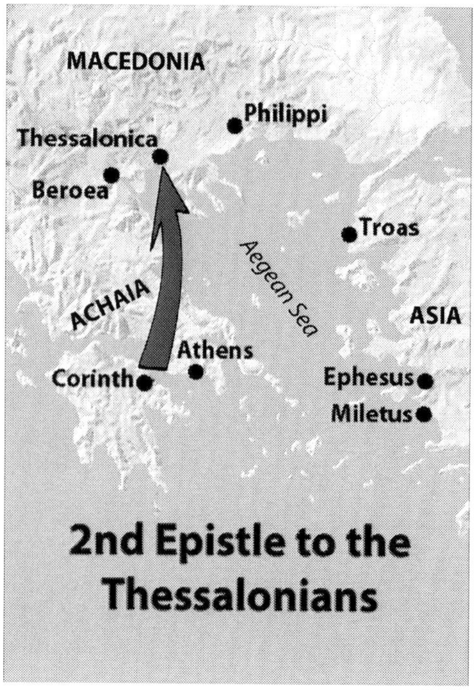

- **2 Thessalonians 1:7–9 The destruction of the wicked at the Second Coming.** Paul assured them that "the Lord Jesus shall be revealed from heaven with his mighty angels," and "in flaming fire taking vengeance on them that know not God, and that obey not the gospel of our Lord Jesus Christ" (vv. 7–8). They will "be punished with everlasting destruction from the presence of the Lord, and from the glory of his power" (v. 9). Elder Bruce R. McConkie said, "[To experience everlasting destruction is to partake of spiritual death], which is to be cast out of the presence of God and to die as pertaining to the things of righteousness."[12]

The Great Apostasy

To end speculation about the precise time of the Second Coming, Paul taught that a great rebellion or apostasy from the Lord's true Church must precede it.

- **2 Thessalonians 2:1–2 The apostasy had already begun in 52 AD as Paul wrote this epistle.** Paul counseled, "That ye be not soon shaken in mind, or be troubled, neither by spirit, nor by word, nor by letter as from us, as that the day of Christ is at hand" (v. 2). A "letter as from us" suggests that phony letters were circulating, purporting to be written by the Apostles, but that were not. We may look with disdain on those who would do this—members of the Church who should know better. But alas, we are guilty of the same thing. I cannot count the number of times I've heard people quote an Apostle by name, who has supposedly said some strange or wonderful thing, but who, when pressed, cannot supply an appropriate reference. Speaking "words as if they are from the Apostles and Prophet" is precisely the same thing of which Paul speaks here.

- **2 Thessalonians 2:3 A great apostasy will precede the Second Coming.** "Let no man deceive you by any means," said Paul, "for that day shall not come, except there come a falling away first, and that man of sin be revealed, the son of perdition." The idea of a "falling away" suggests a gradual decline, but the Greek word from which it is translated, *apostasia*, means to "revolt." Both are probably correct. "That man of sin" is Satan, and "the son of perdition" also means Satan and his followers. The word perdition is derived from the Latin *perditus*, which means "to destroy." This is a title given to Satan (D&C 76:26), and also to Cain (Moses 5:24).

  President Joseph Fielding Smith said, "[Satan and those with him who rebelled against God in heaven and were cast out are known as sons of perdition. These rebellious spirits] 'chose evil by choice after having had the light. While dwelling in the presence of God they knowingly entered into their rebellion. Their mission on earth is to attempt to destroy the souls of men and make them miserable as they themselves are miserable.'"[13]

- **2 Thessalonians 2:4–6 Satan still seeks to be our god.** As he did in the premortal world, on this earth Satan "opposeth and exalteth himself above all that is called God, or that is worshipped; so that he as God sitteth in the temple of God, shewing himself that he is God" (v. 4).

C.H. BLOCH

  "The temple of God" in this case is the body of believers, the Church. Satan would invade the Church with false doctrine and changed ordinances, putting all those who follow these things securely in his power and separated from the true cause and doctrine of Christ. Paul reminded them that he had warned them of these things when he was with them (v. 5). He wanted them to understand clearly "what withholdeth that he might be revealed in his time (v. 6). "What withholdeth" means "the one who possesses, holds firmly in his grasp, or restrains," in other words, Satan. So Paul is saying that now they know that it is Satan who will introduce apostasy in order to take us captive and hold us in his power. And all this will be "revealed" (disclosed, discovered, manifested) in time.

- **2 Thessalonians 2:7 The apostasy is already under way.** Paul says, "the mystery of iniquity doth already work," which means the Great Apostasy was already under way by the time of Paul's ministry. Elder James E. Talmage said, "The expression 'mystery of iniquity' as used by Paul is significant. Prominent among the early perverters of the Christian faith were those who assailed its simplicity and lack of exclusiveness. This simplicity was so different from the mysteries of Judaism and the mysterious rites of heathen idolatry as to be disappointing to many; and the earliest changes in the Christian form of worship were marked by the introduction of mystic ceremonies."[14]

- **2 Thessalonians 2:7–8 Satan will eventually be bound.** The phrase "he who now letteth will let, until he be taken out of the way" (v. 7) is a prime example of how Old English can be torturous to understand. At the time the Bible was translated, to "let" meant to "restrain" or "hinder."[15] Thus, Paul is saying that "he who now possesses and restrains the Church (Satan, through apostasy) will eventually be restrained himself. Satan has and will continue to cause misery, unhappiness, and sin throughout the

ANONYMOUS PAINTING OF SATAN SEEKING TO BIND US

Satan seeks to bind us

world. But he will eventually be "taken out of the way"—bound by the Lord at the beginning of the Millennium.[16] Satan will be revealed for the evil being that he is, and the Lord will "consume [him] with the spirit of his mouth, and shall destroy [him] with the brightness of his coming" (v. 8).

- **2 Thessalonians 2:9 Satan has power to produce false signs and wonders.** Many examples can be found in the scriptures and the words of the prophets:

  — He has the ability to imitate the miracles of God, as in Pharaoh's court (Exodus 7:11).
  — He has power over the elements (Job 1:12–19).
  — He can inflict disease (Job 2:3–7).
  — He is a master of deceit (2 Nephi 9:9).
  — He can appear as an angel of light (2 Cor. 11:14).
  — He has the gift of tongues (*Teachings of the Prophet Joseph Smith*, 162).
  — Those spirits who follow Satan have these same capacities in lesser degrees (Revelation 16:14).

  However, in all of this, "the power of the devil is limited; [and] the power of God is unlimited"[17]

- **2 Thessalonians 2:9–12 Satan will deceive the unrighteous.** He will easily deceive the unrighteous "because they received not the love of the truth, that they might be saved" (v. 10). They suffer from a "strong delusion, that they should believe a lie" (v. 11). And they will be "damned who believed not the truth, [and] had pleasure in unrighteousness (v. 12).

  President David O. McKay said:

  > If man is to be rewarded for righteousness and punished for evil, then common justice demands that he be given the power of independent action. A knowledge of good and evil is essential to man's progress on earth. If he were coerced to do right at all times, or were helplessly enticed to commit sin, he would merit neither a blessing for the first nor punishment for the second . . .
  >
  > God is standing in the shadow of eternity, it seems to me, deploring the inevitable results of the follies, the transgressions and the sins of His wayward children, but we cannot blame Him for these any more than we can blame a father who might say to his son, 'There are two roads, my son, one leading to the right, one leading to the left. If you take the one to the right it will lead you to success and to happiness. If you take the one to the left it will bring upon you misery and unhappiness and perhaps death, but you choose which you will. You must choose; I will not force either upon you . . .'[18]

Separating from the Wicked

- **2 Thessalonians 3:6–7 We are to withdraw from those who "behave disorderly."** These would be members who take pride in upsetting others, who teach false doctrines in order to gain a following, or who behave in any other way that is destructive to the peace we enjoy in the presence of the Spirit. Paul advised them to "withdraw yourselves from every brother that walketh disorderly, and not after the tradition which he received of us" (v. 6). He reminded them that he and his companions did not behave this way when they were with them (v. 7).

Elder Bruce R. McConkie said, "Enemies from within, traitors to the Cause, cultists who pervert the doctrines and practices which lead to salvation, often draw others away with them, and added souls lose their anticipated inheritance in the heavenly kingdom. When cultists and enemies become fixed in their opposition to the Church, and when they seek to convert others to their diverse positions, the course of wisdom is to avoid them, as Paul here directs, and to leave them in the Lord's hands."[19]

- **2 Thessalonians 3:8–15 Some members were living off the labor of others** and did not want to work. But work is a commandment. Paul and his companions "did [not] eat any man's bread for nought; but wrought with labour and travail night and day, that we might not be chargeable to any of you" (v. 8). In this, they sought to be "an ensample unto you to follow us" (v. 9). They had clearly taught the Saints that "if any [man] would not work, neither should he eat" (v. 10). There were among them "some which [were] disorderly, working not at all, but are busybodies" (v. 11). These, Paul said, should "with quietness" [be content] to "work, and eat their own bread" (v. 12).

Paul said those who don't work shouldn't eat

Elder Bruce R. McConkie said, "Even Paul and his ministerial associates, who were in fact entitled to temporal help from the Saints, chose to set an example of self-support. There are perils in a paid ministry."[20]

- **2 Thessalonians 3:13–15 Be not weary in well doing.** Working with imperfect Saints can be difficult and sometimes thankless. "But ye, brethren, be not weary in well doing," said Paul (v. 13). If anyone refuses to keep the commandments Paul had reiterated in his epistles, "note that man, and have no company with him, that he may be ashamed" (v. 14). But in any attempt to correct another, "count him not as an enemy, but admonish him as a brother" (v. 15).

- **2 Thessalonians 3:16 Paul closes with a blessing of the "peace of Christ."** Paul always began his epistles with expressions of love and closed them in the same spirit. He prayed that "the Lord of peace himself give you peace always by all means" and that "the Lord be with you all." This is the end of the actual letter, but additional notes were appended to it (see below).

President David O. McKay said:

> The peace of Christ does not come by seeking the superficial things of life, neither does it come except as it springs from the individual's heart. Jesus said to His disciples: 'Peace I leave with you, my peace I give unto you: not as the world giveth, give I unto you . . . ' (John 14:27). Thus the Son of Man, as the executor of His own will and testament, gave to His disciples and to mankind the 'first of all human blessings.' It was a bequest conditioned upon obedience to the principles of the gospel of Jesus Christ. It is thus bequeathed to each individual. No man is at peace with himself or his God who is untrue to his better self, who transgresses the law of right either in dealing with himself by indulging in passion, in appetite, yielding to temptations against his accusing conscience, or in dealing with his fellow men, being untrue to their trust. Peace does not come to the transgressor of law; peace comes by obedience to law; and it is that message which Jesus would have us proclaim among men.[21]

Important Historical Information

- **2 Thessalonians 3:17–18 Paul usually dictated his epistles to a scribe and then added a few words in his own handwriting at the bottom.** We see here a typical handwritten note from Paul at the end of this epistle: "The salutation of Paul with mine own hand, which is the token in every epistle: so I write. The grace of our Lord Jesus Christ be with you all. Amen."
- **Note at the end of 2 Thessalonians: "The second epistle to the Thessalonians was written from Athens."** This is historical information added later by a scribe rather than by Paul. And it is not correct. Both of Paul's letters to Thessalonica were written from Corinth, not from Athens.

Notes:

1. Adapted from Kelly Ogden & Andrew D. Skinner, *New Testament Apostles Testify of Christ* [1998], 89, 125. For additional information on the sequence of the epistles, see "The Epistles" in the article entitled "New Testament," in Ludlow, *Encyclopedia of Mormonism*, 5 vols. [1992], 3:1013–14.

2. The place from which the book of Hebrews was written is unknown, though a partial clue is furnished by the phrase, "They of Italy salute you" (13:24). Since it was written to the "Hebrews," this author prefers the theory that it was written from Rome to Jerusalem. We also do not know the exact date of the epistle. It seems from references within the epistle that the temple in Jerusalem was still standing, so it would be before 70 AD. Judging from its themes, it appears to have been written after Paul's first imprisonment (61–62 AD), but before his second imprisonment and death (AD 68). A date of about 65 AD seems to fit the known facts.

3. *Mormon Doctrine*, 2nd ed. [1966], 675.

4. "Solemn Assemblies," *Ensign*, November 1994, 14–15.

5. In *Journal of Discourses*, 21:207.

6. "He Loved Them unto the End," *Ensign*, November 1989, 25.

7. *Doctrinal New Testament Commentary*, 3 vols. [1966–1973], 3:58.

8. *Doctrinal New Testament Commentary*, 3:58.

9. *Teachings of the Prophet Joseph Smith*, sel. Joseph Fielding Smith [1976], 141.

10. *Deseret News* [Salt Lake City], 1 May 1861.

11. *Doctrines of Salvation*, comp. Bruce R. McConkie, 3 vols. [1954–1956], 3:52–53.

12. *Doctrinal New Testament Commentary*, 3:61.

13. *Doctrines of Salvation*, 2:219.

14. *The Great Apostasy* [1953], 41–42.

15. *The Great Apostasy*, 41–42.

16. *Doctrinal New Testament Commentary*, 3:63.

17. *Discourses of Brigham Young*, sel. John A. Widtsoe [1941], 68.

18. *Pathways to Happiness* [1957], 90–91, 93.

19. *Doctrinal New Testament Commentary*, 3:66.

20. *Doctrinal New Testament Commentary*, 3:67.

21. In Conference Report, October 1938, 133.

SECTION NINE

Paul's Third Missionary Journey

(54 AD — 58 AD)

Paul's third missionary journey was the longest of the three, covering 3,500 miles and lasting about four years (53–58 AD). Paul departed from Antioch in Syria and traveled overland "through the upper coasts," (Acts 18:23; 19:1), which means along the high road through Galatia and Asia. This took him to Derbe, Lystra, Iconium, and Antioch of Pisidia—three branches that he had visited during each of his first two missionary journeys. He crossed through Asia (modern-day Turkey) to Ephesus, then made a circular route through Troas, Philippi, and Thessalonica on his way to Corinth. He then retraced that route back to Troas, then sailed to Ephesus and Miletus. His journey home from there took him to Lycia and then to Tyre and Caesarea. Paul then returned and reported on his mission to the authorities at Jerusalem.

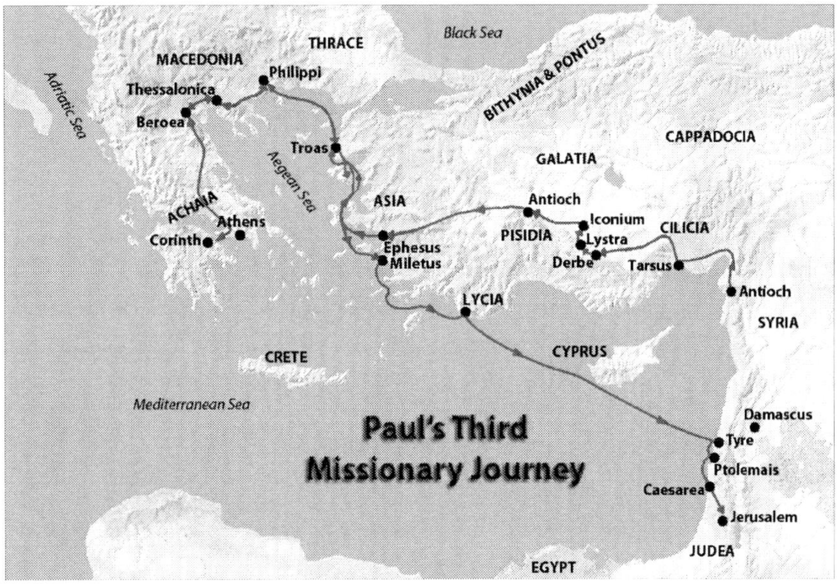

This journey included the following ministries:

GALATIA:	Derbe, Lystra, Iconium, Antioch (Pisidia)
ASIA:	Ephesus, Troas
MACEDONIA:	Philippi, Thessalonica, Beroea
ACHAIA:	Corinth
MACEDONIA:	Farewell return visits to Beroea, Thessalonica, Philippi
ASIA:	Farewell visit to Ephesus, Miletus

The Significance of Paul's Third Missionary Journey

This journey was the last of Paul's three missionary journeys. As such, it would be the last time that he would see the Saints in these cities before his death.

Wickedness and apostasy were increasing, and Paul faced the same forces that we face today in defending truth and right. President Joseph F. Smith said in 1914: "There are at least three dangers that threaten the Church within, and the authorities need to awaken to the fact that the people should be warned unceasingly against them. As I see these, they are flattery of prominent men in the world, false educational ideas, and sexual impurity."[1] Paul sought vigorously to keep the Saints away from these dangers and on the path to exaltation.

Unlike our own day, when digital integration allows instant communication around the globe, Paul had only two options: visit a branch in person or write them a letter. Thus, as he traveled around the cities bordering on the Aegean Sea, if he heard of difficulties in a distant branch, all he could do was write to them and send the letter with a trusted associate like Timothy or Silas. Paul wrote at least four such epistles during this journey.

EPISTLE	WRITTEN FROM	DATE WRITTEN
1 Corinthians	Ephesus	57 AD
2 Corinthians	Macedonia	57 AD
Romans	Corinth	57–58 AD
Galatians	Corinth	58 AD

During this missionary journey, Paul had times when he resided in a certain city for a period of time. He was not always on the move. For example, after he arrived in Ephesus during this journey, he resided there for two years, during which time "all they which dwelt in Asia heard the word of the Lord Jesus, both Jews and Greeks" (Acts 19:10). It was toward the end of his time in Ephesus that Paul wrote what we call his "first" epistle to the Corinthians, in 57 AD.

Paul actually wrote at least three letters to the Corinthian Saints. The first is lost to us, but we have copies of the second and third letters—known as First Corinthians and Second Corinthians, respectively.

In fall of that same year (57 AD), Paul made his way northward to Troas looking for Titus who was supposed to be returning from Corinth. When he did not find him there Paul crossed the Aegean Sea to Philippi in Macedonia and waited there for him to arrive. While waiting, he wrote the "second" epistle to the Corinthians as a follow up to the "first."

Eventually, Paul made his way to Corinth, and once he got there he stayed for three months, probably during the winter months of 57–58 AD, waiting for good sailing conditions before departing for Jerusalem. While waiting, Paul wrote two epistles: one to the Romans in 57–58 AD and another to the Galatians shortly thereafter in early 58 AD.

The Non-Chronological Order of Our Lessons

The descriptions above and the chart at the end of this section show the chronological sequence of events during Paul's third missionary journey. However, Gospel Doctrine lessons do not follow a chronological sequence; they follow a thematic one.

Thus, the first chapter in this section, "Living in the Spirit" includes information from Paul's visit to Ephesus in 55–57 AD, but also includes his epistle to the Galatians, which was not written from Ephesus; it was written a year later from Corinth in 58 AD. The reason they are combined in the Gospel Doctrine lesson is because they share a common theme of "Living in the Spirit."

The intervening chapters are mostly in the order of when each epistle was written. Chronological information will be provided for each chapter in an effort to keep the reader informed as to where and when each epistle was written.

The associated chapters of this book, corresponding to Gospel Doctrine lessons, are:

32. Living in the Spirit (Acts 18-20, Galatians)
33. The Temple of God (1 Corinthians 1-6)
34. Keeping the Ordinances (1 Corinthians 11-16)
35. Reconciliation to God (2 Corinthians)
36. Epistle to the Romans (Acts 20; Romans)

The following is a chronological list of events that took place during this period and the scriptures from Acts and the Epistles that tell the story.

Date	Events	Scriptural References
PAUL'S THIRD MISSIONARY JOURNEY (54–58 AD)		
54	Antioch	
	Paul begins his third missionary journey.	Acts 18:23–24
	He visits Saints in the Branches of Galatia	
55–57	Ephesus	Acts 18–19
	Paul at Ephesus:.	Acts 18:24–28
	Apollos and the Disciples of John	Acts 19:1–7
	All Asia Heard the Gospel.	Acts 19:8–10
	Miracles of Healing	Acts 19:11–12
	Exorcists Cannot Cast Out Devils.	Acts 19:13–20
	The Silversmiths Riot—"Great is Diana!".	Acts 19:21–41
	Priestcraft Fights True Religion	
57	1 Corinthians written from Ephesus	1 Corinthians
	Macedonia (Philippi)	Acts 20:1–2
	2 Corinthians written from Macedonia.	2 Corinthians
	Corinth (Paul Returns to)	Acts 20:2–3
	Romans written from Corinth.	Romans
58	Galatians written from Corinth	Galatians

PAUL'S THIRD MISSIONARY JOURNEY (Cont'd.) (54–58 AD)

58	Troas:		
		Paul Raises Eutychus from Death	Acts 20:4–12
	Miletus:		
		Farewell, Testimony and Counsel	Acts 20:13–38
	Toward Jerusalem:		
		Paul's farewell journey thru Macedonia and Asia	Acts 20:4–38
		Agabus' Prophetic Warnings	Acts 21:1–17

Notes

1. *Gospel Doctrine*, 5th ed. [1939], 312–313.

Chapter 32

Living in the Spirit

(Acts 18–20; Galatians)

INTRODUCTION

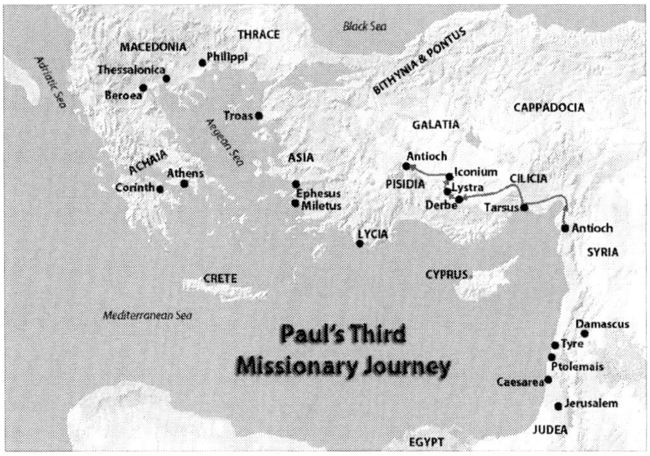

- **Acts 18:23 Paul travels through the Branches in order.** He had only been at home in Antioch of Syria for a while, perhaps through the winter of 53–54 AD, and then "he departed, and went over all the country of Galatia and Phrygia in order, strengthening all the disciples."

  This was a final effort to visit his converts personally. He traveled to Derbe, Lystra, and Iconium in Galatia, and then to Antioch of Pisidia, strengthening the Saints and bearing a final personal witness of Jesus Christ.

THE MISSION TO EPHESUS

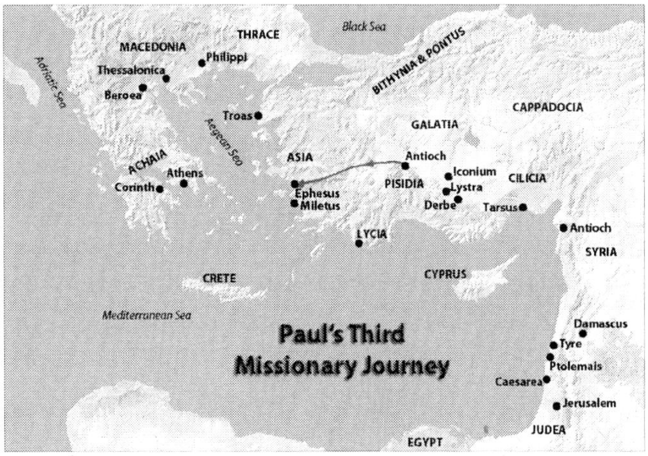

Paul had visited Ephesus only once before, and only briefly on his way home from his second mission.

His teachings were so powerful that they begged him to stay for a while, but he declined, saying, "I must by all means keep this feast that cometh in Jerusalem: but I will return again unto you, if God will" (Acts 18:21). Now, he was keeping his promise.

Ephesus became the headquarters of Paul's third missionary journey. He spent more time there than anywhere else. And eventually, John the Beloved would make his home there and it would become an important new center for the entire Church.

False Baptisms

Baptismal font at Ephesus

- **Acts 18:24–28 Apollos teaches baptism at Ephesus.** During Paul's absence, "a certain Jew named Apollos, born at Alexandria, an eloquent man, and mighty in the scriptures, came to Ephesus" (v. 24). Apollos was knowledgeable of the gospel of repentance and "fervent in the spirit," and "he spake and taught diligently the things of the Lord" (v. 25). But his knowledge was incomplete; he knew only concerning baptism as it had been taught by the Baptist (v. 25). Apollos was brave. He spoke "boldly in the synagogue," causing Aquila and Priscilla to take him in and "expounded unto him the way of God more perfectly" (v. 26). With this new knowledge, he "mightily convinced the Jews, and that publickly, shewing by the scriptures that Jesus was Christ" (v. 28). When Apollos decided to go to Achaia (Athens and Corinth) to preach, the Saints at Ephesus wrote him letters "exhorting the disciples to receive him: who, when he was come, helped them much which had believed through grace" (v. 27).

- **Acts 19:1–7 Paul encounters Apollos' converts at Ephesus.** During the time that Apollos was in Corinth, Paul came into Ephesus (v. 1). Speaking to the disciples there, he asked, "Have ye received the Holy Ghost since ye believed? And they said unto him, We have not so much as heard whether there be any Holy Ghost" (vv. 1–2). This was obviously a problem. He asked, "Unto what then were ye baptized? And they said, Unto John's baptism" (v. 3). These were Apollos' converts, whom he had baptized after teaching them the doctrine of repentance and baptism that John the Baptist had preached. Paul said to them, "John verily baptized with the baptism of repentance, saying unto the people, that they should believe on him which should come after him, that is, on Christ Jesus" (v. 4). This, they had not heard from Apollos, who apparently not only did not know anything beyond baptism, he probably didn't have authority to baptize, either.

Paul baptized these disciples again, "in the name of the Lord Jesus," and then "laid his hands upon them" to confer the Gift of the Holy Ghost (vv. 5–6). And immediately, "the Holy Ghost came on them; and they spake with tongues, and prophesied" (v. 6). There were twelve such disciples that Paul had to re-baptize and confirm (v. 7).

The Prophet Joseph Smith said, "Baptism was the essential point on which [after receiving it] they could receive the gift of the Holy Ghost. It seems that some sectarian Jew had been baptizing like John but had forgotten to inform them that there was one to follow by the name of Jesus Christ, to baptize with fire and the Holy Ghost, which showed these converts that their first baptism was illegal. And when they heard this, they were gladly baptized, and after hands were laid on them they received the gifts, according to promise, and spake with tongues and prophesied."[1]

- **Acts 19:8–10 Paul resides at Ephesus for the next two years.** He spent the first three months in the synagogue, speaking boldly, "disputing and persuading . . . concerning the kingdom of God" (v. 8). But when "divers" [several different] people hardened their hearts against his message, "he departed from them" and took his converts with him (v. 9). Having been rejected by the Jews, Paul then "disput[ed] daily in the school of one Tyrannus," who was most likely a Gentile (v. 9). This state of affairs continued for two years, during which time "all they which dwelt in Asia heard the word of the Lord Jesus, both Jews and Greeks" (v. 10). The word "all" here means a "great quantity" or "large portion," not literally *all* persons.

During this time, Paul wrote 1st Corinthians from Ephesus, in 57 AD

Miracles

- **Acts 19:11–12 Miracles performed at a distance through touching Paul's clothing.** Paul could not be everywhere at the same time, and the demands for his ministrations were many. On more than one occasion, Paul sent handkerchiefs or aprons to the sick via trusted companions, and when the sick received these items "the diseases departed from them, and the evil spirits went out of them."

  These miracles are unusual but not unique. Touching the Savior's clothing healed several persons during His earthly ministry (Matt. 9:20–22; 14:34–36). A person was healed by merely coming under the shadow of the Apostle Peter (Acts 5:15). And on July 22, 1839, a similar miracle occurred during a plague epidemic by the Prophet Joseph Smith sending out a handkerchief to those he could not immediately reach.

  The *History of the Church* records:

  > After healing the sick in Montrose, all the company followed Joseph to the bank of the river, where he was going to take the boat to return home. While waiting for the boat, a man from the West, who had seen that the sick and dying were healed, asked Joseph if he would not go to his house and heal two of his children who were very sick. They were twins and were

three months old. Joseph told the man he could not go, but he would send some one to heal them. He told Elder Woodruff to go with the man and heal his children. At the same time he took from his pocket a silk bandanna handkerchief, and gave to Brother Woodruff, telling him to wipe the faces of the children with it, and they should be healed; and remarked at the same time: "As long as you keep that handkerchief it shall remain a league between you and me." Elder Woodruff did as he was commanded, and the children were healed, and he keeps the handkerchief to this day.[2]

- **Acts 19:13–16 Evil spirits refuse to acknowledge the authority of Jewish exorcists.** The Jews had seen Paul cast out devils, and perhaps had heard of other Apostles doing the same. So, on this occasion "certain of the vagabond Jews, exorcists, took upon them to call over them which had evil spirits the name of the Lord Jesus, saying, We adjure you by Jesus whom Paul preacheth" (v. 13). This is curious, indeed, since they did not even believe in the divinity of Jesus; perhaps they thought the mere mention of His name had some kind of magical power. These "vagabonds" were "seven sons of one Sceva, a Jew, and chief of the priests" (v. 14). The evil spirit was not deceived; he replied, "Jesus I know, and Paul I know; but who are ye?" (v. 15). Then "the man in whom the evil spirit was leaped on them, and overcame them, and prevailed against them, so that they fled out of that house naked and wounded" (v. 16).

- **Acts 19:17–20 The people burn their books about the occult.** Word of the incident spread to "all the Jews and Greeks . . . dwelling at Ephesus; and fear fell on them all" (v. 17). This was because many of them were dabbling in the occult, even members of the Church, and this even clearly showed that (1) evil spirits are real, and (2) they only respond to proper priesthood authority. As a result, "many that believed [Church members] came, and confessed, and shewed their deeds" (v. 18). And "many of them also which used curious arts brought their books together, and burned them before all men: and they counted the price of them, and found it fifty thousand pieces of silver [about $10,000]" (v. 19). And the word of God grew mightily in the minds and hearts of the people of Ephesus because of this event (v. 20).

DORE, 1896

The Prophet Joseph Smith taught, "It is very evident that [evil spirits] possess a power that none but those who have the priesthood can control, as in the case of the sons of Sceva."[3]

I have found this to be true. While serving my mission in England in the 1960s, my companion and I encountered an evil spirit that tried to frighten us away from a particular city in which we were about to baptize 8 persons. There had not been a baptism in that city for many years before, and Satan had great hold on the hearts of the people there. But now, that grip of unbelief was about to be broken, and this spirit came to try to frighten us away. We were in our room and just about ready to go to bed. When the spirit entered the room, it was immediately obvious that an evil presence was there. We looked to the other end of the long room, and it was darker than usual and seemed to contain a personage of some kind in the darkness. Needless to say, we were extremely afraid and immediately dropped to our knees and prayed for the Lord to take this evil influence away from us. As senior companion, I felt an impression in my mind that said, "You hold the priesthood. You cast him out." And so, we did. And the spirit immediately left through the door without opening it. He did not return.

- **Acts 19:21–22 Paul's premonition of his future.** Thinking about his future after he completed this third mission by traveling to Macedonia and Corinth, Paul declared, "I [must] go to Jerusalem, [and] after I have been there, I must also see Rome" (v. 21). This would turn out to be literally true, and he would eventually die at Rome. But for now, "sent into Macedonia two of them that ministered unto him, Timoth[y] and Erastus; but he himself stayed in Asia [Ephesus] for a season" (v. 22).

- **Acts 19:24 The magnificent temple and theater at Ephesus.** There existed in the city of Ephesus a temple built in honor of the Greek goddess Artemis (the Roman Diana). It was four times bigger than the Parthenon in Athens. Pliny the Elder, who wrote in the first century after Christ, described it as 425 long, 225 feet wide, and 60 feet high (bigger than BYU's LaVell Edwards Stadium) with 127 columns.[4] It was full of silver shrines built in Diana's honor, and the craftsmen of the city made a nice living building these shrines to this pagan goddess. It was one of the seven wonders of the world in that day. And nearby, the theater at Ephesus had room for 24,000 people.

The magnificent theater at Ephesus

- **Acts 19:23–28 Artisans angrily proclaim "Great is Diana of the Ephesians."** There was in the city "a certain man named Demetrius, a silversmith, which made silver shrines for Diana, [which] brought no small gain unto the craftsmen" (v. 24). He created "no small stir" among the craftsmen (v. 23) by pointing out to them that "by this craft we have our wealth" (v. 25). He noted that both in Ephesus and "almost throughout all Asia, this Paul hath persuaded and turned away much people, saying that they be no gods, which are made with hands" (v. 26). They feared that their craft would be "set at nought" if the "great goddess Diana should be despised, and her magnificence should be destroyed, whom all Asia and the world worshippeth" (v. 27). Hearing this warning from Demetrius, the craftsmen "were full of wrath, and cried out, saying, Great is Diana of the Ephesians" (v. 28).

A. PIRSCH, THE BIBLE AND ITS STORY, 1908

- **Acts 19:29–34 Great confusion at the theater.** "The whole city was filled with confusion," and the mob caught Paul's two companions, "Gaius and Aristarchus, men of Macedonia" and "rushed with one accord into the theatre" (v. 29). Paul intended to go into the theater to face the people and defend his friends, but "the disciples suffered him not" (v. 30). Some of the "chief [men] of Asia, which were his friends . . . [advised] him that he [should] not adventure himself into the theatre" (v. 31). There was great confusion there, with "some . . . cr[ying] one thing, and some another . . . and the more part knew not wherefore they were come together" (v. 32). Then the Jews put forward Alexander out of the crowd, and he "beckoned with the hand, and would have made his defence unto the people" (v. 33). "But when they knew that he was a Jew, all with one voice [for] about . . . two hours cried out, Great is Diana of the Ephesians" (v. 34).

- **Acts 19:35–41 The town clerk calms the crowd and sends them home.** Seeking peace, "the townclerk . . . appeased the people [by saying], "Ye men of Ephesus, what man is there that knoweth not how that the city of the Ephesians is a worshipper of the great goddess Diana, and of the image which fell down from Jupiter?" (v. 35). He argued that such great things "cannot be spoken against, [so] ye ought to be quiet, and to do nothing rashly" (v. 36). "For ye have brought hither these men, which are neither robbers of churches, nor yet blasphemers of your goddess" (v. 37). He pointed out that if "Demetrius, and the craftsmen which are with him, have a matter against any man, the law is open, and there are deputies [attorneys]" who can "[plead with] one another" (v. 38). If anything was to be done, it should be "determined in a lawful assembly" (v. 39). Otherwise, "we are in danger to be called in question for this day's uproar, there being no cause whereby we may give an account of this concourse" (v. 40). "And when he had thus spoken, he dismissed the assembly" (v. 41).

TRAVELING TO CORINTH

- **Acts 20:1 Paul travels to Troas, then to Macedonia (Philippi).** "Paul called unto him the disciples, and embraced them, and departed for to go into Macedonia." He traveled first to Troas, where he hoped to meet Titus who would be bringing him word from Corinth. When he did not find Titus there, he took ship toward Philippi on the other side of the Aegean Sea, and waited for Titus there. While waiting he "[went] over those parts, and [gave] them much exhortation" (v. 2). He also wrote his "second" epistle to the Corinthians.

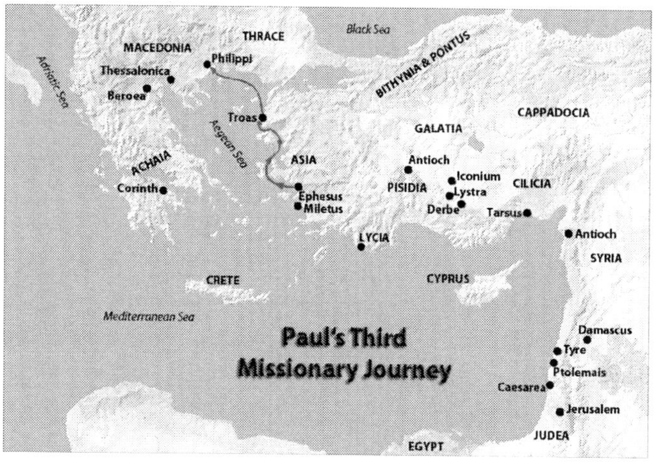

During this time, Paul wrote 2nd Corinthians, from Macedonia, 57 AD

- **Acts 20:2–3 Paul travels to Corinth and stays there 3 months.** The scripture records that "he came into Greece" (Corinth) (v. 2), and "there abode three months" (v. 3). Paul was likely planning to depart from there by sea to return home to Jerusalem. But the weather during the winter of 57–58 AD proved dangerous and he waited for better weather. It would be three months before he could depart.

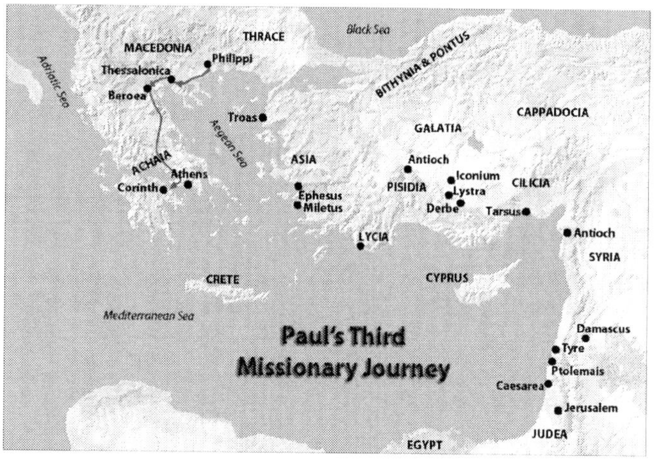

During this time, Paul wrote to the Romans, Probably from Corinth, 57–58 AD

During this time, Paul also wrote to the Galatians, Probably from Corinth, 58 AD

PAUL'S EPISTLE TO GALATIA

When and Where Paul Wrote Galatians

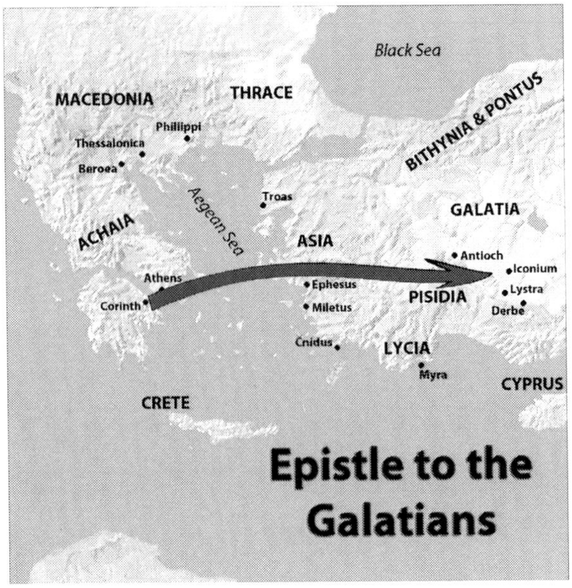

- **Galatians Endnote Says inaccurately that Galatians was written from Rome.** This note was not written by Paul but by a scribe at some time later on. Because of it, many assume that Galatians was written from Rome. But it was not. It was written at the same time as the epistle to the Romans, which of course was not written in Rome but was written elsewhere and sent back to Rome.

  Though neither the place nor date of writing of the letter to the Galatian Saints can be established with certainty, the evidence favors that it was written from Corinth in 58 AD, a few months after the epistle to the Romans, which was written in 57–58 AD.

  While Paul's epistle to the Galatians was written at this time, when Paul was in Corinth, both 1 and 2 Corinthians were written well before it, the previous spring and fall, from Ephesus and Macedonia, respectively. The Gospel Doctrine manual discusses this epistle now, in this chapter, because of the similar content it contains to the events that occurred during Paul's time in Ephesus—namely, "Living in the Spirit." The epistle to the Romans and 1 and 2 Corinthians will be discussed in future chapters.

Why Paul Wrote Galatians

- **Who are the Galatians?** Paul was most likely writing to the southern part of Asia Minor, including the towns of Antioch, Derbe, Lystra, and Iconium—towns he visited on all three of his missionary journeys (Acts 13:13—14:23 and Acts 16:1–9).

  Paul's primary purpose for writing to the Galatians was to remind them that true freedom can be found only in the gospel of Jesus Christ and that holding onto Mosaic ordinances would destroy the freedom they had found in Christ. He demonstrated that although the Mosaic law was of value for the children of Israel prior to Christ's mortal ministry, its need was now superseded by the higher law.

- **Galatians 1:1 Paul is an Apostle.** He begins his epistle to the Galatians by calling himself "an apostle, (not of men, neither by man, but by Jesus Christ, and God the Father, who raised him from the dead)" (v. 1). In other words, this is not just a title for anyone who preaches the gospel (as some claim), or even one that he took upon himself, but a calling from the Lord.

- **Galatians 1:2–5 Paul uses a familiar greeting,** similar to those of all his other epistles. The letter brings greetings from himself and "all the brethren which are with me, unto the churches of Galatia" (v. 2). Then, once again, he makes a clear distinction between the Father and the Son: "Grace be to you and peace from God the Father, and from our Lord Jesus Christ, who gave himself for our sins, that he might deliver us from this present evil world, according to the will of God . . . our Father" (vv. 3–4). "To whom be glory for ever and ever. Amen" (v. 5).

PAUL'S APOSTOLIC AUTHORITY

Paul Chastises the Galatians' Apostasy

- **Galatians 1:6–9 Paul upbraids the Galatians for the apostasy already arising among them.** We see evidence in many epistles of an apostasy already underway during the lifetimes of the Apostles. In light of this evidence, the claim that there was no apostasy is absurd. Paul here speaks plainly of the process. "I marvel that ye are so soon removed from him that called you into the grace of Christ unto another gospel" (v. 6). They were believing things that Paul had not taught them when he was among them. And what they were now believing was not "another" gospel, because there is only one true gospel (v. 7). It was false doctrine. Paul observed that "there be some that trouble you, and would pervert the gospel of Christ" (v. 7). Why would someone do that? To gain a following, for sure, and perhaps for worldly gain or to promote immorality.

THEBIBLEREVIVAL.COM, #22

Paul wrote to stem the tide of apostasy

Paul was very clear in his warning. "Though we, or an angel from heaven, preach any other gospel unto you than that which we . . . preached unto you, let him be accursed" (v. 8). Paul had warned them of this "before, [and] so say I now again, If any man preach any other gospel unto you than that ye have received, let him be accursed" (v. 9).

Tad R. Callister observed:

> The Apostles spoke of wickedness that was occurring in their day and of further wickedness that would yet come to pass. Paul wrote to the Galatians: "O foolish Galatians,

> who hath bewitched you, that ye should not obey the truth" (Galatians 3:1). To Titus he spoke of those who professed God (those who were members of the Church), but were "abominable, and disobedient, and unto every good work reprobate" (Titus 1:16).... These were perilous times and Paul affirmed that some Saints had "already turned aside after Satan" (1 Timothy 5:15). Paul saw it all unraveling before his eyes and could hardly believe it: "I marvel that ye are so soon removed from him that called you into the grace of Christ" (Galatians 1:6)....
>
> However, the overwhelming evil that infected the Church was immorality. It is mentioned again and again by the Apostles. Paul wrote to the Corinthians: "It is reported commonly that there is fornication among you" (1 Corinthians 5:1). He then reprimanded them, but evidently unsuccessfully, for he later wrote to the same Saints: "I shall bewail many which have sinned already, and have not repented of the uncleanness and fornication and lasciviousness which they have committed" (2 Corinthians 12:21)....
> Paul warned the Saints at Galatia: "But now, after that ye have known God, or rather are known of God, how turn ye again to the weak and beggarly elements [meaning, the lesser law of Moses], whereunto ye desire again to be in bondage?" (Galatians 4:9).... So widespread and pervasive was this return to former traditions that Paul lamented: "I am afraid of you, lest I have bestowed upon you labour in vain" (Galatians 4:11)....
>
> So grievous was this backlash of Mosaic formalism that Paul both lamented and warned Titus that "there are many unruly and vain talkers and deceivers, specially they of the circumcision: whose mouths must be stopped, who subvert whole houses, teaching things which they ought not" (Titus 1:10–11). Tertullian (AD 140–230) spoke of false Apostles who "crept in ... insisting upon circumcision and the Jewish ceremonies." Origen also acknowledged the seriousness of this heresy ... "there are some who accept Jesus, and boast on that account of being Christians, and yet would regulate their lives ... in accordance with the Jewish law.".... Paul warned that "of your own selves shall men arise, speaking perverse things, to draw away disciples after them" (Acts 20:30), and spoke of "false brethren unawares brought in" (Galatians 2:4).[5]

Elder Howard W. Hunter said, "From the earliest days of the Christian church, spurious gospels have been taught—not really gospels, as Paul pointed out, for there is only one gospel of Christ. Today is not different. We are surrounded by frustrations and advances in thought and learning which raise questions and doubts. These seem to drag men down and destroy faith and morality. Where, then, is hope in this world of frustration and moral decay? It lies in the knowledge and understanding of the truths taught by the Master, which must be taught by the Church of Christ without deviation and believed in and lived by its membership. These are eternal truths and will be so in perpetuity regardless of changing circumstances in society, development of new scientific achievements, or increase of man's knowledge."[6]

President Harold B. Lee warned about false teachings arising within the Church:

> There are some as wolves among us. By that, I mean some who profess membership in this church who are not sparing the flock. And among our own membership, men are arising speaking perverse things. Now perverse means diverting from the right or correct, and being obstinate in the wrong, willfully, in order to draw the weak and unwary members of the Church away after them.

And as the Apostle Paul said, it is likewise a marvel to us today, as it was in that day, that some members are so soon removed from those who taught them the gospel and are removed from the true teachings of the gospel of Christ to be led astray into something that corrupts the true doctrines of the gospel of Christ into vicious and wicked practices and performances.

These, as have been evidenced by shocking events among some of these splinter groups, have been accursed, as the prophets warned; and they are obviously in the power of that evil one who feeds the gullible with all the sophistries which Satan has employed since the beginning of time.[7]

Paul's Conversion, Doctrine, and Authority

- **Galatians 1:10–14 His gospel is not of man; he learned it by revelation from Jesus Christ.** Especially among Gentiles, conversion was a challenging cultural experience. Their former ways of life still surrounded them. Greek philosophy still dominated all public discourse. They were "outsiders within" who abandoned the doctrines and practices of a pagan world but still lived among those who cherished them. It was easy for someone to preach a less-demanding gospel—one that combined familiar cultural norms with the gospel of Jesus Christ. It was the philosophies of men mingled with scripture.

  Paul asked, "For do I now persuade men, or God? or do I seek to please men?" (v. 10) And "if I yet pleased men, I should not be the servant of Christ" (v. 10). He proclaimed that "the gospel which was preached of me is not after man" (v. 11). He "neither received it of man, neither was I taught it, but by the revelation of Jesus Christ" (v. 12).

ANONYMOUS

Saul was a member of the Sanhedrin

- **Galatians 1:13–17 Paul himself had once preached a false but culturally-embedded religion.** "In time[s] past in the Jews' religion, . . . beyond measure I persecuted the church of God, and wasted it: And profited in the Jews' religion above many . . . in mine own nation, being more exceedingly zealous of the traditions of my fathers" (vv. 13–14). "But when it pleased God . . . to reveal his Son in me, that I might preach him among the heathen; immediately I conferred not with flesh and blood: Neither went I up to Jerusalem to them which were apostles before me; but I went into Arabia, and returned again unto Damascus" (vv. 15–17). Paul is referring here to his first missionary work, which was done in the vicinity of Damascus shortly after the Lord appeared to him on the road to that city. Once an enemy of the Church, Paul was now immediately a witness for it, and bore that witness in all the surrounding area.

- **Galatians 1:18, 20–24 Paul's call to the Apostleship.** It was "after three years" that Paul was summoned and "went up to Jerusalem to see Peter, and abode with him fifteen days." Presumably during those days he received his official call to be an Apostle, and he received it from the Lord's Prophet and President of the Church: Peter.

  After this short visit Paul preached in Syria [Antioch] and Cilicia [Tarsus, his home town], but was personally unknown to Church members in Judea (vv. 20–21). All that they knew about him was that their former persecutor was now preaching faith in Jesus Christ (v. 23). "And they glorified God in me" (v. 24).

ANONYMOUS

James the brother of the Lord

- **Galatians 1:19 James, the Lord's brother, is also an Apostle.** James, the son of Zebedee, who, with his brother John had constituted the rest of the original First Presidency, was now dead. He had been martyred at Jerusalem in 62 AD. In his place, apparently, had been appointed the Lord's half-brother James. Like Paul, this James had received an open vision of the resurrected Lord, shortly after His resurrection. Now, like the James before him, he presided over the local congregation at Jerusalem and acted as a counselor to Peter. Paul observes that while he was as Jerusalem "other of the apostles saw I none, save James the Lord's brother."

- **Galatians 2:1–2 Paul returns and reports to the First Presidency.** Paul's next trip to Jerusalem was 14 years later. He went to report on the work in which he, Barnabas, Titus, and others had been engaged (v. 1). Paul said he "went up by revelation, and communicated unto them that gospel which I [had] preach[ed] among the Gentiles" (v. 2). This report was given "privately to them which were of reputation, lest by any means I should run, or had run, in vain" (v. 2). Paul understood that his work would be in vain unless he had the approval of the Lord's leaders.

- **Galatians 2:6 Paul did not receive the gospel from the Apostles; he already had it.** The brethren he reported to seemed to be "somewhat" [meaning "important"], but "whatsoever they were, it maketh no matter to me: God accepteth no man's person" and as far as knowledge of the gospel is concerned they "added nothing to me." In other words, though he recognized their authority and the need to report to them (see

Galatians 2:1–2 above), they were not the source of his testimony of Christ or his knowledge of the gospel. Those he had obtained on his own. (See Galatians 1:15–17).

- **Galatians 2:7–9 Paul's ministry is to the Gentiles.** The brethren "saw that the gospel of the uncircumcision [meaning to the Gentiles] was committed unto me" (v. 7). The need for this ministry had been made known unto Peter, and now "was mighty in me toward the Gentiles" (v. 8). So, "when James [the brother of the Lord], Cephas [Peter], and John, who seemed to be pillars [the First Presidency], perceived the grace that was given unto me, they gave to me and Barnabas the right hands of fellowship; that we should go unto the heathen" while they focused on "the circumcision" (the Jews) (v. 9). If Paul's ordination as an Apostle did not come 14 years earlier when he first visited with Peter, it certainly came at this time. And now he was set apart, along with Barnabas, to take the gospel to the Gentiles.

Paul also assisted the poor

- **Galatians 2:10 Taking care of the poor.** Paul's responsibilities included more than the preaching of the gospel; it also included "remember[ing] the poor," which work Paul was equally "forward [anxious] to do." Thus, he had both temporal and spiritual responsibilities, and whatever funds for the poor he collected from the Gentiles, he was to use locally and forward the rest to the authorites in Jerusalem.

- **Galatians 2:11–14 A controversy arises between Paul and Peter.** This was not unusual. Several disagreements among early Church leaders are discussed in the book of Acts and in Galatians (Acts 15:36–40; Galatians 2:11–14). But this one is particularly interesting because of who it involved—Peter and Paul—and because of what it involved: Jewish cultural practices that were insulting to the Gentiles. In this case, on one occasion when "Peter was come to Antioch," Paul "withstood him to the face" over an issue for which Paul believed "he was to be blamed" (v. 11).

  Apparently, on a previous occasion, "certain [men] came from [were assigned to visit by] James," and when they arrived at Antioch they observed that Peter "did eat with the Gentiles" (v. 12). When Peter saw that they had come, "he withdrew and separated himself," fearing the disapproval of these Jewish members of the Church (v. 12). When Peter did this, "other Jews dissembled likewise with him; insomuch that Barnabas also was carried away with their dissimulation" (v. 13). We can only imagine how this made the Gentile members of the Church feel on that occasion.

Paul was incensed, believing that they were behaving "not uprightly according to the truth of the gospel," and said to Peter in front of them all, "If thou, being a Jew, livest after the manner of Gentiles, and not as do the Jews, why compellest thou the Gentiles to live as do the Jews?" (v. 14). In other words, if Gentile members have to accommodate Jews, why can't Jews also accommodate Gentiles? Peter was setting a bad example.

Elder Bruce R. McConkie said:

> Peter and Paul—both of whom were apostles, both of whom received revelations, saw angels, and were approved of the Lord, and both of whom shall inherit the fulness of the Father's kingdom—these same righteous and mighty preachers disagreed on a basic matter of church policy. Peter was the President of the Church; Paul, an apostle and Peter's junior in the church hierarchy, was subject to the direction of the chief apostle. But Paul was right and Peter was wrong. Paul stood firm, determined that they should walk "uprightly according to the truth of the gospel"; Peter temporized for fear of offending Jewish semi-converts who still kept the law of Moses.
>
> The issue was not whether the Gentiles should receive the gospel. Peter himself had received the revelation that God was no respecter of persons, and that those of all lineages were now to be heirs of salvation along with the Jews (Acts 10:21–35). Further, the heads of the Church, in council assembled, with the Holy Ghost guiding their minds and directing their decisions, had determined that the Gentiles who received the gospel should not be subject to the law of Moses (Acts 15:1–35).
>
> The Jewish members of the Church, however, had not been able to accept this decision without reservation. They themselves continued to conform to Mosaic performances, and they expected Gentile converts to do likewise. Peter sided with them; Paul publicly withstood the chief apostle and won the debate, as could not otherwise have been the case. Without question, if we had the full account, we would find Peter reversing himself and doing all in his power to get the Jewish Saints to believe that the law of Moses was fulfilled in Christ and no longer applied to anyone either Jew or Gentile.[8]

THE DOCTRINE OF JUSTIFICATION

The Law vs. Grace

- **Galatians 3:11 Justification requires faith in Jesus Christ.** To be "justified" is to be made righteous, holy, or worthy of salvation. Contrary to what Jews had believed for centuries, the Law of Moses was not sufficient for salvation. Paul declared that "no man is justified by the law in the sight of God," and that "the just shall live by faith." And by that he meant faith in Jesus Christ.

- **Galatians 2:16–17, 21 We are not saved by our obedience.** The Jews believed (as do some Church members today) that obedience alone would save them. They were strictly obedient to the commandments as they understood them (the Law of Moses). But Paul clearly taught that obedience was not enough to save them. "A man is not justified by the works of the law, but by the faith of Jesus Christ," he declared, and "by the works of the law shall no flesh be justified" (v. 16). No matter how hard they try to keep the commandments, those who believe in Christ fall short of perfection and are still "found sinners." So will Christ save them "in their sins" because they were obedient to the best of their ability? "God forbid," said Paul (v. 17). While obedience is required, we can ultimately be saved only by "the grace of God," and "if righteousness come by [obedience to] the law, then Christ is dead in vain" (v. 21). In other words, if obedience to the commandments alone saves us, then Jesus' atonement was in vain.

— **2 Nephi 25:23 Christ's atonement saves us "after all we can do."** Nephi said that he "labor[ed] diligently to write, to persuade our children, and also our brethren, to believe in Christ," in order to be "reconciled to God." He explained the relationship between obedience and faith by saying, "it is by grace that we are saved, after all we can do" (emphasis added). Thus, we do all we can do, and then, though we fall short, Christ does the rest through His atonement.

The Gospel of Christ Pre-dated the Law

- **Galatians 3:8 The gospel was preached to Abraham in his day.** If we can inherit salvation by means of obedience alone, then salvation is not obtained by "promise" (covenant). But God "gave it to Abraham by promise." He received the gospel in his day, with all of its ordinances and covenants.

  The Prophet Joseph Smith said:

The Gospel was preached to Abraham

> It will be noticed that, according to Paul, (Gal. 3:8) the Gospel was preached to Abraham. We would like to be informed in what name the Gospel was then preached, whether it was in the name of Christ or some other name. If in any other name, was it the Gospel? And if it was the Gospel, and that preached in the name of Christ, had it any ordinances? If not, was it the Gospel? And if it had ordinances what were they? Our friends may say, perhaps, that there were never any ordinances except those of offering sacrifices before the coming of Christ, and that it could not be possible before the Gospel to have been administered while the law of sacrifices of blood was in force. But we will recollect that Abraham offered sacrifice, and notwithstanding this, had the Gospel preached to him.[9]

- **Galatians 3:16–17 The doctrine and covenants of Christ pre-dated the law of Moses.** Many suppose that the teachings of Christ were new, and that they replaced the Law of Moses. But this is not so. Paul observes that "to Abraham and his seed were the promises made." And Paul explains further that this means that Abraham knew about his "seed" Jesus Christ (v. 16).

Paul further explained that "the covenant [gospel], that was confirmed before of God in Christ, the law, which was four hundred and thirty years after, cannot disannul, that it should make the promise of none effect" (v. 17). This deserves closer examination so that we clearly understand what Paul is saying.

— "the covenant"	The gospel with all its ordinances and covenants.
— "of God"	It was given to Abraham by God.
— "in Christ"	It was given to him in the name of Christ.
— "the law"	The law of Moses, which was given 430 years later.
— "cannot disannul"	Does not replace the gospel of Christ given to Abraham. If it did, then it would make the covenants made to Abraham of "none effect."

The Gospel of Christ Covenants/Ordinances In the name of Christ	➜ 430 yrs ➜	The Law of Moses Lesser ordinances Because of disobedience

- **Hebrews 4:2 The gospel in its fulness was also preached at Mt. Sinai.** The gospel which has been preached unto us was "preached, as well as unto them [the children of Israel]: but the word preached did not profit them, not being mixed with faith in them that heard it." Because of their lack of faith the gospel could do them no good, so God gave them a lesser set of expectations, the law of Moses, until they could learn to have faith in Christ. It is interesting and important to note that all of the ordinances they were given under the law of Moses used symbols clearly pointing them forward to Christ's atonement. Why else would they be required to sacrifice only first-born male lambs without spot or blemish and to shed their blood as an act of atonement for their sins?

- **Galatians 3:19 The law of Moses was added after the gospel was rejected.** What purpose did the law of Moses serve? Paul said, "It was added because of transgressions" and would serve its purpose only until "the seed [Christ] should come to whom the promise was made." And even the law of Moses was given "by angels in the hand of a mediator."

  The Prophet Joseph Smith said:

  > When the Israelites came out of Egypt they had the Gospel preached to them, according to Paul in his letter to the Hebrews, which says: "For unto us was the Gospel preached, as well as unto them: but the word preached did not profit them, not being mixed with faith in them that heard it" (Heb. 4:2). It is said again, in Gal. [3:19], that the law (of Moses, or the Levitical law) was "added" because of transgression. What, we ask, was this law added to, if it was not added to the Gospel? It must be plain that it was added to the Gospel, since we learn that they had the Gospel preached to them. . . .
  >
  > From these few facts, we conclude that whenever the Lord revealed Himself to men in ancient days, and commanded them to offer sacrifice to Him, that it was done that they

might look forward in faith to the time of His coming, and rely upon the power of that atonement for a remission of their sins. And this they have done, thousands who have gone before us, whose garments are spotless, and who are, like Job, waiting with an assurance like his, that they will see Him in the latter day upon the earth, even in their flesh.[10]

- **Galatians 3:24–25 The Law was a "schoolmaster" for the children of Israel.** Paul called it "our schoolmaster to bring us unto Christ, that we might be justified by faith" (v. 24). And, he said, "after that faith is come, we are no longer under a schoolmaster" (v. 25).

A Jewish schoolmaster with young students

  "Schoolmaster" is translated from the Greek word *paidagogus*, from which we also have the word pedagogue or "teacher," and pedagogy or "method of teaching." In Paul's time a *paidagogos* was a special tutor who was responsible for a child's education and was also expected to train the child in all ways necessary to prepare him for adulthood. By using this analogy, Paul explains the purpose of the Mosaic law—to prepare the "children" of Israel for the more mature laws and ordinances of the gospel.

Joint-Heirs with Christ

- **Galatians 3:26–29 Baptized disciples of Christ are children of God and heirs of the blessings of Abraham.** We become "children of God by faith in Christ Jesus" (v. 26) and by being baptized in order to "put on Christ" [take His name upon us] (v. 27). As children of Christ, we cease to be Jew or Gentile, slave or free, or even male or female; we "are all one in Christ Jesus" (v. 28), equally loved by Him as His spiritual offspring. And if we are thus made children of Christ we are also "Abraham's seed, and heirs [of the] promise[s]" made to him (v. 29).

- **Galatians 4:1–7 Through Christ we can also become joint-heirs of God with our Savior-brother.** An heir of any kind, while he is a child, is no different than a servant, being unaware of who he is (v. 1). Such an heir is placed "under tutors and governors until the time appointed of the father" (v. 2). "Even so we, when we were children, were in bondage under the elements of the world" (v. 3). "But when the fulness of the time was come, God sent forth his Son . . . to redeem them that were under the law," in order that they might receive all the privileges of a son who is an heir (vv. 4–5).

Paul said, "because ye are sons, God hath sent forth the Spirit of his Son into your hearts, crying, Abba, Father" (v. 6). "Abba Father" was a term of endearment in Paul's day which meant, essentially, "Daddy." Thus, Paul was saying the Spirit teaches us that we have a very personal relationship with God the Father as His literal children. "Wherefore thou art no more a servant, but a son; and if a son, then an heir of God through Christ" (v. 7). The analogy is clear. We are destined to inherit all that the Father has as His heirs, but only through faith in Jesus Christ.

ADDITIONAL TEACHINGS IN GALATIANS

- **Galatians 3:1–5 Continuing in the faith.** In some of the strongest language he ever used, Paul rebukes the Galatians for forgetting principles of the gospel he taught them. "O foolish Galatians, who hath bewitched you, that ye should not obey the truth?" Paul had taught them concerning Jesus Christ and His atonement. And now he asked of them, "Received ye the Spirit by the works of the law, or by the hearing of faith? Are ye so foolish? Having begun in the Spirit, are ye now made perfect by the flesh?" (vv. 2–3). He wondered whether they had "suffered so many things in vain" and hoped that it would still not be in vain (v. 4). He had ministered to them and worked miracles among them, and now they were turning back to the law of Moses. He asked them whether they believed that he did these things among them "by the works of the law, or by the hearing of faith" (v. 5). This chastisement sounds like it was primarily aimed at Jewish converts who were having trouble giving up their old beliefs and practices.

- **Galatians 4:8–12 Following Paul's personal example.** Paul also expresses his concern about Galatian Saints who had been Gentiles before their conversion. He asked them to follow his personal example of faith. He reminded them that "when ye knew not God, ye did service unto them which by nature are no gods [idols]" (v. 8). How, he wonders, "after . . . ye have known God, or rather are known of God" can they "turn . . . again to the weak and beggarly elements, whereunto ye desire again to be in bondage?" (v. 9). They had returned to such practices as astrology—observing "days, and months, and times, and years" (v. 10). Paul wonders aloud whether he has "bestowed upon you [my] labour in vain" (v. 11). "Brethren, I beseech you, be as I am," he pleads, and remember that Paul is "as ye are"—human—and they are not injuring him by their behavior, they are offending God (v. 12).

- **Galatians 4:21–31 The "allegory" of Hagar and Sara.** To understand this allegory, we must know that Hagar represents the temporal law, as does its place of origin, Mount Sinai. Sara represents the new spiritual law, as does one of its places of origin, the Mount of Beatitudes. Through this figurative story, Paul is teaching about the law of Moses and the gospel of Jesus Christ.

  "It is written, that Abraham had two sons, the one by a bondmaid, the other by a freewoman (v. 22). But he who was of the bondwoman [Ishmael, born of Hagar] was born after the flesh; but he of the freewoman [Isaac, born of Sarah] was by promise" (v.

23). This circumstance provides "an allegory: for these [represent] the two covenants" (v. 24).

The law of Moses came from "mount Sinai [and] gendereth [leads] to bondage" (v. 24). Paul also calls this mountain "Agar." The results of what happened on Mt. Sinai now "answereth to [have affected] Jerusalem which . . . is in bondage with her children" (v. 25). Compare this, Paul suggests, to the "Jerusalem which is above [in heaven] is free, [and] is the mother of us all" (v. 26).

It was never intended that Israel should remain childless and barren with regard to the gospel. "For it is written, Rejoice, thou barren that bearest not; break forth and cry, thou that travailest [labors in childbirth] not" over the fact that "the desolate [unworthy] hath many more children than she which hath an husband [Israel]" (v. 27).

Paul reminds the Saints that "we, brethren, as Isaac was, are the children of promise" (v. 28). And as "he that was born after the flesh [Ishmael] persecuted him that was born after the Spirit [Isaac], even so it is now" (v. 29). "Nevertheless what saith the scripture? Cast out the bondwoman [Hagar] and her son: for the son of the bondwoman [Ishamel] shall not be heir with the son of the freewoman [Isaac]" (v. 30). "So then, brethren, we are not children of the bondwoman, but of the free" (v. 31).

- **Galatians 5:1–6 The burden of the law of Moses is past.** Paul advises them to stand fast in the liberty of the gospel of Christ and not be burdened by taking back the yoke of the Mosaic law. "Stand fast therefore in the liberty wherewith Christ hath made us free, and be not entangled again with the yoke of bondage" (v. 1).

THEBIBLEREVIVAL.COM, #30

Paul always taught the Jews first

Christ will not reward them for being circumcised (v. 2). Paul testifies that those who follow the law of Moses (represented by the idea of being circumcised) are "debtor[s] to do the whole law" (v. 3). And the atonement of Christ will be "of no effect unto you." In other words, if you believe that you are "justified by the law" then you will be "fallen from grace"— unaffected by the atonement because you do not believe in it (v. 4). Those who "through the Spirit wait wait for the hope of righteousness by faith" realize that "in Jesus Christ neither circumcision . . . nor uncircumcision" matters; the only thing that matters is "faith which worketh by love" (vv. 5–6).

Elder Bruce R. McConkie explained, "Circumcision, as a religious ordinance, is the token and sign certifying belief in, acceptance of, and conformity to the whole Mosaic system, and therefore for the Christians of that day it constituted a rejection of Christ and His gospel which replaced the law."[11]

- **Galatians 5:13 Use agency wisely.** Paul reminds us that we have been "called unto liberty," but we should not use that liberty "for an occasion to [satisfy] the flesh, but [instead] by love serve one another."

- **Galatians 5:13–15 The law is fulfilled in one thing: Loving our neighbor.** As Jesus Himself had said, "the law is fulfilled in one word, even in this; Thou shalt love thy neighbour as thyself" (v. 14). And if we choose to "bite and devour one another," we will also be "consumed one of another" (v. 15).

- **Galatians 5:16–23 Comparing natural and spiritual things.** "Walk in the Spirit," Paul advised, "and ye shall not fulfil the lust of the flesh" (v. 16). These two influences are at war with one another. "The flesh lusteth against the Spirit, and the Spirit against the flesh: and these are contrary the one to the other" (v. 17). "Now the works of the flesh are manifest, which are these: adultery, fornication, uncleanness, lasciviousness, idolatry, witchcraft, hatred, variance, emulations, wrath, strife, seditions, heresies, envyings, murders, drunkenness, revellings, and such like" and "they which do such things shall not inherit the kingdom of God" (vv. 19–21). "But the fruit of the Spirit is love, joy, peace, longsuffering, gentleness, goodness, faith, meekness, temperance: [and] against such there is no law" (vv. 22–23).

  President David O. McKay said: "Man is a dual being, and his life a plan of God. That is the first fundamental fact to keep in mind. Man has a natural body and a spiritual body. . . . Man's body, therefore, is but the tabernacle in which his spirit dwells. Too many, far too many, are prone to regard the body as the man, and consequently to direct their efforts to the gratifying of the body's pleasures, its appetites, its desires, its passions."[12]

THEBIBLEREVIVAL.COM, #30

- **Galatians 6:1–3 Show mercy and kindness to the weak.** Real Christians humbly help those who are weaker. Paul said, "Brethren, if a man be overtaken in a fault, ye which are spiritual, restore such an one in the spirit of meekness; considering thyself, lest thou also be tempted. Bear ye one another's burdens, and so fulfil the law of Christ" (vv. 1–2). But all this must be done humbly, not looking down on others, "for if a man think himself to be something, when he is nothing, he deceiveth himself" (v. 3).

- **Galatians 6:7–8 The law of the harvest is an eternal principle.** "Be not deceived," Paul warns, "God is not mocked: for whatsoever a man soweth, that shall he also reap" (v. 7). "For he that soweth to his flesh shall of the flesh reap corruption; but he that soweth to the Spirit shall of the Spirit reap life everlasting" (v. 8).

- **Galatians 6:9–10 "Be [not] weary in well doing,"** said Paul, "for in due season we shall reap, if we faint not" (v. 9). "As we have therefore opportunity, let us do good unto all men, especially unto them who are of the household of faith" (v. 10).

- **Galatians 6:17 Bearing the marks of Jesus Christ.** Our English word *stigma* is translated from the Greek word *stigmata*, which means "a wound or scar, or a brand with which slaves were marked." Paul uses it here to suggest that our "scars" of adversity are marks of faithfulness in the face of persecution. Paul says that he, like we, "bear[s] in [his] body the marks of the Lord Jesus."

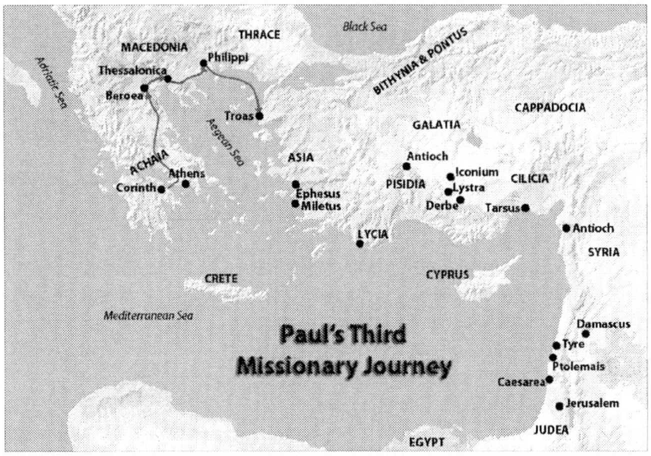

- **Acts 20:3–6 Paul escapes his enemies and returns overland to Philippi, then sails to Troas.** Paul had been in Corinth for 3 months, waiting for favorable weather to sail back to Jerusalem. During this time he had written epistles to the Romans and the Galatians. But apparently, "the Jews laid wait for him, as he was about to sail into Syria," and when he discovered this "he purposed to return [by land] through Macedonia" (v. 3). He and several companions walked back to Philippi and then sailed from there to Troas, where Timothy and others, who had gone ahead of him, waited there for his arrival (vv. 4–5). The trip by boat took 5 days, and then they stayed at Troas for 7 days (v. 6).

Notes:

1. Jackson, *Joseph Smith's Commentary on the Bible,* 151.
2. *History of the Church,* 4:4–5.
3. Jackson, *Joseph Smith's Commentary on the Bible,* 152.
4. *Natural History,* 36.21.95.
5. *The Inevitable Apostasy and the Promised Restoration,* [Salt Lake City, UT: Deseret Book Company, 2006], 27–30, 39.
6. In Conference Report, October 1973, 66; or *Ensign,* January 1974, 56.
7. In Conference Report, October 1972, 125; or *Ensign,* January 1973, 105.
8. *Doctrinal New Testament Commentary,* 3 vols. [1966–1973], 2:463–464.

9. *Teachings of the Prophet Joseph Smith,* sel. Joseph Fielding Smith [1976], 60.

10. *Teachings of the Prophet Joseph Smith,* 60–61.

11. *Doctrinal New Testament Commentary,* 2:479.

12. "The Abundant Life in a Selfish World," *Improvement Era,* September 1949, 558.

Chapter 33

The Temple of God

(1 Corinthians 1–6)

INTRODUCTION

Problems Then, Problems Now

President Joseph F. Smith said in 1914, "There are at least three dangers that threaten the Church within, and the authorities need to awaken to the fact that the people should be warned unceasingly against them. As I see these, they are flattery of prominent men in the world, false educational ideas, and sexual impurity."[1]

These are the same problems faced by the Saints in Paul's day. Nine of Paul's fourteen epistles contain direct instruction about sexual morality. The Corinthian Saints, in particular, struggled with immorality. And it definitely affected their faith. Elder Melvin J. Ballard said, "The easiest way to destroy a man's faith is to destroy his morality."[2]

PAUL'S 1ST CORINTHIAN EPISTLE

Paul's first epistle to the Corinthians was written from Ephesus in 57 AD, during his two-year stay there, prior to going to Corinth. It was probably written in the spring around Passover time. This would make it the first epistle he wrote on his third missionary journey. He would later write a second epistle to the Corinthians from Macedonia, and two epistles, to the Romans and Galatians, from Corinth.

Why Paul Wrote 1st Corinthians

Paul wrote to the Corinthians for three reasons:

- To rebuke the Corinthians for their morally questionable way of living.
- To correct misunderstandings from a former letter, now lost (1 Corinthians 7:1).
- To answer questions posed by the Corinthians in their return letter, also lost.

Elder Howard W. Hunter said:

> One of the fascinating subjects in the life of the Apostle [Paul] is the exchange of communications and news between him and his converts in Corinth. The communications revealed that there were factions forming in the branch with different views regarding moral conduct and doctrine. Some of the converts were assuming a libertine or freethinking attitude with respect to the doctrines which had been taught to them by Paul and the missionaries who worked with him. Some were defending loose sexual standards that were

rampant in the notorious city. These problems came into being because of the background of the new converts and the conditions of the time and place in which they were living. They were reactions to the new faith which had been taught to them against the old background which had been part of their former conduct and thinking.[3]

The City of Corinth

Corinth, an ancient city in Greece, across a sea channel from Athens, was destroyed in 146 BC by the Romans. Julius Caesar rebuilt the city 100 years later with the intent that it would be the capitol city of the province of Achaia. Corinth was a prosperous trading center with a large and growing population who were mostly pagan. It was near the site of the Isthmian games—a major passion for the Greeks which attracted large crowds.

PUBLIC DOMAIN

Ruins at Corinth with the Acrocorinth behind

As at Athens, the love of philosophy and endless questioning without answers was well established at Corinth. Paul also experienced problems at Corinth with the Judaizers who sought to discredit him and destroy the Church he built up at Corinth.

The Saints at Corinth were surrounded with temptations. Corinth had a worldwide reputation in the ancient world for its immorality. It was the site of the famous temple of Aphrodite (Venus), the goddess of love, which sat atop the famous Acrocorinth rock mountain. The temple had 1,000 "priestesses" who were nothing more than glorified prostitutes who performed their acts as an act of worship to Aphrodite. In Paul's day, to "Corinthianize" meant to engage in reckless debauchery. And in stage plays, Corinthians were usually portrayed on the stage as immoral drunkards. Even today, calling someone a Corinthian means that he is given totally over to licentious desires. Thus, it is not surprising that in his letters to Corinth Paul sharply condemns immorality and the lusts of the flesh.

There are interesting and valuable parallels here with the circumstances of our own day. The world has become "Corinthianized" by the overflowing scourge of pornography. Our youth and adults are surrounded with explicit images and loose morals. The message of the Corinthian epistles are very timely today.

AVOIDING FACTIONS

Unity among Members

- **1 Corinthians 1:10–15 Paul warns against divisions, factions, and schisms.** Members were beginning to divide themselves according to the person who taught and baptized them. Paul wrote, "For it hath been declared unto me of you, my brethren, . . . that there are contentions among you" (v. 11). . . . "Every one of you saith, I am of Paul; and I of Apollos; and I of Cephas [Peter]; and I of Christ" (v. 12). Paul firmly reminded them that they were all of "the Church of God" and not of Paul, Apollos, or Peter. "Is Christ divided? was Paul crucified for you? or were ye baptized in the name of Paul? I thank God that I baptized none of you,"—that was done by Crispus and Gaius—"Lest any should say that I had baptized in mine own name" (vv. 13–15). "Now I beseech you, brethren, by the name of our Lord Jesus Christ, that ye all speak the same thing, and that there be no divisions among you; but that ye be perfectly joined together in the same mind and in the same judgment" (v. 10).

- **1 Corinthians 3:2–8 Paul again speaks out against pride and cliquishness in the Church.** Paul had fed these converts "with milk, and not with meat" because they were not able to bear deeper doctrine and still were not able now (v. 2). Paul observed that they were still "carnal" [worldly], with "envying, and strife, and divisions" among them (v. 3). So long as they were declaring themselves to be "of Paul" or "of Apollos" they were showing themselves to be carnal (v. 4). "Who then is Paul, and who is Apollos, but ministers by whom ye believed, even as the Lord gave to every man? I have planted, Apollos watered; but God gave the increase" (vv. 5–6). And those that did the planting and watering were not the cause of their conversion; it was "God that [gave] the increase" (v. 7). Paul observed that he and Apollos "are one" and associating oneself with either one of them will profit them nothing because "every man shall receive his own reward according to his own labour" (v. 8).

Rhetoric vs. Wisdom

The Greeks were a haughty people, relishing in their philosophical associations and debates. They spent endless hours debating the philosophies of men and thought that by doing so they were achieving the highest form of human perfection through their intellect. We should find this situation familiar in our own day, when scholars engage in the same debates, citing their favorite Greek philosophers as they do it. Paul was intelligent and learned, but understood that debate was not the way to teach concerning Christ. Reason must be mixed with Spirit and presented humbly and with testimony.

- **1 Corinthians 1:26–31 "God uses the weak of the world to confound those who are mighty.** Paul noted that among the leaders of the Church in his day "not many wise men after the flesh, not many mighty, not many noble, are called: But God hath chosen the foolish things of the world to confound the wise; and God hath chosen the weak things of the world to confound the things which are mighty" (vv. 26–27). God uses the "base things of the world" to do His work (v. 28). The word "base" which the King James Translators used in this case meant "lowly" or "humble." So what Paul is saying means that God takes the lowly and humble and despised and uses them to confound those who think they are wise (v. 28). Our wisdom comes from God as a result of "righteousness, and sanctification, and redemption" (v. 30). We seek to "glory in the Lord" rather than in men (v. 31).

- **1 Corinthians 2:1–16 Paul did not teach with the "enticing words of man's wisdom."** Though he could have done so, Paul did not come to them "with excellency of speech or of wisdom, declaring unto you the testimony of God" (v. 1). He decided "not to know any thing among you, save Jesus Christ, and him crucified" (v. 2). Paul approached them "in weakness, and in fear, and in much trembling," and his speaking and preaching "was not with enticing words of man's wisdom, but in demonstration of the Spirit and of power" (vv. 3–4). This was done so that their faith would not be based "in the wisdom of men, but in the power of God" (v. 5).

"ONE NIGHT IN CORINTH," G. FOXLEY, PROVIDENCE LITHOGRAPHIC CO.

  The wisdom that Paul and his associates used was "not the wisdom of this world, nor of the princes of this world, that come to nought: But . . . the wisdom of God . . . the hidden wisdom, which God ordained before the world unto our glory" (vv. 6–7). He is speaking here of the plan of salvation and the atonement of Christ, which were determined in the premortal world. This wisdom, said Paul "none of the princes of this world knew: for had they known it, they would not have crucified the Lord of glory" (v. 8).

- **1 Corinthians 2:9; 3:21–23 The glory and blessings that await the righteous.** Man does not comprehend—indeed, cannot comprehend—what awaits us in the celestial kingdom. Paul declared that "eye hath not seen, nor ear heard, neither have entered into the heart of man, the things which God hath prepared for them that love him." Sometimes these things are referred to in scripture as "unspeakable things," because there are no words that can adequately describe what the prophets have seen.

  "For all things are yours," Paul declares a few verses later (v. 21). No matter what it is, whether of "the world, or life, or death, or things present, or things to come; all are yours" (v. 22). "And ye are Christ's; and Christ is God's" (v. 23).

- **1 Corinthians 2:10–13 Teaching by the Spirit.** That which we know and believe has been "revealed . . . unto us by his Spirit: for the Spirit searcheth all things, yea, the deep things of God" (v. 10). Worldly things can be comprehended in worldly ways, using the ideas of men, but "the things of God knoweth no man, but [by] the Spirit of God" (v. 11). In other words, it is not possible to teach or to learn the things of God without the Spirit. Paul declared, "Now we have received, not the spirit of the world, but the spirit which is of God; that we might know the things that are freely given to us of God. Which things also we speak, not in the words which man's wisdom teacheth, but which the Holy Ghost teacheth; comparing spiritual things with spiritual" (vv. 12–13).

THEBIBLEREVIVAL.COM, #21

- **1 Corinthians 2:14 The natural man does not comprehend spiritual things.** "The natural man receiveth not the things of the Spirit of God: for they are foolishness unto him: neither can he know them, because they are spiritually discerned."

- **1 Corinthians 2:15–16 A spiritual man possesses the "mind of Christ."** A man who possesses the Spirit can "judge . . . all things" correctly (v. 15). God knows all things. No man can instruct Him. And when we have the Spirit, we are connected to the "mind of Christ," which makes us wiser than any amount of worldly knowledge can provide" (v. 16).

Elder Marion G. Romney said, "Now, I tell you that you can make every decision in your life correctly if you can learn to follow the guidance of the Holy Spirit. This you can do if you will discipline yourself to yield your own feelings to the promptings of the Spirit."[4]

Elder Bruce R. McConkie said, "There was of old, there is now, and to all eternity there shall be only one approved and proper way to preach the gospel—Preach by the power of the Spirit. Anything short of this is not of God and has neither converting nor saving power. All the religious learning, of all the professors of religion, of all the ages is as nothing compared to the Spirit-born testimony of one legal administrator. . . . There is one formula and one formula only for conveying saving truth to men—Preach by the power of the Spirit."[5]

- **1 Corinthians 3:19–23 From God's perspective, worldly-wise men are fools and their supposed wisdom is "foolishness."** Think about it for a minute. How much does our God know? And if we were to compare His intellect with that of the wisest man on earth, there would be absolutely no comparison. He is on a totally different level of understanding. That is why "the wisdom of this world is foolishness with God" (v. 19). God can "take . . . the wise in their own craftiness" because He "knoweth the thoughts of the wise, that they are vain" (vv. 19–20). "Therefore," said Paul, "let no man glory in men" (v. 21).

RAPHAEL

- **1 Corinthians 8:1 "Knowledge puffeth up, but charity edifieth."** This is one of many powerful declarations which Paul uses in his epistles. The point is that knowledge can lead to pride, and when it does it accomplishes nothing worthwhile. But acts of charity and love do make a difference and are far more important in the heavenly scheme of things.

- **1 Corinthians 4:1–2, 9–16 Paul invites them to follow his personal example.** He urges them to take "account of us, as of the ministers of Christ, and stewards of the mysteries of God," because "it is required in stewards, that a man be found faithful" (vv. 1–2). He and the other apostles are "appointed to death: for we are made a spectacle unto the world, and to angels, and to men" (v. 9). They become "fools for Christ's sake" and "weak" and "despised" so that the Saints might become "strong" and "honourable" (v. 10). "Even unto this present hour we both hunger, and thirst, and are naked, and are buffeted, and have no certain dwellingplace; And labour, working with our own hands: being reviled, we bless; being persecuted, we suffer it: Being defamed, we intreat: we are made as the filth of the world, and are the offscouring of all things unto this day" (vv. 11–13). Paul does not say these things to gain sympathy or to shame the Saints by comparison, but "as my beloved sons I warn you" (v. 14). They might have "ten thousand instructors" in the gospel, but few who will love them like a father; Paul loves them like a father because "I have begotten you through the gospel" (v. 15). So, he urges them to follow his example in enduring difficulties: "be ye followers of me" (v. 16).

- **1 Corinthians 4:17–21 Though Paul cannot come he is sending Timothy, his "beloved son" in the gospel.** Paul had great faith and trust in Timothy, whom he described as "my beloved son, and faithful in the Lord" (v. 17). Though Paul could not, at this time, come personally, he knew that Timothy would "bring [them] into remembrance of my ways which be in Christ," and which "I teach every where in every church" (v. 17). Apparently, some at Corinth had become "puffed up" and were complaining because Paul was not coming (v. 18). "But I will come to you shortly, if the Lord will," and when he does he will want to know "not the speech of them which are puffed up, but the power" [their spiritual strength] (v. 19). The kingdom of God is not built up by rhetoric or speech, "but in power" (v. 20). The choice is up to them. Paul can come "with a rod" [in the spirit of correction], "or in love, and in the spirit of meekness" (v. 21). That will depend on whether they humble themselves and set aside the spirit of criticism and contention, or not.

IMMORALITY

- **1 Corinthians 3:1 Understanding Paul.** Speaking of Paul's writings, the Apostle Peter said they were "hard to be understood" (2 Peter 3:16). There are two reasons for this. First, like the apostle James E. Talmage in our own day, Paul is a highly educated man who uses words and allegories that are not always familiar to the average reader.

REMBRANDT

  Second, his writings were translated by men in the 1600s who also had their own awkward way of saying things, using words that meant one thing in their day and entirely another in ours.

  There is no better example of this than this first verse of 1 Corinthians chapter 3: "And I, brethren, could not speak unto you as unto spiritual, but as unto carnal, even as unto babes in Christ." The key to understanding this is to insert "men and women" after the words "spiritual" and "carnal." If we do, then it reads like this: "And I, brethren, could not speak unto you as unto spiritual men and women, but as unto carnal men and women, even as unto babes in Christ."

- **1 Corinthians 3:16–17 Paul attacks the immorality that is so prevalent in Corinth.** The Corinthians practiced ritual fornication in their temples to Aphrodite. Paul here uses a multi-level metaphor to teach the Saints about the importance of personal morality: "Know ye not that ye are the temple of God, and that the Spirit of God dwelleth in you? If any man defile the temple of God, him shall God destroy; for the temple of God is holy, which temple ye are." This can be understood on two levels: (1) where the "temple" is the Church and its members, and (2) where the "temple" is their individual bodies. Either way, it is true.

Elder Joseph B. Wirthlin taught, "One of the most pervasive deceptions in recent years is the notion that immorality is normal and acceptable and has no negative consequences. In truth, immorality is the underlying cause of much suffering and many other problems that are prevalent today, including rampant disease, abortion, broken families, families without fathers, and mothers who themselves are children."[6]

Elder Boyd K. Packer taught, "[Satan] knows that this power of creation is not just an incident to the plan, but a key to it. He knows that if he can entice you to use this power prematurely, to use it too soon, or to misuse it in any way, you may well lose your opportunities for eternal progression."[7]

- **1 Corinthians 5:1, 6–7** "Fornication" is from the Greek *porneia* (same root as pornography), which means any extramarital sexual relations. Paul tells the Corinthian Saints that he has heard troubling reports that "there is fornication among you" (v. 1). And worse, it is "such fornication as is not so much as named among the Gentiles," namely "that [a man] should have [intercourse with] his father's wife" (v. 1). In this case, someone had married his stepmother, and needed to be excommunicated. Paul warns that "a little leaven leaveneth the whole lump" (v. 6), and that they must "purge out . . . the old leaven, that ye [the Church] may be a new lump [that is] unleavened" [by such wickedness] (v. 7).

  Elder Bruce R. McConkie said, "Apparently a member of the Church in Corinth had married his stepmother, either because she was a widow or had been separated from her prior husband. Such marriages were forbidden by the Mosaic code under penalty of excommunication. (Lev. 18:6–8, 29). Paul endorses the Mosaic prohibition, describes the intimacies resulting from such unions as fornication, condemns his Corinthian brethren for winking at the offense, and directs the excommunication of the offender. If the sinner were left in the Church, Paul reasons, his influence, as leaven, would spread throughout the whole Church."[8]

  The world, as we know, has reached a point where virtually "anything goes" when it comes to sexual relations. Television is full of adultery and fornication, which is treated as a joke or a game. Marriage is denigrated as unnecessary for "modern" couples, yet for homosexuals it is supposedly essential. The traditional family is under attack, and few love the truth about morality. In the midst of this confusion, the Lord has been crystal clear, both in the temple and in the scriptures. The Lord wants us to be a pure people.

  — **D&C 42:23 God's law of sexual morality.** We are not only to avoid immoral acts, but "he that looketh upon a woman to lust after her shall deny the faith, and shall not have the Spirit." And the penalty is severe: "If he repents not he shall be cast out [excommunicated]." Thus, looking at pornography is tantamount to adultery in the eyes of the Lord. So is sexual harassment in the workplace or anywhere else. We are to keep our minds and our bodies free from the taint of immorality.

  — **D&C 59:6 "Nor . . . anything like unto it."** Anything that mimicks intercourse in either its method or its results is also forbidden: masturbation, oral sex, petting, or lengthy and passionate kissing are just a few of the practices that are "like unto" intercourse.

Elder Richard G. Scott said: "Any sexual intimacy outside of the bonds of marriage—I mean any intentional contact with the sacred, private parts of another's body, with or without clothing—is a sin and is forbidden by God. It is also a transgression to intentionally stimulate these emotions within your own body.... Satan tempts one to believe that there are allowable levels of physical contact between consenting individuals who seek the powerful stimulation of emotions they produce, and if kept within bounds, no harm will result. As a witness of Jesus Christ, I testify that is absolutely false.... Decide what you will and will not do. When temptation comes, do not change your standards."[9]

President Spencer W. Kimball said, "He will use his logic to confuse and his rationalizations to destroy. He will shade meanings, open doors an inch at a time, and lead from purest white through all the shades of gray to the darkest black."[10]

- **1 Corinthians 5:11 We should not have contact with immoral persons or places.** Paul said, "I have written unto you not to keep company [with] any man [even if he is a brother in the Church] that is . . . a fornicator, or covetous, or an idolater, or a railer, or a drunkard, or an extortioner; with such an one [we are] not to eat."

- **1 Corinthians 5:12–13 Keep the Church pure and leave the world to God.** It is not our business to "judge them . . . that are without" (the world), but to "judge them that are within" (v. 12). Those "that are without God judgeth," but we are to "put away from among yourselves" any wicked and adulterous member of the Church (v. 13).

- **1 Corinthians 6:15, 19–20 Our bodies belong to Christ.** "It's my body!" say rebellious and immoral persons in every age. "It's nobody else's business what I do with it." Not so. We would not even have a body had it not been created for us in our mother's womb by the miraculous power of the Creator, Jesus Christ. We did not create it ourselves; it is a gift given to us from God. "Ye are not your own," Paul declared (v. 19). "For ye are bought with a price" (the atonement) and should "therefore glorify God in your body, and in your spirit, which are God's" (v. 20).

- **1 Corinthians 6:15–17 We become whatever we join.** "Know ye not that your bodies are the members of [belong to] Christ?" asked Paul. "Shall I then take the members of Christ, and make them the members of an harlot? God forbid" (v. 15). When we are "joined to" (have intercourse with) "an harlot," the two of us become "one body" through that act (v. 16). That makes us a harlot also. On the other hand, when we are "joined unto the Lord" spiritually, our spirit and His become "one spirit" (v. 17). We become like Him.

- **1 Corinthians 6:18–19 Our bodies are the temple of the Spirit.** "Flee fornication," Paul adjures us. Virtually every other sin is done "without the body; but he that committeth fornication sinneth against his own body" (v. 18). And since "your body is the temple of the Holy Ghost which is in you," if you defile your body the Spirit will leave you (v. 19).

Notes:

1. *Gospel Doctrine*, 5th ed. [1939], 312–313.
2. In Conference Report, April, 1929, 65.

3. In Conference Report, April 1969, 136.

4. In Conference Report, October 1961, 60.

5. *Doctrinal New Testament Commentary*, 3 vols. [1966–1973], 2:318.

6. In Conference Report, Oct. 1994, 100–101; or *Ensign*, November 1994, 76.

7. In Conference Report, April 1972, 137; or *Ensign*, July 1972, 112.

8. *Doctrinal New Testament Commentary*, 2:335.

9. In Conference Report, October 1994, 51; or *Ensign*, November 1994, 38.

10. *Faith Precedes the Miracle* [1972], 152.

Chapter 34

Keeping the Ordinances

(1 Corinthians 11–16)

INTRODUCTION

In this part of 1st Corinthians, Paul is responding to questions asked in a previous letter sent to him from the Corinthian Saints that we do not have today. Paul wrote, "Now to deal with the questions you wrote about—Is it good for a man to stay away from women?" (1 Corinthians 7:1; footnotes 1a, 2a). Thus, 1st Corinthians is really the second epistle Paul wrote to the Saints at Corinth.

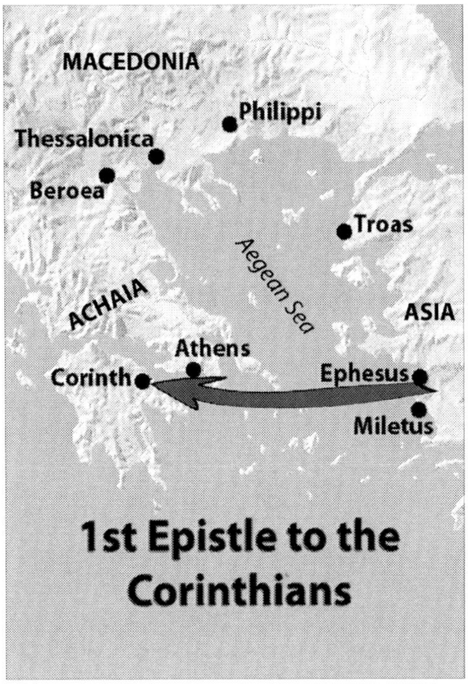

As with our previous chapter taken from 1st Corinthians, these subjects are taken from a letter written by Paul while he was at Ephesus for two years during his 2nd missionary journey. He would soon visit Corinth personally, but in the meantime he had a lively correspondence with them by means of at least three letters that he wrote and at least one letter that they wrote back to him.

Because of the rampant immorality at Corinth, Paul spent much of his letters warning against it.

MARRIAGE AND GENDER ROLES

Paul's Teachings on Marriage

Many misunderstand Paul's teachings in 1 Corinthians 7 because of mistranslation and misinterpretation, taking statements in this chapter out of context. All scriptures—taken together and in context—endorse marriage.

- **1 Corinthians 7:1–2 It is better to marry than to remain single and fornicate.** Paul is answering questions from the Saints at Corinth. He observes first that an unmarried man should avoiding touching a woman (v. 1). This does not suggest that women are somehow evil or untouchable. If we look at the next sentence it is clear what Paul is trying to say. "Nevertheless, to avoid fornication, let every man have his own wife, and let every woman have her own husband" (v. 2). Clearly, this statement endorses sexual contact between married persons. It also makes clear what Paul meant by the first statement: that our natural sex drive is powerful and should be guarded carefully. And it is better to marry than to remain single and fornicate.

- **1 Corinthians 7:3–5 Husbands and wives should love one another and have a normal and frequent sexual relationship.** First and foremost, they are to have "due benevolence" (love and affection) for each other (v. 3). And as it pertains to sexual relations, their bodies are not only their own but belong to their partner as well (v. 4). They are not to "defraud" their partner of sexual contact "except it be with consent for a time, that ye may give yourselves to fasting and prayer." But then they should "come together again, that Satan tempt you not for your incontinency" (lack of sexual contact) (v. 5).

- **1 Corinthians 7:6–9 Unmarried and widowed missionaries should remain single.** This is friendly advice, "not of commandment" (v. 6). Paul is experienced in this area, and "would that all men were even as I myself" (v. 7). What does he mean by this? He is speaking to "the unmarried and widows" who serve missions, and advises "It is good for them if they abide even as I" (v. 8). Paul was clearly not married as he wrote this. But it is possible that Paul was a widower. Being gone for up to four years at a time, his heart was thoroughly set on missionary work, and thus he might have chosen not to re-marry. But he believed that every man could decide this matter using the Spirit, "his proper gift of God," and that one might decide one way and another might decide differently (v. 7). One thing was for sure: "If they cannot contain [their sexual urges], let them marry: for it is better to marry than to burn" (v. 9).

  Elder Spencer W. Kimball said, "Taking such statements in conjunction with others [Paul] made it is clear that he is not talking about celibacy, but is urging the normal and controlled sex [while] living in marriage and total continence outside marriage. There is no real evidence that Paul was never married, as some students claim, and there are in fact indications to the contrary."[1]

- **1 Corinthians 9:5 Paul argues that Apostles have as much right to marry as anyone else.** Lest they think that he had been commanded not to marry, Paul asked, "Have we not power to lead about a sister, a wife, [like] other apostles, and [like] the brethren of the Lord, and Cephas [Peter]?" From this question we can deduce that other apostles and general authorities, including Peter, had wives at that time.

- **1 Corinthians 7:10–19 Paul's advice on special circumstances in marriages.** We can imagine that the questions posed in their letter to Paul covered all kinds of circumstances. Paul provides here a list of advice for particular situations.

  — **v. 10–11 In a troubled marriage, partners should try to persevere and work it out.** Paul declares that it is a commandment from the Lord that the wife should not depart from her husband. "But and if she depart, let her remain unmarried, or be reconciled to her husband: and let not the husband put away his wife." In other words, divorce is not the answer in most circumstances and God wants married partners to stay together. If they set aside selfishness, worldliness, and lust, just about any couple can make things work if they really try. Divorce has become the first resort rather than the last resort, and Paul speaks here against that practice.

— **vv. 12–14** **In part-member families, a member should not divorce a non-member if he or she refuses to convert.** Marriage is sacred, and differences in belief is not a reason to separate. "If any brother hath a wife that believeth not, and she be pleased to dwell with him, let him not put her away" (v. 12). "And the woman which hath an husband that believeth not, and if he be pleased to dwell with her, let her not leave him" (v. 13). "For the unbelieving husband is sanctified by the [believing] wife, and the unbelieving wife is sanctified by the [believing] husband" (v. 14). When divorce ensues in these circumstances, "children [become] unclean" [inactive] by the lack of family unity," but when partners stay together children have a better chance of growing up "holy" (v. 14).

— **v. 15** **If an unbelieving spouse leaves, let him or her go.** In such circumstances, the remaining spouse "is not under bondage" and may move on to another partner without condemnation. "God hath called us to peace," says Paul.

- **1 Corinthians 7:25 Advice to unmarried women.** Paul had not received any commandment from the Lord concerning women who (presumably not by their own choice) remained "virgins" (unmarried). But as one who had himself received mercy from the Lord, he believed that God would be merciful to such women and that their only responsibility is "to be faithful."

- **1 Corinthians 7:26–38 More advice on marriage for missionaries.** Having just spoken of unmarried women, Paul observes that it is "good for the present distress" for young men who serve as missionaries to also remain unmarried (v. 26). "The present distress" would be translated better as "the present necessity," which was the pressing need for missionaries. If they were already married, they should not seek divorce, but if they are not yet married they should not seek a wife (v. 27). There was nothing sinful about marrying, for either the man or the woman, but the circumstances would produce "trouble in the flesh" because of their long separations from each other (v. 28). Paul simply wants them

PROVIDENCE LITHOGRAPHIC CO. 901, #34

to understand that "the time is short" to get the work done, and they will have to work and behave "as though they had [no wife]" (v. 29).

The urgency, of course, was because the Great Apostasy was imminent (see the JST corrections). They had to cover the known world in an era of no rapid communication or transit. Those "that weep" for any reason will have to work "as though they wept not;" those that were rejoicing would have to set that rejoicing aside; and those who had possessions would have to act as if "they possessed not" (v. 30). Those who were engaged in worldly pursuits would have to forget about those pursuits and realize that "the fashion of this world passeth away" (v. 31). In other words, they would have to give their full and undivided attention to the work. "I would have you without carefulness," said Paul, which means "without anxiety about anything" (v. 32). Worries would distract missionaries from their work.

"He that is unmarried careth for the things that belong to the Lord," observed Paul, and would focus on "how he may please the Lord" (v. 32). "But he that is married careth for the things that are of the world, [and] how he may please his wife" (v. 33).

"There is [a] difference also between a wife and a virgin," said Paul. In this case, a man's "virgin" means his fiancee. A fiancee cares more about "the things of the Lord, that she may be holy both in body and in spirit," while a wife "careth for the things of the world, how she may please her husband" (v. 34). This of course, is not doctrine; it is Paul's opinion based on his own experience. He gave the advice "for your own profit; not that I may cast a snare upon you," but simply to ensure that men who engage in missionary work can "attend upon the Lord without distraction" (v. 35).

"If any man think that he [might behave inappropriately] toward his virgin, [or] if she [feels she is] pass[ing] the flower of her age" [getting old], then "let him do what he will," Paul said; it would not be sinful for them to marry (v. 36). But if a man "standeth stedfast in his heart, having no necessity, but hath power over his own will, and hath so decreed in his heart that he will keep [not compromise the virtue of] his virgin" by remaining unmarried, then he "doeth well" (v. 37). Both marrying and not marrying are okay in Paul's eyes (v. 38). But the JST words this last verse differently to get the full meaning of Paul's advice: It says that it is better (for the "present necessity") to be a missionary; but if not, get married, for that is acceptable. (JST corrections).

- **1 Corinthians 7:39–40 Advice for widows.** "The wife is bound by the law as long as her husband liveth; but if her husband be dead, she is at liberty to be married to whom she will" but "only in the Lord" (v. 39). Nevertheless, Paul thinks that she will be happier if she remains a widow. But this, he said, is "after my judgment;" it is only his personal opinion. But, said Paul, "I think also that I have the Spirit of God" (v. 40). So he thinks his advice is correct.

Gender Roles

- **1 Corinthians 11:3 Everyone is accountable to somebody else; even Christ to the Father.** Paul teaches that a woman's head is her husband (see also Ephesians 5:22–33). But in saying this, he would have us remember that "the head of every man is Christ." Each is accountable to somebody, and neither is a law unto themselves. Paul elaborates later on what being "the head" means. And it does not mean "lording over" the wife.

- **1 Corinthians 11:4–6 Cultural practices of the day concerning proper worship.** Cultural practices are not doctrine, but they do affect the spirit of worship when proper rules are ignored or even flaunted. The point is that we should not behave unseemly or draw attention to ourselves.

  For instance, in Paul's day, for a man to leave his hat on while praying or prophesying [speaking] was dishonorable (v. 4). But for a woman, just the opposite was true: to remove her hat would be dishonorable (v. 5). A woman's hair was part of her beauty and flaunting her hair would be inappropriate. So unless she plans to shave her head she ought not to remove her head covering (vv. 5–6). To do so would have been shocking in the culture of Paul's day. But one other important point to be learned from these verses is that Paul acknowledges that women can both pray and testify.

THEBIBLEREVIVAL.COM, #30

- **1 Corinthians 11:11–12 "Neither is the man without the woman, neither the woman without the man, in the Lord."** This is one of the most clear statements in scripture about the necessity of marriage. Paul said, "Nevertheless neither is the man without the woman, neither the woman without the man, in the Lord" (v. 11). Neither is sufficient on their own; "the woman is of the man" and "the man [is] also by the woman." And both of them are created of God (v. 12).

  President Joseph F. Smith said:

  > The house of the Lord is a house of order and not . . . of confusion; and that means that the man is not without the woman in the Lord, neither is the woman without the man in the Lord; and that no man can be saved and exalted in the kingdom of God without the woman, and no woman can reach the perfection and exaltation in the kingdom of God alone. . . . God instituted marriage in the beginning. He made man in his own image and likeness, male and female, and in their creation it was designed that they should be united together in sacred bonds of marriage, and one is not perfect without the other. Furthermore, it means that

there is no union for time and eternity that can be perfected outside of the law of God, and the order of His house. Men may desire it, they may go through the form of it, in this life, but it will be of no effect except it be done and sanctioned by divine authority.[2]

- **1 Corinthians 11:14–15 Proper grooming.** It was the custom in Paul's day for women to have long hair which they kept covered in public. It was considered immodest not to do so. But for men, long hair was considered shameful. Paul argues that "nature itself teach[es] you, that, if a man have long hair, it is a shame unto him, but if a woman have long hair, it is a glory to her: for her hair is given her for a covering." All cultural practices are important with a given culture, and to violate them can seem "unnatural," even weird. But whether or not it is "natural," as Paul claims, it is certainly true that proper grooming according to acceptable cultural norms is important.

- **1 Corinthians 14:34–35 Joseph Smith changed the word "speak" to "rule"** (JST). "Let your women keep silence in the churches," said Paul, "for it is not permitted unto them to speak" (v. 34). This sounds harsh, but is translated incorrectly. The Prophet Joseph Smith changed the word "speak" to "rule," which makes it more plain what Paul was saying—that priesthood holders should preside in meetings, and that women are commanded to be obedient to their priesthood leaders. If women have criticisms or objections to how a congregation is lead, they should tell these matters to "their husbands at home: for it is a shame for women to [attempt to lead] in the church" (v. 35).

  Elder Bruce R. McConkie said: "May women speak in Church? Yes, in the sense of teaching, counseling, testifying, exhorting, and the like; no, in the sense of assuming rule over the Church as such, and in attempting to give direction as to how God's affairs on earth shall be regulated. . . . Paul is here telling the sisters they are subject to the priesthood, that it is not their province to rule and reign, that the bishop's wife is not the bishop."[3]

SPIRITUAL GIFTS

The Diversity and Purpose of Gifts

In 1 Corinthians 12 Paul sought to eliminate the Corinthians' contentions about the importance of various spiritual gifts. His goal was unity among them, which he illustrated by comparing them to the members of the body, all of which are necessary, important, and interdependent.

- **1 Corinthians 12:1–3 A testimony is a gift of the Spirit.** Paul said, "Now concerning spiritual gifts, brethren, I would not have you ignorant" (v. 1). We need to know and understand the gifts of the Spirit in order to use them properly. Paul reminded the Saints at Corinth that they were once "Gentiles, carried away unto [worshiping] dumb idols, even as ye were led" (v. 2). They did not have the Spirit nor understand how it works. "Wherefore I give you to understand, that no man speaking by the Spirit of God calleth Jesus accursed: and that no man can say that Jesus is the Lord, but by the Holy Ghost" (v. 3). The Prophet Joseph Smith changed 1 Corinthians 12:3 in the JST to read, "No man can know that Jesus is the Lord, but by the Holy Ghost."[4]

- **1 Corinthians 12:7 Spiritual gifts are "given to every man to profit withal."** In other words, everybody has at least one gift of the Spirit given unto them, and that gift is given for the purpose of blessing everybody else. In this way, when we come together in congregations we can enjoy all of the gifts of the Spirit.

  Elder Heber J. Grant said: "I rejoice . . . that every Latter-day Saint, every humble son and daughter of God that has embraced the Gospel and become a member of The Church of Jesus Christ of Latter-day Saints has received the witness of the Holy Spirit, that the gift of tongues, the gift of prophecy, of healing, and other gifts and blessings, are found in the Church, and are not confined to men that hold responsible positions in the Church."[5]

  — **D&C 46:8–9 Always remember the reason for which they were given.** People go astray with regard to spiritual gifts when they fail to remember "for what they are given" (v. 8). They are not given as signs to convince the ungodly—those that seek "for a sign that they may consume it upon their lusts" (v. 9). "They are given for the benefit of those who love me and keep all my commandments, and him that seeketh so to do" (v. 9)—in other words they are given as rewards to the already faithful. And when the Lord gives a gift, He intends "that all may be benefited," not just the person who received it. So if I do have the gift of music, I must realize that it was given to me so that I can bless the lives of others with it.

  Elder Orson Pratt said: "Each member does not receive all these gifts; but they are distributed through the whole body [of the Church], according to the will and wisdom of the Spirit. . . . Some may have all these gifts bestowed upon them, so as to understand them all, and be prepared to detect any spurious gifts, and to preside over the whole body of the Church, that all may be benefitted. These spiritual gifts are distributed among the members of the Church, according to their faithfulness, circumstances, natural abilities, duties, and callings; that the whole may be properly instructed, confirmed, perfected, and saved."[6]

  — **D&C 46:9 "They are given for the benefit of those who love me and keep all my commandments, and him that seeketh so to do."** When we are sick, the gift of healing can bring blessed relief. When we need counsel, the gift of wisdom manifested through a loving bishop can help us navigate a problem. The gift of music can lift and bear witness to our souls in a way that few other things can. The gift of teaching can give us understanding of gospel principles. The gift of tongues can help a new missionary master a language. And a hundred other blessings can result from these gifts. Elder Dallin H. Oaks said that gifts of the Spirit "can lead us to God. They can shield us from the power of the adversary. They can compensate for our inadequacies and repair our imperfections."[7]

Elder Bruce R. McConkie said: "They are signs and miracles reserved for the faithful and for none else. . . . Their purpose is to enlighten, encourage, and edify the faithful so that they will inherit peace in this life and be guided toward eternal life in the world to come. Their presence is proof of the divinity of the Lord's work; where they are not found, there the Church and kingdom of God is not."[8]

Thus, spiritual gifts are not given to convince unbelievers or to show off our supernatural power. They are not given to inflate our vanity or as evidence that we are somehow favored of God. Instead, they are blessings of a loving Heavenly Father to His obedient children, as well as manifestations of power through which God accomplishes His purposes.

— **D&C 46:11–12, 26 God gave us our gifts for service, not as a badge of honor.** If we do not share our gifts they are of no benefit to anyone, and like the foolish man who buried his one talent we will find ourselves condemned at the last day.

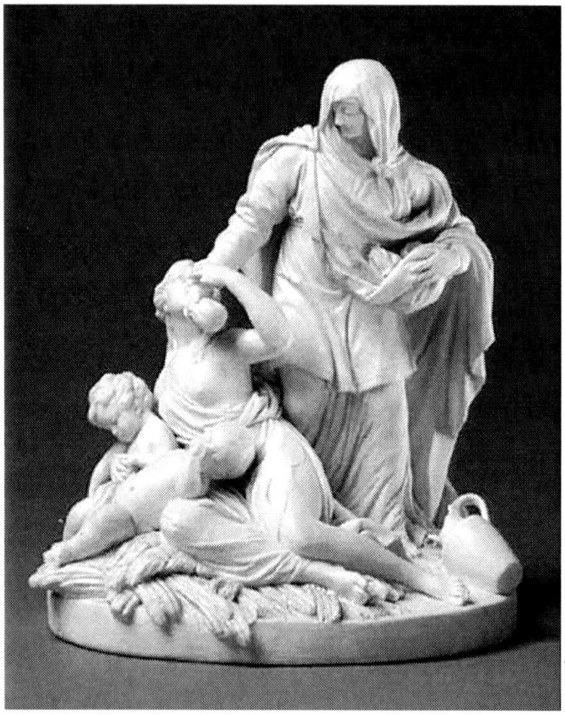
STATUE BY S. L. BOIZOT, 1785

While serving as a bishop I became aware of the fact that every gift of the Spirit was present in our ward through one person or another. Nobody had all of them. But as a group, we did. Thus, by coming together as a ward congregation we were able to bless each other's lives with every spiritual gift. "For all have not every gift given unto them; for there are many gifts, and to every man is given a gift by the Spirit of God. To some is given one, and to some is given another, that all may be profited thereby" (vv. 11–12). "And all these gifts come from God, for the benefit of the children of God" (v. 26).

Elder Robert D. Hales said: "The phrase 'that all may be profited thereby' [D&C 46:12] is a very important concept to understand about the gifts of the Spirit. The gifts given to each individual are given not only for the one who receives, but also for those who can benefit when the gift is shared with others."[9]

- **1 Corinthians 12:4 The Spirit bestows all gifts.** Paul taught there are many gifts of the Spirit—too many to list comprehensively—but all of them are given by "the same

Spirit." Elder Bruce R. McConkie said: "By the grace of God—following devotion, faith, and obedience on man's part—certain special spiritual blessings called gifts of the Spirit are bestowed upon men. Their receipt is always predicated upon obedience to law, but because they are freely available to all the obedient, they are called gifts."[10]

President Joseph Fielding Smith said: "Now, the Lord will give us gifts. He will quicken our minds. He will give us knowledge that will clear up all difficulties and put us in harmony with the commandments that He has given us; He will give us a knowledge that will be so deeply rooted in our souls that it can never be rooted out, if we will just seek for the light and the truth and the understanding that are promised to us and that we can receive if we will only be true and faithful to every covenant and obligation pertaining to the gospel of Jesus Christ."[11]

- **1 Corinthians 12:5–6, 8–11 Paul lists 10 important gifts** as an example of what he meant. It is useful to compare these with the 9 gifts listed by Moroni in the Book of Mormon (Moroni 10:9–16) and the 14 gifts listed in the Doctrine and Covenants (D&C 46:13–25).

1 Corinthians 12:5–11	Moroni 10:9–16	D&C 46:13–25
		To know that Jesus is the Christ
		Believe in Christ by others' word
Differences in administration		Differences in administration
Diversities of operations		Diversities of operations
Word of wisdom	Teach the word of wisdom.	Word of wisdom
Word of knowledge	Teach the word of knowledge.	Word of knowledge
Faith	Great faith	
Gifts of healing	Gifts of healing	Faith to heal and be healed
Working of miracles	Work mighty miracles	Working of miracles
Prophecy	Prophecy	Prophecy
Discerning of spirits	Behold angels/ministering spirits	Discerning of spirits
Diverse tongues	All kinds of tongues	Speak with tongues
Interpretation of tongues	Interpret languages & tongues	Interpretation of tongues

Because this chapter is about Paul's teachings on this topic, we will primarily use the list he provided in 1st Corinthians. But we will start with the first two listed in the Doctrine and Covenants since Paul had already mentioned these before he made his list.

— **D&C 46:13 A personal testimony of Jesus Christ.** Knowing "by the Holy Ghost . . . that Jesus Christ is the Son of God, and that he was crucified for the sins of the world." This is a gift available to everyone. The Lord has promised that everyone can know for himself—by the power of the Holy Ghost—of the divinity of the Savior and the truthfulness of the gospel (Moroni 10:4–7). President David O. McKay said: "Inspiration, revelation to the individual soul, is the rock upon which a testimony should be built, and there is no person living who cannot get it if he will conform to those laws and live a clean life which will permit the Holy Spirit to place that testimony in him."[12]

— **D&C 46:14 Belief in others' testimonies of the Savior.** Believing on the words of those who know Jesus is the Christ is also a gift of the Spirit. Such persons are "given to believe on their words, that they also might have eternal life if they continue faithful."

President Harold B. Lee invited the young people of the Church to "Lean on my testimony until you get your own. Some of you may not have a testimony, and so I have said to other groups like you, if you don't have a testimony today, why don't you cling to mine for a little while? Hold on to our testimonies, the testimonies of your bishops, your stake presidents, until you can develop it. If you can say nothing more today than I believe because my president, or my bishop, believes, I trust him, do this until you can get a testimony for yourselves; but I warn you that won't stay with you unless you continue to cultivate it and live the teachings. You are a temple of God worthy to receive the companionship of the Holy Ghost."[13]

— **1 Corinthians 12:5 Differences of Administration.** Having a knowledge of the "differences of administration," according to Elder Bruce R. McConkie, is a gift "used in administering and regulating the Church."[14] As used in the New Testament by Paul, this term meant literally the different divisions or courses of the priests and Levites engaged in the temple service. In this revelation it refers to the different duties and responsibilities of the priesthood in its two divisions, the Melchizedek and Aaronic. To know and understand this is a gift of the Spirit."[15]

This could be manifested in understanding how the various organizations of the Church function, and being able to manage them in effective ways. There are various styles of leadership; not all leaders do things in precisely the same way. But through this gift of the Spirit, they can know what the proper thing to do might be in a given circumstance. This is also a gift given of the Spirit, and good administrators have this gift.

— **1 Corinthians 12:6 Diversities of Operations (Discernment of Spiritual Gifts).** "Knowing the diversities of operations means being able to discern whether or not a given form of spiritual manifestation is of the Lord."[16] This gift helps us discern whether a teaching or influence comes from God or from some other source. Presiding authorities who hold keys are given this gift as a part of their responsibilities to regulate the spiritual affairs of the Church. Elder Abraham O. Woodruff said: "If the bishop, who is a common judge in Israel, tells a person to restrain this gift, or any other gift, it is the duty of that person to do it. The bishop has a right to the gift of discernment, whereby he may tell whether these spirits are of God or not."[17]

— **1 Corinthians 12:8 Wisdom and Knowledge.** "There is a [fundamental] difference between wisdom, knowledge, and the ability to instruct." Wisdom, in gospel terms, means to follow correct principles and to use knowledge properly. Knowledge is an understanding of the principles—"a carefully-stored-up supply of facts, generally slowly acquired. The ability to instruct is the gift to impart of this supply to others. Each is a gift of God."[18]

— **1 Corinthians 12:9 Faith to be healed.** It is interesting to note that faith is a gift—something given to us from God which is a prerequisite to receiving another gift: to be healed. Therefore, faith is one gift of the Spirit that we should most earnestly seek for because so much else depends upon it. If we have sufficient faith, the Lord is willing to heal all diseases (Psalm 103:3), so long as we are not appointed to death (D&C 42:48).

This gift was evident very early on in the Church's history. The Lord revealed that when Church members were sick they should call for elders to "pray for and lay their hands upon them" in the name of the Lord (D&C 42:43–52). And some months before section 42 was received, Joseph Smith and Oliver Cowdery had been told that they should heal the sick (D&C 24:13–14). These blessings were among the Saints from the very beginning.

Elder Parley P. Pratt wrote of a woman named Chloe Smith who was so ill that she was near death, but was healed by the Prophet Joseph Smith:

Under these circumstances, President Smith and myself, with several other Elders, called to see her. She was so low that no one had been allowed for some days previous to speak above a whisper, and even the door of the log dwelling was muffled with cloths to prevent a noise. We kneeled down and prayed vocally all around, each in turn, after which President Smith arose, went to the bedside, took her by the hand, and said unto her with a loud voice, "in the name of Jesus Christ arise and walk!" She immediately arose, was dressed by a woman in attendance, when she walked to a chair before the fire, and was seated and joined in singing a hymn. The house was thronged with people in a few moments, and the young lady arose and shook hands with each as they came in; and from that minute she was restored to health.[19]

— **1 Corinthians 12:9 Faith to heal.** This is one of the most well-known of the spiritual gifts because our Lord healed so many persons during His mortal ministry. Walter A. Norton said: "Significantly, Christ himself laid on hands to heal the sick (Mark 6:5, 13; Luke 13:12–13), and sent His Apostles out doing the same (Mark 6:7–13). In Mark 6:13, however, we learn something that is revealed in no other place in the four Gospels; that the Apostles 'anointed with oil many that were sick, and healed them'. . . . In only one other place in the entire New Testament do we find an explicit reference to the ordinance of anointing the sick with oil. That reference is given in the epistle of the Apostle James (5:14–16)."[20]

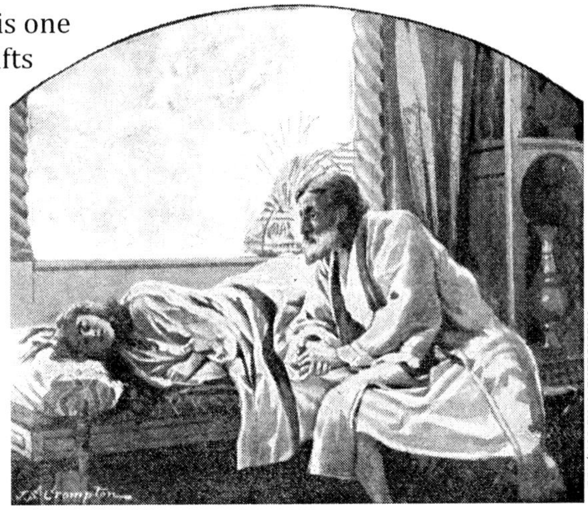
THEBIBLEREVIVAL.COM, #21

The same gift of healing was possessed by Joseph Smith, who used it often to bless the Saints in both Kirtland and Nauvoo. In the spring of 1831 a Methodist preacher named Ezra Booth came with a group of people into Kirtland to investigate the claims of the Prophet and his followers. The party included a well-to-do farmer named John Johnson and his wife, Alice, from Hiram, Ohio. Alice's arm was partially paralyzed from rheumatism, and she could not raise it above her head. As they talked with the Prophet, one of the visitors asked if there was anyone on earth who had the power to cure Alice's lame arm. When the conversation turned to another subject, Joseph went up to Mrs. Johnson, took her by the hand, and with calm assurance said: "Woman, in the name of the Lord Jesus Christ I command thee to be whole." As Joseph went from the room, leaving everyone astonished and speechless, she raised her arm. The next day she hung out her first wash in over six years without any pain. Some members of the Johnson family joined the Church as a result of the healing. The miracle also attracted wide acclaim throughout northern Ohio.[21]

— **1 Corinthians 12:10 Miracles.** The working of miracles is a gift of the Spirit. While they appear surprising—almost magical—to those who witness them, Elder James E. Talmage said that miracles do not violate natural law, but rather they show the operation of higher laws that we may not yet understand.[22] The Lord declared that "signs come by faith, not by the will of men, nor as they please, but by the will of God" (D&C 63:10). He also said: "I am God, and mine arm is not shortened; and I will show miracles, signs, and wonders, unto all those who believe on my name (D&C 35:8). Thus, only those with faith can receive such miracles. Even the Lord Himself had to inquire whether those He healed believed in Him before He could heal them. As President Kimball is famous for saying, "faith precedes the miracle."

— **1 Corinthians 12:10 Prophecy.** Prophecy refers to the right to speak for God—in other words, to be His mouthpiece. It may or may not involve foretelling the future. But in a much broader sense, "the testimony of Jesus is the spirit of prophecy" (Revelation 19:10). And herefore, in a broad sense, every Saint who has a personal witness that Jesus is the Christ is a prophet. If a person has this spirit of prophecy, he or she can better understand the writings of the prophets, such as Isaiah, who wrote by the spirit of prophecy. The fruits of the spirit of prophecy are many: besides being able to understand the writings of the prophets, one who possesses the spirit of prophecy may also have the gifts of discernment, revelation, translation of inspired scripture, and prophecy.

Moses had the gift of prophecy

Elder Bruce R. McConkie said: "Prophets are simply members of the true Church who have testimonies of the truth and divinity of the work. They are the Saints of God who have learned by the power of the Holy Ghost that Jesus is the Christ, the Son of the living God . . . That is, every person who receives revelation so that he knows, independent of any other source, of the divine Sonship of the Savior, has, by definition and in the very nature of things, the spirit of prophecy and is a prophet. . . . Both testimony and prophecy come by the power of the Holy Ghost; and any person who receives the revelation that Jesus is the Lord is a prophet and can, as occasion requires and when guided by the Spirit, 'prophesy of all things.'"[23]

Joseph Smith understood this well and made frequent reference to it in his sermons. On one occasion he explained, "No man can be a minister of Jesus Christ except he has the testimony of Jesus; and this is the spirit of prophecy. Whenever salvation has been administered, it has been by testimony."[24]

Several ancient prophets have connected the spirit of prophecy to the Holy Ghost or the Spirit of God (Alma 5:47), to truth (Alma 5:47; 6:8; 43:2), and to the gifts of the Holy Ghost, including the gift of tongues and the gift of translation (Alma 9:21). Modern prophets view the spirit of prophecy and the Holy Ghost as virtually equivalent. Elder Delbert L. Stapley stated, "The Holy Ghost is the spirit of prophecy."[25] And Elder Wilford Woodruff wrote, "It is the privilege of every man and woman in this kingdom to enjoy the spirit of prophecy, which is the Spirit of God."[26]

— **1 Corinthians 12:10 Discernment of Spirits.** The gift of "discerning of spirits" is one of the most important spiritual gifts, and is the main subject of D&C 50 (below). ". . . the bishop of the church, and . . . such as God shall appoint and ordain to watch over the church . . . have it given unto them to discern all those gifts lest there shall be any among you professing and yet be not of God" (D&C 46:27). This is somewhat related to the gift of "discernment of operations" with which one may discern the source of spiritual gifts (above), but this one has specific reference to discerning the "spirit" of an *individual* rather than *the source of a spiritual gift.*

Elder Stephen L Richards said:

> The gift of discernment is essential to the leadership of the Church. I never ordain a bishop or set apart a president of a stake without invoking upon him this divine blessing, that he may read the lives and hearts of his people and call forth the best within them. The gift and power of discernment in this world of contention between the forces of good and the power of evil is essential equipment for every son and daughter of God. [This gift] arises largely out of an acute sensitivity to impressions—spiritual impressions, if you will—to read under the surface as it were, to detect hidden evil, and more importantly to find the good that may be concealed. The highest type of discernment is that which perceives in others and uncovers for them their better natures, the good inherent within them. It's the gift every missionary needs when he takes the gospel to the people of the world. He must make an appraisal of every personality whom he meets. He must be able to discern the hidden spark that may be lighted for truth. The gift of discernment will save him from mistakes and embarrassment, and it will never fail to inspire confidence in the one who is rightly appraised.[27]

— **1 Corinthians 12:10 Tongues and Interpretation of Tongues.** The gift of tongues may take two forms: (1) one may be able to speak a foreign tongue [language] or (2) one may be able to understand or interpret a foreign tongue [language]. Whenever the gift of tongues is manifest in an unknown tongue (e.g., the Adamic language), another who is present will be given the interpretation of tongues so that the listeners may benefit from what is being said. In other words, there must always be some spiritual benefit to the manifestation; it will not be given as a "show" of some kind with no knowledge being imparted.

The Prophet Joseph Smith counseled the Saints to speak in tongues only when an interpreter was present:

> There are only two gifts that could be made visible—the gift of tongues and the gift of prophecy. These are things that are the most talked about, and yet if a person spoke in an unknown tongue, according to Paul's testimony, he would be a barbarian to those present. They would say that it was gibberish; and if he prophesied they would call it nonsense. The gift of tongues is the smallest gift perhaps of the whole, and yet it is one that is the most sought after.... The greatest, the best, and the most useful gifts would be known nothing about by an observer.... Be not so curious about tongues, do not speak in tongues except there be an interpreter present; the ultimate design of tongues is to speak to foreigners, and if persons are very anxious to display their intelligence, let them speak to such in their own tongues.[28]

The Prophet Joseph Smith said several more things about the gift of tongues:

> Speak not in the gift of tongues without understanding it, or without interpretation. The devil can speak in tongues; the adversary will come with his work; he can tempt all classes; can speak in English or Dutch. Let no one speak in tongues unless he interpret, except by the consent of the one who is placed to preside; then he may discern or interpret, or another may.[29]
>
> The gift of tongues by the power of the Holy Ghost in the Church, is for the benefit of the servants of God to preach to unbelievers, as on the day of Pentecost. When devout men from every nation shall assemble to hear the things of God, let the Elders preach to them in their own mother tongue, whether it is German, French, Spanish or Irish, or any other, and let those interpret who understand the language spoken, in their own mother tongue, and this is what the Apostle meant in First Corinthians 14:27.[30]
>
> If you have a matter to reveal, let it be in your own tongue; do not indulge too much in the exercise of the gift of tongues, or the devil will take advantage of the innocent and unwary. You may speak in tongues for your own comfort, but I lay this down for a rule, that if anything is taught by the gift of tongues, it is not to be received for doctrine.[31]

— **Additional Spiritual Gifts** As pointed out by Elder Bruce R. McConkie, spiritual gifts are endless in number and infinite in variety. Those listed in the scriptures and described above are simply illustrations of how the Spirit may manifest itself through those who possess the Gift of the Holy Ghost.[32] Elder Marvin J. Ashton said: "[Some] less-conspicuous gifts [include] the gift of asking; the gift of listening; the gift of hearing and using a still, small voice; ... the gift of avoiding contention; the gift of being agreeable; .. the gift of seeking that which is righteous; the gift of not passing judgment; the gift of looking to God for guidance; the gift of being a disciple; the gift of caring for others; the gift of being able to ponder; the gift of offering prayer; the gift of bearing a mighty testimony; and the gift of receiving the Holy Ghost."[33]

Other gifts are identified elsewhere in the scriptures:

- Alma 11:21–25 Discernment
- Acts 2:14–41 Teaching
- 1 Nephi 3:7 Faith
- D&C 76:5–13 Knowledge

- **1 Corinthians 12:12–26 The Church has need of all members and their gifts.** Using the analogy of a physical body, Paul said, "For as the body is one, and hath many members, and all the members of that one body, being many, are one body: so also is Christ [His Church]" (v. 12). Every member was baptized into one "body" [Church] "whether we be Jews or Gentiles, whether we be bond or free," and have all enjoyed the blessings of Holy Ghost (v. 13).

PROVIDENCE LITHOGRAPHIC CO., 1901, #34

Every Church member's gifts are needed

Bodies are made up of many parts (v. 14). So, "If the foot shall say, Because I am not the hand, I am not of the body; is it therefore not of the body? And if the ear shall say, Because I am not the eye, I am not of the body; is it therefore not of the body?" (vv. 15–16). And if "the whole body were an eye, where [would be] the hearing? If the whole were hearing, where [would be] the smelling?" (v. 17). "God [has] set the members [body parts] every one of them in the body, as it hath pleased him. And if they were all one member [body part], where [would be] the body?" (vv. 18–19). The answer is, of course, that there are "many members [of the body], yet but one body" (v. 20). "And the eye cannot say unto the hand, I have no need of thee: nor again the head to the feet, I have no need of you" (v. 21). Even the most feeble parts of the body are necessary (v. 22).

Paul now shifted the analogy to a discussion of members of the Church. He said that "those members of the body [Church], which we think to be less honourable [important], upon these we [should] bestow more abundant honour [attention]" (v. 23). If a member of the Church is not so attractive to us as another member, we should see a different kind of beauty in them so that they become more "comely" [important] to us (v. 23). Those members who are more visible and whose gifts are more obvious may have fewer needs; but God has put all of us together in the same congregation in order to "give . . . more abundant honour [attention] to that part [member] which lack[s]" (v. 24). And their gifts, however small and humble, are a blessing to every other member.

Paul summarized his analogy by declaring "that there should be no schism in the body; but that the members should have the same care one for another" (v. 25). When "one member suffer[s], all the members suffer with [him]; or [if] one member be honoured, all the members rejoice with [him]" (v. 26).

- **1 Corinthians 12:27–30 God never intended that we should all be the same or have the same gifts.** "Now ye are the body of Christ, and members in particular. And God hath set . . . in the church, first apostles, secondarily prophets, thirdly teachers," and has bestowed us "miracles, then gifts of healings, helps, governments, diversities of tongues" (vv. 27–28). "Are all apostles? are all prophets? are all teachers? are all workers of miracles? Have all the gifts of healing? do all speak with tongues? do all interpret?" (vv. 29–30). The answer is obviously, "No."

- **1 Corinthians 12:27–31 "Covet earnestly the best gifts."** We are invited to seek after spiritual gifts earnestly. But, at the same time, we must always remember why they are given—so that all members may be benefitted. If we seek a gift from God, we must seek it with a determination to use it to bless others.

  — **D&C 46:8–9 "Seek ye earnestly the best gifts, always remembering for what they are given"** (v. 8). For verily I say unto you, they are given for the benefit of those who love me and keep all my commandments, and him that seeketh so to do; that all may be benefited that seek or that ask of me, that ask . . . not for a sign that they may consume it upon their lusts."

The Gift of Tongues

- **1 Corinthians 14:1–12 Paul's teachings on the gift of tongues and of prophecy.** One of the most visible (and therefore most coveted) gifts of the Spirit is the gift of tongues. Some modern-day believers in Christ claim to have this gift and display it publicly in sometimes lurid fashion. But that kind of display edifies nobody. We learn nothing, we understanding nothing, and the only person who conceivably benefits is the person babbling incoherently before us.

  Paul suggested that the gift of tongues is far less valuable than the gift of prophecy. "Follow after charity, and desire spiritual gifts," he said, "but rather that ye may prophesy. For he that speaketh in an unknown tongue speaketh not unto men, but unto God: for no man understandeth him. . . . But he that prophesieth speaketh unto men to edification, and exhortation, and comfort. He that speaketh in an unknown tongue edifieth himself; but he that prophesieth edifieth the church. I would that ye all spake with tongues, but [would] rather that ye prophesied: for greater is he that prophesieth than he that speaketh with tongues . . ." (vv. 1–5).

  Paul taught that the gift of tongues is not useful unless it is interpreted so that "the church may receive edifying" (v. 5). Paul asked, "If I come unto you speaking with tongues, what shall I profit you?" (v. 6). He profited them more by giving them "revelation, or . . . knowledge, or . . . prophesying, or . . . doctrine" (v. 6). He compared those speaking in an unknown tongue to musical instruments whose notes are meaningless—more like noise—unless we can discern what is played on them (v. 7). And "if the trumpet give an uncertain sound, who shall prepare himself to the battle?" (v. 8). "So likewise ye, except ye utter by the tongue words easy to be understood, how shall it be known what is spoken? for ye shall speak into the air" (v. 9).

Paul observed that "there are . . . so many kinds of voices [languages] in the world, and none of them is without signification" (v. 10). They all mean something to those who understand them. But to those who do not understand what they are saying, their speech sounds more like a barbarian (v. 11). So if we are "zealous of spiritual gifts, [we should] seek that ye may excel to the edifying of the church" (v. 12).

The Prophet Joseph Smith said a number of things about the gift of tongues:

— The devil can speak in tongues, so he can deceive us with this gift.[34]
— Its purpose is to teach unbelievers in their own tongue.[35]
— Don't be too curious about it.[36]
— Don't indulge in it too much.[37]
— Not everything taught by the gift of tongues is doctrine.[38]

- **1 Corinthians 14:21–22 The gift of tongues can be of benefit to unbelievers,** because it is dramatic. They might be impressed that this gift was given so that they could understand what is being taught. But the gift of prophecy is of more benefit to believers because it communicates the mind and will of the Lord (v. 22). The Lord promised in Old Testament times that "with men of other tongues and other lips will I speak unto this people" (v. 21). And yet, the Lord said, "they not hear me" (v. 21).

- **1 Corinthians 14:26 If the gift of tongues causes someone to "lose control," it is not of God.** Whatever gift we bring to our worshiping, whether it is "a psalm, . . . a doctrine, . . . a tongue, . . . a revelation, . . . [or] an interpretation, let all things be done unto edifying." If it is showy or disturbing or undignified, it is not of God. He does not work in that manner.

M. HEEMSKERK, THE BIBLE AND ITS STORY, 1908

The Apostles spoke in tongues on the day of Pentecost

CHARITY

- **1 Corinthians 12:31 Charity is the "more excellent way."** When Paul said earlier that we should "covet earnestly the best gifts," he also said that he would "shew . . . unto you a more excellent way." That way was and is charity, which is the topic of the next chapter of 1 Corinthians: chapter 13.

- **Moroni 7:47–48 Charity is the pure love of Christ.** Mormon taught that "charity is the pure love of Christ" which "endureth forever," and whoever is "found possessed of it at the last day, it shall be well with him" (v. 47). The charity of which he spoke is "the highest, noblest, strongest kind of love, not merely affection [but] the pure love of Christ."[39]

THEBIBLEREVIVAL.COM, #25

This "pure love of Christ" can mean more than one thing.

(1) It can mean loving Christ with a love that is pure, total, and endless.
(2) It can mean being loved by Christ.
(3) It can mean love for others that is like the love that Christ possessed—pure and selfless.

Elder C. Max Caldwell said:

> The phrase "love of Christ" might have meaning in three dimensions: . . . First, love for Christ. This concept proclaims Jesus as the object of our love, and our lives should be an external expression of our gratitude for Him. . . . A second dimension of the meaning of charity is love from Christ (Ether 12:33–34). . . . The Savior's act of redemption for our sins is of no effect without our willingness to comply with the conditions of His Atonement. . . . A third perception of charity is to possess a love that is like Christ (2 Ne. 33:7–9; John 13:34). . . . Charity is not just . . . a word to describe actions or attitudes. Rather, it is an internal condition that must be developed and experienced in order to be understood. . . . People who have charity have a love for the Savior, have received of His love, and love others as He does.[40]

Mormon taught that charity is a gift of God, and one must pray fervently to receive it. He urged Church members to "pray unto the Father with all the energy of heart, that ye may be filled with this love, which he hath bestowed upon all who are true followers of his Son, Jesus Christ" (v. 48). He promised that if we do we "may become the sons of God; that when he shall appear we shall be like him . . . purified even as he is pure" (v. 48). Mormon then closes his sermon with a simple "Amen."

Elder Bruce R. McConkie said, "Above all the attributes of godliness and perfection, charity is the one most devoutly to be desired. Charity is more than love, far more; it is everlasting love, perfect love, the pure love of Christ which endureth forever. It is love so centered in righteousness that the possessor has no aim or desire except for the eternal welfare of his own soul and for the souls of those around him (2 Ne. 26:30; Moro. 7:47; 8:25–26)."[41]

- **1 Corinthians 13:1–3 Charity is more important than any other thing we may say or do.** The beauty of this passage stands on its own; it needs no comment. Paul said:

  > "Though I speak with the tongues of men and of angels, and have not charity, I am become as sounding brass, or a tinkling cymbal. And though I have the gift of prophecy, and understand all mysteries, and all knowledge; and though I have all faith, so that I could remove mountains, and have not charity, I am nothing. And though I bestow all my goods to feed the poor, and though I give my body to be burned, and have not charity, it profiteth me nothing" (vv. 1–3).

- **1 Corinthians 13:4–8 Paul's definition of charity.** He made lists of things that people of charity do—and do not—do.

  The person who possesses the pure love of Christ does not:

  v. 4 Envy
  Vaunt (or exalt) himself—"vaunt" is translated from the Greek for "braggart."
  Have puffed up or inflated ideas of his own worth

  v. 5 Behave himself unseemly.
  Seek his own ends
  Provoke easily—"easily provoked" is translated from the Greek for "irritable."
  Think evil—"think" would be better translated as "reckons" or "takes notice of."

  v. 6 Rejoice in iniquity.

  The person who possesses the love of Christ does:

  v. 4 Suffer long. This means to have patience—to be long-suffering.
  Show kindness.

  v. 6 Rejoice in the truth.

  v. 7 Bear all things. "Beareth" comes from the word meaning "to cover" as with roofs and the hulls of ships—keeping out resentment as the roof does the rain.

  Believe all things (that the Spirit tells him are true).
  Hope for all things.
  Endure all things.

  v. 8 Persist without failing, The word translated faileth really means "to fall off" as happens with leaves or flowers. Such love is never separated from us.

- **1 Corinthians 13:13 Charity is greater than faith and hope.** All three are essential to our happiness and exaltation. But of "these three," Paul declared that "the greatest of these is charity."

- **1 Corinthians 13:9–10, 12 Our understanding of things is only partial.** Paul said, "We know in part, and we prophesy in part" (v. 9). But when Christ comes, our partial understanding "shall be done away" (v. 10). "For now we see through a glass, darkly; but then face to face: now I know in part; but then shall I know even as also I am known" (v. 12).

The word translated "glass" here actually means a "mirror." To readers today who enjoy clear, high-quality mirrors, Paul's imagery might not be clear. "The ancient mirror . . . was of polished metal, and required constant polishing, so that a sponge with pounded pumice-stone was generally attached to it."[42] When such mirrors were not cleaned, then the experience of looking into them was like "seeing images darkly."

RESURRECTION

"THE LIVING CHRIST," © JOSEPH BRICKEY, USED BY PERMISSION

- **1 Corinthians 15:3–4 The centrality of the atonement and resurrection.** Paul had taught the Corinthians about Christ—"how that Christ died for our sins according to the scriptures; and that he was buried, and that he rose again the third day according to the scriptures." These are at the heart of the gospel of Jesus Christ.

- **1 Corinthians 15:5–8 Some appearances of Jesus after His resurrection.** In support of Paul's testimony that Christ had risen from the dead, he offered a list of witnesses that had seen Him as a resurrected being.

  — He was seen by Cephas [Peter] (v. 5).
  — He was seen by the Twelve Apostles (without Thomas) (v. 5).
  — He was seen by "above five hundred brethren at once; of whom the greater part remain unto this present, but some are fallen asleep (v. 6).
  — He was seen by James [the younger brother of the Lord] (v. 7).
  — He was then seen again by "all the Apostles" (v. 7).
  — "And last of all," Paul said, "he was seen of me also" (v. 8).

  Paul's reference to being "born out of due time" (v. 8) means that he became an Apostle later than these others, being both younger and having received his call after the death of Christ.

- **1 Corinthians 15:9–11 Paul's humility concerning his Apostolic calling.** He called himself "the least of the apostles," and felt sometimes that he was not worthy to be called an Apostle "because I persecuted the church of God" (v. 9). "But by the grace of God I am what I am," he said, "and his grace which was bestowed upon me was not in vain" because he was determined to "labour . . . more abundantly than they all: yet not I, but the grace of God which was with me" (v. 10).

- **1 Corinthians 15:12–18 What if there were no resurrection?** The Sadducees denied the reality of the resurrection, possibly because of their close ties with Greek philosophy and culture. The Greeks believed that the body was evil, and while there might be eternal life for the spirit, there certainly was none for the body. Paul's response was that the doctrine of the resurrection is pivotal and all other truths of the gospel of Jesus Christ depend on it.

  Some of the Corinthian Saints were still caught up in Greek philosophy and were saying "that there is no resurrection of the dead" (v. 12). Paul listed all of the things that would be affected if this claim was true:

  — 13 If there be no resurrection of the dead, then is Christ not risen:
  — 14 And if Christ be not risen, then is our preaching vain, and your faith is also vain.
  — 15 Yea, and we are found false witnesses of God; because we have testified of God that he raised up Christ.
  — 16 If the dead rise not, then is not Christ raised:
  — 17 And if Christ be not raised, your faith is vain; ye are yet in your sins.
  — 18 [And] they also which are fallen asleep in Christ are perished.

- **1 Corinthians 15:19–20 Paul's witness of the resurrected Christ.** If this life is it—if there is no life after death or resurrection from the dead—and "in this life only we have hope in Christ, we are of all men most miserable" (v. 19). But "Christ [is] risen from the dead, and [has] become the firstfruits of them that slept" (v. 20). He knew this for himself, having seen the resurrected Lord on his way to Damascus many years before.

- **1 Corinthians 15:21–23 All who ever lived will rise from the dead.** The great plan of our Heavenly Father provided for Adam's fall that we might become mortal, and then Christ's atonement that we might rise from the dead and qualify to return to His presence. "For since by man came death, by man came also the resurrection of the dead. For as in Adam *all die*, even so in Christ shall *all be made alive*" (vv. 21–22, emphasis added). But this must be done in proper order. Christ is the "firstfruits" of the resurrection; then after Him will rise all "they that are Christ's at his coming" (v. 23).

- **1 Corinthians 15:24–28 Christ will put all things "under his feet" including death.** After the Millennium, when Christ will "deliver . . . up the kingdom to God, even the Father," He will have "put down all rule and all authority and power" on the earth (v. 24). "For he must reign, till he hath put all enemies under his feet," including death (vv. 25–26). "And when all things shall be subdued unto him, then shall the Son also himself be subject unto him that put all things under him [meaning God the Father], that God may be all in all" (v. 28).

- **1 Corinthians 15:29 Paul's reasoning concerning resurrection and work for the dead.** As part of his reasoning concerning the necessity of a resurrection, Paul asked, "Else what shall they do which are baptized for the dead, if the dead rise not at all? why are they then baptized for the dead?" The point is clear; if there is no resurrection then doing baptisms for the dead is pointless. This, of course, shows us that they were doing baptisms for the dead in the Church in Paul's day.

  The Prophet Joseph Smith said, "Every man that has been baptized and belongs to the kingdom has a right to be baptized for those who have gone before; and as soon as the law of the Gospel is obeyed here by their friends who act as proxy for them, the Lord has administrators there to set them free. A man may act as proxy for his own relatives; the ordinances of the Gospel which were laid out before the foundations of the world have thus been fulfilled by them."[43]

B. PICART, b. 1728

- **1 Corinthians 15:30–32 If there is no resurrection, then all of Paul's efforts to save souls are pointless.** "Why stand we in jeopardy every hour?" he asked, if there is no life after death and no resurrection. In his effort to bring to them the "rejoicing which I have in Christ Jesus our Lord," he had "die[d] daily" (v. 31) and "fought with beasts at Ephesus," but for what purpose? "What advantageth it me, if the dead rise not?" They might as well "eat and drink; for to morrow we die" as other men do (v. 32).

- **1 Corinthians 15:35–39 Planting a seed illustrates how God can create life from death** (burial). Doubters will ask, "How are the dead raised up? and with what body do they come?" (v. 35). Paul uses the analogy of planting seeds to explain. The seed which we put in the ground "is not quickened, except it die [be planted in the earth]" (v. 36). And yet, when we plant a seed we are not planting a full grown plant (the "body that shall be"), but merely a seed, in hopes that it might "bare grain . . . of wheat, or of some other grain" (v. 37). But God gives the seed "a body as it hath pleased him, and to every seed his own body" (v. 38). The same is true about animals. "There is one kind of flesh of men, another flesh of beasts, another of fishes, and another of birds" (v. 39). Each "bears seed after its own kind" as was decreed at the creation of the earth.

  How does a bean seed know how to grow into a bean stalk? Or a corn seed into a corn plant bearing ears of corn? As we know, it's all in the genetic code contained in the seed. We do not know how or why this happens, but we can observe that it does. It is one of the marvelous miracles of God's creation. From Paul's analogy we can also deduce that from any one cell of our body God can create an entire person according to the genetic code it contains. Some may say this is impossible. But I say He did it once within our mother's womb. And He can do it again, and will do it again at our resurrection, by whatever means He uses to do it.

— **Alma 11:42–44; 40:23 Bodies will be restored to their "perfect frame."** Amulek taught that our resurrected bodies will look precisely as they do now, only in more perfected form. The "perfect frame" of which he speaks is the genetic code that each of us possesses and which is unique from every other person who lives or ever has lived or will live on this earth. Alma called this code our "proper and perfect frame" (40:23).

- **2 Corinthians 12:2–4 Paul's visions of the celestial kingdom and of paradise.** In his second epistle to the Corinthians, Paul returned to a discussion of the three degrees of glory when he spoke of a revelation he had on this subject. "I knew a man in Christ above fourteen years ago," he said, referring to himself in the third person. This man [Paul] had a vision—"whether in the body, I cannot tell; or whether out of the body, I cannot tell: God knoweth"—in which he was "caught up to the third heaven" (v. 2). This means that Paul saw in vision the celestial kingdom [the third heaven] of our God.

ZAMPIERI, THE BIBLE AND ITS STORY, 1908

The same man had another vision—"whether in the body, or out of the body, I cannot tell: God knoweth"—of "paradise" (vv. 3–4), which is the state of the righteous after death while they wait for the resurrection. Notice that Paul speaks of these events as two separate visions of two separate places. The Christian world got these two places confused long ago, in the first few centuries after Christ, and began to teach that upon death we go to "heaven" or "hell" immediately. These states of being actually describe the two parts of the spirit world—paradise and spirit prison—but do not describe what happens after the resurrection. The Book of Mormon and modern revelation have restored a complete understanding, which Paul was trying to explain here.

- **2 Corinthians 12:4 "Unspeakable words."** Paul said that in his visions of the celestial kingdom and of paradise he heard "unspeakable words, which it is not lawful for a man to utter." This can be understood correctly in two ways:

— **Things which are indescribable.** There are things that exist in the heavenly spheres for which we have no adequate words or comparisons in this life. For example, Isaiah had no worthy comparison for missile warfare in the latter days, but attempted to describe them as "fiery flying serpents"—something which the people of his day had experienced and could understand. But the comparison, while somewhat accurate in physical description, is inadequate to convey how missiles work and the destruction they cause.

— **Things which are forbidden to discuss.** Our ability and willingness to control our tongues is directly related to how much revelation the Lord is willing to give us. He cautioned the early Latter-day Saints with these words: "Remember that that which cometh from above is sacred, and must be spoken with care, and by constraint of the Spirit" (D&C 63:64). Promising that marvelous signs and healings would follow true believers in the early Church, the Lord cautioned: "But a commandment I give unto them, that they shall not boast themselves of these things, neither speak them before the world; for these things are given unto you for *your* profit and for salvation" (D&C 84:73, emphasis added).

The Prophet Joseph Smith said, "The reason we do not have the secrets of the Lord revealed unto us, is because we do not keep them but reveal them; we do not keep our own secrets, but reveal our difficulties to the world, even to our enemies, then how would we keep the secrets of the Lord?"[44]

President Brigham Young said, "Should you receive a vision or revelation from the Almighty, one that the Lord gave you concerning yourselves, or this people, but which you are not to reveal on account of your not being the proper person, or because it ought not to be known by the people at present, you should shut it up and seal it as close, and lock it as tight as heaven is to you, and make it as secret as the grave. The Lord has no confidence in those who reveal secrets, for He cannot safely reveal Himself to such persons."[45] He also said, "That man who cannot know things without telling any other living being upon the earth, who cannot keep his secrets and those that God reveals to him, never can receive the voice of his Lord to dictate him and the people on this earth."[46]

Elder Boyd K. Packer said, "It is not wise to continually talk of unusual spiritual experiences. They are to be guarded with care and shared only when the Spirit itself prompts you to use them to the blessing of others. I am ever mindful of Alma's words (Alma 12:9) . . ."[47]

President Marion G. Romney said, "I do not tell all I know. I have not told my wife all I know. I have found that if I tell everything I know and explain every experience that I have had, the Lord will not trust me."[48]

President David O. McKay called special spiritual experiences "heart petals." Surely it would take some special inspiration to share them with others. The spirit of the occasion would have to be right, and the motive would have to be to build another or to build the kingdom, not self-aggrandizement.

- **1 Corinthians 15:40–42 There are different kinds of bodies in the resurrection.** (D&C 88:20–21, 28–31). While still speaking of the resurrection, Paul wrote about the different kinds of bodies that will rise in the resurrection. "There are . . . celestial bodies, and bodies terrestrial," he said, "but the glory of the celestial is one, and the glory of the terrestrial is another" (v. 40). In other words, we will not all rise to the same level of glory. That will depend on our faithfulness in this life. Paul here mentions only two degrees of glory, but in the next two verses, he mentions three. As we know from other scripture they are referred to as celestial, terrestrial, and telestial.

Paul compares the glory of resurrected bodies to heavenly bodies: "There is one glory of the sun [celestial], and another glory of the moon [terrestrial], and another glory of the stars [telestial]," and just as "one star differeth from another star in glory, so also is the resurrection of the dead" (vv. 41–42). And although at our death our bodies are "sown [planted in the earth] in corruption; [they are] raised in incorruption"—to a more glorified state which has no corruption and will never die.

- **Alma 41:1–7 The doctrine of restitution.** Alma explained the principle behind this when he taught that whatever state of righteousness we have obtained at the time we die, it will rise again with that same degree of glory. We cannot live a telestial life and then hope that we will rise with celestial glory. Whatever we are . . . we are. And it will be restored to us again in the resurrection. In this sense, we judge ourselves by the way that we live and according to the "law of the harvest" we will reap what we have sown.

- **1 Corinthians 15:44–49 The nature of resurrected bodies.** Paul continued his discussion of the nature of resurrected bodies by saying that our bodies at death are "sown a natural body; [but] . . . raised a spiritual body. There is a natural body, and there is a spiritual body" (v. 44). When "Adam was made a living soul [by receiving] a quickening spirit," his body was not "spiritual, but . . . natural," and could only later become "that which is spiritual" (vv. 45–46). "The first man [Adam] is of the earth, earthy," and it is from him that we inherited our earthly bodies. But "the second man" [Christ] "is the Lord from heaven" (v. 47), and from Him we will inherit a glorified body. "And as we have borne the image of the earthy, we shall also bear the image of the heavenly" (v. 49).

Elder Howard W. Hunter said, "There is a separation of the spirit and the body at the time of death. The resurrection will again unite the spirit with the body, and the body becomes a spiritual body, one of flesh and bones but quickened by the spirit instead of blood. Thus, our bodies after the resurrection, quickened by the spirit, shall become immortal and never die. This is the meaning of the statements of Paul that 'there is a natural body, and there is a spiritual body' and 'that flesh and blood cannot inherit the kingdom of God.' The natural body is flesh and blood, but quickened by the spirit instead of blood, it can and will enter the kingdom."[49]

- **1 Corinthians 15:50 "Flesh and blood cannot inherit the Kingdom of God."** Where God dwells, no corruption is allowed or could even exist. Thus, our physical bodies in their present state cannot go there. In this sense, death is a blessing because it is the first step toward receiving a more glorified body that can inherit the celestial kingdom. Paul said, "flesh and blood cannot inherit the kingdom of God; neither doth corruption inherit incorruption."

  The Prophet Joseph Smith taught:

  1. The life of the mortal body is in the blood (Leviticus 17:11), and "when our flesh is quickened by the Spirit, there will be no blood in this tabernacle."[50]
  2. "God Almighty Himself dwells in eternal fire; flesh and blood cannot go there, for all corruption is devoured by the fire.... When our flesh is quickened by the Spirit, there will be no blood in this tabernacle."[51]
  3. "Flesh and blood cannot go there [into God's presence]; but flesh and bones, quickened by the Spirit of God, can."[52]
  4. "As concerning the resurrection, ... all will be raised by the power of God, having spirit in their bodies, and not blood."[53]

- **1 Corinthians 15:51–52 Some will not die but be changed instantaneously from mortality to immortality.** Speaking of those who have been translated and also of those who will be mortal at the time of the Millennium, Paul said, "Behold, I shew you a mystery; We shall not all sleep, but we shall all be changed" (v. 51). Those who are so changed will be changed "in a moment, in the twinkling of an eye" from mortality to immortality and a glorified body. For those who have died, "at the last trump: for the trumpet shall sound, ... the dead shall be raised incorruptible, and ... shall be changed" into glorified beings.

OTHER TEACHINGS IN 1 CORINTHIANS

- **1 Corinthians 1:1 Paul's Apostleship.** Paul was an ordained Apostle, having been called to that holy office "through the will of God."

- **1 Corinthians 1:2 Members of the Church were called Saints** (just as in our day). Paul referred to members of the Church at Corinth as "them that are sanctified in Christ Jesus, called to be saints" (v. 2). This applies to "all that in every place call upon the name of Jesus Christ our Lord" (v. 2), wherever they may be ("both theirs and ours").

- **1 Corinthians 1:3 The Father and the Son are separate persons.** In this letter, Paul used his usual greeting, which makes a clear distinction between the Father and Son: "Grace be unto you, and peace, from God our Father, and from the Lord Jesus Christ."

- **1 Corinthians 1:4–9 Saints have personal testimonies.** They have received a powerful witness of Christ's power and of their fellowship with Him. Paul thanked God that His grace had been given to the Saints through Jesus Christ, and that "in every thing ye are enriched by him, in all utterance, and in all knowledge" (v. 5). He observed that "the testimony of Christ was confirmed" in them, and they were "behind in no gift; waiting for the coming of our Lord Jesus Christ" (vv. 6–7). He reminded them that "God is faithful, by whom ye were called unto the fellowship of his Son Jesus Christ our Lord" (v. 9), and that Christ "shall also confirm you unto the end, that ye may be blameless in the day of our Lord Jesus Christ" (v. 8). These are promises to all of the Lord's Saints.

- **1 Corinthians 6:1–3 Lawsuits.** Members should settle their disputes internally without turning to the world for judgment (v. 1). Eventually, we will judge the world, "and if the world shall be judged by you, are ye unworthy to judge the smallest matters" among yourselves? (v. 2). Paul said that "we shall [also] judge angels," so we certainly ought to be able to judge "things that pertain to this life" (v. 3).

  President Joseph F. Smith said:

  > The man who passes through this probation, and is faithful, being redeemed from sin by the blood of Christ, through the ordinances of the gospel, and attains to exaltation in the kingdom of God, is not less but greater than the angels, and if you doubt it, read your Bible, for there it is written that the Saints shall "judge angels," and also they shall "judge the world." And why? Because the resurrected, righteous man has progressed beyond the preexistent or disembodied spirits, and has risen above them, having both spirit and body as Christ has, having gained the victory over death and the grave, and having power over sin and Satan; in fact, having passed from the condition of the angels to that of a God. He possesses keys of power, dominion and glory that the angel does not possess—and cannot possess without gaining them in the same way that he gained them, which will be by passing through the same ordeals and proving equally faithful.[54]

- **1 Corinthians 8:5–6 Godhood:** Many Christians suppose these verses refer only to the gods of the Greek and Roman pantheons, but this is not correct. Paul began by acknowledging that there are many "that are called gods, [both] in heaven [and] in earth. He further explained his statement by saying that in heaven "there be gods many, and lords many" (v. 5). "But to us there is but one God, the Father, of whom are all things [created]." There is also "one Lord Jesus Christ, by whom are all things [created], and [even] we [were created] by him" (v. 6).

RUBENS, 1616-17

Stephen saw two Beings in heaven when he was stoned to death

The Prophet Joseph Smith said, "Paul says there are Gods many and Lords many. I want to set it forth in a plain and simple manner . . . to us there is but one God—that is pertaining to us. . . . Paul had no allusion to the heathen gods in the text."[55] The Prophet also said, "If Jesus had a Father, can we not believe that He had a Father also?"[56] This is only logical. But in imagining such things, we must always remember what Paul said: "to us there is but one God, the Father" (v. 6). We need not concern ourselves with any other gods—on earth or in heaven.

- **1 Corinthians 8:10–13 Idolatry.** The Gentiles did not need to be circumcised or follow the Law of Moses. But they had been commanded not to eat meats that had been spiritually contaminated by being offered to idols. Paul also condemned pagan rituals and sacraments (1 Corinthians 10:19–22). In all these things, they were to avoid even the appearance of evil. This was a challenge, since in Gentile society these events were the cultural events of their cities and nations. Avoiding them made the members of the Church seems stand-offish and perhaps even subversive to those around them.

  Nevertheless, Paul noted that if people saw them participate in events by "sit[ting] at meat in the idol's temple," then members of the Church [those who "have knowledge"] who are "weak" will be "emboldened to eat those things which are offered to idols" (v. 10). And by this process "the weak brother [will] perish, for whom Christ died" (v. 11). Paul taught that when we set a bad example for weaker members of the Church, we "wound their weak conscience, [and] sin against Christ" (v. 12). Paul said that if eating meat would offend any brother, "I will eat no flesh while the world standeth, lest I make my brother to offend" (v. 13).

- **1 Corinthians 9:22–23 Adaptability.** Paul always adapted himself and his message to his audience. "To the weak became I as weak, that I might gain the weak," he said, and "I am made all things to all men, that I might by all means save some" (v. 22). This was not done to be phony or to deceive anyone, but "for the gospel's sake, that I might be partaker thereof with you" (v. 23).

  Elder Bruce R. McConkie said, "Paul here says he made himself all things to all men in an effort to get them to accept the gospel message; that is, he adapted himself to the conditions and circumstances of all classes of people, as a means of getting them to pay attention to his teachings and testimony. And then, lest any suppose this included the acceptance of their false doctrines or practices, or that it in any way involved a compromise between the gospel and false systems of worship, he hastened to add that he and all men must obey the gospel law to be saved."[57]

- **1 Corinthians 9:24 Commitment.** Here Paul used athletic racing as a metaphor for achieving our spiritual goals. "Know ye not that they which run in a race run all, but one receiveth the prize? So run, that ye may obtain."

- **1 Corinthians 10:1–4 Christ is Jehovah and the Rock of our salvation.** Paul reminded the Saints that their "fathers" (the children of Israel) passed through the Red Seas and were guided through the wilderness by a cloud (v. 1). "And [they] were all baptized unto Moses in the cloud and in the sea" (v. 2). With regard to the gospel of Jesus Christ, they "did all eat the same spiritual meat; and did all drink the same spiritual drink: for they drank of that spiritual Rock that followed them: and that Rock was Christ" (vv. 3–4). Thus, though they were worshiping Jehovah, they were really worshiping Christ, and knew of His future coming. The Greek word in verse 4 translated "Rock" (petra) means "bedrock." The Rock of salvation for Israel and for us, is Jesus Christ.

- **1 Corinthians 10:12 Pride.** If you think you are firm in the faith, be careful that you forget your need for the Lord's help, because if you do you will fall (compare with Proverbs 16:18: "Pride goeth before a fall"). "Wherefore let him that thinketh he standeth [is self-sufficient] take heed lest he fall."

- **1 Corinthians 10:13 Temptation.** God protects us against temptations, but if we seek out temptations our protection is weakened (footnote a & Alma 13:28). "There hath no temptation taken you but such as is common to man," Paul observed. "But God is faithful, [and] will not suffer you to be tempted above that ye are able" to resist. No matter what the temptation may be, God will "with the temptation also make a way to escape, that ye may be able to bear it."

- **1 Corinthians 10:24 Service.** This is another confusing statement from Paul. "Let no man seek his own, but every man another's wealth." The JST helps us understand what Paul really meant by rendering it this way: "Let not man therefore seek his own, but every man another's good." The word "wealth" as used in the days of the King James translators conveyed not only the idea of riches but also of well-being and welfare. Paul was teaching true Christian charity, not greed. And Joseph Smith corrected this in his Inspired Version of the Bible.

THEBIBLEREVIVAL.COM, #30

- **1 Corinthians 10:25–28 Avoiding extremism in diet.** Paul taught, "Whatsoever is sold in the shambles [meat markets], that eat, asking no question for conscience sake" (v. 25). Saints were unnecessarily refusing to buy meat in the market because some of it *might* have come from offerings to idols, and there was no way to know. Paul says that this is extreme and uncalled for, because all things come from God: "For the earth is the Lord's, and the fulness thereof" (v. 26).

  Also, "If any of them that believe not bid you to a feast, and ye be disposed to go; whatsoever is set before you, eat, asking no question for conscience sake" (v. 27). But if your host specifies that your food was previously offered to idols, "eat not" as an example before the man that offered it to you ("shewed it"), and also for your own conscience's sake" (v. 28).

- **1 Corinthians 11:19 Heresies.** Doctrine is the great divider. There will always be heresies that separate "sheep" from "goats" in the Church (Matthew 25:32). We can fully expect that "there must be also heresies among you," because Satan will use every device he can to deceive and divide the Saints. But by means of their reaction to such things, "they which are approved" (true Saints) will be "made manifest among you."

  We are not immune to this problem in the latter days. The constant drum-beat of speculation on doctrinal matters in the Church seems never-ending. I was recently challenged by a brother, a High Priest, who insisted that Jesus was married and that we know His wife's name (Mary

Magdalene) and the names of His four children by her. When I cautioned him that those beliefs are not doctrine, he insisted that Brigham Young had said so and it is in the *Journal of Discourses*. Well, so too is the "Adam-God" theory in the *Journal of Discourses*, and neither one of these teachings is Church doctrine. Yet this brother was teaching these things to his High Priests.

This kind of speculation upon the "mysteries" that we do not know for sure is the same process by which the Great Apostasy entered into the Church, even before all the Apostles were dead. That which is true doctrine will be set before the Church members for their sustaining vote, just as the Word of Wisdom was when it became a "doctrine" rather than just a "suggestion." The official position of the Church is that we do not know for sure concerning Christ's marital status, nor is it a saving doctrine for us. When we focus on the heresies, we turn our attention away from saving principles and put in danger both ourselves and all those with whom we share these "mysteries."

Elder Bruce R. McConkie, in a speech at Brigham Young University in 1980, identified seven "deadly heresies" that are frequently taught in the Church.[58] These heresies included:

1. "God is progressing in knowledge and is learning new truths. This is false—utterly, totally, and completely. There is not one sliver of truth in it. It grows out of a wholly twisted and incorrect view of the King Follett Sermon and of what is meant by eternal progression."
2. The relationship between organic evolution and revealed religion." Most members of the Church will tell you that we do not believe in evolution as the means by which Adam's body was created. It was a matter of serious debate among the Apostles[59] in 1931. In the end, they concluded, "As to how were formed the bodies of the first human beings to take tabernacles, the revealed word gives no details . . ."[60] President David O. McKay declared in 1957 that "On the subject of organic evolution the Church has officially taken no position."[61] In the meantime, there is no sin in continuing to explore the matter. McConkie observes that "all truth is in agreement, that true religion and true science bear the same witness, and that in the true and full sense, true science is part of true religion."
3. "Temple marriage assures us of an eventual exaltation. Some have supposed that couples married in the temple who commit all manner of sin, and who then pay the penalty, will gain their exaltation eventually. This notion is contrary to the whole system and plan that the Lord has ordained."
4. "The doctrine of salvation for the dead offers men a second chance for salvation. . . . There is no such thing as a second chance to gain salvation. This is the time and the day of our probation. After this day of life, which is given us to prepare for eternity, then cometh the night of darkness wherein there can be no labor performed."
5. "There is progression from one kingdom to another in the eternal worlds or that lower kingdoms eventually progress to where higher kingdoms once were. . . . This belief lulls men into a state of carnal security. . . . The body we receive in the resurrection determines the glory we receive in the kingdoms that are prepared. . . . They neither progress from one kingdom to another, nor does a lower kingdom ever get where a higher kingdom once was. Whatever eternal progression there is, it is within a sphere."

6. "Adam is our father and our god . . . . He is the father of our spirits and our bodies, and . . . he is the one we worship [this is the Adam-God theory]. The devil keeps this heresy alive as a means of obtaining converts to cultism. It is contrary to the whole plan of salvation set forth in the scriptures, and anyone who has read the Book of Moses, and anyone who has received the temple endowment, has no excuse whatever for being led astray by it. Those who are so ensnared reject the living prophet and close their ears to the apostles of their day."

7. "We must be perfect to gain salvation. This is not really a great heresy, only a doctrinal misunderstanding, that I mention here in order to help round out our discussion and to turn our attention from negative to positive things. . . . There was only one perfect being, the Lord Jesus. If men had to be perfect and live all of the law strictly, wholly, and completely, there would be only one saved person in eternity [Christ Himself]. The prophet taught that there are many things to be done, even beyond the grave, in working out our salvation."

- **1 Corinthians 11:20–22 Selfishness among members.** In the early Church, members came together on Sunday and ate a meal together—not just the sacrament but a meal. It became a tradition among Church members, sort of like a Ward dinner every Sunday.[62] Paul was critical of this practice because when they came together for this purpose it was "not to eat the Lord's supper" (v. 20), which should have been their primary purpose. They had also become selfish, with people seeking to eat before others in order to get the advantage, leaving "one . . . hungry, and another . . . drunken" (v. 21). "What? have ye not houses to eat and to drink in?" asked Paul, "or despise ye the church of God, [as you] shame them that have not? What shall I say to you? shall I praise you in this? I praise you not" (v. 22).

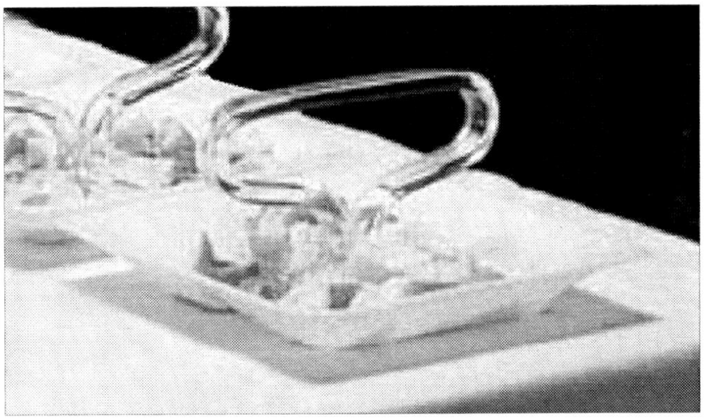

- **1 Corinthians 11:23–30 Partaking of the sacrament worthily.** Paul reminded the Saints that the Lord, on the "same night in which he was betrayed took bread: And when he had given thanks, he brake it, and said, Take, eat: this is my body, which is broken for you: this do in remembrance of me" (v. 24). "After the same manner also he took the cup, when he had supped, saying, This cup is the new testament in my blood: this do ye, as oft as ye drink it, in remembrance of me" (v. 25). Thus, this ordinance was given as a memorial, such that "as often as ye eat this bread, and drink this cup, ye do shew the Lord's death till he come" (v. 26). Paul then reasoned with the Saints concerning the implications of this.

"Wherefore whosoever shall eat this bread, and drink this cup of the Lord, unworthily, shall be guilty of the body and blood of the Lord" (v. 27). To do so would be an act of mocking God, and taking lightly the sacrifice of His Son. "But let a man examine himself," Paul said. They should not prevent anyone from "eat[ing] of that bread, and drink[ing] of that cup" (v. 28). But Paul warned that "he that eateth and drinketh unworthily, eateth and drinketh damnation to himself, not discerning the Lord's body" (v. 29; see also 3 Nephi 18:28–30). And because some were guilty of this at Corinth, "many are weak and sickly among you, and many sleep" (v. 30).

- **1 Corinthians 10:16–17 The unifying power of the sacrament.** Paul refers to both the eating of the bread and the drinking of the cup as our "communion" with Christ (v. 16); it makes us one with Him. But also, it unifies us as Saints because "we being many are one bread, and one body: for we are all partakers of that one bread" (v. 17).

  Elder Melvin J. Ballard said, "[We must] go to those against whom we have sinned or transgressed and obtain their forgiveness and then repair to the sacrament table where, if we have sincerely repented and put ourselves in proper condition, we shall be forgiven, and spiritual healing will come to our souls. It will really enter into our being. You have felt it. I am a witness that there is a spirit attending the administration of the sacrament that warms the soul from head to foot; you feel the wounds of the spirit being healed, and the load being lifted. Comfort and happiness come to the soul that is worthy and truly desirous of partaking of this spiritual food."[63]

- **1 Corinthians 13:11 We need to speak and act like adults.** "When I was a child," Paul said, "I spake as a child, I understood as a child, I thought as a child: but when I became a man, I put away childish things."

- **1 Corinthians 15:33 The importance of peers.** "Be not deceived," Paul warned, "evil communications corrupt good manners." The word "communications" here means companionships or associations. Paul is saying one's standards are determined by the company he keeps. This passage may be a quotation from the Greek poet Menander, Euripides, or Plato. It was a common saying in Paul's day.[64]

- **1 Corinthians 16:22 A colloquialism.** This is another common saying of Paul's time, a common greeting among Christians. "If any man love not the Lord Jesus Christ, let him be Anathema Maran-atha." Anathema means literally "something set apart or consecrated," and came to mean "cursed" or "accursed." Maranatha means "the Lord comes," "the Lord will come," or "the Lord is at hand." Thus it means: "If anyone has no love for the Lord, let him be accursed. Our Lord [will] come!"

- **1 Corinthians 16:1–4 The handling of tithes and offerings:** Paul outlines a plan for tithes and offerings, which Church headquarters in Jerusalem would administer. Paul said to the Corinthian Saints, "Now concerning the collection for the saints, as I have given order to the churches of Galatia, even so do ye. Upon the first day of the week let every one of you lay by him in store, as God hath prospered him" (vv. 1–2). Then, when Paul came to them, "whomsoever ye shall approve by your letters, them will I send to bring your liberality unto Jerusalem" (v. 3). In some cases, Paul would go with them (v. 4).

- **1 Corinthians 16:5–9 Concerning a personal visit to Corinth by Paul.** "I will come unto you," Paul promised, "[after] I shall pass through Macedonia: for I do pass through Macedonia" (v. 5). And once he got there, he intended to "winter with you, that ye may bring me on my journey whithersoever I go" (v. 6). Paul intended to go to Jerusalem by sea from Corinth once the winter weather had passed. Although he would "not see you now," Paul intended to "tarry a while with you, if the Lord permit" (v. 7). For now, however, Paul intended to "tarry at Ephesus until Pentecost" because a great and effectual door had been opened to him there for the preaching of the gospel, along with "many adversaries" (vv. 8–9).

- **1 Corinthians 16:10–11 They must respect Timothy's authority.** Timothy was a young man but very faithful, and Paul trusted him with his most important matters. He said to the Corinthian Saints, "Now if Timotheus come, see that he may be with you without fear: for he worketh the work of the Lord, as I also do. Let no man therefore despise him: but conduct him forth in peace, that he may come unto me: for I look for him with the brethren."

PROVIDENCE LITHOGRAPHIC CO., 1908, #41

Paul often sent Timothy to represent him

- **1 Corinthians 16:12, 15–18 They must also respect other visiting and local authorities.** Paul had also wanted to send Apollos to them, but "his will was not at all to come at this time; but he will come when he shall have convenient time" (v. 12). He also recommended Stephanas, whose family was "the firstfruits of Achaia" [the province in which Corinth lay] and who had "addicted themselves to the ministry of the saints" (v. 15). Paul advised the Corinthians to "submit yourselves unto such, and to every one that helpeth with us, and laboureth" (v. 16). "I am glad of the coming of Stephanas and Fortunatus and Achaicus: for that which was lacking on your part they have supplied" (v. 17). Paul observed that "they have refreshed my spirit and yours: therefore acknowledge ye them" (v. 18).

- **1 Corinthians 16:5–18 Diligence and charity.** "Watch ye, stand fast in the faith, quit you like men, be strong," said Paul. "Let all your things be done with charity" (vv. 13–14). He was pleading for diligence in living gospel principles, especially love, unity, charity, kindness towards leaders, and assisting the Lord's work to move forward. As Elder B. H. Roberts later said: "In essentials let there be unity; in nonessentials, liberty; and in all things, charity."[65]

- **1 Corinthians 16:19 Members held Church meetings in their houses.**"The churches of Asia [Ephesus] salute you," wrote Paul. "Aquila and Priscilla salute you much in the Lord, with the church that is in their house" (v. 19). There were no chapels in which to meet, so members would often congregate at a member's home. In this case, Paul is mentioning the congregation that met at Aquila and Priscilla's home.

- **1 Corinthians 16:20 Traditional greetings included a kiss.** This verse communicates Paul's warm conclusion to his letter. We see again (as in 1 Thes. 5:26) that members of the early Church continued the practice of giving one another a kiss on the cheek as a salutation and demonstration of respect. Jews practiced the custom in ancient times (Proverbs 27:6; Matthew 26:49). "All the brethren greet you," Paul wrote. "Greet ye one another with an holy kiss."

Notes

1. *The Miracle of Forgiveness* [1969], 64.
2. *Gospel Doctrine*, 5th ed. [1939], 272.
3. *Doctrinal New Testament Commentary*, 3 vols. [1965–1973], 2:387–388.
4. *Teachings of the Prophet Joseph Smith*, sel. Joseph Fielding Smith [1976], 223.
5. In Conference Report, April 1901, 64.
6. N. B. Lundwall, *Masterful Discourses of Orson Pratt* [1962], 539–541.
7. "Spiritual Gifts," *Ensign*, September 1986, 72.
8. *Doctrinal New Testament Commentary*, 2:368.
9. *Ensign*, February 2002, 12, 14.
10. *Doctrinal New Testament Commentary*, 2:368.
11. *Ensign*, June 1972, 3.
12. "Individual Testimony," *Improvement Era*, September 1963, 733.
13. *The Teachings of Harold B. Lee*, edited by Clyde J. Williams [1996], 136.
14. *A New Witness for the Articles of Faith* [1985], 278.
15. Smith and Sjodahl, *Doctrine and Covenants Commentary* [1978], 274.
16. Richard O. Cowan, *The Doctrine and Covenants, Our Modern Scripture* [1984], 83.
17. In Conference Report, April 1901, 12.
18. *Doctrine and Covenants Commentary*, 274.
19. *Autobiography of Parley P. Pratt*, edited by his son, Parley P. Pratt (1985), 79–80.
20. *The New Testament and The Latter-day Saints* [1987], 234.

21. *History of the Church*, 1:215–216; *Millennial Star*, 31 December 1864, 834.

22. James E. Talmage, *Articles of Faith* [1981], 220–223.

23. *The Promised Messiah: The First Coming of Christ* [1978], 23–24.

24. *History of the Church*, 3:389–390.

25. In Conference Report, October 1966, 113.

26. In *Journal of Discourses*, 9:324, April 8, 1862.

27. In Conference Report, April 1950, 163.

28. *History of the Church*, 5:30–31.

29. *Teachings of the Prophet Joseph Smith*, 162.

30. *Teachings of the Prophet Joseph Smith*, 195.

31. *Teachings of the Prophet Joseph Smith*, 229.

32. See *A New Witness for the Articles of Faith*, 371.

33. In Conference Report, October 1987, 23; or *Ensign*, November 1987, 20.

34. *Teachings of the Prophet Joseph Smith*, 162.

35. *Teachings of the Prophet Joseph Smith*, 195.

36. *Teachings of the Prophet Joseph Smith*, 247.

37. *Teachings of the Prophet Joseph Smith*, 229.

38. *Teachings of the Prophet Joseph Smith*, 229.

39. *LDS Bible Dictionary*, s.v. "Charity," 632.

40. *Ensign*, November 1992, 29–30.

41. *Mormon Doctrine*, 121.

42. Vincent, *Word Studies*, 2:795–796.

43. *Teachings of the Prophet Joseph Smith*, 367.

44. *Teachings of the Prophet Joseph Smith*, 195.

45. In *Journal of Discourses*, 4:288.

46. In *Journal of Discourses*, 4:287.

47. *Ensign*, January 1983, 53.

48. Quoted by Boyd K. Packer, Church Employees Lecture Series, January 18, 1980.

49. In Conference Report, April 1969, 138.

50. *Teachings of the Prophet Joseph Smith*, 367.

51. *Teachings of the Prophet Joseph Smith*, 367.

52. *Teachings of the Prophet Joseph Smith*, 326.

53. *Teachings of the Prophet Joseph Smith*, 199–200.

54. *Gospel Doctrine*, 18–19.

55. *Teachings of the Prophet Joseph Smith*, 370–371.

56. *Teachings of the Prophet Joseph Smith*, 373.

57. *Doctrinal New Testament Commentary*, 2:353.

58. Fireside Address, BYU Marriott Center, June 1, 1980.

59. *The Personal Journal of James E. Talmage*, Vol. 5, November 2–21, 1931.

60. James E. Talmage, *The Earth and Man*, August 9, 1931.

61. Letter addressed to Professor William Lee Stokes of the University of Utah, February 15, 1957.

62. See *Doctrinal New Testament Commentary*, 2:364.

63. *New Era*, "The Sacramental Covenant," January 1976, 8.

64. Bullinger, *Figures of Speech Used in the Bible*, 801.

65. In Conference Report, October 1912, 30.

Chapter 35

Reconciliation to God

(2 Corinthians)

INTRODUCTION

Paul's Third Missionary Journey Continues

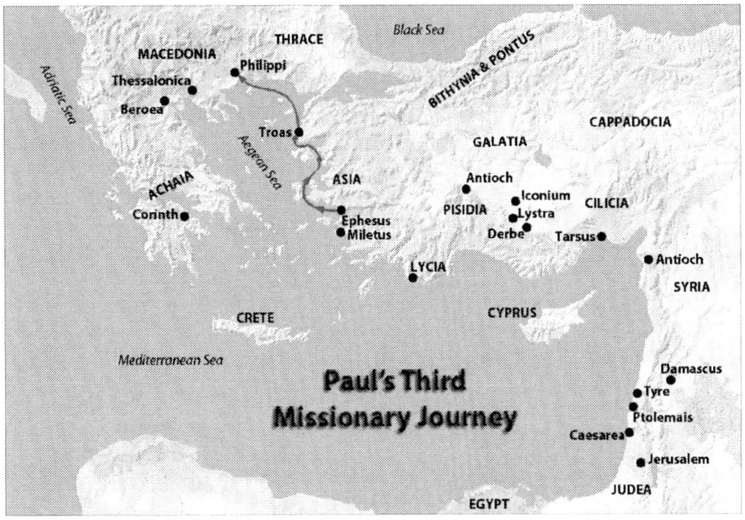

In his first epistle to the Corinthians, written from Ephesus, Paul promised to come to visit the Corinthians "[after] I shall pass through Macedonia: for I do pass through Macedonia" (1 Cor. 16:5).

In Acts 20:1–3 we read that Paul and his companions traveled to Macedonia on their way to Greece (Corinth), preaching the gospel as they went. At the time he wrote this second epistle to Corinth, Paul was in Macedonia at the city of Philippi.

- **2 Corinthians 2:12–13 Events at Troas:** After writing 1st Corinthians, Paul was anxious for word from Corinth. He traveled from Ephesus to Troas hoping to find Titus there with word from Corinth, but was disappointed—Titus was not at Troas.

- **2 Corinthians 7:5–7 Events in Macedonia:** Increasingly anxious for news of the welfare of the Corinthian church, Paul hastened by ship west across the Aegean Sea into Macedonia, where he worked among the branches of the Church and waited for Titus. Finally, in the Fall of 57 AD, Titus arrived at Philippi. Paul received Titus' report with gladness. The Saints at Corinth had repented and were anxious to see Paul again.

At this Point, Paul wrote 2 Corinthians from Macedonia, about 57 AD

PAUL'S 2ND CORINTHIAN EPISTLE

When and Where Paul Wrote 2nd Corinthians

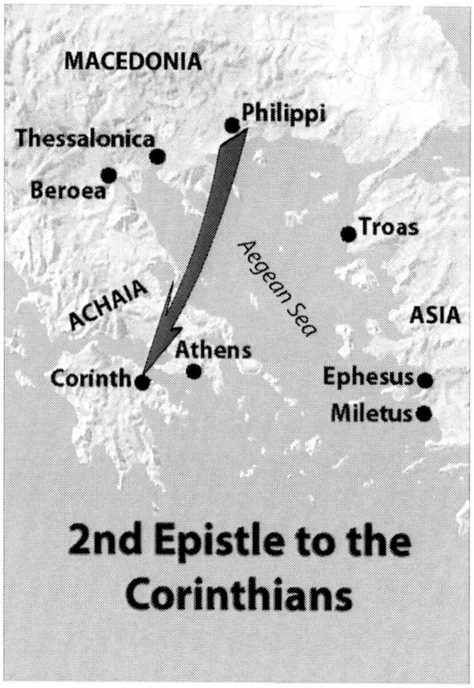

Paul wrote at least three letters to the Corinthian Saints. The first apparently has been lost to us, but we have copies of the second and third letters—known as First Corinthians and Second Corinthians, respectively. Second Corinthians is a follow-up letter to First Corinthians.

Evidence within the epistle itself suggests that Paul wrote 2 Corinthians from Macedonia (2 Cor. 2:13; 7:5–7; 9:2–4). Since Luke places Paul's visit to Macedonia near the end of Paul's third missionary journey, the letter was likely written in 57 AD, a few months after 1st Corinthians.

There is good evidence to suggest that it was written in haste. He wrote tenderly and kindly, explaining his delay and telling them that God would comfort them in tribulation.

Of all of Paul's writings, 2nd Corinthians and Philemon seem to be the most personal. We gain insight into Paul's sensitive nature—how it hurt him to be falsely accused by fair-weather Saints who had not borne the burden of the ministry as he had. Paul vigorously defends his personal character and his conduct as an Apostle of Jesus Christ.

Although Paul had much to discourage him when he wrote 2 Corinthians, he was buoyed up by the news that most members of the Church at Corinth were faithful disciples of Christ.

- **2 Corinthians 1:23–24** To those who criticized him for not yet coming to Corinth, he tempers what he writes, saying if he were there in person he "would use sharpness" (2 Cor. 13:10). This spirit of criticism was a frequent problem at Corinth.

- **2 Corinthians 8:18, 22 Paul sent his letter with Titus, who was returning to Corinth.** Titus was accompanied by 2 companions, one of whom may have been Luke.

Why Paul Wrote 2nd Corinthians

- Paul wrote 2nd Corinthians for at least four reasons:
  - — To counsel the Corinthians.
  - — To defend himself against the accusations of his enemies (1:12—7:16; 10:1—13:10).
  - — To collect money for the Judean poor (8:1—9:15).
  - — To prepare the Corinthians for his next visit (12:20–21; 13:7–10).

His powerful message includes counsel to repent, turn to Jesus Christ, gain true wisdom from inspiration, be reconciled to God, and do what is right.

- **2 Corinthians 2:17 Paul also wrote to counter rising apostasy.** The word "corrupt" is taken from the Greek word for a "peddler," with whom cheating was common. False teachers in the Church were watering down or changing the word of God to further their own selfish ends.

PAUL'S COUNSEL TO CORINTH

The Need for Love and Forgiveness

- **2 Corinthians 2:1–5 Paul expresses his great love for the Saints at Corinth.** Paul had visited Corinth once before—his first visit during his second missionary journey. A lot had happened since then, and the Church at Corinth was experiencing some serious problems. But Paul had "determined this with myself, that I would not come again to you in heaviness" (v. 1). He reasoned that if he made them sorry, there would be nobody to make him glad because they had all been made sorry by him (v. 2). This light-hearted observation reveals much about Paul's character.

PROVIDENCE LITHOGRAPHIC CO., 1897, #30

Paul said that he wrote this to them so that "when I came, I should [not] have sorrow from them of whom I ought to rejoice" (v. 3). Paul expressed his confidence in them, and said that "my joy is the joy of you all" (v. 3). He admitted to writing to them "out of much affliction and anguish of heart [and] with many tears; not that ye should be grieved, but that ye might know the love which I have more abundantly unto you" (v. 4). And as for those who had "caused [him] grief," Paul declared that they were only a small segment of the Saints there and he did not want to "overcharge you all" with that problem (v. 5).

- **2 Corinthians 2:6–8 Counsel concerning an excommunicated member.** Such a punishment was "sufficient to such a man" who had inflicted many with his sins (v. 6). But rather than turn their backs on him now, Paul advised that "ye ought rather to forgive him, and comfort him, lest perhaps such a one should be swallowed up with overmuch sorrow" (v. 7). Members should instead "confirm [their] love toward him" (v. 8).

Faith in Tribulation

- **2 Corinthians 1:1–7 Paul's adversities helped him to bless the Saints.** After his usual greeting, Paul begins this letter with the observation that God "comforteth us [Paul and his missionary companions] in all our tribulation, that we may be able to comfort them which are in any trouble," according to "the comfort wherewith we ourselves are comforted of God" (v. 4). And although "the sufferings of Christ abound in us," so too does "our consolation also abound . . . by Christ" (v. 5). Paul saw his afflictions as being for the consolation and salvation of the Saints, who were suffering the same things for the Gospel's sake (v. 6). And Paul had "steadfast" hope for the Saints, "knowing, that as ye are partakers of the sufferings, so shall ye be also of the consolation" (v. 7).

- **2 Corinthians 1:8–11 Paul's personal adversities at Ephesus.** "For we would not, brethren, have you ignorant of our trouble which came to us in Asia [probably at Ephesus], that we were pressed out of measure, above strength, insomuch that we despaired even of life" (v. 8). We don't know what this difficulty was, but clearly it was a difficult and very depressing event. But from this, Paul and his companions learned that "we should not trust in ourselves, but in God which raiseth the dead: Who delivered us from so great a death, and doth deliver: in whom we trust that he will yet deliver us" (vv. 9–10). Paul also thanked those Saints who prayed for him and his companions in their time of adversity (v. 11).

- **2 Corinthians 1:22 The Spirit is a "down payment" from God toward our eventual salvation.** Paul speaks of the Holy Ghost as "the earnest," which was a technical term in his day in the world of finance. It means "a guarantee" or "caution money"—similar to "earnest money" we pay toward a significant purchase in our own day. Paul said we have been given the Holy Ghost as an initial payment of blessedness and a guarantee of a much fuller payment in the future.

- **2 Corinthians 4:7–9 Paul's faith in the face of serious difficulties.** Paul speaks of having "treasure" hidden in "earthen vessels"—a common way to hide something of value in his day (v. 7). And what was that treasure? It was the "power . . . of God" that could lift them from any difficulty (v. 7). "We are troubled on every side, yet not distressed," said Paul. "We are perplexed, but not in despair; Persecuted, but not forsaken; cast down, but not destroyed" (v. 8). This kind of faith in God provides mental stability, knowing that God is ultimately in charge and all will turn out for the best.

- **2 Corinthians 4:14–18 Keeping an eternal perspective.** Paul testified that "he which raised up the Lord Jesus [the God the Father] shall raise up us also [through] Jesus, and shall present us with you [at the last day]" (v. 14). All of Paul's efforts were "for your sakes, that the abundant grace [of God] might through [their gratitude] . . . redound to the glory of God" (v. 15).

"For which cause we faint not," said Paul, and "though our outward man perish, yet the inward man is renewed day by day" (v. 16). "For our light affliction, which is but for a moment, worketh for us a far more exceeding and eternal weight of glory" (v. 17). Thus, we should "look not at the things which are seen, but at the things which are not seen: for the things which are seen are temporal; but the things which are not seen are eternal" (v. 18).

Becoming Reconciled to God

- **2 Corinthians 5:1–7 Mortality is a time of testing and trials, and requires faith.** Paul testified of the resurrection by saying, "For we know that if our earthly house of this tabernacle [our bodies] were dissolved, we [will yet] have a building of God, an house not made with hands [our resurrected bodies that will live], eternal in the heavens" (v. 1). Yet, in this life, "we groan, earnestly desiring to be clothed upon with our house which is from heaven" (v. 2) and to "not be found naked" of eternal glory when we do rise (v. 3). We groan while on this earth, being burdened, but look forward to the day when we will be "clothed upon" [with glory], that mortality might be swallowed up of life" (v. 4).

  God is also working for the "selfsame thing" for all of us, and has given us the Spirit to help guide us to that end, and "therefore we are always confident" (vv. 5–6). In the meantime, "whilst we are at home in the body, we are absent from the Lord" and we must learn to "walk by faith, not by sight" (vv. 6–7).

- **2 Corinthians 5:9–10 We will be judged according to our deeds while in the flesh.** We all "labour, that . . . we may be accepted of him [God]" (v. 9) because we know that "we must all appear before the judgment seat of Christ; that every one may receive according to "the things done in his body, . . . whether it be good or bad" (v. 10).

"GETHSEMANE." ©JOSEPH BRICKEY. USED BY PERMISSION

- **2 Corinthians 5:17–21 Paul explains reconciliation.** Whenever a man becomes a disciple of Christ, "he is a new creature: old things are passed away; behold, all things are become new" (v. 17). This is because "all things are of God, who hath reconciled us to himself by Jesus Christ, and hath given to us the ministry of reconciliation" (v. 18). The Greek term from which "reconcile" and "reconciliation" are translated means being restored to God's favor. Paul explains reconciliation as follows. "God was in [sent] Christ, reconciling the world unto himself," because He made it possible to "not imput[e] their trespasses unto them"

(v. 19). Thus, we are reconciled to God the Father despite our errors because of Jesus Christ's atonement on our behalf.

Elder Bruce R. McConkie said, "Reconciliation is the process of ransoming man from his state of sin and spiritual darkness and of restoring him to a state of harmony and unity with Deity. . . . Man, who was once carnal and evil, who lived after the manner of the flesh, becomes a new creature of the Holy Ghost; he is born again; and, even as a little child, he is alive in Christ."[1]

Paul calls the missionaries "ambassadors for Christ," who beseech the people on behalf of Christ to be "reconciled to God" (v. 20). And he says that God had imputed our sins to Christ, "who knew no sin; that we might [receive] the righteousness of God [through] Him" (v. 21; see also 2 Nephi 25:23; Jacob 4:10–11). Their sole purpose is to "do you to wit of the grace of God" (2 Cor. 8:1)—another statement from Paul that seems to make no sense unless you understand that "wit" is an old English verb which literally means "to know" or "to find out." So, Paul is saying that "we want you to know of the grace of God."

Godly Sorrow for Sin

- **2 Corinthians 7:8–10 Sorrow that leads to repentance is good.** Hearing that one of his epistles had "made [the Corinthians] sorry," Paul rejoiced because it was the kind of sorrow that leads to repentance. Alma taught the same thing to his son (see also Alma 42:29–30). Paul wrote, "For though I made you sorry with a letter, I do not repent" (v. 8). "I rejoice, not that ye were made sorry, but that ye sorrowed to repentance: for ye were made sorry after a godly manner" (v. 9). They were not harmed by their sorrow, "for godly sorrow worketh repentance" (vv. 9–10). On the other hand, "the sorrow of the world worketh death" (v. 10).

Elder Spencer W. Kimball explained:

> Often people indicate that they have repented when all they have done is to express regret for a wrong act. But true repentance is marked by that godly sorrow that changes, transforms, and saves. To be sorry is not enough. Perhaps the felon in the penitentiary, coming to realize the high price he must pay for his folly, may wish he had not committed the crime. That is not repentance. The vicious man who is serving a stiff sentence for rape may be very sorry he did the deed, but he is not repentant if his heavy sentence is the only reason for his sorrow. That is the sorrow of the world.
>
> The truly repentant man is sorry before he is apprehended. He is sorry even if his secret is never known. . . . Repentance of the godly type means that one comes to recognize the sin and voluntarily and without pressure from outside sources begins his transformation.[2]
>
> If one is sorry only because someone found out about his sin, his repentance is not complete. Godly sorrow causes one to want to repent, even though he has not been caught by others, and makes him determined to do right no matter what happens. This kind of sorrow brings righteousness and will work toward forgiveness.[3]

PAUL DEFENDS HIS MINISTRY

Paul Acknowledges His Weaknesses

- **2 Corinthians 10:1 Paul describes himself as lowly and humble.** He sought to persuade the Saints "by the meekness and gentleness of Christ." In His presence, Paul feels "base"—meaning lowly and humble, but in dealing with the Saints he is "bold."

- **2 Corinthians 10:8, 17–18 Paul "boasts" of his authority.** It was frequently necessary for Paul to defend his authority to preach the Gospel. But he saw that authority as having been given to them for the edification of others and not for their destruction (v. 8). "He that glorieth," declared Paul, "let him glory in the Lord" (v. 17). A man who commends himself is not approved of God, only those "whom the Lord commendeth" (v. 18).

- **2 Corinthians 10:10–12 Paul's antagonists in Corinth criticize his appearance and voice.** Though they conceded that his letters were "weighty and powerful," they mocked his physical weaknesses and his "contemptible" voice (v. 10). Paul warned them that "such as we are in word by letters when we are absent, [so] will we be also in deed [actions] when we are present" (v. 11). Paul refused to behave like those "that commend themselves" because by "measuring themselves by themselves, and comparing themselves among themselves" they showed themselves to be "not wise" (v. 12).

- **A Physical Description of Paul.** In January 1841, Joseph Smith gave a detailed description of the Apostle Paul's physical appearance and mannerisms:

  "Description of Paul:—He is about five feet high; very dark hair; dark complexion; dark skin; large Roman nose; sharp face; small black eyes, penetrating as eternity; round shoulders; a whining voice, except when elevated, and then it almost resembled the oaring of a lion. He was a good orator, active and diligent, always employing himself in doing good to his fellowman."[4]

Bronze Medallion of Paul, 150 AD

- **2 Corinthians 11:6 Paul is characterized by his enemies as "rude in speech."** Paul declared, "But though I be rude in speech, [I am not rude] in knowledge," which had been "throughly made manifest among you in all things."

- **2 Corinthians 11:22–23 Paul ridicules false teachers.** He rejected their specious claims to authority. "Are they Hebrews? so am I. Are they Israelites? so am I. Are they the seed of Abraham? so am I" (v. 22). Paul then admitted that he was speaking like one of them—"a fool"—when he said, "Are they ministers of Christ? . . . I am more" (v. 23).

Paul's Sacrifices

- **2 Corinthians 11:23–33 A summary of Paul's sacrifices while testifying of Christ.** Paul declared that he had been "in labours more abundant, in stripes above measure, in prisons more frequent, in deaths oft" (v. 23).

  "Of the Jews five times received I forty stripes save one," said Paul (v. 24). These painful whippings could have been administered with a scourge, just as with Christ. "Thrice was I beaten with rods" (v. 25). Beating with rods was a Roman punishment. Paul could have claimed Roman citizenship and escaped the scourging and beatings, but that would have meant excommunication and being cut off from the synagogues. Since going into the synagogues to teach was his primary missionary approach, he willingly submitted to these shameful punishments in order to continue teaching his own people.

"PAUL SHIPWRECKED," J. E. SEWARD, PROVIDENCE LITHOGRAPHIC CO.

"Once was I stoned, thrice I suffered shipwreck, a night and a day I have been in the deep [floating helplessly in the sea]; In journeyings often, in perils of waters, in perils of robbers, in perils by mine own countrymen, in perils by the heathen, in perils in the city, in perils in the wilderness, in perils in the sea, in perils among false brethren" (vv. 25–26). Paul had served "in weariness and painfulness, in watchings often, in hunger and thirst, in fastings often, in cold and nakedness" (v. 27). And these trials were all in addition to the responsibility that came upon him daily to take "care of all the churches" (v. 28).

This had been true for Paul from the very beginning of his ministry. "In Damascus the governor under Aretas the king kept the city of the Damascenes with a garrison, desirous to apprehend me: And through a window in a basket was I let down by the wall, and escaped his hands" (vv. 32–33). And Paul had been suffering for Christ's sake ever since that day.

Nobody was justified in comparing their own sufferings because of the work to those suffered by Paul. "Who is weak, and I am not weak? who is offended, and I burn not? If I must needs glory, I will glory of . . . mine infirmities" (vv. 29–30). They were badges of honor for him, evidence of his devotion to duty in spite of difficulty and pain. "The God and Father of our Lord Jesus Christ, which is blessed for evermore, knoweth that I lie not" (v. 31).

Paul's "Thorn in the Flesh"

THEBIBLEREVIVAL.COM, #22

- **2 Corinthians 12:7–10 Paul has a "thorn in the flesh" which keeps him humble.** On three separate occasions he pleaded with the Lord to take it away, but the Lord declined, saying that "strength is made perfect in weakness."

  The word Paul uses here literally means "a pale" (as in impaled) or "a stake." It was used to refer to sharpened stakes, to surgical instruments, or to fishhooks. The term suggests something that was extremely painful and troublesome to Paul. There have been endless debates on what his infirmity was, and the suggestions have included a bitter and shrewish wife, epilepsy, a serious eye affliction, malaria, and a painful hip condition that caused pain with every step.

  Elder Harold B. Lee said:

  > The Lord has told us in the scriptures that Satan is an enemy of all righteousness; because of that fact, those who are standing in high places in our Father's kingdom will become the objects of his attacks. You may well expect, as the Apostle Paul understood, that you who preside in the various places in our Father's kingdom will be subject to the devil's onslaughts. . . .
  >
  > Sometimes there is given infirmity, difficulty, hardship upon you to try your souls; and the powers of Satan seem to be enrolled against you, watching and trying to break down your powers of resistance; but your weakness, through those infirmities, will give you the power of God that shall rest upon you even as the Apostle Paul was reconciled and comforted by the thought that through his trials the power of God might rest upon him.[5]

  — **Ether 12:27 Christ's grace will cover (make up for) all of our weaknesses, if we are humble.** The Lord said that "if men come unto me I will show unto them their weakness." He gives us weaknesses to make us humble, but promises that in spite of those weaknesses, "my grace is sufficient for all men that humble themselves before me." This is a promise of redemption and salvation (through Christ) despite our foolishness and weakness. "For if they humble themselves before me, and have faith in me, then will I make weak things become strong unto them."

Paul's Visions

- **2 Corinthians 12:1–3 Paul describes his vision of the celestial kingdom and of paradise**, which was probably the source of his earlier teaching on three degrees of glory after the resurrection (see the discussion of 1 Cor. 15:35, 40–42 in the previous chapter of this book).

  Paul said, "I knew a man in Christ above fourteen years ago," referring to himself in the third person. This man [Paul] had a vision—"whether in the body, I cannot tell; or whether out of the body, I cannot tell: God knoweth"—in which he was "caught up to the third heaven" (v. 2). This means that Paul saw in vision the celestial kingdom [the third heaven] of our God.

  ZAMPIERI, THE BIBLE AND ITS STORY, 1908

  The same man had another vision—"whether in the body, or out of the body, I cannot tell: God knoweth"—of "paradise" (vv. 3–4), which is the state of the righteous after death while they wait for the resurrection. Notice that Paul speaks of these events as two separate visions of two separate places. The Christian world got these two places confused long ago, in the first few centuries after Christ, and began to teach that upon death we go to "heaven" or "hell" immediately. These states of being actually describe the two parts of the spirit world—paradise and spirit prison—but do not describe what happens after the resurrection. The Book of Mormon and modern revelation have restored a complete understanding, which Paul was trying to explain here.

- **2 Corinthians 12:4 "Unspeakable words."** Paul said that in his visions of the celestial kingdom and of paradise he heard "unspeakable words, which it is not lawful for a man to utter." This can be understood correctly in two ways:

  — **Things which are indescribable.** There are things that exist in the heavenly spheres for which we have no adequate words or comparisons in this life. For example, Isaiah had no worthy comparison for missile warfare in the latter days, but attempted to describe them as "fiery flying serpents"—something which the people of his day had experienced and could understand. But the comparison, while somewhat accurate in physical description, is inadequate to convey how missiles work and the destruction they cause.

  — **Things which are forbidden to discuss.** Our ability and willingness to control our tongues is directly related to how much revelation the Lord is willing to give us. He cautioned the early Latter-day Saints with these words: "Remember that that which cometh from above is sacred, and must be spoken with care, and by constraint of the Spirit" (D&C 63:64). Promising that marvelous signs and healings would follow true believers in the early Church, the Lord cautioned: "But a commandment I give unto them, that they shall not boast themselves of these things, neither speak them before the world; for these things are given unto you for *your* profit and for salvation" (D&C 84:73, emphasis added).

The Prophet Joseph Smith said, "The reason we do not have the secrets of the Lord revealed unto us, is because we do not keep them but reveal them; we do not keep our own secrets, but reveal our difficulties to the world, even to our enemies, then how would we keep the secrets of the Lord?"[6]

President Brigham Young said, "Should you receive a vision or revelation from the Almighty, one that the Lord gave you concerning yourselves, or this people, but which you are not to reveal on account of your not being the proper person, or because it ought not to be known by the people at present, you should shut it up and seal it as close, and lock it as tight as heaven is to you, and make it as secret as the grave. The Lord has no confidence in those who reveal secrets, for He cannot safely reveal Himself to such persons."[7] He also said, "That man who cannot know things without telling any other living being upon the earth, who cannot keep his secrets and those that God reveals to him, never can receive the voice of his Lord to dictate him and the people on this earth."[8]

Elder Boyd K. Packer said, "It is not wise to continually talk of unusual spiritual experiences. They are to be guarded with care and shared only when the Spirit itself prompts you to use them to the blessing of others. I am ever mindful of Alma's words (Alma 12:9) . . ."[9]

President Marion G. Romney said, "I do not tell all I know. I have not told my wife all I know. I have found that if I tell everything I know and explain every experience that I have had, the Lord will not trust me."[10]

President David O. McKay called special spiritual experiences "heart petals." Surely it would take some special inspiration to share them with others. The spirit of the occasion would have to be right, and the motive would have to be to build another or to build the kingdom, not self-aggrandizement.

The Prophet Joseph Smith said, "Paul ascended into the third heavens, and he could understand the three principal rounds of Jacob's ladder—the telestial, the terrestrial, and the celestial glories or kingdoms, where Paul saw and heard things which were not lawful for him to utter."[11]

Preparing the Corinthians for His Visit

- **2 Corinthians 6:1, 3–10 Righteous priesthood service.** Paul and his companions, "workers together with [God]," had striven to "giv[e] no offence in any thing, that the ministry be not blamed" (vv. 1, 3). They had sought, "as the ministers of God," to serve "in much patience, in afflictions, in necessities, in distresses, In stripes, in imprisonments, in tumults, in labours, in watchings, in fastings" (vv. 4–5).

As we have been counseled in our own day (D&C 121), Paul exercised his priesthood "by pureness, by knowledge, by longsuffering, by kindness, by the Holy Ghost, by love unfeigned, by the word of truth, by the power of God, by the armour of righteousness on the right hand and on the left" (vv. 6–7).

Along the way, they had received "honour and dishonour, . . . evil report and good report [being called] deceivers, and yet true" (v. 8). They had been both known and unknown by the people, had come close to "dying, and [yet], behold, we live;" had been "chastened, and [yet] not killed; . . . sorrowful, yet alway[s] rejoicing; . . . poor, yet making many rich; . . . having nothing, and yet possessing all things" (vv. 9–10).

The Prophet Joseph Smith said, "God hath said that He would have a tried people, that He would purge them as gold."[12]

The Prophet also said, "You will have all kinds of trials to pass through. And it is quite as necessary for you to be tried as it was for Abraham and other men of God. . . God will feel after you, and He will take hold of you and wrench your very heart strings, and if you cannot stand it you will not be fit for an inheritance in the Celestial kingdom of God."[13]

President Brigham Young said the Prophet Joseph Smith was perfected by his afflictions: "Joseph could not have been perfected, though he had lived a thousand years, if he had received no persecution. If he had lived a thousand years, and led this people, and preached the Gospel without persecution, he would not have been perfected as well as he was at the age of thirty-nine years. You may calculate, when this people are called to go through scenes of affliction and suffering, are driven from their homes, and cast down, and scattered, and smitten, and peeled, the Almighty is rolling on His work with greater rapidity."[14]

President John Taylor said, "It is necessary that we pass through certain ordeals in order that we may be purified. People sometimes do not comprehend these things. . . . We have learned many things through suffering, we call it suffering; I call it a school of experience. . . . What are these things for? Why is it that good men should be tried? . . . that we may learn to place our dependence upon God, and trust in Him, and to observe His laws and keep His commandments. . . . I have never looked at these things in any other light than trials for the purpose of purifying the Saints of God, that they may be, as the Scriptures say, as gold that has been seven times purified by the fire. [See Psalm 12:6.]"[15]

Elder Marion G. Romney said:

> I say to you and all the rest of us who are being tried in the crucible of adversity and affliction: Take courage; revive your spirits and strengthen your faith. In these lessons so impressively taught in precept and example by our great exemplar, Jesus Christ, and His Prophet of the restoration, Joseph Smith, we have ample inspiration for comfort and for hope.

If we can bear our afflictions with the understanding, faith, and courage, and in the spirit in which they bore theirs, we shall be strengthened and comforted in many ways. We shall be spared the torment which accompanies the mistaken idea that all suffering comes as chastisement for transgression. We shall be comforted by the knowledge that we are not enduring, nor will we be required to endure, the suffering of the wicked who are to "be cast out into outer darkness [where] there shall be weeping, and wailing, and gnashing of teeth." (Alma 40:13).[16]

THEBIBLEREVIVAL.COM, #22

- **2 Corinthians 6:11–13 I have opened my heart freely to you; open yours to me.** Paul pleaded with the Corinthians to receive them with open hearts. "Our mouth is open unto you, our heart is enlarged," he said (v. 11). In fact, he considered them to be his children (v. 13). If their hearts were "straitened" (narrowed) toward Paul and his companions, it was not because of anything they had done to them, "but [because] ye are straitened in your own bowels" (v. 12). "Bowels" represent the center of pity and kindness. Thus, these verses mean, "You are restricted, not by any lack of Paul's kindness, but by your own failure to show love and compassion." To make up for this ("recompense in the same"), he invited them to "be . . . enlarged" in their hearts (v. 13).

- **2 Corinthians 12:14; 13:1–2 Was there another visit?** This verse creates confusion since it mentions that this is "the third time I am ready to come to you." He said it again in 2 Corinthians 13:1, but followed that statement with this one: "I told you before, and foretell you, as if I were present, the *second time*" (v. 2, emphasis added). We know that Paul visited Corinth during his first mission, and again this time during his second mission. If there was a third time, we are not aware of it from the scriptural record.

- **2 Corinthians 12:14–15 You will not have to support me temporally.** "I will not be burdensome to you," Paul promised, "for I seek not yours [your possessions], but you." He observed that "children ought not to lay up for [support] the parents, but the parents for the children" (v. 14). Paul said he would "very gladly spend and be spent for you," although "the more abundantly I love you, the less I be loved" (v. 15).

- **2 Corinthians 12:19–21 All that Paul did, he did in love, for their good.** "We do all things, dearly beloved, for your edifying" (v. 19). Paul hoped that when he came to them he would find them "such as I would [want you to be]"—all that they should be as Saints. But he worried that they would find him "such as ye would not [want me to be]," leading to "debates, envyings, wraths, strifes, backbitings, whisperings, swellings, tumults" (v. 20). This would be very humbling to him, and he would "bewail [mourn] many which have sinned already, and have not repented of the uncleanness and fornication and lasciviousness which they have committed" (v. 21).

- **2 Corinthians 13:2–10 God will give you the power to be righteous if you really want to be.** "Being absent now I write to them which heretofore have sinned, and to all other[s], that, if I come again, I will not spare" (v. 2). They apparently sought a stronger witness from Paul (not one that is "weak" but is "mighty") that "Christ speaking in me" (v. 3). "Examine yourselves," Paul said, "whether ye be in the faith; prove your own selves" (v. 5). He knew that which they did not know—"that Jesus Christ is in you, except ye be reprobates" (v. 5). Paul adjured them to "do no evil," not just for the sake of approving Paul's work among them, "but that ye should do that which is honest, . . . For we can do nothing against the truth, but [only] for the truth" (vv. 7–8). He would gladly be weak if they would be strong, "and this also we wish, even your perfection" (v. 9). Paul was writing these things, "being absent, lest being present I should use sharpness, according to the power which the Lord hath given me" for their "edification," not their "destruction" (v. 10).

- **2 Corinthians 13:11–14 Paul ends his epistle with love.** "Finally, brethren, farewell. Be perfect, be of good comfort, be of one mind, live in peace; and the God of love and peace shall be with you. Greet one another with an holy kiss. All the saints salute you. The grace of the Lord Jesus Christ, and the love of God, and the communion of the Holy Ghost, be with you all. Amen."

ADDITIONAL TEACHINGS IN 2ND CORINTHIANS

- **2 Corinthians 2:14–16 Paul's gratitude to Christ for His mission.** Paul here digresses from his narrative about his travel itinerary to speak out in spontaneous praise and gratitude for the privilege of representing Christ. "Now thanks be unto God, which always causeth us to triumph in Christ, and maketh manifest . . . his knowledge [through] us in every place" (v. 14). He said that to those who are saved, the missionaries brought "a sweet savour [smell] of Christ" unto life, while "in them that perish . . . we are the savour of death unto death" (vv. 15–16). This was an ominous responsibility and blessing for the missionaries, "and who is sufficient for these things?" (v. 16).

- **2 Corinthians 3:1–5 The source of Paul's joy.** Paul doesn't need a letter of thanks from the Corinthian Saints; what is written in their hearts (their faithfulness) is thanks enough. Paul asked, "Do we begin again to commend ourselves? or need we, as some others, epistles of commendation to you, or letters of commendation from you?" (v. 1). No. "Ye are our epistle written in our hearts, known and read of all men . . . the epistle of Christ . . . written not with ink, but with the Spirit of the living God; not in tables of stone, but in fleshy tables of the heart" (vv. 2–3). That's all the commendation that Paul needed or wanted. The missionaries' trust was in God, through Christ (v. 4). They were not self-sufficient; their "sufficiency is of God" (v. 5).

- **2 Corinthians 3:6 "The letter of the law killeth, but the spirit giveth life."** As "ministers of the new testament," Paul and his companions were not ministers "of the letter, but of the spirit: for the letter killeth, but the spirit giveth life."

- **2 Corinthians 3:7–11 The gospel is far more glorious than the law of Moses.** "If the ministration of death [law of Moses], written and engraven in stones, was glorious,. . . how shall not the ministration of the spirit be rather [more] glorious" (vv. 7–8). "If the ministration of condemnation [the lesser law] be glor[ious], . . . the ministration of righteousness [the Gospel] exceed[s it] in glory" (v. 9). By comparison, the law of Moses has no glory to compare with the Gospel" (v. 10). "For if that which is done away was glorious, [how] much more that which remaineth is glorious" (v. 11).

  The word "testament" here is translated from the Greek word *diatheke*, which is used primarily to mean "covenant." Paul is saying here that the new covenant (Gospel) is based on higher principles and priesthood than the old covenant, which if continued after the higher law has been given will kill the Saints spiritually.

- **2 Corinthians 3:12–16 The law of Moses veils the heart from understanding.** Because of the hope the Gospel brings, Paul could "use great plainness of speech" (v. 12). This was different from "Moses, which put a vail over his face, that the children of Israel could not stedfastly [see] to the end of that which is abolished [the laws of Moses]" (v. 13). The children of Israel's "minds were blinded: [and even to] this day remaineth the same vail [when] reading . . . the old testament" (v. 14). But the "vail [that] is upon their heart" is "done away in Christ" (vv. 15, 14). And when people "turn to the Lord, the vail shall be taken away" (v. 16).

- **2 Corinthians 4:16 The outward and inner man.** Paul said that for the cause of Christ "we faint not; [and] though our outward man perish, yet the inward man is renewed day by day." The "outward man" is the natural man, whose body and spirit can grow weary of trying so hard. The "inward man" has the gospel written "in his heart," and can be renewed day by day, regardless of what happens to the outward man.

- **2 Corinthians 5:20 Ambassadors for Christ.** Paul saw the missionaries' duty to be "ambassadors for Christ," through which God could beseech them to "be ye reconciled to God." In this effort, they were acting "in Christ's stead" as His duly-appointed representatives.

- **2 Corinthians 6:14 Marrying within the faith.** With regard to marriage, Paul advised, "Be ye not unequally yoked together with unbelievers: for what fellowship hath righteousness with unrighteousness? and what communion hath light with darkness?"

In order for two animals to plow together, a yoke made of a wooden beam was laid across the top of the animals' necks and fastened under their necks. The Mosaic law prohibited yoking together two different beasts, such as an ox and an ass; the unequal pull could cause the weaker or smaller of the animals discomfort and pain. Paul's counsel, "Be ye not unequally yoked together with unbelievers" was meant to suggest that different-faith marriage partners would experience the unequal pull that could cause serious discomfort and pain to one or the other or both.

Elder Mark E. Petersen said: "What are we to do then? Shall we bring upon ourselves the unhappiness of a divided household? Shall we profit by the voice of experience and marry within own faith? . . . The obvious answer to everyone is, marry within your own faith. If you are a Presbyterian, marry a Presbyterian. If you are a Catholic, marry a Catholic. If you are of the house of Judah, marry within your own faith. If you are a Mormon, marry a Mormon."[17]

- **2 Corinthians 8:9–14 Imparting to others according to their need.** We should impart of our substance to the less fortunate "by an equality"—that is, according to proper needs and wants (D&C 51:3; 82:17). Paul reminded the Saints that "Christ, . . . though he was rich, yet for your sakes . . . became poor, that ye through his poverty might be rich" (v. 9). He advised them, as he had done a year before, to follow Christ's example (v. 10) and give "out of that which ye have" to others (v. 11). In this, they were to "perform the doing of it," not just have "a readiness to will [do it]" (v. 11).

THEBIBLEREVIVAL.COM, #30

If they had "a willing mind," they should give according to that which they had and not according to that which they did not have (v. 12). This suggests they need to be wise in giving and to give of our surplus, not something beyond our means. In this, Paul said, "I mean not that other men be eased, and ye burdened" (v. 13). Rather, there should be more of an "equality, . . . that . . . your abundance may be a supply for their want, that their abundance also may be a supply for your want" (v. 14).

The Lord's way of establishing "equality" does not mean an equal quantity but rather an equal opportunity to satisfy all our needs and wants. Paul was not advocating a dole system, but one in which Saints help each other to be temporally and spiritually secure.

- **2 Corinthians 9:6 The necessity of work.** Paul encouraged the Saints to work for their temporal blessings. He warned that "he which soweth sparingly shall reap also sparingly; and he which soweth bountifully shall reap also bountifully."

- **2 Corinthians 9:7–13 The blessings of being generous.** When we share with others, "every man [should do] according as he purposeth in his heart, [and] give; not grudgingly, or of necessity: for God loveth a cheerful giver" (v. 7). God is able to bless us with "all sufficiency in all things, [if we] abound to every good work" (v. 8). He is also able to provide for the poor (v. 9). But when we give to the poor, we are also blessed, because "he that ministereth seed to the sower . . . minister[s] bread for [his own] food," and also "increase[s] the fruits of [his own] righteousness" (v. 10). Also, when we are "enriched in every thing to all bountifulness," and we share with others, it "causeth through us thanksgiving to God" (v. 11), because our help "not only supplieth the want of the saints, but is abundant also [in producing] thanksgivings unto God" (v. 12). Those who receive "this ministration . . . glorify God for your [living of] the gospel of Christ, and for your liberal distribution unto them, and unto all men" (v. 13).

- **2 Corinthians 11:2 Christ is the Bridegroom.** Christ often used the analogy of a bride and bridegroom to explain the sacred nature of our covenants with Him. Paul uses the same analogy here. "For I am jealous over you with godly jealousy: for I have espoused you to one husband, that I may present you as a chaste virgin to Christ." The Lord's Church is married to her Bridegroom, as the disciples of Christ take upon themselves His name.

- **2 Corinthians 11:3 The plainness and simplicity of the Gospel.** Paul reminded the Saints that "the serpent beguiled Eve through his subtilty." The complex philosophical reasonings of men may corrupt our minds "from the simplicity that is in Christ." Nephi also gloried in plainness, believing that it was the best way to bring souls to Christ (2 Nephi 25:4, 7, 20; 26:33; 31:3; Jacob 4:13; Mosiah 2:40; Alma 5:43; 13:23).

- **2 Corinthians 11:18 Righteous glorying.** Noting that "many [people] glory after the flesh," Paul said the he "will glory also." But he was glorying not over worldly accomplishments but in his successes on behalf of Christ (see also Alma 26).

Notes

1. *Doctrinal New Testament Commentary*, 3 vols. [1965–1973], 2:422–423.
2. *The Miracle of Forgiveness* [1969], 153.
3. *Repentance Brings Forgiveness* [LDS Church pamphlet, 1984], 8.
4. *Teachings of the Prophet Joseph Smith*, sel. Joseph Fielding Smith [1976], 180.
5. In Conference Report, October 1949, 57.
6. *Teachings of the Prophet Joseph Smith*, 195.
7. In *Journal of Discourses*, 4:288.
8. In *Journal of Discourses*, 4:287.

9. *Ensign*, January 1983, 53.

10. Quoted by Boyd K. Packer, Church Employees Lecture Series, January 18, 1980.

11. *Teachings of the Prophet Joseph Smith*, 304–305.

12. *Teachings of the Prophet Joseph Smith*, 135.

13. As reported by John Taylor in *Journal of Discourses*, 24:197.

14. *Discourses of Brigham Young*, sel. John A. Widtsoe [1941], 351.

15. In *Journal of Discourses*, 23:334, 336.

16. In Conference Report, October 1969, 59.

17. In Conference Report, April 1958, 106.

Chapter 36

Epistle to the Romans

(Acts 20; Romans)

INTRODUCTION

Where and When Was the Epistle to the Romans Written?

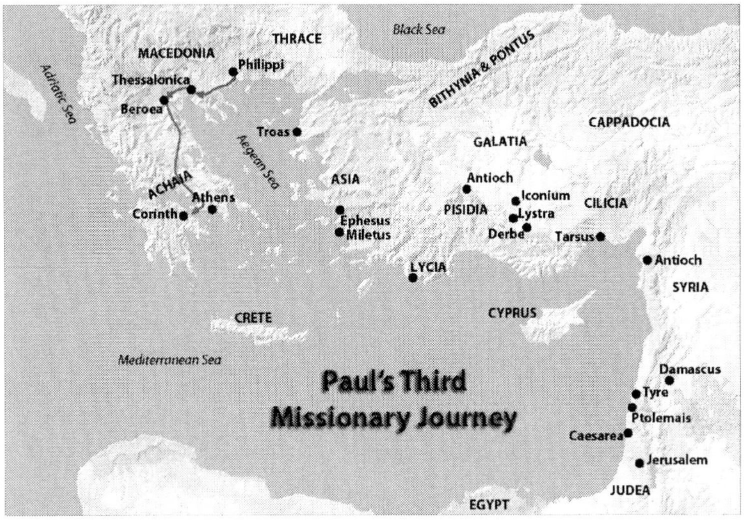

After writing his second epistle to the Corinthians from Macedonia (Philippi), Paul then traveled to Corinth, where he spent 3 months waiting for good sailing conditions before departing for Jerusalem (Acts 20:2–3).

While there, in addition to teaching the Corinthians in person, Paul wrote two epistles to Saints elsewhere: (1) the epistle to the Galatians, which we studied earlier in chapter 32, and (2) the epistle to the Romans, which is the subject of this chapter.

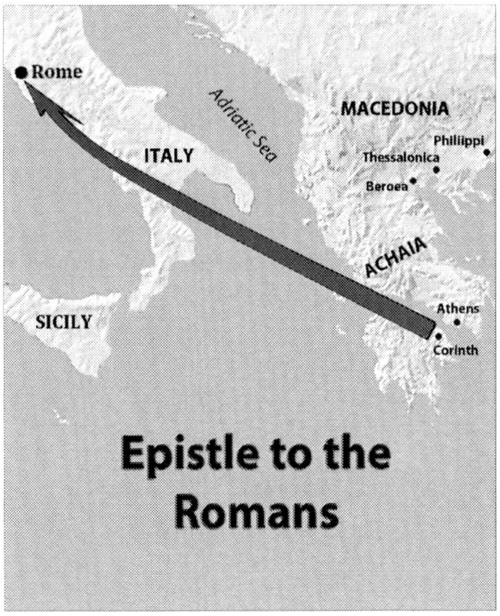

From clues within the epistle (Romans 15:25 says it was just before he returned to Jerusalem), we can tell that the letter to Rome was written from Corinth near the end of Paul's third missionary journey, most likely during the winter months of 57–58 AD.

In this letter, Paul was informing the Saints at Rome of his intent to visit them. He had been thinking about a visit to Rome since earlier in the year when he was still at Ephesus (Acts 19:21). He had no idea at this time that when he did visit Rome he would be under arrest to Roman authorities.

Paul wrote to the Romans from Corinth in 57–58 AD.

- **Romans 16:1–2 Paul sent the epistle to the Roman Saints with Phebe**, a Church member from Cenchrea, a port town south of Corinth. She had assisted Paul in the work before, and now carried his letter to Rome. Paul commended her to the Saints at Rome and asked that they "receive her in the Lord, as becometh saints, and that ye assist her in whatsoever business she hath need of you: for she hath been a succourer of many, and of myself also."
- **Romans 16:3–15** Paul had become acquainted with many Roman Saints, probably in Corinth and Ephesus. In all, 28 individuals, including women, are mentioned by name in this epistle. Some may have been relatives of Paul.

Significant Contributions of the Epistle to the Romans

The reports from Rome were positive. The Saints were believing and testifying, and Church membership was growing. But Paul was already seeing the dark specter of apostasy arising throughout the Church, and he warned the Romans of the threat posed by false teachers.

The theme of the epistle to the Romans is simply this: "For I am not ashamed of the gospel of Christ; for it is the power of God unto salvation to every one that believeth; to the Jew first, and also to the Greek" (Romans 1:16).

In this epistle, Paul provided a powerful defense of righteousness. He defined the gospel and summarized the process through which salvation comes—through faith in Jesus Christ. He spoke plainly of a number of essential doctrines, including:

— Adam's fall, which brought death, and Christ's atoning sacrifice, which brought life.
— The law of justification, which requires faith, works, and the atoning blood of Christ.
— The glorious doctrine of joint-heirship with Christ.
— The election of grace.
— The status of the chosen race.
— Why salvation cannot come by the law of Moses alone.
— Why circumcision was done away in Christ.
— How and why salvation was taken to the Gentiles.

To Whom Was the Epistle to the Romans Written?

The teachings in the epistle to the Romans presuppose gospel knowledge, so they were written to the Saints, not to investigators.

Elder Bruce R. McConkie said:

> The epistle to the Romans is a letter, not a treatise on gospel subjects. It is not written to the world, but to the Saints, to people who already know and understand the doctrines of

salvation. Paul's comments on gospel subjects presuppose an extensive prior knowledge on the part of his readers. He does not here expound doctrines as such; he simply comments about them, leaving unsaid the volumes of gospel understanding already possessed by the Saints. Romans, hence is not a source of gospel knowledge for the spiritually untutored; it is not the initial place to turn to learn of Christ and His laws. In the hands of the sectarian world, Romans is a book on calculus in the hands of students who are still struggling to learn the basics of common arithmetic . . .

In its very nature Romans is an epistle capable of differing interpretations. Those without prior and full knowledge of the doctrines involved find it exceedingly difficult to place Paul's comments about these doctrines into their true perspective. For instance, it is on a misunderstanding of the Apostle's statement about justification by faith alone that the whole sectarian world is led to believe that men are not required to work out their own salvation; and it was this very passage that enabled Martin Luther to justify in his own mind his break with Catholicism, an eventuality of vital importance to the furtherance of the Lord's work on earth . . .

To whom was the Epistle to the Romans written? To the Gentiles in Rome? To the world in general? To sectarian Christians today? Not by any means. If there is any truth the world can gain from this Epistle, such is all to the good. But Paul wrote it to the Saints, to members of the Church, to those who already had the gift of the Holy Ghost, to those who had been born again, to those who held the priesthood and enjoyed the gifts of the Spirit. Hence he was writing to the people who already knew the doctrines of salvation, and his teachings can only be understood by people who have the same background, the same knowledge, and the same experience as the original recipients of the message. Romans is a sealed book to the sectarian world; it is an open volume of inspiring gospel truth to the Saints of God.[1]

PAUL'S EPISTLE TO THE ROMANS

Saints vs. Sinners: The Faithful Roman Saints

THEBIBLEREVIVAL.COM, #22

- **Romans 1:7–13 Paul's love and prayers for the Roman Saints.** The theme and language of Romans is very similar to Galatians, but the tone is very different. Paul began with his usual affectionate greeting: "To all that be in Rome, beloved of God, called to be saints: Grace to you and peace from God our Father, and the Lord Jesus Christ" (v. 7). Then he expressed his gratitude for them and said that their faith "is spoken of throughout the whole world" (v. 8). And he assured them "that without ceasing I make mention of you always in my prayers" (v. 9).

  Paul had also prayed that, "if by any means . . . at length I might have a prosperous journey by the will of God to come unto you. For I long to see you, that I may impart unto you some spiritual gift, to the end ye may be established" (vv. 10–11). And also "that I may be comforted together with you by the mutual faith both of you and me" (v. 12). Paul told them that "oftentimes I purposed to come unto you, . . . that I might have some fruit among you also, even as among other Gentiles" (v. 13). Unfortunately, he was "let" [restrained] "hitherto" [up to this present time]).

The Wicked World

- **Romans 1:18–21 The willfully rebellious receive the wrath of God.** Paul declared that "the wrath of God is revealed from heaven against all ungodliness and unrighteousness of men," but added the caveat "who hold the truth in unrighteousness" (v. 18). Thus willful rebellion brings the wrath of God upon men and nations. Sinning in ignorance is another matter. Why? Because for people who know or have known the truths of the Gospel, "that which may be known of God is manifest in them; for God hath shewed it unto them" (v. 19). In other words, they have received a witness or testimony. Plus, the evidence of God is all around them and has been since "the creation of the world;" they are "clearly seen [in] the things that are made, even his eternal power and Godhead," which leaves them "without excuse" (v. 20). "When they knew God, they glorified him not as God, neither were thankful; but became vain in their imaginations, and their foolish heart was darkened" (v. 21). I have known many apostates who are very aptly described by Paul in these verses. Their minds and even their countenances have become dark, and there is virtually nothing that can reach or change them.

- **Romans 1:22–25 The arrogance and ignorance of those who worship idols.** "Professing themselves to be wise, they became fools, and changed the glory of the uncorruptible God into an image made like to corruptible man, and to birds, and four-footed beasts, and creeping things" (v. 23). In our own time, we might add to this list their cars, boats, jewelry, and homes. They worship "things" rather than God. Many such worldly persons also give themselves up to "uncleanness through the lusts of their own hearts, [and] dishonour their own bodies between themselves" (v. 24). They have "changed the truth of God into a lie, and worshipped and served the creature more than the Creator, who is blessed for ever." (v. 25).

THEBIBLEREVIVAL.COM, #21

- **Romans 1:26–28 A clear declaration against homosexual behavior.** The fashion today is to ignore the clear statements of the Bible concerning homosexuality. Since it has been declared "normal" by social-psychologists, we have slowly but surely tolerated, then accepted, and finally embraced this immoral behavior. Paul spoke clearly against it when he said, "For this cause God gave them up unto vile affections: for even their women did change the natural use into that which is against nature [lesbians]" (v. 26). "And likewise also the men, leaving the natural use of the woman, burned in their lust one toward another; men with men working that which is unseemly, and receiving in themselves that recompence of their error which was meet" (v. 27). Such persons do not "like to retain God in their knowledge," because of what God has clearly said in the scriptures; thus, "God gave them over to a reprobate mind, to do those things which are not convenient" (v. 28). "Convenient" is King James English for the Greek word meaning "fitting" or "proper."

Elder Spencer W. Kimball said:

> Of the adverse social effects of homosexuality none is more significant than the effect on marriage and home. The normal, God-given sexual relationship is the procreative act between man and woman in honorable marriage. . . . Where stands the perversion of homosexuality? Clearly it is hostile to God's purpose in that it negates His first and great commandment to "multiply and replenish the earth." If the abominable practice became universal it would depopulate the earth in a single generation. It would nullify God's great program for His spirit children in that it would leave countless unembodied spirits in the heavenly world without the chance for the opportunities of mortality and would deny to all the participants in the practice the eternal life God makes available to us all . . .
>
> Many have been misinformed that they are powerless in the matter, not responsible for the tendency, and that 'God made them that way.' This is as untrue as any other of the diabolical lies Satan has concocted. It is blasphemy. Man is made in the image of God. Does the pervert think God to be 'that way'? . . . Sometimes not heavenly but earthly parents get the blame. Granted that certain conditions make it easier for one to become [homosexual] . . . he can . . . rise above the frustrations of childhood and stand on his own feet . . . . A man may rationalize and excuse himself till the groove is so deep he cannot get out without great difficulty.[2]

- **Romans 1:29–32 Paul lists characteristics of the reprobate.** The list is very recognizable in our own dispensation. We live in a world that has become saturated with the sins that Paul saw around him in the early Church. "Being filled with all unrighteousness, fornication, wickedness, covetousness, maliciousness; full of envy, murder, debate, deceit, malignity; whisperers [gossipers], backbiters, haters of God, despiteful, proud, boasters, inventors of evil things, disobedient to parents, without understanding, covenant-breakers, without natural affection, implacable, unmerciful" (vv. 29–31). These are people who, "knowing the judgment of God, that they which commit such things are worthy of death, not only do the same, but have pleasure in them that do them" (v. 32). They are proud of their lifestyle and flaunt it openly.

FAITH, JUSTIFICATION AND GRACE

How Our Faith Is Measured

About 20% of the epistle to the Romans deals with faith and grace and about 30% with works. These two terms are used more often in Romans than in any other New Testament scripture. Paul was speaking to both Jewish and Gentile members of the Church, so he emphasized different aspects of the gospel to each group, according to their needs:

— To Jews: Emphasis on justification by grace, apart from the works of the law.
— To Pagans: Emphasis on avoiding evil works and being judged by our actions.

- **Romans 2:6–10 Paul teaches of the importance of works.** Those churches that make much of Paul's doctrines of justification by faith and salvation by grace either skip or gloss over the powerful teaching of Paul in these verses. Paul clearly taught that God "will render to every man according to his *deeds*" (v. 6, emphasis added). "Deeds" comes from from the Greek word *ergon*, which is translated in the New Testament 20 times as "deeds" and more than 150 times as "works."

  "To them who by patient continuance in well doing seek for glory and honour and immortality, [God will grant] eternal life" (v. 7). "But unto them that are contentious, and do not obey the truth, but obey unrighteousness, [God will send] indignation and wrath, tribulation and anguish," which will fall upon "every soul of man that doeth evil, of the Jew first, and also of the Gentile" (vv. 8–9). "But glory, honour, and peace, [will be granted] to every man that worketh good, to the Jew first, and also to the Gentile" (v. 10).

THEBIBLEREVIVAL.COM, #21

- **Romans 2:13 More on the importance of works.** It is "not the *hearers* of the law [that] are just[ified] before God, but the *doers* of the law shall be justified" (v. 13, emphasis added).

- **Romans 2:11–12 Those who "die without law" are judged differently than those who have known the truth.** Paul taught that "there is no respect of persons with God" (v. 11). By this he meant that God does not favor one person over another when judging their sins. "For as many as have sinned without law shall also perish without law" (v. 12). This means that a person who does not know the truth is not judged or punished for not living it; they will die "without law" and be judged according to the light that they had. But "as many as have sinned in the law shall be judged by the law" (v. 12). Where more understanding exists, a higher standard of judgment applies.

- **Romans 2:14–15 Those who live by the light that they have are blessed.** "For when the Gentiles, which have not the law, do *by nature* the things contained in the law, these, having not the law, are a law unto themselves" (v. 14). But in doing so, they "shew the work of the law written in their hearts, their conscience [the light of Christ] also bearing witness" (v. 15).

- **Romans 3:1–2 Are Jews more righteous than Gentiles?** Paul asked "What advantage then hath the Jew? or what profit is there of circumcision?" (v. 1). Then, according to the Bible, he answered that Jews have an advantage, "Much [in] every way" because they had the "oracles of God" among them (v. 2). This verse is not only confusing in the way it is worded, but it is contradictory to what Paul was actually trying to say. Look at the clarification in the JST, which is included in footnote "a": "JST Rom. 3:1–2 What advantage then hath the Jew over the Gentile? or what profit of circumcision, who is not a Jew from the heart? But he who is a Jew from the heart, I say hath much every way." In other words, if a Jew were practicing his religion "from the heart," then God will respect it. Inner motivations and outward motions are both critical in bringing disciples closer to God.

- **Romans 4:15 "Where no law is, there is no transgression."** We cannot violate a commandment of which we have no knowledge. This is discussed many times by the prophets in the Book of Mormon, who shed important additional light on the topic.

  — **2 Nephi 9:25 "Where there is no law given there is no punishment."** Jacob declared that people will not be punished for violating laws that they do not know. He went on to reason that "where there is no punishment there is no condemnation; and where there is no condemnation the mercies of the Holy One of Israel have claim upon them, because of the atonement; for they are delivered by the power of [Christ]."

  — **2 Nephi 2:11–15 Righteousness requires law.** Lehi explained that there can be transgression and punishment only where a law is given. The reason why has much to do with agency. "For it must needs be, that there is an opposition in all things. If not so, . . . righteousness could not be brought to pass, neither wickedness, neither holiness nor misery, neither good nor bad" (v. 11). This condition—the one that Lucifer advocated in the premortal council—would have left "all things [as] a compound in one," meaning that there would have been only one choice. There would have been "no life neither death, nor corruption nor incorruption, happiness nor misery, neither sense nor insensibility" (v. 11). The whole world would have been "created for a thing of naught" and there would have been "no purpose in the end of its creation." It would have "destroy[ed] the wisdom of God and his eternal purposes, and also the power, and the mercy, and the justice of God" (v. 12). Obviously, commandments are essential!

  "And if ye shall say there is no law, ye shall also say there is no sin. If ye shall say there is no sin, ye shall also say there is no righteousness. And if there be no righteousness there be no happiness. And if there be no righteousness nor happiness there be no punishment nor misery. And if these things are not there is no God. And if there is no God we are not, neither the earth; for there could have been no creation of things, neither to act nor to be acted upon; wherefore, all things must have vanished away" (v. 13). Thankfully, "there is a God, and he hath created all things, both the heavens and the earth, and all things that in them are, both things to act and things to be acted upon. And to bring about his eternal purposes . . . [He allowed there to be] an opposition" (vv. 14–15). Opposition creates choice, and choice creates agency. I thank God for the wisdom of His plan and for the commandments He has given us.

Elder Bruce R. McConkie said:

> All men—all living souls, whether they have knowledge of gospel law or not—shall be judged by the law of the gospel. Specifically, [Paul] says, those who sin, having not the law, shall perish, meaning they will be condemned for disobedience to [the] law. . . . They are damned through sin whether they had the gospel law or not. . . .
>
> To show the justice of such a course the Apostle, having previously named the sins of sexual perversion, murder, fornication, and wickedness of every sort, now says that the Gentiles who have not the law given them by revelation, nonetheless have the law written in their hearts so that their minds and consciences bear record that they should not violate the laws of God [verse 15]. This is another and quite an expressive way of saying that "the Spirit of Christ is given to every man, that he may know good from evil" (Moroni 7:16; D&C 84:46). Hence every man, in and out of the Church, whether he has the gospel law or not, is accountable for his deeds and will be judged by gospel standards.[3]

The Law of Justification

What does it mean to be justified? The Greek word means "to be declared righteous." It means to be *reconciled* to God, *pardoned* from punishment for sin, and *declared righteous* and guiltless. Alma explained why this is necessary:

— **Alma 7:21 Unless we are pardoned, we cannot live with God.** God does not "dwell in unholy temples; neither can filthiness or anything which is unclean be received into the kingdom of God." We must be made absolutely clean and sinless in order to return to His presence. And if we do not, "the time shall come, yea, and it shall be at the last day, that he who is filthy shall remain in his filthiness."

The Necessity of Grace

- **Romans 3:10–12, 23 No living soul is sinless.** Paul said it as plainly as it can be said: "There is none righteous, no, not one" (v. 10). We all sin. "There is none that understandeth, there is none that seeketh after God. They are all gone out of the way, they are together become unprofitable; there is none that doeth good, no, not one" (vv. 11–12). In short, "all have sinned, and come short of the glory of God" (v. 23).

- **Romans 3:20 Since we all violate the law, we cannot be justified by our obedience.** There would have been only one Being saved, and that would have been the absolutely perfect one: Jesus Christ. The rest of us would all fall short. "Therefore by the deeds of the law there shall no flesh be justified in his sight . . ."

- **Romans 3:24, 28 We receive justification through Christ's atoning grace.** How, then, can we ever be justified? We are all unworthy of God's presence. Paul provided the answer when he explained that we are "justified freely by his grace through the redemption that is in Christ Jesus" (v. 24). The JST renders this verse a little differently, but with the same essential meaning: An individual is justified only through the grace of Christ. "Therefore we conclude that a man is *justified by faith without the deeds of the* *law*" (v. 28, emphasis added). In other words, our personal righteousness is not sufficient to justify us before God. It falls far short of what is necessary, and we need the grace of Christ to make up the difference.

- **What Is Grace?** Grace is divine help. It allows us to tap into the "goodwill," "favor," or "spiritual generosity" of God in order to be justified (made perfect).

President Joseph Fielding Smith said:

"IN REMEMBRANCE," ©JOSEPH BRICKEY, USED BY PERMISSION

> There is a difference between the Lord Jesus Christ and the rest of mankind. We have no life in ourselves, for no power has been given unto us, to lay down our lives and take them again. That is beyond our power, and so, being subject to death, and being sinners—for we are all transgressors of the law to some extent, no matter how good we have tried to be—we are therefore unable in and of ourselves to receive redemption from our sins by any act of our own.
>
> This is the grace that Paul was teaching. Therefore, it is by the grace of Jesus Christ that we are saved. And had He not come into the world, and laid down His life that He might take it again, or as He said in another place, to give us life that we may have it more abundantly—we would still be subject to death and be in our sins . . .
>
> So it is easy to understand that we must accept the mission of Jesus Christ. We must believe that it is through His grace that we are saved, that He performed for us that labor which we were unable to perform for ourselves, and did for us those things which were essential to our salvation, which were beyond our power; and also that we are under the commandment and the necessity of performing the labors that are required of us as set forth in the commandments known as the gospel of Jesus Christ.[4]

- **Romans 5:1–2 Christ's grace gives us hope despite our weakness.** Knowing how imperfect we are, we might despair of ever receiving exaltation in our Father's kingdom. But because we can be justified (made perfect) by our faith in Christ, "we have peace with God through our Lord Jesus Christ" (v. 1). Through our faith, "we have access . . . [to] this grace [which allows us to] stand, and rejoice in hope of [receiving] the glory of God" (v. 2).

- **Romans 5:1–5 Faith and grace help us bear tribulation with hope.** Knowing that we can be "justified by faith, we have peace [reconciliation] with God through our Lord

Jesus Christ" (v. 1). And because "we have access by faith into this grace," we can "rejoice in [the] hope of [achieving] the glory of God" (v. 2). Furthermore, because of our faith we can "glory in tribulations also: knowing that tribulation worketh patience; And patience, experience; and experience, hope" (vv. 3–4). So, even in the midst of tribulation we can have hope "because the love of God is shed abroad in our hearts by the Holy Ghost which is given unto us" (v. 5).

— **Mosiah 2:20–21 Even our best efforts will not be enough to make us pure.** King Benjamin taught his people of the absolute necessity of the grace of Christ when he said, "I say unto you, my brethren, that if you should render all the thanks and praise which your whole soul has power to possess, to that God who has created you, and has kept and preserved you, and has caused that ye should rejoice, and has granted that ye should live in peace one with another—I say unto you that if ye should serve him who has created you from the beginning, and is preserving you from day to day, by lending you breath, that ye may live and move and do according to your own will, and even supporting you from one moment to another—I say, if ye should serve him with all your whole souls yet ye would be unprofitable servants."

— **Ether 12:26–27 God gave us weaknesses to keep us humble**, then provided a way for us to be forgiven through grace. We may feel inadequate and even mocked by those who think that our quest for perfection is pointless. To this, the Lord said, "Fools mock, but they shall mourn; and *my grace is sufficient for the meek*, that they shall take no advantage of your weakness" (v. 26, emphasis added). This is a beautiful promise, and one that I wish to emphasize: Christ's grace is sufficient to save us all, if we will have faith in Him and do our very best to keep His commandments.

THEBIBLEREVIVAL.COM, #22

There is a Godly purpose in weaknesses. The Lord explained it this way: "And if men come unto me I will show unto them their weakness. I give unto men weakness that they may be humble; and my grace is sufficient for all men that humble themselves before me; for if they humble themselves before me, and have faith in me, then will I make weak things become strong unto them" (v. 27).

— **2 Nephi 2:6–8 Christ's atonement pays the debt for our sins.** Understanding that (1) we must be justified (made perfect) in order to enter God's presence, and (2) that our behavior always falls short of perfection, we then can understand why "redemption cometh in and through the Holy Messiah; [who] is full of grace and truth" (v. 6). "Behold, he offereth himself a sacrifice for sin, to answer the ends of the law, unto all those who have a broken heart and a contrite spirit; and unto none else can the ends of the law be answered" (v. 7).

> "Wherefore, how great the importance to make these things known unto the inhabitants of the earth, that they may know that there is no flesh that can dwell in the presence of God, save it be through the merits, and mercy, and grace of the Holy Messiah, who layeth down his life according to the flesh, and taketh it again by the power of the Spirit, that he may bring to pass the resurrection of the dead, being the first that should rise" (v. 8).

The Importance of Works

We must understand that we do not "save ourselves" by ourselves. Though we might render our total thanks to God through valiant service all the days of our lives, we will still far short of what is needed. So let us never think that we can do it on our own. We need Christ's grace to achieve justification.

However, some Christian churches (so-called) have wrested the scriptures in order to claim that grace is *all* that is necessary. And that is not true. Christ has commanded us to demonstrate our faith in Him and our love for Him by keeping His commandments. That is where works comes into the equation of exaltation.

- **Romans 10:9–10 Is grace obtained merely by profession of faith?** Paul wrote in his epistle to the Romans, "If thou shalt confess with thy mouth the Lord Jesus, and shalt believe in thine heart that God hath raised him from the dead, thou shalt be saved" (v. 9). It is with our heart that we "believe . . . unto righteousness," and with our mouths that "confession is made unto salvation" (v. 10). These two verses of scripture are often quoted by those who believe that we are saved by the grace of God alone, and that we can do nothing to promote our own salvation.

  William Temple summarized this view when he wrote, "The only thing of my very own which I can contribute to my redemption is the sin from which I need to be redeemed."[5] In other words *my sins contribute to my salvation*. This is a gross misinterpretation of what Paul was saying in these verses. Paul was talking about Israel's rejection of the gospel. He pointed out that while the Jews were zealous for God (that is, eagerly trying to be obedient to His commandments), they had missed a vital point of the gospel by trying to rely on their own righteousness alone. And sadly, I've heard members of the Church suggest similar things.

  Paul quoted from the Old Testament to show that no man could accomplish what Christ did in coming down from heaven and overcoming death, no matter how hard he tried. To obtain salvation, Paul said we must confess the Lord openly with a heart that "believeth unto righteousness" (v. 10). The "heart" (*kardia*) in Greek meant a man's inner self. "Believing with the heart" was an idiom (figure of speech) in Paul's day that implied much more than intellectual assent. It implied an inner change as demonstrated by behavior. Confession with the mouth was not sufficient.

  Billy Graham, renowned evangelist, cautioned: "Too often we have tended toward superficiality—an overemphasis on easy-believism or experience rather than on true discipleship. We have sometimes offered cheap grace and cheap conversions without genuine repentance."[6]

Elder Bruce R. McConkie said:

> What price must men pay for this precious gift? Not conformity to Mosaic standards, not compliance with the ordinances and performances of a dead law, but the price of faith, faith in the Lord Jesus Christ, faith that includes within itself enduring works of righteousness, which faith cannot so much as exist unless and until men conform their lives to gospel standards.
>
> Does salvation come, then, by works? No, not by the works of the law of Moses, and for that matter, not even by the more perfect works of the gospel itself. Salvation comes through Christ's atonement, through the ransom He paid, the propitiation He made; without this no good works on the part of men could redeem them from temporal death, which redemption is resurrection, or redeem them from spiritual death, which redemption is eternal life.[7]

— **2 Nephi 25:23 We are saved by the grace of Christ, "after all we can do."** "For we labor diligently to write, to persuade our children, and also our brethren, to believe in Christ, and to be reconciled to God; for we know that it is by grace that we are saved, after all we can do."

- **Romans 3:31 Faith alone is not enough; works demonstrate our faith.** "Do we then make void the law through faith? God forbid: yea, we establish the law."

— **James 2:14–20 We demonstrate our faith by our works.** James asked, "What doth it profit, my brethren, [if] a man say[s] he hath faith, and [has] not works? Can faith save him?" (v. 14). Saying we have faith in the absence of works is as pointless as promising a hungry man food and then doing nothing to help him (vv. 15–16). "Even so faith, if it hath not works, is dead, being alone" (v. 17). "Shew me thy faith without thy works," James said, "and I will shew thee my faith *by my works*" (v. 18, emphasis added).

"I believe!" the rapturous convert may proclaim, but James was not impressed. "Thou doest well: the devils also believe, and tremble" (v. 19). Does it do Satan and his angels any good that they know that Jesus is the Christ? They know this, but it does not save them. "Know, O vain man," said James, "that faith without works is dead" (v. 20).

James, the brother of the Lord explained faith and works

The Prophet Joseph Smith said: "Any person who is exalted to the highest mansion has to abide a celestial law, and the whole law, too.... To get salvation we must not only do some things, but everything which God has commanded.... obey God in just what He tells us to do."[8]

The Prophet also said, "To be justified before God we must love one another: we must overcome evil; we must visit the fatherless and the widow in their affliction, and we must keep ourselves unspotted from the world: for such virtues flow from the great fountain of pure religion, strengthening our faith by adding every good quality that adorns the children of the blessed Jesus. We can pray in the season of prayer; we can love our neighbor as ourselves, and be faithful in tribulation, knowing that the reward of such is greater in the kingdom of heaven. What a consolation! What a joy!"[9]

- **Romans 5:12–21 The connection between Adam, Christ, and the Atonement.** "By one man sin entered into the world," said Paul, "and death [came because of] sin; . . Death passed upon all men, [because] all have sinned" (v. 12). Notice here that the opportunity to sin entered into the world because of Adam's fall, but our *personal* spiritual death occurs because of *our* sins, not Adam's. And for those that "sin" without knowing the commandments, "sin is not imputed" (v. 13). "Death reigned from Adam to Moses," said Paul, but not because men had sinned "after the similitude of Adam's transgression" (v. 14). There is no "original sin" by Adam under which we are cursed or damned. We bring punishment upon ourselves according to our own sins.

Adam and Eve sacrificed in similitude of the Savior's Atonement that would forgive sins

Paul then explained how the "free gift" of the atonement of Jesus Christ paid for the transgression of Adam and overcame death, which Adam had brought into the world. Just as with "the offence, so also is the free gift. For if through the offence of one [Adam] many be dead, [by] the grace of God, and the gift by grace, . . . by one man, Jesus Christ, hath abounded unto many" (v. 15). "For if by one man's offence death reigned . . . grace and of the gift of righteousness shall reign . . . by one, Jesus Christ" (v. 17). "Therefore as by the offence of one [Adam] judgment came upon all men to condemnation; even so by the righteousness of one [Jesus Christ] the free gift came upon all men unto justification" (v. 18). And if "by one man's disobedience many were made sinners, so by the obedience of one shall many be made righteous" (v. 19).

The next teaching of Paul is one of those difficult-to-understand phrases: "The law entered, that the offense might abound." Paul uses a metaphor of the theater here to explain the temporary role of the law of Moses. The Greek word that is translated "entered" here means literally "to come in by the side of." In classical Greek theater, actors who played a supporting role would come onto the stage from the wings, play their part, then disappear again. By using this word to describe the law of Moses, Paul was showing how the role that the law plays was intended to be temporary, not permanent.

The second part of this statement—"that the offence might abound"—suggests that when commandments ("the law") were given to men by God, sin ("offence") began to abound in the world because men would naturally fall short of perfection. But whereas "sin abounded, grace did much more abound" (v. 20). And whereas "sin [had] reigned unto death, even so . . . grace reign[s] through righteousness unto eternal life [because of the atonement of] Jesus Christ our Lord" (v. 21).

HEIRS OF GOD

We Are the Children of God

- **Romans 8:14–16 The nature of our relationship to God the Father.** Paul said that "as many as are led by the Spirit of God . . . are the sons of God" (v. 14). And as His children, we should not feel like we are in bondage to God or be afraid of Him. We should realize, through the Spirit, that we can address Him as "Abba, Father" (v. 15). The word Abba was a term of endearment in Paul's day, similar to calling our fathers "daddy" or "papa" today. "The Spirit itself beareth witness with our spirit, that we are the children of God," Paul declared.

    — **Galatians 3:26–29 As His children, we are all equal and must become "one."** "For ye are all the children of God by faith in Christ Jesus" (v. 26). "For as many of you as have been baptized into [the Church of] Christ have put on [the name of] Christ" (v. 27). And after this is done, in the eyes of God, "There is neither Jew nor Greek, there is neither bond nor free, there is neither male nor female: for ye are all one in Christ Jesus" (v. 28).

Elder Dallin H. Oaks said, "Consider the power of the idea taught in our beloved song 'I Am a Child of God' (*Hymns,* 1985, no. 301). . . . Here is the answer to one of life's great questions, 'Who am I?' I am a child of God with a spirit lineage to heavenly parents. That parentage defines our eternal potential. That powerful idea is a potent antidepressant. It can strengthen each of us to make righteous choices and to seek the best that is within us. Establish in the mind of a young person the powerful idea that he or she is a child of God, and you have given self-respect and motivation to move against the problems of life."[10]

If Children, Then We Are His Heirs

- **Galatians 4:1–7 As God's children, we are heirs.** Paul taught that "the heir, as long as he is a child, differeth nothing from a servant, though he be [a] lord of all" in waiting (v. 1). He is "under tutors and governors until the time appointed of the father" when he will begin to reign (v. 2). "Even so we, [as His] children, [are] in bondage under the elements of the world: But when the fulness of the time was come, God sent forth his Son . . . to redeem [us] . . . that we might receive the [blessings, rights, and privileges of] sons" (vv. 3–5). "And because ye are sons, God hath sent forth the Spirit of his Son into your hearts, crying, Abba, Father. Wherefore thou art no more a servant, but a son; and if a son, then an heir of God through Christ" (vv. 6–7).

Hear it, all ye modern Pharisees who mock our teachings concerning the destiny of man! The early Pharisees sought the death of Jesus Christ primarily for this one reason: He claimed to be the Son of God. "Thou makes thyself god," they said in derision. And then they killed Him. Is it any different today when so-called Christians call us "god-makers" and insist that we are not Christian? I think not. Modern Pharisees are as blind and bigoted as were their predecessors.

On one occasion, when I was serving on the High Council of a stake in Sandy, Utah, I was assigned to speak in a particular ward. When the sacrament meeting was over, I stayed for awhile to get a feeling for how the ward members were doing. Standing in the hallway, I observed a primary class coming out of their room with their teacher. All of the boys and girls had a crown upon heir heads. One particular little boy caught my eye. He could not have been much more than 5 years old, but his mother had him dressed up in a suit and tie like a little missionary. He walked past me with his head held high and a look of satisfaction on his face. I saw that on the front of his crown was written the phrase, "I am a child of God," and on the back of the crown was written, "Future king."

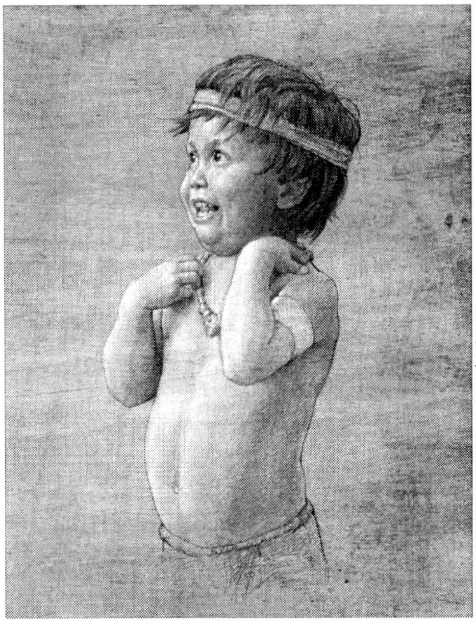

"MAYAN BOY," ©JOSEPH BRICKEY, USED BY PERMISSION

We are the children of a loving Father in Heaven

I leaned against the wall and silently wept. "He's only 5 years old, and he already knows it," I thought. He knows who he is and what he is destined to become. How many children in the world know this? Not many. And how blessed are those that have been taught these things from their youth. I am one of those. I've had the gospel in my life since birth, and my wonderful parents taught me who I am. Later, in my patriarchal blessing, the Lord said to me, "Thou are obligated to act upon the favorable circumstances of thy birth." This constantly reminds me of what a gift it is to know this principle almost from birth. And I am obligated to reach out to those who do not know who they are and help them find their way back to their Father in Heaven.

Joint-Heirs with Christ

- **Romans 8:17–18 If we are God's children, we are joint-heirs with Christ.** Paul taught very clearly that "if children, then [we are] heirs; heirs of God, and joint-heirs with Christ" (v. 17). But this is not automatic. To achieve this, "we suffer with him, that we may be also glorified together" (v. 17). We have no idea how glorious that future inheritance will be. "For I reckon that the sufferings of this present time are not worthy to be compared with the glory which shall be revealed in us," said Paul (v. 18).

Elder Bruce R. McConkie said:

> A joint-heir is one who inherits equally with all other heirs including the Chief Heir who is the Son. Each joint-heir has an equal and an undivided portion of the whole of everything. If one knows all things, so do all others. If one has all power, so do all those who inherit jointly with him. If the universe belongs to one, so it does equally to the total of all upon whom the joint inheritances are bestowed.
>
> Joint-heirs are possessors of all things (D&C 50:26–28). All things are theirs for they have exaltation (D&C 76:50–60). They are made "equal" with their Lord (D&C 88:107). They gain all power both in heaven and on earth and receive the fulness of the Father, and all knowledge and truth are theirs (D&C 93:15–30). They are gods (D&C 132:20). Celestial marriage is the gate to this high state of exaltation (*Doctrines of Salvation,* 2:24, 35–39; D&C 131:1–4; 132)."[11]

Elder Delbert L. Stapley said: "In the important doctrinal discourse known as the 'King Follett Sermon' the Prophet Joseph Smith, referring to those who 'shall be heirs of God and joint-heirs with Jesus Christ,' described joint-heirship as inheriting the same power, the same glory, and the same exaltation, until an individual ascends to the station of Godhood and rises to the throne of eternal power sharing the rewards with all the faithful who have preceded him. A joint-heir legally inherits and shares all equities and gifts in equal interest with all other heirs. Nothing is excluded nor adjusted in value between the participating joint-heirs."[12]

Heirs of What?

- **John 16:15 Christ is an heir to all things that the Father has.** "All things that the Father hath are mine," said Christ, who also said, "He [God the Father] shall take of mine, and shall shew it unto you." What will these things include? We learn most of what we know about that from the Doctrine and Covenants.

  — **D&C 84:33–39 The oath and covenant of the Melchizedek priesthood** (v. 39). As with all covenants, this is a two-way promise. Priesthood holders promise some things, and God promises blessings in return.

  A man shows his faithfulness by doing two things:

PHOTO COURTESY OF NASA

- "Obtaining these two priesthoods of which I have spoken" (v. 33).
- "Magnifying their calling" (v. 34).

The Lord promises blessings in return:

○ "Sanctified by the Spirit" (v. 33).	Forgiven of sins
○ Receive a "renewing of their bodies" (v. 33).	Increased health
○ "Become the sons of Moses and of Aaron" (v. 34).	Priests of these orders
○ "Become . . . the seed of Abraham (v. 34).	Temple blessings
○ "Become . . . the church and kingdom" (v. 34).	Ministers of God's Kingdom
○ "They become . . . the elect of God" (v. 34).	Candidates for exaltation
○ [They] "receive me, saith the Lord" (v. 35)	Witnesses of Christ

Blessings promised to those who receive God's authorized priesthood servants.

- "He that receiveth my servants receiveth me" (v. 36).
- "And he that receiveth me receiveth my Father" (v. 37).
- "And he that receiveth my Father receiveth my Father's kingdom" (v. 38).
- "All that my Father hath shall be given unto him" (v. 38, emphasis added).

— **D&C 88:107 We will be made equal with Christ.** At the final judgment, "the angels [will] be crowned with the glory of his might, and the saints shall be filled with his glory, and receive their inheritance and be made equal with him."

— **D&C 93:19–23 We will receive the glory of the Father.** It is important to "know how to worship, and know what you worship" (v. 19). Only then can we "come unto the Father in [Jesus Christ's] name, and in due time receive of his [the Father's] fulness" (v. 19). "For if you keep my commandments you shall receive of his fulness, and be glorified in me [Jesus Christ] as I am in the Father" (v. 20). But this will not be accomplished all at once or suddenly. "I say unto you, you shall receive grace for grace" (v. 20).

"And now, verily I say unto you, I was in the beginning with the Father, and am the Firstborn" (v. 21). "Ye were also in the beginning with the Father" as is witnessed by the "Spirit, even the Spirit of truth" (v. 23). "And all those who are begotten through me are partakers of the glory of the [Father], and are the church of the Firstborn [those who receive exaltation]" (v. 22).

— **D&C 93:27–28 We will know all things.** "No man receiveth a fulness unless he keepeth his commandments" (v. 27). But "he that keepeth his commandments receiveth truth and light, until he is glorified in truth and knoweth all things" (v. 28).

— **D&C 76:50–53 Who will receive the celestial kingdom?** Joseph Smith and Sidney Rigdon saw a vision of the celestial kingdom in 1832 at Hiram, Ohio, and described those who will receive "the resurrection of the just" (v. 50). This means those who will inherit the celestial kingdom and be exalted in God's presence.

- Those who "received the testimony of Jesus, and believed on his name" (v. 51).
- Those who "were baptized after the manner of his burial" (v. 51).
- Those who kept the Lord's commandments (v. 52).
- Those who "receive the Holy Spirit by the laying on of the hands" (v. 52).

- Those who "overcome [the world] by faith" (v. 53).
- Those who "are sealed by the Holy Spirit of promise" (v. 53).

— **D&C 76:54–59 What do celestial beings inherit?** Here the Lord lists the blessings that are received by those who are exalted in God's presence.

- "They are the church of the Firstborn" (v. 54).
- "They into whose hands the Father has given all things" (v. 55).
- "They are priests and kings" (v. 56).
- "They have received of his [God's] fulness, and of his glory" (v. 56).
- "They are priests of the Most High, after the order of Melchizedek" (v. 57).
- "They are gods, even the sons of God" (v. 58).
- "All things are theirs" (v. 59).
- "They are [belong to] Christ's (v. 59).
- "And Christ is God's" (v. 59).

— **D&C 132:20 We will be gods, with all things subject unto us.** After becoming exalted, we shall . . .

- Be gods, because [we will] have no end.
- Be from everlasting to everlasting, because we will continue.
- Be above all, because all things are subject unto us.
- Be gods, because we will have all power.
- And the angels will be subject unto us.

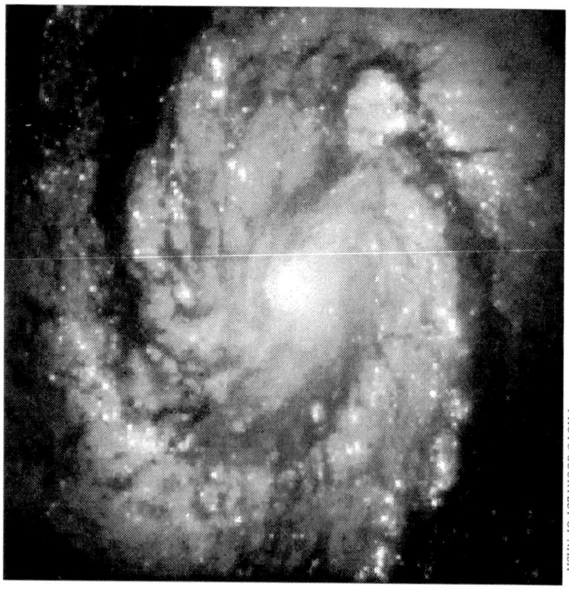

PHOTO COURTESY OF NASA

- **Romans 8:19–23 All creation anticipates a future day of redemption and glory.** Paul said that even the "creature [material universe] waiteth for the manifestation [revelation] of the sons of God" (v. 19). Though material objects like rocks, rivers, planets, and stars are "made subject" to God's will and have no agency, they also will be "delivered from the bondage of corruption into the glorious liberty of the children of God" who will inherit them (vv. 20–21). In the meantime, "the whole creation groaneth and travaileth in pain together" under the weight of fallen man's sins (v. 22). And we also, "which have the firstfruits of the Spirit, even we ourselves groan within ourselves, waiting for the . . . redemption of our body" (v. 23).

- **Romans 8:31, 35–39 Nothing can separate us from the love of Jesus Christ.** Paul asked the simple but profound question, "If God be for us, who can be against us?" (v.

31). "Who [or what] shall separate us from the love of Christ? shall tribulation, or distress, or persecution, or famine, or nakedness, or peril, or sword?" (v. 35). Though we may think that, for the cause of Christ, "we are killed all the day long; we are accounted as sheep for the slaughter," the truth is that "we are more than conquerors through him that loved us" (vv. 36–37). He will bring us through triumphant and guide us back to the presence of God. And He will do this because He loves us. "I am persuaded," said Paul, "that neither death, nor life, nor angels, nor principalities, nor powers, nor things present, nor things to come, nor height, nor depth, nor any other creature, shall be able to separate us from the love of God, which is in Christ Jesus our Lord" (vv. 38–39).

ELECTED BEFORE THE FOUNDATIONS OF THE WORLD

Foreordination, Not Predestination

- **Romans 8:28 All things will work together for our good.** "We know that all things work together for good to them that love God, to them who are the called according to his purpose," said Paul (v. 28). This is similar to the Lord's promise in our own dispensation: "Search diligently, pray always, and be believing, and all things shall work together for your good, if ye walk uprightly and remember the covenant wherewith ye have covenanted one with another" (D&C 90:24).

- **Romans 8:29–30 Knowing our intended destiny helps us to bear tribulation.** "For whom [God] did foreknow, he also did predestinate to be conformed to the image of his Son" (v. 29). The word "predestinate" appears four times in the Bible, but the word predestination is never used. The word that Paul used here (which was translated "predestinate" by the English translators) does not imply a loss of agency. The word means "to determine [our *potential* destiny] beforehand." The word "foreordain" is a better translation of the original Greek. "Moreover whom he did predestinate, them he also called: and whom he called, them he also justified: and whom he justified, them he also glorified" (v. 30).

"THE HUNDRED GREATEST MEN," 1885

John Calvin

John Calvin, the reformer, misunderstood the doctrine when he wrote: "By predestination we mean the eternal decree of God, by which He determined with Himself whatever He wished to happen with regard to every man. All are not created on equal terms, but some are pre-ordained to eternal life, others to eternal damnation. And accordingly, as each has been created for one or other of these ends, we say that he has been predestined to life or to death."[13]

President Joseph Fielding Smith said, "Is it not horrible to contemplate that gospel truth has been perverted and defiled until it has become such an abomination? Justice, as well as mercy, pleads for the dead who have died without a knowledge of the gospel. How could justice be administered if all the untold multitudes who have died without a knowledge of Jesus Christ should be everlastingly consigned, without hope, to the damnation of hell? . . . The scriptures say, 'Justice and judgment are the habitation of thy throne: mercy and truth shall go before thy face' (Psalm 89:14). The mercy and love of a just God are reaching out after all His children."[14]

President Smith also said:

> Just what Paul might have had in mind may not be too clearly expressed in the translation that has come to us. That he taught that some men are destined to be damned must be rejected; likewise that some were predestined to be saved without a trial of their faith. Those who rejected the truth and rebelled were cast out with Lucifer because of the great gift of free agency.
>
> We have reason to believe that all who were privileged to come to this mortal world came because they were entitled by pre-mortal qualifications. It is absurd to think that Paul would teach that in the beginning before the earth was formed, some souls were destined to come to earth, receive tabernacles and then be consigned to perdition and some to be saved. Such a doctrine is contrary to all that has been revealed.[15]

The Doctrine of Election

It is clear from these scriptures that we were *chosen* in the pre-mortal existence to perform a mission or missions upon this earth. Whether or not we do what we were assigned to do is up to us. We can fail in our mission, and some have done so. So, while God knows our needs and talents and has foreordained us in our life's work, we should never take this to mean that everything that happens to us was "supposed to happen." We may, at times, brings difficulties upon ourselves that God would not have wished upon us.

The Prophet Joseph Smith said: "The whole of [Romans 9] had reference to the priesthood and the house of Israel; and unconditional election of individuals to eternal life was not taught by the Apostles. God did elect or predestinate, that all those who would be saved, should be saved in Christ Jesus, and through obedience to the Gospel; but He passes over no man's sins, but visits them with correction, and if His children will not repent of their sins He will discard them."[16]

Elder Bruce R. McConkie said, "The house of Israel was a distinct people in pre-existence."[17] He also said, "This election to a chosen lineage is based on pre-existent worthiness and is thus made 'according to the foreknowledge of God.'"[18]

To be "elected" then means to be "chosen" for some mission or purpose. And with that comes obligations and accountability. It is not a badge of honor. It is an assignment.

THE JEWS' LOST OPPORTUNITY

THEBIBLEREVIVAL.COM, 30

- **Romans 9:1–5 Paul loves the Jews, but sorrows over their rejection of Christ.** The Jews "are Israelites; to whom pertaineth the adoption, and the glory, and the covenants, and the giving of the law, and the service of God, and the promises," so they are a special and chosen people (v. 4). They are also the kinsmen of Christ, who is our King (v. 5). But Paul bears solemn witness that he had "great heaviness and continual sorrow in [his] heart" for "my kinsmen according to the flesh" [the Jews] (vv. 2–3), because of their rejection of Christ.

- **Romans 9:6–8 The Gentiles who accept the gospel become children of Israel.** "They are not all [of] Israel, which are of Israel" (v. 6)—that is, not every covenant-making member of the Church was born an Israelite. Neither does being the literal descendant of Abraham make one chosen (v. 7). "That is, They which are the children of the flesh, these are not the children of God: but the children of the promise (those who have made and kept their covenants with God) are counted [as His] seed" (v. 8).

- **Romans 9:9–14 Jacob was chosen over Esau before they were even born.** Paul reminded the Saints that God had promised Abraham and Sarah a son (v. 9). And Rebecca also bore twins as the wife of Isaac (v. 10). These children, "being not yet born, [had not] done any good or evil" when God called them (in the premortal world) to accomplish His purposes (v. 11). And before they were even born, God said to Rebecca, "The elder shall serve the younger" (v. 12).

  This was not the culturally-correct state of affairs, but God had already determined that "Jacob have I loved, but Esau have I hated" (v. 13). The Greek word that was translated "hated" here is a verb that also means "displeased with" or "rejected." The Lord did not hate Esau. Rather, the Lord's preferential regard for one over the other is based on their righteousness in the premortal life.[19] And if God makes such a judgment, "shall we say then [that] there [is] unrighteousness with God? God forbid" (v. 14).

- **Romans 10:12–13 God does not prefer one nation over another.** Nephi said, "All are alike unto God, both Jew and Gentile" (2 Nephi 26:33). Paul also said, "there is no difference between the Jew and the Greek: for the same Lord over all is rich unto all that call upon him" (v. 12), which means that God will "richly bless all that call upon Him." "For whosoever shall call upon the name of the Lord shall be saved" (v. 13).

- **Romans 9:15–21 God's omnipotence and sovereignty in dealing with man.** God said to Moses, "I will have mercy on whom I will have mercy, and I will have compassion on whom I will have compassion" (v. 15). The matter is not decided by "him that willeth" (whoever wants it), . . . but [by] God that sheweth mercy" (v. 16). For example, God said to Pharaoh, "Even for this same purpose have I raised thee up, that I might shew my power in thee, and that my name might be declared throughout all the earth" (v. 17). It was not Pharaoh's will but God's will that was being done. Likewise, in the matter of mercy, God decides on whom He will have mercy and on whom He will not (v. 18).

  THEBIBLEREVIVAL.COM, #20

  A person might find fault with God for this, but Paul asked, "O man, who art thou that repliest against God?" (vv. 19–20). Paul then used the analogy of a potter and his clay to ask, "Shall the thing formed say to him that formed it, Why hast thou made me thus? Hath not the potter power over the clay, of the same lump to make one vessel unto honour, and another unto dishonour?" (vv. 20–21).

- **Romans 9:23–24 Our lineage does not determine our salvation.** God "make[s] known the riches of his glory on the vessels [children] of mercy, which he had afore prepared unto glory" (v. 23). And who are these whom He chose to receive glory? "Even us," Paul answered, "whom he hath called, not of the Jews only, but also of the Gentiles" (v. 24). In other words, all of God's children were intended to be saved.

- **Romans 9:25–28 Many non-Israelites will become "children of God."** Paul quoted the Old Testament prophet Hosea ("Osee") to whom the Lord said, "I will call them my people, which were not my people; and her beloved, which was not beloved. And it shall come to pass, that in the place where it was said unto them, Ye are not my people; there shall they be called the children of the living God" (vv. 25–26; Hosea 2:23; Zech. 13:9). Paul also quoted Isaiah concerning Israel, "Though the number of the children of Israel be as the sand of the sea, [only] a remnant shall be saved: For he will finish the work, and cut it short in righteousness" (vv. 27–28; Isaiah 10:22)

- **Romans 9:32–33 The stumbling stone for the Jews is Jesus Christ.** And why? "Because they sought it [salvation] not by faith, but . . . by the works of the law [and] they stumbled at that stumblingstone" (v. 32). They really did believe that they would be saved because of their lineage and because of their strict obedience to the law of Moses. And because of this, they saw Christ as an obstacle and not as their Messiah. "As it is written, Behold, I lay in Sion a stumblingstone and rock of offence [but] whosoever believeth on him shall not be ashamed" (v. 33).

- **Romans 10:1–3 Their righteousness was Judaism; the righteousness of God was the gospel.** Paul did not wish for the Jews' destruction. He, himself, was a Jew, as was Christ. In fact, he said, "my heart's desire and prayer to God for Israel is, that they might be saved" (v. 1). "For I bear them record that they have a zeal of God, but not according to knowledge" (v. 2). "For they being ignorant of God's righteousness, and going about to establish their own righteousness, have not submitted themselves unto the righteousness of God" (v. 3). And who would know this better than Paul? He himself had gone around persecuting the Church with great zeal until God intervened in his life.

- **Romans 10:18–21 Why did Israel reject their God?** Paul asks and answers several questions about this problem. "Have they not heard? Yes verily, their sound [the disciples and missionaries] went into all the earth, and their words unto the ends of the world" (v. 18). "Did not Israel know?" They should have, because to Moses the Lord said, "I will provoke you to jealousy by them that are no people, and by a foolish nation I will anger you" (v. 19). To Isaiah the Lord declared, "I was found of them that sought me not; I was made manifest unto them that asked not after me" (v. 20). And "to Israel he saith, All day long I have stretched forth my hands unto a disobedient and gainsaying people" (v. 21). It had been prophesied for centuries and was contained in their scriptures that Israel would reject God and He would turn to the world with His message and His covenants.

- **Romans 11:1–9 Israel rejected God, not the other way around.** "Hath God cast away his people?" Paul asked, then answered, "God forbid. For I also am an Israelite, of the seed of Abraham, of the tribe of Benjamin" (v. 1). "God hath not cast away his people which he foreknew" (v. 2). Paul recalled ("wot ye not," meaning "know ye not") that Isaiah had made "intercession to God against Israel, saying, Lord, they have killed thy prophets, and digged down thine altars; and I am left alone, and they seek my life" (v. 3). And what was God's answer? "I have reserved to myself seven thousand men, who have not bowed the knee to the image of Baal. Even so then at this present time also there is a remnant according to the election of grace" (vv. 4–5). God knows the righteous among the wicked, and He will save them.

  Were these 7,000 righteous persons saved only by grace? If so, said Paul, "then [it is not by] works: otherwise grace is no more grace." On the other hand, "if it be [by] works, then [it is not by] grace: otherwise work is no more work" (v. 6). And the final answer is that it is by both faith and works that "the elect . . . hath obtained it, and the rest were blinded" (v. 7). "God hath given them the spirit of slumber, eyes that they should not see, and ears that they should not hear; unto this day" (v. 8). King David forsaw this when he wrote, "Let their table be made a snare, and a trap, and a stumblingblock, and a recompence unto them" (v. 9).

- **Romans 11:13–14 How Paul magnifies his priesthood.** Paul refers to himself as "the apostle of the Gentiles," and focuses on them, hoping that his own people (Jews) will also listen. In so doing, he "magnifies" his priesthood calling (v. 13). And he hopes that by some means he might "provoke to emulation them which are my flesh [the Jews], and [that he] might save some of them" (v. 14).

- **Romans 11:11, 15 First the Jews, then the Gentiles, then again the Jews.** Did God allow the Jews to stumble so that they would fall and He could destroy them? "God forbid: but rather through their fall salvation is come unto the Gentiles," whom God will use "to provoke them [the Jews] to jealousy" (v. 11). And if the "casting away" of the Jews for a time leads to the "reconciling of the world" [to God], then the "receiving of them" [the Jews] at a later time will be like "life from the dead" (v. 15). They will rise up and worship their God.

- **Romans 11:16–25 The Olive tree allegory.** Members of the Church are familiar with the Olive tree allegory taught by the prophet Zenos in Old Testament times. It is recorded in the book of Jacob in the Book of Mormon (Jacob 5). Paul here makes reference to the same allegory, which may have been an ancient and well-known one in those days. Both Paul and Jacob used it to show how the day of the Gentiles and the day of the Jews will work together to bring about God's purposes.

OLIVE TREES IN GETHSEMANE, DAVID HALL, COLLECTION II, 2002

"If the firstfruit be holy, the lump is also holy" (v. 16). "And if the root be holy, so are the branches" (v. 16). This was the situation of the early Church. It was holy and healthy.

Now, "if some of the branches [of the healthy tree] be broken off," and "graffed in among them [wild olive trees]," the wild olives trees will "partake . . . of the root and fatness of the [original] olive tree" (v. 17). This was the situation as the gospel was grafted into the Gentiles during the last part of the first century after Christ.

To the Gentiles Paul warned, "Boast not against the branches" [that were grafted into you]; remember that "thou bearest not the root, but the root thee" (v. 18). If you think that "the branches were broken off, that I might be graffed in" [in other words, "I am more important than they in God's eyes"], and that you have more faith than they did, "be not highminded, but fear" (vv. 19–20). "For if God spared not the natural branches [the Jews], take heed lest he also spare not thee [the Gentiles]" (v. 21). God is good, but

He is also severe. "On them which fell, severity; but toward thee, goodness, if thou continue in his goodness: otherwise thou also shalt be cut off" (v. 22).

In the future, "if they abide not still in unbelief," the Jews themselves shall receive grafts of righteousness, "for God is able to graff them in again" (v. 23). If God were to do this with grafts from "the olive tree which is wild by nature [the Gentiles], and wert graffed contrary to nature into a good olive tree" it would not work (v. 24). "How much more shall these, which be the natural branches, be graffed into their own olive tree?" (v. 24). In other words, the Gentiles will not heal and save the Jews, but other children of Israel will do so in the latter days. "Blindness in part is happened to Israel, [only] until the fulness of the Gentiles be come in" [accomplished] (v. 25).

Paraphrasing Elder Bruce R. McConkie: "'Until the fullness of the Gentiles be come in,' means that since Paul's day, the gospel has been and will continue to be taught to the Gentiles on a preferential basis until they have had a full opportunity to accept it. That is 'the fullness of the Gentiles.' Then, the message will go again to the Jews."[20]

This analogy uses "grafted branches" as a metaphor for adoption into the house of Israel. "Graffed in," or "grafted in," is an agricultural way of saying "adopted in." Paul uses an analogy from agriculture to make the doctrine clearer. The natural olive tree is Israel; the wild branches are the Gentiles. The natural order of things is that the grafted branches control the destiny of the tree. Thus, a good branch from the natural tree can be grafted into a wild tree and make it good.

The conversion of the Gentiles was contrary to the expected order of things from Israel's viewpoint. They believed that the convert Gentiles did not change the nature and destiny of the house of Israel, but that the Gentiles had simply become part of Israel. This would not work with grafts, because the wild olive branches would make the natural tree worse. Paul makes this point to teach the Gentiles the power, importance, and meaning of the house of Israel in God's view. Even though the gospel was then being taken to the Gentiles on a preferential basis, Israel was still the chosen family and the guardian of the Abrahamic covenant. Eventually, the children of Israel will rise again as their scattered children receive the gospel and rejuvenate the mother tree once again.

OTHER DOCTRINES TAUGHT IN ROMANS

- **Romans 6:1–2 Does sin matter?** Paul asks the logical question, "Shall we continue in sin, that grace may abound?" In other words, doesn't sin just provide a greater opportunity for the grace of Christ to be made manifest among us? Some so-called "Christian" sects actually teach that Paul was giving implicit approval to commit sin because Christ's "free" gift would take care of everything anyway. "God forbid," said Paul. "How shall we, that are dead to sin, live any longer therein?"

- **Romans 6:3–6 The symbolism of baptism.** Paul compares baptism to death, burial, and resurrection. "Know ye not, that [as] many of us as were baptized into Jesus Christ were baptized [in symbolism of] his death?" (v. 3). "We are buried [like] him by baptism," which symbolizes death and laying down in the grave. Then, "like as Christ was raised up from the dead by the glory of the Father, even so we also [rise up and] walk in newness of life" (v. 4). "For if we have been planted [immersed] in the likeness of his death, we shall be also [come up out of the water] in the likeness of his resurrection" (v. 5). In this way, "our old man is crucified with him, that the body of sin might be destroyed, that henceforth we should not serve sin" (v. 6).

Baptismal font at Ephesus

President Joseph Fielding Smith said:

> Baptism cannot be by any other means than immersion of the entire body in water, for the following reasons:
>
> 1. It is in the similitude of the death, burial, and resurrection of Jesus Christ, and of all others who have received the resurrection.
> 2. Baptism is also a birth and is performed in the similitude of the birth of a child into this world.
> 3. Baptism is not only a figure of the resurrection, but also is literally a transplanting or resurrection from one life to another.[21]

- **Romans 6:11–13 We should become dead to sin but alive to righteousness.** After baptism we should "reckon [consider] ye also yourselves to be dead indeed unto sin, but alive unto God through Jesus Christ our Lord" (v. 11). "Let not sin therefore reign in your mortal body, that ye should obey it in the lusts thereof" (v. 12). "Neither yield ye your members [parts of your body] as instruments of unrighteousness unto sin: but yield yourselves unto God, as those that are alive from the dead, and your members as instruments of righteousness unto God" (v. 13).

- **Romans 6:14–18 Righteousness, not sin, should be our master after baptism.** Whom or what should we become subject to after baptism? Paul said, "sin [should] not have dominion over you: for ye are not under the law, but under grace" (v. 14). "Know ye not, that to whom ye yield yourselves servants to obey, his servants ye are to whom ye obey; whether of sin unto death, or of obedience unto righteousness?" (v. 16). Paul thanked God that although "ye were the servants of sin, . . . ye have obeyed from the heart that form of doctrine which was delivered [unto] you" and "being then made free from sin, ye became the servants of righteousness" (vv. 17–18).

- **Romans 6:20–23 Eternal life vs. death.** Before our conversion, "when ye were the servants of sin," we were "free from righteousness" (v. 20). But what were the fruits of that freedom, because "the end [result] of those things is death" (v. 21). "But now being made free from sin, and becom[ing] servants to God, . . . your fruit [is] holiness, and the end [is] everlasting life" (v. 22). "For the wages of sin is death; but the gift of God is eternal life through Jesus Christ our Lord" (v. 23).

  — **D&C 6:13 The gift of God is eternal life**, "which is the greatest of all the gifts of God; for there is no gift greater than the gift of salvation."

- **Romans 8:5–10 The natural man vs. the man of the Spirit.** Those who are "after the flesh do mind [pay attention to] the things of the flesh; but they that are after the Spirit the things of the Spirit" (v. 5). And "to be carnally minded is death; but to be spiritually minded is life and peace" (v. 6). "The carnal mind is [at] enmity against God: for it is not subject to the law of God, neither indeed can be. So then they that are in the flesh cannot please God" (vv. 7–8).

  "But ye are not in the flesh, but in the Spirit, if [it] so be that the Spirit of God dwell in you" (v. 9). If we do not have the Spirit of Christ, we are not His, but "if Christ be in you, the body is dead because of sin; but the Spirit is life because of righteousness" (vv. 9–10). We become a "new creature" in Christ (1 Cor. 2:10–16).

A transvestite man posing with pride

- **Romans 7:1–6 The law of Moses vs. the Spirit.** Speaking to the Jews, Paul said, "Know ye not, brethren, . . . that the law hath dominion over a man as long as he liveth?" (v. 1). Like a woman, who under the law is "bound by the law to her husband so long as he liveth; but if the husband be dead, she is loosed from the law of her husband" (v. 2). In the same manner, the law of Moses was now "dead," and therefore the Jews were free to "be married to another, even to him who is raised from the dead, that we should bring forth fruit unto God" (vv. 3–4). Even before the earthly ministry of Christ, Nephi said, "The law hath become dead unto us, and we are made alive in Christ because of our faith" (2 Nephi 25:25). Paul wanted the Jews to know that they were now "delivered from the law [under which] we were held; that we should serve in newness of spirit, and not in the oldness of the letter" (vv. 5–6).

- **Romans 8:1–3 The law of Moses cannot save anyone.** The law is still important as a set of moral, ethical, and cultural guidelines. But there is no condemnation for moving to the higher law of the Gospel, "walk[ing] not after the flesh, but after the Spirit" (v. 1). "The law of the Spirit of life in Christ Jesus hath made me free from the law of sin and death," said Paul, and "what the law could not do, . . . [was accomplished by] God sending his own Son" in the flesh as a sacrifice for sin (vv. 2–3).

- **Romans 10:14–17 Faith comes by hearing the word of God** preached, and this requires an authorized messenger. Paul pointed out that people cannot worship a God in whom they have not believed. And they cannot believe in God unless they have heard of Him. And they cannot hear of Him unless someone preaches to them concerning Him (v. 14). And any such messenger must be "sent" by proper authority (v. 15). But when all these things are properly done, "then faith cometh by hearing . . . the word of God" (v. 17).

  The Prophet Joseph Smith said, "Faith comes by hearing the word of God, through the testimony of the servants of God; that testimony is always attended by the Spirit of prophecy and revelation."[22]

  Elder John Taylor said, "When truth shall touch the cords of your heart they will vibrate; then intelligence shall illuminate your mind, and shed [its] lustre in your soul, and you shall begin to understand the things you once knew, but which had gone from you; you shall then begin to understand and know the object of your creation."[23]

The "Sermon on the Mount of the Epistles."[24]

Romans 12–15 has become known as the "Sermon on the Mount" of the epistles. More than 50 commandments are listed in this discourse, and we cannot consider them all in our limited space and time for this chapter. But a number of them should be mentioned.

- **Romans 12:1 Being a "living sacrifice."** Paul exhorted the Roman Saints to present themselves as "a living sacrifice, holy, acceptable unto God" through their "reasonable service" (see also 3 Nephi 9:20; D&C 59:8).

- **Romans 12:2 Avoiding worldliness.** Paul counseled the Roman Saints to "be not conformed to this world" but rather "transformed by the renewing of your mind, that ye may prove [discover] that good, and acceptable, and perfect, will of God."

- **Romans 12:3 Humility.** A man is "not to think of himself more highly than he ought to think," but instead should "think soberly [seriously]" and with faith about what great things "God hath dealt [given] to every man" (see also Galatians 6:3; D&C 136:19).

- **Romans 12:9 Sincere love.** Love without "dissimulation" is love without hypocrisy; it is "love unfeigned" (D&C 121:41).

- **Romans 12:9 Abhor evil.** We are to "abhor that which is evil; cleave to that which is good."
- **Romans 12:12 Patience in tribulation.** This is a principle the Lord often taught through the Prophet Joseph Smith (D&C 31:9; 54:10; 58:2). Paul advised the Saints, when they are in tribulation, to be "rejoicing in hope; patient in tribulation; continuing instant in prayer."
- **Romans 12:16, 18 Friendliness to all men.** Paul advised that we not be full of pride and haughtiness but associate with all types of people. "Be of the same mind one toward another. Mind not high things, but condescend to men of low estate. Be not wise in your own conceits" (v. 16). "If it be possible, as much as lieth in you, live peaceably with all men" (v. 18).

- **Romans 12:17 Be honest in your dealings with others.** "Provide things honest in the sight of all men."
- **Romans 12:17, 19 Do not seek revenge but forgive.** Jesus, being reviled, "reviled not again" (1 Peter 2:23), and Paul said, "Recompense to no man evil for evil" (v. 17). He also said, "avenge not yourselves, but rather give place unto [stifle your] wrath: for it is written, Vengeance is mine; I will repay, saith the Lord" (v. 19).
- **Romans 12:20–21 Overcome evil with good.** The Lord said, "Love your enemies, bless them that curse you, do good to them that hate you, and pray for them which despitefully use you, and persecute you" (Matthew 5:44). Paul echoed that advice by saying, "If thine enemy hunger, feed him; if he thirst, give him drink: for in so doing thou shalt heap coals of fire on his head" (v. 20). "Be not overcome of evil, but overcome evil with good" (v. 21).
- **Romans 13:9–10 Having love fulfills the entire law of Moses.** Every other sin—"Thou shalt not commit adultery, Thou shalt not kill, Thou shalt not steal, Thou shalt not bear false witness, Thou shalt not covet; and if there be any other commandment"—is understood fully only in this one: "Thou shalt love thy neighbour as thyself" (v. 9). "Love worketh no ill to his neighbour: therefore love is the fulfilling of the law" (v. 10).
- **Romans 13:1–7 Being subject to the "powers that be."** Every Saint should be "subject unto the higher powers" because all power comes from God and "the powers that be are ordained of [permitted to be in power by] God" (v. 1). "Whosoever therefore resisteth the power, resisteth the ordinance of God: and they that resist shall receive to

themselves damnation" (v. 2). We know by experience that "rulers are not a terror to good works, but to [do] evil. Wilt thou then not be afraid of the power? Do that which is good, and thou shalt have praise of the same" (v. 3).

Political powers can be "the minister of God to thee for good. But if thou do that which is evil, be afraid; for he beareth not the sword in vain" and he can be "a revenger to execute wrath upon him that doeth evil" (v. 4). We should be subject unto such powers out of fear of their "wrath," but "also for conscience sake" (v. 5). And for the same reasons we are to pay our taxes ("tribute") also (v. 6). "Render therefore to [them] all their dues: tribute to whom tribute is due; custom to whom custom; fear to whom fear; honour to whom honour" (v. 7).

- **Romans 13:1–7 Being subject also to Church authorities.** Joseph Smith added some significant phrases to these verses that make it sound like Paul was not speaking of governmental authorities, as is commonly supposed, but of those who are the ruling authorities in the Church.

  Elder Bruce R. McConkie said, "'Let every soul be subject unto the higher powers. For there is no power in the church but of God; the powers that be are ordained of God' (JST Romans 13:1). . . . To gain salvation the Saints must be subject to God's ministers. The doctrines and ordinances of the gospel cannot be separated from those appointed to teach Christ's gospel and perform His ordinances. Those who accept the gospel do so by submitting to the will and dictation of Christ. They come to the legal administrators who teach the doctrines of Christ and who perform the ordinances of salvation in His name and by His authority."[25]

- **Romans 14:23 Maintain your faith.** "He that doubteth is damned if he eat, because he eateth not of faith." This has to do with those who do not recognize the source of their blessings, which all come from God. And "whatsoever is not of faith is sin." Elder Bruce R. McConkie said this scripture applies to members of the Church, not to the world in general, which is without the law.[26]

THEBIBLEREVIVAL.COM, #21

- **Romans 15:1–4 Strengthen others.** We should focus on the needs of others rather than ourselves. "We then that are strong ought to bear the infirmities of the weak, and not to please ourselves. Let every one of us please his neighbour for his good to edification" (vv. 1–2). Christ did not serve Himself; in all of the accounts of His life in the New Testament we can find not a single self-serving act. Instead, He served and saved us, whose sins fell upon Him (v. 3). Even our scriptures are the result of this principle. "For whatsoever things were written aforetime were written for our learning, that we through patience and comfort of the scriptures might have hope" (v. 4).

- **Romans 15:5–7 Maintain unity.** "Now the God of patience and consolation grant you to be likeminded one toward another according to Christ Jesus: That ye may with one mind and one mouth glorify God, even the Father of our Lord Jesus Christ. Wherefore receive ye one another, as Christ also received us to the glory of God."

- **Romans 15:18–22 The geographical extent of Paul's missions.** Paul could not list all of "those things which Christ hath . . . wrought by me, to make the Gentiles obedient, by word and deed" and "through mighty signs and wonders, by the power of the Spirit of God" (vv. 18–19).

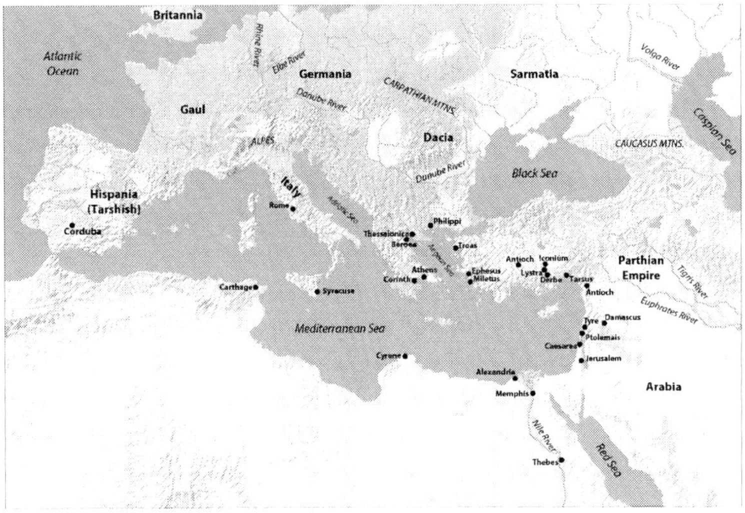

"From Jerusalem, and round about unto Illyricum, I have fully preached the gospel of Christ" (v. 19). Illyricum is present-day Albania and Macedonia. Paul is defining the geographical limits of his missionary work.

Paul specialized in opening new mission fields among the Gentiles, rather than building upon others' previous efforts. "I strived to preach the gospel, not where Christ was named, lest I should build upon another man's foundation: But . . . to whom he was not spoken of . . . and they that have not heard" (vv. 20–21). "For which cause also I have been much hindered from coming to you," Paul said to the Romans (v. 22).

- **Romans 15:24, 28 Paul mentions a possible mission to Spain.** While writing to the Romans, Paul said, "Whensoever I take my journey into Spain, I will come to you: for I trust to see you in my journey, and to be brought on my way thitherward [toward Spain] by you, if first [after] I be somewhat filled with your company" (v. 24). Paul then said again, "When therefore I have performed this, and have sealed to them this fruit, I will come by you into Spain" (v. 28).

Paul probably did go to Spain between his imprisonments. Clement of Rome (about 100 AD) said that Paul had "gone to the extremity of the West,"[27] which implies Spain. Others of the early Christian fathers also reported that he labored in Spain. Thus, Paul's intentions to go to Spain may have been eventually realized.

PAUL'S RETURN TRIP TO JERUSALEM

- **Acts 20:3 Paul discovers a conspiracy against him.** Paul had intended to return to "Syria" (his home base of Antioch there) by sea from the port of Corinth. But after three months at Corinth, during which he wrote the epistles to the Galatians and the Romans, Paul discovered that certain Jews "laid wait for him, as he was about to sail into Syria." Paul therefore altered his plans and decided "to return [by land] through Macedonia."

A Brief Return to Troas

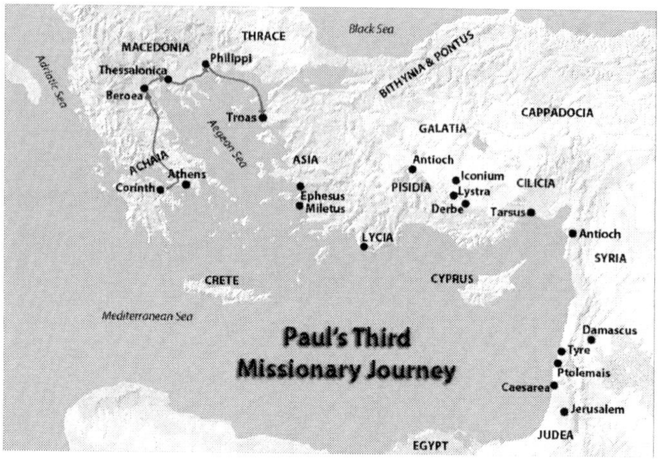

- **Acts 20:4–6 Paul and his companions return to Troas.** Several traveling companions—"Sopater of Berea; and of the Thessalonians, Aristarchus, and Secundus; and Gaius of Derbe, and Timotheus; and of Asia, Tychicus and rophimus"—went ahead of Paul and waited for him at Troas (vv. 4–5).

  Paul and another companion (probably Luke, who wrote the book of Acts—note the "us" and "we" in these verses) remained behind briefly but then walked to Philippi in Macedonia and sailed from there to Troas (v. 6).

A. HOUBRACKEN, THE BIBLE AND ITS STORY, 1908

- **Acts 20:7–12 Paul addresses the Church at Troas for many hours.** It was "the first day of the week, when the disciples came together to break bread," and "Paul preached unto them, ready to depart on the morrow; and continued his speech until midnight" (v. 7). From this we can see that the new Sabbath for Christians had become the first day of the week—Sunday—which they referred to as "the Lord's day."

  They had gathered in an "upper chamber" for their meeting and there were many lights [torches] in the room which produced heat (v. 8). "And there sat in a window a certain young man named Eutychus, being fallen into a deep sleep: and as Paul was long preaching, he sunk down with sleep, and fell down from the third loft, and was taken up dead" (v. 9). Paul came down from his speaking podium and "fell on him, and embracing him said, Trouble not yourselves; for his life is in him" (v. 10). "And they brought the young man alive, and were not a little comforted" (v. 12).

It is interesting to note that, after the young man was revived, Paul "talked a long while, even till break of day, [before] he departed" (v. 11). This may seem excessive, but we should remember that Paul did not know when he might see them again, if ever. He had much to impart to them. And Elder Bruce R. McConkie wrote of this event, "Sermons can and sometimes should be long."[28]

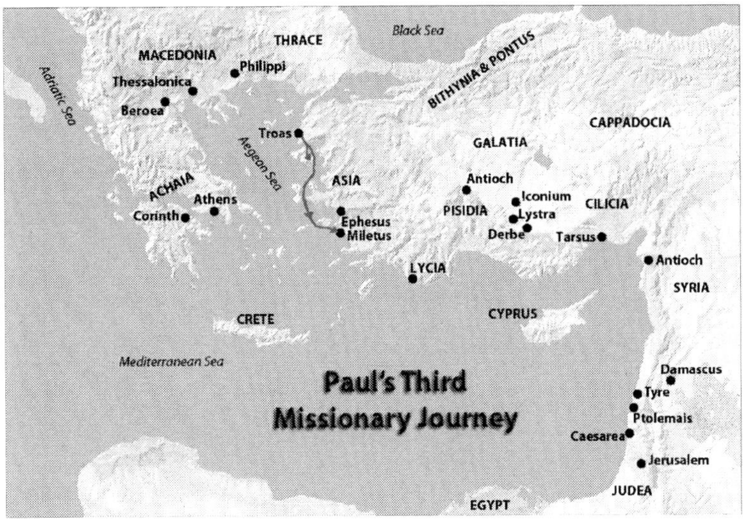

- **Acts 20:13–17 The missionaries travel to Miletus** (vv. 13–15). In the interest of time, the leaders of the Church at Ephesus were called to meet with Paul in Miletus (v. 17), which was a little bit south of Ephesus. Paul chose not to go to Ephesus because he would have had to spend too much time there, and he wanted to get back to Jerusalem by the day of Pentecost (v. 16).

PAUL'S FAREWELL ADDRESS TO EPHESIAN LEADERS

THEBIBLEREVIVAL.COM, #21

- **Acts 20:18–27 Paul rehearses his many labors among them.** This sermon is the only sermon recorded in the book of Acts. Paul began it by saying, "Ye know, from the first day that I came into Asia, after what manner I have been with you at all seasons," he said, "serving the Lord with all humility of mind, and with many tears, and temptations [meaning "trials, ordeals," and "afflictions"], which befell me by the lying in wait of the Jews" (vv. 18–19). "I kept back nothing that was profitable unto you, but have shewed you, and have taught you publickly, and from house to house, testifying both to the Jews, and also to the Greeks, repentance toward God, and faith toward our Lord Jesus Christ" (vv. 20–21).

"Now," said Paul, "I go bound in the spirit unto Jerusalem, not knowing the things that shall befall me there" except that "the Holy Ghost witnesseth in every city, saying that bonds and afflictions abide [await] me" (vv. 22–23). Paul was not intimidated by these things, and said, "neither count I my life dear unto myself, so that I might finish my course with joy, and the ministry, which I have received of the Lord Jesus, to testify the gospel of the grace of God" (v. 24).

Paul said, "And now, behold, I know that ye all . . . shall see my face no more" (v. 25). He was wrong about that. He would yet again return to Ephesus briefly after being released from prison at Rome. But he believed he was giving his last testimony to them, and said, "I take you to record this day, that I am pure from the blood of all men. For I have not shunned to declare unto you all the counsel of God" (vv. 26–27).

- **Acts 20:28–31 Paul predicts that apostasy will come to Ephesus after his departure.** Paul said to the leaders at Ephesus, "Take heed therefore unto yourselves, and to all the flock, over the which the Holy Ghost hath made you overseers, to feed the church of God, which he hath purchased with his own blood" (v. 28). "For I know this, that after my departing shall grievous wolves enter in among you, not sparing the flock" (v. 29). This is a figure of speech of Paul's day wherein wolves represent people from outside the Church who would attack the Saints with perverse (distorted and corrupted) doctrine.

  "Also of your own selves shall men arise, speaking perverse things, to draw away disciples after them" (v. 30). Paul was also predicting an internal threat—that Church members would apostatize and seek followers by changing doctrine.

  "Therefore watch, and remember, that by the space of three years I ceased not to warn every one night and day with tears" (v. 31).

- **Acts 20:32–35 Paul charges them to selflessly protect the Church.** "And now, brethren, I commend you to God, and to the word of his grace [Christ], [who] is able to build you up, and to give you an inheritance among all them which are sanctified" (v. 32).

  Paul had not profited by them (as some of them would later seek to do). "I have coveted no man's silver, or gold, or apparel," he said (v. 33). "Yea, ye yourselves know, that these hands have ministered unto my necessities, and to them that were with me" (v. 34). He had set the example to them of "labouring . . . to support the weak, and to remember the words of the Lord Jesus, how he said, It is more blessed to give than to receive" (v. 35). This quote, by the way, is not found in the Gospels. Paul obtained it from some other source, apparently.

- **Acts 20:36–38 After a tearful farewell, Paul prays with them and departs for Jerusalem.** Paul "kneeled down, and prayed with them all" (v. 36). "And they all wept sore, and fell on Paul's neck, and kissed him, sorrowing most of all for the words which he spake, that they should see his face no more. And they accompanied him unto the ship" (vv. 37–38).

CAROLSFELD, 1852-60

Notes

1. *Doctrinal New Testament Commentary*, 3 vols. [1965–1973], 2:212–213, 216.
2. *The Miracle of Forgiveness* [1969], 80–81, 85–86.
3. *Doctrinal New Testament Commentary*, 2:222.
4. *Doctrines of Salvation*, comp. Bruce R. McConkie, 3 vols. [1954–1956], 2:309, 311.
5. In Anderson, *Understanding Paul* [1983], 179.
6. *Christianity Today*, 17 July 1981, 19.
7. *Doctrinal New Testament Commentary*, 2:231.
8. *Teachings of the Prophet Joseph Smith*, sel. Joseph Fielding Smith [1976], 331–332.
9. *Teachings of the Prophet Joseph Smith*, 76.
10. In Conference Report, October 1995, 31; or *Ensign*, November 1995, 25.
11. *Mormon Doctrine*, 2nd ed. [1966], 395.
12. In Conference Report, April 1961, 66
13. *Institutes of the Christian Religion* [xxxx], 3.21.5
14. *Doctrines of Salvation*, 3:286–287.
15. *Answers to Gospel Questions*, comp. Joseph Fielding Smith Jr., 5 vols. [1957–1966], 4:153.
16. *Teachings of the Prophet Joseph Smith*, 189.
17. *Doctrinal New Testament Commentary*, 2:276.
18. *Mormon Doctrine*, 216.
19. *Doctrinal New Testament Commentary*, 2:277.

20. See *Doctrinal New Testament Commentary*, 2:290.

21. *Doctrines of Salvation*, 2:323–324.

22. *Teachings of the Prophet Joseph Smith*, 148.

23. *The Mormon* [New York City], 29 August 1857.

24. Anderson, *Understanding Paul*, 193.

25. *Doctrinal New Testament Commentary*, 2:296.

26. *Doctrinal New Testament Commentary*, 2:302.

27. 1 Clement 5.5-7.

28. *Doctrinal New Testament Commentary*, 2:175.

SECTION TEN

Paul at Jerusalem and Rome; The Death of Paul

(58 AD — 68 AD)

Many years before in Damascus, at the beginning of Paul's ministry, the Lord declared to Ananias His plans for the future Apostle: He said Paul would preach the gospel "before the Gentiles, and kings, and the children of Israel" (Acts 9:15). Now, toward the end of his ministry, Paul had fulfilled every aspect of this prophecy except for "testifying before kings." The events that occurred during this last period of Paul's life fulfilled the prophecy. He would testify before King Festus, appeal to Caesar, nearly die twice at sea, suffer two imprisonments with some traveling between, then finally be beheaded at Rome.

The events of this period can be divided into thee segments. The first segment was his return to Jerusalem at the end of his third missionary journey. He returned to Jerusalem from Miletus by way of Tyre, Ptolemais, and Caesarea. He wanted to be back in Jerusalem in time for Pentecost (the first week in June).

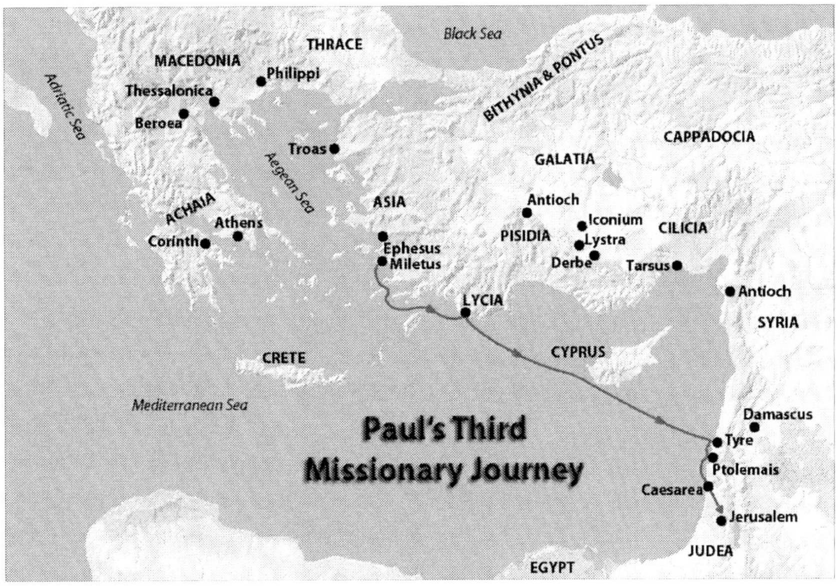

This journey included the following stops along the way:

TYRE:	Where he stayed with some of his converts for a week.
CAESAREA:	Where he stayed with Philip for a while.

The second period includes his arrest and trials at Jerusalem and Caesarea, his trials before Felix and Festus, his perilous sea journey to Rome, and his imprisonment at Rome.

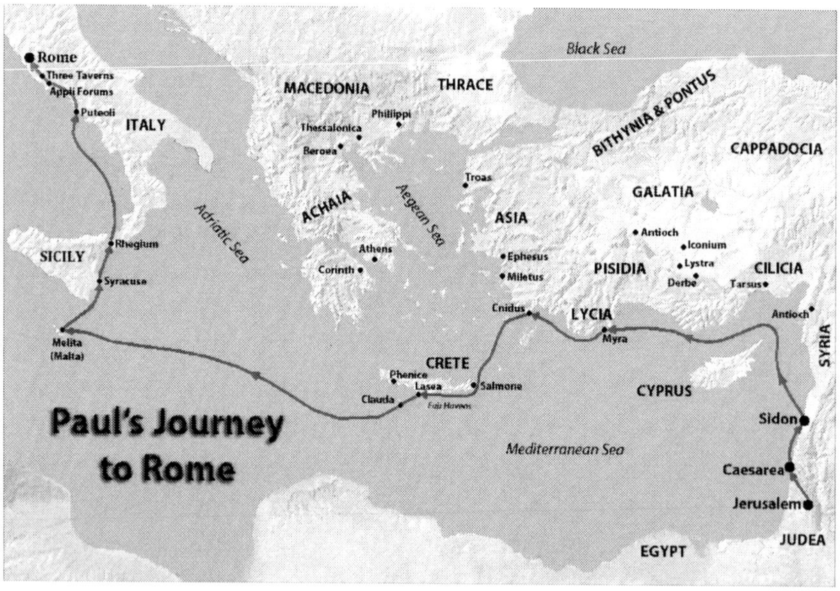

This journey included the following events along the way:

CAESAREA:	Tried before the kings Felix and Festus; his appeal unto Caesar.
SIDON:	A brief visit with friends before sailing on to Rome via Lycia and Cnidus.
CRETE:	Fair Havens, Cnydus, near shipwreck at Claudia, and Paul's prophecy of safety.
MALTA:	Shipwreck, refuge at Melita, and miracles performed by Paul.
SICILY:	Brief stops at Syracuse and Rhegium.
ITALY:	Landing at Puteoli, overland to the Appii forum, Three Taverns, and finally Rome.

The third and final period includes Paul's release from prison and subsequent travels for a short time, and then his re-imprisonment and death at Rome.

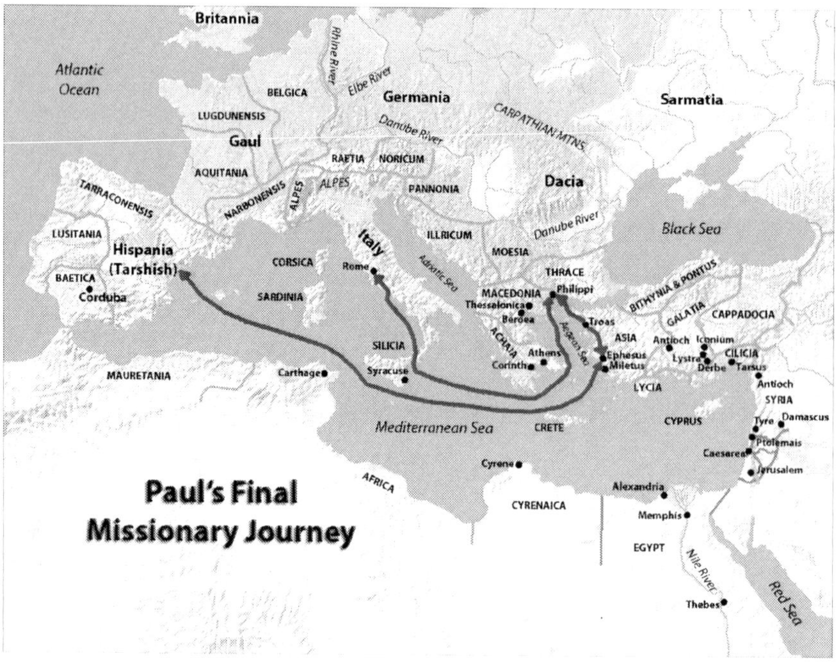

This journey included the following events:

ROME:	Paul's first imprisonment and writing of four epistles.
MACEDONIA:	Paul's respite from prison and writing of two epistles.
ASIA & SPAIN:	Paul's journey to Spain from and returning to Ephesus.
MACEDONIA:	Paul's final visit to Philippi then return to Rome.
ROME:	Paul's final imprisonment, writing of two epistles, and death by beheading.

The Significance of This Final Period of Paul's Life and Ministry

These journeys were the last of Paul's nearly 33-year ministry. The scope of his mission stretched as far west as Spain, and as far east as Ephesus in Asia (modern-day Turkey). Eight of his 14 epistles were written during this time, one a masterful thesis on faith and Jewish history (Hebrews), three very personal letters to young leaders, one letter to a slave, and loving counsel to three groups of Saints in Asia and Macedonia. Thus, a large portion of what we have from Paul comes from this period of time.

EPISTLE	WRITTEN FROM	DATE WRITTEN
Ephesians	Rome	61-62 AD
Colossians	Rome	61-62 AD
Philemon	Rome	61-62 AD
Philippians	Rome	62 AD
Hebrews[1]	Rome	65 AD
1 Timothy	Macedonia	66 AD
Titus	Macedonia	67-68 AD
2 Timothy	Rome	67-68 AD

Hebrews Is Not Presented In Chronological Order

The descriptions above and the chart at the end of this section show the chronological sequence of events during Paul's final journeys. However, Gospel Doctrine lessons do not follow a chronological sequence; they discuss the letter to the Hebrews at the beginning, whose date is uncertain but may have been written as many as 8 years later, in 65 AD. And the two letters to Timothy, though written by as many as 2 years apart, are presented together with the one to Titus.

The associated chapters of this book, corresponding to Gospel Doctrine lessons, are:

37. Faith in Jesus Christ (Hebrews)
38. Jerusalem & Paul's Journey to Rome (Acts 21-28)
39. Perfecting the Saints (Ephesians)
40. Our Possibilities Through Christ (Philippians, Colossians, Philemon)
41. Paul's Pastoral Epistles and Death (1 & 2 Timothy, Titus)

The following is a chronological list of events that took place during this period and the scriptures from Acts and the Epistles that tell the story.

Date	Events	Scriptural References
PAUL'S JOURNEYS TO JERUSALEM AND ROME (58-60 AD)		
58	Jerusalem:	
	The Gradual Process of Conversion	Acts 21:18-26
	Paul Persecuted, Arrested, Bound	Acts 21:27-39
	The Story of Paul's Conversion	Acts 21:40; 22:1-16
	Paul's Vision of Jesus	Acts 22:17-21
	The Protection of Roman Citizenship	Acts 22:22-29
	Appearance Before the Sanhedrin	Acts 22:30; 23:1-10
	The Lord Again Appears to Paul	Acts 23:11
	The Jewish Conspiracy Against Paul	Acts 23:12-22
	Caesarea:	
	Paul Transferred to Caesarea	Acts 23:23-35
	The Case Before Felix	Acts 24:1-27
	Paul Appeals to Caesar	Acts 25:1-22
	Paul Testifies Before King Agrippa	Acts 25:23-27; 26:1-32
	Hebrews written from Caesarea	Hebrews
60	Paul's Departure for Rome	Acts 27:1-8
	Crete:	
	Shipwreck at Fair Havens	Acts 27:9-44
	Melita (Malta):	
	Paul Heals the Sick	Acts 28:1-10
	From Malta to Rome	Acts 28:11-15
PAUL AT ROME		
	Rome:	
61-62	Paul lives in own house 2 yrs at Rome; awaits hearing before Nero.	Acts 28
	Paul Preaches in Rome	Acts 28:16-31
	Colossians written from Rome	Colossians
	Ephesians written from Rome	Ephesians
	Philemon written from Rome	Philemon
62	Philippians written from Rome	Philippians
63	Ministry in Rome and Italy	
PAUL'S JOURNEY TO WESTERN EUROPE		
	Spain, Gaul, Raetia, Noricum:	
64-66	Possible missionary journey to western provinces	
PAUL'S IMPRISONMENT AT ROME		
	Rome:	
66-68	Pastoral Epistles written from Rome	1 & 2 Timothy; Titus
68	Possible date of death; Paul beheaded in Rome	

Notes

1. The place from which the book of Hebrews was written is unknown, though a partial clue is furnished by the phrase, "They of Italy salute you" (13:24). Since it was written to the "Hebrews," this author prefers the theory that it was written from Rome to Jerusalem. We also do not know the exact date of the epistle. It seems from references within the epistle that the temple in Jerusalem was still standing, so it would be before 70 AD. Judging from its themes, it appears to have been written after Paul's first imprisonment (61-62 AD), but before his second imprisonment and death (68 AD). About 65 AD fits the known facts.

Chapter 37

Faith in Jesus Christ

(Hebrews)

INTRODUCTION

Where and When Was Hebrews Written?

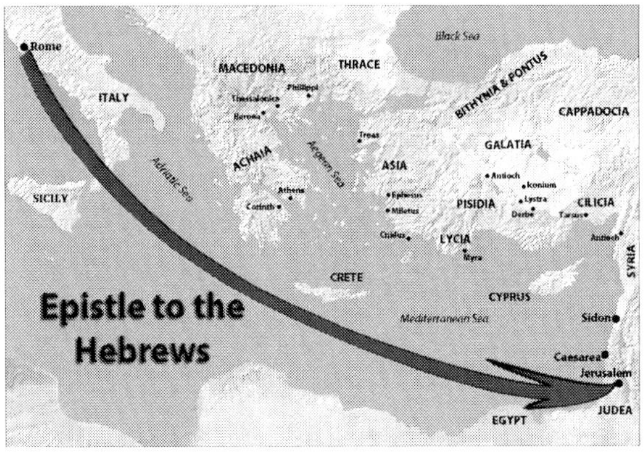

The place from which the book of Hebrews was written is unknown, though a partial clue is furnished by the phrase, "They of Italy salute you" (13:24). This could mean that the author was in Italy and sending greetings from his Italian acquaintances or that he was in some other part of the empire sending greetings to Italy from Italian acquaintances. Since it was written to the "Hebrews," I prefer the theory that it was written from Rome to Jerusalem.

We also do not know the exact date of the epistle. It seems, from the frequent allusions to Mosaic ritual, that the temple in Jerusalem was still standing, and if so the letter's date was before 70 AD. Judging from its themes, it appears to have been written after the epistles written during Paul's first imprisonment (61–62 AD), but before his second imprisonment and death (68 AD). A date of about 65 AD would seem to fit the known facts.

Who Wrote Hebrews?

Scholars also debate the authorship of the epistle to the Hebrews. Some do not accept Paul as its author, though Clement, the bishop of Rome, accepted Paul as its author in 95 AD, only 30 years after it was written. In our dispensation, its authorship was affirmed by revelation.

Elder Bruce R. McConkie said, "The Prophet Joseph Smith says this Epistle was written 'by Paul . . . to the Hebrew brethren'[1], and repeatedly in his sermons he attributes statements from it to Paul. Peter, himself a Hebrew, whose ministry and teachings were directed in large part to his own people, seems to be identifying its authorship when he writes, 'Our beloved brother Paul . . . according to the wisdom given unto him hath written unto you [the Hebrews]; As also in all his [other] epistles, . . . some things hard to be understood' (2 Pet. 3:15–16). In any event, Paul did write Hebrews, and to those who accept Joseph Smith as an inspired witness of truth, the matter is at rest."[2]

Why Was Hebrews Written?

The book of Hebrews discusses Christ's fulfillment of the law of Moses. Jewish converts to Christianity brought with them a tradition of reverent study of the Old Testament and law of Moses. The question was whether Mosaic ritual was done away in Christ's atonement, and whether any value remained in the Old Testament. Paul's letter to the Hebrews was written, at least in part, to answer these questions. Because he was writing to the Jews, Paul used the symbolism of the law of Moses and its rituals to show their fulfillment in Christ.

What Are its Most Significant Contributions?

Because of its focus on these topics, Hebrews became one of the finest scriptural commentaries on the Old Testament. It provides doctrine, knowledge, and enlightenment to the faithful. It also takes revelations from the past, the dead letter of the law, and ties them into the living principles of Christianity. Paul seeks to convince the Hebrews that Jesus is the Messiah for whom they have waited. And he gives evidence that Christ was Jehovah, Lord of the Old Testament and of the earth. Finally, it explains how Christ's atoning sacrifice was symbolically foretold in Old Testament events and practices.

THE ROLE OF CHRIST

Christ Is a God

- **Hebrews 1:1–15 Christ's role and accomplishments.** The majority of this scripture provides titles for Christ that reveal His role and His relationship to us.
  - — He created the world (vv. 2, 10)
  - — He is in the image of God the Father (v. 3)
  - — He atoned for our sins (v. 3)
  - — He is the Firstborn Son of God the Father (vv. 5–6)
  - — His glory and power are eternal and unchanging (vv. 8, 12)
  - — He is greater than the angels (vv. 13–14)

"THE LIVING CHRIST," ©JOSEPH BRICKEY, USED BY PERMISSION

While speaking of the angels, Paul mentioned "ministering spirits" (vv. 13–14). What are ministering spirits, and how, if at all, do they differ from the angels in heaven? The Prophet Joseph Smith said: "The difference between an angel and a ministering spirit [is that] the one [is] a resurrected or translated body, with its spirit ministering to embodied spirits—the other a disembodied spirit, visiting and ministering to disembodied spirits. Jesus Christ became a ministering spirit (while His body was lying in the sepulchre) to the spirits in prison, to fulfill an important part of His mission, without which He could not have perfected His work, or entered into His rest. After His resurrection He appeared as an angel to His disciples."[3]

"These angels are under the direction of Michael or Adam, who acts under the direction of the Lord. From [Hebrews 1:4] we learn that Paul perfectly understood the purposes of God in relation to His connection with man, and that glorious and perfect order which He established in Himself, whereby he sent forth power, revelations, and glory."[4]

Christ Was a Mortal

- **Hebrews 1:4 Christ was "made . . . better than the angels."** People in Paul's day, as well as in ours, think of angels as special and holy persons who minister to our needs. Indeed, some Christian faiths teach that the reward of a good life is to become an angel forever. But Christ, Paul wrote, was "made so much better than the angels," and "hath by inheritance obtained a more excellent name than they."

"HOPE," ©JOSEPH BRICKEY, USED BY PERMISSION

- **Hebrews 2:6–9 He was also "made a little lower than the angels."** Paul quotes King David as saying, "What is man, that thou art mindful of him? or the son of man, that thou visitest him? Thou madest him a little lower than the angels; thou crownedst him with glory and honour, and didst set him over the works of thy hands [and] Thou hast put all things in subjection under his feet" (vv. 6–8; Psalm 8:4–6).

On the surface, this sounds contradictory. How can Christ be both "better" and "lower" than the angels? The problem is partly one of translation. The word that the English translators rendered "angels" is in Hebrew "gods" and only in the Greek "angels." And either way, the idea is that Christ lowered Himself below all things in order to save us through His atonement. "We see Jesus," said Paul, "made a little lower than the angels for the suffering of death," and then later "crowned with glory and honour . . . [because He] taste[d] death for every man" (v. 9).

Elder Bruce R. McConkie said:

> The marginal reading of this quotation from Psalm 8:4–6 recites that man is made, not a little lower than the angels, but a little lower than Elohim, which means that all God's offspring, Jesus included, as children in His family, are created subject to Him, with the power to advance until all things are "in subjection" to them. Of those who gain eternal life, it is written: "Then shall they be above all, because all things are subject unto them. Then

shall they be gods, because they have all power, and the angels are subject unto them" (D&C 132:20).

The only sense in which either men or Jesus are lower than the angels is in that mortal restrictions limit them for the moment; and for that matter, angels themselves become mortals and then in the resurrection attain again their angelic status.[5]

- **Hebrews 2:10 The "captain of [our] salvation " was made "perfect through sufferings."** The same Being for whom and by whom all things were made, brought "many sons unto glory" as the "captain of their salvation," and through that process He became "perfect [glorified] through [His] sufferings."

- **Hebrews 2:16–18 He took upon Himself mortality, becoming just like us.** Christ did not come to earth to take upon Himself "the nature of angels; but he took on him the seed of Abraham" (v. 16). It was appropriate that He be made "like unto his brethren, that he might be a merciful and faithful high priest in things pertaining to God, [and] to make reconciliation for the sins of the people" (v. 17). Thus, by experience, He came to know how "to succour them that are tempted" (v. 18).

- **Hebrews 4:15–16 He suffered and was tempted in every way that we are.** Jesus, our "high priest" was not above the disappointments, infirmities, sorrows, and temptations we experience in life, "but was in all points tempted like as we are, yet without sin" (v. 15). We can "therefore come boldly unto the throne of grace" and know that He will understand and be merciful and that we can "find grace to help in time of need" (v. 16).

    — **Mosiah 13:34–35 He came to earth as a mortal and was subject to pain and death.** The prophet Abinadi said that "God himself [will] come down among the children of men, and take upon him the form of man, and go forth in mighty power upon the face of the earth" (v. 34). He would be "oppressed and afflicted" like we are, and after His own death would "bring to pass the resurrection of the dead" (v. 35).

Christ and the Law of Moses

- **Hebrews 3:1–6 Christ is greater than Moses.** Speaking of Christ, Paul invited the Jewish members of the Church to "consider the Apostle and High Priest of our profession, Christ Jesus" (v. 1). The Savior was "faithful to him that appointed him [God the Father], as also Moses was faithful in all his house" (v. 2). Yet, Jesus was "worthy of more glory than Moses," just like "he who hath builded [a] house hath more honour than the house" (v. 3). "For every house is builded by some man; but he that built all things is God" (v. 4). Moses was a faithful servant of God, and gave "testimony of those things which were to be spoken after [his time]" (v. 5). "But Christ [is] a son over his own house; whose house are we," if we will "hold fast the confidence and the rejoicing of the hope firm unto the end" (v. 6).

    — **Alma 34:13–14 Christ's sacrifice put an end to blood sacrifices.** It was "expedient [necessary] that there should be a great and last sacrifice," after which "there should be a stop to the shedding of blood" (v. 13). With Christ's sacrifice, "the law of Moses [was] fulfilled," as was determined beforehand that it should "be all fulfilled, every jot and tittle, and none shall have passed away" (v. 13). In fact, "the whole meaning of the law, every whit," was to point forward to "that great and last sacrifice [of the] Son of God, [an] infinite and eternal" sacrifice to end all sacrifices (v. 14).

— **3 Nephi 15:1–8 Christ came to fulfill the law of Moses.** After teaching His gospel to the Nephites, Christ discerned that some of them were confused about how the law of Moses related to these new teachings (vv. 1–2). "They understood not the saying that old things had passed away, and that all things had become new" (v. 2). Christ then explained to them that "the law is fulfilled that was given unto Moses. Behold, I am he that gave the law, and I am he who covenanted with my people Israel; therefore, the law in me is fulfilled, for I have come to fulfil the law; therefore it hath an end" (vv. 4–5).

This fulfillment of the law of Moses did not "destroy the [prophecies of the] prophets, for as many as have not been fulfilled in me, verily I say unto you, shall all be fulfilled" (v. 6). The fact that "old things have passed away" does not "destroy that which hath been spoken concerning things which are to come" (v. 7). Indeed, "the covenant which I have made with my people [through Abraham] is not all fulfilled; but the law which was given unto Moses hath an end in me" (v. 8).

- **Hebrews 3:7–12, 16–19 The children of Israel forfeited their blessings.** Paul said that the Holy Ghost was whispering to those Jews who would listen to "harden not your hearts, as in the provocation, in the day of temptation in the wilderness" (vv. 7–8). This referred to the rebellion of the children of Israel in the wilderness, "when your fathers tempted me, proved me, and saw my works forty years," yet "alway[s] err[ed] in their heart; and [had] not known my ways" (vv. 9–10). "So I sware in my wrath, They shall not enter into my rest" (v. 11). "Take heed, brethren, lest there be in any of you an evil heart of unbelief, in departing from the living God" (v. 12).

PROVIDENCE LITHOGRAPHIC CO., 1901, #34

Paul noted that "some, when they had heard, did provoke," but "not all that came out of Egypt by Moses" (v. 16). The ones who grieved the Lord for 40 years were "them that had sinned, whose carcases fell in the wilderness, and to whom [He] sware . . . that they should not enter into his rest, . . . them that believed not" (vv. 17–18). "So we see that they could not enter in because of unbelief" (v. 19). (See also Hebrews 4:1–6, 11; D&C 84:23–24; Alma 13:12–13, 16.)

- **Hebrews 3:11 The righteous enter into the "rest" of the Lord.** What does it mean to "enter into my rest?" And who qualifies for this blessing?
  - **D&C 84:24 The "rest" of the Lord is "the fulness of his glory."** The children of Israel "hardened their hearts and could not endure his presence; therefore, the Lord in his wrath . . . swore that they should not enter into his rest while in the wilderness, which rest is the fulness of his glory."
  - **Alma 40:12 When we leave this life we enter paradise, "a state of rest."** "The spirits of those who are righteous are received into a state of happiness, which is called paradise, a state of rest, a state of peace, where they shall rest from all their troubles and from all care, and sorrow."

    President Joseph F. Smith said, "The ancient prophets speak of 'entering into God's rest'; what does it mean? To my mind, it means entering into the knowledge and love of God, having faith in His purpose and in His plan, to such an extent that we know we are right, and that we are not hunting for something else, we are not disturbed by every wind of doctrine, or by the cunning and craftiness of men who lie in wait to deceive. We know of the doctrine that it is of God, and we do not ask any questions of anybody about it; they are welcome to their opinions, to their ideas and to their vagaries. The man who has reached that degree of faith in God that all doubt and fear have been cast from him, he has entered into 'God's rest.' . . . rest from doubt, from fear, from apprehension of danger, rest from the religious turmoil of the world."[6]

- **Hebrews 4:8 Paul says that the Israelites did not obtain this "rest" under Joshua.** "Jesus" is the Greek form of the Hebrew name "Yeshua" and is translated into English as "Joshua." Paul was speaking here of Joshua, the Old Testament prophet/general who led the children of Israel into the promised land. Paul's point is that the Israelites did not find their "rest" under Joshua, nor under David, their greatest king.

THE PRIESTHOOD

How Priesthood Is Conferred

- **Hebrews 5:4 We cannot "call ourselves" to the priesthood; we must obtain it like Aaron did.** "No man taketh this honour unto himself," Paul wrote. To receive the priesthood, a man must be "called of God, as was Aaron."
  - **Article of Faith 5 What it means to be called of God.** "We believe that a man must be called of God, by prophecy [revelation], and by the laying on of hands by those who are in authority," before he can "preach the Gospel and administer in the ordinances thereof."

THE HOLMAN BIBLE, 1890

- **Hebrews 5:5–6 Jesus Christ holds the Melchizedek priesthood.** Even "Christ glorified not himself to be made an high priest;" rather He received His priesthood office from "he that said unto him, Thou art my Son, to day have I begotten thee" [God the Father] (v. 5). And when He received His priesthood office, the Father said unto Him, "Thou art a priest for ever after the order of Melchisedec" (v. 6; see also Hebrews 6:20). The Prophet Joseph Smith said, "The priesthood is an everlasting principle, and existed with God from eternity, and will to eternity, without beginning of days or end of years."[7] The Prophet also said, "If a man gets a fulness of the priesthood of God he has to get it in the same way that Jesus Christ obtained it, and that was by keeping all the commandments and obeying all the ordinances of the house of the Lord."[8]

- **Hebrews 5:7–8 Christ learned obedience through His suffering.** Speaking of Christ, Paul wrote that "in the days of his flesh, when he had offered up prayers and supplications with strong crying and tears unto him that was able to save him from death, [He] was heard [by God because] he feared [worshiped His Father appropriately]" (v. 7). Yet God did not remove the suffering from His Son, and "though he [was] a Son, yet learned he obedience by the things which he suffered" (v. 8).

Christ prayed frequently for His Father's help

Elder Bruce R. McConkie said:

> These verses make clear reference to Christ and His mortal ministry and are in complete harmony with other scriptures which bear on the same matters, as also with the sermons of the early brethren of this dispensation who quote them as applying to our Lord. However, there is a footnote in the Inspired Version [JST] which says, "The 7th and 8th verses allude to Melchizedek, and not to Christ." Standing alone, and because it is only part of the picture, this footnote gives an erroneous impression. The fact is verses 7 and 8 apply to both Melchizedek and to Christ, because Melchizedek was a prototype of Christ and that prophet's ministry typified and foreshadowed that of our Lord in the same sense that the ministry of Moses did (Deut. 18:15–19; Acts 3:22–23; 3 Ne. 30:23; JS–History 1:40). Thus, though the words of these verses, and particularly those in the 7th verse, had original application to Melchizedek, they apply with equal and perhaps even greater force to the life and ministry of Him through whom all the promises made to Melchizedek were fulfilled.[9]

- **Hebrews 5:8–9 How Jesus was made perfect.** "Though he [was] a Son, yet learned he obedience by the things which he suffered" (v. 8), and "being made perfect" [by that process], he became the author of eternal salvation unto all them that obey him" (v. 9). Elder Bruce R. McConkie said, "Christ always was perfect in that He obeyed the whole law of the Father at all times and was everlastingly the Sinless One (Heb. 4:14–16;

5:1–3). But on the other hand He was made perfect, through the sufferings and experiences of mortality, in the sense that He thereby died and was resurrected in glorious immortality. In that perfected state, possessing at long last a body of flesh and bones, He then had the same eternal perfection possessed by His Father. Hence His pronouncement, after the resurrection, that all power was given Him in heaven and in earth (Matt 28:18)."[10]

Limits of the Aaronic Priesthood

- **Hebrews 7:11–12 The Melchizedek priesthood is necessary to perform all the ordinances necessary for salvation.** "If therefore perfection were by the Levitical priesthood, (for under it the people received the law,) what further need was there that another priest should rise after the order of Melchisedec," asked Paul, instead of being "called after the order of Aaron?" (v. 11). If there had to be a change in priesthood, then there had to be "of necessity a change also of the law" (v. 12). Paul said also that "He [God] taketh away the first [law and associated priesthood], that he may establish the second [or Melchizedek]" priesthood (Hebrews 10:9). It is through that priesthood that "we are sanctified through the offering of the body of Jesus Christ once for all" (Hebrews 10:10). The Melchizedek priesthood, the higher priesthood, can minister to gospel ordinances in their fulness and is therefore capable of purifying our lives so that we can again enter into the presence of the Lord (3 Nephi 27:19–20). The Aaronic priesthood cannot do this.
    - **D&C 84:25–27 The law of Moses had only the Aaronic priesthood**, also called the Levitical, lesser, or preparatory priesthood. "Neither the law of Moses nor the priesthood of Aaron which administered it was capable of bringing God's children unto perfection. The Aaronic priesthood is a lesser authority, and it administers the preparatory gospel only. The Melchizedek priesthood, on the other hand, is the higher priesthood, commissioned to minister the gospel ordinances in their fulness and capable of purifying our lives so that we can again enter into the presence of the Lord."[11]

The Melchizedek Priesthood

- **D&C 107:1–4 The distinction between Aaronic and Melchizedek priesthood.** The Lord explained through the Prophet Joseph Smith that "there are, in the church, two priesthoods, namely, the Melchizedek and Aaronic, including the Levitical Priesthood" (v. 1). The first or higher priesthood "is called the Melchizedek Priesthood is because Melchizedek was such a great high priest. Before his day it was called the Holy Priesthood, after the Order of the Son of God. But out of respect or reverence to the name of the Supreme Being, to avoid the too frequent repetition of his name, they, the church, in ancient days, called that priesthood after Melchizedek, or the Melchizedek Priesthood" (vv. 2–4).

- **Abraham 1:1–4 Abraham sought for the blessings of the higher priesthood.** As he read the ancient scriptures, Abraham realized that he was entitled, if worthy, to the priesthood held by the ancient patriarchs Adam, Seth, Enoch, Noah, and others (vv. 1–3). Therefore, said he, "I sought for mine appointment unto the Priesthood according to the appointment of God unto the fathers concerning the seed" (v. 4).

- **D&C 84:14 Abraham received the priesthood from the high priest Melchizedek.** Modern revelation tells us that "Abraham received the priesthood from Melchizedek, who received it through the lineage of his fathers, even till Noah."

- **Hebrews 7:1–2 Who Was Melchizedek?** He was "king of Salem, [a] priest of the most high God, who met Abraham returning from the slaughter of the kings, and blessed him" (v. 1). Abraham paid his tithing to Melchizedek (v. 2). Other names for this great high priest were "King of righteousness, and after that also King of Salem, which [means], King of peace" (v. 2).

  — Melchizedek was king & high priest of the Lord's people in pre-Israelite Canaan.
  — Thus, he dwelt in the area around Jerusalem, which Abraham inherited.
  — Hebrew Malki-Zedek means "King of righteousness."
  — He was king of Salem (Hebrew, Shalem), which means "King of peace."
  — These are also names of Jesus Christ; Melchizedek was a symbol of Christ.

  — **Alma 13:14–15 Melchizedek turned a wicked people into a celestial people.** He was "a high priest after this same order [of] which I have spoken, who also took upon him the high priesthood forever" (v. 14). "And it was this same Melchizedek to whom Abraham paid tithes" (v. 15).

- **JST Genesis 14:26–27 More about Melchizedek.** The Prophet Joseph Smith restored considerably more to the Bible about Melchizedek than can be found in the King James Version. From the JST, we learn that "Melchizedek was a man of faith, who wrought righteousness; and when a child he feared God, and stopped the mouths of lions, and quenched the violence of fire. And thus, having been approved of God, he was ordained an high priest after the order of the covenant which God made with Enoch."

  — **Alma 13:16–19 Melchizedek turned a wicked people into a celestial people.** He instituted the priesthood ordinances of the gospel "that thereby the people might look forward on the Son of God, it being a type of his order, or it being his order, and this that they might look forward to him for a remission of their sins, that they might enter into the rest of the Lord" (v. 16). He was "a king over the land of Salem; and his people had waxed strong in iniquity and abomination; yea, they had all gone astray; they were full of all manner of wickedness" (v. 17). "But Melchizedek having exercised mighty faith, and received the office of the high priesthood according to the holy order of God, did preach repentance unto his people. And behold, they did repent; and Melchizedek did establish peace in the land in his days; therefore he was called the prince of peace, for he was the king of Salem; and he did reign under his father" (v. 18). "Now, there were many before him, and also there were many afterwards, but none were greater; therefore, of him they have more particularly made mention" (v. 19).

- **JST Hebrews 7:3 The Melchizedek priesthood is conferred only because of righteousness.** This priesthood is "after the order of the Son of God, which order was without father, without mother, without descent, having neither beginning of days, nor end of life." This priesthood is conferred only by a man being "made like unto the Son of God, abiding a priest continually." JST Genesis 14:28–29 says it is conferred "of God" upon men "by the calling of his own voice" [revelation], according to his [God's] own will, unto us many as believe . . . on his name."

PROVIDENCE LITHOGRAPHIC CO., 1902, #41

By comparison, the Aaronic priesthood anciently and in Paul's day was conferred by heredity to the Levites and the direct descendants of Aaron.
Elder Bruce R. McConkie said: "As compared to the Aaronic priesthood, as administered in ancient Israel, the order of Melchizedek did not come 'by descent from father and mother.'[12] That is, the right to this higher priesthood was not inherited in the same way as was the case with the Levites and sons of Aaron. Righteousness was an absolute requisite for the conferral of the higher priesthood."[13]

— **Alma 13:1–5 Those who hold this priesthood were foreordained to do so.** "The Lord God ordained priests, after his holy order, which was after the order of his Son, to teach these things unto the people" (v. 1). This was done so that "the people might know in what manner to look forward to his Son for redemption" (v. 2). "And this is the manner after which they were ordained . . . .

They were "called and prepared from the foundation of the world [in premortal life] according to the foreknowledge of God, on account of their exceeding faith and good works" (v. 3). Alma teaches that "in the first place [premortal world]" they were able "to choose good or evil; [and] therefore . . . having chosen good, and exercising exceedingly great faith, [were] called . . . with that holy calling" (v. 3).

While these were "called to this holy calling on account of their faith, . . . others . . . reject[ed] the Spirit of God on account of the hardness of their hearts and blindness of their minds, while, if it had not been for this they might have had as great privilege as their brethren" (v. 4). There, "in the first place [the premortal world] they were on the same standing with their brethren," but "this holy calling being [was] prepared from the foundation of the world [only] for such as would not harden their hearts" (v. 5).

Elder Bruce R. McConkie said, "Alma taught the great truth that every person who holds the Melchizedek priesthood was foreordained to receive that high and holy order in the pre-existent councils of eternity. . . . Thus, he explains, Melchizedek priesthood holders have been 'prepared from the foundation of the world' for their high callings. The Lord has prepared them 'from eternity to all eternity, according to his foreknowledge of all things.'"[14]

The Prophet Joseph Smith said: "Every man who has a calling to minister to the inhabitants of the world was ordained to that very purpose in the Grand Council of heaven before this world was. I suppose that I was ordained to this very office in that Grand Council."[15]

- **Hebrews 7:19 The Aaronic priesthood cannot make us perfect.** "The law [makes] nothing perfect," said Paul, "but the bringing in of a better hope [through Christ] did; by the which we draw nigh unto God."

- **Hebrews 7:15–17 The Melchizedek priesthood has the power to exalt us.** Christ was "after the similitude of Melchisedec" (v. 15) and was "a priest for ever after the order of Melchisedec" (v. 17). As such, He offered "not . . . the law of a carnal commandment, but . . . the power of an endless life" (v. 16).
  The Melchizedek priesthood is the power of "endless life" because . . .

PHOTO BY C. R. SAVAGE, PUBLIC DOMAIN

  — **D&C 84:19–22 It administers in the Church and in the temples.** In addition to "administer[ing] the gospel" [branch presidents, bishops, stake presidents, etc. must hold this priesthood], the Melchizedek priesthood holds the "key of the mysteries of the kingdom, even the key of the knowledge of God" (v. 19). This means administering the temple and its ordinances. In those ordinances "the power of godliness [how to become like God] is manifest" (v. 20). "And without the ordinances thereof, and the authority of the priesthood, the power of godliness is not manifest unto men in the flesh" (v. 21). Therefore, "without this [the priesthood and temple ordinances] no man can see the face of God, even the Father, and live" (v. 22).

  — **D&C 132:19 It has the power to bind marriages for all eternity.** There are very specific requirements for this to be true.

(1) They must be married according to the Lord's instructions for the "new and everlasting covenant" of marriage; a civil marriage will not do.

(2) That marriage must be "sealed" (verified or ratified like a notary public "seals" a document) "by the Holy Spirit of promise."

(3) The marriage must be performed "by him who is anointed, unto whom I have appointed this power and the keys of this priesthood;" in other words, by one who has been given the sealing keys.

(4) As part of that marriage, the participants must be told that "Ye shall come forth in the first resurrection . . . and shall inherit thrones, kingdoms, principalities, and powers, dominions, all heights and depths," which are the Abrahamic covenant promises.

(5) The participants must "commit no murder whereby to shed innocent blood."

(6) The participants must "abide in [remain and be faithful to the] covenant [of their marriage]," which fact will be verified by the Holy Spirit (see #2 above).

(7) "Then shall it be written in the Lamb's Book of Life [acknowledged in heaven] . . . [that these promises] in time, and through all eternity . . . shall be of full force when they are out of the world."

— **D&C 132:19–20 Persons who marry by this power may obtain godhood and endless spiritual posterity.** There are very specific promises associated with this.

(1) "They shall pass by the angels, and the gods, which are set there, to their exaltation and glory in all things, as hath been sealed upon their heads."

(2) They shall enjoy "a fulness and a continuation of the seeds [posterity] forever and ever."

(3) "Then shall they be gods, because they have no end; therefore shall they be from everlasting to everlasting, because they continue; then shall they be above all, because all things are subject unto them. Then shall they be gods, because they have all power, and the angels are subject unto them."

PROVIDENCE LITHOGRAPHIC CO., 1901, #34

The Saints in Paul's day understood the principles of exaltation

— **D&C 132:21–24 To be exalted we must obtain these ordinances and make these covenants.** "Verily, verily, I say unto you, except ye abide my law ye cannot attain to this glory . . . For strait is the gate, and narrow the way that leadeth unto the exaltation and continuation of the lives" (vv. 21–22). "And few there be that find it, because ye receive me not in the world neither do ye know me. But if ye receive me in the world, then shall ye know me, and shall receive your exaltation; that where I am ye shall be also" (vv. 22–23). "This is eternal lives—to know the only wise and true God, and Jesus Christ, whom he hath sent. I am he. Receive ye, therefore, my law" (v. 24).

— **Celestial marriage is not the same thing as polygamy.** We should note that none of these covenants and promises explained in D&C 132:19–24 say anything at all about polygamy. While the Lord does make clear in this same revelation that multiple wives may be justified when and if He commands it, when we look at these specific requirements and promises for eternal life there is nothing at all that says we must live in polygamy to be exalted.

Priesthood Covenants

- **Hebrews 7:20 The Aaronic priesthood is not received with an oath.** Then, as now, it was received by men "without an oath."

- **Hebrews 7:21 The Melchizedek priesthood is received with an oath.** It is received "with an oath" to God—"him that said unto [Christ] . . . thou art a priest for ever after the order of Melchisedec." The JST version of this verse says that Jesus also received His priesthood with a solemn oath (JST Hebrews 7:21).

THEBIBLEREVIVAL.COM, #22

— **D&C 84:33–44 The oath and covenant of the priesthood.** As with all covenants, this covenant consists of a two-way set of promises between the priesthood holder and God.

- All who receive the Melchizedek priesthood "receive this oath and covenant of my Father, which he cannot break, neither can it be moved [changed]" (vv. 39–40) without forfeiting their promised blessings.
- Things promised by the priesthood holder:
  - He will "obtain . . . these two priesthoods [Aaronic and Melchizedek] (v. 33).
  - He will "magnify" his priesthood callings (v. 33).
  - He will "give diligent heed to the words of eternal life [the gospel]" (v. 43).
  - He will "live by [be obedient to] every word that proceedeth forth from the mouth of God" (v. 44). This would necessarily include the scriptures, instructions from his priesthood leaders at all levels, and any revelation or inspiration given by the Holy Spirit to the priesthood holder.
- Things promised by God to priesthood holders who keep their covenants:
  - They "are sanctified by the Spirit unto the renewing of their bodies" (v. 33).
  - They become "the sons of Moses and of Aaron" (v. 34).

- They become "the seed of Abraham" (v. 34).
- They are recognized by God as His "church and kingdom" (v. 34).
- They become "the elect of God" (v. 34).
- They "receive me, saith the Lord" (vv. 35–36).
- They "receive . . . my Father," which means that they "receive . . . my Father's kingdom" [are exalted] (vv. 37–38).
- All that my Father hath shall be given unto him" (v. 38).

Elder Bruce R. McConkie said, "Every person upon whom the Melchizedek priesthood is conferred receives his office and calling in this higher priesthood with an oath and a covenant. The Covenant is to this effect: 1. Man on his part solemnly agrees to magnify his calling in the priesthood, to keep the commandments of God, to live by every word that proceedeth forth from the mouth of Deity, and to walk in paths of righteousness and virtue; and 2. God on His part agrees to give such persons an inheritance of exaltation and godhood in His everlasting presence. The oath is the solemn attestation of Deity, His sworn promise, that those who keep their part of the covenant shall come forth and inherit all things according to the promise."[16]

— **D&C 84:41 The penalty for breaking this covenant.** "Whoso breaketh this covenant after he hath received it, and *altogether turneth therefrom*, shall not have forgiveness of sins in this world nor in the world to come" (emphasis added).

— **D&C 84:42 The penalty for not receiving the priesthood and this covenant.** The Lord says simply, "And wo unto all those who come not unto this priesthood which ye have received." They will not obtain any of the blessings promised to those who receive the priesthood and keep their covenants and will live forever without them.

— **D&C 132:4–5 To obtain any blessing we must obey the associated covenants.** After revealing the "new and an everlasting covenant" of marriage, the Lord said, "If ye abide not that covenant, then are ye damned; for no one can reject this covenant and be permitted to enter into my glory" (v. 4). "For all who will have a blessing at my hands shall abide the law which was appointed for that blessing, and the conditions thereof, as were instituted from before the foundation of the world" (v. 5).

— **D&C 132:6 If we reject eternal marriage we will be damned.** "As pertaining to the new and everlasting covenant, it was instituted for the fulness of my glory; and he that receiveth a fulness thereof must and shall abide the law, or he shall be damned, saith the Lord God." This would include the scoffers who reject the entire idea of eternal marriage, those who do not keep their eternal marriage covenants, and those who purposefully avoid entering into this covenant. Those who cannot obtain such a marriage in this life (through no fault of their own) will have that opportunity granted unto them in the future and they are not damned.

— **D&C 132:7 The fate of things not sealed by the power of the Melchizedek priesthood.** The list of earthly things that fall into this category is lengthy: "All covenants, contracts, bonds, obligations, oaths, vows, performances, connections, associations, or expectations" that we may have in this life will end at death. Period.

They will be "of no efficacy, virtue, or force in and after the resurrection from the dead; for all contracts that are not made unto this end have an end when men are dead."

— **D&C 132:7 The fate of things that are sealed by the power of the Melchizedek priesthood.** Those things that are (1) "entered into and sealed by the Holy Spirit of promise;" (2) are performed by "him who is anointed" to perform such ordinances; and (3) are approved "by revelation and commandment through the medium of mine anointed [the President of the Church], whom I have appointed on the earth to hold this power," will endure for "time and all eternity" and will not end when we die.
This certainly applies to eternal marriages, which are performed by ordained sealers who have received their authority from the President of the Church. It would also apply to the ordinance of being "sealed up unto eternal life" [having one's calling and election made sure], which ordinance would only come by revelation from God to the Prophet and would be sealed under the Prophet's hand.

— **D&C 132:7 Only the Prophet administers sealing keys.** The Lord said, "I have appointed unto my servant Joseph to hold this power in the last days, and there is never but one on the earth at a time on whom this power and the keys of this priesthood are conferred." That person is the President of the Church. All Apostles are given these keys when ordained, but the only one who is authorized to administer them is the living Prophet, who is the senior Apostle. This is what the Lord meant when He said to Peter, "Whatsoever thou shalt bind on earth shall be bound in heaven" (Matt. 16:19; 18:18).

- **Hebrews 6:10–18 God will keep His promises if we remain faithful to the end.** Paul assured the Saints that "God [will not] forget your work and labour of love, which ye have shewed toward his name" while "minister[ing] to the saints" (v. 10). His promises to us are sure if we "shew the same diligence" with "the full assurance of hope unto the end [of our lives]" (v. 11). "Be not slothful," said Paul, "but [be] followers of them who through faith and patience [have] inherit[ed] the promises" (v. 12).

THEBIBLEREVIVAL.COM, #47

One of those whose example we should follow is Abraham, to whom the Lord promised because of his faith that "I will bless thee, and . . . I will multiply thee" (vv. 13–14). And then, "after he had patiently endured, he obtained the promise" (v. 15).

Men put great confidence in official oaths, covenants, treaties, etc., which we make to each other and by which we seek to obtain "an end of all strife" (v. 16). We can have even greater faith in the covenant promises of God, who demonstrated "unto the heirs of promise the immutability of his counsel [promises]" by "confirm[ing] it by an oath" (v. 17). And since we know that it is "impossible for God to lie," we can have "a strong consolation [peace and confidence]" in what He has promised (v. 18). This confidence is "an anchor of the soul, both sure and stedfast," that we will eventually "enter . . . into that [kingdom] within the veil" (v. 19).

— **D&C 82:10 God is bound by His promises.** He has said with clarity that "I, the Lord, am bound when ye do what I say; but when ye do not what I say, ye have no promise."

- **Hebrews 10:26–31 Those who break their covenants will be damned.** "If we sin wilfully after . . . we have received the knowledge of the truth, there remaineth no more sacrifice [atonement] for sins, but a certain fearful looking for . . . judgment and fiery indignation, which shall devour [the Lord's] adversaries" (v. 27). Paul reminded his Hebrew readers that those of their ancestors who "despised Moses' law died without mercy under two or three witnesses" (v. 28). "Of how much sorer punishment, suppose ye, shall he be thought worthy, who hath trodden under foot the Son of God," by considering "the blood of [His Atonement] . . . an unholy [unimportant] thing" or who has sinned "despite . . . the Spirit of grace" that Christ offers them (v. 29). The Lord has assured us that "vengeance belongeth unto [Him]" and He will both "recompense" and "judge" all men (v. 30). If we are sinful, said Paul, "It [will be] a fearful thing to fall into the hands of the living God" (v. 31).

FAITH

What Is Faith?

- **Hebrews 11:1 Paul's classic definition.** Paul called faith "the substance of things hoped for, the evidence of things not seen."

  In his inspired version of the Bible, the Prophet Joseph Smith substituted "assurance" for the word "substance" (JST Hebrews 11:1) Thus, faith is the assurance we have that we will receive the things for which we hope. For example, faith is my assurance that I will indeed be able to live with my precious wife and children in my Father's kingdom some day.

  Faith is also "the evidence of things not seen." Though I have not seen my Heavenly Father during this life, my faith provides all the evidence I need that He lives. It does this by qualifying me to receive blessings and answers to prayers, which, when I receive them, give me even greater assurance that He is there.

"SEEKING SHILOAH," ©JOSEPH BRICKEY, USED BY PERMISSION

- **Hebrews 11:2 By faith we receive a testimony.** Paul said that by faith "the elders obtained a good report." This means a testimony. First, by faith we believe. Then, in response to that faith we receive witnesses and blessings. And in turn, those witnesses and blessings increase our testimonies. It is an ever-upward spiral of confidence.

- **Hebrews 11:3 Faith is the power by which the worlds were created.** Paul taught that "through faith . . . the worlds were framed by the word of God." For example, when God said "let there be light," the elements responded to the power of His absolute faith and responded by forming an earth off which the sun's light could reflect. He did not need massive earth-moving equipment or other material means to accomplish the miracle of creation. His faith alone drove all the processes which were necessary.

  The Prophet Joseph Smith said:

  > Faith is not only the principle of action, but of power also, in all intelligent beings, whether in heaven or on earth. Thus says the author of the epistle to the Hebrews, xi. 3—"Through faith we understand that the worlds were framed by the word of God; so that things which are seen were not made of things which do appear."
  > By this we understand that the principle of power which existed in the bosom of God, by which the worlds were framed, was faith; and that it is by reason of this principle of power existing in the Deity, that all created things exist; so that all things in heaven, on earth, or under the earth exist by reason of faith as it existed in HIM. Had it not been for the principle of faith the worlds would never have been framed, neither would man have been formed of the dust. It is the principle by which Jehovah works, and through which He exercises power over all temporal as well as eternal things. . . . God spake, chaos heard, and worlds came into order by reason of the faith there was in HIM. . . .
  >
  > Faith, then, is the first great governing principle which has power, dominion, and authority over all things; by it they exist, by it they are upheld, by it they are changed, or by it they remain, agreeable to the will of God. Without it there is no power, and with out power there could be no creation nor existence![17]

- **Hebrews 11:3 The earth was made from existing materials.** Paul added an additional fact that we should not lightly skip over. He said, "Things which are seen were not made of things which do appear." In other words, the earth was not created by chance or by magic out of nothingness ("things which do appear [out of nothingness]").

PHOTO COURTESY OF NASA

  Elder Bruce R. McConkie said:

  > A difficult and obscure passage? Not really. Paul is simply saying that created things were not made of or by "things" which are seen. That is: All created things, this earth and all that is thereon—all things were and are made, not by man's power, not by some undirected forces of nature or of the universe. There was no happenstance in creation, no chance creation of life in primordial swamps, no development up from one species to another by evolutionary processes. The creation was planned, organized, and

> controlled. It came by God's power—by faith! It came by a power that does not appear and is not seen and understood by the carnal mind or the scientific intellect. The creation is God's doing. Things came into being by forces which do not appear to man and can in fact be known only by revelation. And as God created all things by faith, even so His created handiwork can be known and understood only by that same power, the power which is faith.[18]

Faith in Whom?

- **Hebrews 11:6 Our faith must be in Christ.** The world will sometimes acknowledge man's spiritual nature by admitting that some form of belief or faith is healthy. But the kind of faith that saves us eternally is not just any faith—it is faith in Christ. And without that faith "it is impossible to please him: for he that cometh to God must believe that he is, and that he is a rewarder of them that diligently seek him."

Elder Bruce R. McConkie said:

> Faith unto life and salvation centers in Christ. The first principle of the gospel is faith in the Lord Jesus Christ. It matters not who has faith or what age of the earth's history is involved; faith has been, is now, and everlastingly shall be in the Son of God.
>
> When Paul says Abraham, Isaac, and Jacob gained favor with God by faith, he is saying that they believed in Christ and worshiped the Father in His name the same as all the prophets of all the ages have always done. . . . Christ and His gospel laws have been known from the beginning, not just from the meridian of time, and no man has or ever will be saved except through faith in His holy name.[19]

"CHRIST PORTRAIT," ©JOSEPH BRICKEY, USED BY PERMISSION

- **Hebrews 11:4–31 Paul cites multiple examples of faith from the Old Testament.** These are those who have been exalted because of their obedience, sacrifice, and faith. They all exercised faith in Christ, even though they did not live to see Him, and were blessed because of their faith.

  — Abel's faith made his sacrifice more acceptable than Cain's (v. 4).
  — Enoch's faith made it possible for him and his people to be translated (v. 5).
  — Noah's faith led him to make the ark while the wicked condemned him and died (v. 7).
  — Abraham's faith took him to a strange land to establish God's purposes (vv. 8–10).
  — Sarah's faith allowed her to have a child in her old age through whom posterity more numerous than the stars would come to her (vv. 11–12).

"These all died in faith," said Paul, "not having received the promises [in this life], but having seen them afar off, and were persuaded of them, and embraced them" (v. 13). Faith was their "assurance of things hoped for" and their "evidence of things not seen" (v. 1). They readily "confessed that they were strangers and pilgrims on the earth" and they "declare[d] plainly that they [sought for] a country" of promise, not one of this earth (vv. 13–14). If they had "been mindful of [focused on] that country from whence they came out, they might have [sought an] opportunity to have returned" (v. 15). But because of their faith, "they desire[d] a better country, that is, an heavenly: wherefore God is not ashamed to be called their God: for he hath prepared for them a city" (v. 16).

— Abraham by faith nearly offered up his only covenant son Isaac, despite the fact that he had been told that his numerous posterity would come through Isaac (vv. 17–19).
— Isaac by faith prophesied concerning the future seed of Jacob and Esau (v. 20).
— Jacob by faith blessed all of his sons in his old age about the future of their seed (v. 21).
— Joseph by faith prophesied concerning Israel's future departure from Egypt (v. 22).
— Moses by faith rejected Pharaoh's riches to lead the Israelites from bondage (vv. 23–27)
— Moses by faith instituted the Passover in remembrance of Christ's future mission (v. 28)
— Moses by faith parted the Red Sea and performed other great miracles (v. 29).
— Joshua by faith caused the walls of Jericho to fall down (v. 30).
— Rahab by faith helped the Israelites and was spared from Jericho's destruction (v. 31).

- **Hebrews 11:32–38 A list of things endured and accomplished in the past through faith.** "And what shall I more say?" Paul asked. He didn't have sufficient time to discuss Gideon, Barak, Samson, Jephthah, David, Samuel, or any of the great prophets (v. 32).

The Old Testament is full of stories of faith, by which the righteous "subdued kingdoms, wrought righteousness, obtained promises, stopped the mouths of lions, quenched the violence of fire, escaped the edge of the sword, out of weakness were made strong, waxed valiant in fight, [and] turned to flight the armies of the aliens" (vv. 33–34).

"Women received their dead raised to life again: and others were tortured, not accepting deliverance; that they might obtain a better resurrection" (v. 35). Notice that Paul speaks of a "better resurrection" that can be obtained through faithfulness. All of God's children will be resurrected. But some will be resurrected with celestial bodies while others will not.

The Prophet Joseph Smith said: "Now it was evident that there was a better resurrection, or else God would not have revealed it unto Paul. Wherein then, can it be said a better resurrection? This distinction is made between the doctrine of the actual resurrection and translation: translation obtains deliverance from the tortures and sufferings of the body, but their existence will prolong as to the labors and toils of the ministry, before they can enter into so great a rest and glory. On the other hand, those who were tortured, not accepting deliverance, received an immediate rest from their labors. . . . They rest from their labors for a long time, and yet their work is held in reserve for them, that they are permitted to do the same work, after they receive a resurrection for their bodies."[20]

"And others [endured] trial[s] of cruel mockings and scourgings, yea, moreover of bonds and imprisonment: They were stoned, they were sawn asunder, were tempted, were slain with the sword: they wandered about in sheepskins and goatskins; being destitute, afflicted, tormented" (vv. 36–37). All of these—"of whom the world was not worthy"— "wandered in deserts, and in mountains, and in dens and caves of the earth" (v. 38).

And why did they endure these things? Paul said they obtained "a good report [testimony] through faith," and continued to believe, even though they personally "received not the promise" (the fullness of the gospel and its ordinances) (v. 39).

- **Hebrews 11:40 The dead cannot be made perfect without us.** The promises made to these "fathers" must be fulfilled by us. God "provided some better thing for us" by permitting us to do their ordinances for them. And because of this, "they without us [cannot] be made perfect." Nor can we be made perfect without them and their faithful examples, or if we neglect to do our promised work for faithful dead ancestors.

  The Prophet Joseph Smith said:

  > The greatest responsibility in this world that God has laid upon us is to seek after our dead. The Apostle says, "They without us cannot be made perfect;" (Hebrews 11:40) for it is necessary that the sealing power should be in our hands to seal our children and our dead for the fulness of the dispensation of times—a dispensation to meet the promises made by Jesus Christ before the foundation of the world for the salvation of man.
  >
  > Now, I will speak of them. I will meet Paul half way. I say to you, Paul, you cannot be perfect without us. It is necessary that those who are going before and those who come after us should have salvation in common with us; and thus hath God made it obligatory upon man.[21]

ACHIEVING PERFECTION

- **Hebrews 6:1–3 "Let us go on unto perfection."** The Bible reads, "Leaving the principles of the doctrine of Christ, let us go on unto perfection" (v. 1). Joseph Smith changed this to read "*not* leaving the principles of the doctrine of Christ, let us go on unto perfection" (JST Heb. 6:1; emphasis added).

  Paul said we do this by obeying the first principles—repentance, faith in God, baptism, and the laying on of hands—but not stopping there. We must go on to an understanding of the doctrines of "resurrection of the dead, and of eternal judgment" (v. 2). And ultimately, we must "go on unto perfection" (v. 1). "And this will we do, if God permit" (v. 3).

- **Hebrews 5:11–14 Perfection is "meat" compared to the "milk" of the first principles.** Paul had many meaty matters to discuss with the Saints of his day, but found them "hard to be uttered" because the members were "dull of hearing" (v. 11). Although they themselves "ought to be teachers, ye have need that one teach you again . . . the first principles of the oracles [scriptures] of God" (v. 12). Thus they were still in "need of milk, and not of strong meat," and "every one that useth milk is unskilful in the word of righteousness: for he is a babe" (vv. 12–13). The "strong meat" of the doctrines of resurrection, judgment, and degrees of exaltation belong to those that are "of full age" [mature in gospel knowledge] and have by "reason of use" [experience] have learned "to discern both good and evil" (v. 14).

Christ's Example

- **Hebrews 5:8–9 How Christ became perfect (exalted).** Paul taught that "though he were a Son, yet learned he obedience by the things which he suffered" (v. 8). He had to be tried and tested like all of us. "And being made perfect" [by His faithful endurance of those sufferings], he became the author of eternal salvation unto all them that obey him" (v. 9). According to the JST, Paul taught that no one can ever achieve perfection without enduring suffering faithfully (JST Hebrews 11:40).

  Elder Bruce R. McConkie said, "Christ always was perfect in that He obeyed the whole law of the Father at all times and was everlastingly the Sinless One (Heb. 4:14–16; 5:1–3). But on the other hand He was made perfect, through the sufferings and experiences of mortality, in the sense that He thereby died and was resurrected in glorious immortality. In that perfected state, possessing at long last a body of flesh and bones, He then had the same eternal perfection possessed by His Father. Hence His pronouncement, after the resurrection, that all power was given Him in heaven and in earth (Matt 28:18)."[22]

Jesus rejected the temptations of Satan

- **Hebrews 12:1–3 Christ is our example of faith and endurance.** Having summarized "so great a cloud of witnesses" in chapter 11 (see above), Paul invited the Saints to "lay aside every weight, and the sin which doth so easily beset us, and let us run with patience the race that is set before us" (v. 1). We can do this by "looking unto Jesus the author and finisher of our faith; who for the joy that was set before him endured the cross, despising the shame, and is set down at the right hand of the throne of God" (v. 2). Whenever we become "wearied and faint in [our] minds," we should "consider him [Christ] that endured such contradiction of sinners against himself" (v. 3).

The Need for Endurance

- **Hebrews 12:5–11 God tests and chastises those He loves.** Paul reminded the Hebrews of previous counsel they had received: "My son, despise not thou the chastening of the Lord, nor faint when thou art rebuked of him: For whom the Lord loveth he chasteneth, and scourgeth every son whom he receiveth" (vv. 5–6). When we "endure chastening" we should know that God is dealing with us like sons, "for what son is he whom the father chasteneth not?" (v. 7). If we are "without chastisement, whereof all are partakers, then are ye bastards, and not sons" (v. 8).

"Furthermore we have had fathers of our flesh which corrected us, and we gave them reverence: shall we not much rather be in subjection unto the Father of spirits, and live?" (v. 9). Our earthly fathers corrected us for "a few days" of our lives in ways that suited them ("after their own pleasure"), but God corrects us "for our profit, that we might be partakers of his holiness" (v. 10). Of course, "no chastening for the present seemeth to be joyous, but grievous: nevertheless afterward it yieldeth the peaceable fruit of righteousness unto them which are exercised thereby" (v. 11).

— **D&C 136:31 Those who cannot endure chastening will lose their inheritance.** My people must be tried in all things, that they may be prepared to receive the glory that I have for them, even the glory of Zion; and he that will not bear chastisement is not worthy of my kingdom.

Elder Orson F. Whitney said, "No pain that we suffer, no trial that we experience is wasted. It ministers to our education, to the development of such qualities as patience, faith, fortitude and humility. All that we suffer and all that we endure, especially when we endure it patiently, builds up our characters, purifies our hearts, expands our souls, and makes us more tender and charitable, more worthy to be called the children of God . . . and it is through sorrow and suffering, toil and tribulation, that we gain the education that we come here to acquire and which will make us more like our Father and Mother in heaven."[23]

Sanctification Through Christ

- **D&C 101:4–5 We must be tried "even as Abraham" in order to be sanctified.** The Lord declared, "They must needs be chastened and tried, even as Abraham, who was commanded to offer up his only son" (v. 4). And "all those who will not endure chastening, but deny me, cannot be sanctified" (v. 5).

  Elder Bruce R. McConkie said, "To be sanctified is to become clean, pure, and spotless; to be free from the blood and sins of the world; to become a new creature of the Holy Ghost, one whose body has been renewed by the rebirth of the Spirit. Sanctification is a state of saintliness, a state attained only by conformity to the laws and ordinances of the gospel. The plan of salvation is the system and means provided whereby men may sanctify their souls and thereby become worthy of a celestial inheritance. . . . Those who attain this state of cleanliness and perfection are able, as occasion may require, to see God and view the things of His kingdom (D&C 84:23; 88:68; Ether 4:7). The Three Nephites 'were sanctified in the flesh, that they were holy, and that the powers of the earth could not hold them' (3 Ne. 28:39)."[24]

  The Prophet Joseph Smith said, "You will have all kinds of trials to pass through. And it is quite as necessary for you to be tried [even] as . . . Abraham and other men of God . . . God will feel after you, and He will take hold of . . . and wrench your very heart strings, and if you cannot stand it you will not be fit for an inheritance in the Celestial Kingdom of God."[25]

The Prophet Joseph Smith also said, "It is in vain for persons to fancy to themselves that they are heirs with those, or can be heirs with them, who have offered their all in sacrifice, and by this means obtained faith in God and favor with Him so as to obtain eternal life, unless they, in like manner, offer unto Him the same sacrifice, and through that offering obtain the knowledge that they are accepted of Him."[26]

The Promised Reward

- **Hebrews 12:22–24 As members of the Church of the Firstborn, we will dwell with God and Christ in the celestial kingdom.** We will be called by the Lord to "come unto mount Sion [Zion], and unto the city of the living God, the heavenly Jerusalem, and to an innumerable company of angels" (v. 22). We might ask, "How many will be in this 'enumerable company' that will be exalted?" The answer is millions and millions, according to Daniel 7:10 and Revelation 5:11.

  We will become part of "the general assembly and church of the firstborn [those who have been exalted], which are written in heaven," and will dwell with "God the Judge of all, and . . . the spirits of just men made perfect" (v. 23). These will be our fellow-citizens in God's holy dwelling place.

  This "Church of the Firstborn" has no reference to the apostate group of the same name. It is the congregation of the exalted in our Father's presence.

  Elder Bruce R. McConkie said: "Members of The Church of Jesus Christ of Latter-day Saints who so devote themselves to righteousness that they receive the higher ordinances of exaltation become members of the Church of the Firstborn. . . . The Church of the Firstborn is made up of the sons of God, those who have been adopted into the family of the Lord, those who are destined to be joint-heirs with Christ in receiving all that the Father hath."[27]

  There we will meet "Jesus the mediator of the new covenant" (v. 24). Our presence there will be possible because of the "blood of sprinkling"—a reference to a symbolic act in the law of Moses that represented the people being cleansed of their sins by being sprinkled with the blood of a lamb that was sacrificed. Of course, this represented the blood of Christ that was shed so that we can repent and be forgiven of our sins. It is His blood and suffering, and that alone, that makes our sanctification and exaltation possible.

- **Hebrews 12:25–27 Unlike the children of Israel, when God calls to us we must listen and obey.** In another reference to the children of Israel at Mt. Sinai, Paul warns, "See that ye refuse not him that speaketh"—a reference to the fact that when the Lord invited the Israelites to come up on the mount to meet Him, they refused Him out of fear. "For if they escaped not who refused him that spake on earth, much more shall not we escape, if we turn away from him that speaketh from heaven" (v. 25). In those days, the Lord's voice "shook the earth," but at His Second Coming it will "shake not the earth only, but also heaven" (v. 26). This shaking of the earth is symbolic; it represents the process by which "things that are made" will be destroyed, while "those things which cannot be shaken may remain" (v. 27).

- **Hebrews 12:28–29 "Our God is a consuming fire."** As Saints who have "receiv[ed] a kingdom which cannot be moved," Paul warned that we must "have grace [charity]," and "serve God acceptably with reverence and godly fear: For our God is a consuming fire." What does it mean to say that "God is a consuming fire?"[28]
  - "God Almighty Himself dwells in eternal fire."[29]
  - The "fire" of the Second Coming is the actual presence of the Savior, a celestial glory comparable to the glory of the sun (D&C 76:70) or a "consuming fire" (Hebrews 12:29; Malachi 3:2; 4:1)
  - "So great shall be the glory of his presence that the sun shall hide his face in shame" (D&C 133:49)
  - "The presence of the Lord shall be as the melting fire that burneth, and as the fire which causeth the waters to boil" (D&C 133:41; Isaiah 64:2; JS-History 1:37)
  - "Element shall melt with fervent heat" (D&C 101:25) and "the mountains flow down at thy presence" (D&C 133:44)

TISSOT, 1904

- **Hebrews 12:12–15 We must maintain hope and faith, and help others to do so.** We are to "lift up the hands which hang down [the discouraged], and the feeble knees [the weak]" (v. 12). We are to "make straight paths for your feet" [set the example in our behavior], lest that which is lame [those who are weak] be turned out of the way [led astray]" (v. 13). "But let it rather be healed" means to help the "lame" [those who are weak] become stronger.

  "Follow peace with all men, and holiness, without which no man shall see the Lord" (v. 14). As leaders and fellow Saints we are to "look . . . diligently" [be careful] lest any man fail of the grace of God [turn away from Christ and His Atonement]" and "lest any root of bitterness springing up trouble you, and thereby many be defiled" (v. 15).

- **Hebrews 10:35–39 If we have patience and faith, we will inherit eternal life.** Life can be discouraging with all of its challenges and disappointments. But Paul counseled us to "cast not away . . . your confidence," because we will receive a "great recompence of reward" (v. 35). "For ye have need of patience, that, after ye have done the will of

God, ye might receive the promise" (v. 36). It will be "yet a little while" before Christ will come again and no longer tarry (v. 37). Until then, "the just shall live by faith" (v. 38). If some "draw back" from their progress toward salvation, "my soul shall have no pleasure in him" (v. 39). It will be very sad for them and for us. "But we are not of them who draw back unto perdition; but of them that believe to the saving of the soul" (v. 39).

OTHER CONCEPTS IN HEBREWS

Doctrinal Concepts

- **Hebrews 6:4–6 The fate of the sons of Perdition.** Paul taught that "it is impossible for those who were once enlightened, and have tasted of the heavenly gift, and were made partakers of the Holy Ghost, and have tasted the good word of God, and the powers of the world to come, . . . If they shall fall away, to renew them again unto repentance." This is because by their behavior "they crucify to themselves the Son of God afresh [again], and put him to an open shame" (v. 6). In other words, they deliberately deny the Lord and His atonement despite the fact that they have "tasted of the heavenly gift" [received revelation] by which they *know* that Christ lives and that He suffered for our sins. In this way, they "crucify to themselves the Son of God afresh, and put him to an open shame" (v. 6).

  The Prophet Joseph Smith said:

  > All sins shall be forgiven, except the sin against the Holy Ghost; for Jesus will save all except the sons of perdition.
  >
  > What must a man do to commit the unpardonable sin? He must receive the Holy Ghost, have the heavens opened unto him, and know God, and then sin against Him. After a man has sinned against the Holy Ghost, there is no repentance for him. He has got to say that the sun does not shine while he sees it; he has got to deny Jesus Christ when the heavens have been opened unto him, and to deny the plan of salvation with his eyes open to the truth of it; and from that time he begins to be an enemy. This is the case with many apostates of the Church of Jesus Christ of Latter-day Saints.
  >
  > When a man begins to be an enemy to this work, he hunts me, he seeks to kill me, and never ceases to thirst for my blood. He gets the spirit of the devil—the same spirit that they had who crucified the Lord of Life—the same spirit that sins against the Holy Ghost. You cannot save such persons; you cannot bring them to repentance; they make open war, like the devil, and awful is the consequence.[30]

- **Hebrews 6:8–9 A metaphor of fruitfulness.** Paul observed that "that which beareth thorns and briers is rejected, and is nigh unto cursing; whose end is to be burned" (v. 8). But to the Saints Paul said, "Beloved, we are persuaded [of] better things of you," because they did those "things that accompany salvation" (v. 9).

  A great number of thistles and thorns grew in the Holy Land and everywhere else around the Mediterranean Sea. Thus, they became useful as symbols for teaching by Jesus and His Apostles. Thistles and thorns represented affliction, distraction, and annoyance. They also sometimes represented the cares of this world and the deceitfulness of riches (Matthew 13:22; Mark 4:18–19; Luke 8:14). Thorns were never used to symbolize something good or positive. They were good for nothing except to be burned. Paul encouraged the Saints not to be "thorns."

- **Hebrews 8:8–12 The Gospel must be "written in our hearts."** Paul quoted a prophecy made by Jeremiah: "Behold, the days come, saith the Lord, when I will make a new covenant with the house of Israel and with the house of Judah: Not according to the covenant that I made with their fathers in the day when I took them by the hand to lead them out of the land of Egypt; because they continued not in my covenant, and I regarded them not, saith the Lord" (vv. 8–9; Jeremiah 31:31–32).

  Instead, "this is the covenant that I will make with the house of Israel [in] those days, saith the Lord; I will put my laws into their mind, and write them in their hearts: and I will be to them a God, and they shall be to me a people" (v. 10; Jeremiah 31:33).

  The Prophet Joseph Smith said:

  > This covenant has never been established with the house of Israel, nor with the house of Judah [until our day], for it requires two parties to make a covenant, and those two parties must be agreed, or no covenant can be made... Christ, in the days of His flesh, proposed to make a covenant with them, but they rejected Him and His proposals, and in consequence thereof, they were broken off, and no covenant was made with them at that time . . .
  >
  > Thus after this chosen family had rejected Christ and His proposals, the heralds of salvation said to them, 'Lo we turn unto the Gentiles'; and the Gentiles received the covenant, and were grafted in from whence the chosen family were broken off: but the Gentiles have not continued in the goodness of God, but have departed from the faith that was once delivered to the Saints, and have broken the covenant in which their fathers were established [see Isaiah 24:5]; and have become high-minded, and have not feared; therefore, but few of them will be gathered with the chosen family.[31]

  "And they shall not teach every man his neighbour, and every man his brother, saying, Know the Lord: for all shall know me, from the least to the greatest. For I will be merciful to their unrighteousness, and their sins and their iniquities will I remember no more" (vv. 11–12; Jeremiah 31:34–35).

  If we are truly God's people in this dispensation, the Gospel must be "written in our hearts," which means that it guides our every thought, word, and deed. We do not need to be commanded in all things like the children of Israel were in Moses' day. Nor do we have to have somebody else tell us that Christ lives and is our Head. We can and will know this for ourselves. And if we do these things, then the Lord will mercifully forgive us of our shortcomings and exalt us on high.

- **Hebrews 8:6–7 Christ is our Mediator with the Father.** His ministry is far "more excellent" than the law of Moses. He has become "the mediator of a better covenant, which was established upon better promises" (v. 6). A mediator is one who resolves differences between two parties. The Atonement of Christ reconciles us to God the Father, which the law of Moses could not do. "For if that first covenant [the law of Moses] had been faultless, then should no place have been sought for the second [the gospel of Jesus Christ]" (v. 7). We need a Mediator who can plead on our behalf and who has paid the price of our sins. That Mediator is the Lord, Jesus Christ.

- **Hebrews 9:15–17 "Where a testament is, there must also of necessity be the death of the testator."** Christ became "the mediator of the new testament" so that "by means of [His] death, . . . redemption [could be made for] the transgressions that were [committed] under the first testament [the law of Moses]," so that "they which [were] called [in Old Testament times as well as our own] might receive the promise of eternal inheritance" (v. 15). In other words, He died to save us all. And why did He need to die? Paul said that "where a testament is, there must also of necessity be the death of the testator" (v. 16). And such a testament must be "of force after men are dead"— "otherwise it is of no strength at all while the testator liveth" (v. 17).

CARL BLOCH

Elder Bruce R. McConkie said:

> In legal usage, a testator is one who leaves a valid will or testament at his death. The will or testament is the written document wherein the testator provides for the disposition of his property. As used in the gospel sense, a testament is a covenant. Jesus is the Mediator of the new covenant or testament, that is of the gospel which came to replace the law of Moses. . . .
>
> In other words, Christ had to die to bring salvation. The testament or covenant of salvation came in force because of the Atonement worked out in connection with that death. Christ is the Testator. His gift, as would be true of any testator, cannot be inherited until His death. Christ died that salvation might come; without His death, He could not have willed either immortality or eternal life to men.[32]

- **Hebrews 12:2 The shame of the cross.** Paul testified that "Jesus the author and finisher of our faith," out of pure love ("joy") "endured the cross, despising the shame [of such a death], and is set down at the right hand of the throne of God."

The fact that Jesus was crucified was "a stumbling block" to Jews and a sign of great folly to the Gentiles (1 Cor. 1:23; Gal. 5:11). Christians testified that Christ was chosen and sent by God and anointed to sit on the Father's right hand. But in the culture of the Jews, a person who was crucified was understood to be cursed by God (Deut. 21:23; Galatians 3:13). To the Gentiles it was "sheer folly" to proclaim the crucified Jesus as God's Son (1 Cor. 1:18) because of the extremely dishonorable form of His death—crucifixion. Only criminals and vagabonds were consigned to such a publicly humiliating execution.

- **Hebrews 13:4 Marriage is honorable.** Sexual intercourse is not evil; it is a vital part of God's great plan for us and for those spirits who are waiting for their opportunity to come to earth. "Marriage is honourable [for] all, and the bed undefiled," said Paul. In fact, Elder Bruce R. McConkie said that "to deliberately refrain from assuming marital or parental obligation is to fail the most important test of this mortal probation."[33]

  However, the illicit use of sex outside of marriage is evil, and "whoremongers" [those who sell sex acts] and adulterers will receive the judgments of God.

- **Hebrews 13:8 Christ is unchangeable.** He is "the same yesterday, and to day, and for ever." This eternal consistency is part of what gives us confidence in His promises. The same great Being who suffered for our sins will greet us with the same loving charity in our Father's kingdom in a future day. And the same Lord who revealed Himself to His apostles after the resurrection and taught them, is the same Lord who does likewise with His apostles today. Neither His love nor His methods of ministering to our needs have—or ever will—change.

- **Hebrews 13:22 The importance of being teachable.** Paul's only method of continuing to minister to Saints in far-away places was to "writ[e] a letter to you in a few words." So he pleaded with the Saints to "suffer the word of exhortation." This means to be teachable and to accept correction and chastening with humility.

- **Hebrews 13:9 Avoid false doctrines and false traditions.** Apostasy was already sweeping through the Church in Paul's day. He counseled the Saints to "be not carried about with divers and strange doctrines." He also advised them not to put their trust in the "meats" of sacrifice "which have not profited them that have been occupied therein" (v. 9). Going back to the old ways might feel comfortable, but it would not save them. Instead, he urged them to let their "heart[s] be established with grace"—seeking for forgiveness through the great sacrifice performed by our Savior.

- **Hebrews 13:10 "We have an altar,"** Paul said to the Christians, "whereof they have no right to eat which serve the tabernacle." The altar Paul refers to is the sacrament table upon which are placed the tokens of the Atonement of Jesus Christ, which may be partaken of by those who wish to make a covenant with Christ. Those who "serve the tabernacle" refers to the Levitical priests who performed ordinances in the ancient tabernacle and in the temple, and by extension, to unconverted Jews who still relied on the sacrifice of animals to obtain mercy from God.

Symbols of Christ in the Law of Moses

- **Hebrews 8:5 The ceremonies in the tabernacle and temple symbolized "heavenly things."** Paul called them a "shadow of heavenly things" which Moses was commanded to establish in and around the tabernacle in the wilderness. And because of the importance of the symbolism of these things Moses was charged "that thou make all things according to the pattern shewed to thee in the mount."

Ordinance in the tabernacle:	What it symbolized:
— The priests offered animals as sacrifices to God (Hebrews 10:1–4, 11).	Jesus offered Himself as a sacrifice for our sins (Hebrews 9:26–28; 10:4–12).
— The priests placed blood from the sacrificed animals on the altar to symbolize the cleansing and purification of the people (Hebrews 9:11–15).	Jesus' blood, shed during the Atonement, cleanses and purifies us from sin (Hebrews 9:6–7, 19–23).
— The high priest went through the veil into the Holy of Holies (Hebrews 9:1–7).	Jesus, the great high priest, went through the veil into heaven itself (Hebrews 9:24).

Elder Bruce R. McConkie said, "The form of the ordinance was always so arranged as to point attention to our Lord's sacrifice. The sacrificial offering made in connection with the Passover, the killing of the Paschal Lamb, for instance, was so arranged that a male lamb of the first year, one without spot or blemish, was chosen; in the offering the blood was spilled and care was taken to break no bones—all symbolical of the manner of Christ's death (Ex. 12). Many sacrificial details were added to the law as it operated in the Mosaic dispensation, but the basic principles governing sacrifices are part of the gospel itself and preceded Moses and the lesser order which came through him."[34]

- **Hebrews 9:22 The necessity of blood atonement.** According to the immutable laws of justice "almost all things are . . . purged with blood; and without shedding of blood [there] is no remission [of sins]."

  Remission of sins under the law of Moses required the shedding of an animal's blood. The Lord explained: "For the life of the flesh is in the blood: and I have given it to you upon the altar to make an atonement for your souls: for it is the blood that maketh an atonement for the soul" (Leviticus 17:11). In other words, blood is symbolic of life, and it was the life of Christ that was required to remit sins. (Mosiah 3:14–15).

- **Hebrews 13:11–13 Temple sacrifices symbolized Christ's atonement.** To show that animal sacrifices were symbolic of Christ's atonement, Paul noted that "the bodies of those beasts, whose blood is brought into the sanctuary [temple] by the high priest for sin, are burned without [outside of] the camp [city]" (v. 11). Likewise, "Jesus also, that he might sanctify the people with his own blood, suffered [outside of] the gate" (v.

12). "Let us go forth therefore unto him [outside of] the [city], bearing his reproach [with Him]" (v. 13).

- **Hebrews 6:19–20 The temple high priest passing through the veil of the temple was a symbol of Christ.** Christ is our "hope [and the] anchor of the soul, both sure and stedfast," when He "entereth . . . within the veil" (v. 19). This has reference to the one day per year when the High Priest would enter the Holy of Holies and sprinkle the blood of a sacrificed lamb upon the lid of the Ark of the Covenant. It is not coincidence that the lid was called the "mercy seat" and was the place where God and man were symbolically reconciled through this ordinance (see Exodus 25–40 and Leviticus 16). Where in the past a "forerunner [the high priest] . . . for us entered" in and made an offering for the people, so also "Jesus," who was "made an high priest for ever after the order of Melchisedec" (v. 20) enters into our Father's presence and makes an offering of His own blood on our behalf to make recompense for our sins.

THE HOLMAN BIBLE, 1890

- **Hebrews 8:1–3 Christ is our great High Priest.** Speaking of the supreme priesthood officer of the Aaronic and Levitical priesthoods, Paul declared that "we have such an high priest, who is set on the right hand of the throne of the Majesty in the heavens" (v. 1). Just as the temple high priest was the minister of the Jerusalem Temple (an earthly sanctuary), Christ is the minister of the heavenly sanctuary (celestial kingdom) who offered the ultimate sacrifice of Himself on our behalf (v. 2).

  Elder Bruce R. McConkie said, "As the high priest in Israel passed through the veil into the holy of holies on the day of atonement, as part of the cleansing rites which freed Israel from sin (Lev. 16), so Jesus has entered into heaven to prepare the way for those who through obedience to His laws become clean and pure."[35]

- **Hebrews 10:19–22 Christ is our High Priest and Mediator.** Because of His Atonement, we can with "boldness . . . enter into the holiest [place] by the blood of Jesus" (v. 19). The CES Institute manual for the New Testament says that "Paul capitalizes upon the Hebrew understanding of these things to indicate symbolically the role of Jesus in making it possible for us to enter into heaven, our 'holy of holies.' As in ancient times the high priest entered the earthly sanctuary through rites of purification, so we too are privileged to enter the heavenly sanctuary through the blood of Christ, which cleanses us from sin."[36]

"The ancient tabernacle and the temples patterned thereafter had veils which separated one portion of the structure from another. To pass the first veil was to move from the outer court into an inner sanctuary known as the Holy Place. To pass the second veil was to enter the Holy of Holies, or the Most Holy Place."[37]

Paul said the "new and living way" to enter into God's kingdom is the way that Christ "consecrated for us," which is by means of the suffering, death, and resurrection of His own body (v. 20). He is the "high priest over the house of God," to whom we should "draw near with a true heart in full assurance of faith, having our hearts sprinkled [cleansed] from an evil conscience, and our bodies washed with pure water" (vv. 21–22).

Elder Bruce R. McConkie said, "Atonement for sin is no longer made by the high priest in Israel when he passes through the veil of the temple into the holy of holies (Lev. 16). See Heb. 6:19–20. Now there is a new way, a living way, for the veil of the old temple was rent with the crucifixion (Matt. 27:50–51). Now Jesus has passed through the veil into heaven itself. While He lived, His mortal flesh stood between Him and the eternal holy of holies, for 'flesh and blood cannot inherit the kingdom of God' (1 Cor. 15:50), but now He has, as it were, rent the veil of His flesh through death and entered into the fulness of His Father's kingdom through resurrection."[38]

Notes

1. *Teachings of the Prophet Joseph Smith*, sel. Joseph Fielding Smith [1976], 59.
2. *Doctrinal New Testament Commentary*, 3 vols. [1965–1973], 3:133.
3. *Teachings of the Prophet Joseph Smith*, 191.
4. *Teachings of the Prophet Joseph Smith*, 168.
5. *Doctrinal New Testament Commentary*, 3:143.
6. *Gospel Doctrine*, 5th ed. [1939], 58.
7. *Teachings of the Prophet Joseph Smith*, 157.
8. *Teachings of the Prophet Joseph Smith*, 308.
9. *Doctrinal New Testament Commentary*, 3:157.
10. *Doctrinal New Testament Commentary*, 3:158.
11. *The Life and Teachings of Jesus and His Apostles* [CES manual, 1979], 385–386.
12. *Mormon Doctrine*, 2nd ed. [1966], 478. See *Teachings of the Prophet Joseph Smith*, 323.
13. *Mormon Doctrine*, 478.
14. *Mormon Doctrine*, 290–291.

15. *Teachings of the Prophet Joseph Smith*, 365.

16. *Mormon Doctrine*, 480.

17. *Lectures on Faith*, Lecture First, 13–16, 22, 24.

18. *Doctrinal New Testament Commentary*, 3:195.

19. *Doctrinal New Testament Commentary*, 3:211.

20. *Teachings of the Prophet Joseph Smith*, 170–171.

21. *Teachings of the Prophet Joseph Smith*, 356.

22. *Doctrinal New Testament Commentary*, 3:158.

23. As cited in Spencer W. Kimball, *Faith Precedes the Miracle* [1972], 98.

24. *Mormon Doctrine*, 675–676.

25. As quoted by John Taylor in *Journal of Discourses*, 24:197.

26. *Lectures on Faith*, Lecture Sixth, 8.

27. *Mormon Doctrine*, 139.

28. "Jesus Christ: Second Coming of Jesus Christ," in Daniel H. Ludlow, ed., *Encyclopedia of Mormonism*, 5 vols. [1992], 2:738.

29. *Teachings of the Prophet Joseph Smith*, 367.

30. *Teachings of the Prophet Joseph Smith*, 358.

31. *Teachings of the Prophet Joseph Smith*, 14–15.

32. *Mormon Doctrine*, 784–785.

33. *Doctrinal New Testament Commentary*, 3:236.

34. *Mormon Doctrine*, 665.

35. *Doctrinal New Testament Commentary*, 3:165.

36. *The Life and Teachings of Jesus and His Apostles* [CES manual, 1979], 391.

37. *The Life and Teachings of Jesus and His Apostles* [CES manual, 1979], 391.

38. *Doctrinal New Testament Commentary*, 3:190–191.

Chapter 38

Jerusalem & the Journey to Rome

(Acts 21–28)

INTRODUCTION

Many years before in Damascus, at the beginning of Paul's ministry, the Lord declared to Ananias His plans for Paul. He said Paul would preach the gospel "before the Gentiles, and kings, and the children of Israel" (Acts 9:15). Now, toward the end of his ministry, Paul had fulfilled every aspect of this prophecy except for "testifying before kings." The events that occurred on this fifth and final visit to Jerusalem fulfilled the prophecy. He returned to Jerusalem from the Greek city of Corinth, apparently late in February of 58 AD, after visiting with Church leaders at Ephesus. He wanted to be back in Jerusalem in time for Pentecost (approximately the first week in June).

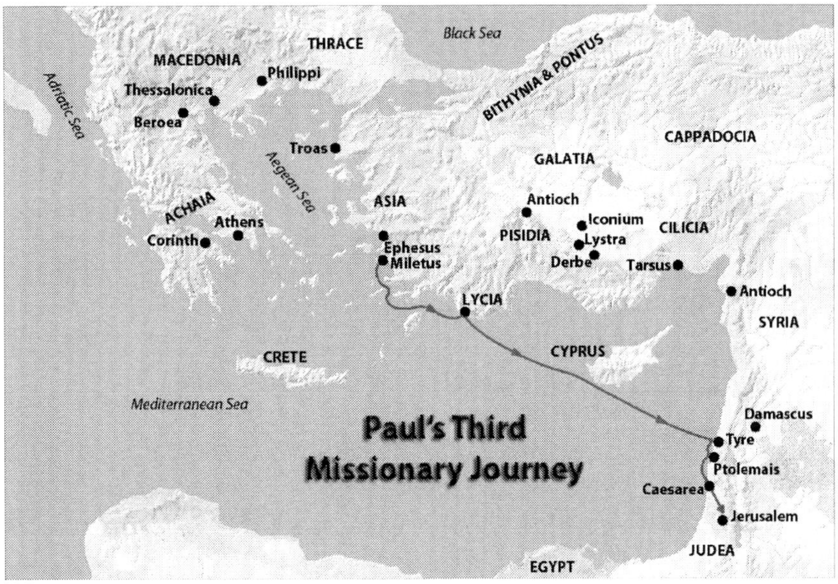

- **Acts 20:22–24 Paul is aware of the dangers he faces when he returns to Jerusalem.** He said to the leaders at Ephesus, "I go bound in the spirit unto Jerusalem, not knowing the things that shall befall me there: Save that the Holy Ghost witnesseth in every city, saying that bonds and afflictions abide me" (vv. 22–23). But he was not afraid to face these things. "None of these things move me, neither count I my life dear unto myself, so that I might finish my course with joy, and the ministry, which I have received of the Lord Jesus, to testify the gospel of the grace of God" (v. 24).

- **Acts 21:1–4 Paul sails to Tyre.** From Miletus, Paul sailed to Lycia, then past the island of Cyprus and on to Tyre on the Mediterranean coast of Phoenicia (see map on previous page). He stayed there for a week with several convert friends.

- **Acts 21:4–6 The Saints in Tyre try to discourage Paul from going to Jerusalem.** When Paul left Tyre, his friends, troubled by promptings from the Spirit that he might be in danger, tried to dissuade him from going on to Jerusalem (v. 4). Nevertheless, he departed, and as he did so, his friends and their wives and children followed him "out of the city" where they "kneeled down on the shore, and prayed" (v. 5). Then Paul "took ship" and set sail for home (v. 6).

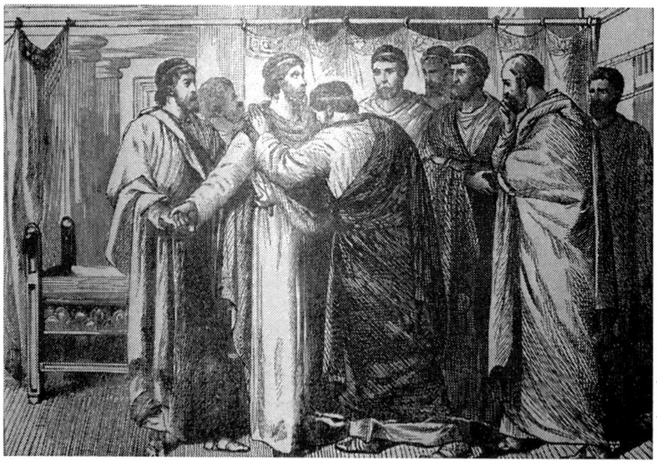

THE HOLMAN BIBLE, 1890, #55

- **Acts 21:7–9 Paul visits with Philip in Caesarea.** His ship stopped briefly at Ptolemais, and then at Caesarea (see map on previous page). While there, he stayed with Philip, a well-known Church leader and missionary (v. 8; Acts 6:5; 8:5–13, 26–40). By this time, Philip had become an "evangelist" (Patriarch) in the Church (v. 8). Philip also had four spiritually-sensitive daughters who had the gift of prophecy (v. 9).

  Elder Bruce R. McConkie said, "Though men are appointed to hold rule in the home and in the Church, women are not one whit behind them in spiritual endowments. They prophesy, receive visions, entertain angels (Alma 32:23), enjoy the gifts of the Spirit, and qualify with their husbands for full exaltation in the highest heaven."[1]

- **Acts 21:10–12 The prophet Agabus predicts Paul's imprisonment at Jerusalem.** We have read of this prophet before, when he came to Antioch and predicted a severe worldwide drought (Acts 11:28). On this occasion he came to Caesarea from Judea, "took Paul's girdle, and bound his own hands and feet, and said, Thus saith the Holy Ghost, So shall the Jews at Jerusalem bind the man that owneth this girdle, and shall deliver him into the hands of the Gentiles" (v. 11). That was enough to cause Luke (the writer of Acts) and the others who were there to plead with him "not to go up to Jerusalem" (v. 12).

- **Acts 21:13–14 Paul is willing to die for Christ.** He said to his friends at Caesarea, "What mean ye to weep and to break mine heart? for I am ready not to be bound only, but also to die at Jerusalem for the name of the Lord Jesus" (v. 13). And so, Luke wrote, "when he would not be persuaded, we ceased," saying to him, "The will of the Lord be done" (v. 14).

Events at the Temple

James, the Lord's brother

- **Acts 21:17–19 Paul reports to the Apostles, including James the brother of Jesus.** Remembering that it was Luke who wrote the Acts of the Apostles, we are getting his report of what happened. He said, "And when we were come to Jerusalem, the brethren received us gladly. And the day following Paul went in with us unto James [the brother of the Lord]; and all the elders were present" (vv. 17–18). This would seem to indicate that James was now an apostle himself and a member of the First Presidency. Perhaps he replaced the first James, the brother of John, who was martyred by Herod Agrippa at Jerusalem in 44 AD. The James that Paul went in to see on this occasion was the brother of the Lord. "And when he [Paul] had saluted them, he declared particularly what things God had wrought among the Gentiles by his ministry" (v. 19).

- **Acts 21:20–26 Paul satisfies Jewish members of the Church by publicly performing an ordinance belonging to the law of Moses.** The brethren were pleased when they heard Paul's report and "glorified the Lord" for his success. But they had a problem. They said to Paul, "Thou seest, brother, how many thousands of Jews there are which believe; and they are all zealous of the law: And they are informed of thee, that thou teachest all the Jews which are among the Gentiles to forsake Moses, saying that they ought not to circumcise their children, neither to walk after the customs" (vv. 20–21). This ought not to have been an issue; it had already been decided many years before in the first Jerusalem Council. That Council ruled that Gentile converts did not need to be circumcised but should not eat meat offered to idols or commit adultery (Acts 15:28–29).

  Nevertheless, some Jewish converts still held on to their traditional ways and considered "unclean" any member who had not first obeyed the law of Moses by being circumcised. "What is it therefore?," the brethren asked Paul, meaning "What shall we do?" "The multitude must needs come together: for they will hear that thou art come" (v. 22). They feared a disturbance.

  "Do therefore this," they said unto Paul: "We have four men which have a vow on them; Them take, and purify thyself with them, and be at charges [pay their expenses] with them, that they may shave their heads" (vv. 23–24). These four men, like Paul, were all Jews. They were about to enter the temple to make a Nazarite vow, which required their purification over a number of days and the shaving of their heads at the end of those days. The authorities advised Paul to go in with them and do the same thing so that "all may know that those things, whereof they were informed concerning thee, are nothing; [and] that thou thyself also walkest orderly, and keepest the law" (v. 24).

The brethren admitted that "as touching the Gentiles which believe, we have written and concluded that they observe no such thing, save only that they keep themselves from things offered to idols, and from blood, and from strangled, and from fornication" (v. 25). But they wanted to perform these ordinances publicly to avoid conflict and allow him to teach the gospel. "Then Paul took the men, and the next day purifying himself with them entered into the temple, to signify the accomplishment of the days of purification, until that an offering should be offered for every one of them" (v. 26).

- **Acts 21:27–30 Paul is accused of bringing Gentiles into the sacred precincts very near the Temple.** This was beyond the Court of the Gentiles, the general area on the temple mount where anyone could go; it was in the immediate area surrounding the temple itself, which was protected by walls. Jews believed that if any Gentile entered that area they would pollute or desecrate the holy place.

There were in the city at that time some "Jews which were of Asia," the area around Ephesus where Paul taught and was viciously opposed by the Jews there. "When they saw him in the temple, [they] stirred up all the people, and laid hands on him, Crying out, Men of Israel, help: This is the man, that teacheth all men every where against the people, and the law, and this place: and further brought Greeks also into the temple, and hath polluted this holy place" (vv. 27–28).

DORÉ, 1896

This was not true. "They had seen . . . with him in the city Trophimus an Ephesian, whom they supposed that Paul had brought into the temple" (v. 29). Nevertheless, despite their error, "all the city was moved, and the people ran together: and they took Paul, and drew him out of the temple: and forthwith the doors were shut" (v. 30).

Arrested by the Roman Guards

- **Acts 21:31–36 The prompt action of a Roman captain saves Paul's life but also makes him a Roman prisoner.** As the mob sought to kill Paul, word was sent to the captain of the Roman garrison there, Claudius Lysias, that "all Jerusalem was in an uproar" (v. 31). He "immediately took soldiers and centurions, and ran down unto them: and when they saw the chief captain and the soldiers, they left beating of Paul" (v. 32). The chief captain then took Paul and "bound [him] with two chains; and demanded who he was, and what he had done" (v. 33). Members of the crowd cried out conflicting information, so the captain commanded his soldiers to take Paul into the castle (v. 34). He did this because of "the violence of the people," who continued to follow after them, crying, "Away with him" (vv. 35–36).

- **Acts 21:37–40 Paul requests permission to speak again to the people of Jerusalem.** As Paul was being led into the castle, he said in Greek unto the chief captain, "May I speak unto thee?" The captain was astonished and asked, "Canst thou speak Greek?" (v. 37). The captain had mistaken Paul for an "Egyptian, which before these days madest an uproar, and leddest out into the wilderness four thousand men that were murderers" (v. 38). Paul answered that he was not that man, but was "a Jew of Tarsus, a city in Cilicia, a citizen of no mean city: and, I beseech thee, suffer me to speak unto the people" (v. 39). The captain agreed, after which "Paul stood on the stairs, and beckoned with the hand unto the people. And when there was made a great silence, he spake unto them in the Hebrew tongue" (v. 40). We are reminded by this incident that Paul was multilingual—he knew Hebrew, Greek, and probably Aramaic, which was the common spoken language of the people.

- **Acts 22:1–21 Paul testifies again concerning his conversion to Christianity.** Paul was a well-known figure in Jerusalem. He had once been a member of the Jewish Sanhedrin and actively worked to suppress the Christians. To many Jews in the city he was probably considered to be a traitor. Paul wanted them to hear his story (this was the third time during his ministry that he told it), and to testify of his vision of the Savior.

"Men, brethren, and fathers, hear ye my defence which I make now unto you. . . . I am verily a man which am a Jew, born in Tarsus, a city in Cilicia, yet brought up in this city at the feet of Gamaliel, and taught according to the perfect manner of the law of the fathers, and was zealous toward God, as ye all are this day. And I persecuted this way unto the death, binding and delivering into prisons both men and women. As also the high priest doth bear me witness, and all the estate of the elders: from whom also I received letters unto the brethren, and went to Damascus, to bring them which were there bound unto Jerusalem, for to be punished" (vv. 1–5).

DORÉ, 1896

"And it came to pass, that, as I made my journey, and was come nigh unto Damascus about noon, suddenly there shone from heaven a great light round about me. And I fell unto the ground, and heard a voice saying unto me, Saul, Saul, why persecutest thou me? And I answered, Who art thou, Lord? And he said unto me, I am Jesus of Nazareth, whom thou persecutest. And they that were with me saw indeed the light, and were afraid; [and] they heard not the voice of him that spake to me" (vv. 6–9). This statement corrects Acts 9:7, which says that they heard the voice but saw nothing.

"And I said, What shall I do, Lord? And the Lord said unto me, Arise, and go into Damascus; and there it shall be told thee of all things which are appointed for thee to do. And when I could not see for the glory of that light, being led by the hand of them that were with me, I came into Damascus. And one Ananias, a devout man according to the law, having a good report of all the Jews which dwelt there, came unto me, and stood, and said unto me, Brother Saul, receive thy sight. And the same hour I looked up upon him. And he said, The God of our fathers hath chosen thee, that thou shouldest know his will, and see that Just One, and shouldest hear the voice of his mouth. For thou shalt be his witness unto all men of what thou hast seen and heard. And now why tarriest thou? arise, and be baptized, and wash away thy sins, calling on the name of the Lord" (vv. 10–16).

"And it came to pass, that, when I was come again to Jerusalem, even while I prayed in the temple, I was in a trance; And saw him saying unto me, Make haste, and get thee quickly out of Jerusalem: for they will not receive thy testimony concerning me. And I said, Lord, they know that I imprisoned and beat in every synagogue them that believed on thee: And when the blood of thy martyr Stephen was shed, I also was standing by, and consenting unto his death, and kept the raiment of them that slew him. And he said unto me, Depart: for I will send thee far hence unto the Gentiles" (vv. 17–21).

- **Acts 22:22–29 Paul declares his Roman citizenship.** The Jews had listened to his testimony but were not moved. They "lifted up their voices, and said, Away with such a fellow from the earth: for it is not fit that he should live. And as they cried out, and cast off their clothes, and threw dust into the air" (vv. 22–23). Lysias then ordered him taken into the castle for questioning by torture—specifically scourging (v. 24). But "as they bound him with thongs, Paul said unto the centurion that stood by, Is it lawful for you to scourge a man that is a Roman, and un-condemned?" (v. 25). The answer is "no, it is not lawful," and had they proceeded they would have been condemned to great suffering themselves. The centurion hurried to the captain and informed him that Paul was a Roman citizen (v. 26).

  The chief captain came to Paul and asked him, "Art thou a Roman?" to which Paul replied, "Yea" (v. 27). The chief captain was also a Roman citizen, but had paid "a great sum [to] obtain . . . this freedom. And Paul said, But I was free born" (v. 28). All those around Paul immediately departed "and the chief captain also was afraid, after he knew that he was a Roman, and because he had bound him" (v. 29). The next day, "he loosed him from his bands, and commanded the chief priests and all their council to appear, and brought Paul down, and set him before them" (v. 30).

Tried Before the Sanhedrin

- **Acts 23:1–5 Paul speaks of his clear conscience before both God and men.** Paul, as he "earnestly [beheld] the council, said, Men and brethren, I have lived in all good conscience before God until this day. And the high priest Ananias commanded them that stood by him to smite him on the mouth" (vv. 1–2). "Then said Paul unto him, God shall smite thee, thou whited wall: for sittest thou to judge me after the law, and commandest me to be smitten contrary to the law?" (v. 3). Of course, Paul knew the law quite well and knew that what they had just done was contrary to the teachings of Moses. But this group of men were far more concerned about their good-standing with the Romans and their lucrative positions of power among the Jews, than they were about the law they so hypocritically pretended to defend. One of them "that stood by said, Revilest thou God's high priest?" (v. 4). And Paul answered, "I wist [knew] not, brethren, that he was the high priest: for it is written, Thou shalt not speak evil of the ruler of thy people" (v. 5).

  — **Acts 24:16–17 Paul was not a trouble-maker.** He strove to "have always a conscience void of offence toward God, and toward men" (v. 16). He viewed his visit to Jerusalem as a chance to "bring alms to my nation, and offerings" (v. 17).

- **Acts 23:6–10 Paul cleverly narrows the focus of the accusation to belief in the resurrection**—a subject on which the Sanhedrin did not agree. The Saducees among them did not believe in the resurrection, but the Pharisees did. Knowing this, Paul "cried out in the council, Men and brethren, I am a Pharisee, the son of a Pharisee: of the hope and resurrection of the dead I am called in question" (v. 6). This immediately produced "a dissension between the Pharisees and the Sadducees: and the multitude was divided" (v. 7).

"The Sadducees say that there is no resurrection," Paul declared, "neither angel, nor spirit: but the Pharisees confess both" (v. 8). This set off another argument, during which "the Pharisees . . . arose, and strove, saying, We find no evil in this man: [and] if a spirit or an angel hath spoken to him, let us not fight against God" (v. 9). This set off another "great dissension"—so much so that the chief captain, fearing that Paul might be pulled into pieces by them, "commanded the soldiers to go down, and to take him by force from among them, and to bring him into the castle" (v. 10).

THEBIBLEREVIVAL.COM, #23

- **Acts 23:11 Jesus appears to Paul for the third time.** The first had been on the road to Damascus. The second was in the temple before he departed on his mission. Now, on this night, as Paul sat in his cell in the castle, "the Lord stood by him, and said, Be of good cheer, Paul: for as thou hast testified of me in Jerusalem, so must thou bear witness also at Rome." This was an assurance that his life would be spared, but also a prophecy that he would yet testify in the capital city of the Roman Empire: Rome.

- **Acts 23:12–22 The plot against Paul involves conspiracy, secret oaths, and curses.** We are told that "certain of the Jews [about 40 of them] banded together, and bound themselves under a curse, saying that they would neither eat nor drink till they had killed Paul" (vv. 12–13). They went to the chief priests and elders, and said, "We have bound ourselves under a great curse, that we will eat nothing until we have slain Paul. Now therefore ye with the council signify to the chief captain that he bring him down unto you to morrow, as though ye would enquire something more perfectly concerning him: and we, or ever he come near, are ready to kill him" (vv. 14–15).

Paul's sister lived in Jerusalem, as did her son, Paul's nephew. Hearing of this conspiracy, he brought word of it to Paul (v. 16). Paul asked one of the guards to take his nephew to the chief captain because he had something important to tell him (v. 17). "So he took him, and brought him to the chief captain, and said, Paul the prisoner called me unto him, and prayed me to bring this young man unto thee, who hath something to say unto thee. Then the chief captain took him by the hand, and went with him aside privately, and asked him, What is that thou hast to tell me?" (vv. 18–19).

Paul's nephew informed the chief captain of their plot and of the fact that 40 people were lying in wait to kill Paul when and if the captain took him back down among them (v. 20). "[They] have bound themselves with an oath, that they will neither eat nor drink till they have killed him: and now are they ready, looking for a promise from thee" (v. 21). The chief captain sent Paul's nephew away with strict instructions to "tell no man that thou hast shewed these things to me" (v. 22).

- **Acts 23:23–24** Believing that he could not protect Paul forever among such blood-thirsty enemies, the chief captain sent Roman officers to escort Paul to Caesarea with 400 infantry and 70 cavalry.

  Then, to avoid a possible ambush, the contingent departed Jerusalem at the "third hour of the night" (9 PM). Paul was on his way to testify before two governors and a king.

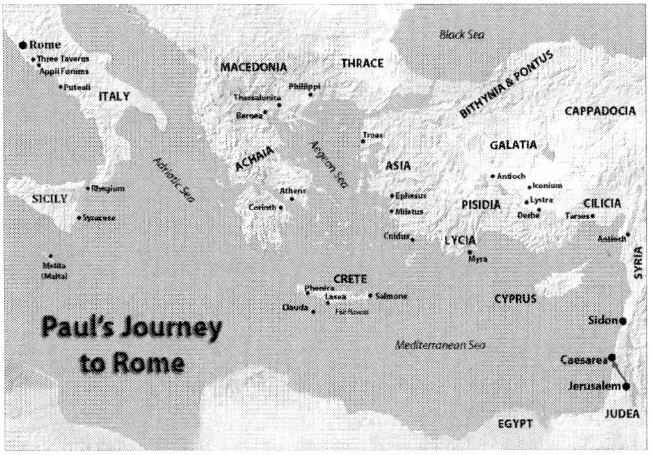

TESTIFYING BEFORE GOVERNORS AND KINGS

The Governor Felix

- **Acts 23:25–35 Paul is delivered to Antonius Felix.** Felix was appointed procurator [governor] of the territory that included Jerusalem in 52 AD. His wife was Drusilla, a sister of Herod Agrippa II and also a Jew. They were living in an adulterous relationship because Drusilla had left her husband and "married" Felix, thus violating Jewish law.

  The chief captain at Jerusalem sent a letter to Felix, explaining all the circumstances that now brought Paul to stand before him (vv. 25–28). He wrote that he did not believe that Paul had done anything "worthy of death or of bonds" (v. 29), but was sending both Paul and some of his accusers to Felix "to say before thee what they had against him" (v. 30). All of this was done (vv. 31–33). When Felix learned that Paul had been born in Cilicia, he agreed to hear the case (vv. 34–35). But he would not hear from Paul until his accusers had arrived, so he put him into Herod's judgment hall for safe-keeping (v. 35).

- **Acts 24:1–9 An eloquent orator accuses Paul.** Hired by the high priest and the elders, this man named Tertullus was supposed to "inform . . . the governor against Paul" (v. 1). He started by flattering the Roman Governor, "saying, Seeing that by thee we enjoy great quietness, and that very worthy deeds are done unto this nation by thy providence, We accept it always, and in all places, most noble Felix, with all thankfulness" (vv. 2–3). Then he began with his accusations against Paul. "We have found this man a pestilent fellow, and a mover of sedition among all the Jews throughout the world, and a ringleader of the sect of the Nazarenes" (v. 5). Furthermore, he accused Paul of "[going] about to profane the temple" (v. 6).

Tertullus complained that when they might have taken Paul and punished him for violating their religious laws, "the chief captain Lysias came upon us, and with great violence took him away out of our hands" (v. 7). He had now sent Paul and his accusers to Felix, who, by examining the case, could obtain "knowledge of all these things, whereof we accuse him" (v. 8). "And the Jews [who were there with Tertullus] also assented, saying that these things were so" (v. 9).

- **Acts 24:10–21 Paul energetically defends himself.** Paul began his response with a compliment to the governor for having "been of many years a judge unto this nation," and expressed his eagerness to defend himself (v. 10). He said to the governor, "There are yet but twelve days since I went up to Jerusalem for to worship. And they neither found me in the temple disputing with any man, neither raising up the people, neither in the synagogues, nor in the city: Neither can they prove the things whereof they now accuse me" (vv. 11–13). Paul did admit that "after the way which they call heresy, so worship I the God of my fathers" (v. 14). He believed "all things which are written in the law and in the prophets: and [had] hope . . . that there shall be a resurrection of the dead, both of the just and unjust" (vv. 14–15). Thus, Paul could not be convicted of creating a public disturbance or of believing in heresies since they themselves believed and taught these things.

  "I . . . have always a conscience void of offence toward God, and toward men," said Paul (v. 16). He had come back to Jerusalem "after many years . . . to bring alms to my nation, and offerings" (v. 17). His accusers were "certain Jews from Asia" (the same who had followed him from city to city for several years), and they "found me purified in the temple, neither with multitude, nor with tumult" (v. 18). They would only be justified in being "here before thee . . . if they had ought against me . . . [or] if they [had] found any evil doing in me, while I stood before the council, [but only] for this [charge], that I cried standing among them, [concerning] the resurrection of the dead [am I] called in question by you this day" (vv. 19–21).

- **Acts 24:22–27 Felix realizes that the accusations are matters of Jewish law and defers judgment on Paul** until "Lysias the chief captain shall come down, [and] I will know the uttermost of your matter" (v. 22). He placed Paul under house arrest, with liberty to move about and to receive visitors (v. 23). After a few days, "Felix came with his wife Drusilla, which was a Jewess, . . . and heard him concerning . . . faith in Christ" (v. 24). But after hearing Paul teach concerning "righteousness, temperance, and judgment to come, Felix trembled, and [said], Go thy way for this time; when I have a convenient season, I will call for thee" (v. 25). The truth is, Felix hoped that if he held onto Paul for awhile that Paul would bribe him, and for this reason "he sent for him the oftener, and communed with him" (v. 26). But after two years, no bribe had been forthcoming from Paul and "Porcius Festus came into Felix' room" [replaced him as governor]. In order to please the Jews, Felix left Paul bound as he left office, but Porcius Festus, the new procurator, agreed to hear Paul's case (v. 27).

The Governor Festus

THEBIBLEREVIVAL.COM, #20

- **Acts 25:1–8 Jewish leaders accuse Paul before Festus without any evidence.** Three days after coming into office, Festus visited Jerusalem (v. 1). There, "the high priest and the chief of the Jews informed him against Paul," and sought a favor from the new governor "that he would send for [Paul to come] to Jerusalem, laying [in] wait [along] the way to kill him" (vv. 2–3). But Festus declined, saying that "Paul should be kept at Cæsarea, and that he himself would depart shortly thither" (v. 4). If there were any among them who were able, he invited them to "go down with me, and accuse this man, if there be any wickedness in him" (v. 5).

  Ten days later, Festus returned to Cæsarea, and, "sitting on the judgment seat commanded Paul to be brought" (v. 6). "And when he was come, the Jews which came down from Jerusalem stood round about, and laid many and grievous complaints against Paul, which they could not prove" (v. 7). Paul "answered for himself, [that] neither against the law of the Jews, neither against the temple, nor yet against Cæsar, have I offended any thing at all" (v. 8).

- **Acts 25:9–12 "I appeal unto Caesar."** Willing to appease the Jews, Festus asked Paul if he would go to Jerusalem. The governor would go also, and Paul could then "be judged of these things before me" (v. 9). But Paul knew his life would be in danger and that the Lord intended for him to go to Rome. So he replied, "I stand at Cæsar's judgment seat, where I ought to be judged: to the Jews have I done no wrong, as thou very well knowest. For if I be an offender, or have committed any thing worthy of death, I refuse not to die: but if there be none of these things whereof these accuse me, no man may deliver me unto them. I appeal unto Cæsar" (vv. 10–11).

  Under Roman law, each citizen accused of crime had the right to be heard before the imperial seat. Paul was a Roman citizen, and now, for the second time, he used that citizenship to protect his life. After conferring with the Jews, Festus answered, "Hast thou appealed unto Cæsar? Unto Cæsar shalt thou go" (v. 12). He really had no other choice. And the Jews would be forever denied their wish to kill him.

King Herod Agrippa II

- **Acts 25:13–27 Herod Agrippa II visits Caesarea.** Before Paul could be sent to Rome, Agrippa (grandson of Herod the great) and his sister (and wife), Bernice, visited Festus at Caesarea (v. 13). While the king was there, Festus recounted Paul's case to him (vv. 14–19). He also said, "And because I doubted of such manner of questions, I asked him whether he would go to Jerusalem, and there be judged of these matters. But when Paul had appealed to be reserved unto the hearing of Augustus, I commanded him to be kept till I might send him to Cæsar" (vv. 20–21). "Then Agrippa said unto Festus, I would also hear the man myself," and Festus promised, "Tomorrow . . . thou shalt hear him" (v. 22).

  The next day Agrippa and Bernice came "with great pomp, and was entered into the place of hearing, with the chief captains, and principal men of the city, [and] at Festus' commandment Paul was brought forth" (v. 23). Festus introduced Paul as "this man, about whom all the multitude of the Jews have dealt with me, both at Jerusalem, and also here, crying that he ought not to live any longer" (v. 24). "But when I found that he had committed nothing worthy of death, and [because] he himself hath appealed to Augustus, I have determined to send him" (v. 25). The problem was, Festus had nothing to write by way of accusation in his letter to the emperor. Paul was guilty of no crime. He told Agrippa that he had "brought him forth before you, and specially before thee, O king Agrippa, that, after examination . . . I might have somewhat to write" (v. 26). He could hardly send a prisoner to Rome without "signify[ing] the crimes laid against him" (v. 27).

- **Acts 26:1–29 Paul relates his conversion story to Herod Agrippa II.** Agrippa said unto Paul, "Thou art permitted to speak for thyself," whereupon "Paul stretched forth the hand, and answered for himself" (v. 1). Here was the fulfillment of prophecy, as Paul now stood before a king to testify concerning Christ. He began by telling his own conversion story, which is so beautifully written that we will include it all here.

THEBIBLEREVIVAL.COM, #27

> I think myself happy, king Agrippa, because I shall answer for myself this day before thee touching all the things whereof I am accused of the Jews: Especially because I know thee to be expert in all customs and questions which are among the Jews: wherefore I beseech thee to hear me patiently.

My manner of life from my youth, which was at the first among mine own nation at Jerusalem, know all the Jews; Which knew me from the beginning, if they would testify, that after the most straitest sect of our religion I lived a Pharisee.

And now I stand and am judged for the hope of the promise made of God unto our fathers: Unto which promise our twelve tribes, instantly serving God day and night, hope to come. For which hope's sake, king Agrippa, I am accused of the Jews.

Why should it be thought a thing incredible with you, that God should raise the dead? I verily thought with myself, that I ought to do many things contrary to the name of Jesus of Nazareth. Which thing I also did in Jerusalem: and many of the saints did I shut up in prison, having received authority from the chief priests; and when they were put to death, I gave my voice against them. And I punished them oft in every synagogue, and compelled them to blaspheme; and being exceedingly mad against them, I persecuted them even unto strange cities. Whereupon as I went to Damascus with authority and commission from the chief priests,

"WHAT SHLL I DO LORD?" ©WALTER RANE, USED BY PERMISSION

At midday, O king, I saw in the way a light from heaven, above the brightness of the sun, shining round about me and them which journeyed with me. And when we were all fallen to the earth, I heard a voice speaking unto me, and saying in the Hebrew tongue, Saul, Saul, why persecutest thou me? it is hard for thee to kick against the pricks.

And I said, Who art thou, Lord? And he said, I am Jesus whom thou persecutest. But rise, and stand upon thy feet: for I have appeared unto thee for this purpose, to make thee a minister and a witness both of these things which thou hast seen, and of those things in the which I will appear unto thee; Delivering thee from the people, and from the Gentiles, unto whom now I send thee, To open their eyes, and to turn them from darkness to light, and from the power of Satan unto God, that they may receive forgiveness of sins, and inheritance among them which are sanctified by faith that is in me.

Whereupon, O king Agrippa, I was not disobedient unto the heavenly vision: But shewed first unto them of Damascus, and at Jerusalem, and throughout all the coasts of Judæa, and then to the Gentiles, that they should repent and turn to God, and do works meet for repentance. For these causes the Jews caught me in the temple, and went about to kill me.

Having therefore obtained help of God, I continue unto this day, witnessing both to small and great, saying none other things than those which the prophets and Moses did say should come: That Christ should suffer, and that he should be the first that should rise from the dead, and should shew light unto the people, and to the Gentiles [vv. 2–23).

At this juncture, Festus interrupted with a loud voice, saying, "Paul, thou art beside thyself; much learning doth make thee mad" (v. 24). But Paul continued his witness.

> But he said, I am not mad, most noble Festus; but speak forth the words of truth and soberness. For the king knoweth of these things, before whom also I speak freely: for I am persuaded that none of these things are hidden from him; for this thing was not done in a corner [vv. 25–26].

Then, turning to the king, Paul asked a piercing question:

> King Agrippa, believest thou the prophets? I know that thou believest. Then Agrippa said unto Paul, Almost thou persuadest me to be a Christian.
>
> And Paul said, I would to God, that not only thou, but also all that hear me this day, were both almost, and altogether such as I am, except these bonds [vv. 27–29].

Elder Neal A. Maxwell noted that "Agrippa's comment ["almost thou persuadest me to be a Christian"] was not [a] flippant [one; he was seriously touched]."[2] Paul's testimony also touched the Prophet Joseph Smith, who had similar experiences of accusation after he told people about his first vision. Indeed, Joseph Smith compared himself to Paul on many occasions (see JS–History 1:23–25).

- **Acts 26:30–32 Festus and Agrippa agree that Paul is "not guilty."** When Paul concluded his defense, "the king rose up, and the governor, and Bernice, and they that sat with them: And when they were gone aside, they talked between themselves, saying, This man doeth nothing worthy of death or of bonds" (vv. 30–31). Indeed, he might have been set free at this point if he had not appealed to Caesar (v. 32).

JOURNEY TO ROME

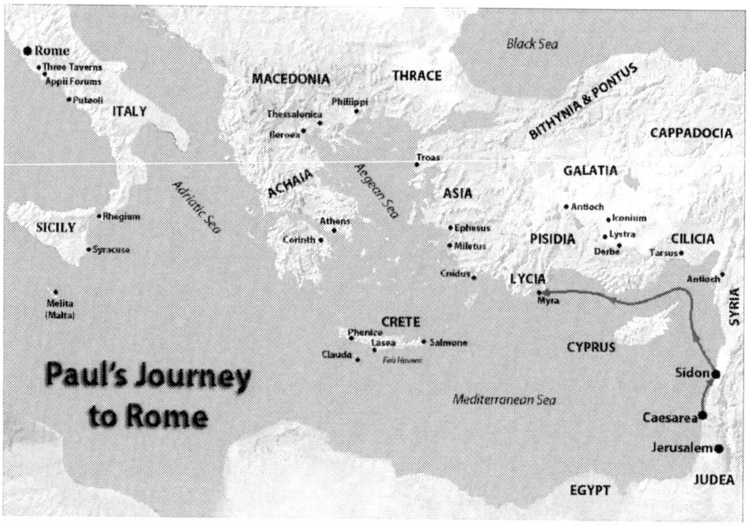

- **Acts 27:1–5 The journey to Myra.** Paul traveled with other prisoners and with a man named Aristarchus on a ship bound for Italy. They were guarded by a man named "Julius, a centurion of Augustus' band" (v. 1).

  The ship left Caesarea and sailed north to Sidon, where they rested for a day. "Julius courteously entreated Paul, and gave him liberty to go unto his friends to refresh himself" (v. 3).

After their day's rest, they sailed on toward Italy. Because of unfavorable wind conditions they did not take the direct route, but sailed around the north side of the island of Cyprus and landed at Myra in the province of Lycia (vv. 4–5).

- **Acts 27:6–8 The journey to Lasea.** Boarding a different ship at Myra, Paul and his fellow-travelers sailed west toward Cnidus. "And there the centurion found a ship of Alexandria sailing into Italy; and he put us therein" (v. 6).

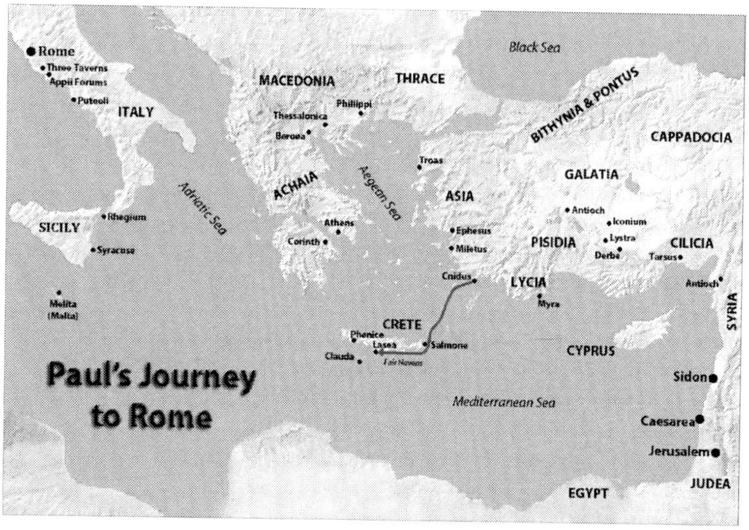

They continued their journey toward Italy, but sailed very slowly because the winds were not favorable. After many days they had hardly left the vicinity of Cnidus (v. 7). So, once again, they could not take the direct route toward Italy and decided to sail under rather than over the island of Crete, and they landed at Lasea (v. 8).

Heeding a Prophet's Voice

- **Acts 27:9–11 Paul's warnings of danger are ignored.** The ship and its passengers was forced to spend many days at Lasea because "the fast was now already past" and sailing was dangerous (v. 9). "The fast" Paul refers to is Yom Kippur, the Day of Atonement, which occurs each year between September and October. After that date, ocean waters were very unsafe for travel until weather moderated again early the next spring.

Paul warned them, "Sirs, I perceive that this voyage will be with hurt and much damage, not only of the lading and ship, but also of our lives" (v. 10). But the master and owner of the ship did not agree with Paul and the centurion guard "believed [him] more than those things which were spoken by Paul" (v. 11). So, they sailed on.

- **Acts 27:12–20 Difficulties at sea from Clauda to Malta.** Lasea was "not commodious to winter in" so they sailed west toward Phenice on the western end of the island of Crete (v. 12). They set forth from Lasea in fair weather, and hoped to stay close to the island as they went. But shortly thereafter they encountered vicious winds, and were forced to "let her drive" on her own and the ship traveled "under a certain island which is called Clauda" (vv. 14–16).

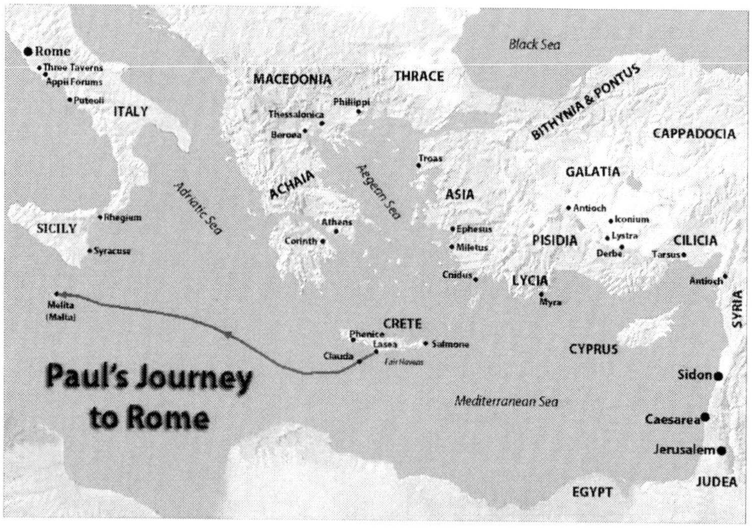

The men onboard "had much work" to try to gain control of the ship, and fearing that they might be driven into quicksands they "strake sail, and so were driven" (vv. 16–17). Then, "being exceedingly tossed with a tempest, the next day they lightened the ship" by throwing things overboard (v. 18). By the third day, "we cast out with our own hands the tackling of the ship" (v. 19). They had not seen the sun or the moon in "many days," and since "no small tempest lay on us, all hope that we should be saved was then taken away" (v. 20). They felt certain that they were going to die. But Paul knew better.

THEBIBLEREVIVAL.COM, #20

- **Acts 27:21–26 Paul prophesies that they will not die based on the words of an angel.** Paul had long abstained from saying anything, but finally "stood forth in the midst of them, and said, Sirs, ye should have hearkened unto me, and not have loosed from Crete, and to have gained this harm and loss" (v. 21). But now he exhorted them to "be of good cheer: for there shall be no loss of any man's life among you;" only the ship would be harmed (v. 22).

Paul had been promised by the Lord while at Jerusalem that he would yet testify in Rome. But additionally, he told the men that "there stood by me this night the angel of God, whose I am, and whom I serve, Saying, Fear not, Paul; thou must be brought before Cæsar: and, lo, God hath given thee all them that sail with thee" (vv. 23–24). Paul concluded, "Wherefore, sirs, be of good cheer: for I believe God, that it shall be even as it was told me" (v. 25), and he prophesied that they would "be cast upon a certain island" (v. 26).

- **Acts 27:27–32 When they are about to flee the ship, Paul advises them to stay.** Despite Paul's prophecy of eventual safety, after 14 days they were still being "driven up and down in Adria [the Adriatic Sea], [and] about midnight the shipmen deemed that they drew near to some country" (v. 27). They "sounded" to determine their distance from shore, and found that they were indeed heading toward land (v. 28). "Then fearing lest we should [fall] upon rocks, they cast four anchors out of the stern, and wished [waited] for the day" (v. 29). The tempest continued, and "the shipmen were about to flee out of the ship," lowering down a small boat into the sea while pretending to be "cast[ing] anchors" out of the ship (v. 30). Paul warned "the centurion and . . . the soldiers, [that] except these abide in the ship, ye cannot be saved" (v. 31). So "the soldiers cut off the ropes of the boat" that they had hoped to escape in, "and let her fall off" (v. 32).

- **Acts 27:41–44 As promised, they find land—the island of Melita (Malta).** The "violence of the waves" eventually "ran the ship aground; and the forepart stuck fast, and remained unmoveable, but the hinder part was broken" (v. 41). They now had no choice but to leave the ship, and "the soldiers' counsel was to kill the prisoners, lest any of them should swim out, and escape" (v. 42).

  "But the centurion, willing to save Paul, kept them from their purpose; and commanded that they which could swim should cast themselves first into the sea, and get to land" (v. 43). Those who could not swim, "some on boards, and some on broken pieces of the ship" floated to safety; "and so it came to pass, that they escaped all safe to land" (v. 44). Paul's prophecy was fully fulfilled.

DORE, 1896 IN THEBIBLEREVIVAL.COM, #27

Elder Spencer W. Kimball said, "The authorities which the Lord has placed in His Church constitute for the people of the Church a harbor, a place of refuge, a hitching post, as it were. No one in this Church will ever go far astray who ties himself securely to the Church Authorities whom the Lord has placed in His Church. . . . And those people who stand close to them will be safe."[3]

Miracles on Malta

- **Acts 28:1–6 Paul receives no harm from a snake bite.** Learning that the island on which they found safety was "Melita" (Malta), they received "no little kindness" from the "barbarous people" who lived there; "they kindled a fire, and received us every one, because of the present rain, and because of the cold" (vv. 1–2).

  THEBIBLEREVIVAL.COM, #20

  Paul "gathered a bundle of sticks, and laid them on the fire, [when] there came a viper [poisonous snake] out of the heat, and fastened on his hand" (v. 3). Seeing the snake "hang on his hand," the locals "said among themselves, No doubt this man is a murderer, whom, though he hath escaped the sea, yet vengeance suffereth not to live" (v. 4). But Paul "shook off the beast into the fire, and felt no harm" (v. 5).

  They fully expected that he would become "swollen, or fall . . . down dead suddenly: but after they had looked a great while, and saw no harm come to him, they changed their minds, and said that he was a god" (v. 6).

- **Acts 28:7–10 Paul uses his priesthood to heal Publius' father and others.** The "chief man of the island" was named Publius, and he had a home in the same area where Paul and his shipmates had landed. He invited them to stay at his home and "lodged us three days courteously" (v. 7). At that time, "the father of Publius lay sick of a fever and of a bloody flux," so "Paul entered in, and prayed, and laid his hands on him, and healed him" (v. 8). Seeing this, "others also, which had diseases in the island, came, and were healed" by Paul (v. 9). Because of this, the inhabitants of the island "honoured us with many honours; and when we departed [after three months], they laded us with such things as were necessary" (v. 10).

On to Rome

Because of Paul's miracles, the islanders treated Paul and the others kindly. They stayed on the island for three months until the weather improved. Then it was time to move on to their final destination: Rome. The Lord's promise, given many months earlier at Jerusalem, that Paul would "bear witness also at Rome" (Acts 23:11) would now be fulfilled.

- **Acts 28:11–14 Journey to Puteoli.** The missionaries boarded a ship and continued their journey to Rome. They sailed first to Syracuse on the island of Sicily, then after three days rest they passed between Sicily and Italy at Rhegium, and sailed north to Puteoli, a port on the western side of southern Italy. They found Church members there, who invited them to stay for seven days rest, after which they continued on foot toward Rome (v. 14).

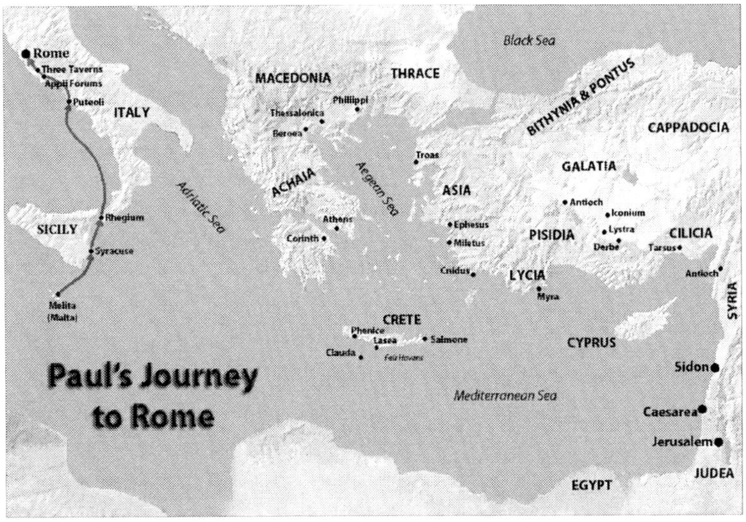

- **Acts 28:15 The journey north toward Rome on the Appian Way.** The Appian Way is perhaps the most famous of all Roman roads, stretching from Capua to Rome. Once, after a slave rebellion led by Spartacus, 6,000 slaves were crucified on poles along the whole length of this road.

  Paul's party traveled north along this road, and "when the brethren [in Rome] heard of us, they came to meet us as far as Appii forum, and The three taverns: whom when Paul saw, he thanked God, and took courage."

CAROLSFELD, 1852-60

EVENTS AT ROME

- **Acts 28:16–19 At Rome, Paul is allowed relative freedom, which he uses to teach the gospel.** When they arrived at Rome, "the centurion delivered the prisoners to the captain of the guard: but Paul was suffered to dwell by himself with a soldier that kept him" (v. 16).

THEBIBLEREVIVAL.COM, #30

After three days rest, as was always his practice, Paul began preaching first to the Jews of the city. He "called the chief of the Jews together: and when they were come together, he said unto them, Men and brethren, though I have committed nothing against the people, or customs of our fathers, yet was I delivered prisoner from Jerusalem into the hands of the Romans. Who, when they had examined me, would have let me go, because there was no cause of death in me. But when the Jews spake against it, I was constrained to appeal unto Cæsar; not that I had ought to accuse my nation of" (vv. 17–19).

- **Acts 28:20–29 Paul teaches them concerning Jesus, the Messiah, and some of them believe.** Paul testified to the Jews that "for the hope of Israel [Christ] I am bound with this chain" (v. 20). "And they said unto him, We neither received letters out of Judæa concerning thee, neither any of the brethren that came shewed or spake any harm of thee. But we desire to hear of thee what thou thinkest: for as concerning this sect, we know that every where it is spoken against" (vv. 21–22). And they "appointed him a day," when he could preach to them (v. 23).

PROVIDENCE LITHOGRAPHIC CO., 1897, #41

When that day came, "there came many to him into his lodging; to whom he expounded and testified the kingdom of God, persuading them concerning Jesus, both out of the law of Moses, and out of the prophets, from morning till evening. And some believed the things which were spoken, and some believed not" (vv. 23–24). So, seeing that "they agreed not among themselves, they departed" (v. 25).

As they departed, Paul said to them, "Well spake the Holy Ghost by Esaias the prophet unto our fathers, Saying, Go unto this people, and say, Hearing ye shall hear, and shall not understand; and seeing ye shall see, and not perceive: For the heart of this people is waxed gross, and their ears are dull of hearing, and their eyes have they closed; lest they should see with their eyes, and hear with their ears, and understand with their heart, and should be converted, and I should heal them" (vv. 25–27). "Be it known therefore unto you, that the salvation of God is sent unto the Gentiles, and that they will hear it" (v. 28). "And when he had said these words, the Jews departed, and had great reasoning among themselves" (v. 29).

- **Acts 28:30–31 For two more years, Paul preaches in Rome.** The Lord had promised that Paul would preach the Gospel at Rome, and although officially a prisoner, he was able to teach and testify, "no man forbidding him." He lived in "his own hired house, and received all that came in unto him, Preaching the kingdom of God, and teaching those things which concern the Lord Jesus Christ, with all confidence."

THE EPISTLES FROM ROME

Paul also had time during these two years to write many epistles to Saints in other areas where he had taught. He wrote at least four epistles while in Rome.

Paul Wrote to the Colossians from Rome, about AD 61

Paul Wrote to Philemon from Rome, AD 61

Paul Wrote to the Ephesians from Rome, AD 61

Paul Wrote to the Philippians from Rome, AD 62

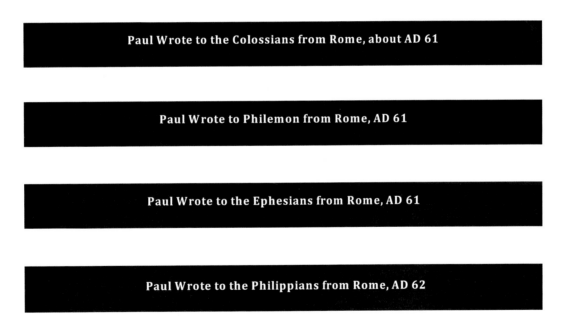

Notes

1. *Doctrinal New Testament Commentary*, 3 vols. [1965–1973], 2:181.

2. "Taking Up the Cross," BYU Fireside Address, 4 January 1976. In Neal A. Maxwell, *The Inexhaustible Gospel: Speeches of Neal A. Maxwell* [2004].

3. In Conference Report, April 1951, 104.

Chapter 39

Perfecting the Saints

(Ephesians)

EPHESIANS

When and Where Was Ephesians Written?

The epistle to the Ephesians was written during Paul's first imprisonment in Rome, 61–62 AD.

Why Was Ephesians Written?

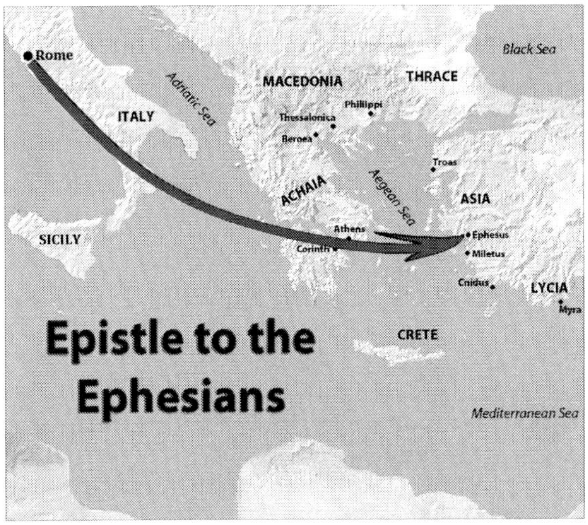

Ephesians may have been an epistle for a variety of branches in Asia. It provides a summary of Church doctrine and organization., but its deeper purpose is to teach how we can set aside the things of this world in order to seek for greater godliness. It is a deeply spiritual sermon that is directed to members of the Church who have considerable spiritual maturity and understanding. The depth of its teachings can be appreciated more when we realize that many of the Saints at Ephesus were righteous enough to have been sealed up to eternal life (Ephesians 1:13).

Many of the doctrines taught in Ephesians are very familiar to the Latter-day Saints. It speaks of foreordination, the dispensation of the fulness of times, the importance of apostles and prophets in the Church, the idea that there is only one true and unified church, and that the proper organization of the Church is essential. We also find some of the most clear teachings on the roles of the members of a family and the importance of family life itself. Also Paul writes about "grace" twelve times and "peace" seven times in Ephesians.

OUR PAST AND OUR DESTINY

God and Our Pre-Mortal Life

- **Ephesians 1:1, 3 As usual, Paul opens with a distinction between the Father and the Son** and with a statement of his apostolic authority. "Paul, an apostle of Jesus Christ by the will of God," wrote to "the saints which are at Ephesus, and to the faithful in

Christ Jesus" (v. 1). He wishes both grace and peace for them (v. 2), and he acknowledges that God "hath blessed us with all spiritual blessings in heavenly places in Christ" (v. 3).

- **Ephesians 1:3, 17 He refers to the Father as the "God of our Lord, Jesus Christ."** (John 20:17). He speaks of our Heavenly Father as "the God and Father of our Lord Jesus Christ," making it clear that the two are not the same person (v. 3). This idea is repeated in verse 17 where he calls the Father "the God of our Lord Jesus Christ, the Father of glory," and prays that the Father "may give unto you the spirit of wisdom and revelation in the knowledge of him" (v. 17).

- **Ephesians 1:4–5 "Predestinated" means foreordained.** Paul taught that God "hath chosen us in him before the foundation of the world, that we should be holy and without blame before him in love" (v. 4). The phrase "before the foundation of this world" clearly speaks of things before the world was made—our premortal life. The idea of being "chosen" does not mean "selected by decree to succeed;" that would be predestination. To be chosen is to be given a particular calling or responsibility. Based upon our actions in premortal life, God called us to serve Him in this life. We exercise our agency by accepting or rejecting that call; it is a matter determined by our choices in this life.

  Paul said that God had "predestinated us unto the adoption of children by Jesus Christ to himself, according to the good pleasure of his will" (v. 5). We must read this phrase carefully to understand what he meant.

  — Predestinated. In King James' time, predestination did not have the same connotation as it does today. Most modern versions translate the Greek word as "foreordain." It is not an irrevocable decree of destiny but rather a divine declaration of trust.

  — Unto the adoption of children. This phrase is taken from the Abrahamic covenant, whereby the Gentiles can become "adopted" children of Abraham and entitled to all his blessings. Paul's calling (and ours), given to us in the premortal life, is to seek out and bring into the Church those who are born outside of it.

  — By Jesus Christ to Himself. The way that we all become purified and exalted enough to dwell in the Father's presence is through the Atonement of Jesus Christ.

  — According to the good pleasure of His will. God's will has always been and will always be the salvation and exaltation of His children. This phrase does not refer to predestination but to the overall plan by which we are saved.

  Thus, what Paul is saying in his unique and difficult-to-understand way, is that God has chosen [foreordained, assigned] us to work for the salvation of people not of this Church, and, through Christ, to return them back to Him again. That is the plan of salvation.

The Dispensation of the Fullness of Times

"JOSEPH SMITH PORTRAIT," ©JOSEPH BRICKEY, USED BY PERMISSION

- **Ephesians 1:9–10 Paul speaks of our own latter-day dispensation**, and suggests that what is happening to them will have an important role in the restoration. God had made known to the early Saints, and Paul in particular, the "mystery" of what would happen in the latter days (v. 9). They had been taught that "in the dispensation of the fulness of times he might gather together in one all things in Christ, both which are in heaven, and which are on earth" (v. 10).

  President Gordon B. Hinckley taught, "You and I are experiencing the profound and wonderful blessings of the dispensation of the fulness of times. In this day and time there have been restored to the earth all of the principles, powers, blessings, and keys of all previous dispensations."[1]

Sealed by the Holy Spirit

- **Ephesians 1:11–14 Being "sealed with that Holy Spirit of promise" is having one's calling and election made sure.**[2] Paul taught that members of the Church have "obtained an inheritance" in God's kingdom, "being predestinated [foreordained] to serve in that kingdom "according to the purpose of him who worketh all things after the counsel of his own will" (v. 11). And as we do this, we become "the praise of his glory" (v. 12).

  Those early Saints "who first trusted in Christ" after hearing "the word of truth, the gospel of your salvation," were afterward ["after that ye believed"] "sealed with that holy Spirit of promise" (vv. 12–13). This blessing—which comes only to those who have demonstrated their faith under all circumstances—was to have their calling and election in God's kingdom "made sure." The Holy Spirit "seals" (verifies, like a notary public does) that a person has achieved this state of righteousness. We will discuss this doctrine more fully in 2 Peter 1:4–19.

  Such a sealing "is the earnest of [down payment on] our inheritance—an assurance that we will, indeed, be saved. And such a person remains in that state "until the redemption of the purchased possession [the saved soul] unto the praise of his glory" (v. 14).

- **Ephesians 1:18 "The eyes of your understanding being enlightened"** is a phrase that comes from a Greek figure of speech which means "the enlightenment of the whole man" through the gospel of Jesus Christ. Paul prayed that "the eyes of your understanding [may be] enlightened; that ye may know . . . the hope of his calling [what it means to be chosen of God], and . . . the riches of the glory of his inheritance" [the glorious blessings that await all faithful Saints].

- **Ephesians 1:21–23 Paul emphasizes the exalted status of Christ.** Christ is "far above all principality, and power, and might, and dominion, and every name that is named, not only in this world, but also in that which is to come: And hath put all things under his feet" (vv. 21–22). God our Father "gave him [Christ] to be the head over all things to the church" (v. 22), which Paul metaphorically called "his body, the fulness of him that filleth all in all" (v. 23). Thus, the Church in this instance is called the "body of Christ."

  Elder Bruce R. McConkie said: "In the Lectures on Faith, Joseph Smith describes the Father and the Son as 'filling all in all' because the Son, having overcome, has 'received a fulness of the glory of the Father,' and possesses 'the same mind with the Father.' Then he announces the conclusion to which Paul here only alludes: 'And all those who keep His commandments shall grow up from grace to grace, and become heirs of the heavenly kingdom, and joint-heirs with Jesus Christ; possessing the same mind, being transformed into the same image or likeness, even the express image of Him who fills all in all; being filled with the fulness of His glory, and become one in Him, even as the Father, Son and Holy Spirit are one'[3]."[4]

Saved by the Grace of Christ

- **Ephesians 2:1–5 The Saints are made alive in Christ.** Though we may have been "dead in trespasses and sins," yet we are "quickened" [made alive] through Christ (v. 1).

  "In time[s] past ye walked according to the course of this world, according to the prince of the power of the air [Satan]," who is "the spirit that now worketh in the children of disobedience" (v. 2). In those times past, we have had "conversation" [a relationship with] "the lusts of our flesh, fulfilling the desires of the flesh and of the mind; and were by nature the children of wrath, even as others" (v. 3).

  "But God, who is rich in mercy, [because of] his great love [for] us, even when we were dead in sins, hath quickened us together with Christ" (vv. 4–5). Then Paul appended a note to this teaching: "(by grace ye are saved)." The point of this statement is to remind us that the only way we can be rescued from our sins is through the saving grace of Christ's Atonement. We do not save ourselves.

- **Ephesians 2:6–7 The full extent of God's love and grace** will be apparent when we find ourselves in the celestial kingdom. As His children, God has "raised us up together, and made us sit together in heavenly places in [through] Christ Jesus" (v. 6). "That in the ages to come he might shew the exceeding riches of his grace in his kindness toward us" (v. 7). These riches of eternity, according to Paul, are beyond our imagining. Only when we see and receive them will we fully know the extent of God's love for us.

- **Ephesians 2:8–10 Ultimately, we are saved by grace.** Paul next clarified his earlier statement about being saved through grace. "For by grace are ye saved through faith" means that our faith in Christ is what saves us. This is because His Atonement can remove the stain and liability we would otherwise have to bear for all the sins that we have committed.

  Paul wants us to understand that, in the end, salvation is "not of yourselves: it is the gift of God" (v. 8). And it does not come by works "lest any man should boast" (v. 9). But God has also "ordained" [intended] that we should do "good works" also (v. 10). Those works alone cannot save us, but obedience to God's commandments cannot be ignored. Paul taught that there must be a balance.

  The grace versus works controversy that has arisen out of Paul's words is never-ending. But if one were to claim that grace is more important than works, or that works are more important than grace, they would have to ignore one-half of what Paul actually said. As in this verse, Paul consistently taught that both are necessary. C. S. Lewis said that arguing that one of these elements is more important than the other is "like asking which blade in a pair of scissors is [more] necessary."[5]

- **Ephesians 4:8–9 Christ made death subject to Him, thereby freeing us from its bonds.** When Christ "ascended up on high, he led captivity captive" as a "gift . . . unto men" (v. 8). This means that He conquered death through His resurrection, and by so doing provided the same opportunity for all of our Father's children.

"THE LIVING CHRIST," ©JOSEPH BRICKEY, USED BY PERMISSION

  This also applies to those in spirit prison, whom Christ visited before He ascended up on high. Paul taught that before He ascended, "he also descended first into the lower parts of the earth" [the place where people in Paul's day believed that the spirits of the dead live]" (v. 9).

LIVING LIKE SAINTS

The Church of Jesus Christ

- **Ephesians 2:11–12 The condition of those who are without the gospel.** Paul asked the Gentiles to remember the days when they were "Gentiles in the flesh" and were called the "Uncircumcis[ed]" by those who called themselves the "Circumcis[ed]" [the Jews], who believed in the importance of this token "in the flesh made by hands" (v. 11). "At that time ye were without Christ, being aliens from the commonwealth of Israel, and strangers from the covenants of promise, having no hope, and without God in the world" (v. 12). This is a clear statement of the state of those in any age who do not know the truth about who they are and what they might become.

- **Ephesians 2:19–22 The condition of those who have been baptized into the Church of Jesus Christ.** When a man or woman chooses to be baptized, they are "no more strangers and foreigners, but fellowcitizens with the saints, and of the household of God" (v. 19). To be of one's "household" was to be a family member or dear friend. Paul extends the metaphor by talking about what makes a house strong: "[Ye] are built upon the foundation of the apostles and prophets, Jesus Christ himself being the chief corner stone" (v. 20).

  Thus, without apostles and prophets and the direct participation of Christ in a church, it will not be the household of God and will eventually fall. It is through the apostles and prophets that "all the building fitly framed together groweth unto an holy temple in the Lord"—one that can be "an habitation of God through the Spirit" (vv. 21–22).

- **Ephesians 3:3–8 Christ's Church is led by revelation.** Paul did not receive his call to the apostleship or his doctrine from school or from another man. He said that "by revelation he [Christ] made known unto me the mystery [revealed teachings] . . . of Christ," which Paul was now delivering to the Saints (vv. 3–4). A "mystery" is a sacred truth made known by revelation.

  Some of these teachings "in other ages [were] not made known unto the sons of men, as it is now revealed unto his holy apostles and prophets by the Spirit" (v. 5). For example, by revelation the Church in Paul's day learned "that the Gentiles should be fellowheirs, and of the same body, and partakers of his promise in Christ by the gospel" (v. 6). That was new doctrine, received by revelation from Jesus Christ.

  By that same process—revelation—Paul was "made a minister, according to the gift of the grace of God given unto me by the effectual working of his power" (v. 7). He marveled that "unto me, who am less than the least of all saints, is this grace given, that I should preach among the Gentiles the unsearchable riches of Christ" (v. 8). We get a glimpse here of Paul's humility and the sacredness of his calling.

- **Ephesians 4:11–14 The officers of the Church and its mission or purpose.** Paul did not insert the commas in these verses; the King James Translators did that. And they were wrong. Paul is talking about the various officers of Christ's Church, not a host of different churches being led by a different type of leader. In order to perfect the organization of His Church, Christ provided "some apostles; and some prophets; and some evangelists; and some, pastors and teachers" (v. 11). We know what most of these officers do, but Paul uses three terms that need explanation.

  — <u>Evangelist</u>: The Prophet Joseph Smith said: "An Evangelist is a Patriarch. . . . Wherever the Church of Christ is established in the earth, there should be a Patriarch for the benefit of the posterity of the Saints, as it was with Jacob in giving his patriarchal blessing unto his sons, etc."[6]

— Pastor: The Latin word means "shepherd," one who leads a flock, as does a bishop or stake president. The term is translated variously in the English New Testament as "pastor," "shepherd," or "bishop."

— Saints: The English word "saint" comes from the Latin *sanctus* and is used to translate the Greek *hagios* in the New Testament. All of these terms mean "holy ones"—those who are trying to become a holy people. The term in no way conveys sinlessness or any suggestion of superiority over other people. The members of the Church are given the name because they are attempting to live a holy life.

Richard Lloyd Anderson developed the following chart to compare all of the officers of the Church in Paul's day to their present-day equivalents. Dr. Anderson's information is taken from the scriptures indicated in the chart.

Church Officers In Paul's Time[7]

Scripture Refs:	Office Titles, Meanings, and Present-Day Equivalents:				
Ephesians 4:11	**Apostle**	**Prophet**	**Evangelist**	**Pastor**	**Teacher**
Greek term:	*apóstolos*	*prophétēs*	*evangelistēs*	*poimén*	*didáskalos*
Meaning:	"one sent;" special messenger	"forthteller" or "foreteller"	bringer of good news	shepherd	teacher
Equivalent:	Apostles	Prophets	Patriarchs	Quorum & Aux Presidents	Teachers
1 Cor. 12:28	**Apostle**	**Prophet**	**Help**	**Government**	**Teacher**
Greek term:	*apóstolos*	*prophétēs*	*antílēmpsis*	*kubérnēsis*	*didáskalos*
Meaning:	"one sent;" special messenger	"forthteller" or "foreteller"	help or aid	director or administrator	teacher
Equivalent:	Apostles	Prophets	Church workers	Presidents	Teachers
Local officers *		**Deacon**	**Elder**	**Bishop**	* These offices taken from 1 Tim.3; Titus; Acts 14:23; Philippians 1:1
Greek term:		*diákonos*	*presbúteros*	*epískopos*	
Meaning:		servant	elder (civic office)	overseer	
Equivalent:		Deacons	Elders	Bishops	

All of these were necessary "for the perfecting of the saints, for the work of the ministry, for the edifying of the body of Christ" (v. 12). They will continue to be necessary "till we all come in the unity of the faith, and [with a] knowledge of the Son of God, [having achieved the status of] a perfect man, [who has achieved the] measure of the stature of the fulness of Christ" (v. 13). That will not happen until the Millennium, and so these named officers are still necessary in our own time and will be until Christ comes again. Their purpose is to ensure that "we henceforth be no more children, tossed to and fro, and carried about with every wind of doctrine, by the sleight of men, and cunning craftiness, whereby they lie in wait to deceive" (v. 14). They are Christ's bulwark against heresy and apostasy.

- **Ephesians 4:5 "One Lord, one faith, one baptism."** There is only one Savior for all mankind: Jesus Christ. And He has only one faith [Church] that represents Him. And if we want membership in that Church we must submit to the one method of baptism He requires, as performed by one who is authorized by Christ to do so. Already in Paul's day there were "wolves" among the members who were teaching false doctrines and leading people away into false churches with false and unauthorized ordinances. That is why Paul made this statement.

Being Children of Light

- **Ephesians 4:18–19 The state of the wicked.** They have had their "understanding darkened, being alienated from the life of God through the ignorance that is in them, because of the blindness of their heart" (v. 18). And eventually, "being past feeling have given themselves over unto lasciviousness, to work all uncleanness with greediness" (v. 19). People of the world alienate themselves from God by refusing to look to Him, by becoming "past feeling," and by giving themselves over to lasciviousness [immoral desires]. Members of Christ's Church are expected to do better—to live by the light they have been given.

- **Ephesians 5:4–6 A list of sins to avoid.** Paul warned the Ephesians against "filthiness" [immoral behavior] and against "foolish talking" and "jesting," which means, among other things, the use of polished and clever speech to accomplish evil things. Instead, Paul advises "convenient" [appropriate] speech and the giving of thanks (v. 4).

  "For this ye know, that no whoremonger, nor unclean person, nor covetous man, who is an idolater, hath any inheritance in the kingdom of Christ and of God. Let no man deceive you with vain words: for because of these things cometh the wrath of God upon the children of disobedience" (vv. 5–6).

- **Ephesians 5:8–13 The righteous are children of light; the wicked are children of darkness.** Speaking to converts, Paul reminded them that they "were sometimes [full of] darkness, but now are ye [full of] light in the Lord" and counseled them to "walk as children of light" (v. 8). He said that the Spirit would lead them to "all goodness and righteousness and truth," and would "Prov[e] [test and testify of] what is acceptable unto the Lord" (vv. 9–10).

  Paul counseled that Saints should "have no fellowship with the unfruitful works of darkness, but rather reprove them. For it is a shame even to speak of those things which are done of them in secret" (vv. 11–12). Such things "are made manifest by the light" [of Christ] and "whatsoever doth make manifest is light" (v. 13).

Righteous Relationships

- **Ephesians 4:25–32 Practical advice on how to dwell together in love as Saints.** Paul made many lists in his epistles. This one is a list of things we should remember as we live together with our neighbors and fellow members of the Church.

  — "Put . . . away lying, speak every man truth with his neighbour" (v. 25).

  — If you are angry, "sin not: let not the sun go down upon your wrath" (v. 26).

  — "Neither give place to the devil" (v. 27).

  — "Let him that stole steal no more: but . . . let him labour, working with his hands [that] which is good, that he may have to give to him that needeth" (v. 28).

  — "Let no corrupt communication proceed out of your mouth, but that which is good [and] edifying, that it may minister grace unto the hearers" (v. 29).

  — "Grieve not the holy Spirit of God, whereby ye are sealed unto the day of redemption" (v. 30).

  — "Let all bitterness, and wrath, and anger, and clamour, and evil speaking, be put away from you, [along] with all malice" (v. 31).

  — "And be ye kind one to another, tenderhearted, forgiving one another, even as God for Christ's sake hath forgiven you" (v. 32).

- **Ephesians 5:15–21 Characteristics of good relationships.** This list by Paul mentions wisdom, respect for time, spiritual inspiration, good music, and a willingness to submit to others.

  — "See then that ye walk circumspectly, not as fools, but as wise" (v. 15).

  — "Redeeming [making good use of] time, because the days are [full of] evil" (v. 16).

  — "Be ye not unwise, but understanding what the will of the Lord is" (v. 17).

  — "Be not drunk with wine, wherein is excess; but be filled with the Spirit" (v. 18).

  — "Speak . . . [among] yourselves in psalms and hymns and spiritual songs, singing and making melody in your heart to the Lord" (v. 19).

  — "Giv[e] thanks always for all things unto God and the Father in the name of our Lord Jesus Christ" (v. 20).

  — "Submit . . . yourselves one to another in the fear of [reverence for] God" (v. 21).

- **Ephesians 5:22–24 The relationship of wives to their husbands.** Paul counseled wives to "submit yourselves unto your own husbands" in the same way you would submit "unto the Lord" (v. 22). The comparison Paul makes in this verse is important to understanding what he meant. For example, "submitting as you would submit unto the Lord" means "following in righteousness," not blindly agreeing to every word or act without thought. And if a husband is doing evil, then he is not at all like the Lord, and the wife's need to follow him ceases when he chooses evil.

THEBIBLEREVIVAL.COM, #22

  In a family of Christians, "the husband is the head of the wife, even as [in the same way that] Christ is the head of the church" (v. 23). Again, we may look to the example Paul provided in order to understand his counsel. How did the Lord lead the Church? That is how Paul taught that husbands should preside in a home. Paul also said that the husband is "the saviour of [provider for] the body [family]" (v. 23).

  "Therefore as [in the same way that] the church is subject unto Christ, so let the wives be to their own husbands in every thing" (v. 24).

- **Ephesians 5:25–33 The relationship of husbands to their wives.** Paul continued the metaphor of Christ-like leadership as he turned to the duties of husbands. He began with the most important: "Husbands, love your wives, even as Christ also loved the church, and gave himself for it" (v. 25). Am I willing to sacrifice myself for the good of my wife? Do I love her as deeply as Christ loved the Church? If not, then I am not a righteous husband.

  Christ worked with the members of His Church "that he might sanctify and cleanse it with the washing of water by the word, [and] that he might present it to himself a glorious church, not having spot, or wrinkle, or any such thing; but that it should be holy and without blemish" (vv. 26–27). My care for the welfare and perfection of my wife should be as continuous and consistent as were Christ's efforts to bless the Church.

  Men "ought . . . to love their wives as their own bodies. He that loveth his wife loveth himself. For no man ever yet hated his own flesh; but nourisheth and cherisheth it, even as the Lord the church" (vv. 28–29). "For this cause shall a man leave his father and mother, and shall be joined unto his wife, and they two shall be one flesh" (vv. 30–31). This metaphor of husband and wife being "one body" goes all the way back to the Garden of Eden. It was there that the Lord taught Adam that his wife was "his rib" [which meant "very best friend" in Hebrew culture]. The rib symbolized that he was to treat her as if she were his own flesh. And where does a rib come from? It is to the side, under the arm, and near the heart—exactly where his wife should be in his life.

Paul admitted that understanding how fully Christ loved the Church is "a great mystery" (v. 32). "Nevertheless let every one of you in particular so love his wife even as himself; and the wife see that she reverence her husband" (v. 33).

President Spencer W. Kimball taught, "Can you find in all the holy scriptures where the Lord Jesus Christ ever failed His church? . . . Was He faithful? Was He true? Is there anything good and worthy that He did not give? Then that is what we ask—what He asks—of a husband. . . . Can you think of how He loved the Church? Its every breath was important to Him. Its every growth, its every individual was precious to Him. He gave to those people all His energy, all His power, all His interest. He gave His life—and what more could one give?"[8]

- **Ephesians 6:1–3 The relationship of children to their parents.** Paul's advice to children is short and sweet. "Children, obey your parents in the Lord: for this is right" (v. 1). But again, children are only required to obey their parents if what their parents are teaching them is "in the Lord." The next requirement is not conditional like the first one. "Honour thy father and mother; (which is the first commandment with promise;) That it may be well with thee, and thou mayest live long on the earth" (vv. 2–3). Honoring suggests respecting and not fault-finding and blaming. I know perfectly well that my parents were not perfect; they made many mistakes. But neither am I perfect, and I also make mistakes. I honor them as the people who agreed to bring me into this life and who nurtured me through my childhood. I honor them as people who did their very best and sacrificed greatly for me. I have, from time to time, heard criticism from my siblings toward them. But I choose to love and honor them, as Paul counseled.

PROVIDENCE LITHOGRAPHIC CO., 1901

- **Ephesians 6:4 The relationship of parents to their children.** Paul was particularly concerned about fathers' behavior toward their children. "Ye fathers, provoke not your children to wrath: but bring them up in the nurture and admonition of the Lord." Abuse of both wives and children is an abomination in the Lord's eyes. Shouting, bullying, hitting, humiliating, and the like, are as sinful as adultery. Christ taught that a person who takes the light of innocence out of a child's eyes by abusing them would have been better off if he had never been born because the punishment will be severe. Instead, fathers are counseled by Paul to bring up children in the admonition [commandments] and nurture [love] of the Lord.

- **Ephesians 6:5–9 The relationship of masters to servants.** Slavery was a reality in the culture of Paul's time. So he spoke of the duties of servants and slaves to their masters. In our time, this advice would apply to the relationship between employers and their employees.

  "Servants, be obedient to them that are your masters according to the flesh, with fear and trembling, in singleness of your heart, as unto Christ" (v. 5). They should not work only "with eyeservice" [when they are being watched] or as "menpleasers" [showing fake loyalty for some personal gain], "but as [in the same manner as] the servants of Christ, [who] do . . . the will of God from the heart" (v. 6). They should work "with good will," doing their service as if they were serving the Lord, and not men (v. 7). Such service will not go unrewarded by the Lord. "Knowing that whatsoever good thing any man doeth, the same shall he receive of the Lord, whether he be bond or free" (v. 8).

  Paul also spoke to the "masters" [employers]. "And, ye masters, do the same things unto them, forbearing threatening" (v. 9). All masters should remember that their Master in heaven is watching, and He will not favor you because of your position. "Neither is there respect of persons [any favoritism for one man over another] with him" (v. 9).

Putting on the Whole Armor of God

- **Ephesians 6:10–18 The best defenses against the world and Satan.** Paul encouraged the Saints to be "strong in the Lord, and in the power of his might" (v. 10). Then he used the metaphor of a Roman solider to illustrate how they might do this most effectively.

  "Put on the whole armour of God, that ye may be able to stand against the wiles of the devil" (v. 11). "For we wrestle not against flesh and blood, but against principalities, against powers, against the rulers of the darkness of this world, against spiritual wickedness in high places" (v. 12). "Wherefore take unto you the whole armour of God, that ye may be able to withstand in the evil day, and having done all, to stand" (v. 13).

  — Truth will protect our virtue and chastity (our "loins") (v. 14).
  — Righteousness, like a breastplate, will protect our conduct and desires (v. 14).
  — The gospel will direct our paths and objectives in life (our "feet") (v. 15).
  — Faith will be our shield against the fiery darts of the wicked (v. 16).
  — Salvation will be on our minds like a "helmet" covering our head (v. 17).
  — The Spirit is our weapon, calling to memory the word of God (scriptures) (v. 17).

- **Ephesians 6:18–20 Paul also advises prayer, both for ourselves and for our leaders.** Persistent prayer that is accompanied by the Spirit is the method by which we can make supplication for all the Saints (v. 18). As he served as an "ambassador in bonds" for the cause of Christ, Paul continually prayed "that utterance may be given unto me, that I may open my mouth boldly, to make known the mystery of the gospel" and that "I may speak boldly, as I ought to speak" (vv. 19–20).

Notes

1. In Conference Report, April 1992, 98; or *Ensign,* May 1992, 70.
2. *Teachings of the Prophet Joseph Smith*, sel. Joseph Fielding Smith [1976], 149; *Doctrinal New Testament Commentary,* 3 vols. [1965–1973], 2:493–495.
3. *Lectures on Faith,* Lecture Fifth, 2.
4. *Doctrinal New Testament Commentary*, 2:497.
5. *Mere Christianity* [2001], 129.
6. *Teachings of the Prophet Joseph Smith*, 151.
7. Adapted from Richard Lloyd Anderson, *Understanding Paul* [1983], 281.
8. "Men of Example." Address to religious educators, 12 September 1975, 4–5.

Chapter 40

Possibilities Through Christ

(Philippians; Colossians; Philemon)

PHILIPPIANS

When and Where Was Philippians Written?

The epistle to the Philippians was written during Paul's first imprisonment in Rome (61–62 AD).

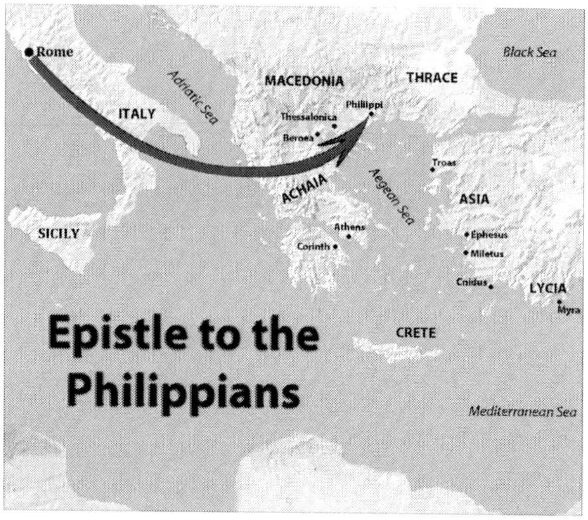

Although Colossians, Philemon, and Ephesians appear to have been sent at the same time (Colossians 4:7–9; Philemon 10; Ephesians 6:21), when Paul wrote Philippians he was in his own rented house, suggesting it was slightly later than the other three (perhaps 62 AD).

At the time the letter was written, it had been ten years since Paul's first visit to the city and the conversion of Lydia, the jailer, and others (Acts 16).

Why Was Philippians Written?

The city of Philippi was named after King Philip II of Macedon, father of Alexander the Great. It was a prosperous Roman colony, and its inhabitants were Roman citizens who prided themselves on the superiority of Roman customs (Acts 16:21).

Some of the Saints worked in "Caesar's household," a possible reference to the emperor's palace. These had been converted through Paul's preaching (Philippians 4:22; Philippians 1:13). This is perhaps the reason for Paul's exhortation to the Saints to look to heaven as the source of their lasting citizenship (Philippians 3:17–21).

The letter to Philippi may be the happiest, most positive, and most personal of all Paul's writings. The Philippian Saints showed great concern about Paul's temporal needs, not just in Philippi but also in Thessalonica, Corinth, and Rome (Philippians 4:15–18). He called the Philippian Saints "my joy and crown" (Philippians 4:1), and they seem to have been the most faithful branch in the Church.

FOLLOWING JESUS CHRIST

Persevering in a Wicked World

REMBRANDT, THE BIBLE AND ITS STORY, 1908

- **Philippians 1:21–24 Life has its rewards, but death is also a blessing.** Paul considered living to be a blessing from Christ, and death to be not a loss but a "gain" (v. 21). He knew that if he lived he could enjoy "the fruit of my labour" but still did not know which was the greater blessing: to live or to die (v. 22). "For I am in a strait betwixt [the] two [hard pressed to choose], having a desire to depart, and to be with Christ; which is far better: Nevertheless to abide in the flesh is more needful for you" (vv. 23–24).

- **Philippians 1:27 The Saints must unitedly maintain their standards in the midst of a wicked world.** Their daily conversation was to be that which is becoming to a follower of Christ and His gospel. They must "stand fast in one spirit, with one mind striving together for the faith of the gospel."

Submitting to Christ

- **Philippians 2:2–3 The importance of unity and love.** Paul encouraged the Saints to be "likeminded, having the same love, being of one accord, of one mind" (v. 2). They were also to be humble, "let[ting] nothing be done through strife or vainglory; but in lowliness of mind [and] each esteem[ing the] other better than themselves" (v. 3).

- **Philippians 2:5–6 Becoming like God does not diminish His Godhood.** With regard to this doctrine, the Saints were to have the same attitude that Christ had, "Who, being in the form of God, thought it not robbery to be equal with God" (vv. 5–6).

- **Philippians 2:7–8 Follow Christ's example of humility and service.** Though He was the Son of God, Christ "made himself of no reputation, and took upon him the form of a servant, and was made in the likeness of men: And being found in fashion as a man, he humbled himself, and became obedient unto death, even the death of the cross."

- **Philippians 2:9–11 Eventually every knee will bow and every tongue confess Christ.** Because of His obedience, God the Father has exalted Christ "and given him a name which is above every name" (v. 9). And to that name "every knee should bow, of things in heaven, and things in earth, and things under the earth," and "every tongue should confess that Jesus Christ is Lord, [all] to the glory of God the Father" (vv. 10–11).
    — **2 Nephi 25:20** There is no other name whereby we can be saved.

- **Philippians 2:12 Salvation comes through obedience.** By this means we are to work out our own salvation with "fear and trembling." Paul complimented the Philippians by saying, "ye have always obeyed, not . . . in my presence only, but now much more in my absence," and he encouraged them to "work out your own salvation with fear and trembling."

  President David O. McKay said, "'Work out your own salvation' is an exhortation to demonstrate by activity, by thoughtful, obedient effort the reality of faith. But this must be done with a consciousness that absolute dependence upon self may produce pride and weakness that will bring failure. With 'fear and trembling' we should seek the strength and grace of God for inspiration to obtain the final victory."[1]

- **Philippians 2:14–15 Avoid murmuring and disputations.** "Do all things without murmurings and disputings," said Paul, "that ye may be blameless and harmless, the sons of God, without rebuke, in the midst of a crooked and perverse nation, among whom ye shine as lights in the world."

Sacrificing for Christ

- **Philippians 3:6–8 Paul reflects on what he might have had as a Pharisee.** Paul said that "concerning zeal, persecuting the church; [and regarding] the righteousness which is in the law [of Moses]" he was "blameless" among the Jews (v. 6). But although the accolades he received were "gain" to him, he now "counted [them as a] loss for Christ" (v. 7). Paul now considered all the things he had as a Pharisee a "loss for the excellency of the knowledge of Christ Jesus my Lord: for whom I have suffered the loss of all things, and do count them but dung, that I may win Christ" (v. 8). This included friends, family, fame, income, and the comforts of life.

  The Prophet Joseph Smith said, "A religion that does not require the sacrifice of all things never has power sufficient to produce the faith necessary unto life and salvation; for, from the first existence of man, the faith necessary unto the enjoyment of life and salvation never could be obtained without the sacrifice of all earthly things."[2]

- **Philippians 3:12–14 Obtaining salvation is a long, hard struggle.** Paul did not believe that he had "already attained" or was "already perfect;" he continued to "follow after" these things in order to "apprehend that for which also I am apprehended of

Christ Jesus" [namely, salvation] (v. 12). He did not claim to have already attained salvation, but, "forgetting those things which are behind, and reaching forth unto those things which are before, I press toward the mark for the prize of the high calling of God in Christ Jesus" (vv. 13–14).

- **Philippians 3:20–21 Our resurrected bodies will look like Christ's.** As Christians, "our conversation [focus] is [on] heaven; from whence also we look for the Saviour, the Lord Jesus Christ" (v. 20). And when He does come, He will "change our vile body, that it may be fashioned like unto his glorious body," because of the power He has to "subdue all things [including death] unto himself" (v. 21). As my own body and the bodies of my friends deteriorate with age, we often say to each other that we can't wait until we get to "trade them in on a newer model." It's a joke, but also a reality that will one day come.

Seeking the Peace of Christ

- **Philippians 4:2–3 Paul asks members to help two sisters work out a dispute.** These two women, named Euodias and Syntyche, needed to be "of the same mind in the Lord" (v. 2). So Paul asked others, as "true yokefellow[s] to "help those women which laboured with me in the gospel, [and] with Clement also, and with other my fellow-labourers, whose names are in the book of life" (v. 3).

  — There were several early "fathers" of the Church who wrote during the years after the deaths of the Apostles. A number of them make mention of Clement, who is mentioned only this once in the New Testament.

  - Origen (185–254 AD)
  - Eusebius of Caesarea (260–339 AD)
  - Epiphanius (315–403 AD)
  - Jerome (331–420 AD)

Clement of Rome

  — All indicate that Clement was a younger contemporary of Peter and Paul and that eventually he became the Bishop of Rome. Eusebius said, "Clement . . . who became the third bishop of Rome, was, as the Apostle himself testifies, Paul's fellow-worker and fellow-combatant."[3]

- **Philippians 4:6–7 Do not "stress out" over things, but seek the peace of Christ.** Paul advised that we should "be careful [concerned] for nothing; but in every thing by prayer and supplication with thanksgiving let your requests be made known unto God" (v. 6). In that way, "the peace of God, which passeth all understanding, shall keep your hearts and minds [at ease] through Christ Jesus" (v. 7).

- **Philippians 4:8 Seek for and embrace every good thing the world has to offer.** All good things come from God for our benefit. Paul's list of these things was used by Joseph Smith in the 13th Article of Faith: "Finally, brethren, whatsoever things are true, whatsoever things are honest, whatsoever things are just, whatsoever things are pure, whatsoever things are lovely, whatsoever things are of good report; if there be any virtue, and if there be any praise, think on these things."

- **Philippians 4:11–13 Everything we experience teaches us.** "I have learned," Paul said, "in whatsoever state I am, therewith to be content" (v. 11). Being dissatisfied with our lot may lead to increased effort and desire to do better, but it can also lead to no good if we become unhappy, anxious, or angry over our situation.

  "I know both how to be abased, and I know how to abound," said Paul. Certainly he had been in both circumstances multiple times. But here was the key for his benefit: "every where and in all things I am instructed" (v. 12). In other words, he learned from every situation and experience of his life, "both to be full and to be hungry, both to abound and to suffer need" (v. 12). And he had learned that he could "do all things through Christ which strengtheneth me" (v. 13).

COLOSSIANS

When and Where Was Colossians Written?

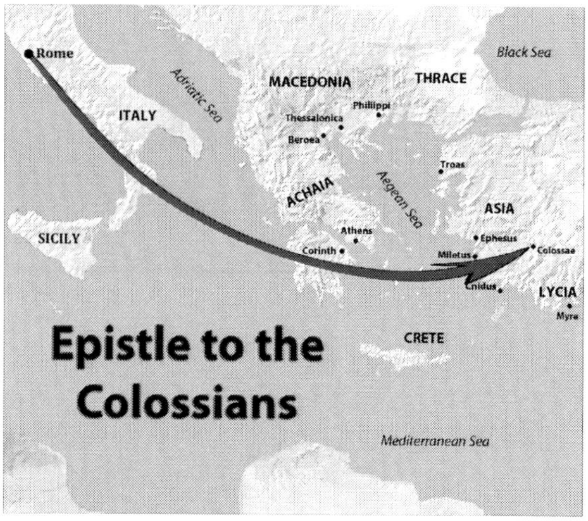

The epistle to the Colossians was written during Paul's first imprisonment in Rome (61–62 AD).

It was written to Colosse, Laodicea, and Hierapolis in western Asia Minor (Colossians 4:12–13, 16). Colosse was a small, unimportant town in Phrygia (it's not even shown on our Bible maps). Philemon and his slave Onesimus lived in Colosse (see the epistle to Philemon). All three cities were located in the Lycus Valley about one hundred miles east of Ephesus.

Though small and relatively unimportant, Colosse lay on the famous trade route which connected East with West through the province of Phyrgia. In the fifth century BC, the city had achieved some degree of commercial importance but was later eclipsed in importance by Hierapolis and Laodicea.

Some scholars say that Paul never visited Colosse prior to his Roman imprisonment (Colossians 2:1). They believe that Epaphras, who was a native of Colosse, may have been converted when Paul preached at Ephesus on his third missionary journey, and that Epaphras then spread the gospel message in Colosse and the surrounding area (Colossians 1:7, 8; 4:12, 13). Others say Paul did visit Colosse on his third missionary journey, either to establish the Church or to lend his support to an already existing branch (Acts 18:23; 19:1).

Either way, it is apparent that Paul greatly desired to visit Colosse after his Roman imprisonment (Philemon 22).

Why Was Colossians Written?

Colossians is one of the shortest of Paul's epistles, yet it contains important doctrines. It was written to counteract the effects of Jewish and Gentile thought on the members there. There were false doctrines concerning the Godhead and worship of angels (Colossians 2:18). Some members or apostates were denying the physical nature of Christ and a bodily resurrection. They argued whether Jesus was a God (monophysitism) or a man (arianism) or both at the same. Some were also attempting to displace the preeminence of God by teaching that we needed mediating angels for our prayers.

These false doctrines were a result of the Greek philosophy that permeated society in Paul's day. The Greeks taught that the body was vile, the spirit had no need for it, and that losing the body through death was a good thing so that the soul could be set free from corruption. This led to arguments about whether Christ, as a holy being, would lower Himself to the status of having a body, and whether resurrection was a physical event or a spiritual event. These questions were still dogging the Church when the Nicene Council met to decided these issues in 325 AD.

SOUND DOCTRINE

The Godhead

- **Colossians 1:1–3 Paul refers to two beings in the Godhead:** "God our Father and the Lord Jesus Christ," as he often did at the first of his epistles. He also gave thanks to "God . . . the Father of our Lord Jesus Christ" when he was praying for the Colossians (v. 3). The letter was sent by "Paul, an apostle of Jesus Christ by the will of God, and Timotheus our brother," to "the saints and faithful brethren in Christ which are at Colosse" (vv. 1–2).

- **Colossians 1:12–14 God made us worthy of exaltation through Jesus Christ.** Paul thanked our Father for making us "meet" [able, worthy] "to be partakers of the inheritance of the saints in light," and "deliver[ing] us from the power of darkness" (vv. 12–13). He said the Father had "translated us into the kingdom of his dear Son," and that "we have redemption through his blood, even the forgiveness of sins" (vv. 13–14).

- **Colossians 1:15 Jesus Christ is the express image of the Father.** Paul said that Jesus was "the image of the invisible God, the firstborn of every creature." The word "image" is translated from the Greek word *icon*, which is something that looks like the thing for which it stands. The word "invisible" means "unseen." Therefore, Paul is saying that Jesus looks like the Father, who is the unseen God. He is not saying that they are one and the same being. Paul adds that Jesus was the "firstborn" of our Father. This is true in the spirit, where He was the first spirit child of God. It is also true in the flesh, where He was the first (and only) child of God in the flesh.

HUBBLE TELESCOPE DEEP FIELD PHOTO COURTESY OF NASA

- **Colossians 1:16–19 Jesus Christ is the creator of all things.** Still speaking of Jesus Christ, Paul said that "by him were all things created, that are in heaven, and that are in earth, visible and invisible, whether they be thrones, or dominions, or principalities, or powers: all things were created by him, and for him" (v. 16). As the Firstborn, Christ was "before all things," and because He is the Creator "by him all things consist" (v. 17). He is the head of the Church (v. 18). And He was the "firstborn from the dead" through resurrection. All of these things were done so that "he might have the preeminence" over us and all other things (v. 18). And "it pleased the Father that in him should all fulness dwell" (v. 19).

Remaining Steadfast

- **Colossians 1:23 Remain steadfast in the Church and in its doctrines.** Paul knew that the Saints would face many difficulties in the years ahead, not only from the Romans but also from apostates. He urged them as their "minister" to "continue in the faith grounded and settled, and be not moved away from the hope of the gospel, which ye have heard, and which was preached to every creature [person] which is under heaven."

- **Colossians 2:2–3 The Saints should have their hearts "knit together in love" and in their knowledge of God the Father and Jesus Christ.** In the times of trouble that were now coming upon them, in order that "their hearts might be comforted," Paul advised them to be "knit together in love," and to maintain "the full assurance of understanding" with regard to the "mystery of [revelations concerning] God, and of the Father, and of Christ" (v. 2), "in whom are hid all the treasures of wisdom and knowledge" (v. 3). These are the two major threats which the early Church would face: dissensions among themselves and false doctrines concerning God and Christ.

- **Colossians 2:7 We are to be "rooted and built up" in Christ.** Paul used the analogy of roots nourishing a tree to show our dependence on Christ for spiritual strength. He counseled the Saints to be "rooted and built up in him [Christ], and [e]stablished in the faith, as ye have been taught, abounding therein with thanksgiving."

- **Colossians 2:8 A warning against intellectualism.** The philosophies of men have no saving grace. We cannot rely on them for salvation nor should we mix them with the words of the scriptures when teaching the Gospel. Intellectualism can be stimulating, but is all too often used as a tool to build up and maintain pride. Paul said, "Beware lest any man spoil you through philosophy and vain deceit, after the tradition of men, after the rudiments of the world, and not after Christ." The truths of God are far superior to the philosophies of men. As the poet John Milton said, "The end of all learning is to know God, and out of that knowledge to love and imitate Him."[4]

THE PHILOSOPHICAL SCHOOL AT ATHENS, RAPHAEL

The philosophies of men have no saving grace

- **Colossians 2:14–16 The ordinances and performances of the law of Moses were fulfilled in Christ.** Calling the law of Moses "the handwriting of ordinances" that had been "blotted out" by the Gospel of Christ, Paul suggested that the law "was against us" and "was contrary to us" and that Christ "took it [the law of Moses] out of the way, nailing it to his cross" (v. 14). Christ "spoiled principalities and powers" and "made a shew [example] of them" by openly "triumphing over them" through His death and resurrection. The Saints, therefore, needed not to follow the doctrine, traditions, and rituals of the law of Moses because they were all only a type and a shadow of Christ and his Gospel" (vv. 15–16).

- **Colossians 2:18 Paul denounces the idea of worshiping angels.** The heresy had already begun to creep into the Church that man could not talk directly to God. Gnostic philosophy held that God had to be contacted through angelic mediators or spirits. This was the forerunner of the doctrine still taught today that we must pray through Mary or one of the designated Saints. Paul spoke clearly against this idea. "Let no man beguile you of [steal] your reward" through "voluntary [fake] humility and worshipping of angels" (v. 18). Those who taught this were teaching about things "which he hath not seen, vainly puffed up by his fleshly mind" (v. 18).

  Elder Bruce R. McConkie said in our own day concerning such doctrines, "This is plain sectarian nonsense. Our prayers are addressed to the Father, and to Him only. They do not go through Christ, or the Blessed Virgin, or St. Genevieve or along the beads of a rosary. We are entitled to "come boldly unto the throne of grace, that we may obtain mercy, and find grace to help in time of need" (Hebrews 4:16).[5]

The Elect of God

PROVIDENCE LITHOGRAPHIC CO. 1901, #34

- **Colossians 3:2–3 Having our election made sure.** Some Colossian Saints had their calling and election made sure; that is, they were sealed up unto eternal life because of their faithfulness. To these Saints Paul counseled, "Set your affection on things above, not on things on the earth. For ye are dead [meaning "saved through the suffering and death of Christ], and your life is hid with Christ in God."

  The Prophet Joseph Smith used the same language on 16 May 1843 when he declared that William Clayton had his calling and election made sure. Later, the Prophet wrote: "Putting my hand on the knee of William Clayton, I said: Your life is hid with Christ in God, and so are many others. Nothing but the unpardonable sin can prevent you from inheriting eternal life."[6]

- **Colossians 3:5–17 Characteristics of the elect.** Paul instructed the Saints to "mortify" [kill] all those tendencies that come from being mortal: "fornication, uncleanness, inordinate affection, evil concupiscence, and covetousness, which is idolatry," because these are the things that bring "the wrath of God . . . [up]on the children of disobedience" (vv. 5–6). He reminded them that they were guilty of these things in the past "when ye lived in them" (v. 7). They were also to "put off all these: anger, wrath, malice, blasphemy, [and] filthy communication out of your mouth" (v. 8). "Lie not one to another, seeing that ye have put off the old man with his deeds; and have put on the new man, which is renewed in knowledge after the image of him that created him" (vv. 9–10).

  Among such people, who are the elect of God, "there is neither Greek nor Jew, circumcision nor uncircumcision, Barbarian, Scythian, bond nor free" because "Christ is all [that matters], and [He is] in all" (v. 11). "Put on therefore, as the elect of God, holy and beloved, bowels of mercies, kindness, humbleness of mind, meekness, longsuffering; forbearing one another, and forgiving one another, if any man have a quarrel against any: even as Christ forgave you, so also do ye" (vv. 12–13).

  "And above all these things put on charity, which is the bond of perfectness. And let the peace of God rule in your hearts, to the which also ye are called in one body; and be ye thankful. Let the word of Christ dwell in you richly in all wisdom; teaching and admonishing one another in psalms and hymns and spiritual songs, singing with grace in your hearts to the Lord. And whatsoever ye do in word or deed, do all in the name of the Lord Jesus, giving thanks to God and the Father by him" (vv. 14–17).

- **Colossians 3:16 The importance of music to our spiritual nourishment.** We should take special note of the importance that Paul gave to music in the spiritual lives of the Saints. "Let the word of Christ dwell in you richly in all wisdom; teaching and admonishing one another in psalms and hymns and spiritual songs, singing with grace in your hearts to the Lord."

  — **D&C 25:11–12 "The song of the righteous is a prayer unto me."** In our own day, the Lord instructed Emma Smith that "it shall be given thee, also, to make a selection of sacred hymns . . . which is pleasing unto me, to be had in my church. For my soul delighteth in the song of the heart; yea, the song of the righteous is a prayer unto me, and it shall be answered with a blessing upon their heads."

Elder Dallin H. Oaks said, "We need to make more use of our hymns to put us in tune with the Spirit of the Lord, to unify us, and to help us teach and learn our doctrine. We need to make better use of our hymns in missionary teaching, in gospel classes, in quorum meetings, in home evenings, and in home teaching visits. Music is an effective way to worship our Heavenly Father and His Son, Jesus Christ. We should use hymns when we need spiritual strength and inspiration."[7]

Personal Relationships

- **Colossians 3:18–21 Family Relationships.** This counsel is identical to that given in Ephesians 5:25–33 (see previous chapter). It is beautiful counsel to members of the family. A more detailed exploration of these principles is provided in the chapter on Ephesians, and that will not be repeated here. But a quick summary is as follows.

  — Wives, submit yourselves unto your own husbands, as it is fit in the Lord (v. 18).
  — Husbands, love your wives, and be not bitter against them (v. 19).
  — Children, obey your parents in all things: for this is well pleasing unto the Lord (v. 20).
  — Fathers, provoke not your children to anger, lest they be discouraged (v. 21).

- **Colossians 3:22; 4:1 Work/Employment Relationships.** The is also a repeat of the advice given in Ephesians 5. While Paul speaks of masters and servants, it would apply in our day to the relationship between employers and employees.

  — Servants, obey in all things your masters according to the flesh; not with eyeservice, as menpleasers; but in singleness of heart, fearing God (3:22).

  — Masters, give unto your servants that which is just and equal; knowing that ye also have a Master in heaven.

- **Colossians 4:5–6 Relationships with Nonmembers.** Paul advises us to "walk in wisdom toward them that are without [nonmembers], redeeming [making wise use of] the time" (v. 5). He also says that we should behave toward them with "grace" and improve ("salt") the world by our behavior (v. 6).

PHILEMON

When, Where, and Why Was Philemon Written?

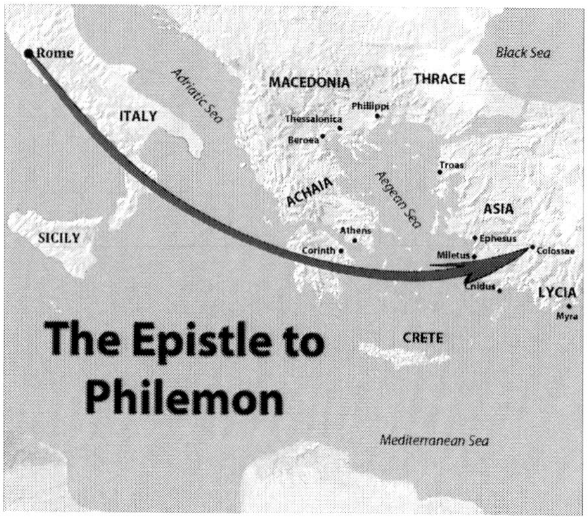

The epistle to Philemon was written during Paul's first imprisonment in Rome (61–62 AD). It was written to convince a man named Philemon to accept back his runaway slave, Onesimus. Philemon was apparently a rich and faithful member of the Church, a resident of Colosse. Philemon appears to have been converted by Paul (vv. 19–20).

Onesimus, Philemon's runaway Greek slave, had apparent also joined the Church by this time. Slavery, or servitude, was not viewed as evil by the cultures at the time of Christ. Slaves actually constituted 20–30% of the population of the Roman empire. Under Roman law, Paul was legally bound to encourage Onesimus to return to Philemon.

Paul says Onesimus would be coming back different—not as a slave but as a brother (v. 16). Paul's tender Christlike feelings reveal themselves as he pleads the cause of a poor runaway who has nobody but Paul to recommend him.

PAUL'S FRIENDS IN COLOSSE

Faithful Colossian Friends

- **Philemon 1:2, 17 Paul mentions several faithful Saints.** He sent greetings to "our beloved Apphia, and Archippus our fellowsoldier, and to the church in thy house" (v. 2). He also recommends Onesimus, and pleads to his friends at Colosse, "If thou count me therefore a partner, receive him as myself" (v. 17).

  These were all people Paul would have met during his third missionary journey while he lived at Ephesus and preached in the surrounding area. They may also have been his own converts. Some have suggested that Apphia was Philemon's wife and Archippus, his son. Ancient tradition holds that Philemon became bishop of Colosse and, during the persecution under Nero when Peter and Paul met their deaths, was martyred in Colosse with his wife Apphia, his son Archippus, and his slave Onesimus.

Paul's Appeal Concerning Onesimus

- **Philemon 1:7, 12, 20 Paul asks the Colossian Saints to extend charity to Onesimus.** First, he complemented them for their example of charity: "We have great joy and consolation in thy love, because the bowels [emotions, feelings] of the saints are refreshed by thee" (v. 7). Now, he was sending Onesimus back to them, whom he refers to as "mine own bowels," suggesting the personal nature of his feelings. And he pleads with Philemon to "let me have joy of thee in the Lord: refresh my bowels in the Lord" by treating Onesimus with charity.

- **Philemon 1:8–9 Paul asks Philemon to do the right thing.** He admitted that he might be "much bold in Christ to enjoin [ask] thee [to do] that which is convenient" (v. 8). The Greek word translated as "convenience" means "to measure up" to a certain standard. Paul is suggesting that Philemon's forgiveness of his runaway slave would be the most appropriate thing for a true follower of Christ to do. "Yet for love's sake I rather beseech thee, being such an one as Paul the aged, and now also a prisoner of Jesus Christ" (v. 9). "The aged" is more properly translated as "the elder"—a priesthood office or title.

- **Philemon 1:10–11 Paul himself is in bonds, and has compassion for Onesimus.** "I beseech thee for my son Onesimus, whom I have begotten in my bonds" suggests that Paul felt for him as he would for his own son. He admitted that, in the past, Onesimus "was to thee unprofitable, but now [had become] profitable to thee and to me" (v. 11). The Greek name Onesimus means "helpful" or "profitable" and was a common name for slaves. Paul uses an interesting play on his name in verse 11.

- **Philemon 1:15–19 There may have been a purpose in Onesimus' escape.** Under Roman law runaway slaves were put to death. But Paul suggested that "perhaps he therefore departed for a season, that thou shouldest receive him for ever; Not now as a servant, but above a servant, a brother beloved" (vv. 15–16). This does not mean that he cannot continue as a slave, but that he was now a brother in the Gospel sense. Onesimus had become a brother to Paul, "but how much more unto thee, both in the flesh, and in the Lord?" (v. 16). "If thou count me therefore a partner, receive him as myself" (v. 17).

  Paul offers to pay Philemon back for any financial loss suffered by this incident. "If he hath wronged thee, or oweth thee ought, put that on mine account; I Paul have written it with mine own hand, I will repay it" (vv. 18–19). And in doing so, Paul wished

Philemon to know that the only payment he hoped to receive in return for his kindness to Onesimus was his friendship ("thine own self besides") (v. 19).

Other Information from Philemon

- **Philemon 1:22 Paul is interested in making a personal visit soon.** He asked them to "prepare me also a lodging: for I trust that through your prayers I shall be given unto you." In fact, Paul did get to return to Ephesus after his first imprisonment at Rome, and no doubt he did spend time with Philemon during that visit.

- **Philemon 1:23 Epaphras, a resident of Colosse, carried Paul's letter to them.** Paul calls him "my fellowprisoner in Christ Jesus."

- **Philemon 1:24 Paul's companions and fellow missionaries at the time of his first imprisonment at Rome.** He mentions Marcus (John Mark, whom we know as Mark) and Aristarchus as fellow-prisoners (Colossians 4:10). He also mentions Lucas (Luke) and Demas, whom he calls "my fellowlabourers." The name Demas is probably a contraction of Demetrius or Demarchus. He was imprisoned with Paul, but later apostatized (2 Timothy 4:10).

Notes

1. In Conference Report, April 1957, 7.
2. *Lectures on Faith,* Lecture Sixth, 7.
3. Eusebius, *History of the Church*, 67.
4. *A Puritan Golden Treasury*, compiled by I.D.E. Thomas, by permission of Banner of Truth, Carlisle, PA [2000], 164.
5. "Our Relationship With The Lord," BYU Devotional Address, 2 March 1982.
6. *History of the Church*, 5:391.
7. In Conference Report, October 1994, 13; or *Ensign*, November 1994, 12.

Chapter 41

Paul's Pastoral Epistles and Death

(1 & 2 Timothy, Titus)

INTRODUCTION

Paul's First Imprisonment at Rome

Because of his Roman citizenship, Paul had the privilege of "appealing to Caesar" when he was accused of a crime at Jerusalem. After doing so, he was brought to Rome to stand trial in Nero's court. While waiting for trial, Paul was placed in house arrest at a home near the Imperial Palace, where he remained under house arrest for two years. During that time, although guarded continually, he preached the gospel to everyone he could and converted some of the soldiers and others of the royal household. When his case was finally heard, we have reason to believe he was acquitted and released because he subsequently wrote letters from Philippi in Macedonia.

A Brief Interval of Freedom

After his release, Paul went to Philippi (in Macedonia) to rest. Then he went to Ephesus to strengthen the Church. There is some evidence he went to Spain and then returned to Ephesus before finally returning to Macedonia.

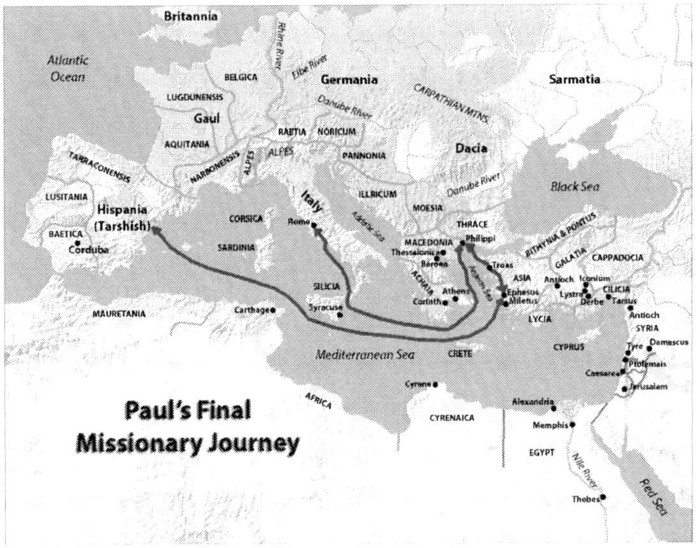

It was from Macedonia that he wrote his first epistle to Timothy and probably his epistle to Titus, between 66–68 AD.

Paul later traveled back to Rome, where he was imprisoned a second time.

Paul's Second Imprisonment at Rome

Paul's second imprisonment was different from the first in that the Roman authorities did not treat Paul with the same deference which they had shown to him before. The attitude of the Roman government toward the early Church had undergone a radical shift. Nero blamed the Christians for the great fire of Rome (which he probably set himself) and launched a series of intense persecutions against them in Rome. Paul and Peter were caught up in this new hostility and were martyred along with many other Christians.

During his second imprisonment, friends still visited Paul, but his freedom to preach the gospel was greatly restricted. At his trial no one came forth to plead his cause, and only Luke remained with him. In spite of these adverse circumstances, he remained optimistic and was buoyed up by his faith in Christ.

Contributions of the Pastoral Epistles

These three letters are called Pastoral Epistles because they were written to Church leaders. Timothy was a Church leader and teacher at Ephesus (1 Timothy 1:3). Because he appointed bishops, Timothy was apparently a regional officer (area authority). Titus was a Church leader and teacher on the island of Crete, probably a bishop.

With death approaching, Paul's counsel reflects eternal perspective. He speaks movingly of the trials which the youthful Timothy must face. He counsels both men concerning Church leadership, doctrine, and spirituality. And now, before his impending death, he speaks confidently of his own exaltation to come.

- **1 Timothy 1:12–13 Paul is thankful for his ministry.** He considered it a great privilege to be "enabled" by the Lord to be His minister (v. 12). He confessed that he was "before a blasphemer, and a persecutor, and injurious: but I obtained mercy, because I did it ignorantly in unbelief" (v. 13). Paul worked his entire life after his first vision to show to the Lord that he was a changed man and would serve Him at all costs.

1ST EPISTLE TO TIMOTHY

Who Was Timothy?

Timothy was a very young man when he was converted by Paul in Lystra. Paul always spoke of him with great pride, calling him a "dearly beloved son" (2 Timothy 1:2). Paul also gave Timothy important assignments (1 Cor. 4:17; 1 Thess. 3:1–2). Paul mentions Timothy in the beginning verses of seven of his letters, and commends Timothy's faithfulness and trustworthiness in three of them.

THEBIBLEREVIVAL.COM, #30

- **1 Timothy 1:2 "Unto Timothy, my own son in the faith."** Paul's way of addressing Timothy reveals his great affection for him. He called him "my own son" and wished him "grace, mercy, and peace, from God our Father and Jesus Christ our Lord."

- **1 Timothy 1:3 Timothy is charged to fight against apostasy in Ephesus.** Paul had asked Timothy to "abide still at Ephesus, when I went into Macedonia" so that Timothy could fight against apostasy there and "charge some that they teach no other doctrine." This was the nature of Timothy's ministry and is discussed in both of Paul's epistles to him.

When and Where Was 1st Timothy Written?

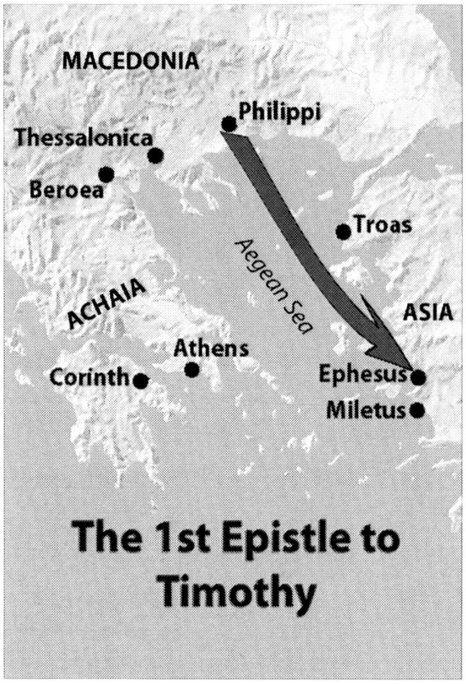

It appears to have been written from Macedonia between Paul's first and second Roman imprisonments. The year was approximately 66 AD.

Why Was 1st Timothy Written?

The central theme is "proper care of the Church" by Church leaders. Paul challenges Timothy and other leaders to be true to their trust in the ministry. He encourages Timothy to teach true doctrines, keep the faith, pray diligently, and walk in holiness.

At the time, Timothy was a priesthood leader at Ephesus with major administrative responsibility. He was a Church leader of proven worth whom Paul regarded highly. Paul himself had placed Timothy in charge of the Ephesian Church. Some prominent members were older than Timothy and had difficulty accepting his authority. This appears to have been a major reason why Paul sent Timothy this letter.

What Are 1st Timothy's Significant Contributions?

Church administration, the conscientious performance of duties, the teaching of correct doctrine, the faithful conduct of an appointed servant in Christ's Church are some of the topics. Interwoven into the text are some references to Jesus Christ, to salvation, to the great latter-day apostasy, and to the necessity for obedience to the principles of the gospel.

ADVICE TO CHURCH MEMBERS

- **1 Timothy 1:5, 15–16; 2 Timothy 2:19 Paul identifies eight virtues that are "the end [purpose] of the commandment[s]"** in his two epistles to Timothy:

  — Charity or pure love (1:5).
  — A good conscience (1:5).
  — Faith unfeigned [not pretended] (1:5).
  — Patience and long-suffering (1:15–16).

— Soberness (2:19).
— Obedience (2:19).
— Sincerity (2:19).
— Knowledge of sound doctrine (2:19).

- **1 Timothy 1:5–7 The most important of all these virtues is charity.** "Now the end of the commandment is charity out of a pure heart," said Paul (v. 5). "From which some having swerved have turned aside unto vain jangling [fruitless intellectual arguing]" (v. 6). These people, "desiring to be teachers of the law; understand . . . neither what they say, nor whereof they affirm" (v. 7).

- **1 Timothy 2:1–3 Pray for those in authority in the Church and the nation.** Paul encouraged "supplications, prayers, intercessions, and giving of thanks" on behalf of "all men" (v. 1). But especially for "kings, and for all that are in authority; that we may lead a quiet and peaceable life in all godliness and honesty" (v. 2). "For this is good and acceptable in the sight of God our Saviour" (v. 3).

- **1 Timothy 2:4–6 Remember that God wants to save everyone.** Should we be surprised that our Heavenly Father wants "all men to be saved, and to come unto the knowledge of the truth"? (v. 4). They are all, after all, the children of our "one God" and Father, and He loves every one of them. And in order to save them, the Father appointed "one mediator between God and men, the man Christ Jesus; Who gave himself a ransom for all, to be testified in due time" (vv. 5–6).

- **1 Timothy 2:9–15 Grooming and behavioral standards for women.** In every age and dispensation, prophets have had to comment on appropriate grooming and dress when believers come before God to worship Him. The overall principle is that we should never try to call attention to ourselves in a place where the focus should be on God and our worship of Him. Thus, while long white beards might have been a sign of dignity in one generation, today they would appear to be strange and would divert people's attention unnecessarily.

  Paul faced this same problem when he advised how women should dress. His advice is clearly tied to the culture of his day. But it is interesting to read and shows the importance of avoiding vain or distracting or immodest dress. Paul advised the following with regard to this.

  — "Women [should] adorn themselves in modest apparel, with shamefacedness [humility] and sobriety; not with broided hair, or gold, or pearls, or costly array" (v. 9).

  — Instead, they should dress in a way that "becometh women professing godliness [and] good works" (v. 10).

  — "Let the woman learn in silence with all subjection [respect for authority]." (v. 11). "Suffer not a woman to teach, nor to usurp authority over the man, but to be in silence" (v. 12). The Greek word translated here as "silence" means tranquillity—to support their leaders and not try to usurp authority.

— "For Adam was first formed, then Eve. And Adam was not deceived, but the woman being deceived was in the transgression" (vv. 13–14). The Greek word *parabasis* used here does not mean "transgression" as that word is understood today. It means "to overstep." Eve overstepped her bounds by usurping authority to make a decision that affected both herself and Adam, without first counseling with Adam about it.

"Notwithstanding she shall be saved in childbearing, if they continue in faith and charity and holiness with sobriety" (v. 15).

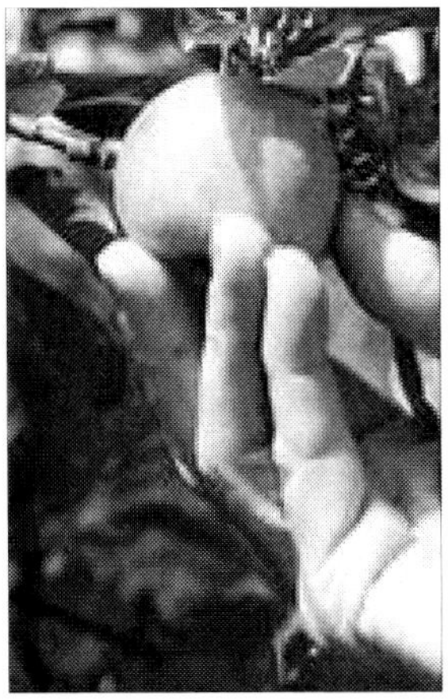

ADVICE FOR TIMOTHY

Maintaining Confidence and Judgment

- **1 Timothy 4:12–16 Timothy was not to be intimidated by those who "despised his youth."** His call came by prophecy and the laying on of hands, and God would support him if he would lead righteously. "Let no man despise thy youth," said Paul, "but be thou an example of the believers, in word, in conversation [conduct, behavior], in charity, in spirit, in faith, in purity" (v. 12).

  Until Paul could come to him, Timothy was to "give attendance to reading, to exhortation, to doctrine" (v. 13). And he was to "neglect not the gift that is in thee, which was given thee by prophecy, with the laying on of the hands of the presbytery." This gift is his ordination to office and the Holy Ghost that would unfailingly guide his decisions and actions.

  "Meditate upon these things; give thyself wholly to them; that thy profiting [progress, advancement] may appear [be apparent] to all" (v. 15). "Take heed unto thyself, and unto the doctrine; continue in them: for in doing this thou shalt both save thyself, and them that hear thee" (v. 16).

- **1 Timothy 5:1–2 How Timothy should respond to men and women of all ages.** Paul advised Timothy to "rebuke not an elder, but intreat him as a father," and when dealing with younger men he was to treat them "as brethren" (v. 1). "The elder women" should be treated "as mothers; [and] the younger as sisters, with all purity" (v. 2).

- **1 Timothy 5:19–21 Judging righteous judgment as a "judge in Israel."** Timothy was not to judge based on rumor. Paul said, "Against an elder receive not an accusation, but before two or three witnesses" (v. 19). When someone was shown to be guilty of a sin, Timothy was to "rebuke [him] before all, that others also may fear" (v. 20). And in all judgments, Timothy was to be fair and unbiased. "I charge thee before God, and the Lord Jesus Christ, and the elect angels, that thou observe these things without preferring one before another, doing nothing by partiality" (v. 21).

- **1 Timothy 5:24–25 Be thoroughly familiar with your people.**
  - "Some men's sins are open beforehand [conspicuous], going [appearing] before ... judgment; and [with] some men they follow after" (v. 24). Leaders must be thoroughly familiar with their people's weaknesses.
  - "Likewise also the good works of some are manifest beforehand; and they that are otherwise cannot be hid" (v. 25). Leaders must also be thoroughly familiar with their people's strengths and faithfulness.

Qualifications for Church Callings

- **1 Timothy 3:1–7 Qualifications for a Bishop.** A bishop is one who watches over the flock; the title "bishop" derives from the Greek *episcopos*—to oversee or watch. Since Timothy would need to call bishops in his area, Paul gave him a list of qualifications for this office in the Church. "This is a true saying, If a man desire the office of a bishop, he desireth a good work" (v. 1). But a bishop must be all of the following.

v. 2	"Husband of one wife"	Not practicing polygamy
	"Vigilant"	Watchful
	"Sober"	Serious-minded
	"Of good behavior"	Well behaved
	"Hospitable"	Friendly
	"Apt to teach"	Able to teach
v. 3	"Not given to wine"	Temperate, Not a drinker of alcohol
	"No striker, Not a brawler"	Not violent
	"Patient"	
	"Not covetous"	
	"Not greedy of filthy lucre"	Does not obtain money by dishonorable means. Note that not all money is "filthy."

vv. 4–5 "One that ruleth well his own house, having his children in subjection in all gravity" means with all due diligence, not abuse or dominance. His pattern in the home will translate to his "fatherhood" of the ward.

v. 6 "Not a novice" is translated from neophyton—one who is newly "born" (baptized). A bishop should be an experienced priesthood holder.

v. 7 "Hav[ing] a good report of [those] without" means having a good reputation with people outside the Church—the community at large.

- **1 Timothy 3:8–13 Qualifications for a Deacon.** A deacon in Paul's day was more likely to be a man than a young boy, and the duties of a deacon were somewhat different than today. Being an Aaronic priesthood office, deacons assisted the bishop in temporal affairs and in watching over the Church in general. Therefore, a deacon should be all of the following.

v. 8 "Grave [serious], not doubletongued [duplicitous], not given to much wine, not greedy of filthy lucre."

v. 9 "Holding the mystery [revelations] of the faith in a pure conscience."

v. 10 "Let these also first be proved; then let them use the office of a deacon, being found blameless."

v. 11 "Even so must their wives be grave, not slanderers, sober, faithful in all things."

v. 12 "The husbands of one wife, ruling their children and their own houses well."

v. 13 "For they that have used the office of a deacon well purchase [acquire] to themselves a good degree [standing among the people], and great boldness in the faith which is in Christ Jesus."

Selecting Priesthood Leaders

PROVIDENCE LITHOGRAPHIC CO. 902, #41

- **1 Timothy 5:22 The process by which Timothy was to select and ordain priesthood leaders.** These instructions show Paul's wisdom and experience in organizing Church units during each of his mission journeys.
  - "Lay hands suddenly on no man" (v. 22). Elder Bruce R. McConkie said, "Brethren should be seasoned, tried, and found worthy before they are ordained and set apart to serve in positions of power and influence in the Church."[1]
- **1 Timothy 5:23 The attitude with which leaders should lead.** There was to be no "holier-than-thou" aloofness, as the proud tend to do. Leaders should eat and drink with the common people.
  - "Drink no longer water, but use a little wine for thy stomach's sake and thine often infirmities" (v. 23). "Water-drinker" was a title used in Paul's day for a rigid ascetic. Timothy was to avoid such extremes of behavior.

Righteous Temporal Welfare

- **1 Timothy 5:3–4, 8, 16 Families must support their own needy and widows.** As a bishop, Timothy was to "honour widows that are widows indeed" (v. 3). However, if they have family—"children or nephews"—that could take care of them, he was to ensure that these family members "learn first to shew piety at home, and to requite [take care of] their parents: for that is good and acceptable before God" (v. 4). "If any man or woman that believeth have widows, let them relieve them, and let not the church be charged; that it may relieve them that are widows indeed" (v. 16). This is the same principle taught and practiced in the Church today; we turn first to the family for our needs and then to the Church. And "if any provide not for his own, and specially for those of his own house, he hath denied the faith, and is worse than an infidel" (v. 8).

- **1 Timothy 5:5–7, 9–10 Widows must also be worthy to receive help.** "Now she that is a widow indeed, and desolate, trusteth in God, and continueth in supplications and prayers night and day" (v. 5). "But she that liveth in pleasure is dead while she liveth" (v. 6). When assisting widows, Timothy was to "give in charge" [with judgment and requiring faithfulness], that they may be blameless" (v. 7).

  A widow would qualify for assistance if she was older than "threescore years" (60) and had been "the wife of one man" (v. 9). She must also be "well reported of for good works; if she have brought up children, if she have lodged strangers, if she have washed the saints' feet, if she have relieved the afflicted, if she have diligently followed every good work" (v. 10).

- **1 Timothy 5:11–13 Younger widows should remarry.** Paul said younger widows should be refused Church assistance, because while under assistance they will become "wanton against Christ" and then "they will marry" (v. 11). This will happen if they "learn to be idle, wandering about from house to house; and not only idle, but tattlers also and busybodies, speaking things which they ought not" (v. 13). Such behavior will bring them "damnation [condemnation from God], because they have cast off their first faith" (v. 12). Rather than do this, they should immediately remarry.

- **1 Timothy 5:14–15 Advice to young, marriageable women in the Church.** Paul said, "I will therefore that the younger women marry, bear children, guide the house, [and] give none occasion to the adversary to speak reproachfully" (v. 14). Unfortunately, said Paul, "some are already turned aside after Satan" (v. 15).

Avoiding Apostate Doctrines

- **1 Timothy 4:1–9 A revelation on conditions in the "latter times."** Whether Paul was speaking of the "latter times" of his own dispensation—when the Church would be overcome with apostasy—or whether he was speaking of our own latter days, is not clear. The prophecy is likely dualistic: applying to both periods of time.

  "Now the Spirit speaketh expressly," said Paul, "that in the latter times some shall depart from the faith, giving heed to seducing spirits, and doctrines of devils; Speaking lies in hypocrisy; having their conscience seared with a hot iron; Forbidding to marry, and commanding to abstain from meats, which God hath created to be received with thanksgiving of them which believe and know the truth" (vv. 1–3).

  — "Forbidding to marry." There is no special holiness in celibacy. Marriage is ordained of God and one of life's great purposes. The Gnostics of Paul's day were already preaching against it.

— "Commanding to abstain from meats." This has reference to restrictions in the law of Moses on eating certain meats and foods. Some apostates would continue to insist on the rituals and rules of the law of Moses. This doctrine concerning meat was unnecessary, said Paul, because "every creature of God is good, and nothing to be refused, if it be received with thanksgiving . . . [and] sanctified by the word of God and prayer" (vv. 4–5).

Paul asked Timothy to "put the brethren in remembrance of these things" as a "good minister of Jesus Christ" who has "nourished up in the words of faith and of good doctrine," which status Timothy had already attained (v. 6).

Paul counseled Timothy to "refuse profane and old wives' fables, and exercise thyself rather unto godliness. For bodily exercise profiteth little: but godliness is profitable unto all things, having promise of the life that now is, and of that which is to come" (vv. 7–8). The meaning of this statement in Greek is not that physical exercise is worthless, but rather that its usefulness is limited.

- **1 Timothy 6:20–21 Avoid Gnostic heresies.** "O Timothy, keep that which is committed to thy trust, avoiding profane and vain babblings, and oppositions of science falsely so called: Which some [while] professing have erred concerning the faith." The word "science" here is translated from *gnosis* ("knowledge") in Greek. The problem is Gnostic heresies, which are pseudo-knowledge.

Material Possessions

- **1 Timothy 6:5 Material gain is not godliness.** Paul observed all around him "perverse disputings of men of corrupt minds," who are "destitute of the truth," and who "suppos[e] that gain is godliness" (v. 5). His counsel? "From such withdraw thyself" (v. 5). In my own patriarchal blessing, the patriarch prophesied of "hatred and selfishness" being "everywhere apparent." This condition, fully evident all around us, is what Paul was talking about here.

PROVIDENCE LITHOGRAPHIC CO., 1909, #39

- **1 Timothy 6:6–10 The love of money is the root of all evil.** Paul said, "Godliness with contentment is great gain" (v. 6). Possession of material things brings us neither contentment nor godliness. "For we brought nothing into this world, and it is certain we can carry nothing out" (v. 7). As my good friend Joe Judd likes to say, "There is never a U-Haul behind or a luggage rack on top of a hearse."

Paul advised, "Having food and raiment let us be therewith content" (v. 8). If we have sufficient for our needs, we have enough. When such contentment is combined with godliness great blessings result. Those who are intent on being rich will "fall into temptation and a snare, and into many foolish and hurtful lusts, which drown men in destruction and perdition. For the love of money is the root of all evil: which while some coveted after, they have erred from the faith, and pierced themselves through with many sorrows" (vv. 9–10). Notice that it is not *money* that is evil, it is *the love of money* that is evil. One can covet material possessions while rich or while poor. And in either case, the soul is cankered.

Elder Dallin H. Oaks taught, "There is nothing inherently evil about money. The Good Samaritan used the same coinage to serve his fellowman that Judas used to betray the Master. It is 'the love of money [which] is the root of all evil' (1 Timothy 6:10). The critical difference is the degree of spirituality we exercise in viewing, evaluating, and managing the things of this world."[2]

Elder Spencer W. Kimball said:

> The possession of riches does not necessarily constitute sin. But sin may arise in the acquisition and use of wealth. . . . Book of Mormon history eloquently reveals the corrosive effect of the passion for wealth. . . . Had the people used their wealth for good purposes they could have enjoyed a continuing prosperity. But they seemed unable for a sustained period to be simultaneously wealthy and righteous. For a limited time some people can "hold the line," but they deteriorate spiritually when money is abundant.[3]
>
> Now, my beloved friends, . . . Are you too wealthy and fettered with the cares of this world to accept the difficult demands of Christ's church? Are you so influential as to fear prejudice to your position or local influence? Are you too weak to accept and carry a load of service? Are you too busy to study and pray and learn of Christ and His program? Are you too materialistically trained to accept the miracles, visions, prophets, and revelations?[4]
>
> Many people build and furnish a home and buy the automobile first—and then find they "cannot afford" to pay tithing. Whom do they worship? Certainly not the Lord of heaven and earth, for we serve whom we love and give first consideration to the object of our affection and desires. Young married couples who postpone parenthood until their degrees are attained might be shocked if their expressed preference were labeled idolatry. Their rationalization gives them degrees at the expense of children. Is it a justifiable exchange? Whom do they love and worship—themselves or God?[5]

- **1 Timothy 6:11–12, 17–19 Follow after righteousness and trust not in riches.** "But thou, O man of God, flee these things," said Paul, "and follow after righteousness, godliness, faith, love, patience, meekness. Fight the good fight of faith, lay hold on eternal life, whereunto thou art also called, and hast professed a good profession before many witnesses" (vv. 11–12).

  Paul said to Timothy, "Charge them that are rich in this world, that they be not highminded, nor trust in uncertain riches, but in the living God, who giveth us richly all things to enjoy; That they do good, that they be rich in good works, ready to distribute, willing to communicate; Laying up in store for themselves a good foundation against the time to come, that they may lay hold on eternal life" (vv. 17–19). This means that those who are rich should not be arrogant, but should bless the lives of others as an "investment" in the life to come, where they will have the true riches of eternal life.

EPISTLE TO TITUS

Who Was Titus?

Titus was apparently converted by Paul in Antioch (of Syria). He attended the Jerusalem Council with Paul and was his missionary companion at times. He carried the 1st and 2nd Corinthian epistles to the city of Corinth on behalf of Paul. He was in Crete when he received this letter from Paul. He later served a mission to Dalmatia.

- **Titus 1:4 Paul's calls Titus his "son after the . . . faith."** His love and confidence in Titus is shown by this greeting and by the blessings he wishes for him: "Grace, mercy, and peace, from God the Father and the Lord Jesus Christ our Saviour."

When, Where, and Why Was the Epistle to Titus Written?

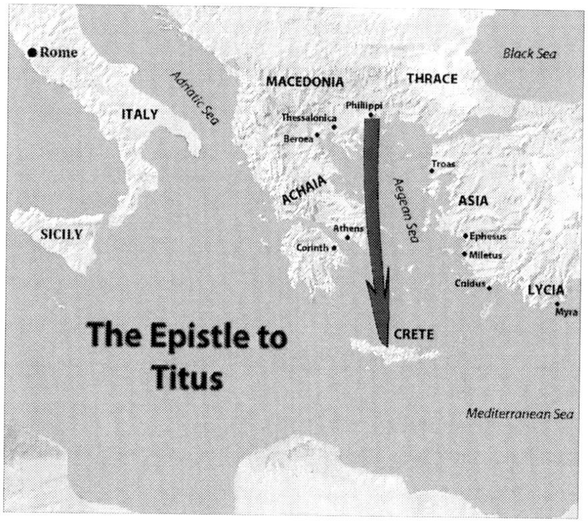

We do not know for sure the letter's point of origin, but it was probably written at or very near the same time as 1st Timothy, about 67–68 AD. This would put it sometime between his first and second imprisonments at Rome. If so, then it was most likely written at Philippi in Macedonia, where Paul rested for a time after being released from his first imprisonment.

Titus was an early Greek convert to the Church. He was present with Paul at the Jerusalem Council (Galatians 2:1). Paul had left Titus on Crete (Titus 1:5) and Titus became the first bishop of the Cretans. Crete is an island approximately 160 miles long and 25 miles wide, with many cities. This epistle was written to strengthen and encourage Titus.

What Are the Epistle to Titus' Most Significant Contributions?

Like 1 Timothy, this letter deals with priesthood organization and the duties of leaders in the Church. Specifically, Paul warns Titus to beware of false ministers and doctrines. He also speaks regarding the character and conduct of those called to priesthood leadership.

Elder Bruce R. McConkie said: "Titus is the epistle of obedience. Writing in his old age, Paul seems increasingly impressed by the Spirit to counsel his beloved Titus, and through him all the Saints, of the overpowering need to walk in paths of truth and righteousness. . . . Titus is written to and for the Saints. It is a sermon of practical exhortation to those in the fold, a common sense approach to the problem of living in the world without being of the world."[6]

- **Titus 1:1–3 God's premortal promise of eternal life.** In the opening to his letter to Titus, Paul called himself "a servant of God, and an apostle of Jesus Christ," who had been testifying "according to the faith of God's elect," and "acknowledging . . . the truth which is after [leads to] godliness" (v. 1). Paul said he served "in hope of eternal life, which God, that cannot lie, promised before the world began" (v. 2). This is clearly a reference to the plan of salvation instituted by God in the premortal world. The same God "hath in due times manifested his word through preaching, which [assignment] is committed unto me according to the commandment of God our Saviour" (v. 3).

CONTENDING AGAINST EVIL

- **Titus 1:6–9 Paul again outlines qualifications for a bishop** (compare to 1 Timothy 3:2–7). He did this in the epistle to Titus as part of explaining the evils that Titus and the Saints must contend against. In this list, Paul says a bishop must be:

Paul made Titus the Bishop of Crete

  - — Blameless (vv. 6, 7).
  - — The husband of one wife (v. 6).
  - — Having faithful children (v. 6).
  - — Not accused of riot [debauchery, insubordination] or [of being] unruly (v. 6).
  - — Not self-willed (v. 7).
  - — Not soon angry (v. 7).
  - — Not given to wine (v. 7).
  - — No striker (v. 7).
  - — Not given to filthy lucre (v. 7).
  - — A lover of hospitality (v. 8).
  - — A lover of good men [meaning a lover of what is good] (v. 8).
  - — Sober (v. 8).
  - — Just (v. 8).
  - — Holy (v. 8).
  - — Temperate [self-controlled] (v. 8).
  - — Holding fast the faithful word as he hath been taught, that he may be able by sound doctrine both to exhort and to convince (v. 9).

- **Titus 1:9–11 Gainsaying for filthy lucre's sake.** Paul warned Titus that he would have to confront and convince the "gainsayers" (v. 9), which is an old Anglo-Saxon word that means "contrary to" or "in opposition of." Today we would translate it "those who speak against something in order to enrich themselves at the expense of others." Paul said, "There are many unruly [insubordinate, rebellious] and vain talkers [idle speakers, disputers] and deceivers, [e]specially they of the circumcision [the Jews]" (v. 10). The opponents' "mouths must be stopped," because they "subvert whole houses, teaching things which they ought not, for filthy lucre's sake" (v. 11).

Elder Spencer W. Kimball said:

> Now, all money is not lucre—all money is not filthy. There is clean money—clean money with which to buy food, clothes, shelter, and other necessities and with which to make contributions toward the building of the kingdom of God.
>
> Clean money is that compensation received for a full day's honest work. It is that reasonable pay for faithful service. It is that fair profit from the sale of goods, commodities, or service. It is that income received from transactions where all parties profit.
>
> Filthy lucre is blood money; that which is obtained through theft and robbery. It is that obtained through gambling or the operation of gambling establishments. Filthy lucre is that had through sin or sinful operations and that which comes from the handling of liquor, beer, narcotics and those other many things which are displeasing in the sight of the Lord. Filthy lucre is that money which comes from bribery, and from exploitation.
>
> Compromise money is filthy, graft money is unclean, profits and commissions derived from the sale of worthless stocks are contaminated as is the money derived from other deceptions, excessive charges, oppression to the poor and compensation which is not fully earned. I feel strongly that men who accept wages or salary and do not give commensurate time, energy, devotion, and service are receiving money that is not clean. Certainly those who deal in the forbidden are recipients of filthy lucre.[7]

- **Titus 1:12–13 Cretans were will known for their greed and dishonesty.** Paul quoted "one of themselves, even a prophet of their own," who said, "The Cretians are alway[s] liars, evil beasts, slow bellies" (v. 12). The early Church Father Jerome thought that the "prophet" Paul was quoting was the poet Epimenides. Cretans were well known for their greed and dishonesty, according to Cicero and Plutarch. "Slow bellies" is better translated "idle bellies," suggesting laziness and gluttony. Titus was to "rebuke them [the liars and slow bellies] sharply, that they may be sound in the faith" (v. 13).

- **Titus 1:14 The Jews on Crete were teaching fables.** Titus was "not [to] giv[e] . . . heed to Jewish fables, and commandments of men, that turn from the truth. Evidently, Jewish apostates from the Church were preaching "fables" concerning Mosaic law.

- **Titus 1:15–16 The pure are compared to those for whom nothing is pure.** "Unto the pure all things are pure: but unto them that are defiled and unbelieving is nothing pure; but even their mind and conscience is defiled" (v. 15). "They profess that they know God; but in works they deny him, being abominable, and disobedient, and unto every good work reprobate" (v. 16).

Elder Bruce R. McConkie said, "The pure in heart are those who are free from moral defilement or guilt; who have bridled their passions, put off the natural man and become Saints through the Atonement (Mosiah 3:19); who have been born again, becoming the sons and daughters of Christ (Mosiah 5:7); who are walking in paths of uprightness and virtue and seeking to do all things that further the interests of the Lord's earthly kingdom.... One of the chief identifying characteristics of a Saint is that he has a pure mind (2 Peter 3:1)."[8]

AVOIDING HERESY

The Sin of Heresy

Heresy is the belief and espousal of false doctrine. Heretics belong to the Church yet adhere to religious opinions which are contrary to the official doctrine of the Church.

- **Titus 3:3–7 Our "good works" do not save us; we are saved by the grace of Christ.** Paul confesses that "we ourselves also [have been] sometimes foolish, disobedient, deceived, serving divers lusts and pleasures, living in malice and envy, hateful, and hating one another" (v. 3). Each of us has plenty to be ashamed of in our lives. But then "the kindness and love of God our Saviour toward man appeared" and saved us (v. 4).

  We are saved "not by works of righteousness which we have done, but according to his [Christ's] mercy ..., by the washing of regeneration [baptism], and renewing [receiving] of the Holy Ghost" (v. 5).

  Elder Bruce R. McConkie said, "There is no salvation in good works as such. That is: There are no good works which men may do which—standing alone—will cause them to be resurrected or to gain eternal life. Immortality and eternal life come through the Atonement of Christ, the one being a free gift, the other being offered freely to all who [are] baptized and ... keep the commandments."[9]

Heretical writings circulated

- **Heresies in our own day.** The heresies of Paul's time eventually took the Church into full apostasy. They are dangerous and deadly if not corrected by the Apostles, whose job it is to ensure "sound doctrine" in the Church (Ephesians 4:14). One such Apostle, Elder Bruce R. McConkie, identified "seven deadly heresies" of our own day:[10]

  — God is still progressing in knowledge and learning new truths.
  — Organic evolution and the restored gospel can be harmonized.
  — Temple marriage assures us of eventual exaltation.
  — Work for the dead offers a "second chance" for salvation.
  — There is progression from one kingdom to another after resurrection.
  — Adam is one of our gods as well as our father (the "Adam-god" theory).
  — We must be perfect to gain salvation.

- **Titus 3:9–11 Saints should avoid the foolish questions and contentious debates that heretics espouse.** Paul said, "Avoid foolish questions, and genealogies, and contentions, and strivings about the law; for they are unprofitable and vain" (v. 9). If a man continues teaching heresy after he has been warned twice, we should "reject," because such a man is "subverted, and sinneth, being condemned of himself" (vv. 10–11).

Elder Bruce R. McConkie said:

> There is no converting power in debate and contention. Christ's ministers are to teach, not to argue. Missionaries go forth, for instance, to "declare glad tidings," with this restriction: "Of tenets thou shalt not talk" (D&C 19:20–31), meaning they are to teach and explain the basic doctrines of salvation and not engage in contentions and strivings about the doctrines of sectarianism. . . .
>
> There comes a time when it is wise to shun and avoid those who rebel against the light and whose hearts are set on promulgating false and damning doctrines. A modern illustration of such is those cultists who leave the Church to advocate and practice plural marriage in a day when the President of the Church has withdrawn from all men the power to perform these marriages.[11]

— **2 Timothy 2:23–25 Debate, argumentation, and criticism stir up ill feelings; instead, teach with gentleness and meekness.** Paul said, "Foolish and unlearned questions avoid, knowing that they do gender strifes (v. 23). "The servant of the Lord must not strive; but be gentle unto all men, apt to teach, patient, in meekness instructing those that oppose themselves; if God peradventure will give them repentance to the acknowledging of the truth" (vv. 24–25).

Elder Bruce R. McConkie said,"Contention and division are of the devil. Agreement and unity are of God. Since true religion comes by revelation, man's sole purpose in trying to understand and interpret gospel principles should be to find out what the Lord means in any given revelation. This knowledge can be gained only by the power of the Spirit. Hence, there is no occasion to debate, to argue, to contend, to champion one cause as against another. 'Those who have the Spirit do not hang doggedly to a point of doctrine or philosophy for no other reason than to come off victorious in a disagreement. Their purpose, rather, is to seek truth by investigation, research, and inspiration. "Cease to contend one with another," the Lord has commanded (D&C 136:23; Titus 3:9).'"[12]

2ND EPISTLE TO TIMOTHY

More Information about Timothy

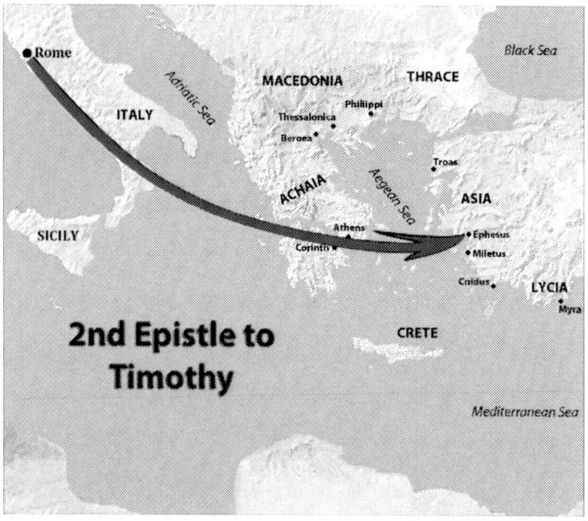

- **2 Timothy 1:3–5 The righteousness of Timothy's family spanned three generations.** Paul loved Timothy very much and had him continually in his prayers (v. 3). He also greatly desired to see him again "that I may be filled with joy" (v. 4).

  Paul recalled the "unfeigned faith" that was in Timothy, "which dwelt first in thy grandmother Lois, and thy mother Eunice; and I am persuaded that in thee also" (v. 5).

- **2 Timothy 3:14–15 Paul admonishes Timothy to do those things he had been taught since childhood**—in particular, to read the scriptures. "Continue thou in the things which thou hast learned and hast been assured of, knowing of whom thou hast learned them; and that from a child thou hast known the holy scriptures, which are able to make thee wise unto salvation through faith which is in Christ Jesus."

  Bishop H. Burke Peterson has counseled, "There shouldn't be—there mustn't be—one family in this Church that doesn't take the time to read from the scriptures every day."[13]

When and Where Was 2nd Timothy Written?

Paul wrote 2nd Timothy during his second Roman imprisonment, just prior to his execution. This imprisonment was different; he was not treated with deference by the Roman authorities. Friends still visited Paul, but his freedom to preach the gospel was greatly restricted.

Nero blamed the great fire of Rome (which he himself probably set) on the Christians. Both Paul and Peter were caught up in this new hostility, as were many Church members. Facing certain execution, Paul's friends deserted him in fear, and others betrayed him. At his trial no one came forth to plead his cause. Apparently only Luke remained with him. Yet he remained calm and even exultant. "I am now ready to be offered," he writes without remorse or pity. "The time of my departure is at hand" (2 Timothy 4:6).

We believe Paul was executed in Rome around 67 or 68 AD by being beheaded. Peter was also executed about that same time by being crucified upside down.

Why Was 2nd Timothy Written?

The 2nd epistle to Timothy is a letter of encouragement to Timothy and to all priesthood leaders. Paul challenged him to magnify the calling to which he had been ordained and to endure to the end. Paul warned Timothy against the spiritual apostasy that was rising in the Church. In chapter 2 of 2nd Timothy, Paul counseled his young friend in the ministry to:

— Be strong in the faith (v. 1).
— Endure persecution and opposition (vv. 2–3).
— Study the holy scriptures (v. 15).
— Shun contention (vv. 16, 23–24).
— Keep the commandments (v. 22).
— Strive for complete victory over the temptations of the world (v. 22).
— Preach the word with power (v. 25).

What Are 2nd Timothy's Most Significant Contributions?

This epistle shows clearly the tremendous faith of the Apostle Paul. In spite of the adverse circumstances (being imprisoned for the second time), he was optimistic and buoyed up by his faith in Christ. This epistle is a monument to his faith and hope in the face of loneliness and adversity.

It also provides a concise and powerful description of the great apostasy that was already descending upon the Church. Paul provides a graphic and prophetic picture of the spiritual confusion that existed during his time and that will exist in the latter days. As Paul's final letter, it is a poignant farewell to all believers and to all mankind.

PERSONAL ADVICE FOR TIMOTHY

Do Not Be Afraid

- **2 Timothy 1:6–7 Righteousness replaces fear with power, love, and a sound mind.** Paul admonishes Timothy to "stir up the gift of God, which is in thee by the putting on of my hands" (v. 6). This would refer to both the Holy Spirit he received after his baptism and to his priesthood ordination and callings. Those were troubling times for priesthood leaders who might become discouraged with the progress and pace of apostasy that was destroying the Church. But Paul reminded Timothy that "God hath not given us the spirit of fear; but of power, and of love, and of a sound mind" (v. 7).

THEBIBLEREVIVAL.COM, #43

Be Devoted to the Work

- **2 Timothy 1:8–12 Be not ashamed of Christ.** "Be not thou therefore ashamed of the testimony of our Lord, nor of me his prisoner: but be thou partaker of the afflictions of the gospel according to the power of God" (v. 8). Paul reminded Timothy that Christ "hath saved us, and called us with an holy calling, not according to our works, but according to his own purpose and grace," and that their ministry "was given us in Christ Jesus before the world began" (v. 9). This is another reference to foreordination to priesthood callings during the premortal council in Heaven. That heavenly plan was "made manifest by the appearing of our Saviour Jesus Christ, who hath abolished death, and hath brought life and immortality to light through the gospel" (v. 10).

  Of those events and principles Paul said he was "appointed a preacher, and an apostle, and a teacher of the Gentiles" (v. 11). "For the which cause I also suffer these things: nevertheless I am not ashamed: for I know whom I have believed, and am persuaded that he is able to keep [remember] that which I have committed unto him [Paul's entire life following his conversion] against that day [the day of judgment]" (v. 12).

- **2 Timothy 1:16–18 A tribute to Onesiphorus.** This member of the Church from Ephesus showed devotion to Paul by visiting and helping him while he was in prison. "He oft refreshed me, and was not ashamed of my chain," said Paul, "But, when he was in Rome, he sought me out very diligently, and found me" (v. 17). "The Lord grant unto him that he may find mercy of the Lord in that day: and in how many things he ministered unto me at Ephesus, thou knowest very well" (v. 18).

- **2 Timothy 2:1–7 Three metaphors of faith.** Calling Timothy "my son" again, Paul urged him to "be strong in the grace that is in Christ Jesus. And the things that thou hast heard of me among many witnesses, the same commit thou to faithful men, who shall be able to teach others also" (v. 2). Then Paul used three different metaphors to illustrate the level of faith that would be required.

  First, Paul provided a military metaphor of a soldier. "Endure hardness [affliction], as a good soldier of Jesus Christ," Paul said. "No man that warreth [goes to war] entangleth himself with the affairs of this life," but remains single-minded to his work "that he may please him who hath chosen him to be a soldier" (vv. 3–4).

  Next, Paul provided an athletic metaphor. "If a man . . . strive for masteries [competes in a contest], . . . he [is] not crowned [wins], except he strive lawfully [obeys the rules of the contest]" (v. 5).
  Finally, Paul provided an agricultural metaphor. "The husbandman [farmer] that laboureth must [will] be first partaker of the fruits" (v. 6). In other words, if Timothy labors diligently in the Lord's vineyard, he will reap salvation to his own soul.

  For each of these metaphors, Paul asked Timothy to "consider what I say; and the Lord give thee understanding in all things" (v. 7).

DEALING WITH APOSTASY

Be Vigilant Against Apostasy

THEBIBLEREVIVAL.COM, #22

- **2 Timothy 1:13–15 Hold fast against apostasy with sound doctrine and the guidance of the Holy Ghost.** Paul lamented the scope and rapid pace of apostasy. To Timothy he observed that "all they which are in Asia [the area over which Timothy presided from Ephesus] be turned away from me; of whom are Phygellus and Hermogenes" (v. 15). Against this onslaught, Paul advised Timothy to "hold fast the form of sound words [teachings], which thou hast heard of me, in faith and love which is in Christ Jesus" (v. 13). "That good thing which was committed unto thee [the gospel and Timothy's testimony] keep by the Holy Ghost which dwelleth in us" (v. 14).

Know the Truth

- **2 Timothy 2:14–16 Be knowledgeable of the gospel and avoid vain arguments.** Those who teach false and heretical things to Church members "strive . . . about words to no profit" [disputing over words and trivial things], which leads to the "subverting of the hearers" (v. 14). To counter this, Paul counseled Timothy to "study to shew thyself approved unto God, a workman that needeth not to be ashamed, rightly dividing the word of truth" (v. 15). "But shun profane and vain babblings [disputations]: for they will increase unto more ungodliness" (v. 16).

- **2 Timothy 2:23–25 Avoid arguments about things that do not matter to our salvation.** Paul said that "foolish and unlearned questions" only "[en]gender strifes" (v. 23). Timothy should avoid such things because "the servant of the Lord must not strive; but be gentle unto all men, apt to teach, patient, in meekness instructing those that oppose themselves; if God peradventure will give them repentance to the acknowledging of the truth" (vv. 24–25).

  Elder Bruce R. McConkie said: "Not all truth is of equal value. Some scientific truths may benefit men in this life only; the truths of revealed religion will pour out blessings upon them now and forever. But even revealed truth is not all of the same worth. Some things apply only to past dispensations, as the performances of the Mosaic system; others are binding in all ages, as the laws pertaining to baptism and celestial marriage."[14]

- **2 Timothy 2:17–18 Heresy destroys faith as it spreads.** False doctrine "will eat as doth a canker," Paul said. The word "canker" is from the Greek word *gangreina*—gangrene. Gangrene kills living cells as it spreads, and apostates do the same to the faith of believers. Paul identifies two such apostates as "Hymenæus and Philetus" (v. 17). These two, "concerning the truth have erred, saying that the resurrection is past already; and overthrow the faith of some" (v. 18).

Elder Bruce R. McConkie said, "Satan's ministers delight in spiritualizing away the prophecies and doctrines of the gospel. Probably what was here involved was the allegorical teaching that the resurrection consisted in imparting new life to the soul through acceptance of the gospel. Such a view is on a par with the sectarian heresy that the Second Coming is past, meaning that the Lord already has returned to dwell in the hearts of the faithful."[15]

Turn Away from Apostates

- **2 Timothy 3:1–7 Conditions in the "latter days" (our day).** Lest Timothy should think that apostasy was only an issue in his day, Paul gave him a larger perspective. He prophesied with stunning accuracy how people would be in the latter days. "This know also, that in the last days perilous times shall come" (v. 1). Paul then listed the character of godless people that would arise in our time. "Men shall be . . .

v. 2	—	Lovers of their own selves [selfish]
	—	Covetous
	—	Boasters
	—	Proud
	—	Blasphemers
	—	Disobedient to parents
	—	Unthankful
	—	Unholy
v. 3	—	Without natural affection [homosexuals]
	—	Truce-breakers
	—	False accusers [slanderers]
	—	Incontinent [without self-control]
	—	Fierce
	—	Despisers of those that are good

President Spencer W. Kimball said, "We see our world sinking into depths of corruption. Every sin mentioned by Paul is now rampant in our society. Men and women are 'lovers of their own selves.' They boast in their accomplishment. They curse. They blaspheme. Another sin is disobedience of children to parents and parents' disobedience to law. Many are without the natural affection, which seems to be eroding family life as they seek to satisfy their own selfish wants. There are said to be millions of perverts who have relinquished their natural affection and bypassed courtship and normal marriage relationships. This practice is spreading like a prairie fire and changing our world. They are without 'natural affection' for God, for spouses, and even for children."[16]

v. 4 — Traitors
— Heady [rash or reckless]
— Highminded [conceited]
— Lovers of pleasures more than lovers of God

President Spencer W. Kimball said, "Paul speaks of 'lovers of pleasure more than lovers of God.' Does that not describe the wanton sex permissiveness of our day? Paul speaks of those who 'creep into houses, and lead captive silly women laden with sins, led away with divers lusts' (2 Tim. 3:6). Immorality seems to now receive the wink of approval of the once honorable people. Debauchery never gave birth to good of any kind, and Paul said: 'But she that liveth in pleasure is dead while she liveth' (1 Tim. 5:6). But now comes a heavenly voice. 'Thou shalt not commit adultery; and he that committeth adultery, and repenteth not, shall be cast out' (D&C 42:24)."[17]

v. 5 — Having a form of godliness; but denying the power thereof

Elder Bruce R. McConkie said, "A form of godliness without saving power! A hollow shell shattered into many fragments! An illusive image without substance! An imitation of what God had aforetime revealed through Peter and Paul! A system of so-called Christianity which worshiped a God without a power, a God who gave no revelations, unfolded no visions, worked no miracles, and had forgotten the unchangeable pattern of the past! All Christendom wallowing in the mire and filth of apostasy!"[18]

"From such turn away," said Paul, "For of this sort are they . . .

v. 6 — Which creep into houses, and lead captive silly women laden with sins, led away with divers lusts [adulterers].

v. 7 — Ever learning, and never able to come to the knowledge of the truth.

President Joseph Fielding Smith said, "Among the signs of the last days was an increase of learning. . . . Is not knowledge increased? Was there ever a time in the history of the world when so much knowledge was poured out upon the people? But sad to say, the words of Paul are true—the people are 'ever learning and never able to come to the knowledge of the truth' (2 Tim. 3:7)."[19]

- **2 Timothy 3:8–9 Apostates resist and challenge the prophets.** According to Jewish tradition, Jannes and Jambres were two magicians who opposed Moses in the court of Pharaoh. Paul said, "Now as Jannes and Jambres withstood Moses, so do these also resist the truth: men of corrupt minds, reprobate concerning the faith" (v. 8). Such men think they will out-smart the prophets and that they know so much better what is right and good and correct. "But they shall proceed no further," said Paul, "for their folly shall be manifest unto all men, as theirs [Jannes and Jambres] also was" (v. 9).

- **2 Timothy 3:10–13 Those who follow Christ will be persecuted by the wicked.** The world will become increasingly wicked over time. "Yea, . . . all that will live godly in

Christ Jesus shall suffer persecution" as "evil men and seducers . . . wax worse and worse, deceiving, and being deceived" (vv. 12–13). But Paul reminded Timothy that he had "fully known my doctrine, manner of life, purpose, faith, longsuffering, charity, patience, persecutions, [and] afflictions, which came unto me at Antioch, at Iconium, at Lystra; [which] persecutions I endured: but out of them all the Lord delivered me" (vv. 10–11). Those who are similarly persecuted should expect such things from the ungodly, but should also know that the Lord will be with them and deliver them.

Read and Follow the Scriptures

- **2 Timothy 3:14–15 Timothy was raised in a home where the scriptures were valued.** "Continue thou in the things which thou hast learned and hast been assured of, knowing of whom thou hast learned them; And that from a child thou hast known the holy scriptures, which are able to make thee wise unto salvation through faith which is in Christ Jesus." What a blessing this is! Those of us who have been raised in the Church should have praise in our hearts continually that "from a child" we have known these things.

Timothy's mother Lydia was a righteous woman

I reflect often on the days of my childhood, being taught by my parents, attending Primary and Sacrament meetings. I was taught from the beginning who I am as a child of God and what my potential destiny could be. On one occasion I laid in a field of grain with my father, sleeping out under the stars during his water turn on his farm. The whole expanse of the sky was lit up with stars and the path of the Milky Way. As I expressed my amazement, my Father said to me, "Son, if you keep your covenants with the Lord, all of that is yours." It blew my mind. It still does. But I know that it is true.

Later, when I received my patriarchal blessing, the Lord made mention of my idyllic upbringing. The patriarch spoke of my "goodly parents" who had taught me concerning "the deep values of life" and of the gospel. Then, he added this very profound statement: "Thou art obligated to act upon the favorable circumstances of thy birth." And so it is. If God has granted us so much, we are obligated to serve Him faithfully in teaching these truths to others. That is my primary motivation in writing these books. And it has been my life's desire ever since.

- **2 Timothy 3:15–17 The benefits of scripture.** "From a child thou hast known the holy scriptures," said Paul to Timothy, "which are able to make thee wise unto salvation through faith which is in Christ Jesus. All scripture is given by inspiration of God, and is profitable for doctrine, for reproof, for correction, for instruction in righteousness" (vv. 15–16). Through the scriptures "the man of God may be perfect, throughly furnished unto all good works" (v. 17). This is an excellent summary of what scriptures provide:

  — They make us wise unto salvation through faith in Christ.
  — They are given by inspiration from God.
  — They are a good source for doctrine.
  — They are a good source for reproof and correction.
  — They are a good source for instruction in righteousness.
  — Through them we learn how to be perfect.
  — Through them we learn to do good works.

  Nevertheless, the scriptures alone do not save us. The Jews believed that in their scriptures they had eternal life (John 5:39), but they failed to live the principles taught by the scriptures or to believe in the Messiah of whom the scriptures testified.

  President Joseph F. Smith said, "'But,' says an objector, 'have we not the Bible, and are not the Holy Scriptures able to make us wise unto salvation?' Yes, provided we obey them. 'All Scripture is given by inspiration of God, and is profitable for doctrine, for reproof, for correction, for instruction in righteousness; that the man of God may be perfect, thoroughly furnished unto all good works.' The 'good works' are the great desideratum. The Bible itself is but the dead letter; it is the Spirit that giveth life. The way to obtain the Spirit is that which is here marked out so plainly in the Scriptures. There is no other. Obedience, therefore, to these principles is absolutely necessary, in order to obtain the salvation and exaltation brought to light through the gospel."[20]

PAUL'S FINAL WORDS

- **2 Timothy 4:1–2 Paul's final charge to Timothy.** "I charge thee therefore before God, and the Lord Jesus Christ, who shall judge the quick and the dead at his appearing and his kingdom," he said, to "preach the word; be instant in season, [and] out of season" (v. 2). "Instant" means urgent, serious, or diligent. Timothy was to diligently "reprove, rebuke, [and] exhort with all longsuffering and doctrine" (v. 2).

  The Prophet Joseph Smith revised this verse to read, "Preach the word. Be instant in season; those who are out of season reprove, rebuke, exhort with all long-suffering and doctrine" (JST v. 2).[21]

PROVIDENCE LITHOGRAPHIC CO., 1909, #39

- **2 Timothy 4:3–5 Another prediction of apostasy.** How difficult it must have been for Paul, Timothy, and other faithful leaders to know that eventually their efforts would fail. "Watch thou in all things," said Paul to Timothy; "endure afflictions, do the work of an evangelist, make full proof of thy ministry" (v. 5). Yet, despite their best efforts, the apostasy was inevitable. They could only hope to keep some of the Saints faithful to the ends of their lives. But the Church itself would not endure.

  "For the time will come when they will not endure sound doctrine; but after their own lusts shall they heap to themselves teachers, having itching ears [those who will teach whatever you want to hear rather than the truth]" (v. 3). "And they shall turn away their ears from the truth, and shall be turned unto fables [false doctrines]" (v. 4).

  Elder Bruce R. McConkie said, "All false doctrines are fables. That is, they are stories which have been imagined, fabricated, and invented as opposed to the gospel which is real and true (2 Pet. 1:16). Apostasy consists in turning from true doctrine to fables."[22]

- **2 Timothy 4:6–8 Paul knew that his work on earth was now complete.** "I am now ready to be offered, and the time of my departure is at hand," he wrote to Timothy (v. 6). "I have fought a good fight, I have finished my course, I have kept the faith" (v. 7). "Henceforth there is laid up for me a crown of righteousness, which the Lord, the righteous judge, shall give me at that day: and not to me only, but unto all them also that love his appearing" (v. 8).

  REMBRANDT, THE BIBLE AND ITS STORY, 1908

  Elder Spencer W. Kimball said, "It will be recalled that Peter was released from prison by an angel and protected in many ways till his work was finished. And Paul likewise. No violence could take his life until he had borne his testimony to Rome and Greece and other lands. But finally he made the prophetic statement to Timothy: 'For I am now ready to be offered, and the time of my departure is at hand. I have fought a good fight, I have finished my course, I have kept the faith' (2 Tim. 4:6–7). There was no fear in his approach to eternity—only assurance and calm resignation to the inevitable martyrdom which he faced. He did not want to die but was willing thus to seal his testimony of the Redeemer."[23]

  Elder Bruce R. McConkie said, "Paul's calling and election had been made sure. He was sealed up unto eternal life. He had kept the commandments, been tried at all hazards, and the Lord had given him the promise: 'Son, Thou shalt be exalted.' And since no man is or can be exalted alone, this is one of the crowning reasons why we know Paul was married."[24]

OTHER CONCEPTS IN THE PASTORAL EPISTLES

- **1 Timothy 1:4; 4:7 Avoid "fables and endless genealogies".** Endless genealogies is a reference to the claims of some (particularly Jews) that they were saved because of their race or ancestry. Are we guilty of this? Do we think that because we descend from a famous leader of the Church that we are somehow more special than others? Do we believe that our race or ethnic background makes us better than others? We should avoid such prideful arrogance. God is no respecter of persons.

  When we focus on "fables" [mysteries and false doctrines] it only generates "questions, rather than godly edifying" which is obtained only through faith (1:4). We should "refuse profane and old wives' fables, and exercise thyself rather unto godliness" (4:7).

- **1 Timothy 1:8–10 The law of Moses was given by God, but it was a lesser law** given to those who were not spiritually ready for a higher law. Paul declared that the law of Moses "is good, if a man use it lawfully" (v. 8). But we should remember that it is "not made for a righteous man, but for the lawless and disobedient, for the ungodly and for sinners, for unholy and profane, for murderers of fathers and murderers of mothers, for manslayers, for whoremongers [pimps], for them that defile themselves with mankind [homosexuals], for menstealers [kidnappers, slave traders], for liars, for perjured persons, and if there be any other thing that is contrary to sound doctrine" (vv. 9–10).

  Reflect for a moment on how many of these things the people of our world are doing. Such are not ready for the higher principles of the Gospel of Jesus Christ or His temples. They are living a telestial law and can only be governed by the law of Moses, which they regularly violate. Though they may consider themselves more "progressive" and "enlightened," they are not much different than the children of Israel in the wilderness.

- **1 Timothy 1:13–17 Paul's personal example of repentance and forgiveness.** He confessed that he "was before a blasphemer, and a persecutor, and injurious: but I obtained mercy, because I did it ignorantly in unbelief" (v. 13). "The grace of our Lord was exceeding abundant" when he exercised "faith" and received of the "love which is in Christ Jesus" (v. 14). "Christ Jesus came into the world to save sinners; of whom I am chief" (v. 15). "Howbeit for this cause I obtained mercy, that in me first Jesus Christ might shew forth all longsuffering, for a pattern to them which should hereafter believe on him to life everlasting" (v. 16). For this, Paul praised "the King eternal, immortal, invisible, the only wise God, be honour and glory for ever and ever. Amen" (v. 17).

- **1 Timothy 1:18–20 Excommunication.** Paul charged Timothy to give heed to "the prophecies which went before on thee," and to use them to "war a good warfare" against evil (v. 18). He was to do this with "faith, and a good conscience; which some having put away concerning faith have made shipwreck" (v. 18). Two such "shipwrecked" souls were Hymenæus and Alexander, whom Paul had "delivered unto Satan" [excommunicated], that they may learn not to blaspheme" (v. 20).

- **1 Timothy 6:1–5 Servants should honor their masters and serve honestly.** Whether a slave or a hired servant, Paul taught that they out to "count their own masters worthy of all honour, that the name of God and his doctrine be not blasphemed" (v. 1). Especially when "they . . . have believing masters, let them not despise them, because they are brethren; but rather do them service, because they are faithful and beloved, partakers of the benefit [Church members]. These things teach and exhort" (v. 2).

  "If any man teach otherwise, and consent not to wholesome words, even the words of our Lord Jesus Christ, and to the doctrine which is according to godliness; He is proud, knowing nothing, but doting about questions and strifes of words, whereof cometh envy, strife, railings, evil surmisings, perverse disputings of men of corrupt minds, and destitute of the truth, supposing that gain is godliness: from such withdraw thyself" (vv. 3–5).

  These verses apply also to employees who sometimes steal from their employers by embezzling, taking supplies for personal use, or not giving a full day's work (see also Titus 2:9–10).

Living as Saints

- **Titus 2:1–3 Values for older men and women.** Paul counseled that "aged men be sober, grave, temperate, sound in faith, in charity, in patience" (v. 2). "The aged women likewise, that they be in behaviour as becometh holiness, not false accusers, not given to much wine, teachers of good things" (v. 3).

SUNRAYS, 1908, #40

- **Titus 2:4–6 Values for young men and women.** Paul advised Titus to "teach the young women to be sober, to love their husbands, to love their children, to be discreet, chaste, keepers at home, good, obedient [subject to] to their own husbands, that the word of God be not blasphemed. Young men likewise exhort to be sober minded [serious]."

- **Titus 2:7–8 As a bishop, Titus should be a good example to others.** "In all things shew . . . thyself a pattern of good works: in doctrine shewing uncorruptness, gravity, sincerity, [and] sound speech, that cannot be condemned" so that "he that is of the contrary part may be ashamed, having no evil thing to say of you."

- **Titus 2:11–14 Living as a "peculiar people" in a wicked world.** "Denying ungodliness and worldly lusts, we should live soberly, righteously, and godly, in this present world; Looking for that blessed hope, and the glorious appearing of the great God and our Saviour Jesus Christ; Who gave himself for us, that he might redeem us from all iniquity, and purify unto himself a peculiar people, zealous of good works."

- **Titus 3:1–2 Obeying the law, setting good examples, and being meek with others.** Paul told Titus to teach Church members "to be subject to principalities and powers, to obey magistrates, to be ready to every good work, to speak evil of no man, to be no brawlers, but gentle, shewing all meekness unto all men."

Paul's Final Requests

THE HOLMAN BIBLE, 1890

- **2 Timothy 4:11, 21 "Only Luke is with me."** Of the others who had been with him previously, Demas had apostatized and Titus was serving a mission in Dalmatia, north of modern-day Greece. Eubulus, Pudens, Linus, and Claudia remained faithful in Rome (v. 21), but only Luke was at Paul's side in prison (v. 11). Paul asked Timothy to come to him before winter (v. 21) and to bring John Mark [Mark] with him. Linus, whom Paul mentions here, later became the bishop of Rome.
- **2 Timothy 4:13 Paul's needs while in jail.** "The cloke that I left at Troas with Carpus, when thou comest, bring with thee, and the books, but especially the parchments." The "cloke" was probably needed for the winter in his cold prison (see v. 21). The "parchments" could have been copies of the scriptures, copies of his own writings, or memos, membership lists, or other administrative documents.
- **2 Timothy 4:16 At Paul's arraignment in Nero's court, all his friends abandoned him.** When Paul was finally arraigned before Nero (his "first answer"), "no man stood with me, but all men forsook me: I pray God that it may not be laid to their charge."
- **2 Timothy 4:17–18, 22 Paul's final testimony and goodbye.** "The Lord stood with me, and strengthened me; that by me the preaching might be fully known, and that all the Gentiles might hear: and I was delivered out of the mouth of the lion. And the Lord shall deliver me from every evil work, and will preserve me unto his heavenly kingdom: to whom be glory for ever and ever" (v. 18). "The Lord Jesus Christ be with thy spirit. Grace be with you. Amen" (v. 22).
- **Paul is beheaded by Nero in Rome.** Sydney B. Sperry wrote, "The tradition is that Paul was conducted about two miles from Rome on the Ostian Way, southwest of the city, where he was beheaded by the sword. His Roman citizenship saved him from the suffering sustained by many Christians in being crucified or in being smeared with pitch and set on fire."[25] Paul met his death sometime between October and June, 67–68 AD.

Notes

1. *Doctrinal New Testament Commentary*, 3 vols. [1965–1973], 3:92.
2. In Conference Report, October 1985, 78; or *Ensign*, November 1985, 63.
3. *The Miracle of Forgiveness* [1969], 47–48.
4. *Faith Precedes the Miracle* [1972], 19.
5. *The Miracle of Forgiveness*, 41.
6. *Doctrinal New Testament Commentary*, 3:119.
7. In Conference Report, October 1953, 52.
8. *Mormon Doctrine*, 2nd ed. [1966], 612, 613.
9. *Doctrinal New Testament Commentary*, 3:126–127.
10. "The Seven Deadly Heresies," Fireside Address, BYU Marriott Center, June 1, 1980.
11. *Doctrinal New Testament Commentary*, 3:127, 128.
12. *Doctrinal New Testament Commentary*, 3:105; *Mormon Doctrine*, 161.
13. In Conference Report, April 1975, 79; or *Ensign*, May 1975, 53–54.
14. *Doctrinal New Testament Commentary*, 3:105–106.
15. *Doctrinal New Testament Commentary*, 3:106.
16. In Conference Report, April 1971, 7; or *Ensign*, June 1971, 17.
17. In Conference Report, April 1971, 8; or *Ensign*, June 1971, 17.
18. *Doctrinal New Testament Commentary*, 3:111.
19. In Conference Report, April 1966, 13–14.
20. *Gospel Doctrine*, 5th ed. [1939], 101–102.
21. Taken from the original manuscript by Robert J. Matthews. Note the punctuation changes in addition to the word changes made by the Prophet.
22. *Mormon Doctrine*, 261.
23. In Conference Report, April 1946, 46.
24. *Doctrinal New Testament Commentary*, 3:116.
25. *Paul's Life and Letters* [1955] 303.

SECTION ELEVEN

The Epistles of James, Peter, Jude & John

(50 AD — 96 AD)

The epistles and events described in this section include those of James (the brother of the Lord), Peter, Jude, and John. These men were scattered around the Mediterranean area at the time they wrote—from Jerusalem to Ephesus to Rome. Their epistles were sometimes intended for a specific audience, but some were intended for all Saints everywhere.

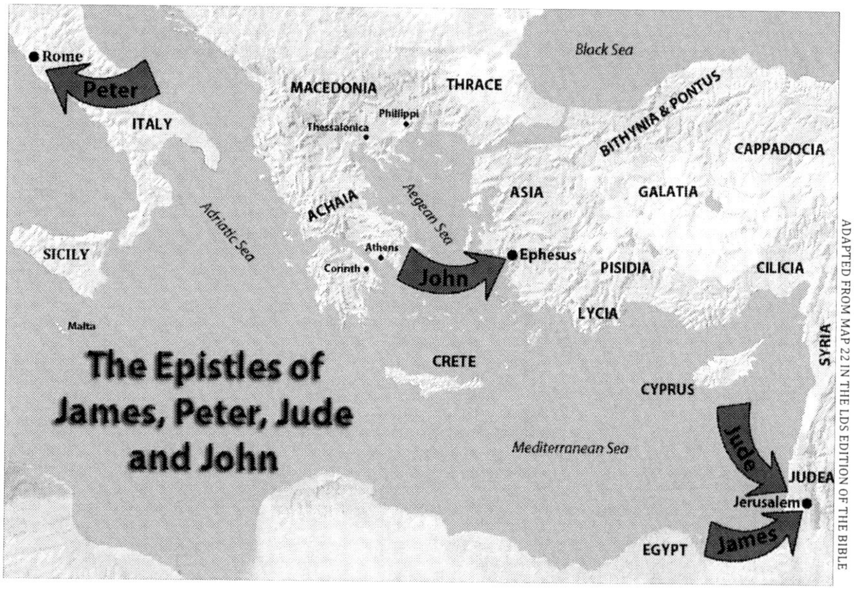

ADAPTED FROM MAP 22 IN THE LDS EDITION OF THE BIBLE

The associated chapters of this book, corresponding to Gospel Doctrine lessons, are:

42. The Epistle of James
43. The Epistles of Peter (1 & 2 Peter)
44. The Epistles of John & Jude (1–3 John & Jude)

These epistles both pre-dated and post-dated the Gospels:[1]

Epistle:	Author:	Date:	Written From:
James	James	50–51	Jerusalem
1 Peter	Peter	63	Rome
2 Peter	Peter	64	Rome
— Matthew, Mark, Luke, & Acts		60s–70s —	
Jude	Jude	80	Jerusalem
1 John	John	96	Ephesus
2 John	John	96	Ephesus
3 John	John	96	Ephesus
— Gospel of John & Revelation		90-96 —	

The following is a summary of topics covered in these epistles.

THE EPISTLE OF JAMES (50-51 AD)
To Christians Everywhere
From Jerusalem. ca. 50-51 AD

Subject:	Scriptural References
Trials Are a Privilege—Ask God for Wisdom	James 1:1-7
God Tempts No One to Do Wrong	James 1:8-18
"Be Ye Doers of the Word"	James 1:19-27
We Commit Sin If We Show Favoritism	James 2:1-9
The Entire Law Must Be Kept	James 2:10-13
"Faith Without Works Is Dead"	James 2:14-26
Controlled Language Aids Perfection	James 3:1-11
Envy and Strife Are of Evil	James 3:13-18
The Source of War and Strife	James 4:1-3
Identifying the Enemies of God	James 4:4-6
Becoming a Friend of God	James 4:7-12
What Is Sin?	James 4:13-17
A Warning for the Wealthy	James 5:1-6
Await the Lord's Coming with Patience	James 5:7-11
Elders Anoint and Heal the Sick	James 5:12-20

THE 1ST EPISTLE OF PETER (62-64AD)
To Saints in Five Provinces
Apparently Written from Rome

Subject:	Scriptural References
Salvation Conies by Faith in Christ	1 Pet. 1:1-16
Christ Was Foreordained to Be the Redeemer	1 Pet. 1:17-21
Converts Experience a New Birth in Christ	1 Pet. 1:22-25; 2:1-3
Christ, the Cornerstone for a Holy Nation	1 Pet. 2:4-10
The Obligation of Christians Towards Gentiles	1 Pet. 2:11-12
Saints to Accept Civil Authority	1 Pet. 2: 13-25
Husbands and Wives Should Honor Each Other	1 Pet. 3:1-7
"Be Followers of That Which Is Good"	1 Pet. 3:8-2x
Christ Preached the Gospel to Spirits in Prison	1 Pet. 4:1-6
"Speak as an Oracle of God"	1 Pet. 4:7-11
Saints to Be Tried in All Things	1 Pet. 4:12-1x
Elders to Feed the Flock of God	1 Pet. 5:1-4
God Refuses the Proud and Favors the Humble	1 Pet. 5:5-1x

THE 2ND EPISTLE OF PETER (Prior to his death in 68 AD)
Written from Rome

Subject:	Scriptural References
"Make Your Calling and Election Sure"	2 Pet. 1:1-19
Prophecy Comes by the Holy Ghost	2 Pet. 1:20-21
False Teachers Are Damned	2 Pet. 2:1-9
The Fallen State of Lustful Saints	2 Pet. 2:10-22
Latter-day Scoffers Shall Deny the 2nd Coming	2 Pet. 3:1-10
Holy and Saintly Lives Are Prepared for the Lord	2 Pet. 3:11-18

THE 1ST EPISTLE OF JOHN (96 AD)
To the Christian Communities
Probably from Ephesus

Subject:	Scriptural References
Walk in the Light of Christ	1 John 1:1–7
We Must Break from Our Sins	1 John 1:8–10; 2:1–2
The Saints May know God and Christ	1 John 2:3–6
Abide in the Light Through the Law of Love	1 John 2:7–14
"Love Not the World"	1 John 2:15–17
Anti-Christs to Come in Latter Days	1 John 2:18–26
The Holy Ghost Leads Saints to Truth	1 John 2:27–29
The Sons of God Shall Be like Christ	1 John 3:1–3
Saints Must Not Continue in Sin	1 John 3:4–9
Love the Brethren and Gain Eternal Life	1 John 3:10–18
Gaining Answers to Prayers	1 John 3:19–24
"Try the Spirits"	1 John 4:1–6
"God Is Love"	1 John 4:7–21
"Who Is Born of God?"	1 John 5:1–4
Many Witnesses Testify of Eternal Life in Christ	1 John 5:5–21

THE 2nd EPISTLE OF JOHN (96 AD)
To a Branch of the Church
Probably from Ephesus

Subject:	Scriptural References
Saints Are Commanded to Teach the Law of Love	2 John 1:1–6
Do Not Aid the Enemies of Christ	2 John 1:7–13

THE 3rd EPISTLE OF JOHN (96 AD)
To Gaius, a Christian Convert
Probably from Ephesus

Subject:	Scriptural References
Gaius Praised for His Labors	3 John 1:1–8
Beware of the Example of Diotrephes	3 John 1:9–11
Demetrius Commended	3 John 1:12–14

THE EPISTLE OF JUDE (80 AD)
To Jewish Christians
From Jerusalem

Subject:	Scriptural References
"Contend for the Faith"	Jude 1:1–5
Certain Angels Kept Not Their First Estate	Jude 1:6
The Disputation of Michael the Archangel	Jude 1:7–13
Enoch Prophesied of Christ's Second Coming	Jude 1:14–16
"Keep Yourselves in the Love of God"	Jude 1:17

Notes

1. Adapted from *Charting the New Testament*, © 2002 Welch, Hall, FARMS Chart 13-2.

Chapter 42

The Epistle of James

(James)

INTRODUCTION

Who Is This James?

There were three men named James in Church leadership:

- — James, the brother of John, son of Zebedee, and a member of the First Presidency.
- — James, the son of Alphaeus, an Apostle concerning whom we know very little.
- — James, the son of Joseph and Mary, and half-brother of the Lord, Jesus Christ.

Who Wrote the Epistle of James?

This James calls himself "a servant of God and of the Lord Jesus Christ" (James 1:1), but gives no other identifying information. He cannot be James the brother of John and son of Zebedee; that James was "killed with the sword" (beheaded) by Herod in 44 AD, five or six years before the great Jerusalem Council attended by the Apostle Paul. It is unlikely that it was James, the son of Alpaheus, about whom we have little information. Therefore, many scholars believe that this James was the Lord's brother, who presided over the Church in the Jerusalem area after the death of the first James and until his own martyrdom. (Acts 12:17; Acts 15:13–20).

The World's Confusion about James

The Apostle Paul called him "the Lord's brother" (Gal. 1:19). The Catholic church teaches that Mary had no other children after Jesus, because to have done so would defile her. They insist that "brother of the Lord" would mean "cousin" or some other non-sibling relationship. Others teach that James was a "step-brother"—the son of Joseph (by a previous marriage) but not of Mary. And those who do not believe that Jesus was divine say that James was simply Jesus' full brother, and that both of them were children of Joseph and Mary.

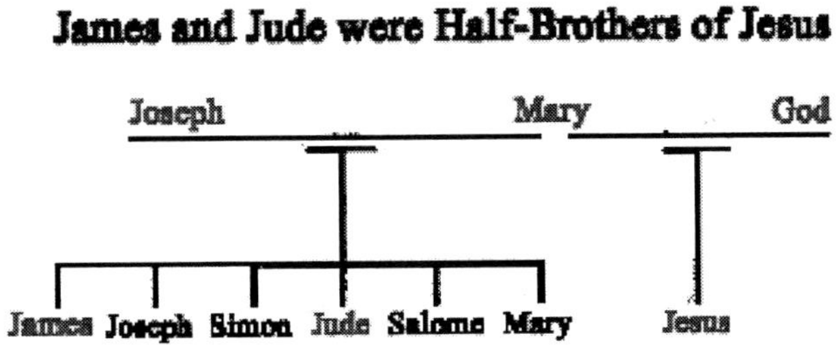

The Martyrdom of James, the Brother of the Lord

The historian Josephus says that this James, who was the leader at Jerusalem, was taken before the Sanhedrin, sentenced to death, and executed by being tossed from a Temple tower and then stoned to death in 62 AD. A recent discovery of a bone ossuary bearing the inscription "James, son of Joseph, brother of Jesus" has created some controversy about whether Jesus Christ had a brother named James.

When and Where Was the Epistle of James Written?

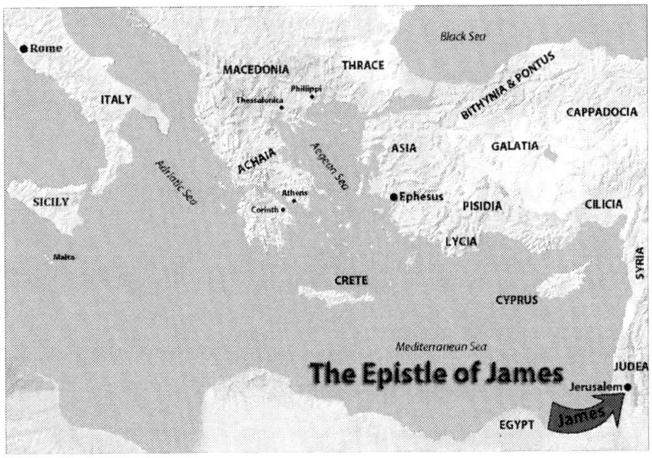

James gives no clues concerning the date or location of the epistle. Many assume that it was written from Jerusalem, since that is where James resided.

The tone of the letter (e.g., no mention of the Jewish-Gentile controversy) suggests that it was written early in the Church's history, perhaps around 50–51 AD. If this is true, it would be one of the earliest of the New Testament epistles.

Why Was the Epistle of James Written?

- **James 1:1 James addresses his letter to the "twelve tribes which are scattered abroad."** It is a general letter—not sent to a specific Church branch but to all Saints. This generality is reflected by the lack of personal references, personal greetings, or mention of any items of news that are so typical in the letters of Paul. The introduction is very brief, and there is no formal closing.

  Elder Bruce R. McConkie said:

  > [James set forth] "the practical operation of the doctrines taught by his Elder Brother [Jesus Christ]. . . . James—religious by nature; schooled in the strict Judaism of the day; converted after our Lord's resurrection; and said to have died a martyr's death—took upon himself

> the awesome responsibility to write an epistle to the Saints in the dispensation of the fulness of times.
>
> Paul wrote to the Saints of his own day, and if his doctrine and counsel blesses us of later years, so much the better. But James addressed himself to those of the Twelve scattered tribes of Israel who belonged to the Church; that is, to a people yet to be gathered, yet to receive the gospel, yet to come into the fold of Christ; and if his words had import to the small cluster of Saints of Judah and Benjamin who joined the Church in the meridian of time, so much the better.[1]

What Are the Most Significant Contributions of the Epistle of James?

James was the younger half-brother of Jesus, so he knew the Master as intimately as anyone. Later in life, James was also a witness of the resurrected Christ, who visited him.

James teaches that we must demonstrate our faith in our day-to-day lives. He teaches that the essence of pure religion is found in very practical, down-to-earth activities. Religion, he teaches, is what we do because of testimony and love.

Elder David O. McKay said, "There is no one great thing that we can do to obtain eternal life, and . . . the great lesson to be learned . . . is to apply in the little acts and duties of life—the glorious principles of the Gospel. . . . Life after all, is made up of little things. . . . The true Christian life is made up of little Christ-like acts performed this hour, this minute, in the home, in the quorum, in the organization, in the town, wherever our life and acts may be cast."[2]

ASKING IN FAITH

How to Obtain Wisdom

- **James 1:5 If we lack wisdom we can ask God for help.** This is certainly one of the best known and loved verses in all of scripture for Latter-day Saints. "If any of you lack wisdom, let him ask of God, that giveth to all men liberally, and upbraideth not; and it shall be given him."

- **James 1:6–7 We must "ask in faith, nothing wavering."** Casual or rote prayer is not enough. James said we must "ask in faith, nothing wavering. For he that wavereth is like a wave of the sea driven with the wind and tossed" (v. 6). If we are wavering in our faith, we should not "think that [we] shall receive any thing of the Lord" (v. 7).

The Impact of James' Teachings

Martin Luther said, "The epistle of James is an epistle full of straw, because it contains nothing of the gospel."[3] The reason that Martin Luther felt this way was because he had already decided that salvation came by grace alone. He had great resentment toward the priesthood of the Catholic Church, and anything that suggested that a man would need anything other than his own faith to be saved was anathema to Luther.

The Prophet Joseph Smith, on the other hand, said, "Never did any passage of scripture come with more power to the heart of man than this did at this time to mine. It seemed to enter with great force into every feeling of my heart. I reflected on it again and again."[4]

Elder Bruce R. McConkie said:

"JOSPEH SMITH IN THE GROVE," ©WALTER RANE, USED BY PERMISSION

> This single verse of scripture [James 1:5] has had a greater impact and a more far reaching effect upon mankind than any other single sentence ever recorded by any prophet in any age. It might well be said that the crowning act of the ministry of James was not his martyrdom for the testimony of Jesus, but his recitation, as guided by the Holy Ghost, of these simple words which led to the opening of the heavens in modern times.
>
> And it might well be added that every investigator of revealed truth stands, at some time in the course of his search, in the place where Joseph Smith stood. He must turn to the Almighty and gain wisdom from God by revelation if he is to gain a place on that strait and narrow path which leads to eternal life.[5]

President Spencer W. Kimball said, "Because the fourteen-year-old boy went out in the woods to pray, having read in the scriptures, . . . because he did live the revelations from on high, we have The Church of Jesus Christ of Latter-day Saints. We have all of the blessings that can make us the happiest people in the whole world, because a boy of fourteen went out into the woods to pray."[6]

TRIALS AND AFFLICTIONS

Enduring Affliction Patiently

- **James 1:2–4 Our faith is tried through affliction and trials.** James advised us to "count it all joy when ye fall into divers temptations [JST: many afflictions]" (v. 2). "Know . . . this, that the trying of your faith worketh patience. But let patience have her perfect work, that ye may be perfect and entire, wanting nothing." (vv. 3–4).

  Elder Neal A. Maxwell said all of the following on the subject of patience:[7]

> Patience is not indifference. Actually, it is caring very much, but being willing, nevertheless, to submit to the Lord and to what the scriptures call the "process of time."

Patience is tied very closely to faith in our Heavenly Father. Actually, when we are unduly impatient, we are suggesting that we know what is best—better than does God. Or, at least, we are asserting that our timetable is better than His. Either way we are questioning the reality of God's omniscience. . . .

Paul, speaking to the Hebrews, brings us up short by writing that even after faithful disciples have "done the will of God, . . . ye have need of patience" (Heb. 10:36). How many times have good individuals done the right thing only to break, or wear away, under the subsequent stress, canceling out much of the value of what they had already so painstakingly done? Sometimes that which we are doing is correct enough but simply needs to be persisted in—patiently—not for a minute or a moment but sometimes for years. . . .

The Lord has twice said: "And seek the face of the Lord always, that in patience ye may possess your souls, and ye shall have eternal life" (D&C 101:38; Luke 21:19). Could it be that only when our self-control has become total do we come into true possession of our own souls? . . .

There is also in patience a greater opportunity for that discernment which sorts out the things that matter most from the things that matter least. . . .

Patience is not only a companion of faith but is also a friend to free agency. Inside our impatience there is sometimes an ugly reality: We are plainly irritated and inconvenienced by the need to make allowances for the free agency of others. In our impatience, which is not the same thing as divine discontent, we would override others. . . . When we are unduly impatient, however, we are, in effect, trying to hasten an outcome when acceleration would abuse agency. . . .

Patience also helps us to realize that while we may be ready to move on, having had enough of a particular learning experience, our continuing presence is often a needed part of the learning environment of others. Patience is thus closely connected with two other central attributes of Christianity—love and humility. Paul said to the Saints at Thessalonica, "Be patient toward all men" (1 Thess. 5:14), clearly a part of keeping the second commandment.

The patient person assumes that what others have to say is worth listening to. . . . In true humility, we do some waiting upon others. We value them for what they say and what they have to contribute. Patience and humility are special friends. . . .

There is also a dimension of patience which links it to a special reverence for life. Patience is a willingness, in a sense, to watch the unfolding purposes of God with a sense of wonder and awe—rather than pacing up and down within the cell of our circumstance.

Too much anxious opening of the oven door and the cake falls instead of rising! So it is with us. If we are always selfishly taking our temperature to see if we are happy, we won't be. . . . Whereas faith and patience are companions, so are selfishness and impatience. . . .

Therefore, if we use the process of time well, it can cradle us as we develop patient humility. Keats tenderly observed: "Time, that aged nurse, rock'd me to patience". . . . Clearly, patience so cradles us amidst suffering. . . .

Patience permits us to cling to our faith in the Lord when we are tossed about by suffering as if by surf. When the undertow grasps us, we will realize that even as we tumble we are somehow being carried forward; we are actually being helped even as we cry for help!

One of the functions of the tribulation of the righteous is that "tribulation worketh patience" (Romans 5:3). What a vital attribute patience is, if tribulation is worth enduring to bring about its development! . . .

Patience is, therefore, clearly not fatalistic, shoulder-shrugging resignation; it is accepting a divine rhythm to life; it is obedience prolonged. Patience stoutly resists pulling up the daisies to see how the roots are doing!

Patience is never condescending or exclusive; it is never glad when others are left out. Patience never preens itself; it prefers keeping the window of the soul open. . . .

Thus . . . patience is a vital virtue in relation to our faith, our free agency, our attitude toward life, our humility, and our suffering. Moreover, patience will not be an obsolete attribute in the next world! . . . There is simply no other way for true growth to occur. . . .

How could we learn about obedience if we were shielded from the consequences of our disobedience? And how could we learn patience under pressure if we did not experience pressure and waiting? . . . God's court is filled with those who have patiently overcome—whose company we do not yet deserve.

- **James 1:9–11 Riches and exaltation.** James taught that poor ["of low degree"] but faithful Saints should"rejoice in that [they are] exalted" (v. 9). The rich should rejoice *when* they are made low "because as the flower of the grass he shall pass away" (v. 10). Wealth has been and always will be a fleeting possession. James described how when the sun is "risen with a burning heat, . . . it withereth the grass, and the flower thereof falleth, and the grace [and] the fashion of it perisheth." This is a metaphor for how riches, and the rich themselves, will "fade away" (v. 11).

  Elder Bruce R. McConkie said: "Let wealthy Saints who are stripped of their goods because of their allegiance to the gospel also rejoice, for worldly riches are fleeting and not to be compared with the riches of eternity. Or, let them rejoice when, through trials, they become lowly in spirit and no longer trust in those things which wither and die in the day's heat."[8]

  — **Romans 5:3–5 Tribulation produces patience, experience, and hope.** Paul also said that we ought to "glory in tribulations . . . knowing that tribulation worketh patience; and patience, experience; and experience, hope: and hope maketh [us] not ashamed; because the love of God is shed abroad in our hearts by the Holy Ghost which is given unto us."

"ICY CRUCIBLES," ©JOSEPH BRICKEY, USED BY PERMISSION

— **JST Heb. 11:40 Without suffering we cannot be made perfect.** Speaking of the sufferings of the faithful in Old Testament times, Paul said that "God . . . provided some better things for them through their sufferings, for without sufferings they could not be made perfect."

Elder Orson F. Whitney wrote, "No pain that we suffer, no trial that we experience is wasted. It ministers to our education, to the development of such qualities as patience, faith, fortitude and humility. All that we suffer and all that we endure, especially when we endure it patiently, builds up our characters, purifies our hearts, expands our souls, and makes us more tender and charitable, more worthy to be called the children of God."[9]

— **D&C 98:12–14 The Lord will prove us in all things, that we may be found worthy.** The Lord "give[s] unto the faithful line upon line, precept upon precept; and [He] will try you and prove you herewith. And whoso layeth down his life in my cause, for my name's sake, shall find it again, even life eternal. Therefore, be not afraid of your enemies, for I have decreed in my heart, saith the Lord, that I will prove you in all things, whether you will abide in my covenant, even unto death, that you may be found worthy."

— **D&C 101:4–5 Those who will not endure chastening cannot be sanctified.** When the Saints were driven from their Zion in Missouri, and wondered why, the Prophet Joseph inquired of the Lord. His answer was that "they must needs be chastened and tried, even as Abraham, who was commanded to offer up his only son. For all those who will not endure chastening, but deny me, cannot be sanctified."

— **D&C 136:31 The Lord's people must be tried in all things.** As the Saints were heading west across the plains and wondering why they had once again been driven from their homes, Brigham Young inquired of the Lord. The answer was, "My people must be tried in all things, that they may be prepared to receive the glory that I have for them, even the glory of Zion; and he that will not bear chastisement is not worthy of my kingdom."

- **James 5:1–3 Riches can corrupt us.** Speaking to those who glory in their riches, James said "Go to now, ye rich men, weep and howl for your miseries that shall come upon you. Your riches are corrupted, and your garments are motheaten. Your gold and silver is cankered; and the rust of them shall be a witness against you, and shall eat your flesh as it were fire. Ye have heaped treasure together for [and will be judged for it in] the last days." These words are reminiscent of the Savior's statements in the Sermon on the Mount: "Lay not up for yourselves treasures upon earth, where moth and rust doth corrupt" (Matthew 6:19–21).

  Elder Boyd K. Packer said, "Some are tested by poor health, some by a body that is deformed or homely. Others are tested by handsome and healthy bodies; some by the passion of youth; others by the erosions of age. Some suffer disappointment in marriage, family problems; others live in poverty and obscurity. Some (perhaps this is the hardest test) find ease and luxury. All are part of the test, and there is more equality in this testing than sometimes we suspect."[10]

- **James 5:7–9 Wait patiently for the Lord's Second Coming.** "Be patient therefore, brethren, unto the coming of the Lord" (v. 7). A farmer waits patiently "for the precious fruit of the earth, and hath long patience for it" (v. 7). "Be ye also patient; [e]stablish your hearts: for the coming of the Lord draweth nigh" (v. 8). We must also "grudge not one against another," or do anything sinful because "the judge [Christ, who] standeth before the door [is coming soon]" (v. 9).

- **James 5:10–11 The prophets are examples of patience in affliction.** James offered the prophets as examples "of suffering affliction, and of patience" (v. 10). As we do so we might think of Abraham waiting patiently for the birth of Isaac until well into his nineties; Joseph in Egypt waiting faithfully for vindication of his righteousness; or Moses enduring the bad behavior of the children of Israel for 40 years in the wilderness. All of these and more have been rewarded for their patience. James offered as an example "the patience of Job," and pointed out that his reward in the end showed that "the Lord is very pitiful, and of tender mercy" (v. 11).

    — **Alma 36:3 God will support us in our trials.** Experience with the Lord showed Alma that "whosoever shall put their trust in God shall be supported in their trials, and their troubles, and their afflictions, and shall be lifted up at the last day."

Job waited patiently upon the Lord for deliverance

Avoiding Temptation

- **James 1:12–17 The source and process of temptation.** "Blessed is the man that endureth [JST: resisteth] temptation: for when he is tried, he shall receive the crown of life, which the Lord hath promised to them that love him" (v. 12)."Let no man say when he is tempted, I am tempted of God: for God cannot be tempted with evil, neither tempteth he any man" (v. 13). God is neither the source nor the cause of our bad choices (v. 16). We might hear someone say, after they find themselves paying the price of their sins, "It was all part of the plan." This is not so. God does not tempt us. Only "good" and "perfect" gifts "cometh down from the Father of lights, with whom is no variableness, neither shadow of turning" (v. 17).

  When a man is tempted, "he is drawn away of his own lust, and enticed" (v. 14). The word translated "drawn away" describes what hunters do—lure wild game out of safety and into the open. The word translated "entice" describes what fishermen do—"catch with bait." "Then when lust hath conceived, it bringeth forth sin: and sin, when it is finished, bringeth forth death" (v. 15).

FAITH WITHOUT WORKS IS DEAD

- **James 1:22–25 We must be more than "hearers only" of the word.** James advised that we be "doers of the word, and not hearers only, deceiving your own selves" (v. 22). "For if any be a hearer of the word, and not a doer, he is like unto a man beholding his natural face in a glass [mirror]: For he beholdeth himself, and goeth his way, and straightway forgetteth what manner of man he was" (vv. 23–24). "But whoso looketh into the perfect law of liberty, and continueth therein, he being not a forgetful hearer, but a doer of the work, this man shall be blessed in his deed" (v. 25).

    — **Romans 3:23–24 Luther's view: We are justified by the grace of Christ alone.** Luther cited these verses in defending his claim: "For all have sinned, and come short of the glory of God; Being justified freely by his grace through the redemption that is in Christ Jesus."

    — **2 Nephi 25:23 Nephi's view: We are saved by grace after doing all that we can.** Nephi agreed that, in the end, we need the grace of Christ to make us perfect. But he also taught that we are required to do all we can do first. "For we labor diligently to write, to persuade our children, and also our brethren, to believe in Christ, and to be reconciled to God; for we know that it is by grace that we are saved, after all we can do."

- **James 2:14–17 Faith without works is dead.** James asked, "What doth it profit, my brethren, though a man say he hath faith, and have not works? can faith save him?" (v. 14). Then he illustrated his answer with an example: "If a brother or sister be naked, and destitute of daily food, and one of you say unto them, Depart in peace, be ye warmed and filled; notwithstanding ye give them not those things which are needful to the body; what doth it profit?" (vv. 15–16). "Even so faith, if it hath not works, is dead, being alone" (v. 17).

- **James 2:18–20 We show our faith through our works.** If a man claims that he has faith in Christ, James asked how such a man can demonstrate his faith without works; meanwhile, James said, "I will shew thee my faith by my works" (v. 18). The man without works may profess Christ with his lips, but that is clearly not enough. "Thou believest that there is one God; thou doest well: the devils also believe, and tremble" (v. 19). What good does it do Satan that he *knows* that Jesus is the Christ? Clearly, more is required than a testimony or even a knowledge of the Savior. James said, "Know, O vain man, that faith without works is dead" (v. 20).

    — **3 Nephi 27:14–15 We are saved by the grace of Christ, but will be judged by our works.** Christ told the Nephites, "My Father sent me that I might be lifted up upon the cross; and after that I had been lifted up upon the cross, that I might draw all men unto me, that as I have been lifted up by men even so should men be lifted up by the Father, to stand before me, to be judged of their works, whether they be good or whether they be evil. . . ."

Larry E. Dahl concluded, "In the final analysis, our works (our thoughts, feelings, and actions) identify the object or objects of our faith."[11]

- **James 2:21–24 Abraham was saved by his works.** James asked, "Was not Abraham our father justified by works, when he had offered Isaac his son upon the altar?" (v. 21). His faith "wrought with [produced] his works, and by works was [his] faith made perfect" (v. 22). "Ye see then how that by works a man is justified, and not by faith only" (v. 24).

  James said that "Abraham believed God, and it was imputed unto him for righteousness: and he was called the Friend of God" (v. 23; see also 2 Chronicles 20:7; Isaiah 41:8). The Savior said His disciples would be His friends if they *did whatsoever He commanded them* (John 15:14, emphasis added). Therefore, actions [works] are critical to demonstrating our faith.

DORÉ, 1896

- **James 2:25 Rahab was saved by her works.** Rahab, the woman who assisted Israel's "spies" during their undercover visit to Jericho just before its destruction, was cited by Paul for her example of faith and works (Hebrews 11:31). James here agrees, saying that she was "justified by works, when she . . . received the messengers, and . . . sent them out another way."

CONTROLLING OUR SPEECH

Bridling Our Tongues

- **James 1:26 We must "bridle" our tongues.** "If any man among you seem to be religious, and bridleth not his tongue," then he "deceiveth his own heart" and his "religion is [in] vain." To "bridle" means to control. Speaking in anger, cursing, shouting, or abusing with words all reveal the true spirit that inhabits a man. He may pretend to be religious, but his words will reveal the truth about him.

- **James 1:19–20 We should be "swift to hear" and "slow to speak," especially in anger.** "Let every man be swift to hear, slow to speak, slow to wrath," said James. "For the wrath of man worketh not the righteousness of God."

  Elder Theodore M. Burton said: "Whenever you get red in the face, whenever you raise your voice, whenever you get 'hot under the collar,' or angry, rebellious, or negative in spirit, then know that the Spirit of God is leaving you and the spirit of Satan is beginning to take over."[12]

- **James 3:3–6 Metaphors for the tongue.** Returning to the "bridling" metaphor, James said, "Behold, we put bits in the horses' mouths, that they may obey us; and we turn about their whole body" (v. 3). Ships also, "though they be so great, and are driven of fierce winds, yet are they turned about with a very small helm, whithersoever the governor [captain of the ship] listeth" (v. 4). "Even so the tongue is a little member, and boasteth great things" (v. 5).

  James also compared the tongue to the spread of fire. "Behold, how great a matter a little fire kindleth!" (v. 5). The word translated as "matter" here is "wood." In other words, "How great a fire a tiny spark can start." The tongue is like a fire, spreading a "world of iniquity," and though it is small "among our members, . . . it defileth the whole body, and setteth on fire the course of nature; and it is set on fire of hell" (v. 6).

- **James 3:7–8 Unruly tongues are full of deadly poison.** All the animals of the earth —"every kind of beasts, and of birds, and of serpents, and of things in the sea"—has been "tamed of mankind" (v. 7). "But the tongue can no man tame; it is an unruly evil, full of deadly poison" (v. 8).

  Elder Hugh B. Brown said: "[Speaking of] self-control . . . many of the cases which I review started with uncontrolled appetites and tempers, leading often to cruelty, mental and physical. When in a temper the tongue may be venomous. The Apostle James said, ' . . . it is an unruly evil, full of deadly poison' (James 3:8). That is only potential, but it is often true. The tongue, with which we say our prayers and pledge our troth is sometimes used to wound those we love best. 'Boys flying kites haul in their white winged birds; we can't do that when we're flying words.'"[13]

- **James 3:9–13 Blessing and cursing with the same tongue.** With our tongues we "bless . . . God, even the Father," and with our tongues we "curse . . . men, which are made after the similitude of God" (v. 9). "Out of the same mouth proceedeth blessing and cursing. My brethren, these things ought not so to be" (v. 10). Do we realize what we are doing when we say to someone, "Damn you!" especially if we hold the priesthood? It is inconsistent that we would wish this on anyone with the same mouth that prays for forgiveness and praises God with speech and singing.

  "Doth a fountain send forth at the same [time] sweet water and bitter?" (v. 11). "Can the fig tree . . . bear olive berries? [Or] a vine, figs? So can no fountain both yield salt water and fresh" (v. 12). James said that "a wise man . . . endued with knowledge" will "shew out of a good conversation his works with [the] meekness of wisdom" (v. 13).

- **James 3:14–16 Envy and strife come from Satan.** James advised, "If ye have bitter envying and strife in your hearts, glory not, and lie not against the truth" (v. 14). Envy is resentment over the good fortune of others. Strife is contention for superiority. These are characteristics of Satan (Moses 4:1) and come from him. They "descend . . . not from above, but [are] earthly, sensual, devilish" (v. 15). "For where envying and strife is, there is confusion and every evil work" (v. 16).

- **James 3:17–18 Controlling our tongues leads to peace.** The wisdom that we receive from God "is first pure, then peaceable, gentle, and easy to be intreated, full of mercy and good fruits, without partiality, and without hypocrisy" (v. 17). "And the fruit of righteousness is sown in peace" (v. 18), not through argument, competition, or anger.

  There is not a single instance in all of scripture where God the Father or the Holy Ghost are depicted as shouting. Though they penetrate to our souls, their promptings are peaceful and quiet. The Lord comforted Elijah on Mount Horeb, speaking to him through a "still, small voice" (1 Kings 19:11–13). God's voice is similarly described in the Book of Mormon (1 Nephi 17:45; 3 Nephi 11:3). President Gordon B. Hinckley called these promptings "the whisperings of the Spirit."[14]

  President Ezra Taft Benson said, "Do you take time to listen to the promptings of the Spirit? Answers to prayer come most often by a still voice and are discerned by our deepest, innermost feelings. I tell you that you can know the will of God concerning yourselves if you will take the time to pray and to listen."[15]

  Elder Boyd K. Packer said, "Inspiration comes more easily in peaceful settings. Such words as quiet, still, peaceable, Comforter abound in the scriptures: 'Be still, and know that I am God' (Ps. 46:10). And the promise, 'You shall receive my Spirit, the Holy Ghost, even the Comforter, which shall teach you the peaceable things of the kingdom' (D&C 36:2). Elijah felt a great wind, an earthquake, a fire. The Lord was not in any of them; then came 'a still small voice' (1 Kings 19:12)."[16]

- **James 4:11–12 Gossip is a form of unrighteous judgment.** "Speak not evil one of another," James counseled. "He that speaketh evil of his brother, and judgeth his brother, speaketh evil of the law, and judgeth the law [meaning that we accuse others of doing wrong]" (v. 11). But when we are so judging our fellow men, we are "not a doer of the law," as we should be, "but [pretending to be] a judge" (v. 11). "There is one lawgiver, who is able to save and to destroy," and that of course is God; "who art thou that judgest another?" (v. 12).

  Elder Spencer W. Kimball said: "Lies and gossip which harm reputations are scattered about by the four winds like the seeds of a ripe dandelion held aloft by a child. . . . The degree and extent of the harm done by the gossip is inestimable."[17]

Keeping Sacred Confidences

Another form of gossip, though not specifically mentioned by James, is equally inappropriate. That is to share sacred experiences unnecessarily. This is often done in a hushed tone, pretending piety, with the intent to convince others of our righteousness or special favor with the Lord. The Lord is offended when we do this.

— **D&C 63:64 Sacred experiences should not generally be shared.** "Remember that that which cometh from above is sacred, and must be spoken with care, and by constraint of the Spirit." There is no condemnation in doing this if we are instructed to do so by the Spirit after prayer, but "without this there remaineth condemnation."

— **D&C 84:73 Do not boast of spiritual experiences.** "But a commandment I give unto them, that they shall not boast themselves of these things, neither speak them before the world; for these things are given unto you for your profit and for salvation."

The Prophet Joseph Smith said: "The reason we do not have the secrets of the Lord revealed unto us, is because we do not keep them but reveal them; we do not keep our own secrets, but reveal our difficulties to the world, even to our enemies, then how would we keep the secrets of the Lord?"[18]

President Brigham Young said, "That man who cannot know things without telling any other living being upon the earth, who cannot keep his secrets and those that God reveals to him, never can receive the voice of his Lord to dictate him and the people on this earth. . . . Should you receive a vision or revelation from the Almighty, one that the Lord gave you concerning yourselves, or this people, but which you are not to reveal on account of your not being the proper person, or because it ought not to be known by the people at present, you should shut it up and seal it as close, and lock it as tight as heaven is to you, and make it as secret as the grave. The Lord has no confidence in those who reveal secrets, for He cannot safely reveal Himself to such persons."[19]

Elder Boyd K. Packer said: "It is not wise to continually talk of unusual spiritual experiences. They are to be guarded with care and shared only when the Spirit itself prompts you to use them to the blessing of others."[20]

Elder Packer also said:

> A teacher must be wise also in the use of his own spiritual experiences. I have come to believe that deep spiritual experiences are given to individuals for the most part for their own instruction and edification, and they are not ordinarily to be talked about. . . .
>
> There is also a scripture that says: "Give not that which is holy unto the dogs, neither cast ye your pearls before swine, lest they trample them under their feet, and turn again and rend you" (Matthew 7:6). Sacred personal experiences are to be related only on rare occasions. I made a rule for myself a number of years ago with reference to this subject. When someone relates a spiritual experience to me, personally or in a small, intimate group, I make it a rigid rule not to talk about it thereafter. I assume that it was told to me in a moment of trust and confidence, and therefore I never talk about it. If, however, on some future occasion I hear that individual talk about it in public in a large gathering, or where a number of people are present, then I know that it has been stated publicly and I can feel free under the right circumstances to relate it. But I know many, many sacred and important things that have been related to me by others that I will not discuss unless I am

privileged to do so under the rule stated above. I know that others of the Brethren have the same feeling.[21]

President Marion G. Romney said, "I do not tell all I know; I have not told my wife all I know, for I have found that if I talked to lightly of sacred things and tell everything I know and explain every experience that I have had, thereafter the Lord would not trust me."[22]

LIVING THE GOSPEL

Pure Religion

- **James 1:27 James defines pure religion.** "Pure religion and undefiled before God and the Father is this, To visit the fatherless and widows in their affliction, and to keep himself unspotted from the world."

President Joseph F. Smith said:

> This may be interpreted as meaning that a person who is religious is thoughtful to the unfortunate, and has an inner spirit that prompts to deeds of kindness and to the leading of a blameless life; who is just, truthful; who does not, as Paul says, think more highly of himself than he ought to think; who is affectionate, patient in tribulation, diligent, cheerful, fervent in spirit, hospitable, merciful; and who abhors evil and cleaves to that which is good. The possession of such a spirit and feeling is a true sign that a person is naturally religious.
>
> The Church's outward ordinances and requirements are but necessary—yet they are necessary—aids to the inner spiritual life. The Church itself, the organization, meetings, ordinances, requirements, are only helps, but very necessary helps, to the practice of true religion—schoolmasters to direct us in the way of eternal light and truth.[23]

We may think that if we are seen taking the sacrament or going to the temple or serving in a Church calling that we are practicing our religion; and indeed, doing these things is part of fulfilling our duty to God. But this is not what James calls "true religion."

— **Alma 34:27–28 The requirements of "keeping the faith.**" Alma counseled that we should "let [our] hearts be full, drawn out in prayer unto him continually for your welfare, and also for the welfare of those who are around you" (v. 27). But we should "not suppose that this is all; for after ye have done all these things, if ye turn away the needy, and the naked, and visit not the sick and afflicted, and impart of your substance, if ye have, to those who stand in need—I say unto you, if ye do not any of these things, behold, your prayer is vain, and availeth you nothing, and ye are as hypocrites who do deny the faith" (v. 28).

— **Mosiah 4:26–27 King Benjamin's teachings on this subject.** "And now, for the sake of . . . retaining a remission of your sins from day to day, that ye may walk guiltless before God—I would that ye should impart of your substance to the poor, every man according to that which he hath, such as feeding the hungry, clothing the naked, visiting the sick and administering to their relief, both spiritually and temporally, according to their wants" (v. 26). "And see that all these things are done in wisdom and order; for it is not requisite that a man should run faster than he has strength" (v. 27).

Elder George Q. Cannon said: "I sometimes think that we, as Latter-day Saints, come short of doing that which is incumbent upon us. We allow our religion to be too theoretical, and do not practice it to the extent that is required by the teachings of the Gospel."[24]

- **James 4:17 James' definition of sin: Knowing how to do good but doing it not.** Thus, sins of omission (failing to act) are just as serious as sins of commission (acting sinfully). "To him that knoweth to do good, and doeth it not, to him it is sin," said James.

  Elder Orson F. Whitney said, "Sin is the transgression of divine law, as made known through the conscience or by revelation. A man sins when he violates his conscience, going contrary to light and knowledge—not the light and knowledge that has come to his neighbor, but that which has come to himself. He sins when he does the opposite of what he knows to be right. Up to that point he only blunders. One may suffer painful consequences for only blundering, but he cannot commit sin unless he knows better than to do the thing in which the sin consists. One must have a conscience before he can violate it."[25]

Avoiding Double-Mindedness

- **James 1:8 To be "double-minded" is to try to "have it both ways" spiritually.** We cannot lead a double-life, nor can we serve two masters equally well. We will be forever having to choose between the two. Thus, James taught that "a double minded man is unstable in all his ways." The faith of such persons will never be stable or sufficient.

- **James 4:4–7 "Submit yourselves . . . to God."** When we seek "the friendship of the world" we put ourselves at "enmity with God [and] whosoever therefore will be a friend of the world is the enemy of God" (v. 4). "The spirit that dwelleth in us lusteth to envy" (v. 5). This is the natural man that seeks ease and pleasure and fame. But when we are thus tempted, James warns us to remember that "God resisteth the proud, but giveth grace unto the humble" (v. 6). "Submit yourselves therefore to God" (v. 7).

  Elder Harold B. Lee said, "The world to which the Apostles James and John and the Master make reference is that moral and spiritual system which is hostile to God and which seeks to delude us into thinking that we and mankind generally do not need God. It is a society which in every age has operated and is operating on wrong principles, from selfish desires, from improper motives, unworthy standards, and false values. Those who do not accept God's revelation through His prophets have devised numerous philosophies from their limited human reasoning and seemingly think that they can find happiness and the satisfaction of their souls by ignoring God's plan of salvation."[26]

- **James 4:7–10 "Resist the devil, and he will flee from you"** (v. 7). "Draw nigh to God, and he will draw nigh to you. Cleanse your hands, ye sinners; and purify your hearts, ye double minded" (v. 8). If we have taken joy in our sinful ways then James' counsel is to "be afflicted, and mourn, and weep: let your laughter be turned to mourning, and your joy to heaviness. Humble yourselves in the sight of the Lord, and he shall lift you up" (vv. 9–10). The Saints have been informed to "let the solemnities of eternity rest upon your minds" (D&C 43:34). The Prophet Joseph stated that levity is inconsistent to those called of God (JS-H 1:28). This does not mean that there is no place for amusement or laughter, but uncontrolled loud laughter or frivolity are offensive to God (D&C 88:69).

  Elder Spencer W. Kimball said:

  > James gave a formula for conquering: "Submit yourselves therefore to God. Resist the devil, and he will flee from you" (James 4:7). In abandoning evil, transforming lives, changing personalities, molding characters or remolding them, we need the help of the Lord, and we may be assured of it if we do our part. The man who leans heavily upon his Lord becomes the master of self and can accomplish anything he sets out to do, whether it be to secure the brass plates, build a ship, overcome a habit, or conquer a deep-seated transgression.
  >
  > He who has greater strength than Lucifer, He who is our fortress and our strength, can sustain us in times of great temptation. While the Lord will never forcibly take anyone out of sin or out of the arms of the tempters, He exerts His Spirit to induce the sinner to do it with divine assistance. And the man who yields to the sweet influence and pleadings of the Spirit and does all in his power to stay in a repentant attitude is guaranteed protection, power, freedom and joy.[27]

Living Together in Faith

- **James 5:13 The antidote for adversity, fear, and sadness is prayer.** "Is any among you afflicted? let him pray." We are not alone. Faith in God's redeeming power and hope for His everlasting charity and kindness are essential keys for rising above our adversity. And we express that faith and hope when we pray for relief.

Elder Marvin J. Ashton said, "Even the chains of fear can be broken by those who will humbly seek God's help and strength."[28] What the Lord said to Joseph Smith when he prayed during his deepest hour of affliction in Liberty Jail applies also to us, if we will keep our covenants and follow principles of righteousness: "Thy days are known, and thy years shall not be numbered less; therefore, fear not what man can do, for God shall be with you forever and ever" (D&C 122:9).

President Ezra Taft Benson said:

> I often think of the Prophet Joseph—to me the greatest prophet who has ever lived upon the face of the earth, save Jesus only, whom he represented and served. I think of his trials and tribulations. I thought of them as I once stood in Liberty Jail. He was in that filthy jail, surrounded by vile men, not for a period of days or weeks, but months. And finally, when it seemed as though he could stand it no longer, Joseph cried out and asked Heavenly Father why He would not intervene. The answer came in revelation to the Prophet in these words: "My son, peace be unto thy soul; thine adversity and thine afflictions shall be but a small moment: And then, if thou endure it well, God shall exalt thee on high; thou shalt triumph over all thy foes" (D&C 121:7–8). Later the Lord uttered this significant statement: "Know thou, my son, that all these things shall give thee experience, and shall be for thy good" (D&C 122:7). God help us to be grateful for our blessings and never to be guilty of the sin of ingratitude. "And he who receiveth all things with thankfulness shall be made glorious; and the things of this earth shall be added unto him, even an hundred fold, yea, more" (D&C 78:19).[29]

Elder Neal A. Maxwell said, "Separated from them though he was, Joseph was further assured that the people of the Church 'shall never be turned against [him] by the testimony of traitors' (D&C 122:3). It is a comfort that this promise is as valid today as when it was given in March of 1839. Such defectors and other detractors caused trouble then (D&C 122:4) as they do now. Nevertheless such troubles and afflictions, comparatively speaking, will be 'but for a small moment' (D&C 122:4; 2 Cor. 4:17)."[30]

President Gordon B. Hinckley said, "If as a people we will build and sustain one another, the Lord will bless us with the strength to weather every storm and continue to move forward through every adversity."[31]

Elder Jeffrey R. Holland said:

> No, it is not without a recognition of life's tempests but fully and directly because of them that I testify of God's love and the Savior's power to calm the storm. Always remember in that biblical story that He was out there on the water also, that He faced the worst of it right along with the newest and youngest and most fearful. Only one who has fought against those ominous waves is justified in telling us—as well as the sea—to "be still." Only one who has taken the full brunt of such adversity could ever be justified in telling us in such times to "be of good cheer." Such counsel is not a jaunty pep talk about the power of positive thinking, though positive thinking is much needed in the world. No, Christ knows better than all others that the trials of life can he very deep and we are not shallow people if we struggle with them. But even as the Lord avoids sugary rhetoric, He rebukes faithlessness and He deplores pessimism. He expects us to believe![32]

- **James 5:13 Music and singing are proper expressions of joy.** "Is any merry? let him sing psalms." The psalms of David gave him both peace and joy during his life's challenges. And the singing of hymns blesses us also in many ways:

THE PSALMIST KING DAVID, THEBIBLEREVIVAL.COM

  — Hymns lift our spirits.
  — Hymns inspire us to live more righteously.
  — Hymns remind us of our blessings.
  — Hymns give us an opportunity to sing praises to the Lord.
  — Hymns give us a way to bear testimony.
  — Hymns help us recommit ourselves to the Lord.
  — Hymns help us feel the Spirit.
  — Hymns help us be more in tune with our Heavenly Father.
  — Hymns help us learn and teach the gospel.

The First Presidency has said, "Inspirational music is an essential part of our church meetings. The hymns invite the Spirit of the Lord, create a feeling of reverence, unify us as members, and provide a way for us to offer praises to the Lord. Some of the greatest sermons are preached by the singing of hymns. Hymns move us to repentance and good works, build testimony and faith, comfort the weary, console the mourning, and inspire us to endure to the end."[33]

Elder Bruce R. McConkie said:

> Music is part of the language of the Gods. It has been given to man so he can sing praises to the Lord. It is a means of expressing, with poetic words and in melodious tunes, the deep feelings of rejoicing and thanksgiving found in the hearts of those who have testimonies of the divine Sonship and who know of the wonders and glories wrought for them by the Father, Son, and Holy Spirit. Music is both in the voice and in the heart. Every true Saint finds his heart full of songs of praise to his Maker. Those whose voices can sing forth the praises found in their hearts are twice blest. "Be filled with the Spirit," Paul counseled, "speaking to yourselves in psalms and hymns and spiritual songs, singing and making melody in your heart to the Lord" (Eph. 5:18–19). Also: "Let the word of Christ dwell in you richly in all wisdom; teaching and admonishing one another in psalms and hymns and spiritual songs, singing with grace in your hearts to the Lord" (Col. 3:16).... In view of all that the Lord Jesus Christ has done for us, ought we not to sing praises to His holy name forever?[34]

- **James 5:14–15 The sick should seek a priesthood anointing and blessing.** "Is any sick among you? let him call for the elders of the church; and let them pray over him, anointing him with oil in the name of the Lord" (v. 14). "And the prayer of faith shall save the sick, and the Lord shall raise him up; and if he have committed sins, they shall be forgiven him" (v. 15).

Why do we call for the elders, if it is faith that heals us? Could we not simply pray in faith and receive relief? The answer is yes, you could, and in some cases that may be the only option. But if Melchizedek priesthood holders are available we are commanded to call on them for a blessing. They stand in the stead of the Lord as they minister unto us. Like the believers of Jesus' day who sought Him out for a blessing, we should seek out His anointed servants for the same thing. This shows our faith in Christ and His priesthood holders, whom He has commanded to anoint and bless us.

- **James 5:16–18 The effect of fervent prayer.** James taught that we should pray for each other and that "the effectual fervent prayer of a righteous man availeth much" (v. 16). Experience teaches us continually that prayer really does make a difference.

In our stake recently we were experiencing a dry spell in missionary work. It seemed that none of our investigators were making progress, and new teaching opportunities were arising. The ward mission leaders gathered together to consider the matter and chose to fast and pray for more investigators and baptisms. They were doing all that they could and now sought the Lord's help. In the weeks following that fast, individuals that had resisted baptism for months—in one case, years—suddenly requested baptism. Four new investigators came forward through the fellowshipping program that was organized in their wards. And one family of five literally walked through the doors of a church and asked for missionaries to teach them. Coincidence? No. This sudden progress was the result of "effective fervent prayer."

Elias [Elijah] is given as an example of effective prayer: he prayed for no rain, and no rain fell for three and a half years (v. 17). "And he prayed again, and the heaven gave rain, and the earth brought forth her fruit" (v. 18). Could the Lord have done these things without Elijah's prayer? Yes. But God makes us participants in His work, and waits in patience for us to ask Him for the things we need. Then, having been freely invited, He can bring about those things that we seek in our lives or the lives of others.

- **James 5:19–20 When we save others, our own sins are forgiven too**. When we reach out to rescue one of God's children who has drifted away from the Church, or when we befriend a nonmember and gently lead them to a knowledge of the truth, it does not go unnoticed by our God. "Let him know," said James, "that he which converteth the sinner from the error of his way shall [not only] save a soul from death,

[but] shall hide a multitude of [his own] sins." The same is true about bearing our testimonies (D&C 62:3).

President Spencer W. Kimball said, "James indicated that each good deed, each testimony, each proselyting effort, each safeguard thrown about others is like a blanket over one's own sins, or like a deposit against an overdraft in the bank."[35]

Elder Spencer W. Kimball also said:

> Every person who is beginning the long journey of emancipating himself from the thralldom of sin and evil will find comfort in the thought expressed by James. We could expand it somewhat and remind the transgressor that every testimony he bears, every prayer he offers, every sermon he preaches, every scripture he reads, every help he gives to stimulate and raise others—all these strengthen him and raise him to higher levels.
>
> The proper motivation for missionary work of any kind, as for all Church service, is of course love for fellowmen, but always such work has its by-product effect on one's own life. Thus as we become instruments in God's hands in changing the lives of others our own lives cannot help being lifted. One can hardly help another to the top of the hill without climbing there himself.[36]

OTHER CONCEPTS IN JAMES

- **James 1:21 "Superfluity of naughtiness.**" James advised that we "lay apart all filthiness and superfluity of naughtiness." Naughtiness in our day means petty or mischievous acts, such as the pranks of children. However, this use of the word is an inadequate translation of the word that James used. *Kakias* not only meant evil in a general sense but, specifically, hatred or bitterness toward another. Thus "malice" is probably a better translation. The Greek word translated "superfluity" means abundance. Thus, James is really telling us to avoid "an abundance of malice," and instead to "receive with meekness the engrafted word, which is able to save your souls."

- **James 2:1–9 Judging others and the "royal law."** If we claim to follow "the faith of our Lord Jesus Christ, the Lord of glory," then we should not judge "with respect of persons" (v. 1). "For if there come unto your assembly a man with a gold ring, in goodly apparel, and there come in also a poor man in vile raiment; And ye have respect to him that weareth the gay [bright and colorful] clothing, and say unto him, Sit thou here in a good place; and say to the poor, Stand thou there, or sit here under my footstool: Are ye not then partial in yourselves, and are become judges of evil thoughts?" (vv. 2–4).

  "God [hath] chosen the poor of this world rich in faith [to be] heirs of the kingdom which he hath promised to them that love him. . . . But ye have despised the poor." (vv. 5–6). "Do not rich men oppress you, and draw you before the judgment seats?" (v. 6). And when they do this, "do not they blaspheme that worthy name by the which ye are called?" (v. 7).

James said "the royal law" is "thou shalt love thy neighbour as thyself" (v. 8). "But if ye have respect to persons, ye commit sin, and are . . . transgressors" (v. 9).

— **1 Nephi 17:35 God only favors those who do His will.** The only aristocracy that counts with the Lord is the aristocracy of righteousness. Men often have much less lofty reasons for their partiality, and if we are partial for any of the following reasons, among others, we need to make changes in our attitude.

  - Color of skin (2 Nephi 26:33)
  - Opportunities for learning (3 Nephi 6:12)
  - Expensiveness of clothes (James 2:2–5)
  - Economic standing (Alma 32:5)
  - National heritage-origin (Matthew 3:8–10; 2 Nephi 26:33)
  - Religious exclusiveness (Alma 31:12–18).

— **1 Samuel 16:7 Look beyond the outward appearance and into people's hearts.** The Lord said unto Samuel, "Look not on his countenance, or on the height of his stature. . . . For the Lord seeth not as man seeth; for man looketh on the outward appearance, but the Lord looketh on the heart."

— **D&C 38:25–27 "Let every man esteem his brother as himself."** "For what man among you having twelve sons, and is no respecter of them, and they serve him obediently, . . . saith unto the one: Be thou clothed in robes and sit thou here; and to the other: Be thou clothed in rags and sit thou there—and . . . saith I am just?" (vv. 25–26). "Behold, this I have given unto you as a parable, and it is even as I am. I say unto you, be one; and if ye are not one ye are not mine."

- **James 2:10 One sin can damn us.** "For whosoever shall keep the whole law, and yet offend in one point, he is guilty of all." This illustrates a principle that I have taught to my classes for years: *"One sin, deliberately committed and un-repented, can keep us out of the celestial kingdom."* This is because (1) To dwell with God we must be cleansed from all sin (D&C 50:28–29). (2) We can never achieve perfection on our own, but will have to rely on the Savior's atonement. And (3) the Savior's atonement can only take effect when we repent of our sins. Thus, a single sin that we choose to commit, unless it is repented of, will damn us from exaltation.

  The Prophet Joseph Smith said: "Any person who is exalted to the highest mansion has to abide a celestial law, and the *whole* law too"[37] (emphasis added).

- **James 4:1–2 The causes of war are envy and lust.** "From whence come wars and fightings among you?" James asked. Then he answered that they come "of your lusts that war in your members [body]." This does not refer to sexual lust but envy—the lust for power and possessions that leads us to violence against others who have what we want to possess or whom we wish to subject to our wishes. And these lusts always come up empty in the end: "Ye lust, and have not: ye kill, and desire to have, and cannot obtain: ye fight and war, yet ye have not" (v. 2).

- **James 4:2–3 Two principles of prayer.** James observed, "Ye have not, because ye ask not. Ye ask, and receive not, because ye ask amiss, that ye may consume it upon your lusts" (vv. 2–3). There are two principles of prayer in these sayings.

  — **"Ye have not, because ye ask not"** (v. 2) We are required to ask God for the things we need. This, despite the fact that "your Father knoweth what things ye have need of, before ye ask him" (Matthew 6:8). Why? Because of our agency. God will not violate our agency by forcing any blessing upon us. We must first ask Him, thus freely opening our hearts and lives to receive the help we desire.

  President Spencer W. Kimball said, "Your Savior said, 'Behold, I stand at the door, and knock: if any man hear my voice, and open the door, I will come in to him, and will sup with him, and he with me' (Revelation 3:20). . . . The Lord stands knocking. He never retreats. But He will never force Himself upon us."[38]

  — **"Ye ask, and receive not, because ye ask amiss"** (v. 3). James says we ask amiss "that ye may consume it upon [our] lusts." In other words, we ask selfishly and without proper thought, and sometimes to obtain things that may not be good for us. Prayer must be more thoughtful and serious than that. Elder Harold B. Lee said, "If you want the blessing, don't just kneel down and pray about it. Prepare yourselves in every conceivable way you can in order to make yourselves worthy to receive the blessing you seek."[39]

  President Spencer W. Kimball said, "Do you get answers to your prayers? If not, perhaps you did not pay the price. Do you offer a few trite words and worn-out phrases, or do you talk intimately to the Lord? Do you pray occasionally when you should be praying regularly, often, constantly? . . . When you pray, do you just speak, or do you also listen? . . . If we ever move apart, it is we who move and not the Lord. And should we ever fail to get an answer to our prayers, we must look into our lives for a reason."[40]

- **James 4:13–14 "Ye know not what shall be tomorrow."** James said that we go about living our lives, saying, "To day or to morrow we will go into such a city, and continue there a year, and buy and sell, and get gain," even though "ye know not what shall be on the morrow" (vv. 13–14). Our mortal lives will not last forever. Life is "a vapour, that appeareth for a little time, and then vanisheth away" (v. 14). We should keep this in mind as we rise each morning, by thanking the Lord for another day of life in which to learn and improve. We should also keep it in mind when we make choices each day that could affect our eternal standing before the Lord.

- **James 5:4 The Lord of Sabaoth.** Speaking of the seriousness of defrauding those who work for us, James said, "Behold, the hire of the labourers who have reaped down your fields, which is of you kept back by fraud, crieth: and the cries of them which have reaped are entered into the ears of the Lord of sabaoth." Often this phrase is read carelessly as the "Lord of the Sabbath." Sabaoth has nothing to do with "sabbath." The word in Hebrew is *tzava'o*t, which means "hosts." Thus, the Lord of Sabaoth is the Lord of Hosts—a familiar title for Jehovah (Isaiah 51:15; 2 Nephi 8:15; D&C 64:24; D&C 88:2).

- **James 5:12 Our word should be our bond.** It was common practice in James' day to verify the truth of ones' words or your intentions by "swearing" [making an oath] in the name of some great or holy thing or person. But James said, "My brethren, swear not, neither by heaven, neither by the earth, neither by any other oath: but let your yea be yea; and your nay, nay; lest ye fall into condemnation." This is similar to what our Lord (and James' half-brother) said in the Sermon on the Mount (Matthew 5:33–37). It means that a simple "yes" or "no" should be sufficient for our promises, without swearing oaths. In our day, the same could be said about written contracts. We require them as evidence of our intentions, to which we can be legally held. But if we are followers of Christ, our word should be as good as any written bond or contract.

- **James 5:16 Confessing our sins to one another.** James counseled us to "confess your faults one to another, and pray one for another, that ye may be healed [of those faults]. When we injure someone we are to confess our error to the injured one immediately. In some cases, we must also confess to a proper Church authority. And if we are the one who has been harmed, we ought to pray for the person who harmed us "that he may be healed."

  Elder Spencer W. Kimball said:

  > The confession of his major sins to a proper Church authority is one of those requirements made by the Lord. These sins include adultery, fornication, other sexual transgressions, and other sins of comparable seriousness. This procedure of confession assures proper controls and protection for the Church and its people and sets the feet of the transgressor on the path of true repentance.
  >
  > Many offenders in their shame and pride have satisfied their consciences, temporarily at least, with a few silent prayers to the Lord and rationalized that this was sufficient confession of their sins. "But I have confessed my sin to my Heavenly Father," they will insist, "and that is all that is necessary." This is not true where a major sin is involved. Then two sets of forgiveness are required to bring peace to the transgressor—one from the proper authorities of the Lord's Church, and one from the Lord Himself. . . .
  >
  > When one has wronged another in deep transgression or in injuries of lesser magnitude, he, the aggressor, who gave the offense, regardless of the attitude of the other party, should immediately make amends by confessing to the injured one and doing all in his power to clear up the matter and again establish good feelings between the two parties.[41]

- **James 5:17 Elias or Elijah?** When talking about the effectiveness of the prayers of a righteous man, James cited the example of "Elias," saying that he was "a man subject to like passions as we are, and he prayed earnestly that it might not rain: and it rained not on the earth by the space of three years and six months."

Anyone who knows the Old Testament well also knows that this is describing an event in Elijah's ministry. So why did James call him "Elias"? The name and title Elias is often confusing, since it can refer to an office, a function, or a person.[42] It is further confused by the fact that the common Greek spelling for the name of the famous Old Testament prophet Elijah is also Elias. In this verse, James is obviously referring to Elijah, who had the power to stop the rains for three years and six months as a warning to Israel (1 Kings 17; 18).

Notes

1. *Doctrinal New Testament Commentary*, 3 vols. [1965–1973], 3:243.
2. In Conference Report, October 1914, 87–88.
3. Dillenberger, *Martin Luther* [1961], 19.
4. JS-History 1:12.
5. *Doctrinal New Testament Commentary*, 3:246–247.
6. In Conference Report, Melbourne Australia Area conference, 1976, 23.
7. Address to BYU students, November 27, 1979; *Ensign*, October 1980, 28–31.
8. *Doctrinal New Testament Commentary*, 3:248.
9. Quoted in Spencer W. Kimball, *Faith Precedes the Miracle* [1972], 98.
10. "The Choice," *Ensign*, November 1980, 21.
11. *Studies in Scripture*, Vol. 6, Acts to Revelation [1987], 212.
12. *Ensign*, November 1974, 56.
13. In Conference Report, October 1954, 16.
14. In Conference Report, October 1996, 71; or *Ensign*, November 1996, 51.
15. In Conference Report, October 1977, 46; or *Ensign*, November 1977, 32.
16. "Reverence Invites Revelation," *Ensign*, November 1991, 21.
17. *The Miracle of Forgiveness* [1969], 54.
18. *Teachings of the Prophet Joseph Smith*, sel. Joseph Fielding Smith [1976], 195.
19. In *Journal of Discourses*, 4:287, 288.
20. *Ensign*, January 1983, 53.

21. *Teach Ye Diligently* [1975], 326.

22. Quoted by Boyd K. Packer, Church Employees Lecture Series, January 18, 1980.

23. *Gospel Doctrine*, 5th ed. [1939], 121.

24. In *Journal of Discourses*, 20:288.

25. *Saturday Night Thoughts* [1921], 239.

26. In Conference Report, October 1968, 59.

27. *The Miracle of Forgiveness*, 176.

28. *Be of Good Cheer* [1987], 68.

29. *New Era*, November 1991, 4.

30. *But For A Small Moment* [1986], 11.

31. *Teachings of Gordon B. Hinckley* [1997], 7.

32. *Ensign*, November 1999, 36–37.

33. *Hymns*, page ix.

34. *The Promised Messiah: The First Coming of Christ* [1978], 553–554.

35. *Faith Precedes the Miracle* [1972], 184.

36. *The Miracle of Forgiveness*, 205.

37. *Teachings of the Prophet Joseph Smith*, 331.

38. "Prayer," *New Era*, March 1978, 16–17.

39. "How to Receive a Blessing from God," *Improvement Era*, October 1966, 862–863, 896.

40. "Prayer," *New Era*, March 1978, 16–17.

41. *The Miracle of Forgiveness*, 179, 186.

42. *Mormon Doctrine*, 2nd ed. [1966], 219–222.

Chapter 43

The Epistles of Peter

(1 and 2 Peter)

INTRODUCTION

Who Was Simon Peter?

G.B. CARLONE, 16th–17th CENTURY

Simon Peter, or Cephas (Aramaic, "stone"), was the chief Apostle of Jesus Christ and the equivalent of the Prophet-President of the Church today (Acts 1:15–22; Galatians 2:7–9). He functioned in this capacity when he directed the Apostles in their efforts to choose a successor to Judas Iscariot (Acts 1:15–26). On the day of Pentecost, Peter was the chief spokesman for the Apostles and Saints (Acts 2:14). He received the revelation authorizing missionary efforts among the Gentiles (Acts 10:1–11:18), and he declared the new policy of the Church regarding circumcision (Acts 15:1–29; Galatians 2:1–10).

Peter became a spiritual rock of a man. He healed the lame and the sick through the power of the priesthood (Acts 3; 5:15–16). Though at one point in his life he denied knowing the Lord, yet his faith in the Lord Jesus Christ became so powerful that when he was threatened, beaten, and maligned by his Sanhedrin persecutors, he boldly testified, "We ought to obey God rather than men" (Acts 5:29).

Peter's ministry was in Jerusalem, Antioch, and Corinth, and later in Rome. As with many of the ancient Saints, Peter suffered much from persecution, first in Jerusalem (Acts 5:29–32, 40; Acts 12) and later in Rome.

President Spencer W. Kimball said: "[Peter was] a man who had grown perfect through his experiences and sufferings—a man with vision, a man of revelations, a man fully trusted by his Lord Jesus Christ."[1]

THE 1ST EPISTLE OF PETER

When and Where Was 1st Peter Written?

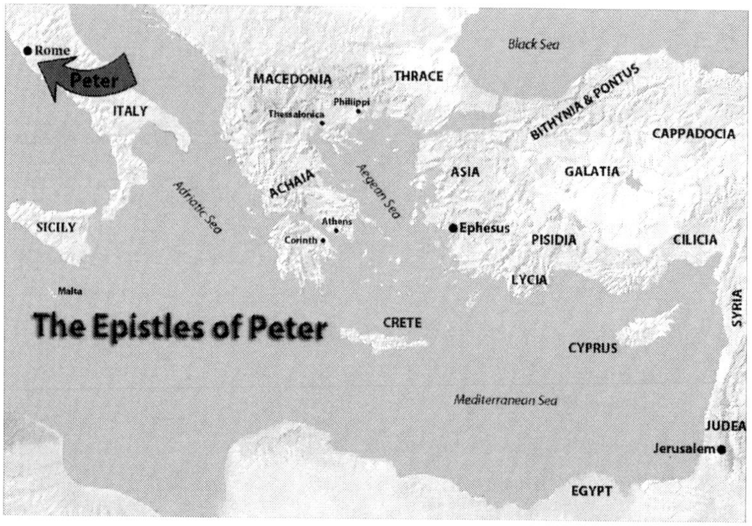

Peter wrote this first of his two surviving epistles sometime before or during the worst of the Roman Emperor Nero's persecutions in 62–64 AD (Nero ruled from 54 to 68 AD).

His reference to "Babylon" (1 Peter 5:13) is a scriptural designation for the wickedest city in the empire (Rev. 18:10, 21).

This epistle was written to members of the Church in Asia (modern-day Turkey), which was headquartered at Ephesus.

The Apostle Paul was also in Rome at this time, and both Paul and Peter were in prison. Shortly after this epistle was written, Peter was crucified in Rome—insisting on being crucified upside down so as not to suggest that he was anywhere near as great as his Lord. The Apostle Paul was also martyred by Nero who beheaded him.

What Are 1st Peter's Most Significant Contributions?

At first, the Roman government displayed tolerance toward all religions, including Christianity, so long as they posed no threat to Rome. Under the emperor Nero, misunderstanding, hatred, and accusations were fostered toward the Saints in Rome and throughout the empire. The change from tolerance to hostility provoked fear and apprehension among the Saints throughout the empire, including Asia.

Therefore, the theme of this letter is: how the Saints ought to react to suffering and persecution. Peter reminded the Saints that they were a "chosen generation" and "a royal priesthood." Peter tells the Saints of a coming "fiery trial"—an ominous warning for the days ahead. And it contains some of the most clear and revealing statements in the Bible about salvation for the dead.

The Prophet Joseph Smith quoted Peter often and said of his writings: "Peter penned the most sublime language of any of the Apostles."[2]

LIVING LIKE SAINTS

Faith Is More Precious than Gold

- **1 Peter 1:2–5 Faith and obedience bring salvation.** Peter addressed his first epistle to the "Elect according to the foreknowledge of God the Father," explaining that they had become elect "through sanctification of the Spirit, [and] obedience and sprinkling of the blood of Jesus Christ" (v. 2). Peter said Christ would raise us from our graves "to an inheritance incorruptible, and undefiled, and that fadeth not away, reserved in heaven for you" (v. 4), and said we are "kept by the power of God through faith unto salvation" (v. 5). All of these wonderful things will "be revealed in the last time [days]" (v. 5).

  Peter wished the Saints grace and peace, then praised "the God and Father of our Lord Jesus Christ, which according to his abundant mercy hath begotten us again unto a lively hope by the resurrection of Jesus Christ from the dead" (v. 3). Note Peter's reference here to God the Father as the "God and Father" of Jesus Christ—showing again that they are two separate beings.

- **1 Peter 1:6–9 Faith is "much more precious than gold."** Though we are "now for a season . . . in heaviness [difficulty] through manifold temptations," we will eventually "greatly rejoice" (v. 6). Our faith, which is "much more precious than of gold" will be "tried with fire" but will carry us through to that day of "praise and honour and glory at the appearing of Jesus Christ" (v. 7). Because of our faith, though we have not seen Christ, we love Him and believe in Him, "rejoic[ing] with joy unspeakable and full of glory" (v. 8). And when He comes again, we will "receiv[e] . . . the end of your faith, even the salvation of your souls" (v. 9).

  — **Hebrews 11:6 Faith is a requirement of exaltation.** "Without faith it is impossible to please him: for he that cometh to God must believe that he is, and that he is a rewarder of them that diligently seek him."

  — **1 Nephi 7:12 God can do anything if we exercise faith in Him.** "The Lord is able to do all things according to his will, for the children of men, if it so be that they exercise faith in him. Wherefore, let us be faithful to him."

- **1 Peter 1:10–12 The prophets "enquired and searched diligently" concerning Christ and His atonement.** The Old Testament "prophets . . . enquired and searched diligently, [and] prophesied of the grace that should come unto you" (v. 10). They possessed "the Spirit of Christ," and searched to understand the meaning "beforehand [of] the sufferings of Christ, and the glory that should follow" (v. 11). And "it was revealed unto them "that not unto themselves, but unto us" would Christ minister on this earth, teaching concerning "things [that even] the angels desire to look into" (v. 5). And these things "are now reported unto you by them that have preached the gospel unto you with the Holy Ghost sent down from heaven" (v. 12).

Being "The People of God"

- **1 Peter 2:5, 9–10 Peter describes the Lord's people.** The Saints in Peter's day were different than the Jews and Gentiles that surrounded them, looking rather peculiar because of the things the did and did not do. Peter called the Saints:

  — Lively "stones" (compared to the Chief Corner Stone of Christ) (v. 5).
  — A spiritual house (speaking of the Church) (v. 5).
  — A holy priesthood making spiritual sacrifices (v. 5).
  — A chosen generation (v. 9).
  — A royal priesthood (v. 9).
  — A holy nation (v. 9).
  — A peculiar people (v. 9). "A peculiar people" in Hebrew is from *segulla*, meaning "a valued property," "a special treasure," or "jewels."
  — The people of God (v. 10).

  We face a similar circumstance today, being quite different from the people of the world. Peter encouraged them [and us] to take righteous pride in who and what they were, "that ye should shew forth the praises of him who hath called you out of darkness into his marvellous light: Which in time[s] past were not a people, but are now the people of God: which had not obtained mercy, but now have obtained mercy" (vv. 9–10).

  Elder Bruce R. McConkie said: "[A chosen generation is] not those living in a particular period or age, but . . . the house of Israel both anciently, in the meridian of time, and now in these latter days. . . . [It includes] faithful members of the Church who have taken upon themselves the name of Christ and been adopted into His family."[3]

Peter's Eight Admonitions

- **1 Peter 1:13–16 Live in holiness and behave like Saints.** Peter counseled the Saints to "gird up the loins of your mind" (v. 13). This figure of speech means the same thing as the modern idiom "roll up your sleeves"—which is to "prepare yourselves." This preparation, coupled with soberness and hope will carry us "to the end" when we will receive "the grace that is to be brought unto you at the revelation of Jesus Christ" (v. 13)

  We should live like "obedient children, not fashioning yourselves according to the former lusts [we indulged in] in your ignorance" (v. 14). And because the God we seek is holy, "so be ye holy in all manner of conversation" (v. 15).

THEBIBLEREVIVAL.COM, #23

The word translated "holy" here is from the Greek word *hagios*, meaning "saintly." And "conversation" is the translation of a Greek word meaning "conduct." Thus, Peter was saying, "Act like Saints in all your conduct."

- **1 Peter 1:22 Love one another fervently with a pure heart.** If we have "purified [our] souls in obeying the truth through the Spirit," then we should show "unfeigned love of the brethren," and "love one another with a pure heart fervently."

- **1 Peter 2:11–12 As "strangers and pilgrims" in the world, we must live as examples.** Because we are different, "abstain[ing] from fleshly lusts, which war against the soul," we will necessarily feel like "strangers and pilgrims" among the worldly (v. 11). Through honest "conversation" [conduct] among the Gentiles, we put ourselves in a position where, even as "they speak against you as evildoers," they will have to acknowledge our good works, and "glorify God in the day of visitation" (v. 12).

- **1 Peter 2:13–16 Submit to the laws of the land.** Followers of Christ are not social revolutionaries, seeking "social justice" through political means. Instead, Peter counseled the Saints to "submit yourselves to every ordinance [law] of man for the Lord's sake" (v. 13). This is true "whether it be to the king, as supreme [ruler]; or unto governors, as [those] that are sent by [the king] for the punishment of evildoers, and for the praise of them that do well" (v. 14). Peter declares this principle of civil obedience to be "the will of God, that with well doing ye may put to silence the ignorance of foolish men" (v. 15). And if we are free we should "not us[e] . . . your liberty for a cloke of maliciousness, but as the servants of God" (v. 16).

- **1 Peter 2:18 Servants: submit to your masters.** Just as Paul had counseled in several of his epistles (Col. 3:22; 1 Tim. 6:1–2; Titus 2:9–10; Eph. 6:5–8), Peter instructed "servants" to "be subject to your masters with all fear; not only to the good and gentle, but also to the froward [demanding]."

- **1 Peter 3:1–6 Wives: be an example to your husbands.** Peter advised wives who are married to husbands that "obey not the word" [are nonbelievers or inactive], to be in subjection to them so that "they [who are] without the word [might] be won [over] by the conversation [conduct] of the[ir] wives" (v. 1). This way, such a husband will "behold your chaste conversation [conduct] coupled with fear [worship]" (v. 2). Peter further advised women not to focus on the kind of outward adorning that involves "plaiting the hair, and of wearing of gold, or of putting on of apparel" (v. 3). Instead, he advised women to focus on the inward adorning of "a meek and quiet spirit, which is in the sight of God of great price" (v. 4). "For after this manner in the old time the holy women also, who trusted in God, adorned themselves, being in subjection unto their own husbands" (v. 5). Peter then cited Sarah's relationship with Abraham as a righteous example of these principles (v. 6).

- **1 Peter 3:7 Husbands: honor your wives.** Peter advised husbands to dwell with their wives "according to knowledge," meaning according to gospel principles. Men should "giv[e] . . . honour unto the wife," and take care of her "as unto the weaker vessel"—meaning weaker in physical strength. A man should also remember that he and his wife are "heirs together of the grace of life [exaltation]" and that if they do not follow the counsel Peter gave them their "prayers [will be] hindered."

W.C.T. DOBSON, THE BIBLE AND ITS STORY, 1908

- **1 Peter 3:8–11 Fellow Saints: be of one mind, compassionate, courteous and peaceful.** Among our fellow members of the Church, we should be "all of one mind, having compassion one of another, lov[ing] as brethren, be[ing] pitiful, be[ing] courteous: Not rendering evil for evil, or railing for railing: but contrariwise blessing; knowing that ye are thereunto called, that ye should inherit a blessing" (v. 9). If we "love life" and hope to see "good days," we must "refrain [our] tongue[s] from evil, and [our] lips that they speak no guile; . . . eschew evil, and do good; . . . seek peace, and ensu[r]e it." We can imagine the increased importance of this counsel in Peter's day when Saints faced tremendous persecution and the temptation to turn on their fellow Saints in the face of such pressures.

Suffering for Christ's Sake

- **1 Peter 2:21–25 The Savior set an example of righteousness despite suffering.** Peter reminded the Saints that "Christ . . . suffered for us, leaving us an example, that ye should follow his steps: Who did no sin, neither was guile found in his mouth: Who, when he was reviled, reviled not again; when he suffered, he threatened not; but committed himself to him that judgeth righteously [the Father]" (vv. 21–23). Peter also testified that Christ "bare our sins in his own body on the tree, that we, being dead to sins, should live unto righteousness: by whose stripes ye were healed. For ye were as sheep going astray; but are now returned unto the Shepherd and Bishop of your souls" (vv. 24–25).

- **1 Peter 3:12–17 Do not fear persecution; bear it with a good conscience.** "The eyes of the Lord are over the righteous, and his ears are open unto their prayers," but He is always "against them that do evil" (v. 12). Peter asked, "Who is he that will harm you, if ye be followers of that which is good?" (v. 13). And "if ye suffer for righteousness' sake, happy are ye: and be not afraid of their terror, neither be troubled . . . but sanctify the Lord God in your hearts" (vv. 14–15). When evildoers "speak evil of you" behave with "a good conscience" so that "they may be ashamed that falsely accuse your good conversation [behavior] in Christ" (v. 16). If it is "the will of God . . . that ye suffer for well doing," that is better than to suffer "for evil doing" (v. 17).

- **1 Peter 3:15 Be ready always to testify and teach.** As the Lord's Saints, we should "be ready always to give an answer to every man that asketh you a reason of the hope that is in you with meekness and fear [worship]" (v. 15; see also Alma 38:10–12).

- **1 Peter 2:19–20 Suffering for our own stupidity vs. suffering for doing well.** Peter taught that we should be thankful if "for conscience toward God [we] endure grief, suffering wrongfully" (v. 19). Peter asked, "what glory is it, if, when ye be buffeted for your faults, ye shall take it patiently?" (v. 20). "Buffeted" means, literally, to be "struck with fists." So, in other words, if we are knocked around or suffer because of our own stupidity and sins, we won't receive much credit. However, "when ye do well, and suffer for it, [if] ye take it patiently, this is acceptable with God" (v. 20). Thus, suffering for doing good and enduring it, is commendable before God (v. 20; see also D&C 54:10).

- **1 Peter 4:7–11 "The end of all things [for those early Saints] is at hand" so they must support one another** in soberness and prayerfulness (v. 7). If they will maintain "fervent charity among yourselves" then that "charity shall cover [a] multitude of [your] sins" (v. 8; see further explanation at the end of this chapter). They should show "hospitality one to another without grudging" (v. 9). Since all of them had "received the gift" [of forgiveness from Christ], even so minister the same one to another, as good stewards of the manifold [bountiful] grace of God" (v. 10). They should behave toward each other like the oracles [prophets and scriptures] teach, to their very best ability "that God in all things may be glorified" (v. 11).

- **1 Peter 4:12–16 Peter predicts "fiery trials" for Christians and urges them to be faithful.** The Saints should "think it not strange" when " fiery trial[s]" come, "as [if] some strange thing happened unto you" (v. 12). "But rejoice, inasmuch as ye are partakers of Christ's sufferings; that, when his glory shall be revealed, ye may be glad also with exceeding joy" (v. 13). "If ye be reproached for the name of Christ, happy are ye; for the spirit of glory and of God resteth upon you" (v. 14). Though God may be "evil spoken of" by the wicked, "on your part he is glorified" (v. 14). If we suffer "as a murderer, or as a thief, or as an evildoer, or as a busybody in other men's matters," then there is no reward (v. 15). But "if any man suffer as a Christian, let him not be ashamed; but let him glorify God on this behalf" (v. 16).

- **1 Peter 4:17–19 Judgments will come first upon the Saints, then the wicked.** God always, as we like to put it, "cleans house" first (see further discussion at the end of this chapter). "And if it first begin at us, what shall the end be of them that obey not the gospel of God? And if the righteous [will] scarcely be saved," what will be the fate of "the ungodly and the sinner . . . ?" (vv. 17–18). Therefore, if we "suffer according to the will of God," we should save our souls through "well doing" unto God our "faithful Creator" (v. 19).

- **Peter's prophecies fulfilled.** It is important to know that, shortly after Peter penned these warnings, a devastating fire burned down roughly one-third of Rome. Though he probably started the fire himself, Nero blamed the Christians and some other unpopular groups, and he started a wave of persecutions and terror toward them in the city and, to a certain extent, throughout the empire.

- **1 Peter 5:6–11 We may cast all our cares upon Christ, who loves us.** "Humble yourselves therefore under the mighty hand of God, that he may exalt you in due time" (v. 6). "Cast . . . all your care upon him; for he careth for you" (v. 7). "Be sober, be vigilant; because your adversary the devil, as a roaring lion, walketh about, seeking whom he may devour" (v. 8). We should resist Satan by remaining "stedfast in the faith, knowing that the same afflictions are [being born by] your brethren that are in the world" (v. 9). Peter promised that "the God of all grace, who hath called us unto his eternal glory by Christ Jesus, after that ye have suffered a while, [will] make you perfect, [e]stablish, strengthen, [and] settle you" (v. 10). "To him be glory and dominion for ever and ever. Amen" (v. 11).

CHRIST'S VISIT TO THE SPIRIT WORLD

Christ Fulfilled His Promise

- **John 5:25 Jesus promised, ". . . the dead shall hear the voice of the Son of God: and they that hear shall live."** These "dead" are those who are physically dead, not just those that are spiritually dead. And when the dead hear the gospel preached unto them, "they that hear shall live."

- **1 Peter 3:18–20 Peter speaks of Christ's ministry to the "spirits in prison."** Peter reminded the Saints that "Christ . . . suffered for [our] sins, the just for the unjust, that he might bring us to God" (v. 18). That was His mission and purpose in our Father's plan. Peter also testified that He was "put to death in the flesh," but was "quickened" [made alive, continued to live] in the Spirit" (v. 18). And while a spirit being, "he went and preached unto the spirits in prison" (v. 19). Lest we should misunderstand this teaching, Peter clarified that these spirits in prison were the spirits of those people who were "disobedient, when . . . the longsuffering of

"SOULS REMOVED FROM PURGATORY," RUBENS, 1635

Painting of the rescue of the dead

God waited in the days of Noah" (v. 20). In other words, they were those who had been disobedient in the days of Noah.

- **1 Peter 4:6 Why Christ preached to the spirits in prison.** Peter said this was done so that they might have an equal opportunity for salvation—"that they might be judged [like] men in the flesh, [while] living . . . in the spirit."

  President Joseph Fielding Smith said: "Why did He [Jesus] preach to these disobedient spirits? Surely not to increase their torments, to taunt them for not accepting of His truth in the days of the prophets! . . . He took the glorious message of the gospel and proclaimed it to the dead with the promise that they, if they would obey it, should partake of its blessings."[4]

  The Prophet Joseph Smith said: "All who have died without a knowledge of this gospel, who would have received it if they had been permitted to tarry, shall be heirs of the celestial kingdom of God; also all that shall die henceforth without a knowledge of it, who would have received it with all their hearts, shall be heirs of that kingdom, for I, the Lord, will judge all men according to their works, according to the desire of their hearts."[5]

  Elder Bruce R. McConkie said: "Salvation for the dead is limited expressly to those who do not have opportunity in this life to accept the gospel but who would have taken the opportunity had it come to them."[6]

  President Joseph F. Smith, near the end of his life, received a vision of Christ's visit to the spirit world. This vision is recorded in Doctrine and Covenants as section 138.

  — **D&C 138:16–18 The spirits of the dead "were assembled awaiting the advent of the Son of God into the spirit world,** to declare their redemption from the bands of death" (v. 16). They knew that after their conversion, "their sleeping dust [would] be restored unto its perfect frame, bone to his bone, and the sinews and the flesh upon them, the spirit and the body to be united never again to be divided, that they might receive a fulness of joy" (v. 17). Then, "while this vast multitude waited and conversed, rejoicing in the hour of their deliverance from the chains of death, the Son of God appeared, declaring liberty to the captives who had been faithful" (v. 18).

  — **D&C 138:19–21 Christ Himself did not go among the wicked. He sent righteous spirits to preach unto them.** Christ preached the everlasting gospel, the doctrine of the resurrection, and the redemption of mankind from the Fall and from their individual sins (v. 19). "But unto the wicked he did not go, and among the ungodly and the unrepentant who had defiled themselves while in the flesh, his voice was not raised" (v. 20). "Neither did the rebellious who rejected the testimonies and the warnings of the ancient prophets behold his presence, nor look upon his face" (v. 21).

  — **D&C 138:57–59 Faithful elders of this dispensation, when they die, preach the gospel in the spirit world** "among those who are in darkness and under the bondage of sin in the great world of the spirits of the dead" (v. 57). "The dead who repent will be redeemed, through obedience to the ordinances of the house of God, and after they have paid the penalty of their transgressions, and are washed clean, shall receive a reward according to their works, for they are heirs of salvation" (vv. 58–59).

- **Early Christian literature speaks of missionary work in the spirit world.** Hermas, whose brother was bishop in Rome, wrote in the early second century AD that Jesus' Apostles died and then preached the name of the Son of God to those who had died before them.[7]

OTHER CONCEPTS IN FIRST PETER

"MESSENGER OF THE COVENANT," ©JOSEPH BRICKEY. USED BY PERMISSION

- **1 Peter 1:20 Christ was foreordained.** Peter taught that Christ "was foreordained before the foundation of the world" to be the Savior. This teaches important doctrine about the pre-existence and about the Savior's role in the great plan of salvation (Revelation 13:8; Moses 4:1–4; Abraham 3:27–38). Christ's future atonement operated retroactively on our behalf even before we came to this earth (D&C 93:38).

  The Prophet Joseph Smith said: "At the first organization in heaven we were all present, and saw the Savior chosen and appointed and the plan of salvation made, and we sanctioned it."[8]

- **1 Peter 1:24–25 "All flesh is grass,"** Peter said, "and all the glory of man [is] as the flower of grass. The grass withereth, and the flower thereof falleth away" (v. 24). "But the word of the Lord endureth for ever. And this is the word which by the gospel is preached unto you" (v. 25). The symbolism of withering grass was clear to people of Peter's day. The heavy rains of wintertime caused grass to flourish and spread over the wilderness. But it withered and died quickly when the east wind started to blow. The blades could be vigorous one day and withered the next. This reminds us that the things of this world, including our own bodies, are perishable and will fade away (see also Isaiah 40:6–8). But the word of the Lord endures forever, and we must be obedient to it.

- **1 Peter 4:1 Gain the mind of Christ.** "Christ hath suffered for us in the flesh," Peter reminded the Saints, so they [and we] should "arm yourselves likewise with the same mind." Peter said we should do this because when we have "suffered in the flesh" we "cease . . . from sin."

  Elder Bruce R. McConkie explained that we should: "Gain the mind of Christ (1 Cor. 2:16), thereby thinking what He thought, saying what He said, and doing what He did, which course of life will stand as a defense against the evils of the world."[9]

- **1 Peter 4:8 Charity prevents sin.** Peter said, "And above all things have fervent charity among yourselves: for charity shall cover the multitude of sins." The Prophet Joseph Smith revised this verse to read: "And above all things have fervent charity among yourselves; for charity preventeth a multitude of sins" (JST v. 8) It is clear that only repentance truly covers or takes away sin because of Christ's atoning sacrifice.

- **1 Peter 4:17 Judgments will begin within the Church.** Peter warned the early Saints that God's judgments would fall first upon the ungodly in the Church, then upon the wicked of the world. The same can be said about the judgments that will come upon the world at the Second Coming. Notice the close relationship between Peter's comment and a revelation given for Thomas B. Marsh, president of the Quorum of the Twelve, in 1837 (D&C 112:24–26).

- **1 Peter 5:1–4 Feed the flock of God.** Peter called himself "an elder, and a witness of the sufferings of Christ, and also a partaker of the glory that shall be revealed" (v. 1). And in that capacity, he warned the other elders in the Church to "feed the flock of God which is among you, taking the oversight thereof, not by constraint, but willingly; not for filthy lucre, but of a ready mind; Neither as being lords over God's heritage, but being ensamples to the flock. And when the chief Shepherd shall appear, ye shall receive a crown of glory that fadeth not away" (vv. 2–4). This is the same advice that he himself received from the Savior after His resurrection (see also D&C 42:12–14).

- **1 Peter 5:13 "Babylon" is Rome.** Peter referred to the Church in Rome as "the church that is at Babylon." "Babylon" is also used figuratively for Rome in John's Revelation, chapters 17–18.

- **1 Peter 5:13 Mark was with Peter in Rome.** Marcus is John Mark, who had left Paul's company during the latter's first missionary journey (Acts 13:13). He wrote the Gospel of Mark. According to tradition (Papias, circa 140 AD), Mark received some of his information from his association with Peter (hearing Peter preach). Mark was also the cousin of Barnabas.[10]

THE 2ND EPISTLE OF PETER

When and Where Was 2nd Peter Written?

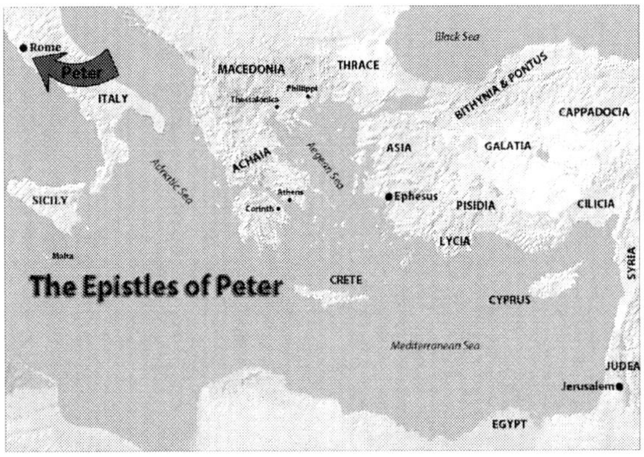

Though some scholars have questioned whether Peter was the author of this epistle, most of the evidence favors it. We cannot say with certainty where Peter wrote his second letter, but we suppose it was Rome, from whence he wrote his first epistle earlier.

This letter was written to a more select audience—to Saints who had obtained the same faith in Christ as had Peter and the Apostles. Because the threat of persecution seems past in this letter (there is no mention of persecution or suffering), it is assumed that the letter was written around 68 AD, between the Nero persecutions and the date of Peter's death.

What Are 2nd Peter's Most Significant Contributions?

Peter's second epistle combines his usual straight-forward simplicity of language with a rich outpouring of the Spirit to produce words which McConkie says, "rank in grandeur and insight with those in the Vision of the degrees of glory and the sermons of the Lord Himself."[11]

Peter expressed concern that Paul had written "some things hard to be understood," enabling the unlearned and unstable to "wrest" his meaning to their own destruction (2 Peter 3:16). Thus we may understand the simplicity and directness of Peter's epistles. Furthermore, he wrote with the awareness that his own death was imminent, and at such a time one would not expect Peter to trifle with words (2 Peter 1:14).

The dominant theme in this letter is how one comes to a knowledge of our Lord Jesus Christ. Peter also speaks forcefully against false teachers and apostates who have arisen everywhere.

DIVINE NATURE

The Attributes of Godliness

- **2 Peter 1:1–3 The early Saints knew all things pertaining to life and godliness,** just as we do. In greeting the Saints at the beginning of this epistle, Peter called them those "that have obtained like precious faith with us through the righteousness of God and our Saviour Jesus Christ" (v. 1). He wished them "grace and peace," and said that God had "given unto us all things that pertain unto life and godliness" through the gospel of Jesus Christ (vv. 2–3).

PROVIDENCE LITHOGRAPHIC CO., 1901, #34

- **2 Peter 1:4 Peter challenged them to achieve a "divine nature" (godhood).** This means becoming more like God by escaping "the corruption that is in the world through lust." For doing so they would receive "exceeding great and precious promises" from the Lord.

- **2 Peter 1:5–7 Peter lists the attributes of godliness.** If we are seeking to become more like God, then we might ask, "What is God like?" Peter here listed the attributes of God that we are expected to seek.

— Faith	=	Active belief.
— Virtue	=	Purity and goodness.
— Knowledge	=	Testimony.
— Temperance	=	Self-control.
— Patience	=	Ability to endure in faith.
— Godliness	=	Devotion, or closeness, to God.
— Brotherly love	=	Fellowship.
— Charity	=	A Christ-like life.
— Perfection	=	Being made perfect through Christ's grace.

President David O. McKay said, "[Peter] wrote on one occasion: '. . . that we might be partakers of the divine nature.' . . . He realized what it means to be in touch with the spiritual, to rise above the temporal, the sensual, and partake of the divine Spirit of God. . . . That is the purpose of making us more capable of responding to the Spirit and subduing the sensual . . . . That is why we like to have every young man and every young woman utilize his or her time intelligently, usefully, to bring the soul in harmony with the spirit, that we all might be partakers of God's Spirit, partakers of His divine nature."[12]

President McKay also said, "Happy is the man who has experienced that relationship to his Maker, wherein we are 'partakers of the divine nature.' That is a reality, and I so testify to you here in this sacred hour."[13]

- **2 Peter 1:8–9 By seeking these virtues we come to know the Savior**, which is essential to the achievement of eternal life. Peter said, "For if these things be in you, and abound, they make you that ye shall neither be barren nor unfruitful in the knowledge of our Lord Jesus Christ" (v. 8). "But he that lacketh these things is blind, and cannot see afar off, and hath forgotten that he was purged from his old sins" (v. 9).

Making Our Calling and Election Sure

On at least two occasions the Prophet Joseph Smith preached with 2 Peter 1 as his text, specifically on making one's calling and election sure.[14]

The Prophet Joseph Smith said: "[The doctrine of making one's calling and election sure] ought (in its proper place) to be taught, for God hath not revealed anything to Joseph, but what He will make known unto the Twelve, and even the least Saint may know all things as fast as he is able to bear them."[15]

Elder Bruce R. McConkie said of 2 Peter 1, "Nowhere else in ancient writ do we find the door so frankly opened to a knowledge of the course men must pursue to have their calling and election made sure."[16]

- **2 Peter 1:16–18 Peter's experience on the Mount of Transfiguration.** He declared to the Saints that "we [the Apostles] have not followed cunningly devised fables, when we made known unto you the power and coming of our Lord Jesus Christ, but were eyewitnesses of his majesty" (v. 16). This refers to the events on the Mount of Transfiguration (v. 18), where Christ "received from God the Father honour and glory, [and] when there came . . . a voice to him [out of] the excellent glory [that surrounded Him on that occasion], This is my beloved Son, in whom I am well pleased" (v. 17).

CARL BLOCH

- **2 Peter 1:19 Peter's even more sure witness of Christ.** In addition to what the Apostles saw on the Mount of Transfiguration, they had received "also a more sure word of prophecy" to which the Saints should "take heed, as unto a light that shineth in a dark place, until the day dawn, and the day star arise in your hearts."

  — **D&C 131:5 What is the "more sure word of prophecy?"** (May 17th, 1843.) The more sure word of prophecy means a man's knowing that he is sealed up unto eternal life, by revelation and the spirit of prophecy, through the power of the Holy Priesthood.

A person who receives a "more sure word of prophecy" knows that he or she is "sealed up unto eternal life, by revelation and the spirit of prophecy." In other words, their calling and election is made sure.

The Prophet Joseph Smith said, "Now, wherein could they have a more sure word of prophecy than to hear the voice of God saying, This is my beloved Son. . . . Though they might hear the voice of God and know that Jesus was the Son of God, this would be no evidence that their election and calling was made sure, that they had part with Christ, and were joint heirs with Him. They then would want that more sure word of prophecy, that they were sealed in the heavens and had the promise of eternal life in the kingdom of God. Then, having this promise sealed unto them, it was an anchor to the soul, sure and steadfast. Though the thunders might roll and lightnings flash, and earthquakes bellow, and war gather thick around, yet this hope and knowledge would support the soul in every hour of trial, trouble and tribulation."[17]

- **2 Peter 1:10 Peter said, "Give diligence to make your calling and election sure,** for if ye do these things, ye shall never fall." We will better understand this saying if we explore the elements of it separately.

— What does it mean to be called?

Elder Bruce R. McConkie said, "To be called is to be a member of the Church and kingdom of God on earth; it is to be numbered with the Saints; . . . it is to be on the path leading to eternal life and to have the hope of eternal glory; it is to have a conditional promise of eternal life. . . . provided there is continued obedience to the laws and ordinances thereof."[18]

— What does it mean be elected? Who are the "elect"?

The Bible Dictionary says, "Election is an opportunity for service and is both on a national and an individual basis. On a national basis the seed of Abraham carry the gospel to the world. But it is by individual faithfulness that it is done. . . . Those who are faithful and diligent in the gospel in mortality receive an even more desirable election in this life, and become the elect of God. These receive the promise of a fulness of God's glory in eternity (D&C 84:33–41)."[19]

— What does it mean to have our calling and election made sure?

Elder Bruce R. McConkie said, "To have one's calling and election made sure is to be sealed up unto eternal life; it is to have the unconditional guarantee of exaltation in the highest heaven of the celestial world; it is to receive the assurance of godhood; it is, in effect, to have the day of judgment advanced, so that an inheritance of all the glory and honor of the Father's kingdom is assured prior to the day when the faithful actually enter into the divine presence to sit with Christ in His throne, even as He is 'set down' with His 'Father in his throne' (Rev. 3:21)."[20]

— What must we do to have our calling and election made sure?

The Prophet Joseph Smith taught, "After a person has faith in Christ, repents of his sins, and is baptized for the remission of his sins and receives the Holy Ghost (by the laying on of hands). . . . then let him continue to humble himself before God, hungering and thirsting after righteousness, and living by every word of God, and the Lord will soon say unto him, Son, thou shalt be exalted. When the Lord has thoroughly proved him, and finds that the man is determined to serve Him at all hazards, then the man will find his calling and his election made sure."[21]

Elder Bruce R. McConkie said: ". . . making one's calling and election sure comes after and grows out of celestial marriage. Eternal life does not and cannot exist for a man or a woman alone, because in its very nature it consists of the continuation of the family unit in eternity."[22]

— It also involves a priesthood ordinance—beyond the ordinance of eternal marriage—presumably also performed in the temple under the authority of God's prophet.

The Prophet Joseph Smith said: "It is the established order of the high priesthood that we have power given unto us to seal the Saints up unto eternal life."[23]

— **D&C 132:49 Joseph Smith received this promise from the Lord.** "For I am the Lord thy God, and will be with thee even unto the end of the world, and through all eternity; for verily I seal upon you your exaltation, and prepare a throne for you in the kingdom of my Father, with Abraham your father."

Others who have had their calling and election made sure include:

— Abraham	(Genesis 22:17)
— Paul	(2 Timothy 4:8)
— Alma	(Mosiah 26:20)
— Nephite Twelve	(3 Nephi 28:1–3)
— Mormon	(Mormon 2:19)
— Moroni	(Ether 12:37).

Elder Marion G. Romney said: "In this dispensation many have received like assurances."[24]

THE FATE OF THE WICKED

Some Signs of Apostasy

Earlier in the Church's history, the greatest threat was persecution from without. The danger now seems to be apostasy from within, which Peter addresses in his second epistle.

- **2 Peter 1:20–21 Peter warns against spurious interpretations of the scriptures.** "Know . . . this first, that no prophecy of the scripture is of any private interpretation" (v. 20). This is because the prophecies within them "came not in old time by the will of man: but holy men of God spake as they were moved by the Holy Ghost" (v. 21).

"Private" is used here to translate the Greek *idios*. This word occurs 113 times in the New Testament but only here is *idios* translated "private." In 77 other instances it is translated "his own" which would lead us to understand this passage as meaning that "no prophecy of the scripture is of his (any prophet's) own interpretation."

Elder Delbert L. Stapley said: "If prophets speak by the power of the Holy Ghost, then the Holy Ghost is required to interpret correctly the teachings of holy men. Therefore, those who do not possess the Spirit of God cannot comprehend the things of God."[25]

- **2 Peter 3:16 This had already happened with the writings of the Apostle Paul.** Peter admitted that Paul wrote in his epistles "some things hard to be understood." And because they were difficult to interpret, "they that are unlearned and unstable wrest [stretch or convolute them], as they do also the other scriptures, unto their own destruction."
- **2 Peter 2:1–3 Peter warns of false teachers who "shall bring in damnable heresies, even denying the Lord."** This was not new among men because "there were false prophets also among the people [of the past], even as there shall be false teachers among you" (v. 1). Peter prophesied that these false teachers would "privily [privately, secretly] . . . bring in damnable heresies, even denying the Lord that bought them, and bring upon themselves swift destruction" (v. 1). "And many shall follow their pernicious ways; by reason of whom the way of truth [the true Gospel] shall be evil spoken of" (v. 2). "And through covetousness shall they with feigned words make merchandise of you" (v. 3). This is a clear, unmistakable prophecy of a coming apostasy in the Church.

- **2 Peter 2:4–5, 9 God will judge and punish apostates.** Peter said that their "judgment [before God] . . . lingereth not, and their damnation slumbereth not. For if God spared not the angels that sinned, but cast them down to hell, and delivered them into chains of darkness, to be reserved unto judgment; And spared not the old world, but saved Noah . . . , a preacher of righteousness, bringing in the flood upon the world of the ungodly" (vv. 4–5), then we can be sure that "the Lord knoweth how to deliver the godly out of temptations, and to reserve the unjust unto the day of judgment to be punished" (v. 9).

- **2 Peter 2:10–19 The brashness of apostate teachers.** Peter said that apostate teachers "walk after the flesh in the lust of uncleanness, and despise government. Presumptuous are they, selfwilled, they are not afraid to speak evil of dignities [authorities]" (v. 10). Even angels "which are greater in power and might, bring not railing accusation against them [the Lord's chosen leaders] before the Lord. But these, as natural brute beasts, made to be taken and destroyed, speak evil of the things that they understand not; and shall utterly perish in their own corruption" (vv. 11–12) and "receive the reward of unrighteousness" (v. 13).

  Peter compared apostates to those "that count it pleasure to riot in the day time. Spots they are and blemishes, sporting themselves with their own deceivings while they feast with you; Having eyes full of adultery, and that cannot cease from sin; beguiling unstable souls: an heart they have exercised with covetous practices" (v. 14). He also called them "cursed children: Which have forsaken the right way, and are gone astray" (vv. 14–15). He compared them to the prophet "Balaam the son of Bosor, who loved the wages of unrighteousness; But was rebuked for his iniquity: the dumb ass speaking with man's voice forb[idding] the madness of the prophet" (v. 16; see also Num. 22:5; Deut. 23:4; Rev. 2:12–17).

Peter continued by calling apostate teachers "wells without water, clouds that are carried with a tempest; to whom the mist of darkness is reserved for ever. For when they speak great swelling words of vanity, they allure through the lusts of the flesh, through much wantonness, those that were clean escaped from them who live in error. While they promise them liberty, they themselves are the servants of corruption: for of whom a man is overcome, of the same is he brought in bondage" (vv. 17–19).

- **2 Peter 2:20–21 Apostasy is worse than never accepting the Gospel in the first place.** Peter said that if "after they have escaped the pollutions of the world through the knowledge of the Lord and Saviour Jesus Christ, they are again entangled therein, and overcome, the latter end is worse with them than the beginning" (v. 20). The reason for this is because when they become knowledgeable they also become responsible and accountable. Peter said it would have been "better for them not to have known the way of righteousness, than, after they have known it, to turn from the holy commandment delivered unto them" (v. 21).

Scoffers in the Last Days

- **2 Peter 3:3–7 In the last days, men will scoff at the idea of a Second Coming.** Apostasy would again be a problem in the last days. Peter prophesied "that there shall come in the last days scoffers, walking after their own lusts, And saying, Where is the promise of his coming? for since the fathers fell asleep, all things continue as they were from the beginning of the creation" (vv. 3–4). How literally do we see this prediction fulfilled in our day! These arrogant scoffers are "willingly . . . ignorant of . . . the word of God [in times] of old" (v. 5). They will deny the story of the flood in the days of Noah (v. 6), and will not believe that "the heavens and the earth, . . . are now, by the same word [of God] . . . reserved unto fire [in] the day of judgment" when "ungodly men" will be assigned to "perdition" (v. 7).

- **2 Peter 3:8 The Lord's time.** Peter declared that "one day is with the Lord as a thousand years, and a thousand years [on earth is] as one day" with Him. Alma declared to the Nephites that "all is as one day with God, and time only is measured unto men" (Alma 40:8), suggesting that there is *no* measuring of time in God's celestial kingdom. But on the planet Kolob, which is nearby where God dwells, the Lord said "one revolution was a day unto the Lord, after his manner of reckoning, it being one thousand years according to the time appointed unto that [world] whereon thou standest [earth]. This is the reckoning of the Lord's time, according to the reckoning of Kolob" (Abraham 3:4).

  Thus, in God's kingdom time is irrelevant and all things are present with Him (D&C 38:2). But by way of comparison, Kolob's revolution (1 day) takes 1,000 earth years to accomplish.

- **2 Peter 3:9 The Lord is patient and wants all to be saved.** "The Lord is not slack concerning his promise [to come again] . . . but is longsuffering . . . , not willing that any should perish, but that all should come to repentance." If God were as vengeful as some claim, He would have destroyed the wicked long ago. But He waits and waits and waits, and He warns and warns and warns, in order to give every one of His children ample opportunity to repent. Only when they reach a "fullness of iniquity" does He permit their destruction (Ether 2:10). And even then, it can be argued, their destruction moves them into a spirit world where they might still respond to the message of salvation.

- **2 Peter 3:10 Christ will come "as a thief in the night."** President Joseph Fielding Smith said, "I do not know when He is going to come. No man knows. Even the angels of heaven are in the dark in regard to that great truth [See Matthew 24:36, 37]. But this I know, that the signs that have been pointed out are here. The earth is full of calamity, of trouble. The hearts of men are failing them. We see the signs as we see the fig tree putting forth her leaves; and knowing this time is near, it behooves you, and all men upon the face of the earth, to pay heed to the words of Christ, to His apostles and watch, for we know not the day nor the hour. But I tell you this, it shall come as a thief in the night, when many of us will not be ready for it."[26]

- **2 Peter 3:10, 12 Great destructions will accompany Christ's coming.** Peter prophesied that "the heavens shall pass away with a great noise, and the elements shall melt with fervent heat, the earth also and the works that are therein shall be burned up" (v. 10), and "the heavens being on fire shall be dissolved, and the elements shall melt with fervent heat" (v. 12).

- **2 Peter 3:11–13 New heavens and a new earth.** Peter asked, "If all these things shall be dissolved, what manner of persons ought ye to be in all holy conversation [behavior] and godliness, looking for and hasting unto the coming of the day of God" (vv. 11–12). For the righteous, that great day will not be fearful but will bring "new heavens and a new earth, wherein dwelleth righteousness" (v. 13).

  Elder Spencer W. Kimball said, "Just as surely as Jesus was born in Bethlehem, just so surely will He come again, a resurrected, glorified being, and with Him will come hosts, and there will be many spectacular changes. It will not be the end of the world in the sense of annihilation, but the end of its present relationships, and there will be many,

many changes. Beginning with the Bridegroom's coming will come the celestializing of this earth and tremendous changes which we can hardly think of or believe."[27]

President Joseph Fielding Smith said: "Let us not misunderstand this expression. The new heaven and new earth will be the same heaven and the same earth on which we now sojourn, for this earth is to receive the resurrection after this day of mortality and be the abode of the righteous in eternity. Without the revelations of the Lord given to men, this truth would not be made known. Neither would we have knowledge of the final glory to which this earth will be assigned. Even now, where men are without the divine guidance and revelation, this truth would not be known."[28]

- **2 Peter 3:14, 17–18 We must be diligent and worthy when that day comes.** As the Lord's Saints, who are looking forward to the great day of His coming, Peter said that we must "be diligent that ye may be found of him in peace, without spot, and blameless" (v. 14). All that is corrupt will be destroyed, so we must "beware lest ye also, being led away with the error of the wicked, fall from your own stedfastness" (v. 17). Until that great day we must "grow in grace, and in the knowledge of our Lord and Saviour Jesus Christ" (v. 18).

  — **D&C 45:56–59 The great promises to those who remain faithful unto the end.** "And at that day, when I shall come in my glory, shall the parable be fulfilled which I spake concerning the ten virgins. For they that are wise and have received the truth, and have taken the Holy Spirit for their guide, and have not been deceived—verily I say unto you, they shall not be hewn down and cast into the fire, but shall abide the day. And the earth shall be given unto them for an inheritance; and they shall multiply and wax strong, and their children shall grow up without sin unto salvation. For the Lord shall be in their midst, and his glory shall be upon them, and he will be their king and their lawgiver."

- **Peter is crucified upside-down in Rome.** David O. Mckay said, "By reading [Peter's] epistles, we get a little insight into the nature of his labors and travels during the last years of his life. Undoubtedly, he visited every country where there were organized branches of the Church, even to the "seven churches in Asia." We do not know for sure where he died, though tradition says he died in Rome where he was crucified—insisting that it be done upside down so as not to provide any comparison to the crucifixion of our Lord.[29] It is evident that the end was not far off when he wrote his second epistle to the churches. That was about 35 years after he first met the Savior. He was in the ministry then, approximately 35 years, perhaps longer."[30] Peter died in about 67–68 AD.

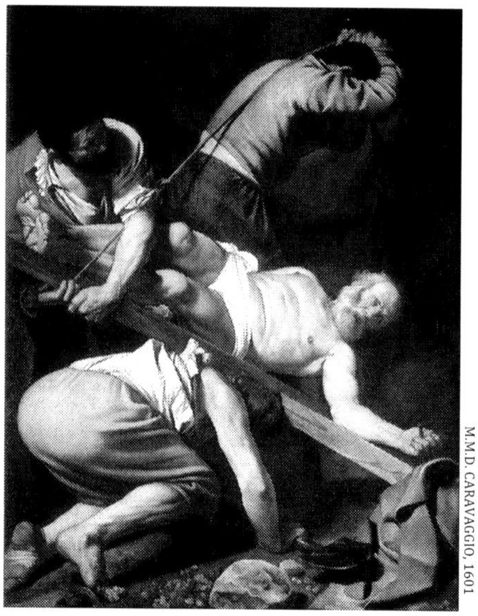

M.M.D. CARAVAGGIO, 1601

OTHER CONCEPTS IN SECOND PETER:

- **2 Peter 2:6 The fate of Sodom and Gomorrah.** Peter said that God "turn[ed] the cities of Sodom and Gomorrah into ashes [and] condemned them with an overthrow, making them an e[x]ample unto those that . . . live ungodly." The Hebrew word *mahapekha*, which is translated here as "overthrow" means "catastrophe." It is used frequently in the Old Testament, and in every case where it refers to Sodom and Gomorrah it suggests an earthquake.

  — **Jude 1:7 Jude suggested that fire destroyed Sodom and Gomorrah.** "Even as Sodom and Gomorrha, and the cities about: them in like manner, giving themselves over to fornication, and going after strange flesh, are set forth for an example, suffering the vengeance of eternal fire." This "eternal fire" was possibly some form of radiance or "fire from the Lord" that consumed them (see Genesis 19:24; Exodus 3:2; 13:21; Leviticus 10:2; Numbers 16:35; Hebrews 12:29).

- **2 Peter 2:12–14 Living a self-indulgent life.** Peter called those that revel in their wickedness "natural brute beasts, made to be taken and destroyed, speak[ing] evil of the things that they understand not" (v. 12). "They . . . count it pleasure to riot in the day time. Spots they are and blemishes, sporting themselves with their own deceivings while they feast with you" (v. 13). "Having eyes full of adultery, and that cannot cease from sin; beguiling unstable souls: an heart they have exercised with covetous practices; cursed children" (v. 14). These, Peter said, "shall utterly perish in their own corruption; And shall receive the reward of unrighteousness" (v. 13).

  We understand these characterizations better when we understand what some of these terms mean, which are quite different from what they mean today.

  — "Riot" (v. 13). The translators used this word because there is no single word in English that carries the exact meaning of the Greek word *truphay*. The actual meaning is "to live delicately, live luxuriously, be given to a soft and luxurious life." So to "riot" was not to make a public disturbance but to live a soft, self-indulgent life, pampering the flesh.

  — "Sporting themselves with their own deceivings while they feast with you" (v. 13) means to show off their religiosity—pretend to be faithful Saints—while inwardly being out of harmony with the Church.

  — "Eyes full of adultery" (v. 14) is a figure of speech that represents the personification of lust. It would have been used to describe those who revel in pornography today.

Notes

1. "Peter, My Brother," *Speeches of the Year*, 1971, 1.
2. *Teachings of the Prophet Joseph Smith*, sel. Joseph Fielding Smith [1976], 301.
3. *Doctrinal New Testament Commentary*, 3 vols. [1965–1973], 3:294.
4. *Doctrines of Salvation*, comp. Bruce R. McConkie, 3 vols. [1954–1956], 2:159–160.

5. *Teachings of the Prophet Joseph Smith*, 107.

6. *Mormon Doctrine*, 2nd ed. [1966], 686.

7. *Shepherd of Hermas, Similitudes* 9:16, in *Ante-Nicene Fathers*, 2:49.

8. *Teachings of the Prophet Joseph Smith*, 181.

9. *Doctrinal New Testament Commentary*, 3:315.

10. Eusebius, *History of the Church*, 390–391.

11. *Doctrinal New Testament Commentary*, 3:325.

12. In Conference Report, October 1961, 90.

13. In Conference Report, April 1957, 130.

14. *Teachings of the Prophet Joseph Smith*, 298–299; 303–306.

15. *Teachings of the Prophet Joseph Smith*, 149.

16. *Doctrinal New Testament Commentary*, 3:323.

17. *Teachings of the Prophet Joseph Smith*, 298.

18. *Doctrinal New Testament Commentary*, 3:326.

19. *Bible Dictionary*, 662–663.

20. *Doctrinal New Testament Commentary*, 3:330–331.

21. *Teachings of the Prophet Joseph Smith*, 150.

22. *Doctrinal New Testament Commentary*, 3:343.

23. October 1831 General conference of the Church.

24. In Conference Report, October 1965, 22.

25. In Conference Report, October 1966, 113.

26. *Doctrines of Salvation*, 3:52–53.

27. *Teachings of Spencer W. Kimball* [1982], 440–441.

28. *Seek Ye Earnestly* [1970], 262.

29. Attested to by Origen, in Eusebius, *Church History* III.1.

30. "Apostleship in the Ancient Church," Chapter 17 in *Gospel Ideals* [1976], 229–251.

Chapter 44

The Epistles of John and Jude

(1–3 John; Jude)

INTRODUCTION

Who Is John?

G. RENI, 1575–1642

There is some evidence that John and his brother James, the sons of Zebedee, were cousins of Jesus, though this has not been proven. John lived—and was probably born—in Bethsaida, the home of Peter and Andrew and Philip. He was a fisherman by trade and worked with his father and brother James. He was a seeker after truth and one of the earliest disciples of John the Baptist. When the Baptist bore witness that Jesus was the "Lamb of God," John immediately left the Baptist and followed Christ.

Among the Twelve, John was one of the three who constituted the First Presidency of that quorum. They were present at all of the Lord's raisings of the dead, and were with Jesus on the Mount of Transfiguration. John was on the Mount of Olives when Jesus taught concerning the destruction of the temple and the Second Coming. He and Peter made preparations for Jesus' final Passover. At that Last Supper, he occupied the position of greatest affection—"in the Lord's bosom"—which means in front of the Savior, with his back to the Lord's chest, as they reclined inward toward the center of the table.

He was present in the Garden of Gethsemane during the Atonement. When Jesus was arrested the other disciples fled, but John followed his Master to the high priest's house. He saw his Savior nailed to the cross—the only Apostle mentioned as being there when the Savior died. As Mary and John stood by the cross, Jesus said to His mother, "Behold thy son!" and to John, "Behold thy mother!" "And from that hour that disciple took her unto his own home" (John 19:27). This is one thing that argues for John being a relative to Jesus.

John was with Peter when Mary Magdalene reported that the Master's body was missing. They ran to the tomb, with John arriving first and being the first to see the empty tomb. John was with the Apostles on both occasions when Christ appeared to them in the upper room and also on the shores of the Sea of Galilee. He was present during the Savior's entire 40-day ministry following His resurrection.

For about 15 years after the Savior's ascension John stayed at Jerusalem as a true son to Mary. During this period, he was imprisoned several times, but never once wavered in his witness. He was with Peter at the Gate Beautiful when he healed a poor man who had never walked.

When the Samaritans received the gospel through the preaching of Philip, John accompanied Peter to Samaria, and conferred the Holy Ghost by the laying on of hands. When the question arose about the Gentiles joining the Church, John was one who sat in the council held at Jerusalem. Paul called him one of three "pillars" of the Church (Galatians 2:9).

After the disciples were forced from Jerusalem, John resided at Ephesus with Mary for a while, preaching the gospel for 18 years among the Churches in Asia (Turkey). While at Ephesus, John was arrested by the cruel Roman emperor Domitian and taken to Rome. There he was condemned to death and plunged into boiling oil, but was preserved through the power of God.

John was then banished to the isle of Patmos. While on Patmos, John beheld a vision of the Savior, who commanded him to write Revelation. Upon the death of Domitian, John was permitted to return to Ephesus, where he continued his preaching, writing, and testimony. Besides "Revelation," he wrote his gospel and his three epistles.

He was probably the last living witness of the Savior's miracles and teachings, with reports of his ministry continuing in various historical documents until the time of the emperor Trajan (98 AD). After that time, we have no record of John's activities, though Joseph Smith tells us that he was sent to minister among the lost ten tribes. He appeared, along with James and John, in 1830, to confer the Melchizedek priesthood upon Joseph Smith and Oliver Cowdery.

THE EPISTLES OF JOHN

When and Where Were They Written?

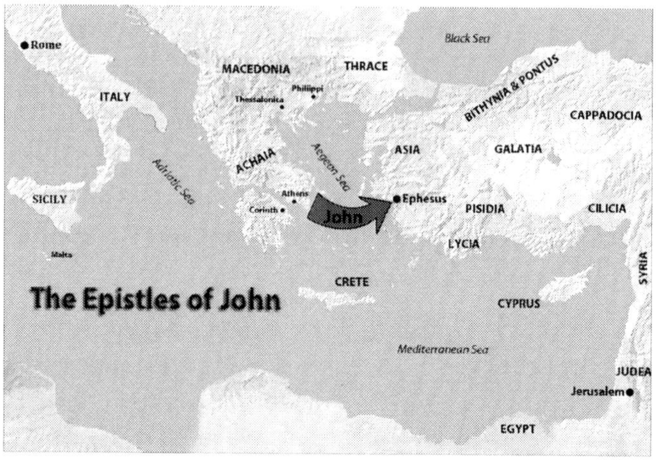

The epistles of John provide little or no evidence of their place of writing. Although John spent the major portion of his life in the Holy Land, Christians as well as Jews were unwelcome there following the destruction of Jerusalem and its temple in 70 AD. If traditions regarding John's long residence in Ephesus are true, they may have come from there.

The epistles of John seem to belong to a period in which Gnostic philosophy was on the rise. They also bear a close relationship to the fourth Gospel, which is dated about 90 or 95 AD. This means they were probably written between 70–100 AD, and likely around 96 AD.

What Are The Most Significant Contributions of John's Epistles?

Elder Bruce R. McConkie said the following about 1 John:

> Written by the Disciple whom Jesus loved, and who in turn had such great love for his Lord and his fellowmen that he gained permission to remain on earth and seek to save souls until the Second Coming—this Epistle has as its essential theme:
>
> That God is love;
> That love is the foundation upon which all personal righteousness rests;
> That all the purposes and plans of Deity are based on his infinite and eternal love; and
> That if men will personify that love in their lives, they will become like the Lord Himself and have eternal life with Him.
>
> The doctrines expounded include how to gain fellowship with God; how to know God and Christ; how to become the sons of God; how to abide in the light and love the brethren; how to dwell in God and have Him dwell in us; how to be born again and gain eternal life.[1]

Second and Third John are more intimate than 1 John; they are addressed to "the elect lady and her children" (2 John 1:1) and to "the well-beloved Gaius, whom I love in the truth" (3 John 1:1). Elder Bruce R. McConkie believes that these two epistles were personal letters to members of John's own immediate family, and summarizes their contributions as follows:

> Why these two brief, personal epistles?
>
> Their doctrinal content and historical recitations are, of course, minimal. But they do add a unique contribution to the revealed word which well pays for their preservation. . . .
>
> Brief, less significant than some portions of Holy Writ, these two lesser epistles of the Beloved John are yet of eternal worth, and the Saints rejoice in the added perspective they give to the Bible as a whole.[2]

THE DARK EVE OF APOSTASY

Those who deny the apostasy of the early Church are simply not reading the scriptures. The best evidence for the reality of the apostasy can be found in Acts and in the epistles of the New Testament. Paul spoke of "all Asia" being turned away from the Gospel (2 Timothy 1:15). Peter spoke of false teachers within the Church who were teaching "damnable heresies, even denying the Lord that bought them" (2 Peter 2:1). And John, in his first epistle speaks plainly about the spiritual degradation that had occurred even before the end of the first century. If it was that bad before the Apostles were gone, what can we think happened after there were no living witnesses of Christ to teach and guard true doctrine?

Gnostic Anti-Christs

Some apostate Christians—called Gnostics (meaning "to know")—claimed "special knowledge" which others were not privileged to know. The Gnositcs taught that Jesus could not have truly come in the flesh, for God is holy and could have nothing to do with contaminating matter such as a physical body. To explain the Savior's presence on earth, the Gnostics set forth two arguments:

Docetism (from the Greek word dokeo, meaning "to seem" or "to appear") taught:

- Jesus didn't really suffer for anyone's sins but merely seemed to do so.
- He wasn't really a partaker of mortality but only appeared to be.
- The physical body the Lord displayed after the resurrection was an illusion.

Cerinthianism (named for the man Cerinthus, its primary proponent) taught:

- The spirit which inhabited Jesus' mortal body descended into the man Jesus at the time of His baptism and departed just prior to His suffering on the cross.
- Thus Christ did not suffer for our sins; only the man Jesus was crucified.

- **1 John 2:18 John cites evidence of the approaching end of the early Church.** John refers to this period as the "last time," which should not be confused with the "last days" before Christ's Second Coming. The days John is referring to are the last years of the early Church, as evidenced by the influence of anti-christs and apostates, which had been prophesied by both Paul and Peter. "And as ye have heard that antichrist shall come, even now are there many antichrists; whereby we know that it is the last time" (v. 18).

PROVIDENCE LITHOGRAPHIC CO., 1904

John wrote to thwart apostate antichrists

- **1 John 2:19 Who were the antichrists?** John said they were apostate members of the Church. "They went out from us, but they were not of us; for if they had been of us, they would no doubt have continued with us: but they went out, that they might be made manifest that they were not all of us" (v. 19).

  — The prefix anti means the same thing in Greek as it does in English—that which is against something else. An anti-Christ is one who stands in *opposition to* or in *substitution for* Christ, or seeks to *amend, change, add to, or undermine* His doctrine.

  — **2 Thess. 2:4 The devil is the best example of an anti-Christ.** He "opposeth and exalteth himself above all that is called God, or that is worshipped."

- **1 John 2:20, 26–27 The "anointing" [Gift of the Holy Ghost] is a guide and protection to the Saints.** "But ye have an unction [anointing] from the Holy One, and ye know all things," John said to the Saints of his day. Elder Bruce R. McConkie said, "This unction, this holy anointing, is the gift of the Holy Ghost, which gives them access to the infinite wisdom of the Father and the Son so that they may know all things as fast as they are able to bear them."[3] Because of it, these Saints could know "all things" that were necessary for their salvation and exaltation. "I have not written unto you because ye know not the truth, but because ye know it, and that no lie is of the truth" (v. 20).

  "These things have I written unto you concerning them that seduce you," said John (v. 26). Because of "the anointing which ye have received of him" which "abideth in you, . . . ye need not that any man teach you" (v. 27). The anointing "teach[es] . . . you of all things, and is truth, and is no lie, and even as it hath taught you, ye shall abide in him [Christ]" (v. 27).

John's Witness for Christ

- **1 John 1:1–2 To Docetists John testified he had personally "handled" the Savior.** Docetists did not believe that Christ ever took upon Himself a physical body because all things having to do with the body were corrupt. Christ only appeared to be mortal. And the physical body He displayed after the resurrection was an illusion.

  John testified that "That which was from the beginning [Christ], . . . we have heard, . . . we have seen with our eyes, . . . we have looked upon, and our hands have handled" (v. 1). John called Christ the "Word of life; (For the life was manifested, and we have seen it, and bear witness, and shew unto you that eternal life, which was with the Father, and was manifested unto us)" (v. 2).

RUBENS, 1615

- **1 John 2:22 The spirit of antichrist.** John wrote that anyone who "denieth that Jesus is the Christ" is "a liar," and anyone "that denieth the Father and the Son" is antichrist (v. 22). Though in our day we associate the prefix *anti* with opposition and antagonism, the base meaning of the word in Greek is "instead of" or "in place of." We have three classic examples of such "antichrists" in the Book of Mormon: Sherem (Jacob 7), Nehor (Alma 1), and Korihor (Alma 30).
  - **1 John 4:1–3 To believe in a disembodied Christ is to become an antichrist.** Since there were many Docetists among them, John urged the Saints to "believe not every spirit, but try the spirits whether they are of God: because many false prophets are gone out into the world" (v. 1). "Ye have heard that it should come; and even now already is it in the world" (v. 2).

Then John gave them the test by which they could "try the spirits" of such teachers. "Every spirit that confesseth that Jesus Christ is come in the flesh is of God: And every spirit that confesseth not that Jesus Christ is come in the flesh is not of God" (v. 2). To teach this false doctrine "is that spirit of antichrist" (v. 2).

Satan has attempted from the beginning to set himself up in the place of God our Father and/or His Son Jesus Christ. He has sought to substitute his wicked plan in place of the Father's plan of salvation. And he leads men into false doctrines concerning Christ and the Father to cause them to worship things that are antichrist. The most dangerous form of apostasy is always that which appears to be true and thus provides a false sense of security and salvation to those who believe it.

— **2 John 1:7–10 Do not listen to or welcome any antichrist who seeks to teach you.** "Many deceivers are entered into the world," John warned, "who confess not that Jesus Christ is come in the flesh. This is a deceiver and an antichrist" (v. 7). He counseled the Saints to "look to yourselves" [be careful] "that [they] lose not those things [teachings] which we [the Apostles] have wrought [taught]," so that, in the end, they might "receive a full reward" (v. 8). If anyone fails to "abide . . . in the doctrine of Christ," then he "hath not God," while "he that abideth in the doctrine of Christ, . . . hath both the Father and the Son" (v. 9). "If there come any unto you, [who] bring not this doctrine, receive him not into your house, neither bid him God speed" (v. 10).

- **1 John 2:23 We receive the Father by receiving His Son.** "Whosoever denieth the Son, the same hath not the Father," said John, but "he that acknowledgeth the Son hath [acknowledged] the Father also."

- **1 John 5:20 Knowing the truth concerning Christ is essential to eternal life.** John testified that "we know that the Son of God is come, and hath given us an understanding," so that "we may know him that is true" (v. 20). In other words, Christ came to earth and made it very clear what His nature was—physical and yet divine. When we have the Spirit "we are in him that is true" [the Father] and "in his Son Jesus Christ." "This is the tru[th] about God, and eternal life" (see also John 17:3; D&C 132:24).

CHILDREN OF A LOVING HEAVENLY FATHER

- **1 John 3:1, 10 God loves us as His children.** John wanted us to consider the depth of God's love for us "that we should be called the sons of God" (v. 1). This family relationship explains how He feels about us—like a Father to a child. The world, which does not literally believe this, "knoweth us not, because it [knows] him not" (v. 1). And how should we, as His children, live our lives? "In this the children of God are manifest, and the children of the devil: whosoever doeth not righteousness is not of God, neither he that loveth not his brother" (v. 10).

- **1 John 3:2 Our destiny is to become like Him.** John assured us that we are the children of God, and while "it doth not yet appear [it is not clear to us] what we shall be," we do know that "when he [Christ] shall appear, we shall be like him" (v. 2). That would necessarily mean that we will have a resurrected and glorified body like He does. "We shall see him as he is," not as the world philosophizes that He might be.

Spiritual Rebirth

- **Being "Born of God".** The metaphor (and reality) of being God's children leads to another metaphor of spiritual birth. When we finally realize who we are and when we worship Him with proper knowledge and in truth, then we are spiritually "born again."

  Throughout his epistles, John defines the characteristics of those who are born again:

  — **1 John 2:28–29 Those who are righteous.** John said, "And now, little children, abide in him; that, when he shall appear, we may have confidence, and not be ashamed before him at his coming" (v. 28). And because "he is righteous, . . . every one that doeth righteousness is born of him" (v. 29).

  — **1 John 4:7 Those who love others.** John taught also that we should "love one another: for love is of God," and that "every one that loveth is born of God, and knoweth God."

  — **1 John 5:1 Those who believe in Christ.** If we believe that "Jesus is the Christ" then our spirits have been born again through that belief.

  — **1 John 5:1 Those who love God the Father and His Son.** If we "loveth him that begat" [the Father], and we "love . . . him also that is begotten of him" [the Christ], then we are born again.

  — **1 John 5:4–5 Those who overcome the world.** We become born of God when we "overcome . . . the world," and this victory is accomplished through our faith in Christ.

  — **1 John 5:18 Those who do not sin.** "Whosoever is born of God sinneth not; but he that is begotten of God keepeth himself, and that wicked one toucheth him not."

  — **1 John 3:9 Spiritual rebirth causes us to forsake sin.** "Whosoever is born of God doth not commit sin; for his seed [his heavenly parentage] remaineth in him: and he cannot sin, because he is born of God."

  In the JST, Joseph Smith translates the passage as follows: "Whosoever is born of God doth not continue in sin; for the Spirit of God remaineth in him; and he cannot continue in sin, because he is born of God, having received that holy Spirit of promise."

- **Moses 6:64–68 How Adam was "born again" and became "a son of God."** After being taught by the Lord, Adam "cried unto the Lord, and he was caught away by the Spirit of the Lord, and was carried down into the water, and was laid under the water, and was brought forth out of the water. And thus he was baptized, and the Spirit of God descended upon him, and thus he was born of the Spirit, and became quickened in the inner man" (vv. 64–65).

  The Lord spoke out of heaven, saying, "Thou art baptized with fire, and with the Holy Ghost. This is the record of the Father, and the Son, from henceforth and forever; And thou art after the order of him who was without beginning of days or end of years, from all eternity to all eternity. Behold, thou art one in me, a son of God; and thus may all become my sons. Amen."

God Is Love

- **1 John 4:7–8 God is the very personification of love.** John taught us to "love one another: for love is of God; and every one that loveth is born of God, and knoweth God" (v. 7). If we do not love others, we do not know God because "God is love" (v. 8).

MICHELANGELO

- **1 John 1:5 God is also "light."** John and the other Apostles had heard from the Lord Himself that "God is light, and in him is no darkness at all."

  Elder Bruce R. McConkie said, "'Our God is a consuming fire' (Heb., 12:29). 'God is light' (1 John 1:5). Similarly, God is also faith, hope, charity, righteousness, truth, virtue, temperance, patience, humility, and so forth. That is, God is the embodiment and personification of every good grace and godly attribute—all of which dwell in His person in perfection and in fulness."[4]

- **1 John 4:19, 9–11 We love God because He first loved us** (v. 19). He manifested that love by sending "his only begotten Son into the world, that we might live through him" (v. 9). Had He not done that, we could never have had a chance to return to Him and His kingdom. We are imperfect, but He "sent his Son to be the propitiation for our sins" (v. 10). Knowing this, John observed, "if God so loved us, we ought also to love one another" (v. 11).

  President Thomas S. Monson said, "Our Heavenly Father's plan contains the ultimate expressions of true love. All that we hold dear—even our families, our friends, our joy, our knowledge, our testimonies—would vanish were it not for our Father and His Son, the Lord Jesus Christ. . . . The world has witnessed no greater gift, nor has it known more lasting love."[5]

  — **D&C 18:10 "Remember the worth of souls is great in the sight of God."** Speaking of the Father's love for every one of His children, President Brigham Young said, "The least, the most inferior person now upon the earth . . . is worth worlds."[6]

    President Spencer W. Kimball said, "God is your Father. He loves you. He and your Mother in heaven value you beyond any measure. . . . You are unique. One of a kind, made of the eternal intelligence which gives you claim upon eternal life. Let there be no question in your mind about your value as an individual. The whole intent of the gospel plan is to provide an opportunity for each of you to reach your fullest potential, which is eternal progression and the possibility of godhood."[7]

- **1 John 4:12 God's love is "perfected" in our love for one another.** "If we love one another, God dwelleth in us, and his love is perfected in us." How is God's love perfected in us? President Spencer W. Kimball said, "God does notice us, and he watches over us. But it is usually through another mortal that He meets our needs. Therefore, it is vital that we serve each other in the kingdom."[8]

The Savior Also Loves Us

"CHRIST WITH CHILDREN," ©JOSEPH BRICKEY, USED BY PERMISSION

- **1 John 3:16 Christ showed His love by laying down His life for us.** Just as the Father loves us and showed that love by sending His Son (1 John 4:10), we can perceive the love of the Savior for us "because he laid down his life for us," and knowing this, "we ought to lay down our lives for the brethren."

- **1 John 1:7 When we walk in the light, the Atonement cleanses us.** "If we walk in the light, as he [the Father] is in the light, we have fellowship one with another, and the blood of Jesus Christ his Son cleanseth us from all sin."

- **1 John 1:8–9 We all need the Atonement of Jesus Christ.** John observed, "If we say that we have no sin, we deceive ourselves, and the truth is not in us" (v. 8). Paul said the same thing to the Roman Saints when he said we all sin "and come short of the glory of God" (Romans 3:23). We are therefore unworthy to live in God's presence, but "if we confess our sins, he is faithful and just to forgive us our sins, and to cleanse us from all unrighteousness" (v. 9).

- **1 John 2:1 Christ is our advocate with the Father if we repent.** John hoped, of course, that the Saints would "sin not." But if we do sin, "we have an advocate with the Father, Jesus Christ the righteous."
  - **D&C 45:3–5 Christ describes how He will advocate for us.** "Listen to him who is the advocate with the Father, who is pleading your cause before him—Saying: Father, behold the sufferings and death of him who did no sin, in whom thou wast well pleased; behold the blood of thy Son which was shed, the blood of him whom thou gavest that thyself might be glorified; Wherefore, Father, spare these my brethren that believe on my name, that they may come unto me and have everlasting life."
  - **D&C 18:11–12 Only those who truly repent will benefit from the Atonement.** The "Lord your Redeemer suffered death in the flesh [and] suffered the pain of all men, that

all men might repent and come unto him" (v. 11). He has also "risen again from the dead," in an effort to "bring all men unto him, *on conditions of repentance*" (v. 12, emphasis added). That final statement is significant, because although He suffered for every sin for every person, in the case of those who reject Him and do not repent, His suffering will have been in vain.

The Universality of the Atonement

"GETHSEMANE," ©JOSEPH BRICKEY, USED BY PERMISSION

- **1 John 2:2 Christ suffered for the sins of all men.** John said the Christ "is the propitiation for our sins: and not for ours only, but also for the sins of the whole world." Can we image the depth of suffering that would be necessary to pay the price of the sins of every child of God who ever lived or will live on this earth?

  Christ truly suffered. W. Jeffrey Marsh said, "Spiritual anguish and physical pain pressed down upon Him so greatly that blood oozed from every pore in His body (JST Luke 22:44; Mosiah 3:7; D&C 19:18). The medical term for such a condition is hematodrosis. Under extreme distress and pressure the capillaries burst and produce a bloody sweat. Christ's was the most severe instance of hematodrosis ever experienced."[9]

  Elder B. H. Roberts said:

  > Let the severity of the Christ's Atonement for man's sin bear witness; for it required all that the Christ gave in suffering and agony of spirit and body, to lay the grounds for man's forgiveness and reconciliation with God.
  >
  > The severity of the Atonement should impress men with the fact that we live in a world of stern realities; that human actions draw with them tremendous consequences that may not be easily set aside if the actions in which they have their origin are wrong. . . . Violations of moral law are attended by shame and suffering; suffering is the consequence or the penalty of violating divine, moral law; and the penalty must be paid, either by the one sinning or by another who shall suffer vicariously for him.[10]

  Modern revelation describes the universality of Christ's atonement.

  — **D&C 76:43 Christ suffered for all of God's creations on this earth.** His atonement "save[d] all the works of his hands, except those sons of perdition who deny the Son after the Father has revealed him." This means that the Savior glorifies the Father by saving all the works of His hands—human, animal, plant, even the earth itself.

  — **D&C 88:43 Christ suffered for all men and all creations on all planets in the universe.** The Lord said the courses of all His creations "are fixed, even the courses of the heavens and the earth, which comprehend [includes] the earth and all the planets."

The "earth and all the planets" are referred to here as "kingdoms," and the Lord visits and saves all of them.

Clement (one of the early Christian "fathers") wrote: "God is the Father of all the worlds. ... As the Father of greatness is in the glorious world, so His Son rules among those cosmoses as first chief lord of all the powers."[11] And Elder Russell M. Nelson said, "The mercy of the Atonement extends not only to an infinite number of people, but also to an infinite number of worlds created by Him."[12]

— **D&C 88:58–60 Christ has visited all of His Father's children throughout the universe."** All of the Father's children have received "the light of the countenance of their lord [Christ], every man in his hour, and in his time, and in his season—Beginning at the first, and so on unto the last, and from the last unto the first. Every man in his own order, ... that his lord might be glorified in him, and he in his lord, that they all might be glorified" (vv. 58 –60).

— **D&C 88:61 Christ has also visited every planet and its creations.** "Every kingdom in its hour, and in its time, and in its season, even according to the decree which God hath made" (v. 61).

WE MUST ALSO SHOW LOVE

Showing Love for God and His Son

- **1 John 5:3 To love God is to keep His commandments.** "For this is the love of God, that we keep his commandments: and his commandments are not grievous" to us.

- **1 John 2:3–6 To know Christ is to keep His commandments.** John said, "He that saith, I know him, and keepeth not his commandments, is a liar, and the truth is not in him" (v. 4). We can say "we know him" only "if we keep his commandments" (v. 3). As we learn to keep His commandments "the love of God [is] perfected" in us (vv. 3–5). Also, "hereby know we that we are in him," if we "walk, even as he walked" (vv. 5–6).

Elder Bruce R. McConkie said, "It is by obedience to the laws and ordinances of the gospel! and in no other way! ... Since the very fact of knowing God, in the ultimate and full sense, consists of thinking what He thinks, saying what He says, doing what He does, and of being like Him, thus having exaltation or godhood—it follows that saved souls must advance and progress until they acquire His character, perfections, and attributes, until they gain His eternal power, until they themselves become gods."[13]

Elder Howard Hunter said: "Merely saying, accepting, believing are not enough. They are incomplete until that which they imply is translated into the dynamic action of daily living. This, then, is the finest source of personal testimony. One knows because he has experienced. He does not have to say, 'Brother Jones says it is true, and I believe him.' He can say, 'I have lived this principle in my own life, and I know through personal experience that it works. I have felt its influence, tested its practical usefulness, and know that it is good. I can testify of my own knowledge that it is a true principle.'"[14]

- **1 John 2:15–17 If we love the transient things of this world, we do not love God.** "Love not the world," said John, "neither the things that are in the world. If any man love the world, the love of the Father is not in him" (v. 15). "For all that is in the world, the lust of the flesh, and the lust of the eyes, and the pride of life, is not of the Father, but is of the world" (v. 16). All these things of the world "passeth away, and the lust thereof: but he that doeth the will of God abideth for ever" (v. 17).

- **3 John 1:4 Our faithfulness brings joy to our Heavenly Father**, in much the same way that we have joy when our children keep the commandments. John expressed this idea when he said, "I have no greater joy than to hear that my children walk in truth."

Obtaining Fellowship with God

- **1 John 1:3–4 Obtaining fellowship with the Apostles and with the Father and Son.** John testified again that "that which we have seen and heard declare we unto you." This the Apostles did so that "ye also may have fellowship with us" and that all might have "fellowship . . . with the Father, and with his Son Jesus Christ." The Greek word *koinonia* ("fellowship") means partnership and the sharing of things in common. Fellowship with God means eternal life. In that way, and in that way only, could their joy be full (v. 4).

  Elder Bruce R. McConkie said, "To have fellowship with the Lord in this life is to enjoy the companionship of His Holy Spirit, which makes us one with Him; and to have fellowship with Him in eternity is to be like Him, having that eternal life of which He is the possessor and originator."[15]

"SEEKING SHILOAH," ©JOSEPH BRICKEY, USED BY PERMISSION

- **1 John 3:21 The source of our confidence.** John said, "If our heart condemn us not, then have we confidence toward God." And in our own day, the Lord said that our "confidence [will] wax strong in the presence of God" (D&C 121:45). In this world, this means the presence of the Spirit in our lives.

  The Prophet Joseph Smith said, "An actual knowledge to any person, that the course of life which he pursues is according to the will of God, is essentially necessary to enable him to have that confidence in God without which no person can obtain eternal life. It was this that enabled the ancient Saints to endure all their afflictions and persecutions, and to take joyfully the spoiling of their goods, knowing (not believing merely) that they had a more enduring substance" [Hebrews 10:34].[16]

- **1 John 3:24 Through the Spirit we can know whether God is with us.** Those that keep the commandments "dwelleth in him [Christ], and he in him." This is accomplished through the Spirit, which "abideth in us" and "which he hath given us."

Love for Our Fellow Man

- **1 John 2:9–11 When we show love for others we maintain the "light" of God within us.** John observed that "he that saith he is in the light, and hateth his brother, is in darkness" (v. 9). But "he that loveth his brother abideth in the light, and there is none occasion of stumbling in him" (v. 10). "He that hateth his brother is in darkness, and walketh in darkness, and knoweth not whither he goeth, because that darkness hath blinded his eyes" (v. 11).

- **1 John 3:17 If others have needs and we ignore them, we are not of God.** When a man possesses "this world's good[s], and seeth his brother have need, and shutteth up his bowels of compassion from him," we cannot say that the love of God is in him.

- **1 John 4:20–21 If we love God we will love His children—our brothers and sisters.** "If a man say, I love God, and hateth his brother, he is a liar," said John. If a man "loveth not his brother whom he hath seen, how can he love God whom he hath not seen?" (v. 20). God has commanded all those "who loveth God [to] love his brother also" (v. 21).

OTHER CONCEPTS IN THE EPISTLES OF JOHN

- **1 John 1:5, 7 Walking in the light.** In Primary, the children sing, "Teach Me to Walk in the Light."[17] One of John's most important themes is that Christ is the Light of the World (see 1 John 2:9–11; John 1:4–9; 8:12; 9:1–5; D&C 50:23–24; 88:67–68). In these two verses, John declared "that God is light, and in him is no darkness at all" (v. 5). And "walking in the light" is defined as obtaining forgiveness of sin and having a love of God in our hearts.

- **1 John 3:4 A definition of sin: "transgression of the law."** John taught that "whosoever committeth sin transgresseth also the law: for sin is the transgression of the law." Not all transgression is sin. One might transgress the law of gravity and fall precipitously if he steps off a porch. Adam and Eve transgressed the law of amortality by partaking of the forbidden fruit and becoming mortal. But all sins constitute a "transgression of the law (God's commandments)."

- **1 John 5:17 Another definition of sin: "all unrighteousness."** Later on in his first epistle, John defined sin as "all unrighteousness."

- **1 John 3:5–8 Christ destroys Satan's works.** "For this purpose the Son of God was manifested, that he might destroy the works of the devil" (v. 8). Satan rebelled against

God in the beginning and was thrust down to earth to deceive and tempt the rest of Heavenly Father's children (Moses 4:1–4; Abraham 3:24–28). Christ was sent into the world to destroy the works of Satan, which are the works of sin.

John taught that He was sent "to take away our sins; and in him is no sin" (v. 5). Those who abide in Christ seek to "sin not," but "whosoever sinneth hath not seen him, neither known him" (v. 6). The righteous seek to be righteous "even as he [Christ] is righteous" (v. 7). But "he that committeth sin is of the devil; for the devil sinneth from the beginning" (v. 8).

Elder Bruce R. McConkie said, "All men sin, before and after baptism, but those Saints who strive to keep the commandments and are continually repenting and returning to the Lord, no longer continue in that course of sinful rebellion against God and His laws which was not their lot before they were baptized for the remission of sins. Church members in name only; they do not receive the companionship of the Holy Ghost, through whose revelations alone can the Lord be 'known.'"[18]

- **1 John 4:12 Has any man seen God?** The Bible records that John said, "No man hath seen God at any time." Yet we know this is not correct and have to suspect that some Docetetic philosophers meddled with these words to further their "bodiless God" heresies.

  The Prophet Joseph Smith re-translated this verse in the Joseph Smith Translation as: "No man hath seen God at any time, *except them who believe*" (JST 1:4:12, emphasis added). This is more consistent with what John said in his Gospel: "Not that any man hath seen the Father, save he which is of God, he hath seen the Father" (John 6:46). Every scripture reader knows that many prophets of God have seen and conversed with God. And we may all see God for ourselves if we are worthy (D&C 67:10–12).

Many prophets have seen God

- **1 John 3:22 Obtaining answers to prayer.** John taught that "whatsoever we ask, we receive of him, [if] we keep his commandments, and do those things that are pleasing in his sight." Thus, the secret of gaining answers to prayers is prior obedience to the Lord's commandments,[19] and asking according to God's will (see 1 John 5:14–15).

- **1 John 5:7 A spurious addition to the Bible.** The Bible reads, "For there are three that bear record in heaven, the Father, the Word, and the Holy Ghost: and these three are one. And there are three that bear witness in earth." But this verse is a late addition.

The King James translators added words in this verse that are not found in any Greek manuscripts nor in any translation prior to the sixteenth century.

This is an example of scribes adding things that they think make the scriptures more accurate according to their understanding of things. The truth is that the members of the Godhead are one in purpose, not in physicality or entity.

- **1 John 5:6, 8 The symbolism of water, blood and spirit.** John taught that Christ "came by water and blood, . . . not by water only, but by water and blood. And it is the Spirit that beareth witness, because the Spirit is truth" (v. 6). Also, "there are three that bear witness in earth, the Spirit, and the water, and the blood: and these three agree in one" (v. 8).

  These three elements are present in our mortal birth as well as in our spiritual re-birth when we are "born again." They were also present in the Atonement that Christ performed for all of us. All three of these elements have eternal significance in our lives.

  Elder Bruce R. McConkie said:

  > Just as there can be no mortal birth without:
  >
  > > Water (the viable fetus being immersed in such in its mother's womb); and
  > >
  > > Blood (the life of the mortal body is in the blood, without which there is immediate death; and there can be no mortal birth as such without the loss of blood by the mother); and
  > >
  > > Spirit (the offspring of God which comes from premortal existence to dwell in the tabernacle of clay formed from the dust of the earth in the womb of the mother);
  >
  > So there can be no spiritual birth into the kingdom of heaven without:
  >
  > > Water (baptism by immersion under the hands of a legal administrator);
  > >
  > > Spirit (the cleansing power of the Holy Spirit which burns sin and iniquity out of the human soul as though by fire, thus making the soul fit to dwell with holy and pure beings in God's kingdom); and
  > >
  > > Blood (the shed blood of Him who poured out His soul unto death so that all of the terms and conditions of the plan of salvation would have force and validity and so that mortal man might be ransomed from the temporal and spiritual death brought into the world by the fall of Adam.[20]

- **1 John 5:9–10 The witness of the Father concerning His Son.** John reasoned, "If we receive the witness of men, the witness of God is greater," and "God . . . hath testified of his Son" (v. 9). Therefore, "he that believeth not God hath made him a liar; because he believeth not the record that God gave of his Son" (v. 10).

- **1 John 5:10–12 We have our own witness that Jesus is the Christ: our testimonies.** "He that believeth on the Son of God hath the witness in himself," said John (v. 10). And this is the testimony that we have: "that God hath given to us eternal life [through] his Son" (v. 11), and that "he that hath [believes in] the Son hath life; and he that hath not [believes not in] the Son of God hath not [eternal] life" (v. 12).

THE EPISTLE OF JUDE

Who Was Jude?

JUDE, BROTHER OF THE LORD, TISSOT, 1904

Instead of saying he was the brother of the Lord, which he was (Matt. 13:55), Jude introduced himself as a servant of the Lord and brother of James the Apostle, another brother of the Lord (Gal. 1:19).

The Greek name "Judas" is rendered "Jude" in English to distinguish him from the traitor and from the patriarch Judah of the tribe of Israel. The Greek version of Luke 6:16 and Acts 1:13 lists one of the Apostles as "Judas of James," which is translated "Jude . . . brother of James" (JST, Jude 1:1). However, this was not the Jude who wrote this epistle. It was an earlier Jude who was an Apostle and probably the brother of "James the Less," who was also an Apostle.

The Jude who wrote this epistle was married and apparently traveled with his wife in his Church duties (1 Cor. 9:5). He was probably not an Apostle. The Prophet Joseph Smith adds to this verse, "Jude, the servant of God, called of Jesus Christ, and brother of James." We have no other indication that he held an office of importance in the early Church, but the epistle seems to suggest he held a position where a letter from him would carry some weight.

Where and When Was Jude Written?

Jude is the third-shortest letter in the New Testament (2–3 John are shorter). We know little about its intended audience. Jude merely addresses his writing "to them that are sanctified by God the Father, and preserved in Jesus Christ, and called" (v. 1). It was most likely written from Jerusalem, where Jude's brother James was an Apostle and leader of the local Branch of the Church.

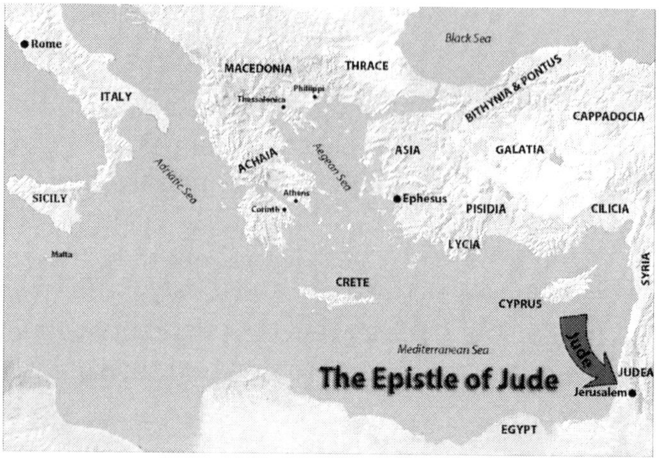

There are many similar passages in Jude and 2 Peter, but whereas Peter's letter points to the future when serious apostasy will infest the Church, Jude's letter conveys the urgent crisis of an immediately-present apostasy.

If Jude indeed quoted Peter's letter, he must then have written sometime after 67 AD. The fourth century historian Eusebius quotes Hegesippus as saying that the Roman emperor Domitian (81–96 AD) searched for survivors of the family of the Lord to determine whether they posed any threat to his reign. He found grandsons of Jude, simple farmers, whom he dismissed as harmless. Since Jude was apparently dead when Domitian went searching for members of the Lord's family, the letter may be dated roughly at 80 AD.

What Are Jude's Most Significant Contributions?

Jude wrote that the purpose in his letter was to urge his readers to "earnestly contend for the faith which was once delivered unto the Saints" (v. 3). Jude's primary concern was apostasy. He wrote of "certain men" who crept into the Church unnoticed, "ungodly men, turning the grace of our God into lasciviousness, and denying the Lord God, and our Lord Jesus Christ" (v. 4) As he discussed these problems, Jude also mentioned important doctrines and teachings not mentioned elsewhere in the Bible.

Elder Bruce R. McConkie said:

> In the whole Bible, it is Jude only who preserves for us the concept that pre-existence was our first estate and that certain angels failed to pass its tests.
>
> It is to him that we turn for our meager knowledge of the disputation between Michael and Lucifer about the body of Moses.
>
> He alone records Enoch's glorious prophecy about the Second Coming of the Son of Man.
>
> And he is the only inspired writer to express the counsel that the Saints should hate even the garments spotted with the flesh.[21]

SPREADING APOSTASY

God Will Punish Disbelievers

- **Jude 1:3–4 Ungodly men crept secretly into the Church.** Jude pleaded with the Saints to "earnestly contend for the faith which was once delivered unto the saints" (v. 3). His concern was that "there are certain men crept in unawares, . . . ungodly men, turning the grace of our God into lasciviousness, and denying the only Lord God, and our Lord Jesus Christ" (v. 4).

- **Jude 1:5–7 Jude cites three scriptural precedents of how God destroys the wicked.** "I will . . . put you in remembrance," he said, "though ye once knew this."

  — Destruction of those who came out of Egypt and couldn't enter the Promised Land because of their disobedience (v. 5).

— Destruction of the angels "who kept not their first estate." These He "hath reserved in everlasting chains under darkness unto the judgment of the great day" (v. 6).

— Destruction of the inhabitants of Sodom and Gomorrah "and the cities [round] about them" who, after "giving themselves over to fornication, and going after strange flesh," were "set forth for an example, suffering the vengeance of eternal fire" (v. 7).

The Nature of Apostates

- **Jude 1:8, 10 They defile the flesh.** Jude called them "filthy dreamers" who "defile the flesh, despise dominion, and speak evil of dignities" (v. 8). They "speak evil of those things which they know not," and seem to know only about "what they know naturally, as brute beasts, in those things they corrupt themselves" (v. 10).

THEBIBLEREVIVAL.COM, #21

— **2 Peter 2:10 Apostates are often also anarchists.** Peter wrote that "them that walk after the flesh in the lust of uncleanness [also] despise government. Presumptuous are they, selfwilled, they are not afraid to speak evil of dignities."

- **Jude 1:11 Jude describes apostates by comparing them to ancient traitors.**

— They "have gone in the way of Cain." Cain knowingly turned his back on Christ and chose Satan instead.

— They "ran greedily after the error of Balaam for reward." Balaam is the Old Testament prophet who accepted money to prophesy against the children of Israel.

— They will perish in the gainsaying of Core [Korah]. The sin of Korah was twofold: (1) He openly rebelled against Moses and Aaron, seeking to turn the congregation away from them; and (2) he usurped the priestly office that belonged to Aaron (Num. 16: 3, 9, 10). For these things, the Lord opened up the earth and it swallowed them alive (Num. 16:25–30).

- **Jude 1:12 Jude calls apostates "spots in your feasts of charity,** when they feast with you, feeding themselves without fear." The Saints were commanded to gather together in fellowship, to provide for needy Saints, and to take the sacrament. They did this by holding fellowship suppers (like our Ward dinners today) after their sacrament meetings. Jude was here warning of licentious persons who came to these gatherings, pretending to be good members but being inwardly wicked.

- **Jude 1:12–13 Jude uses metaphors similar to those used by Peter to describe apostates.**
  - Jude called them "clouds . . . without water, carried about of winds" (v. 12), while Peter called them "wells without water" and "clouds that are carried with a tempest" (2 Peter 2:17).
  - Jude also called them "trees whose fruit withereth, without fruit, twice dead, plucked up by the roots" (v. 12), and "raging waves of the sea, foaming out their own shame," two metaphors that Peter did not use.
  - Finally, Jude called them "wandering stars, to whom is reserved the blackness of darkness for ever," only the latter part of which was used by Peter (2 Peter 2:17).
  - **1 Enoch 2:1–10; 18:14–16** Jude was also alluding to metaphors from the apocryphal book of 1 Enoch, where water and clouds and trees and the motions of stars and seas obey God according to divine law and harmony, but blasphemers and harsh speakers of the Lord are out of harmony with eternal law and must perish.
  - **Moses 7:62–66** The book of Enoch is not included in our present standard works of scripture, but the book of Moses contains some of the writings of Enoch.
- **Jude 1:16 Apostates are dishonest and corrupt.** Jude called them "murmurers, complainers, walking after their own lusts." The Greek word *epithumia*, translated here as "lusts," does not mean simply sexual desire, but any strong worldly desire. To say that "their mouth speaketh great swelling words, having men's persons in admiration because of advantage" means that such persons will say or do anything to get what they want.
- **Jude 1:17–19 The Apostles prophesied of the coming of these apostates.** Jude asked the Saints to "remember . . . the words which were spoken before of the apostles of our Lord Jesus Christ; How that they told you there should be mockers in the last time, who should walk after their own ungodly lusts. These be they who separate themselves, sensual, having not the Spirit."
  - **Ephesians 6:12–13 Paul described the nature of the apostate enemy.** "For we wrestle not against flesh and blood, but against principalities, against powers, against the rulers of the darkness of this world, against spiritual wickedness in high places. Wherefore take unto you the whole armour of God, that ye may be able to withstand in the evil day, and having done all, to stand."

THE LOVE OF GOD

Jude's epistle is full of words and images of preservation, salvation, and protection as a result of God's love. He also identifies love as an effective weapon against apostasy.

- **Jude 1:1–2 Jude begins his epistle with a greeting full of love.** He reminded the Saints that they are "sanctified" by God the Father and "preserved" by Jesus Christ (v. 1). The Greek word translated "sanctified" here should read "loved" instead. Thus, the

Saints are loved by God the Father, and Jude wishes them continued "mercy . . . and peace, and love . . . multiplied" (v. 2).

- **Jude 1:20–21 Jude also ends his epistle with an expression of the love.** Jude invited the Saints to "build . . . up yourselves [in] your most holy faith, [by] praying [under the influence of] the Holy Ghost" (v. 20). He advised them to "keep yourselves in the love of God, looking for the mercy of our Lord Jesus Christ unto eternal life" (v. 21).

- **Jude 1:22–23 Treat people according to their needs and personalities.** "Of some have compassion," Jude advised, in order to "mak[e] . . . a difference" (v. 22). "And others save with fear, pulling them out of the fire; hating even the garment spotted by the flesh" (v. 23).

  President Brigham Young gave similar counsel to the Saints in his day:

  > There are degrees of feeling and degrees of chastisement, and you are led to chastise one man differently to what you do another. You may, figuratively speaking, pound one Elder over the head with a club, and he does not know but what you have handed him a straw dipped in molasses to suck. There are others, if you speak a word to them, or take a straw and chasten them, whose hearts are broken; they are as tender in their feelings as an infant, and will melt like wax before the flame. You must not chasten them severely; you must chasten according to the spirit that is in the person. Some you may talk to all day long, and they do not know what you are talking about. There is a great variety. Treat people as they are.[22]
  >
  > I tell the mothers not to allow the children to indulge in evils, but at the same time to treat them with mildness. . . . Bring up your children in the love and fear of the Lord; study their dispositions and their temperaments, and deal with them accordingly, never allowing yourself to correct them in the heat of passion; teach them to love you rather than to fear you, and let it be your constant care that the children that God has so kindly given you are taught in their early youth the importance of the oracles of God, and the beauty of the principles of our holy religion, that when they grow to the years of man and womanhood they may always cherish a tender regard for them and never forsake the truth.[23]
  >
  > Parents should never drive their children, but lead them along, giving them knowledge as their minds are prepared to receive it. Chastening may be necessary betimes [immediately], but parents should govern their children by faith rather than by the rod, leading them kindly by good example into all truth and holiness.[24]

OTHER DOCTRINAL CONCEPTS IN JUDE

Fallen Angels in Our First Estate

- **Jude 1:6 Angels who did not keep their first (pre-mortal) estate.** This is language that is unique in all of the Bible. The world has no idea what Jude is talking about here, and generally they spiritualize his words to bend them to their sectarian dogmas. But Jude was clearly talking about angels (spirits without bodies) and about their "first estate," which suggests a time when they first came to be. If we reason, then, that they have never been born on this earth, then certainly they must have had a life somewhere else beforehand. That is the first estate of our premortal existence, where we were all spirit children of our Heavenly Father.

The angels "who kept not their first estate" are those who failed to be faithful in that sphere and were forced to leave "their own habitation." These God has "reserved in everlasting chains under darkness unto the judgment of the great day." They are Satan and his followers who rebelled against God and sought to destroy His eternal plan. Jude's teachings here are a significant corroboration of the doctrine taught in Abraham 3:24–28.

COVER TO "THE BOOK OF ENOCH," TRANSLATED BY G.H. CHARLES, 1917

- **Similar doctrines in the Book of Enoch.** Since Jude frequently references the teachings of Enoch, we should not be surprised to find similar discussions of a premortal world and fallen angels in the apocryphal book of Enoch 1.
  - **1 Enoch 12:4** "Enoch, scribe of righteousness, go and make known to the Watchers of heaven who have abandoned [same Greek word as in Jude 1:6, apolipontes] the high heaven, the holy eternal place.... There shall not be peace unto them even forever."
  - **1 Enoch 10:11–14** "And to Michael God said . . . 'Bind [the Watchers] . . . underneath the rocks of the ground until the day of their judgment and of their consummation, until the eternal judgment is concluded. In those days they will lead them into the bottom of the fire—and in torment—in the prison (where) they will be locked up forever.'" "The Watchers" is Enoch's name for Fallen angels.

- **D&C 91:1–6 A caution concerning Apocryphal writings.** The book of Enoch was rejected by those who first assembled the Bible that we have today because they did not believe its teachings. All this talk of premortal life and of fallen angels was contrary to what the sectarians had decided among themselves would be the accepted truth.

  The original book of Enoch is long gone, but apocryphal versions of it have come forth over the years. The Prophet Joseph Smith was told to be cautious with the Apocrypha because "there are many things contained therein that are true, and it is mostly translated correctly," but "there are many things contained therein that are not true, which are interpolations by the hands of men" (vv. 1–2). "Therefore, whoso readeth it, let him understand, for the Spirit manifesteth truth; And whoso is enlightened by the Spirit shall obtain benefit therefrom; And whoso receiveth not by the Spirit, cannot be benefited" (vv. 3–6).

Elder Bruce R. McConkie said: "[1 Enoch] contains many remarkable and inspired teachings and also considerable trashy nonsense."[25]

Sodom and Gomorrah

- **Jude 1:7 How Sodom and Gomorrah were destroyed.** Jude described the destroying power that was sent against these two cities as "eternal fire" (see Genesis 19:24; Exodus 3:2; 13:21) and "fire from the Lord" that consumed other nearby cities also (see Leviticus 10:2; Numbers 16:35; 2 Peter 2:6, Hebrews 12:29). Whether this was a fire started by earthquakes, an asteroid streaking down from the skies, or some sort of nuclear blast, we can only speculate. All we know for sure is that it came from God as a punishment for their lasciviousness.

Michael and Satan

- **Jude 1:9 The role of Michael (Adam).** Jude clarified another story found in 2 Peter about a dispute between Michael and Satan over the body of Moses.

  — **2 Peter 2:11** Peter said that "angels, which are greater in power and might, bring not railing accusation against [others] before the Lord."

Jude was apparently quoting an apocryphal work, The Assumption of Moses, the teachings of which Elder Bruce R. McConkie summarized as follows:

— Moses was translated at the end of his mortal life.

— Before his translation, Michael was commissioned to bury Moses.

— Satan opposed the burial on the ground (a) that he was the lord of matter and that accordingly the body should be rightfully handed over to him; and (b) that Moses was a murderer, having slain the Egyptian.

— Michael charged Satan with having instigated the serpent to tempt Eve.

— Finally, all opposition having been overcome, Moses' translation occurred in the presence of Joshua and Caleb.[26]

A. CARRACCI 1604-05

Michael overcomes Satan

The Prophet Joseph Smith taught, "The priesthood was first given to Adam; he obtained the First Presidency, and held the keys of it from generation to generation .... He had dominion given him over every living creature. He is Michael the archangel, spoken of in the Scriptures. . . . The keys have to be brought from heaven whenever the Gospel is sent. When they are revealed from heaven, it is by Adam's authority. . . . He (Adam) is the father of the human family, and presides over the spirits of all men. . . . Christ is the Great high priest; Adam next."[27]

Enoch's Prophecies of Christ

- **Jude 1:14–15 Enoch's prophecy about apostates and the Second Coming of the Lord.** Jude wrote that Enoch prophesied concerning apostates by saying, "Behold, the Lord cometh with ten thousands of his saints, To execute judgment upon all, and to convince all that are ungodly among them of all their ungodly deeds which they have ungodly committed, and of all their hard speeches which ungodly sinners have spoken against him" (vv. 14–15). This is another unique contribution from Jude to the New Testament, and it may be a direct quotation from the Book of Enoch.

  The Prophet Joseph Smith said that Enoch himself appeared to Jude and thus Jude was able to bear record of the vision of Enoch.[28]

  — **Moses 7:60, 63, 65–66 Enoch's vision of the coming of the Lord as contained in the Book of Moses.** The Lord said unto Enoch: "As I live, even so will I come in the last days, in the days of wickedness and vengeance, to fulfil the oath which I have made unto you concerning the children of Noah" (v. 60). . . . "Then shalt thou and all thy city meet them there, and we will receive them into our bosom, and they shall see us; and we will fall upon their necks, and they shall fall upon our necks, and we will kiss each other" (v. 63).

  "And it came to pass that Enoch saw the day of the coming of the Son of Man, in the last days, to dwell on the earth in righteousness for the space of a thousand years; But before that day he saw great tribulations among the wicked; and he also saw the sea, that it was troubled, and men's hearts failing them, looking forth with fear for the judgments of the Almighty God, which should come upon the wicked" (vv. 65–66).

Notes

1. *Doctrinal New Testament Commentary*, 3 vols. [1965–1973], 3:371.
2. *Doctrinal New Testament Commentary*, 3:409.
3. *Doctrinal New Testament Commentary*, 3:383.
4. *Doctrinal New Testament Commentary*, 3:398.
5. In Conference Report, April 1993, 77.
6. In *Journal of Discourses*, 9:124.
7. "Privileges and Responsibilities of Sisters," *Ensign*, November 1978, 105.

8. *The Teachings of Spencer W. Kimball* [1982], 252.

9. *His Final Hours*, 47–48.

10. *The Seventy's Course in Theology*, 5 vols. [1907–1912], Fourth Year, 127–129.

11. 1 Clement, as quoted by Hugh Nibley in *Old Testament and Related Studies (The Collected Works of Hugh NIbley, Volume 1)*, John Welch, Gary P. Gillium, & Done E. Norton, eds. [1986], 143.

12. "The Atonement," *Ensign*, November 1996, 35.

13. *Doctrinal New Testament Commentary*, 3:377.

14. In Conference Report, April 1967, 116.

15. *Doctrinal New Testament Commentary*, 3:374

16. *Lectures on Faith*, Lecture Sixth, 2.

17. *Hymns* #304; *Children's Songbook* #177.

18. *Doctrinal New Testament Commentary*, 3:386.

19. *Doctrinal New Testament Commentary*, 3:391, 393.

20. *Doctrinal New Testament Commentary*, 3:403–405.

21. *Doctrinal New Testament Commentary*, 3:415.

22. "Rebuking Evil." An address delivered in the Tabernacle, Salt Lake City, March 17, 1861. In *Journal of Discourses*, 8:367.

23. April 22, 1877; in *Journal of Discourses*, 19:223; or *Discourses of Brigham Young* [1954], 207, 323, 320.

24. *Discourses of Brigham Young*, 208.

25. *Doctrinal New Testament Commentary*, 3:423

26. *Doctrinal New Testament Commentary*, 3:421.

27. *Teachings of the Prophet Joseph Smith*, sel. Joseph Fielding Smith [1976], 157–158.

28. *Teachings of the Prophet Joseph Smith*, 170.

SECTION TWELVE

The Book of Revelation

(96 AD)

The events described in the Revelation of John include those that occurred during the Apostle John's exile to the Isle of Patmos.

After the disciples were forced from Jerusalem, John resided at Ephesus with Mary for a while, preaching the gospel for 18 years among the Churches in Asia (Turkey). While at Ephesus, John was arrested by the cruel Roman emperor Domitian and taken to Rome. There he was condemned to death and plunged into boiling oil, but was preserved through the power of God.

John was then banished to the isle of Patmos, where he beheld a vision of the Savior, who commanded him to write Revelation.

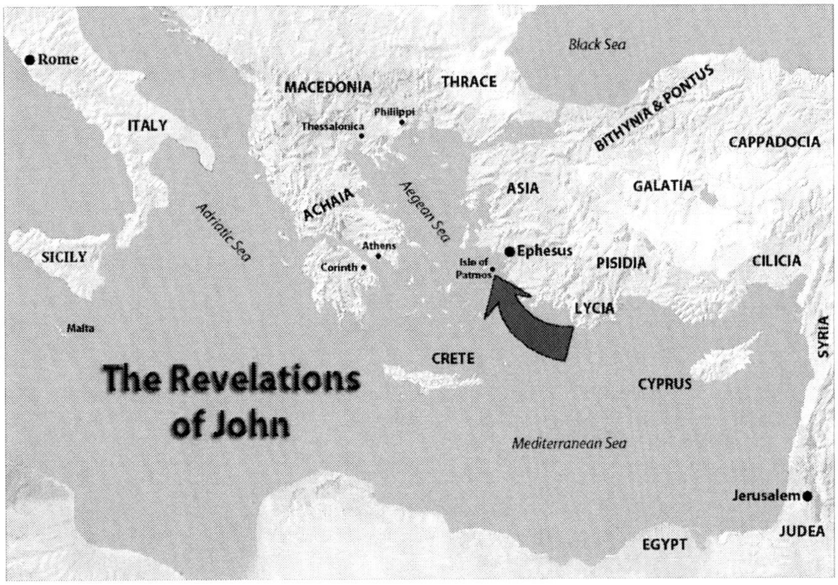

The associated chapters of this book, corresponding to Gospel Doctrine lessons, are:

45. Revelation, Pt. 1 — Understanding & Introduction (Revelation 1-3)
46a. Revelation, Pt. 2 — Visions & Prophecies (Revelation 4-7,10-12,14)
46b. Revelation, Pt. 3 — End of the World & the Millennium (Revelation 8-9, 13-22)

The following is a summary of topics covered in the Revelation of John.

THE BOOK OF REVELATION (The Revelation of John) (96 AD)
To Seven Branches of the Church in Asia
While exiled on the island of Patmos, off the coast of Asia (modern-day Turkey)

Subject:	Scriptural References
From the Isle of Patmos:	
Earth Receives Its Paradisiacal Glory	Rev. 21:1–6
Men May Become Sons of. God.	Rev. 21:6–7
The Second Death	Rev. 21:8
Earth Attains Its Celestial Glory.	Rev. 21:9–27
Saints Will Reign as Gods	Rev. 22:1–5
Christ Comes to Bless the Worthy Saints	Rev. 22:6–16
"Come unto Christ"	Rev. 22:17–21

Chapter 45

Revelation of John, Pt. 1: Understanding & Introduction

(Revelation 1–3; 12)

INTRODUCTION

Who Wrote Revelation?

The book of Revelation was written by John, brother of James, son of Zebedee, and one of the original Twelve called by Jesus. He came to be known as John the Beloved because of the special fondness Jesus felt for him. He was in the First Presidency of the early Church with Peter and James. He stood fearlessly at Peter's side during the early persecutions which followed the Savior's death. He is the author of the Gospel of John, the three epistles of John, and the book of Revelation.

John was given the privilege of continuing to live on the earth as a translated being until the Savior's Second Coming. Little more is recorded of his life except a mention in Revelation of his being on the isle of Patmos. In 1831 the Prophet Joseph Smith said John is now laboring among the lost ten tribes.[1]

John saw symbolic visions on Patmos

Where Was Revelation Written?

- **Revelation 1:9–11 John received these revelations on the isle of Patmos** (96 AD). Patmos is a small, rocky island that lies a short distance off the coast of present-day Turkey, in the Aegean Sea.

  In Roman times, its barren isolation made it ideal as a site for the banishment of political prisoners, ambitious enemies, or others whom the state

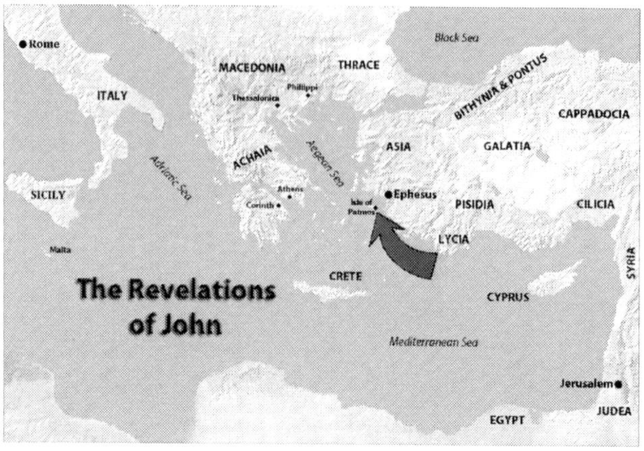

considered undesirable. John was sent there in the last years of the first century AD during a wave of anti-Christian persecution under the emperor Domitian.

To Whom Was Revelation Written?

John addressed his Revelation to seven churches (branches of the Church) in Asia. John was familiar with these seven churches and had priesthood responsibility for them as an Apostle. Sir William Ramsay, a renowned scholar of New Testament geography, once noted that all seven of the cities to whom John addressed the revelation lay on a great circular road that anciently ran through Asia. If one were to start at Ephesus and travel to the others in the order in which they were named, he would travel along this circular route.

There were other branches of the Church in Asia that are not addressed in this revelation. Troas (Acts 20:6–12), Colosse (Colossians 1:2), and Hierapolis (Colossians 4:13) are mentioned elsewhere but not named by John in this revelation. It may be that by the time of John's revelation, the apostasy had eliminated all but these seven. In 68 AD, Paul told Timothy "all they which are in Asia [are] turned away from me" (2 Tim. 1: 15). What we know for sure is that by 95 AD, these seven branches had things of which they needed to repent.

The book of Revelation is not solely for the Saints of the seven churches in Asia. It was also written for the Saints in our day—the dispensation of the fulness times.

What Are the Most Significant Contributions of John's Revelation?

The theme of the Revelation of John is stated in the first verse—it is a revelation of Jesus Christ. The book of Revelation symbolically shows Christ's dealings with men throughout the earth's history. Nowhere else in all of the standard works do we receive such a detailed and comprehensive picture of the whole scope of the Lord's plan as we do in the book of Revelation.

For our benefit in the latter days, Revelation describes the Second Coming of Jesus Christ, the judgment of mankind, the destruction of the wicked, the Millennium, and the ultimate celestialization of the world. John gives us "the big picture"—a view of the ultimate triumph of good and the ultimate victory of God.

Scholars debate whether the book of Revelation depicted events before John's day, during his day, or long after his day. The answer is probably "during and after his day" because . . .

- **Revelation 1:1 It was written to describe "things which must shortly come to pass."** "THE Revelation of Jesus Christ, which God gave unto him, to shew unto his servants things which must shortly come to pass; and he sent and signified it by his angel unto his servant John."

- **Revelation 4:1 It was also written to describe "things which must be hereafter."** John saw "a door . . . opened in heaven: and the first voice which I heard was as it were of a trumpet talking with me; which said, Come up hither, and *I will shew thee things which must be hereafter*" (emphasis added).

  Elder Bruce R. McConkie said, "This is one of the great keys which opens the door to an understanding of the book of Revelation. What is recorded therein is to transpire in the future, mainly in a day subsequent to New Testament times. The revelations promised are to come to the Saints of latter days, not to those in the meridian of time. All the promised events shall transpire 'shortly'; they are soon to be in the perspective of Him with whom one day is 'as a thousand years, and a thousand years as one day' (2 Pet. 3:8).[2]

  The Prophet Joseph Smith said, "The things which John saw had no allusion to the scenes of the days of Adam, Enoch, Abraham or Jesus, only so far as is plainly represented by John, and clearly set forth by him. John saw that only which was lying in futurity and which was shortly to come to pass."[3]

  The Prophet Joseph Smith also said, "John had the curtains of heaven withdrawn, and by vision looked through the dark vista of future ages, and contemplated events that should transpire throughout every subsequent period of time, until the final winding up scene."[4]

UNDERSTANDING JOHN'S REVELATION

Symbolic Images and Language

On practically every page of the Bible we find parables, allegories, similes, or metaphors. These are divine teaching aids used by the Lord and His prophets to teach with power. Symbols are useful in teaching because . . .

— They help the learner understand by comparing unfamiliar things to those that are more familiar.

— They help the mind not only to understand but also to retain.

— They can convey different levels of spiritual truth to those with different levels of spiritual maturity.

— They can encourage the learner to think more deeply about what is being taught.

— For those who are unworthy, they lock the message away, thus assuring that sacred pearls are not cast before swine.

M. SCHEITS, 1672

The Use of Symbolism in Revelation

H. MEMLING, 1474–1479.

The Apostle John, author of the book of Revelation, came from a culture that used symbolism extensively in its language and literature. Thus, the book of Revelation is written primarily in symbolic language.

East Asian peoples, of which the Jews were a part, tend to use language more artistically than we do. Words are colors with which the artist paints verbal pictures. Thus, the East Asian is usually more concerned with effect than with form and detail. Westerners say the sun "is rising," while an East Asian may say that it "leaps from its bed of sleeping."

Readers today (primarily from Western cultures) have difficulty with the symbolism in John's writings because they want to interpret the images literally. This makes the book seem strange and confusing, with its baffling and sometimes grotesque images. But if we remember that many of the images are "simply figurative," they become easier to understand.

In East Asian culture, John's depiction of the Savior as having a sharp, two-edged sword protruding from His mouth is perfectly acceptable, even though the Western mind may find it strange and confusing. But if one remembers the East Asian's love of imagery, such things as beasts with seven heads and ten horns, armies compared to locusts, and prophets with fire coming from their mouths (11:5; 19:15) will become beautiful and profound symbols of eternal truth.

Other Prophets Also Saw John's Revelation

Many prophets have seen visions similar to John's—Adam, Enoch, the brother of Jared, Abraham, Joseph, Moses, Isaiah, Nephi, Daniel, Ezekiel, and others. Most of these received an immediate command to seal it up.

— **1 Nephi 14:19–26** Nephi was told that the recording of the vision was reserved for John.

— **Daniel 12:4** Daniel was told to "shut up the words, and seal the book." It was not meant to be fully understood until the end of time.

— **Daniel 12:8–9** Even Daniel did not understand all that he saw. His symbolic visions, like John's, were very "apocalyptic"—full of strange images of beasts and hard to decipher.

Apocalyptic Visions

J.C. WEIGEL, 1695

The book of Revelation is apocalyptic. Indeed, another name for Revelation is "the Apocalypse," from the Greek "uncovering or unveiling." Its purpose, therefore, is to explain and reveal to the spiritually minded person, not to confuse. Of course, to the unspiritual mind, it remains a mystery.

Other prophets have received apocalyptic visions, including Isaiah, Ezekiel, Daniel, Zechariah, Joel, and Nephi. All apocalyptic visions are highly symbolic, with images of beasts, men, stars, floods, and books that are sealed.

The primary message of Revelation is that "there will be an eventual triumph on this earth of God over the devil; a permanent victory of good over evil, of the Saints over their persecutors, of the kingdom of God over the kingdoms of men and of Satan. . . . The details about the beasts, the wars, the angels, the men, etc., contribute to the development of this theme."[5]

A Book for the Saints

John did not intend to keep the message of the vision veiled from the Saints. Those who prayerfully receive and ponder the book can understood the full significance of each symbol used and are able to comprehend the fulness of his message. In addition, today, through modern revelation, the Lord has provided help in comprehending Revelation.

Peter taught that we may not interpret scriptural messages in any way we wish (2 Peter 1:20–21). So we must seek, through the Spirit, to understand what John was seeing and saying, and not be satisfied with uninspired speculations.

Elder Bruce R. McConkie said, "It is not a book for the theological novice, nor for the uninspired theological speculators of the world. It is written to the Saints who already have a knowledge of the plan of salvation, to say nothing of the interpreting power of the Holy Spirit in their hearts."[6]

Elder McConkie also said:

> As a matter of fact, we are in a much better position to understand those portions of Revelation which we are expected to understand than we generally realize. Thanks be to the interpretive material found in sections 29, 77, 88, and others of the revelations in the Doctrine and Covenants; plus the revisions given in the Inspired Version [Joseph Smith Translation] of the Bible; plus the sermons of the Prophet; plus some clarifying explanations in the Book of Mormon and other latter-day scripture; plus our over-all

knowledge of the plan of salvation—thanks be to all of these things (to say nothing of a little conservative sense, wisdom and inspiration in their application), the fact is that we have a marvelously comprehensive and correct understanding of this otherwise hidden book. . . .

. . . Let us remember that the book of Revelation was written to be understood; true, there are many things in it which we cannot now comprehend; but its true and full meaning will someday be revealed to the faithful and obedient Saints; and the more we can learn now, with the interpretive insight already available to us, the better off we are.[7]

The Organization of John's Revelation

Revelation is presented in what one author calls "kaleidoscopic structure." It consists of disjointed scenes, conversations, and images—each of them always in motion. "Each plays out its brief moment and then shifts to another, jumping from one time period to another, back and forth, constantly refocusing. There seems to be no smooth flow of narrative."[8]

This is what Nephi calls "the manner of prophesying among the Jews" (2 Nephi 25:1). It relates the present to the past and the future, but still maintains a unifying structure overall.

— **Revelation 1 John's testimony of the truthfulness of the revelation** and John's instructions from the Lord.

— **Revelation 2–3 The Lord's counsel to the seven Church branches in Asia.**

— **Revelation 4 John's symbolic vision of heaven.**

— **Revelation 5–20 John's symbolic vision of the triumphant destiny of God's kingdom,** the battles against Satan's kingdom, the destruction of Satan's kingdom, and final scenes in the world's history.

This vision was intended to reassure the Saints during one of the blackest moments of the Church's history. They lived in fear daily of Roman soldiers. Peter had been crucified, Paul beheaded, Bartholomew skinned alive, Thomas and Matthew run through with spears. John was the only surviving Apostle; all the others had died violently because of their faith. By the time of this vision on Patmos, the emperor Nero had lined his colonnade with crucified Christians and savage mobs had screamed for blood in the Coliseum. In the midst of these terrifying persecutions, this vision revealed a Savior still living, still loving, still triumphing over the power of satanic forces.

— **Revelation 21:1–5 John's vision of the new heavens and new earth**—the world in its celestial state.

— **Revelation 21:5–22 The angel's testimony and additional counsel from the Lord.**

JOHN'S VISION OF CHRIST

The Nature, Circumstances, and Purpose of John's Revelation

- **Revelation 1:1–3 "Things which must shortly come to pass."** John titled this book "the Revelation of Jesus Christ," and gave as its purpose "to shew unto his servants things which must shortly come to pass" (v. 1). John said it was "sent and signified . . . by his angel unto his servant John: who bare record of the word of God, and of the testimony of Jesus Christ, and of all things that he saw" (vv. 1–2). "Blessed is he that readeth, and they that hear the words of this prophecy," wrote John, "and [who] keep those things which are written [herein]: for the time is at hand" (v. 3).

- **Revelation 1:4 Addressed "to the seven churches which are in Asia,"** John began this writing by wishing them grace and peace "from him which is, and which was, and which is to come; and from the seven Spirits which are before his throne."

- **Revelation 1:5–6 God makes men kings and priests in heaven.** John dedicated the book to "Jesus Christ, who is the faithful witness, and the first begotten of the dead, and the prince of the kings of the earth. Unto him that loved us, and washed us from our sins in his own blood" (v. 5). He testified that Christ "hath made us kings and priests unto God and his Father," and said "to him be glory and dominion for ever and ever. Amen" (v. 6).

  The Prophet Joseph Smith said, "Those holding the fullness of the Melchizedek priesthood are kings and priests of the Most High God, holding the keys of power and blessings. In fact, that priesthood is a perfect law of theocracy, and stands as God to give laws to the people, administering endless lives to the sons and daughters of Adam."[9]

- **Revelation 1:7 Christ will come again.** "Behold, he cometh with clouds; and every eye shall see him, and they also which pierced him: and all kindreds of the earth shall wail because of him. Even so, Amen" (v. 7).

- **Revelation 1:8 Names of Jesus Christ.** John called the Lord "Alpha and Omega, the beginning and the ending, . . . which is, and which was, and which is to come, the Almighty" (v. 8). These are just some of His names. So far in this revelation John has referred to the Lord as:

  — The faithful witness.
  — The first begotten of the dead.
  — The Prince of the kings of the earth.
  — Him that loved us and washed us from our sins in His own blood.
  — Alpha and Omega, the beginning and the ending.
  — He who is, who was, and who is to come.
  — The Almighty.

- **Revelation 1:9–10 The author, location, and circumstances of the vision.** "I John . . . am your brother, and companion in tribulation, and in the kingdom and patience of Jesus Christ." He said that he "was in the isle that is called Patmos," for the purpose of receiving "the word of God, and for the testimony of Jesus Christ" (v. 9). John said that he "was in the Spirit on the Lord's day [Sunday]" when the vision occurred (v. 10).

Jesus Christ Appears

CAROLSFELD, 1852–60

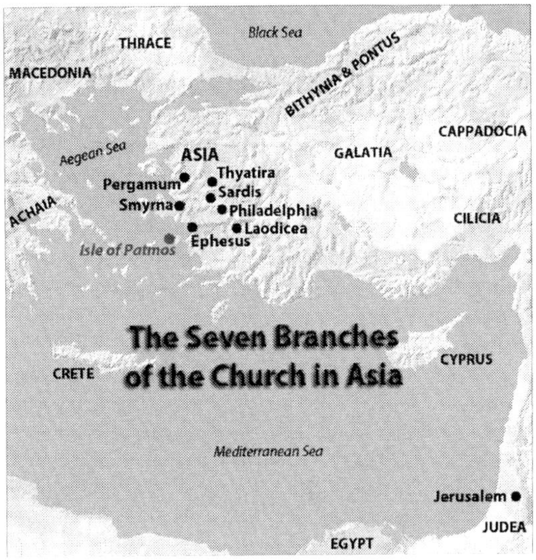

- **Revelation 1:10–11 Christ appears with symbols of the Church.** The vision began with the sound of a voice that was as loud as a trumpet blast (v. 10). John turned toward the noise, and the glorified Savior appeared in the midst of seven golden candlesticks saying, "I am Alpha and Omega, the first and the last" (v. 11).

- **Revelation 1:11 The seven branches of the Church in Asia.** John was commanded to write the vision and "send it unto the seven churches which are in Asia"—Ephesus, Smyrna, Pergamos, Thyatira, Sardis, Philadelphia, and Laodicea.

- **Revelation 1:12 Seven golden candlesticks signify the branches of the Church.** John "turned to see the voice that spake with me. And being turned, I saw seven golden candlesticks." These were symbolic of the seven Church branches in Asia.

  Elder Bruce R. McConkie said: "Candlesticks carry light; they do not create it. Their function is to make it available, not to bring it into being. So by using seven candlesticks to portray the seven churches to whom John is now to give counsel, the Lord is showing that His congregations on earth are to carry His light to the world. Christ is the Light of the world (John 8:12). 'Hold up your light that it may shine unto the world. Behold I am the light which ye shall hold up—that which ye have seen me do' (3 Ne. 18:24; Matt. 5:14–16)."[10]

- **Revelation 1:13–16 John's description of the glorified Christ.** Fifty years earlier John had seen the Lord crucified and then resurrected. Now Christ stood in brightly-blazing glory before John, saying, "I am he that liveth, and was dead, and, behold, I am alive for evermore" (v. 18). John's description of Christ is very much like those given by other prophets in similar circumstances (Ezekiel 1:26–28; Daniel 12:5–8; D&C 110:2–3; Moses 1:9–10; JS–History 1:20).

  — He was "clothed with a garment down to the foot" (v. 13).
  — He was "girt about the paps with a golden girdle" (v. 13).
  — "His head and his hairs were white like wool, as white as snow" (v. 14).

— "His eyes were as a flame of fire" (v. 14).
— "His feet [were] like unto fine brass, as if they burned in a furnace" (v. 15).
— "His voice as the sound of many waters" (v. 15).
— "He had in his right hand seven stars" (v. 16).
— "Out of his mouth went a sharp two-edged sword" (v. 16).
— "His countenance was as the sun shineth in his strength" (v. 16).

- **Revelation 1:17–19 The Lord commands John to write the vision.** John fell to the earth as though dead, but the glorious Christ touched and comforted him (v. 17). The Lord told him to write those things which he was about to see and hear (v. 19).

- **Revelation 1:16, 18, 20 Symbolic elements of the vision.** The Lord identified Himself to John in this manner: "I am the first and the last; I am he that liveth, and was dead; and, behold, I am alive for evermore, . . . and have the keys of hell and of death" (v. 18). This added two more symbolic elements to the vision, all of which deserve explanation.

  — **Candlesticks.** The seven candlesticks represented the seven churches in Asia (v. 20).

  — **Stars:** The Savior was holding seven stars in his right hand when He stood in the midst of the seven candlesticks (v. 16). The seven stars represented "the angels of the seven churches" (v. 20). In the Joseph Smith Translation of Revelation, the word "angels" is changed to "servants," making it clear that the stars represent the leaders of the seven branches of the Church (footnote 20B; Rev. 3:1, footnote 1A).

  Elder Bruce R. McConkie said, "[The seven stars are] the presiding officers of the seven congregations who, as with all His ministers, are in the hands of the Lord. They do not speak or act of themselves; they represent their Master, whose words they speak, whose acts they perform, and in fact whose they are."[11]

  — **Sword:** A sword came out of the Savior's mouth in this vision. This sword represents the word of the Lord (v. 16; see also D&C 6:2; Hebrews 4:12; Helaman 3:29).

  — **Keys:** The Savior was also holding keys. With these keys He will deliver all people from physical death, and He will deliver the righteous from spiritual death (v. 18; see also 2 Nephi 9:10–13).

  — **Keys of Hell and Death:** Hell is that portion of the spirit world where the wicked suffer torment until they have satisfied the strict demands of God's justice. It is Christ alone who releases them from their awful state when their torments are over (v. 18; see also 1 Peter 3:18–20; 4:6).

CHRIST'S MESSAGES TO THE SEVEN CHURCHES

Revelation 2–3 contains the words of the Lord to each of the seven branches of the Church in Asia. The Lord reviewed some of the strengths and weaknesses in each branch and warned the Saints to correct their weaknesses. To each of the Churches the Lord gave a commendation, a warning, and a promise.

The Message to Ephesus

Though not the capital of the Roman province of Asia, Ephesus was one of the major cities of the Empire—fourth largest in population and the largest city in Asia Minor. Its strategic location made it not only an important harbor but also the junction for important highways and trade routes. It was famous throughout the world for its magnificent temple of Diana (Artemis, in Greek), one of the seven wonders of the ancient world.

The temple was the center of the riot in Ephesus involving the Apostle Paul. His preaching threatened to destroy the business of the local artisans who made silver models of the temple to sell to tourists and worshipers (Acts 19:23). At the time of Paul, the port was filling with silt from the river Cayster, and, while still a major city, Ephesus was in a state of gradual decline. After the Fall of Jerusalem in 70 AD, the city became the center of the Christian church for many years until the center gradually shifted to Rome.

- **Revelation 2:2–3, 6 The commendation:** "I know thy works, and thy labour, and thy patience, and how thou canst not bear them which are evil: and thou hast tried them which say they are apostles, and are not, and hast found them liars: And hast borne, and hast patience, and for my name's sake hast laboured, and hast not fainted" (vv. 2–3). The Lord also said, "This thou hast, that thou hatest the deeds of the Nicolaitans, which I also hate" (v. 6).

    — "The Nicolaitans" were a sect in Asia Minor that claimed license for sensual sin (see Rev. 2:6, 15).

- **Revelation 2:4–5 The warning:** "Nevertheless I have somewhat against thee, because thou hast left thy first love. Remember therefore from whence thou art fallen, and repent, and do the first works; or else I will come unto thee quickly, and will remove thy candlestick out of his place, except thou repent."

    — "Left thy first love." This is a suggestion that the kingdom was no longer their first priority. They were not serving with all their heart, might, mind, and strength (see D&C 4:2).

- **Revelation 2:7 The promise: The tree of life.** "To him that overcometh will I give to eat of the tree of life, which is in the midst of the paradise of God." The tree of life represents the love of God as manifested by the Atonement of Jesus Christ and eventual eternal life in the kingdom of the Father.

The Message to Smyrna

Smyrna was called by many ancient writers "The Jewel of Asia." It competed with Ephesus to be called the most important city of Asia. Situated on an excellent harbor that is still one of the major ports of Turkey (present-day Izmir), Smyrna was an important trade center. Destroyed by an earthquake in 627 BC, it was completely rebuilt by Lysimachus, one of the successors of Alexander the Great, about 290 BC. Thus it was one of the few "planned" cities of the ancient world.

As early as 195 BC, Smyrna built a temple to the goddess of Rome and thereafter was one of the first and most important cities to heartily embrace the Imperial Cult (emperor worship). In light of the special encouragement given to the angel ("servant" in the JST) of the Church at Smyrna, it is interesting to note that Polycarp was the bishop of Smyrna. He was martyred in the city when he refused to deny Christ. He was burned at the stake and slain with a sword as the flames encircled him.

- **Revelation 2:9 The commendation:** "I know thy works, and tribulation, and poverty, (but thou art rich) and I know the blasphemy of them which say they are Jews, and are not, but are the synagogue of Satan."
- **Revelation 2:10 The warning:** "Fear none of those things which thou shalt suffer: behold, the devil shall cast some of you into prison, that ye may be tried; and ye shall have tribulation ten days [meaning for a short while]."
- **Revelation 2:10–11 The promises:** "Be thou faithful unto death, and I will give thee a crown of life" (v. 10). "He that overcometh shall not be hurt of the second death" (v. 11).
    — "Avoiding the Second Death." Though the Saints in Smyrna would suffer physical tribulation and possibly death, the Lord promised they would " not be hurt of the second death," which is spiritual death—eternal separation from God and His Son.

The Message to Pergamos

Also called Pergamum, Pergamos was the provincial capital of Asia, but was clearly eclipsed in importance by both Ephesus and Smyrna. Pergamos became a major center for emperor worship and was most famous for its library which housed over 200,000 scrolls. It was also the major center for the worship of the serpent god Aesculapius, whose temple stood in the city. Pergamos was known as a place of much wickedness.

- **Revelation 2:13 The commendation:** "I know thy works, and where thou dwellest, even where Satan's seat is: and thou holdest fast my name, and hast not denied my faith, even in those days wherein Antipas was my faithful martyr, who was slain among you, where Satan dwelleth."
- **Revelation 2:14–16 The warning:** "I have a few things against thee, because thou hast there them that hold the doctrine of Balaam, who taught Balac to cast a stumblingblock before the children of Israel, to eat things sacrificed unto idols, and to commit fornication" (v. 14). "So hast thou also [among you] them that hold the doctrine of the Nicolaitans, which thing I hate" (v. 15). "Repent; or else I will come unto thee quickly, and will fight against them with the sword of my mouth" (v. 16).
    — "The doctrine of Balaam." Balaam was the prophet who desired riches and earthly honors by pretending to curse the children of Israel. In the end, he helped Israel's enemies to overcome them by suggesting they tempt them with fornication.

Apparently there were those in Pergamos who were tempting the Saints with the meat of idols and adultery.

Elder Bruce R. McConkie said: "[The doctrine of Balaam is] to divine for hire; to give counsel contrary to the divine will; to pervert the right way of the Lord—all with a view to gaining wealth and the honors of men. In effect, to preach for money, or to gain personal power and influence. In the very nature of things such a course is a perversion of the right way of the Lord."[12]

- **Revelation 2:17 The promises:** "To him that overcometh will I give to eat of the hidden manna, and will give him a white stone, and in the stone a new name written, which no man knoweth saving he that receiveth it."
  - "The hidden manna." The word hidden in this context means "sacred" or "not evident to everyone." The manna represents Christ. (John 6:35, 49–51).
  - "The stone with a new name." This has reference to the ordinances of the temple and also to the individual Urim and Thummim that will be given to all who are exalted.

The Message to Thyatira

In spite of the fact that Thyatira was the smallest of the seven cities, the Church there received the longest letter. The city was best known as a center for many crafts, including the dyeing of wool. Lydia, "a seller of purple" and a convert of Paul's, was from Thyatira (Acts 16:17). The city was a garrison city that lay on the road from Smyrna. A military spirit prevailed there, and its chief deity, Tyrimnos, a sun-god, was typically portrayed in ways that emphasized his military prowess.

- **Revelation 2:19 The commendation:** "I know thy works, and charity, and service, and faith, and thy patience, and thy works; and the last to be more than the first."
- **Revelation 2:20–23 The warning:** "I have a few things against thee, because thou sufferest that woman Jezebel, which calleth herself a prophetess, to teach and to seduce my servants to commit fornication, and to eat things sacrificed unto idols" (v. 20). The Lord said that He "gave her space to repent of her fornication; and she repented not," so He would now "cast her into a bed, and them that commit adultery with her into great tribulation, except they repent of their deeds" (vv. 21–22). "And I will kill her children with death; and all the churches shall know that I am he which searcheth the reins and hearts: and I will give unto every one of you according to your works" (v. 23).
  - "Searching reins and hearts." The word reins means kidneys. To the Hebrews, the word signified strength and vigor. The phrase is a figure of speech that means that the Lord knows all things about the inner man—his strengths, weaknesses, character, and thoughts—and will "give unto every one of you according to your works."
- **Revelation 2:24–28 The promises:** "Unto the rest in Thyatira, as many as have not this doctrine, and which have not known the depths of Satan, as they speak; I will put upon you none other burden [than] that which ye have already" (vv. 24–25). "Hold fast

till I come. And he that overcometh, and keepeth my works unto the end, to him will I give power over the nations: And he shall rule them with a rod of iron; as the vessels of a potter shall they be broken to shivers: even as I received of my Father. And I will give him the morning star" (vv. 25–28).

— "Power over the nations." This promise refers to the blessings of eternal life and exaltation, when the righteous will rule over heavenly kingdoms.

— "The rod of iron." The rod of iron "the word of God" meaning His gospel and priesthood. (1 Nephi 11:25; JST 2:27). It is by these means that the righteous will rule.

— "The morning star." The morning star is Christ (Revelation 22:16). To receive Christ is to receive Him into our lives and to receive the blessings of His Atonement.

The Message to Sardis

Sardis was located at the crossroads of five major land routes and was an important inland trade center. It was renowned for its great wealth, and its citizens for their inner weakness and corruption. The Lord referred to this condition when He said they were "spiritually dead" (v. 1).

- **Revelation 3:4 The commendation:** "Thou hast a few names . . . in Sardis which have not defiled their garments . . . for they are worthy.
- **Revelation 3:1–3 The warning:** "I know thy works, that thou hast a name that thou livest, and art dead" (v. 1). "Be watchful, and strengthen the things which remain, that are ready to die: for I have not found thy works perfect before God" (v. 2). "Remember therefore how thou hast received and heard, and hold fast, and repent. If therefore thou shalt not watch, I will come on thee as a thief, and thou shalt not know what hour I will come upon thee" (v. 3).

— "Thou art [spiritually] dead." These Saints had a "name" (reputation) as being worthy, but because of the way they were living, they were spiritually dead.

Elder Spencer W. Kimball said: "There are many people in this Church today who think they live, but they are dead to the spiritual things. And I believe even many who are making pretenses of being active are also spiritually dead. Their service is much of the letter and less of the spirit."[13]

- **Revelation 3:4–5 The promises:** "Thou hast a few names . . . in Sardis which have not defiled their garments; and they shall walk with me in white: for they are worthy" (v. 4). "He that overcometh, the same shall be clothed in white raiment; and I will not blot out his name out of the book of life, but I will confess his name before my Father, and before his angels" (v. 5).

— "Clothed in white raiment." This has reference to participation in temple ordinances, which prepare us to understand what it means to be "clothed in white" eternally.

— "The book of life." The book of life is the one that contains the names of those who will inherit our Father's glory and kingdoms through the Atonement of Jesus Christ (D&C 128:7; Exodus 32:33; Alma 5:58).[14]

— "I will not blot out his name." Those whose names are written in the book and then blotted out are those who lose their inheritance because of wickedness (Revelation 21:10, 23–27; Alma 5:58; D&C 88:2).

The Message to Philadelphia

Philadelphia was located 28 miles southeast of Sardis, and was called "the Gateway to the East" because of its location. It was in the midst of an active volcanic region and had several hot springs in the area. Bacchus, the god of wine, was the primary deity worshiped there, since Philadelphia lay in a rich area of vineyards. It was probably second only to Thyatira in smallness and unimportance.

- **Revelation 3:7 The key of David.** As part of introducing Himself, the Lord makes reference to the key of David.

  Elder Bruce R. McConkie explained this key:

  > From the day of Adam the term key has been used . . . as a symbol of power and authority. Keys are the right of presidency, and the one holding them holds the reigns of government within the field and sphere of his appointment. In ancient Israel, David was a man of blood and battle whose word was law and whose very name was also a symbol of power and authority. Accordingly, when Isaiah sought to convey a realization of the supreme, directive control and power resident in our Lord, the Son of David, he spoke these words in the Lord's name: 'And the key of the house of David will I lay upon his shoulder; so he shall open, and none shall shut; and he shall shut, and none shall open' (Isaiah 22:22). . . . Thus, the key of David is the absolute power resident in Christ whereby His will is expressed in all things both temporal and spiritual.[15]

- **Revelation 3:8 The commendation:** "I know thy works: behold, I have set before thee an open door, and no man can shut it: for thou hast a little strength, and hast kept my word, and hast not denied my name."
- **Revelation 3:9, 11 The warnings:** "Behold, I will make them of the synagogue of Satan, which say they are Jews, and are not, but do lie; behold, I will make them to come and worship before thy feet, and to know that I have loved thee" (v. 9). "Behold, I come quickly: hold that fast which thou hast, that no man take thy crown" (v. 11).

- **Revelation 3:10, 12–13 The promises:** "Because thou hast kept the word of my patience, I also will keep thee from the hour of temptation, which shall come upon all the world, to try them that dwell upon the earth" (v. 10). "Him that overcometh will I make a pillar in the temple of my God, and he shall go no more out: and I will write upon him the name of my God, and the name of the city of my God, which is new Jerusalem, which cometh down out of heaven from my God: and I will write upon him my new name" (v. 12).

— "Having God's name written on us." Elder Bruce R. McConkie said, "God's name is God. To have His name written on a person is to identify that person as a god. How can it be said more plainly? Those who gain eternal life become gods! Their inheritance is both a fulness of the glory of the Father and 'a continuation of the seed forever and ever. Then shall they be gods, because they have no end; therefore shall they be from everlasting to everlasting, because they continue; then shall they be above all, because all things are subject unto them. Then shall they be gods, because they have all power, and the angels are subject unto them' (D&C 132:19–20)."[16]

The Message to Laodicea

Located at the junction of two important valleys and three major roads, Laodicea was one of the richest commercial centers in the ancient world. It was especially noted for its banking, its manufacture of a unique black wool, and for a medical school that was famous for an eye salve made from Phrygian stone (Rev. 3:18).

The region around Laodicea was an active earthquake zone. From some of the fissures in the earth hot springs emerged that provided wonderful relaxation to any who immersed themselves in them. The hot springs at Hierapolis, a short distance to the north, deposited their steaming waters into the streams that flowed southward. Those waters were still lukewarm when they reached Laodicea (3:15–16).

Because of their sulfurous content, drinking these lukewarm waters had an emetic effect (it made people vomit), which was a very unpleasant experience and gives rise to the Lord's metaphor of being "spued out of the mouth." Not too far away from the city were other springs of pure cold water that refreshed all who partook of it.

The city was often called "the City of Compromise," a title that was probably meant to be a compliment, but which also describes the problem of lukewarm commitment that affected the Laodicean members of the Church.

- **Revelation 3:14 Christ as the "Amen."** As part of introducing Himself, the Lord makes reference to Himself as the "Amen." The English word "amen" is derived from the Hebrew verb meaning to "prop or make firm." Anciently as well as now, "amen" is a statement of acceptance of the truthfulness and correctness of a prayer or a vow. When used at the beginning, it signified truthfulness and surety. When used after the end of a prayer or statement, it signified that the speaker and listener accepted what had been said as binding and valid for him. That is how it is still used today.

  Through Christ all acts, doctrines, and ordinances are given the stamp of truth and validity; thus the Savior is characterized as the Great Amen. The title takes on additional meaning when it is remembered that the Saints at Laodicea were troubled with lukewarmness, lack of commitment—the very opposite of the affirmation "Amen."

- **Revelation 3:15 The commendation:** "I know thy works, that thou art neither cold nor hot." This is a lukewarm commendation for a lukewarm people, using the metaphor of their lukewarm spring water to make the point.

- **Revelation 3:15–19 The warning:** "I would thou wert cold or hot. So then because thou art lukewarm, and neither cold nor hot, I will spue thee out of my mouth" (vv. 15–16). "Thou sayest, I am rich, and increased with goods, and have need of nothing; and knowest not that thou art wretched, and miserable, and poor, and blind, and naked" (v. 17). "I counsel thee to buy of me gold tried in the fire, that thou mayest be rich; and white raiment, that thou mayest be clothed, and that the shame of thy nakedness do not appear; and anoint thine eyes with eyesalve, that thou mayest see" (v. 18). "As many as I love, I rebuke and chasten: be zealous therefore, and repent" (v. 19).

    — "Being lukewarm." The Lord is here using the local landscape to contrast the benefits of either hot or cold water with the lukewarm vomit-inducing waters of Laodicea.

- **Revelation 3:20–21 The promise:** "Behold, I stand at the door, and knock: if any man hear my voice, and open the door, I will come in to him, and will sup with him, and he with me" (v. 20). "To him that overcometh will I grant to sit with me in my throne, even as I also overcame, and am set down with my Father in his throne" (v. 21).

    — "Sit with me in my throne." This is a direct promise of exaltation. The Lord promises the faithful that they will inherit the same blessings that He has obtained—to "set down with my Father in his throne"—the throne of godhood (Romans 8:16–17).

"Behold, I Stand at the Door"

- **Revelation 3:20 "Behold, I stand at the door and knock."** The promises given to the Laodiceans apply to us all: "Behold, I stand at the door, and knock: if any man hear my voice, and open the door, I will come in to him, and will sup with him, and he with me" (v. 20). From this we may know that Christ is actively trying to come into our lives. It is up to us whether we will open the door and let Him in.

- **Revelation 1–3 Promises to faithful Saints who overcome the world.** From the Lord's promises to the seven branches of the Church in Asia, we can summarize the blessings He has in store for faithful Saints.

    — Eat of the fruit of the tree of life.
    — Be protected from the second death.
    — Eat of the hidden manna.
    — Receive a white stone with a new name on it.
    — Be given power over the nations and rule them with a rod of iron.
    — Receive the morning star (Christ).
    — Be clothed in white raiment.
    — Have their names left in the Book of Life.
    — Have their names confessed by Jesus to the Father.
    — Have the names of God, New Jerusalem, and Christ written on them.

— Sit down with Jesus and the Father on the throne of heaven.

- **D&C 132:20 More promises of the Lord to the faithful.** In our own day, the Lord has promised great and eternal blessings to those who will love and serve Him. These may be summarized as follows.
  - — They shall be gods.
  - — They shall have no end, but continue "from everlasting to everlasting."
  - — They shall be above all, with all things subject unto them.
  - — They shall have all power, and the angels will be subject unto them.

Notes

1. *History of the Church*, 1:176.
2. *Doctrinal New Testament Commentary*, 3 vols. [1965–1973], 3:435.
3. *Teachings of the Prophet Joseph Smith*, sel. Joseph Fielding Smith [1976], 289.
4. *Teachings of the Prophet Joseph Smith*, 247.
5. *Bible Dictionary*, "Revelation of John," 762.
6. *Doctrinal New Testament Commentary*, 3:432.
7. *Doctrinal New Testament Commentary*, 3:431.
8. Ryken, *How to Read the Bible as Literature* [1984], 170.
9. *History of the Church*, 5:555.
10. *Doctrinal New Testament Commentary*, 3:442.
11. *Doctrinal New Testament Commentary*, 3:444.
12. *Doctrinal New Testament Commentary*, 3:450.
13. In Conference Report, April 1951, 104–105.
14. *Bible Dictionary*, "Book of Life," 626–627.
15. *Mormon Doctrine*, 2nd ed. [1966], 409.
16. *Doctrinal New Testament Commentary*, 3:458.

Chapter 46a

Revelation of John, Pt. 2: Visions and Prophecies

(Revelation 4–7, 10–12, 14)

INTRODUCTION

TITIAN, circa 1547

The Prophet Joseph Smith said. "When John had the curtains of heaven withdrawn, and by vision looked through the dark vista of future ages, and contemplated events that should transpire throughout every subsequent period of time, until the final winding up scene—while he gazed upon the glories of the eternal world, saw an innumerable company of angels and heard the voice of God—it was in the Spirit, on the Lord's day, unnoticed and unobserved by the world."[1]

These final chapters are full of John's adoration for the Gospel and for Christ's glorious Atonement. John testified of the glorification of the earth and the righteous Saints who will finally inherit it. As is always the case, words are poor vehicles to convey the fulness of such a vision. Nephi, who received a similar vision, was commanded to "seal it up" (1 Nephi 14:18–27). John was commanded to "seal not . . . the prophecy of this book" (Revelation 22:10), and thus we have it in our Bibles today.

JOHN'S VISION OF HEAVEN

In Revelation 5–20 John recorded his symbolic vision of the triumphant destiny of God's kingdom, the battles against Satan's kingdom, the destruction of Satan's kingdom, and the final scenes in the world's history.

This vision was intended to reassure the Saints during one of the blackest moments of the Church's history. They lived in fear daily of Roman soldiers. Peter had been crucified, Paul beheaded, Bartholomew skinned alive, Thomas and Matthew run through with spears. John was the only surviving Apostle; all the others had died violently because of their faith. By the time of this vision on Patmos, the emperor Nero had lined his colonnade with crucified Christians and savage mobs had screamed for blood in the Coliseum. In the midst of these terrifying persecutions, this vision revealed a Savior still living, still loving, still triumphing over the power of satanic forces.

D.V.D. PLAATS, THE BIBLE AND ITS STORY, 1908

- **Revelation 4:1–8 God on His throne, and many other things.** John said, "I looked, and, behold, a door was opened in heaven: and the first voice which I heard was as it were of a trumpet talking with me; which said, Come up hither, and I will shew thee things which must be hereafter" (v. 1). This means that the visions recorded here are not of "things which must shortly come to pass," as was the vision recorded in Revelation chapter 1. The visions recorded here by John are of things in the future.

  "Immediately I was in the spirit" John said, indicating that, like many previous prophets, he had been transfigured to allow him to stand in the presence of God. "And, behold, a throne was set in heaven, and one sat on the throne" (v. 2). "And he that sat was to look upon like a jasper [diamond-like] and a sardine [bright red] stone: and there was rainbow round about the throne, in sight like unto an emerald [green]" (v. 3).

  "And round about the throne were four and twenty seats: and upon the seats I saw four and twenty elders sitting, clothed in white raiment; and they had on their heads crowns of gold" (v. 4).

  — **D&C 77:5** "The elders whom John saw, were elders who had been faithful in the work of the ministry and were dead; who belonged to the seven churches, and were then in the paradise of God."

  "And out of the throne proceeded lightnings and thunderings and voices: and there were seven lamps of fire burning before the throne, which are the seven Spirits [JST: servants] of God" (v. 5).

  "And before the throne there was a sea of glass like unto crystal" (v. 6).

  — **D&C 77:1** The sea of glass is "the earth in its sanctified, immortal, eternal state."

  — **D&C 130:6–9** "The angels ... reside in the presence of God, on a globe like a sea of glass and fire, where all things for their glory are manifest, past, present, and future, and are continually before the Lord" (vv. 6–7). "The place where God resides is a great Urim and Thummim" (v. 8). "This earth, in its sanctified and immortal state, will be made like unto crystal and will be a Urim and Thummim to the inhabitants who dwell thereon, whereby all things pertaining to an inferior kingdom, or all kingdoms of a lower order, will be manifest to those who dwell on it; and this earth will be Christ's" (v. 9).

"And in the midst of the throne, and round about the throne, were four beasts full of eyes before and behind. And the first beast was like a lion, and the second beast like a calf, and the third beast had a face as a man, and the fourth beast was like a flying eagle" (vv. 6–7).

— **D&C 77:2** These are actual beasts, exalted and praising God on his throne. "They are figurative expressions, used by the Revelator, John, in describing heaven, the paradise of God, the happiness of man, and of beasts, and of creeping things, and of the fowls of the air; that which is spiritual being in the likeness of that which is temporal; and that which is temporal in the likeness of that which is spiritual; the spirit of man in the likeness of his person, as also the spirit of the beast, and every other creature which God has created."

— **D&C 77:3** These four beasts "represent the glory of the [four] classes of [animals] in their destined order or sphere of creation, in the enjoyment of their eternal felicity."

"And the four beasts had each of them six wings about him; and they were full of eyes within: and they rest not day and night, saying, Holy, holy, holy, Lord God Almighty, which was, and is, and is to come" (v. 8).

— **D&C 77:4** The wings of the beasts represent their "power, to move, to act, etc.," and to say that they had six wings is to say that they could move anywhere they wanted instantaneously and with ease.

— **D&C 77:4** The eyes of the beasts represent "light and knowledge," and to say that they are "full of eyes" is to say that "they are full of knowledge."

THE ONGOING WAR WITH SATAN

Important Insights from the JST

Joseph Smith made many significant changes in the book of Revelation while writing the Joseph Smith Translation (JST). And of all the chapters, chapter 12 was the most revised. Every verse, with the exception of verse 12, received some change. Following are two examples of changes from chapter 12. The changes made in the JST are indicated in italicized [*brackets*] for additions and ~~line-outs~~ for things removed.

- **JST Revelation 12:1** (compared to Revelation 12:1). "And there appeared a great ~~wonder~~ [*sign*] in heaven, [*in the likeness of things on the earth*]; a woman clothed with the sun, and the moon under her feet, and upon her head a crown of twelve stars."
- **JST Revelation 12:6–8** (compared to Revelation 12:7–9). "And there was war in heaven; Michael and his angels fought against the dragon; and the dragon ~~fought~~ and his angels [*fought against Michael*]; And [*the dragon*] prevailed not [*against Michael, neither the child, nor the woman which was the Church of God, who had been delivered of her*

pains, and brought forth the kingdom of our God and his Christ]. Neither was ~~their~~ [*there*] place found ~~any more~~ in heaven [*for*] the great dragon, [*who*] was cast out; that old serpent called the devil, and [*also called*] Satan, which deceiveth the whole world; he was cast out into the earth; and his angels were cast out with him."

The War in Heaven

- **Revelation 8:10–11 Satan falls from heaven.** "And the third angel sounded, and there fell a great star from heaven, burning as it were a lamp, and it fell upon the third part of the rivers, and upon the fountains of waters" (v. 10). "And the name of the star is called Wormwood: and the third part of the waters became wormwood; and many men died of the waters, because they were made bitter" (v. 11).
  - "A star" is a symbol of a great and important person.
  - "The great star" that fell from heaven was Lucifer, which was his name in heaven.
  - "Wormwood" is a plant with an extremely bitter taste. To eat or drink of it was fatal.
  - "A third part" in Jewish culture meant "a great many." Whether in this case it was 1/3 of our Father's children who followed Lucifer or just "a great many" we do not know.
  - "Many men died." Those who followed Satan (drank of his waters) experienced only bitterness and spiritual death.

- **Revelation 12:1–2, 5 A woman symbolizing the Church of God.** As with all Jewish prophecies, the symbols used in this vision are dualistic—they can apply to more than one time or one circumstance. This symbol could mean the Church established by Christ during His mortal ministry. But it can also represent the restored Church established in the latter days through the Prophet Joseph Smith.

RUBENS, 1628

"And there appeared a great wonder in heaven; a woman clothed with the sun, and the moon under her feet, and upon her head a crown of twelve stars" (v. 1).

  - "The woman" represents the Church of God, established on earth by the Savior. She can also represent the restored Church in the latter days.
  - "Clothed with the sun" could mean that she was surrounded by much light and glory. It could also represent a state of celestial exaltation.

— "The moon under her feet" can represent the idea that her light was greater than the moon. It can also mean that terrestrial glory is less than the glory she possessed.

— "The crown of twelve stars" is usually interpreted as the 12 tribes of Israel. It could also represent the 12 Apostles who lead the Church.

"And she being with child cried, travailing in birth, and pained to be delivered" (v. 2). "And she brought forth a man child, who was to rule all nations with a rod of iron: and her child was caught up unto God, and to his throne" (v. 5).

— "The man child" represents the kingdom of God and His Christ, who eventually will rule all nations. Ultimately, this means the kingdom and government that will exist on the earth during Jesus Christ's millennial reign.

— "The rod of iron" is a representation of the Word of God (Christ) and/or the word of God (the scriptures).

— "Being caught up to God's throne" means that the kingdom will eventually be exalted to God's throne, as will its worthy members.

Elder Bruce R. McConkie said, "A woman ('the Church of God') gives birth to a man child (the kingdom of our God and his Christ) which shall hold sway during the Millennial Era ... (Rev. 11:14–19). Such is the Prophet's [Joseph Smith's] inspired interpretation. Among Biblical scholars of the world, the man child is presumed to be Christ, a speculative conclusion which, though seemingly persuasive, is refuted by the obvious fact that the Church did not bring forth Christ; He [was] the Creator of the Church."[2]

- **Revelation 12:3 A great red dragon symbolizes Satan.** "And there appeared another wonder in heaven; and behold a great red dragon, having seven heads and ten horns, and seven crowns upon his heads."

  — "The great red dragon" represents "that old serpent, called the Devil, and Satan, which deceiveth the whole world" (v. 9).

  — "The seven heads" represent a multi-faceted threat, not just a single entity, church, or government.

  — "The seven crowns" represent political rule by multiple men and nations.

  — "The ten horns" represent the military power at the command of Satan through these nations and kings.

DORÉ, 1896

- **Revelation 12:7 There was war in Heaven.** Lucifer and his followers waged a war against our Father in heaven and His faithful children. "Michael and his angels fought against the dragon; and the dragon fought and his angels." And eventually, Michael (Adam) was victorious over Satan. However, unlike this painting, it was not a war fought with knives, swords, or guns. This was a war of words—a philosophical battle over how we would be tested on this earth and who would be our God and King.

  The Prophet Joseph Smith said, "The contention in heaven was—Jesus said there would be certain souls that would not be saved; and the devil said he could save them all, and laid his plans before the grand council, who gave their vote in favor of Jesus Christ. So the devil rose up in rebellion against God, and was cast down, with all who put up their heads for him."[3]

A. CARRACCI, 1604-05

  — **D&C 29:36–37 With their agency, 1/3 of Father's children chose to follow Satan.** "For, behold, the devil . . . rebelled against me, saying, Give me thine honor, which is my power; and also a third part of the hosts of heaven turned he away from me because of their agency; And they were thrust down, and thus came the devil and his angels."

  — **Moses 4:1–2 Satan sought to seize God's throne by promising exaltation to everyone without any effort on their part.** "And I, the Lord God, spake unto Moses, saying: That Satan, whom thou hast commanded in the name of mine Only Begotten, is the same which was from the beginning, and he came before me, saying—Behold, here am I, send me, I will be thy son, and I will redeem all mankind, that one soul shall not be lost, and surely I will do it; wherefore give me thine honor" (v. 1). "But, behold, my Beloved Son, which was my Beloved and Chosen from the beginning, said unto me—Father, thy will be done, and the glory be thine forever" (v. 2).

  — **Abraham 3:27–28 Satan was angry that his plan was not adopted, and rebelled.** "And the Lord said: Whom shall I send? And one answered like unto the Son of Man: Here am I, send me. And another answered and said: Here am I, send me. And the Lord said: I will send the first. And the second was angry, and kept not his first estate; and, at that day, many followed after him."

  — **Moses 4:3 Satan's plan would have denied us our agency.** The only way Lucifer could ensure exaltation without effort was to force everyone to be obedient. There would be no agency. "Wherefore, because that Satan rebelled against me, and sought to destroy the agency of man, which I, the Lord God, had given him, and also, that I should give unto him mine own power; by the power of mine Only Begotten, I caused that he should be cast down." The power exerted by Christ was the power of the Gospel plan and the Atonement, which the vast majority of God's children accepted as the better course.

- **Revelation 12:4, 8–9 Satan and his followers were cast out of heaven.** "And his tail drew the third part of the stars of heaven, and did cast them to the earth" (v. 4).

  — "The third part of the stars of heaven" represent the spirits who rejected the plan of salvation and followed Lucifer in the premortal world. Satan and these spirits were cast out of heaven and down to the earth (v. 9).

  Satan "prevailed not; neither was their place found any more in heaven" (v. 8). "And the great dragon was cast out, that old serpent, called the Devil, and Satan, which deceiveth the whole world: he was cast out into the earth, and his angels were cast out with him" (v. 9). In these verses we encounter three of the most common names for Satan:

  — "Devil" means "slanderer" (he spoke evil of God and His plan).
  — "Satan" is a Hebrew word that means "adversary."
  — "Lucifer" means "light-bearer." He was once a righteous son of God.

- **Revelation 12:4, 15 Satan sought to destroy the Church.** "And the dragon stood before the woman which was ready to be delivered, for to devour her child as soon as it was born" (v. 4). "And the serpent cast out of his mouth water as a flood after the woman, that he might cause her to be carried away of the flood." Against both the early Church and the latter-day Church, Satan has used every stratagem, including violence, to stop the work from progressing.

Continuation of the War on Earth

- **Revelation 12:12 Satan is very angry and his time is short.** Those that dwell in the heavens might rejoice that Satan can no longer afflict them with his anger and lies. But "Woe to the inhabiters of the earth and of the sea! for the devil is come down unto you, having great wrath, because he knoweth that he hath but a short time."

- **Revelation 12:13–14 Satan persecutes the Church, which flees for its safety.** "And when the dragon saw that he was cast unto the earth, he persecuted the woman which brought forth the man child" (v. 13). "And to the woman were given two wings of a great eagle, that she might fly into the wilderness, into her place, where she is nourished for a time, and times, and half a time, from the face of the serpent."

- **Revelation 12:6 John prophesies of the Great Apostasy.** Fleeing from the violence of Satan's opposition, "the woman [the Church] fled into the wilderness, where she hath a place prepared of God, that they should feed her there a thousand two hundred and threescore days."
  - **D&C 86:3** "Fled into the wilderness" means the Great Apostasy. "And after they [the Apostles] have fallen asleep [died] the great persecutor of the church, the apostate, the whore, even Babylon, that maketh all nations to drink of her cup, in whose hearts the enemy, even Satan, sitteth to reign—behold he soweth the tares; wherefore, the tares choke the wheat and drive the church into the wilderness."
  - "1260 days." In the JST, Revelation 2:5 says that these days represent 1260 years—the period of the Great Apostasy. During this period the kingdom was caught up unto God [taken off the earth] until its restoration in the latter days.

- **Revelation 12:17 Satan continues to make war on the Saints today.** "And the dragon was [and is still] wroth with the woman, and went to make war with the remnant of her seed, which keep the commandments of God, and have the testimony of Jesus Christ."

  President Wilford Woodruff said, "There are two powers on the earth and in the midst of the inhabitants of the earth—the power of God and the power of the devil. . . . When God has had a people on the earth, it matters not in what age, Lucifer, the son of the morning, and the millions of fallen spirits that were cast out of heaven, have warred against God, against Christ, against the work of God, and against the people of God. And they are not backward in doing it in our day and generation. Whenever the Lord set His hand to perform any work, those powers labored to overthrow it."[4]

  President Gordon B. Hinckley said:

  > That war, so bitter, so intense, has gone on, and it has never ceased. It is the war between truth and error, between agency and compulsion, between the followers of Christ and those who have denied Him. His enemies have used every stratagem in that conflict. They've indulged in lying and deceit. They've employed money and wealth. They've tricked the minds of men. They've murdered and destroyed and engaged in every other unholy and impure practice to thwart the work of Christ. . . .
  >
  > [Opposition] has been felt in the undying efforts of many, both within and without the Church, to destroy faith, to belittle, to demean, to bear false witness, to tempt and allure and induce our people to practices inconsistent with the teachings and standards of this work of God. . . .
  >
  > The war goes on. It is waged across the world over the issues of agency and compulsion. It is waged by an army of missionaries over the issues of truth and error. It is waged in our own lives, day in and day out, in our homes, in our work, in our school associations; it is waged over questions of love and respect, of loyalty and fidelity, of obedience and integrity. We are all involved in it.[5]

President Ezra Taft Benson said, "Each day the forces of evil and the forces of good enlist new recruits. Each day we personally make many decisions showing the cause we support. The final outcome is certain—the forces of righteousness will win. But what remains to be seen is where each of us personally, now and in the future, will stand in this battle—and how tall we will stand. Will we be true to our last days and fulfill our foreordained missions?"[6]

- **Revelation 12:11 The Church and kingdom of God will overcome Satan.** They will do this "by the blood of the Lamb, and by the word of their testimony; and [loving] not their lives unto the death." This means that through the Atonement, the strength of our testimonies, and through our sacrifices we will eventually be triumphant over Satan.

THE BOOK WITH SEVEN SEALS

The Meaning of the "Seals"

J.C. WEIGEL, 1695

- **Revelation 5:1 John sees a book with seven seals in the Father's right hand.** "I saw in the right hand of him that sat on the throne a book written within and on the backside, sealed with seven seals" (v. 1).
  - — **D&C 77:6 The book contains the entire history of the earth—past, present, and future.** "It contains the revealed will, mysteries, and the works of God; the hidden things of his economy concerning this earth during the seven thousand years of its continuance, or its temporal existence.
  - — **D&C 77:7 The seals symbolize the seven 1,000-year "days" of the earth's temporal existence.** "The first seal contains the things of the first thousand years, and the second also of the second thousand years, and so on until the seventh."
  - — **2 Peter 3:8 One day with the Lord is as a thousand years to us.** Peter taught that "one day is with the Lord as a thousand years, and a thousand years as one day."

Elder Orson F. Whitney said:

> "The book which John saw" represented the real history of the world what the eye of God has seen, what the recording angel has written; and the seven thousand years, corresponding to the seven seals of the Apocalyptic volume, are as seven great days during which Mother Earth will fulfill her mortal mission, laboring six days and resting upon the seventh, her period of sanctification. These seven days do not include the period of our

> planet's creation and preparation as a dwelling place for man. They are limited to Earth's "temporal existence," that is, to Time, considered as distinct from Eternity . . .
>
> . . . According to received chronology admittedly imperfect, yet approximately correct four thousand years, or four of the seven great days given to this planet as the period of its "temporal existence," had passed before Christ was crucified; while nearly two thousand years have gone by since. Consequently, Earth's long week is now drawing to a close, and we stand at the present moment in the Saturday Evening of Time, at or near the end of the sixth day of human history. Is it not a time of thought, a season for solemn meditation? Morning will break upon the Millennium, the thousand years of peace, the Sabbath of the World![7]

We can divide the earth's history into seven 1,000-year periods, during which the great events recorded in the book took place. If we did, it would look something like this:

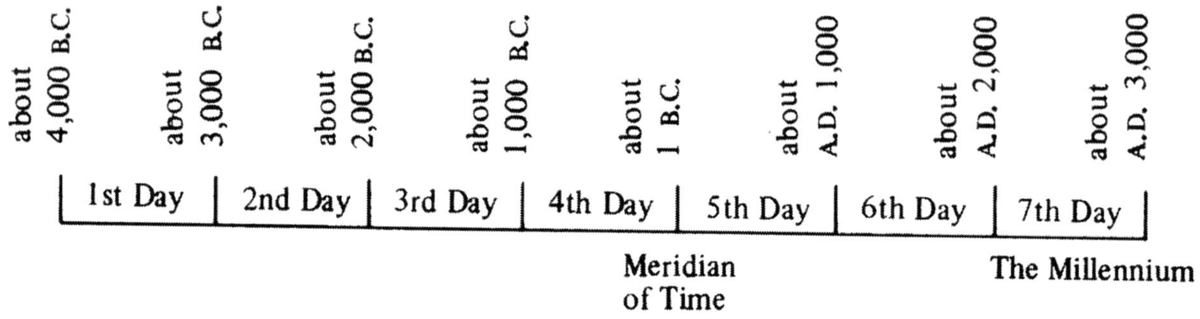

These dates are only approximate. No one knows exactly how many years elapsed between the Fall of Adam and the birth of Christ. Through numerous changes from one calendar system to another through the centuries, many years have been either added or lost. But the chart is useful in visualizing what the seven seals of the book mean.

- **Revelation 5:2–5 Only Christ can open the book.** "And I saw a strong angel proclaiming with a loud voice, Who is worthy to open the book, and to loose the seals thereof? And no man in heaven, nor in earth, neither under the earth, was able to open the book, neither to look thereon. And I wept much, because no man was found worthy to open and to read the book, neither to look thereon" (vv. 2–4). Then, "one of the elders saith unto me, Weep not: behold, the Lion of the tribe of Juda[h], the Root of David, hath prevailed to open the book, and to loose the seven seals thereof" (v. 5). Both of these names refer to Jesus Christ, the literal royal descendant of David in the tribe of Judah.

All Creation Shouts Praises to God

- **Revelation 5:11–14 John beholds "creatures" as well as men worshiping Christ.** John both saw and heard "many angels round about the throne" along with "beasts and the elders: and the number of them was ten thousand times ten thousand, and thousands of thousands" (v. 11). These numbers are symbolic, meaning that the size of the gathering was innumerable. In our day, we would say "there must have been a billion of them."

All of the angels, beasts, and elders that John saw were "saying with a loud voice, Worthy is the Lamb that was slain to receive power, and riches, and wisdom, and strength, and honour, and glory, and blessing" (v. 12). This included "every creature which is in heaven, and on the earth, and under the earth, and such as are in the sea, and all that are in them" all shouting praise to God by saying, "Blessing, and honour, and glory, and power, be unto him that sitteth upon the throne, and unto the Lamb for ever and ever" (v. 13). "And the four beasts said, Amen. And the four and twenty elders fell down and worshipped him that liveth for ever and ever" (v. 14).

The Prophet Joseph Smith said:

> John saw curious looking beasts in heaven; he saw every creature that was in heaven,— all the beasts, fowls and fish in heaven,—actually there, giving glory to God. . . .
>
> I suppose John saw beings there of a thousand forms, that had been saved from ten thousand earths like this—strange beasts of which we have no conception [but] all might be seen in heaven. The grand secret was to show John what there was in heaven. John learned that God glorified Himself by saving all that His hands had made, whether beasts, fowls, fishes or men; and He will glorify Himself with them. . . .
>
> Any man who would tell you that this could not be, would tell you that the revelations are not true. John heard the words of the beasts giving glory to God, and understood them. God who made the beasts could understand every language spoken by them. The four beasts were four of the most noble animals that had filled the measure of their creation, and had been saved from other worlds, because they were perfect; they were like angels in their sphere. We are not told where they came from, and I do not know; but they were seen and heard by John praising and glorifying God.[8]

The First Five Seals

A. DURER, THE BIBLE AND ITS STORY, 1908

As each of the first four seals of the book were opened, John saw horsemen on horses of different colors going forth. These had symbolism as follows:

- **Revelation 6:1–2 The first seal: The time from Adam through Enoch.** "And I saw when the Lamb opened one of the seals, and I heard, as it were the noise of thunder, one of the four beasts saying, Come and see. And I saw, and behold a white horse: and he that sat on him had a bow; and a crown was given unto him: and he went forth conquering, and to conquer."
  - "The white horse" is symbolic of victory over evil.

    Elder Bruce R. McConkie said, "Such of these events as John saw pertained to someone on a white horse (the emblem of victory); who had a bow (weapons of war); wore a crown (the garland or wreath of a conqueror); and who went forth conquering and to conquer (that is, was victorious in war). " . . . it is clear that the most transcendent happenings involved Enoch and his ministry. And it is interesting to note that what John saw was not the establishment of Zion and its removal to heavenly spheres, but the unparalleled wars in which Enoch, as a general over the armies of the Saints, 'went forth conquering and to conquer'. . . . Truly, never was there a ministry such as Enoch's, and never a conqueror and general who was his equal! How appropriate that he should ride the white horse of victory in John's apocalyptic vision!"[9]

- **Revelation 6:3–4 The second seal: Noah's day**, which was full of great wickedness. "And when he had opened the second seal, I heard the second beast say, Come and see. And there went out another horse that was red: and power was given to him that sat thereon to take peace from the earth, and that they should kill one another: and there was given unto him a great sword."

  — "The red horse" is symbolic of bloodshed and the sword.

  Elder Bruce R. McConkie said, "Who rode the red horse, the red horse of war and bloodshed and a sword, during the second seal? Perhaps it was the devil himself, for surely that was the great day of his power, a day of such gross wickedness that every living soul (save eight only) was found worthy of death by drowning, which wickedness caused the Lord God of Heaven to bring in the floods upon them. Or if it was not Lucifer, perhaps it was a man of blood, or a person representing many murdering warriors, of whom we have no record. Suffice it to say that the era from 3000 BC, to 2000 BC, was one of war and destruction, these being the favorite weapons of Satan for creating those social conditions in which men lose their souls."[10]

- **Revelation 6:5–6 The third seal: Abraham, Isaac, Jacob, Joseph, and Moses.** "And when he had opened the third seal, I heard the third beast say, Come and see. And I beheld, and lo a black horse; and he that sat on him had a pair of balances in his hand. And I heard a voice in the midst of the four beasts say, A measure of wheat for a penny, and three measures of barley for a penny; and see thou hurt not the oil and the wine."

  — "The black horse" is symbolic of famine and hunger.

  — A measure (Greek *choenix*) was about 1 quart, a day's allowance.
  — The penny (*denarius*) was a small silver coin, a day's pay.
  — Thus, it cost 1 day's wages to buy 1 day's food for 1 person.
  — Barley for 3 people was inferior, used only in times of great hunger.
  — The balances in the rider's hand means food had to be doled out.

  — "Hurt not the oil and the wine" meant that enough food should be preserved so that man would not utterly perish in the famine conditions of that time.[11]

  Elder Bruce R. McConkie said:

  > As famine follows the sword, so the pangs of hunger gnawed in the bellies of the Lord's people during the third seal. From 2000 BC to 1000 BC, as never in any other age of the

earth's history, the black horse of hunger influenced the whole history of God's dealings with His people.

In the beginning years of this seal, the famine in Ur of the Chaldees was so severe that Abraham's brother, Haran, starved to death, while the father of the faithful was commanded by God to take his family to Canaan. (Abra. 1:29–30; 2:15)....

This search for sustenance was yet burdening the Lord's people in the days of Jacob, who sent his sons to Egypt to buy corn from the granaries of Joseph his son. In that day "the famine was over all the face of the earth," and it was only through divine intervention that Jacob and the beginning members of the house of Israel were saved from the fate of Haran (Gen. 41:53–57; 42; 43; and 44). And in the days of their sojourn in the wilderness, the millions of Jacob's seed who had followed Moses out of Egyptian bondage, lest they perish for want of bread, were fed for forty years with manna from heaven. [Ex. 16.]....

... Truly the third seal was a millennium in which hunger among men affected the whole course of God's dealings with His people.[12]

- **Revelation 6:7–8 The fourth seal: Wicked Israel is conquered, captured, and killed.** "And when he had opened the fourth seal, I heard the voice of the fourth beast say, Come and see. And I looked, and behold a pale horse: and his name that sat on him was Death, and Hell followed with him. And power was given unto them over the fourth part of the earth, to kill with sword, and with hunger, and with death, and with the beasts of the earth."

DORÉ, 1896

  — "The pale horse" is symbolic of death and hell.

  Elder Bruce R. McConkie said, "During the fourth seal, from 1000 BC to the coming of our Lord, death rode roughshod through the nations of men, and hell was at his heels. Thus, the slain among the ungodly in this age of bloodshed whether by sword or by famine or by pestilence or by wild beasts—were, at their death, cast down to hell. This is the millennium of those great kingdoms and nations whose wars and treacheries tormented and overran, again and again, the people whom Jehovah had chosen to bear His name. This is also the general era in which the Lord's own people warred among themselves and sent countless numbers of their own brethren to untimely graves."[13]

- **Revelation 6:9–11 The fifth seal: The Lord's earthly witnesses are martyred,** receive their exaltation and rest awhile. "And when he had opened the fifth seal, I saw under the altar the souls of them that were slain for the word of God, and for the testimony which they held: And they cried with a loud voice, saying, How long, O Lord, holy and true, dost thou not judge and avenge our blood on them that dwell on the earth? And white robes were given unto every one of them; and it was said unto them, that they should rest yet for a little season, until their fellowservants also and their brethren, that should be killed as they were, should be fulfilled."

Elder Bruce R. McConkie said:

> Where the Lord's people are concerned, the events of the fifth seal, that period from our Lord's birth down to 1000 AD, which are of unspeakable worth are:
>
> 1. The birth into mortality of God's only Son; His ministry among men and the atoning sacrifice which He wrought by the shedding of His own blood.
> 2. The spread and perfection of the Church which was set up by Him whose Church it is, and the unbelievable fanaticism among unbelievers that made acceptance of martyrdom almost synonymous with acceptance of the gospel.
> 3. And then, of course, the complete falling away from true and perfect Christianity, which sad eventuality ushered in the long night of apostate darkness on all the face of the earth.
>
> Our Lord's work and ministry are everywhere taught in holy writ; the facts relative to the post-meridian apostasy and the perversion of the saving truths and powers are also abundantly taught in other sacred writings. And so what is more natural than to find the Lord revealing here, that portion of the sealed book which deals with the doctrine of martyrdom. Among the ancient Saints martyrdom was an ever present possibility, one which completely occupied their thoughts and feelings. They knew that by forsaking all to follow Christ, they might, if fate so decreed, be called to lay down their lives for Him who had laid down His life for them. In an almost death inviting sense, the meridian of time was the dispensation of martyrdom.[14]

The Sixth Seal

F. DANBY, THE BIBLE AND ITS STORY, 1908

- **Revelation 6:12–17 The sixth seal: Earth's temporal existence ends with destruction.** "And I beheld when he had opened the sixth seal, and, lo, there was a great earthquake; and the sun became black as sackcloth of hair, and the moon became as blood; And the stars of heaven fell unto the earth, even as a fig tree casteth her untimely figs, when she is shaken of a mighty wind. And the heaven departed as a scroll when it is rolled together; and every mountain and island were moved out of their places; And the kings of the earth, and the great men, and the rich men, and the chief captains, and the mighty men, and every bondman, and every free man, hid themselves in the dens and in the rocks of the mountains; And said to the mountains and rocks, Fall on us, and hide us from the face of him that sitteth on the throne, and from the wrath of the Lamb: For the great day of his wrath is come; and who shall be able to stand?"

Elder Bruce R. McConkie said, "We are now living during the final years of the sixth seal, that thousand year period which began in 1000 AD and will continue through the Saturday night of time and until just before the Sabbatical era when Christ shall reign person ally on earth, when all of the blessings of the Great Millennium shall be poured out upon this planet. This, accordingly, is the era when the signs of the times shall be shown forth, and they are in fact everywhere to be seen."[15]

CAROLSFELD, 1852-60

- **Revelation 7:1–3 The four angels of destruction must wait until the righteous are sealed.** "And after these things I saw four angels standing on the four corners of the earth, holding the four winds of the earth, that the wind should not blow on the earth, nor on the sea, nor on any tree. And I saw another angel ascending from the east, having the seal of the living God: and he cried with a loud voice to the four angels, to whom it was given to hurt the earth and the sea, Saying, Hurt not the earth, neither the sea, nor the trees, till we have sealed the servants of our God in their foreheads."

  — "Sealing in the forehead." It was a common practice in John's day for devotees of the various heathen gods to mark their foreheads with the name or symbol of their god. Being sealed or marked in the forehead would be a vivid metaphor of devotion to God. (See also the discussion of Revelation 13:16 at the end of this chapter.)

  The Prophet Joseph Smith said, "Four destroying angels holding power over the four quarters of the earth until the servants of God are sealed in their foreheads, which signifies sealing the blessing upon their heads, meaning the everlasting covenant, thereby making their calling and election sure."[16]

  — **D&C 77:8 Four angels of destruction.** "They are four angels sent forth from God, to whom is given power over the four parts of the earth, to save life and to destroy; these are they who have the everlasting gospel to commit to every nation, kindred, tongue, and people; having power to shut up the heavens, to seal up unto life, or to cast down to the regions of darkness."

  — **D&C 77:9 The angel ascending from the east.** "The angel ascending from the east is he to whom is given the seal of the living God over the twelve tribes of Israel; wherefore, he crieth unto the four angels having the everlasting gospel, saying: Hurt

> not the earth, neither the sea, nor the trees, till we have sealed the servants of our God in their foreheads. And, if you will receive it, this is Elias which was to come to gather together the tribes of Israel and restore all things."

President Wilford Woodruff said:

> Can you tell me where the people are who will be shielded and protected from these calamities and judgments which are even now at our doors? I'll tell you. The priesthood of God who honor their priesthood, and who are worthy of their blessings are the only ones who shall have this safety and protection. No other people have a right to be shielded from these judgments. They are at our very doors; not even this people will escape them entirely. They will come down like the judgments of Sodom and Gomorrah. And none but the priesthood will be safe from their fury. God has held the angels of destruction for many years, lest they should reap down the wheat with the tares.
>
> But I want to tell you now, that those angels have left the portals of heaven, and they stand over the earth waiting to pour out the judgments. And from this very day they shall be poured out. Calamities and troubles are increasing in the earth, and there is a meaning to these things. Remember this, and reflect upon these matters. If you do your duty, and I do my duty, we'll have the protection, and shall pass through the afflictions in peace and in safety. Read the scriptures and the revelations. They will tell you about these things.[17]

President Joseph Fielding Smith said, "[Wilford Woodruff's statement] was said in June, 1894. Twenty years later, plus one month, the great war broke out. President Woodruff says twenty years would bring changes. We have had trouble and calamities ever since."[18]

Elder Bruce R. McConkie said, "These angels have now begun their work. This we learn through the spirit of inspiration that rested upon President Wilford Woodruff. June 24, 1894, he said: '. . . From this very day they shall be poured out. Calamities and troubles are increasing in the earth, and there is a meaning to these things. . . . Great changes are at our doors. The next 20 years will see mighty changes among the nations of the Earth.' It is interesting to note that almost 20 years later to the day, June 28, 1914, the Archduke Ferdinand of Austria was assassinated, thus initiating the first World War."[19]

- **Revelation 7:4–12 John sees 144,000 sealed.** "And I heard the number of them which were sealed: and there were sealed an hundred and forty and four thousand of all the tribes of the children of Israel" (v. 4). He then enumerated them by tribe, with each of the twelve tribes having 12,000 each (vv. 5–8).
  - — **D&C 77:11 The identity of the 144,000** has been debated extensively by the world. The Prophet Joseph Smith said, "Those who are sealed are high priests, ordained unto the holy order of God, to administer the everlasting gospel; for they are they who are ordained out of every nation, kindred, tongue, and people, by the angels to whom is given power over the nations of the earth, to bring as many as will come to the church of the Firstborn."

- **Revelation 7:9–12 A great multitude in white robes shout praises to God.** "After this I beheld, and, lo, a great multitude, which no man could number, of all nations, and kindreds, and people, and tongues, stood before the throne, and before the Lamb, clothed with white robes, and palms in their hands; And cried with a loud voice, saying, Salvation to our God which sitteth upon the throne, and unto the Lamb. And all the angels stood round about the throne, and about the elders and the four beasts, and fell before the throne on their faces, and worshipped God, Saying, Amen: Blessing, and glory, and wisdom, and thanksgiving, and honour, and power, and might, be unto our God for ever and ever. Amen."

- **Revelation 10:1–2, 8–11 John eats a little book—symbolic of his mission to the lost ten tribes.** "And I saw another mighty angel come down from heaven, clothed with a cloud: and a rainbow was upon his head, and his face was as it were the sun, and his feet as pillars of fire. And he had in his hand a little book open: and he set his right foot upon the sea, and his left foot on the earth" (vv. 1–2).

A. DURER, 1496-98

  "And the voice which I heard from heaven spake unto me again, and said, Go and take the little book which is open in the hand of the angel. . . . And I went unto the angel, and said unto him, Give me the little book. And he said unto me, Take it, and eat it up; and it shall make thy belly bitter, but it shall be in thy mouth sweet as honey" (vv. 8–9).

  "And I took the little book out of the angel's hand, and ate it up; and it was in my mouth sweet as honey: and as soon as I had eaten it, my belly was bitter. And he said unto me, Thou must prophesy again before many peoples, and nations, and tongues, and kings" (vv. 10–11).

  — **D&C 77:14 The meaning of the book.** "It was a mission, and an ordinance, for him to gather the tribes of Israel; behold, this is Elias, who, as it is written, must come and restore all things."

Elder Joseph Fielding Smith said:

> A great mission was given unto John because of his desire, and he is even now laboring as "a flaming fire and a ministering angel, for those who are heirs of salvation." In the tenth chapter of Revelation we read that John was given a little book by the angel and

commanded to eat it up, which he did, and he said "it was in my mouth sweet as honey; and as soon as I had eaten it, my belly was bitter." And the angel said by way of interpretation of this act: "Thou must prophesy again before many peoples, and nations, and tongues, and kings." When this mission was given, John was an old man far beyond the allotted years of three score and ten. . . . It was a mission . . . for John to gather the tribes of Israel (D&C 77:14). At a conference of the Church, held June, 1831, Joseph Smith said "that John the Revelator was then among the ten tribes of Israel who had been led away by Shalmaneser, king of Assyria, to prepare them for their return from their long dispersion."[20] [21]

- **Revelation 14:6–7 John sees an angel bringing the everlasting gospel.** "And I saw another angel fly in the midst of heaven, having the everlasting gospel to preach unto them that dwell on the earth, and to every nation, and kindred, and tongue, and people, Saying with a loud voice, Fear God, and give glory to him; for the hour of his judgment is come: and worship him that made heaven, and earth, and the sea, and the fountains of waters."

Elder Bruce R. McConkie said:

Now, as to the actual work of restoration what angel performed this mighty deed, this work which involves the salvation of all men on earth in these latter days? Who restored the everlasting gospel? Was it one angel or many?

It is traditional (and true!) to reply: "Moroni, son of Mormon, the now resurrected Nephite prophet, who holds the keys of 'the stick of Ephraim' (D&C 27:5), the one through whose ministry the Book of Mormon was again brought to light." The reasoning that the Book of Mormon contains "the fulness of the everlasting gospel" (D&C 135:3); that therein is God's message of salvation for all of the earth's inhabitants; and that this gospel message is now being taken by the Lord's witnesses to one nation, and kindred, and tongue, and people after another.

. . . But other angels were yet to come—Moses, Elias, Elijah, Gabriel, Raphael, and "diverse angels . . . all declaring their dispensation, their rights, their keys, their honors, their majesty and glory, and the power of their priesthood; giving line upon line, precept upon precept; here a little, and there a little" (D&C 128:21).

Thus the angel Moroni brought the message, that is, the word; but other angels brought the keys and priesthood, the power. And in the final analysis the fulness of the everlasting gospel consists of all of the truths and powers needed to enable men to gain a fulness of salvation in the celestial heaven.[22]

OTHER CONCEPTS IN REVELATION, PT. 2

- **Revelation 5:10 We will be kings and priests.** John taught that the Savior "hast made us unto our God kings and priests: and we shall reign on the earth."

  I would ask, "Who will consider me their king?" Certainly not you. You will be a king or queen yourself. So who would consider me to be their king in the world to come? The answer is my own spirit posterity that will bless our eternal home and then head off into their own earthly adventure and test. The circle of eternal life will continue on, and we will all have our place of honor if we live faithfully and keep our covenants (D&C 76:50–56).

  This scripture refutes any notion that we will be angels forever, sitting on clouds, strumming harps, and singing praises to God. We will inherit the same status, glory, and power as Jesus Christ, and indeed as God the Father Himself (Revelation 3:21). This fact does not diminish God; it is the way by which His dominions will grow forever.

- **Revelation 14:12–13 The righteous will rest from their labors.** John said, "Here is the patience of the saints, [that] they that keep the commandments of God, and the faith of Jesus" (v. 12). Then he heard "a voice from heaven saying unto [him], Write, Blessed are the dead which die in the Lord from henceforth: Yea, saith the Spirit, that they may rest from their labours; and their works do follow them" (v. 13).

Notes

1. *Teachings of the Prophet Joseph Smith*, sel. Joseph Fielding Smith [1976], 247.
2. *Doctrinal New Testament Commentary*, 3 vols. [1965–1973], 3:511.
3. *Teachings of the Prophet Joseph Smith*, 357.
4. *Deseret Evening News*, 17 October 1896, 9; quoted by President Gordon B. Hinckley in Conference Report, October 1986, 56; or *Ensign*, November 1986, 43.
5. In Conference Report, October 1986, 55–58; or *Ensign*, November 1986, 42, 44–45.
6. "In His Steps," *Ensign*, September 1988, 2.
7. *Saturday Night Thoughts* [1921], 12.
8. *Teachings of the Prophet Joseph Smith*, 291–292.
9. *Doctrinal New Testament Commentary*, 3:476–478.
10. *Doctrinal New Testament Commentary*, 3:478.
11. *Doctrinal New Testament Commentary*, 3:480.
12. *Doctrinal New Testament Commentary*, 3:479–480.

13. *Doctrinal New Testament Commentary*, 3:481.

14. *Doctrinal New Testament Commentary*, 3:482–483.

15. *Doctrinal New Testament Commentary*, 3:485–486.

16. *Teachings of the Prophet Joseph Smith*, 321.

17. *The Young Woman's Journal*, 5:512–513.

18. *Signs of the Times* [1952], 115.

19. *Mormon Doctrine*, 2nd ed. [1966], 2nd ed., 728.

20. *History of the Church*, 1:176; *Essentials in Church History*, 27th ed. [1974], 126.

21. *Church History and Modern Revelation*, 4 vols. [1946–1949], 1:48.

22. *Doctrinal New Testament Commentary*, 3:528–530.

Chapter 46b

Revelation of John, Pt. 3: End of the World and Millennium

(Revelation 8–9, 13–22)

THE SEVENTH SEAL

The Destruction of Satan's Kingdom

Of all the seals, John's description of events in the seventh seal is the most extensive. This emphasis should teach us of the extreme importance of these events during the Millennium and afterward.

— The first five seals	Covered in 11 verses.
— The sixth seal	Covered in 14 verses.
— The seventh seal	Covered in 226 verses.

- **Revelation 8:1–6 The destruction of the wicked begins.** "And when he had opened the seventh seal, there was silence in heaven about the space of half an hour. And I saw the seven angels which stood before God; and to them were given seven trumpets. And another angel came and stood at the altar, having a golden censer; and there was given unto him much incense, that he should offer it with the prayers of all saints upon the golden altar which was before the throne. And the smoke of the incense, which came with the prayers of the saints, ascended up before God out of the angel's hand. And the angel took the censer, and filled it with fire of the altar, and cast it into the earth: and there were voices, and thunderings, and lightnings, and an earthquake. And the seven angels which had the seven trumpets prepared themselves to sound."

A. DURER, 1496-98

— **D&C 43:17–20 Preparing for the great day of the Lord.** "Hearken ye, for, behold, the great day of the Lord is nigh at hand. For the day cometh that the Lord shall utter his voice out of heaven; the heavens shall shake and the earth shall tremble, and the trump of God shall sound both long and loud, and shall say to the sleeping nations: Ye saints arise and live; ye sinners stay and sleep until I shall call again. Wherefore gird up your loins lest ye be found among the wicked. Lift up your voices and spare not. Call upon the nations to repent, both old and young, both bond and free, saying: Prepare yourselves for the great day of the Lord."

- **Revelation 8:7–13 The sounding of seven trumpets of judgment before the coming of the Lord.** The seven angels who stood before the throne of God with their trumpets represent the judgments that will be poured out upon the earth prior to the coming of the Lord.

— **The 1st angel's trumpet: Natural disasters and death.** "The first angel sounded, and there followed hail and fire mingled with blood, and they were cast upon the earth: and the third part of trees was burnt up, and all green grass was burnt up" (v. 7).

— **The 2nd angel's trumpet: A great volcano in the sea.** "And the second angel sounded, and as it were a great mountain burning with fire was cast into the sea: and the third part of the sea became blood; And the third part of the creatures which were in the sea, and had life, died; and the third part of the ships were destroyed" (vv. 8–9).

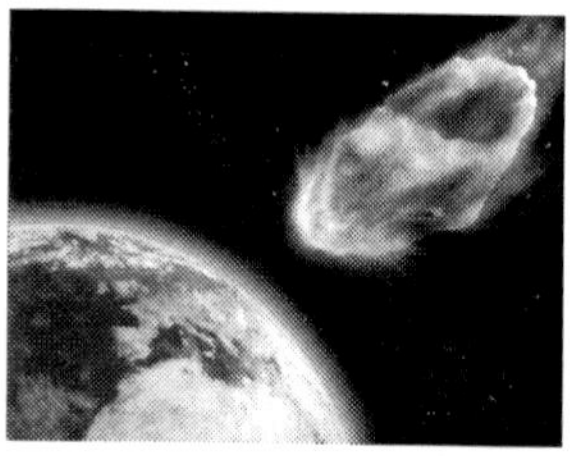

— **The 3rd angel's trumpet: A comet slams into the earth.** "And the third angel sounded, and there fell a great star from heaven, burning as it were a lamp, and it fell upon the third part of the rivers, and upon the fountains of waters; And the name of the star is called Wormwood: and the third part of the waters became wormwood; and many men died of the waters, because they were made bitter" (vv. 10–11).

— **The 4th angel's trumpet: The atmosphere is darkened.** "And the fourth angel sounded, and the third part of the sun was smitten, and the third part of the moon, and the third part of the stars; so as the third part of them was darkened, and the day shone not for a third part of it, and the night likewise" (v. 12).

— This is only the beginning of woes to be poured out upon the earth. "And I beheld, and heard an angel flying through the midst of heaven, saying with a loud voice, Woe, woe, woe, to the inhabiters of the earth by reason of the other voices of the trumpet of the three angels, which are yet to sound!" (v. 13).

The Battle of Armageddon

The valley of Esdraelon, below Har Magiddo, where 200 million men will gather to battle against Israel

- **Revelation 16:16 "A place called in the Hebrew tongue Armageddon."** About 60 miles north of Jerusalem is the site of the hill Megiddo, a great mound that towers over the northern entrance to a broad plain called the valley of Esdraelon. The mountain or hill of Megiddo (*Har Meggido* in Hebrew, *Armageddon* in Greek) also guards a strategic pass that cuts through a mountain range that separates the coastal plains from the inland plains and hills of Galilee. One of the most important highways of the ancient world, which connected Egypt to Asia, ran through this valley and past the fortress of Megiddo. Because of its strategic location, Megiddo and the valley of Esdraelon have seen many bloody conflicts. Egyptian pharaohs, Roman legions, British troops, and Israeli tanks all have battled there in the past.

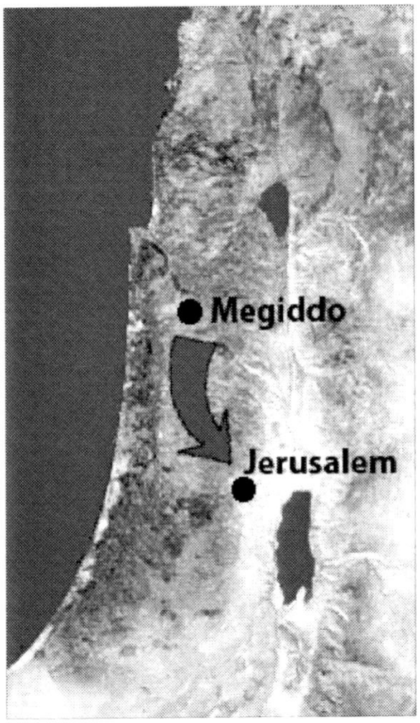

  Prior to the Second Coming of Christ, all the nations of the earth will gather at Armageddon to make war against Jerusalem. This great war has been described in detail by many of the Lord's ancient prophets (See Ezekiel 38–39; Joel 2–3; Isaiah 34; Jeremiah 25; Daniel 11–12; Zechariah 12–14). Jerusalem will be put under siege and great suffering will fill the city. And then, when all will seem lost for Jerusalem, the Lord will appear on the Mt. of Olives and the armies of Armageddon will be destroyed by the plagues of the seventh vial, described above.

  President Joseph Fielding Smith said, "During this siege, when the nations are gathered and the Lord comes, there will be great destruction. The armies will become so confused they will fight among themselves. There will be great slaughter. Then the Lord comes to the Jews. He shows Himself. He calls upon them to come and examine His hands and His feet, and they say, 'What are these wounds?' And He answers them, 'These are the wounds with which I was wounded in the house of my friends. I am Jesus Christ.' Then they will accept Him as their Redeemer, which they have never been willing to do."[1]

- **Revelation 9:1–11 The 5th angel's trumpet: The battle of Armageddon.** "And the fifth angel sounded, and I saw a star fall from heaven unto the earth: and to him was given the key of the bottomless pit. And he opened the bottomless pit; and there arose a smoke out of the pit, as the smoke of a great furnace; and the sun and the air were darkened by reason of the smoke of the pit" (vv. 1–2).

17th-century painting of Armageddon

The bottomless pit is the symbolic dwelling place of Satan. The verses which follow describe the army that will rise up and do his bidding in the battle of Armageddon.

> And there came out of the smoke locusts upon the earth: and unto them was given power, as the scorpions of the earth have power. And it was commanded them that they should not hurt the grass of the earth, neither any green thing, neither any tree; but only those men which have not the seal of God in their foreheads. And to them it was given that they should not kill them, but that they should be tormented five months: and their torment was as the torment of a scorpion, when he striketh a man. And in those days shall men seek death, and shall not find it; and shall desire to die, and death shall flee from them" (vv. 3–6).
>
> "And the shapes of the locusts [airplanes?] were like unto horses prepared unto battle; and on their heads were as it were crowns like gold, and their faces were as the faces of men. And they had hair was the hair of women, and their teeth were as the teeth of lions. And they had breastplates, as it were breastplates of iron; and the sound of their wings was as the sound of chariots of many horses running to battle. And they had tails like unto scorpions, and there were stings in their tails: and their power was to hurt men five months" (vv. 7–10).
>
> "And they had a king over them, which is the angel of the bottomless pit, whose name in the Hebrew tongue is Abaddon, but in the Greek tongue hath his name Apollyon" (v. 11).

The more likely scenario

— Their leader is Abaddon or Apollyon—"Destroyer" (names for Satan).

— A related name is Perdition—meaning "utter loss" or "destruction."

Elder Bruce R. McConkie said:

> During this particular period of the war and desolation the evil forces will be directed against all men, save those sealed up unto eternal life, for those in Zion shall be preserved. The plagues and torments of this era shall so afflict men that they shall desire to die rather than to suffer more.
>
> In prophetic imagery John here seeks to describe a war fought with weapons and under circumstances entirely foreign to any experience of his own or of the people of that day. Joel, subject to the same limitations of descriptive ability, attempted [with difficulty] to portray the same scenes.
>
> It is not improbable that these ancient prophets were seeing such things as men wearing or protected by strong armor; as troops of cavalry and companies of tanks and flame throwers; as airplanes and airborne missiles which explode, fire shells and drop bombs; and even other weapons yet to be devised in an age when warfare is the desire and love of wicked men.[2]

- **Revelation 9:13–21 The 6th angel's trumpet: An army of two hundred million men rise up against God and His people.** "And the sixth angel sounded, and I heard a voice from the four horns of the golden altar which is before God, Saying to the sixth angel which had the trumpet, Loose the four angels which are bound in the great river Euphrates. And the four angels were loosed, which were prepared for an hour, and a day, and a month, and a year, for to slay the third part of men."

John saw the size of the army, which was "two hundred thousand thousand" (200 million) men. And he also saw "the horses in the vision, and them that sat on them, having breastplates of fire, and of jacinth, and brimstone: and the heads of the horses were as the heads of lions; and out of their mouths issued fire and smoke and brimstone" (v. 17).

The verses which follow tell the tale of mass slaughter among a bloodthirsty and unrepentant army. John saw that "the third part of men" were killed—1/3 of 200 million men is 66 million—and yet the wicked will still not repent.

> Death came to these combatants "by the fire, and by the smoke, and by the brimstone, which issued out of their mouths. For their power is in their mouth, and in their tails: for their tails were like unto serpents, and had heads, and with them they do hurt" (vv. 18–19).
>
> "And the rest of the men which were not killed by these plagues yet repented not of the works of their hands, that they should not worship devils, and idols of gold, and silver, and

brass, and stone, and of wood: which neither can see, nor hear, nor walk: Neither repented they of their murders, nor of their sorceries, nor of their fornication, nor of their thefts" (vv. 20–21).

What are we to understand from the sounding of all these trumpets?

— **D&C 77:12 They are the finishing of God's work before the Millennium.** Just "as God made the world in six days, and on the seventh day he finished his work, and sanctified it, and also formed man out of the dust of the earth, even so, in the beginning of the seventh thousand years will the Lord God sanctify the earth, and complete the salvation of man, and judge all things, and shall redeem all things, except that which he hath not put into his power, when he shall have sealed all things, unto the end of all things; and the sounding of the trumpets of the seven angels are the preparing and finishing of his work, in the beginning of the seventh thousand years—the preparing of the way before the time of his coming.

When will all these things be? The Prophet Joseph Smith said, "They are to be accomplished after the opening of the seventh seal, before the coming of Christ" (D&C 77:13).

Two Great Beasts Rise up to Destroy the Church

John used stunning and vivid images to represent the kingdom of Satan, with all its opulent and wicked splendor. Old Testament prophets called this "Babylon." John depicts this system initially as two beasts—one from the sea and the other from the land. The people of Babylon worship this second beast.

John's vision of these two beasts refers to the same worldly organization as the Great and Abominable Church that Nephi saw. They are also the same as the "whore of all the earth"—the world and all its unholy attitudes and practices. Ultimately, these "beasts" are Satan's creations. Those who have drunk of the "poisonous wine of the whore's fornication" will suffer and will be denied God's rest and glory, while those who did not worship the beast will be blessed.

There has been much speculation about these ugly beasts. Many suppose that they represent the Roman Empire, which reigned with blood and horror against the Christians under two different emperors, including during the time that John was banished to the Isle of Patmos. There are a number of details in the description of the beast that could lead to this conclusion. But others prefer a broader interpretation, saying that they represent all of the degenerate worldly powers that have arisen and will arise in the future. Either way, the beasts are servants of Satan and cause much grief to the Saints until they are defeated.

- **Revelation 13:1–3 A great beast rises out of the sea.** John saw a symbolic vision in which "a beast [rose] up out of the sea, having seven heads and ten horns, and upon his horns ten crowns, and upon his heads the name of blasphemy." We can immediately detect the source of this beast, because its appearance is exactly like the "great red dragon" that symbolizes Satan—"having seven heads and ten horns, and seven crowns upon his heads" (Revelation 12:3; see discussion earlier in this chapter).

W. BLAKE, 1805

John described the beast as "like unto a leopard, and his feet were as the feet of a bear, and his mouth as the mouth of a lion: and the dragon [Satan] gave him his power, and his seat, and great authority" (vv. 1–2). Satan also performed miracles for this dragon, healing it of a deadly wound and causing "all the world" to "wonder" [be amazed] concerning it (v. 3).

- **Revelation 13:4–6, 8 The world worships the beast and the dragon [Satan] who gives it power,** "saying, Who is like unto the beast? who is able to make war with him? And there was given unto him a mouth speaking great things and blasphemies; and power was given unto him to continue forty and two months. And he opened his mouth in blasphemy against God, to blaspheme his name, and his tabernacle, and them that dwell in heaven" (vv. 4–6). "And all that dwell upon the earth shall worship him, whose names are not written in the book of life of the Lamb slain from the foundation of the world" (v. 8).

- **Revelation 13:9–10 The beast makes war upon the Saints.** "And it was given unto him to make war with the saints, and to overcome them: and power was given him over all kindreds, and tongues, and nations." John then invited all who "have an ear, [to] let him hear" (v. 9)—a signal to those who possess the Holy Spirit to listen and interpret carefully—then said the following:

  "He that leadeth into captivity shall go into captivity: he that killeth with the sword must be killed with the sword. Here is the patience and the faith of the saints" (v. 10). This is a coded prediction that the force that was now oppressing them would eventually fall, and they must endure with patience and faith.

- **Revelation 13:11–15 Another beast rises from the earth "like a Lamb."** Satan attempts to imitate and counterfeit the true order of things to confuse and deceive mankind. Satan imitated the miraculous power of God when healing the first beast. Now he attempts to deceive by appearing as the Lamb of God.

  John "beheld another beast coming up out of the earth; and he had two horns like a lamb, and he spake as a dragon [Satan]" (v. 11). This is Satan, rising as "the horn" to afflict and torment the Saints.

The Prophet Joseph Smith said, "The 'Horn' made war with the Saints and overcame them, until the Ancient of Days came; judgment was given to the Saints of the Most High from the Ancient of Days; the time came that the Saints possessed the Kingdom. This not only makes us ministers here, but in eternity."[3]

W. BLAKE, 1805

Elder Joseph Fielding Smith said, "Daniel and John each saw the opposition the little horn made against The Church of Jesus Christ of Latter-day Saints. This opposition will continue until the grand council is held at Adam-ondi-Ahman. This "little horn"... is making a renewed and determined effort today to destroy the Church. The Lord has decreed otherwise and while its power will last until Michael comes and the Son of Man receives His rightful place, this great power will endure. It must, however, fall, and according to the scriptures its end will come rather suddenly (D&C 29:21; 1 Nephi 13:1–9; Revelation 17–18)."[4]

B. PICART, THE BIBLE AND ITS STORY, 1908

John said that this horned beast [Satan] exercised "all the power of the first beast before him, and causeth the earth and them which dwell therein to worship the first beast, whose deadly wound was healed. And he doeth great wonders, so that he maketh fire come down from heaven on the earth in the sight of men, And deceiveth them that dwell on the earth by the means of those miracles which he had power to do in the sight of the beast; saying to them that dwell on the earth, that they should make an image to the beast, which had the wound by a sword, and did live" (vv. 11–14).

Satan "had power to give life unto the image of the beast, that the image of the beast should both speak and cause that as many as would not worship the image of the beast should be killed" (v. 15).

- **Revelation 13:16–18 The beast's mark is placed n their right hand or foreheads.** It was a common practice in John's day for devotees of the various heathen gods to mark their foreheads with the name or symbol of their god. Thus followers of Zeus would mark their foreheads with the thunderbolt; those of Poseidon, the trident, and so on. Being sealed or marked in the forehead signaled great devotion to a god.

  Another common practice in John's day was the marking of slaves with a "brand" on their foreheads or on their right hands to indicate to whom they belonged. A similar desire to mark ourselves may be seen in the common practice today of tattooing worldly symbols into our bodies, indicating what we worship and/or whom we wish to be identified with.

  John said that the beast [Satan] "causeth all, both small and great, rich and poor, free and bond, to receive a mark in their right hand, or in their foreheads: And [he caused that] no man might buy or sell, save he that had the mark, or the name of the beast, or the number of his name" (vv. 15–17). Then John provides another coded message: "Here is wisdom. Let him that hath understanding count the number of the beast: for it is the number of a man; and his number is Six hundred threescore and six [666]" (v. 18).

A Whore Who Rides Upon the Beast

W. BLAKE, 1809

John also saw a harlot, lavishly dressed and riding on a beast. The obvious suggestion is that she is impure, evil, and wicked. But the symbolism can be deeper if we see the harlot as a metaphor for Satan's efforts to prostitute (sell for a price) all that is noble and good. And we can see also that she depends upon the beast for her worldly riches.

The ideal relationship between God and man is often symbolized in scripture as a marriage. In the Old Testament, Jehovah is the husband and Israel the bride. In the New Testament Christ is the bridegroom and the Church is the bride (Matthew 25:1–13; Revelation 19:7–9). Whenever His people prove unfaithful to their covenants, they can be likened to a faithless woman who has sold herself to immorality and sin.

The whore represents the same worldly organization that is elsewhere identified as Babylon and/or as the Great and Abominable Church, which, in Revelation 18, we are commanded to flee.

Nephi called these forces "the whore of all the earth," that "[sits] upon many waters; and [has] dominion over all the earth, among all nations, kindreds, tongues, and people (1 Nephi 14:10–11). This imagery of a whore is contrasted in Revelation to the "bride" of Christ (the Church) which is putting on her robes of righteousness in preparation for the "wedding feast" at His Second Coming.

Nephi also called this organization "the great and abominable church," and the word "church" has confused some into thinking it is a religious organization. But in fact, anyone or any organization or thing that "belongeth not to the church of the Lamb of God belongeth to that great church, which is the mother of abominations; and . . . the whore of all the earth" (1 Nephi 14:10).

Elder Bruce R. McConkie said, "The titles church of the devil and great and abominable church are used to identify all churches or organizations of whatever name or nature—whether political, philosophical, educational, economic, social, fraternal, civic, or religious—which are designed to take men on a course that leads away from God and His laws and thus from salvation in the kingdom of God."[5]

Thus, we can conclude that the "whore of all the earth," as described by both John and Nephi, represents the entirety of forces in this world that lead us away from Christ. Whether it be the Docetism of John's day that led to the notion of a "three-in-one" bodiless and immaterial God, or whether it be the greed for power of a dictator with a great army and weapons of mass destruction, or whether it be a false religion that teaches for commandments the philosophies of men—all of these combine into one Satan-inspired whole that is bent on destroying the work of God and the eternal lives of His children.

- **Revelation 17:1–6 The whore of all the earth.** An angel spoke with John, offering to show him "the judgment of the great whore that sitteth upon many waters: With whom the kings of the earth have committed fornication, and the inhabitants of the earth have been made drunk with the wine of her fornication" (vv. 1–2).

  John was "carried . . . away in the spirit into the wilderness" where he "saw a woman sit upon a scarlet coloured beast, full of names of blasphemy, having seven heads and ten horns" (v. 3). These heads and horns reveal that this woman is connected with Satan, as were the beasts of Revelation 13. "And the woman was arrayed in purple and scarlet colour, and decked with gold and precious stones and pearls, having a golden cup in her hand full of abominations and filthiness of her fornication" (v. 4). "And upon her forehead was a name written, MYSTERY, BABYLON THE GREAT, THE MOTHER OF HARLOTS AND ABOMINATIONS OF THE EARTH" (v. 5).

  This whore was "drunken with the blood of the saints, and with the blood of the martyrs of Jesus: and when I saw her, I wondered with great admiration" (v. 6).

  This great and splendiferous whore might have looked impressive, but she was a fraud —a counterfeit to the kingdom of God, whose days were numbered.

- **Revelation 17:14 "And the Lamb shall overcome."** After painting the picture of the harlot and the beast in all of their power and wickedness, John testifies that although they will "make war with the Lamb, . . . the Lamb shall overcome them: for he is Lord of lords, and King of kings: and they that are with him are called, and chosen, and faithful."

  Latter-day revelation confirms this. Just before the organization of the Church in this dispensation, the Lord said that because of His obedience to the Father's will He had subdued all things, including "retaining all power, even to the destroying of Satan and his works at the end of the world" (D&C 19:3).

- **Revelation 18:8 The whore will be destroyed in a day.** "Therefore shall her plagues come in one day, death, and mourning, and famine; and she shall be utterly burned with fire: for strong is the Lord God who judgeth her" (v. 8).

- **Revelation 18:9–10 Kings will bewail her destruction.** "And the kings of the earth, who have committed fornication and lived deliciously with her, shall bewail her, and lament for her, when they shall see the smoke of her burning, Standing afar off for the fear of her torment, saying, Alas, alas, that great city Babylon, that mighty city! for in one hour is thy judgment come" (vv. 9–10).

- **Revelation 18:11–18 Merchants will weep over a destroyed economy.** "And the merchants of the earth shall weep and mourn over her; for no man buyeth their merchandise any more" (v. 11). To make the point, John listed every kind of commodity: precious metals, textiles, manufactured goods, things made from wood, metal, and ivory; perfumes; wine; oil; agricultural goods; meat; and even slaves and "the souls of men" would be available "no more at all" (vv. 12–14).

  The merchants who made money from these things "shall stand afar off for the fear of her torment, weeping and wailing, And saying, Alas, alas, that great city, that was clothed in fine linen, and purple, and scarlet, and decked with gold, and precious stones, and pearls! For in one hour so great riches is come to nought. And every shipmaster, and all the company in ships, and sailors, and as many as trade by sea, stood afar off, And cried when they saw the smoke of her burning, saying, What city is like unto this great city!" (vv. 15–18).

- **Revelation 14:8–11 The fall of Babylon.** John saw and heard "another angel, saying, Babylon is fallen, is fallen, that great city, because she made all nations drink of the wine of the wrath of her fornication" (v. 8). A third angel declared "with a loud voice, If any man worship the beast and his image, and receive his mark in his forehead, or in his hand, the same shall drink of the wine of the wrath of God, which is poured out without mixture into the cup of his indignation; and he shall be tormented with fire and brimstone in the presence of the holy angels, and in the presence of the Lamb" (vv. 9–10). And the smoke of their torment ascendeth up for ever and ever: and they have no rest day nor night, who worship the beast and his image, and whosoever receiveth the mark of his name" (v. 11).

The Destruction of the Wicked

- **Revelation 16:16–21 The seven vials.** To cleanse the world of the wicked, seven angels are instructed to pour out their plagues upon the wicked, as follows:

  — Vial 1 Grievous sores (v. 2).
  — Vial 2 Sea turned to blood (v. 3).
  — Vial 3 Rivers and fountains turned to blood (v. 4).

  At this point, an angel comments on the appropriateness of this curse: "For they have shed the blood of saints and prophets, and thou hast given them blood to drink" (vv. 5–7).

  — Vial 4 Scorching heat (vv. 8–9).
  — Vial 5 Darkness and pain (vv. 10–11).
  — Vial 6 Unclean spirits manifested (vv. 12–16).

  These spirits are described as "like frogs come out of the mouth of the dragon [Satan], and out of the mouth of the beast [Satan's servant], and out of the mouth of the false prophet" (v. 13). T hey are also called "the spirits of devils, working miracles, which go forth unto the kings of the earth and of the whole world, to gather them to the battle of that great day of God Almighty" (v. 14), which will be "into a place called in the Hebrew tongue Armageddon" (v. 16; see more details below).

  — Vial 7 Thunder, lightning, earthquake and hail (vv. 17–18, 21).

  This plague bursts forth after God's voice is heard from heaven, declaring, "It is done" (v. 17). Spiritual Babylon is destroyed as its citizens come "in remembrance before God, to give unto her the cup of the wine of the fierceness of his wrath" (v. 19).

  The earthquake is "such as was not since men were upon the earth, so mighty an earthquake, and so great" (v. 18). "And every island fled away, and the mountains were not found" (v. 20). This has reference to the massive convulsions in the earth's tectonic plates that will bring the continents back together into one land mass. The hailstorm fell "out of heaven, every stone about the weight of a talent [130 lbs]: and men blasphemed God because of the plague of the hail; for the plague thereof was exceeding great" (v. 21).

Elder Bruce R. McConkie said, "God in His mercy shall pour out destructive plagues upon the wicked and ungodly in the last days. These diseases and calamities shall sweep great hosts of men from the face of the earth, preparatory to that final Millennial cleansing which shall prepare our planet as an abode for the righteous."[6]

— **Revelation 16:6** John assures us that they are "worthy" (meaning "deserving") of these plagues.

The Second Coming of Christ

- **Revelation 19:6–9 Great multitudes shout praise at the coming of the Bridegroom.** John "heard as it were the voice of a great multitude, and as the voice of many waters, and as the voice of mighty thunderings, saying, Alleluia: for the Lord God omnipotent reigneth. Let us be glad and rejoice, and give honour to him: for the marriage of the Lamb is come, and his wife hath made herself ready" (vv. 6–7).
    - — In contrast to the image of the "whore," the Church is described as a "wife."
    - — Christ is the Bridegroom.
    - — Our relationship to Him is sacred—like a covenant of marriage.
    - — His coming is symbolized as a "marriage supper."

CAROLSFELD, 1852-60

Elder Bruce R. McConkie said, "'In this dispensation the Bridegroom, who is the Lamb of God, shall come to claim His bride, which is the Church composed of the faithful Saints who have watched for His return. As He taught in the parable of the marriage of the king's son, the great marriage supper of the Lamb shall then be celebrated."[7]

"The elders of Israel are now issuing the invitations to the marriage supper of the Lord; those who believe and obey the gospel thereby accept the invitation and shall sit in due course with the King's Son at the marriage feast."[8]

John saw that "to her [the Church] was granted that she should be arrayed in fine linen, clean and white: for the fine linen is the righteousness of saints" (v. 8). The Lord commanded him to write, "Blessed are they which are called unto the marriage supper of the Lamb," and he testified that "these are the true sayings of God" (v. 9).

- **Revelation 22:12–17 Christ invites all to come to the wedding supper and be exalted.** The Lord said to John, "Behold, I come quickly; and my reward is with me, to give every man according as his work shall be. I am Alpha and Omega, the beginning and the end, the first and the last" (vv. 12–13).

  John wrote that "Blessed are they that do his commandments, that they may have right to the tree of life, and may enter in through the gates into the city. For without are dogs, and sorcerers, and whoremongers, and murderers, and idolaters, and whosoever loveth and maketh a lie" (vv. 14–15).

  And the Lord concluded that "I Jesus have sent mine angel to testify unto you these things in the churches. I am the root and the offspring of David, and the bright and morning star. And the Spirit and the bride say, Come. And let him that heareth say, Come. And let him that is athirst come. And whosoever will, let him take the water of life freely" (vv. 16–17).

The First Resurrection

- **Revelation 20:4–6 The First Resurrection will begin at the Savior's Second Coming.** John saw "thrones, and they [the Saints] sat upon them, and judgment was given unto them: and I saw the souls of them that were beheaded for the witness of Jesus, and for the word of God, and which had not worshipped the beast, neither his image, neither had received his mark upon their foreheads, or in their hands; and they lived and reigned with Christ a thousand years" (v. 4). "This is the first resurrection," said John, but "the rest of the dead lived not again until the thousand years were finished" (v. 5).

  "Blessed and holy is he that hath part in the first resurrection: on such the second death hath no power, but they shall be priests of God and of Christ, and shall reign with him a thousand years" (v. 6).

  The Prophet Joseph Smith said:

  > Would you think it strange that I relate what I have seen in vision in relation [to] this interesting theme? Those who have died in Jesus Christ, may expect to enter into all that fruition of Joy when they come forth, which they have pursued here.
  >
  > So plain was the vision I actually saw men before they had ascended from the tomb as though they were getting up slowly. They take each other by the hand. It was my father and my son, my Mother and my daughter, my brother and my sister. . . .
  >
  > All your losses will be made up to you in the resurrection provided you continue faithful. By

the vision of the Almighty I have seen it. . . . God has revealed His Son from the heavens and the doctrine of the resurrection also. We have a knowledge that those we bury here God [will] bring them up again, clothed upon and quickened by the spirit of the Great God.[9]

— **D&C 88:98–99 The first resurrection.** Those who will receive a celestial or terrestrial reward will come forward in this resurrection. "They are Christ's, the first fruits, they who shall descend with him first, and they who are on the earth and in their graves, who are first caught up to meet him; and all this by the voice of the sounding of the trump of the angel of God" (v. 98).

"And after this another angel shall sound, which is the second trump; and then cometh the redemption of those who are Christ's at his coming; who have received their part in that prison which is prepared for them, that they might receive the gospel, and be judged according to men in the flesh" (v. 99). These are those who did not receive the Gospel while on the earth but received it fully in the spirit world.

— **D&C 88:100–102 The second resurrection**, or the resurrection of the unjust, will not begin until the end of the Millennium. Those who will receive a telestial reward and the sons of perdition will come forward in this resurrection. "And again, another trump shall sound, which is the third trump; and then come the spirits of men who are to be judged, and are found under condemnation; And these are the rest of the dead; and they live not again until the thousand years are ended, neither again, until the end of the earth" (vv. 100–101).

"And another trump shall sound, which is the fourth trump, saying: There are found among those who are to remain until that great and last day, even the end, who shall remain filthy still" (v. 102). These are the sons of perdition, who will be resurrected but will not receive a kingdom of glory because they "remain filthy still."

The Millennium

RUBENS, 1617

- **Revelation 20:1–3 Satan is bound for a thousand years and cannot tempt mankind.** Next, John saw "an angel come down from heaven, having the key of the bottomless pit and a great chain in his hand. And he laid hold on the dragon, that old serpent, which is the Devil, and Satan, and bound him a thousand years, And cast him into the bottomless pit, and shut him up, and set a seal upon him, that he should deceive the nations no more, till the thousand years should be fulfilled: and after that he must be loosed a little season."

  Elder Eldred G. Smith said:

  > Many other scriptures refer to the thousand years of wonderful, glorious conditions on the earth, because Lucifer, Satan, the devil, will be bound. The scriptures say he will be "bound with a chain"

and "put into a bottomless pit." To me, these are symbolical terms. I cannot quite conceive of steel chains or pits that could hold Satan. The only power I know of that will bind Satan, or render him powerless, is righteous living.

The war that started in heaven has not ended yet and shall not end until everyone has proved the extent of his ability to resist Satan. Even Jesus Christ had to bind Satan when He was tempted in the wilderness. Satan had no power over Him, because Jesus resisted his temptations. Then the record says, "... he departed from him for a season" (Luke 4:13).[10]

— **D&C 88:110 Satan will be bound for 1,000 years.** "The seventh angel shall sound his trump; and he shall stand forth upon the land and upon the sea, and swear in the name of him who sitteth upon the throne, that there shall be time no longer; and Satan shall be bound, that old serpent, who is called the devil, and shall not be loosed for the space of a thousand years."

— **1 Nephi 22:26 Satan will be bound because of the righteousness of the people.** "And because of the righteousness of his people, Satan has no power; wherefore, he cannot be loosed for the space of many years; for he hath no power over the hearts of the people, for they dwell in righteousness, and the Holy One of Israel reigneth."

— **D&C 45:55, 58 Little children will grow up without sin unto salvation.** "Satan shall be bound, that he shall have no place in the hearts of the children of men" (v. 55). "And the earth shall be given unto them [the righteous] for an inheritance; and they shall multiply and wax strong, and their children shall grow up without sin unto salvation" (v. 58).

President Joseph Fielding Smith said:

> After Christ comes, all the peoples of the earth will be subject to Him, but there will be multitudes of people on the face of the earth who will not be members of the Church; yet all will have to be obedient to the laws of the kingdom of God, for it will have dominion upon the whole face of the earth. These people will be subject to the political government, even though they are not members of the ecclesiastical kingdom which is the Church.
>
> This government which embraces all the peoples of the earth, both in and out of the Church, is also sometimes spoken of as the kingdom of God, because the people are subject to the kingdom of God which Christ will set up; but they have their agency and thousands will not be members of the Church until they are converted; yet at the same time they will be subject to the theocratic rule.[11]

- **Revelation 20:10 The lake of fire and brimstone.** Satan, at the end of the world, will be "cast into the lake of fire and brimstone, where the beast and the false prophet are, and shall be tormented day and night for ever and ever." Of the eight instances of fire and brimstone in the New Testament, seven are in the book of Revelation, where its use suggests torment and punishment for the wicked.

  Brimstone is sulphur—a yellow-green, highly combustible element that is commonly found along the shores of the Dead Sea. The same substance is used to make matches and gunpowder. When ignited with fire, sulphur liquefies and produces a sharp and suffocating burning odor that can sicken and kill. Apparently in those days, no harsher image of the suffering of the wicked existed than being thrown into a lake of fire, burning with brimstone (See Revelation 21:8; D&C 63:17).

The Battle of Gog and Magog

- **Revelation 20:7–8 When the Millennium is over, Satan will be loosed again for a time.** John saw that "when the thousand years are expired, Satan shall be loosed out of his prison, And shall go out to deceive the nations which are in the four quarters of the earth, Gog and Magog, to gather them together to battle: the number of whom is as the sand of the sea."

  This may be surprising to some, but if we think about it and compare it to the situation of the Nephites after Christ's visit among them, we should not be so surprised. One thousand years is a long time, and in that amount of time some people in scattered parts of the earth could easily become more and more wicked over the generations. That is what happened among the Nephites, who after a little more than 200 years declined from a pure and Zion people into a state of utter apostasy. The same will be true of the Millennium, and by the end of it there will be a need for one more and final cleansing of the earth and destruction of the wicked.

  President Joseph Fielding Smith clarified the difference between the battle of Armageddon and the battle of Gog and Magog: "Before the coming of Christ, the great war, sometimes called Armageddon, will take place as spoken of by Ezekiel, chapters 38 and 39. Another war of Gog and Magog will be after the millennium."[12]

  — **D&C 88:111–113 Satan will be loosed for a season.** "And then he [Satan] shall be loosed for a little season, that he may gather together his armies. And Michael, the seventh angel, even the archangel, shall gather together his armies, even the hosts of heaven. And the devil shall gather together his armies; even the hosts of hell, and shall come up to battle against Michael and his armies."

  — **D&C 88:114–116 The "battle of the great God."** "And then cometh the battle of the great God; and the devil and his armies shall be cast away into their own place, that they shall not have power over the saints any more at all. For Michael shall fight their battles, and shall overcome him who seeketh the throne of him who sitteth upon the throne, even the Lamb. This is the glory of God, and the sanctified; and they shall not any more see death."

- **Revelation 20:9 The wicked will be destroyed again.** John observed that those who chose to follow Satan in the great final battle "went up on the breadth of the earth, and compassed the camp of the saints about, and the beloved city," but "fire came down from God out of heaven, and devoured them."

- **Revelation 20:10–11 The final fate of Satan and his followers.** "And the devil that deceived them was cast into the lake of fire and brimstone, where the beast and the false prophet are, and shall be tormented day and night for ever and ever" (v. 10). John saw "a great white throne, and him [Satan] that sat on it" but he had nothing to reign over and no place to dwell because "the earth and the heaven fled away; and there was found no place for them" (v. 11). They will remain in outer darkness (space) without an inheritance of any kind for ever and ever.

The Final Judgment

- **Revelation 20:12–15 All will stand before God and be judged by their works.** John saw "the dead, small and great, stand before God; and the books were opened: and another book was opened, which is the book of life: and the dead were judged out of those things which were written in the books, according to their works" (v. 12).

  "And the sea gave up the dead which were in it; and death and hell delivered up the dead which were in them: and they were judged every man according to their works" (v. 13).
  "And death and hell were cast into the lake of fire. This is the second death. And whosoever was not found written in the book of life was cast into the lake of fire" (vv. 14–15).

  Elder Joseph Fielding Smith said, "We are informed that the books will be opened. One of these books will be the record of our lives as it is kept in heaven. Other books which will be opened are records which have been kept on earth. From the very organization of the Church the Lord has given instruction that records should be kept of the members of the Church."[13]

  McConkie and Millet commented on the "book" that is within us:

  > Mankind is judged out of the books that the Father has caused to be written, both earthly and heavenly records. We do not know precisely what role the various types of records kept on earth or in heaven will play in the final judgment. As we have already discussed, the scriptures are the primary book or standard of judgment against which we are judged "according to our works."
  >
  > What record has the Father caused to be written that contains our works? Some have the mistaken notion that we are followed around by some guardian angel with a large notebook who diligently keeps track of all our deeds. We often view it as some type of spiritual ledger, with our assets of righteousness in one column and our liabilities of wickedness in the other. In reality, the record of our deeds which the Father has caused to be written is kept within our own souls.[14]

President John Taylor said that our own memories will serve as a record of our lives:

> My understanding of the thing is that God has made each man a register within himself, and each man can read his own register, so far as he enjoys his perfect faculties. . . .
> Let your memories run back, and you can remember the time when you did a good action; you can remember the time when you did a bad action; the thing is printed there, and you can bring it out and gaze upon it whenever you please. . . . Where do you read all this? In your own book. You do not go to somebody else's book or library; it is written in your own record, and you there read it. Your eyes and ears have taken it in, and your hands have touched it; and then your judgment, as it is called, has acted upon it. . . .[15]
>
> The spirit lives where the record of his deeds is kept—that does not die—man cannot kill it; there is no decay associated with it, and it still retains in all its vividness the remembrance of that which transpired before the separation by death of the body and the ever-living spirit. . . . It would be in vain for a man to say then, I did not do so-and-so; the command would be, Unravel and read the record which he has made of himself, and let it testify in relation to these things and all could gaze upon it. . . . That record will stare him in the face; he tells the story himself, and bears witness against himself.[16]
>
> Man himself is a self-registering machine, his eyes, his ears, his nose, the touch, the taste, and all the various senses of the body are so many media whereby man lays up for himself a record which perhaps nobody else is acquainted with but himself; and when the time comes for that record to be unfolded, all men that have eyes to see, and ears to hear will be able to read all things as God Himself reads them and comprehends them, and all things, we are told, are naked and open before Him with whom we have to do.[17]

President Joseph F. Smith said the same thing:

> In reality a man cannot forget anything. He may have a lapse of memory; he may not be able to recall at the moment a thing that he knows or words that he has spoken; he may not have the power at his will to call up these events and words; but let God Almighty touch the mainspring of the memory and awaken recollection, and you will find then that you have not even forgotten a single idle word that you have spoken! I believe the word of God to be true, and, therefore, I warn the youth of Zion, as well as those who are advanced in years, to beware of saying wicked things, of speaking evil, and taking in vain the name of sacred things and sacred beings. Guard your words, that you may not offend even man, much less offend God.[18]

Elder Bruce R. McConkie said our resurrected bodies will also judge us:

> The book of life is the record of the acts of men as such record is written in their own bodies. It is the record engraven on the very bones, sinews, and flesh of the mortal body. That is, every thought, word, and deed has an effect on the human body; all these leave their marks, marks which can be read by Him who is Eternal as easily as the words in a book can be read.
>
> By obedience to telestial law men obtain telestial bodies; terrestrial law leads to terrestrial bodies; and conformity to celestial law—because this law includes the sanctifying power of the Holy Ghost—results in the creation of a body which is clean, pure, and spotless, a celestial body. . . . Men's bodies will show what law they have lived.[19]

The record of our deeds, kept within our own souls, will not only show what we have done, but what we are. Appearing as we really are—our lives in comparison to the words the Father commanded to be recorded in the scriptures—will provide the means by which the Father can judge us out of the books "according to our works."

- **Revelation 21:8 Those not found in the Lamb's "book of life" will suffer spiritual death and eternal disappointment.** John said, "The fearful, and unbelieving, and the abominable, and murderers, and whoremongers, and sorcerers, and idolaters, and all liars, shall have their part in the lake which burneth with fire and brimstone: which is the second death" (see also Revelation 20:14).

  The Prophet Joseph Smith said, "A man is his own tormentor and his own condemner. Hence the saying, They shall go into the lake that burns with fire and brimstone. The torment of disappointment in the mind of man is as exquisite as a lake burning with fire and brimstone. I say, so is the torment of man."[20]

  Elder Bruce R. McConkie said:

  > After the separation of the body and spirit, which is the natural death, the wicked and ungodly die a second death, a spiritual death, meaning they are cast out of the presence of the Lord and are dead as pertaining to the things of righteousness, which are the things of the Spirit [D&C 63:17, 18].
  >
  > But when those here designated have suffered for their own sins, after they have paid the utmost farthing in hell, after they have suffered "the wrath of Almighty God, until the fulness of times," they shall come forth in the second resurrection and receive their inheritance in the telestial kingdom (D&C 76:103–106). That is, the allotted period of their spiritual death shall cease; death and hell shall deliver up the dead which are in them; and all men, except the sons of perdition, shall receive their part in the kingdoms which are prepared. Thus these vessels of wrath are "the only ones on whom the second death shall have any power after the resurrection."[21]

THE CELESTIAL CITY OF OUR GOD

- **Revelation 21:1 A new heaven and a new earth.** John saw in vision "a new heaven and a new earth: for the first heaven and the first earth were passed away; and there was no more sea."

  Elder Joseph Fielding Smith said, "We discover from the word of the Lord that the earth, like mankind upon it, is passing through various stages of development, or change. It was created and pronounced good.

J. MARTIN, 1841

It partook of the decree of mortality coming through the Fall. It is now passing through the telestial condition, in which telestial beings predominate and rule. It will then pass into the 'renewed,' or restored state, for a thousand years as a terrestrial earth and the abode of terrestrial inhabitants. Then comes the end. The earth like all creatures living on it must die. Then it will, like all creatures, receive its resurrection and be celestialized because it obeys its law."[22]

- **Revelation 21:2–3 The heavenly city of Jerusalem will descend.** "And I John saw the holy city, new Jerusalem, coming down from God out of heaven, prepared as a bride adorned for her husband. And I heard a great voice out of heaven saying, Behold, the tabernacle of God is with men, and he will dwell with them, and they shall be his people, and God himself shall be with them, and be their God."

DORÉ, 1865

Elder Bruce R. McConkie said:

> To envision what is meant by this title, we must know these five facts:
>
> 1. Ancient Jerusalem, the city of much of our Lord's personal ministry among men, shall be rebuilt in the last days and become one of the two great world capitals, a millennial city from which the word of the Lord shall go forth.
> 2. A New Jerusalem, a new Zion, a city of God shall be built on the American continent.
> 3. Enoch's city, the original Zion, "the City of Holiness, . . . was taken up into heaven." (Moses 7:13–21).
> 4. Enoch's city, with its translated inhabitants now in their resurrected state, shall return, as a New Jerusalem, to join with the city of the same name which has been built upon the American continent.
> 5. When this earth becomes a celestial sphere "that great city, the holy Jerusalem," shall again descend "out of heaven from God," as this earth becomes the abode of celestial beings forever. (Rev. 21:10–27).[23]

The Prophet Joseph Smith said, "And now, I ask, how righteousness and truth are going to sweep the earth as with a flood [Moses 7:62–64]? I will answer. Men and angels are to be coworkers in bringing to pass this great work, and Zion is to be prepared, even a new Jerusalem, for the elect that are to be gathered from the four quarters of the earth, and to be established an holy city, for the tabernacle of the Lord shall be with them. I discover by this quotation, that John upon the isle of Patmos, saw the same things concerning the last days, which Enoch saw."[24]

- **Revelation 21:4 There will be no sorrow or death.** "And God shall wipe away all tears from their eyes; and there shall be no more death, neither sorrow, nor crying, neither shall there be any more pain: for the former things are passed away."

- **Revelation 21:6–8 "It is done."** John saw the Lord declare, "It is done" (v. 6). And he heard Him also say, "I am Alpha and Omega, the beginning and the end. I will give unto him that is athirst of the fountain of the water of life freely. He that overcometh shall inherit all things; and I will be his God, and he shall be my son" (vv. 6–7). "But the fearful, and unbelieving, and the abominable, and murderers, and whoremongers, and sorcerers, and idolaters, and all liars, shall have their part in the lake which burneth with fire and brimstone: which is the second death" (v. 8).

- **Revelation 21:9–14 The celestial city of God described.** One of the seven angels John had seen carrying vials full of the seven last plagues spoke to him, saying, "Come hither, I will shew thee the bride, the Lamb's wife. And he carried me away in the spirit to a great and high mountain, and shewed me that great city, the holy Jerusalem, descending out of heaven from God" (vv. 9–11).

  John described the city as "having the glory of God: and her light was like unto a stone most precious, even like a jasper stone, clear as crystal; And had a wall great and high, and had twelve gates, and at the gates twelve angels, and names written thereon, which are the names of the twelve tribes of the children of Israel: On the east three gates; on the north three gates; on the south three gates; and on the west three gates. And the wall of the city had twelve foundations, and in them the names of the twelve apostles of the Lamb" (vv. 12–14).

- **Revelation 21:22 There is no temple in the city of God.** John said, "I saw no temple therein: for the Lord God Almighty and the Lamb are the temple of it." Being in the presence of God and Christ, there will be no need for a temple.

- **Revelation 21:23–24 There will be no need for the sun to provide light.** "The city had no need of the sun," said John, "neither of the moon, to shine in it: for the glory of God did lighten it, and the Lamb is the light thereof. And the nations of them which are saved shall walk in the light of it: and the kings of the earth do bring their glory and honour into it."

- **Revelation 22:5 There will be no night there.** "There shall be no night there; and they need no candle, neither light of the sun; for the Lord God giveth them light."

- **Revelation 21:25–27 Its gates will never be shut.** John said, "The gates of it shall not be shut at all by day. . . . And they shall bring the glory and honour of the nations into it. And there shall in no wise enter into it any thing that defileth, neither whatsoever worketh abomination, or maketh a lie: but they which are written in the Lamb's book of life."

- **Revelation 22:1–2 The tree of life will be there.** John saw, "a pure river of water of life, clear as crystal, proceeding out of the throne of God and of the Lamb." And "in the midst of the street of it, and on either side of the river, was there the tree of life, which bare twelve manner of fruits, and yielded her fruit every month: and the leaves of the tree were for the healing of the nations."

- **Revelation 22:3–5 The throne of God will be there.** "The throne of God and of the Lamb shall be in it," John said, "and his servants shall serve him: And they shall see his face; and his name shall be in their foreheads. . . . and they shall reign for ever and ever."

  President David O. McKay received a similar vision of the city of God:

  > The city, I understood, was [the Savior's]. It was the City Eternal; and the people following Him were to abide there in peace and eternal happiness. But who were they?
  >
  > As if the Savior read my thoughts, He answered by pointing to a semicircle that then appeared above them, and on which were written in gold the words: These Are They Who Have Overcome the World—Who Have Truly Been Born Again!"[25]

- **Revelation 22:7 "Behold, I come quickly"** said the Lord, and "blessed is he that keepeth the sayings of the prophecy of this book."

  Elder Bruce R. McConkie said, "Not soon, but in a quick manner; that is, with speed and suddenness after all of the promised conditions precedent have occurred. 'I am Jesus Christ, who cometh quickly, in an hour you think not' (D&C 51:10)."[26]

- **Revelation 22:20 "Even so, come, Lord Jesus."** John responded to the Lord's promise that would "come quickly" with this poignant plea: "Even so, come, Lord Jesus."

  As we reach the end of our study of the New Testament, may I share with you my own feelings on this topic? I have been told by our Master that I would live in days that are filled with darkness, hatred, and selfishness. That has certainly turned out to be true. Wickedness is all around us, and the world seems to be spiraling deeper and deeper into abomination and sorrow. I know that this will not end until our Savior comes, and my heart yearns for that great day. I pray for it to come every morning and night. And it cannot come too quickly for me. I am led to say in my own heart the words of the hymn:

  "Come, O thou King of Kings. We've waited long for Thee."[27]

OTHER CONCEPTS IN REVELATION, PT. 3

- **Revelation 14:2–3 A new song of redemption.** John said he "heard a voice from heaven, as the voice of many waters, and as the voice of a great thunder" accompanied by "harpers harping with their harps" (v. 2). "And they [sang] . . . a new song before the throne, and before the four beasts, and the elders: and no man could learn that song but the hundred and forty and four thousand, which were redeemed from the earth" (v. 3).

— **D&C 84:98–102 The lyrics to this song of redemption.** The Lord said that all who love Him, "from the least unto the greatest, . . . shall be filled with the knowledge of the Lord, and shall see eye to eye, and shall lift up their voice, and with the voice together sing this new song. . . ."

> The Lord hath brought again Zion;
> The Lord hath redeemed his people, Israel,
> According to the election of grace,
> Which was brought to pass by the faith
> And covenant of their fathers.
>
> The Lord hath redeemed his people;
> And Satan is bound and time is no longer.
> The Lord hath gathered all things in one.
> The Lord hath brought down Zion from above.
> The Lord hath brought up Zion from beneath.
>
> The earth hath travailed and brought forth her strength;
> And truth is established in her bowels;
> And the heavens have smiled upon her;
> And she is clothed with the glory of her God;
> For he stands in the midst of his people.
>
> Glory, and honor, and power, and might,
> Be ascribed to our God; for he is full of mercy,
> Justice, grace and truth, and peace,
> Forever and ever, Amen.

- **Revelation 16:20 "And every island fled away."** The earthquakes that accompany these great shifts in the earth's tectonic plates will be extremely violent and frightening. But these changes to the earth's surface will be in preparation for the celestialization of this planet. The continents will reunite into one great land mass and the earth's surface will become smooth.
  Elder Joseph Fielding Smith said:

> When that day comes great changes shall take place upon the earth. We believe this is a day of restoration, and that the earth is to be renewed (Tenth Article of Faith). In this renewal we are informed that the Lord "shall command the great deep, and it shall be driven back into the north country, and the islands shall become one land; and the land of Jerusalem and the land of Zion shall be turned back into their own place, and the earth shall be like as it was in the days before it was divided" (Gen. 10:25).
>
> The notion prevails quite generally that the dividing of the earth in the days of Peleg was a division politically among the people, but from this word of the Lord we gain the idea that the earth itself was divided and that when Christ comes it will again be brought back to the same conditions physically as prevailed before this division took place. The sea is to be driven back into the north. The land is to be brought back as it was originally and the lands of Zion (America) and Jerusalem (Palestine and all the land pertaining unto it) will be restored to their own place as they were in the beginning.
>
> The Savior will stand in the midst of His people, and shall reign over all flesh. We have discovered in our study that the wicked, or all things that are corruptible (Section

101:23–35), will be consumed and therefore will not be permitted to be on the earth when this time comes.[28]

- **Revelation 19:10 "The testimony of Jesus is the spirit of prophecy."** When an angel appeared to John on the Isle of Patmos, John "fell at his feet to worship him. And he said unto me, See thou do it not: I am thy fellowservant, and of thy brethren that have the testimony of Jesus." The angel instructed John to "worship God," and then gave the following important definition:

  "The testimony of Jesus is the spirit of prophecy"—that is, testifying of Jesus is what prophecy is all about. "None of the prophets have written, nor prophesied, save they have spoken concerning this Christ" (Jacob 7:11). "All the prophets who have prophesied ever since the world began—have they not spoken more or less concerning these things?" (Mosiah 13:33). "All the prophets prophesied only of the days of the Messiah."[29]

  The Prophet Joseph Smith said, "If any person should ask me if I were a prophet, I should not deny it, as that would give me the lie; for, according to John, the testimony of Jesus is the spirit of prophecy; therefore, if I profess to be a witness or teacher, and have not the spirit of prophecy, which is the testimony of Jesus, I must be a false witness; but if I be a true teacher and witness, I must possess the spirit of prophecy, and that constitutes a prophet; and any man who says he is a teacher or a preacher of righteousness, and denies the spirit of prophecy, is a liar, and the truth is not in him; and by this key false teachers and impostors may be detected."[30]

- **Revelation 22:18–19 "If any man shall add unto these things."** John wrote Revelation at a time when apostates were active everywhere in the Church, preaching false doctrines, writing fake letters that were supposedly from the Apostles, and changing the words of genuine epistles to fit their own false ideas. Concerned about this trend, John wrote the following at the end of Revelation.

  "I testify unto every man that heareth the words of the prophecy of this book, If any man shall add unto these things, God shall add unto him the plagues that are written in this book: And if any man shall take away from the words of the book of this prophecy, God shall take away his part out of the book of life, and out of the holy city, and from the things which are written in this book."

  The world wants to interpret this scripture as a prohibition against any other scripture but the Bible. However, John wrote his Gospel <u>after</u> he wrote Revelation, so he himself would have violated any such prohibition. The warning speaks only of the marvelous Revelation he has just written, with which no man should tamper. Moses gave a similar warning concerning the law of Moses in Deuteronomy 4:2–3.

Notes

1. *Signs of the Times*, 171.

2. *Doctrinal New Testament Commentary*, 3:502–503.

3. *History of the Church*, 3:389.

4. *Church History and Modern Revelation*, 4:44.

5. *Mormon Doctrine*, 137–138.

6. *Doctrinal New Testament Commentary*, 3:359.

7. *Mormon Doctrine*, 469.

8. *Doctrinal New Testament Commentary*, 3:563–564.

9. 16 April 1843. In S.H. Faulring (ed.), *The Diaries and Journals of Joseph Smith: An American Prophet's Record*, 366–367.

10. In Conference Report, April 1970, 142.

11. *Doctrines of Salvation*, comp. Bruce R. McConkie, 3 vols. [1954–1956], 1:229.

12. *Doctrines of Salvation*, 3:45.

13. *The Way to Perfection* [1949], 342.

14. *Doctrinal Commentary on the Book of Mormon*, 4 vols. [1986–1992], 4:182.

15. In *Journal of Discourses*, 11:77–78.

16. In *Journal of Discourses*, 11:77–79.

17. *Latter-day Prophets Speak*, Daniel H. Ludlow (ed.) [1988], 57.

18. *Latter-day Prophets Speak*, 56–57.

19. *Mormon Doctrine*, 97.

20. *History of the Church*, 6:314.

21. *Doctrinal New Testament Commentary*, 3:583–584.

22. *Church History and Modern Revelation*, 1:295.

23. *Doctrinal New Testament Commentary*, 3:580–581.

24. *Teachings of the Prophet Joseph Smith*, 84.

25. *Cherished Experiences from the Writings of President David O. McKay*, comp. Clare Middlemiss [1976], 60.

26. *Doctrinal New Testament Commentary*, 3:590.

27. *Hymns*, [1985], no. 59.

28. *Church History and Modern Revelation*, 1:264.

29. *Talmud*, "Sanhedrin," 99a.

30. *History of the Church*, 5:215–16.

About the Author

Randal S. Chase spent his childhood years in Nephi, Utah, where his father was a dry land wheat farmer and a businessman. In 1959 their family moved to Salt Lake City and settled in the Holladay area. He served a full-time mission in the Central British (England Central) Mission from 1968 to 1970. He returned home and married Deborah Johnsen in 1971. They are the parents of six children—two daughters and four sons—and an ever-expanding number of grandchildren.

He was called to serve as a bishop at the age of twenty-seven in the Sandy Crescent South Stake area of the Salt Lake Valley. He served six years in that capacity and has since served as a high councilor, a stake executive secretary and clerk, and in many other stake and ward callings. Regardless of whatever other callings he has received over the years, one was nearly constant: he has taught Gospel Doctrine classes in every ward he has ever lived in as an adult—for a total of thirty-five years.

Dr. Chase was a well-known media personality on Salt Lake City radio stations in the 1970s. He left on-air broadcasting in 1978 to develop and market computer-based management, sales, and music programming systems to radio and television stations in the United States, Canada, South America, and Australia. After the business was sold in 1984, he supported his family as a media and business consultant in the Salt Lake City area.

Having a great desire to teach young people of college age, he determined in the late 1980s to pursue his doctorate, and he received his PhD in communication from the University of Utah in 1997. He has taught communication courses at that institution as well as at Salt Lake Community College and Dixie State College of Utah for twenty-one years. He is currently a full-time tenured faculty member in the Communication Department at Dixie State College in St. George, Utah.

Concurrently with his academic career, Dr. Chase has served as a volunteer LDS Institute and Adult Education instructor in the CES system since 1994, both in Salt Lake City and St. George, where he currently teaches a weekly Adult Education class for three stakes in the Washington area. He has also conducted multiple Church history tours and seminars. During these years of gospel teaching, he has developed an extensive library of lesson plans and handouts that are the predecessors to these study guides.